124	01111100	157	10011101	190	10111110	223	11011111
125	01111101	158	10011110	191	10111111	224	11100000
126	01111110	159	10011111	192	11000000	225	11100001
127	01111111	160	10100000	193	11000001	226	11100010
128	10000000	161	10100001	194	11000010	227	11100011
129	10000001	162	10100010	195	11000011	228	11100100
130	10000010	163	10100011	196	11000100	229	11100101
131	10000011	164	10100100	197	11000101	230	11100110
132	10000100	165	10100101	198	11000110	231	11100111
133	10000101	166	10100110	199	11000111	232	11101000
134	10000110	167	10100111	200	11001000	233	11101001
135	10000111	168	10101000	201	11001001	234	11101010
136	10001000	169	10101001	202	11001010	235	11101011
137	10001001	170	10101010	203	11001011	236	11101100
138	10001010	171	10101011	204	11001100	237	11101101
139	10001011	172	10101100	205	11001101	238	11101110
140	10001100	173	10101101	206	11001110	239	11101111
141	10001101	174	10101110	207	11001111	240	11110000
142	10001110	175	10101111	208	11010000	241	11110001
143	10001111	176	10110000	209	11010001	242	11110010
144	10010000	177	10110001	210	11010010	243	11110011
145	10010001	178	10110010	211	11010011	244	11110100
146	10010010	179	10110011	212	11010100	245	11110101
147	10010011	180	10110100	213	11010101	246	11110110
148	10010100	181	10110101	214	11010110	247	11110111
149	10010101	182	10110110	215	11010111	248	11111000
150	10010110	183	10110111	216	11011000	249	11111001
151	10010111	184	10111000	217	11011001	250	11111010
152	10011000	185	10111001	218	11011010	251	11111011
153	10011001	186	10111010	219	11011011	252	11111100
154	10011010	187	10111011	220	11011100	253	11111101
155	10011011	188	10111100	221	11011101	254	11111110
156	10011100	189	10111101	222	11011110	255	11111111

CCNP Practical Studies: Routing

Henry Benjamin CCIE #4695

Cisco Press

Cisco Press
201 West 103rd Street
Indianapolis, IN 46290 USA

CCNP Practical Studies: Routing

Henry Benjamin

Copyright © 2002 Cisco Systems, Inc.

Published by:
Cisco Press
201 West 103rd Street
Indianapolis, IN 46290 USA

Printed in the United States of America 1 2 3 4 5 6 7 8 9 0

First Printing April 2002

Library of Congress Cataloging-in-Publication Number: 2001098198

ISBN: 1-58720-054-6

Warning and Disclaimer

This book is designed to provide information about Cisco routing. Every effort has been made to make this book as complete and as accurate as possible, but no warranty or fitness is implied.

The information is provided on an "as is" basis. The author, Cisco Press, and Cisco Systems, Inc. shall have neither liability nor responsibility to any person or entity with respect to any loss or damages arising from the information contained in this book or from the use of the discs or programs that may accompany it.

The opinions expressed in this book belong to the author and are not necessarily those of Cisco Systems, Inc.

Feedback Information

At Cisco Press, our goal is to create in-depth technical books of the highest quality and value. Each book is crafted with care and precision, undergoing rigorous development that involves the unique expertise of members from the professional technical community.

Readers' feedback is a natural continuation of this process. If you have any comments regarding how we could improve the quality of this book, or otherwise alter it to better suit your needs, you can contact us through e-mail at feedback@ciscopress.com. Please make sure to include the book title and ISBN in your message.

We greatly appreciate your assistance.

Trademark Acknowledgments

All terms mentioned in this book that are known to be trademarks or service marks have been appropriately capitalized. Cisco Press or Cisco Systems, Inc. cannot attest to the accuracy of this information. Use of a term in this book should not be regarded as affecting the validity of any trademark or service mark.

Publisher	John Wait
Editor-in-Chief	John Kane
Executive Editor	Brett Bartow
Cisco Systems Management	Michael Hakkert
	Tom Geitner
	William Warren
Production Manager	Patrick Kanouse
Acquisitions Editor	Michelle Stroup
Development Editor	Andrew Cupp
Project Editor	San Dee Phillips
Copy Editor	Sydney Jones
Technical Editors	Frank Arteaga
	Eddie Chami
	Davin Gibb
Team Coordinator	Tammi Ross
Book Designer	Gina Rexrode
Cover Designer	Louisa Klucznik
Composition	Octal Publishing, Inc.
Indexer	Tim Wright

CISCO SYSTEMS

Corporate Headquarters
Cisco Systems, Inc.
170 West Tasman Drive
San Jose, CA 95134-1706
USA
http://www.cisco.com
Tel: 408 526-4000
       800 553-NETS (6387)
Fax: 408 526-4100

European Headquarters
Cisco Systems Europe
11 Rue Camille Desmoulins
92782 Issy-les-Moulineaux
Cedex 9
France
http://www-europe.cisco.com
Tel: 33 1 58 04 60 00
Fax: 33 1 58 04 61 00

Americas Headquarters
Cisco Systems, Inc.
170 West Tasman Drive
San Jose, CA 95134-1706
USA
http://www.cisco.com
Tel: 408 526-7660
Fax: 408 527-0883

Asia Pacific Headquarters
Cisco Systems Australia,
Pty., Ltd
Level 17, 99 Walker Street
North Sydney
NSW 2059 Australia
http://www.cisco.com
Tel: +61 2 8448 7100
Fax: +61 2 9957 4350

Cisco Systems has more than 200 offices in the following countries. Addresses, phone numbers, and fax numbers are listed on the Cisco Web site at www.cisco.com/go/offices

Argentina • Australia • Austria • Belgium • Brazil • Bulgaria • Canada • Chile • China • Colombia • Costa Rica • Croatia • Czech Republic • Denmark • Dubai, UAE • Finland • France • Germany • Greece • Hong Kong Hungary • India • Indonesia • Ireland • Israel • Italy • Japan • Korea • Luxembourg • Malaysia • Mexico The Netherlands • New Zealand • Norway • Peru • Philippines • Poland • Portugal • Puerto Rico • Romania Russia • Saudi Arabia • Scotland • Singapore • Slovakia • Slovenia • South Africa • Spain • Sweden Switzerland • Taiwan • Thailand • Turkey • Ukraine • United Kingdom • United States • Venezuela • Vietnam Zimbabwe

About the Author

Henry Benjamin is a dual Cisco Certified Internet Expert (CCIE #4695), having been certified in Routing and Switching in May 1999 and ISP Dial in June 2001. His other Cisco certifications include CCNA and CCDA.

He has more than 10 years experience in Cisco networks, including planning, designing, and implementing large IP networks running IGRP, EIGRP, BGP, and OSPF. Recently, Henry worked for Cisco Systems, Inc. in the internal IT department as a key network designer, designing and implementing networks all over Australia and Asia.

In the past two years, Henry has been a key member of the CCIE global team based in Sydney, Australia. As a senior and core member of the team, his tasks include writing new laboratory examinations and written questions for the coveted CCIE R/S certification, recertification examinations, and ISP laboratory examinations.

Proctoring candidates from all parts of the world is a favorite pastime of his. Henry has authored another book, *CCIE Routing and Switching Exam Cram: Exam: 350-001,* for the CCIE qualification examination and helped edit many other titles.

Henry holds a bachelor of aeronautical engineering degree from Sydney University in Australia.

About the Technical Reviewers

Frank Arteaga works as a support engineer for Cisco Systems, Inc. in Sydney, Australia. He holds a bachelor of engineering in telecommunications degree as well as a masters degree in multichannel communications, a Graduate Diploma in Information Systems, and a Graduate Certificate in Internetworking. Frank has 11 years of experience in the computer industry and is also a CCNP, CCNA, CNE, and CNA. Prior to working at Cisco, Frank has done consulting, design, and support work for companies, such as EDS, Qantas, Schindler Lifts, The University of New South Wales, and PDVSA.

Eddie Chami has three years of networking experience. Eddie entered Cisco Systems two years ago, where he joined the Technical Assistance Center (TAC) at Cisco Systems in Australia. During this period, he attained his CCIE in Routing and Switching and has also proctored CCIE R/S exams. With his extensive knowledge in the networking field, Eddie found great satisfaction in not only learning from others but also teaching others. He is currently working with the WAN team, helping customer deployments and troubleshooting day-to-day network connectivity. Eddie's other interests are in the areas of optical, DSL, wireless, and high-speed networks. Eddie has a diploma in aviation studies and a commercial pilot license. His hobbies are sports, reading, and flying. Currently, Eddie is broadening his knowledge in the optical space field; he also has great interests in GMPLS. He can be contacted at echami@cisco.com.

Dedication

January 19, 2001, 5:30 a.m., life changed for my family and me forever. My dear mum passed away after a long battle with cancer. This book is dedicated to my loving mum Anna Philip Benjamin and the memory of her wonderful life. I also dedicate this book to Our Lady, Mary the Mother of God and the Mother of the Eucharist.

Acknowledgments

Cisco Press was wonderful to work with—no bones about it. The team at Cisco Press includes an amazing family of hard-working people. It has been a true pleasure to be invited to write this book. Any aspiring author in this field should seriously consider working with Cisco Press. In particular, at Cisco Press, I'd like to thank Michelle Stroup for introducing me to this project and Andrew Cupp for the tireless work on this book and complete trust in me. Thank you Tammi Ross for being such a great help. I'd also like to thank San Dee Phillips, Sydney Jones, Tim Wright, and Octal Publishing, Inc. for all of their expert work on this book. If I ever write another book, it will be only with the fine folks at Cisco Press.

The technical editors, Eddie, Frank, and Davin, provided valuable technical expertise, and all three showed they have the technical expertise and keen eye for detail to become accomplished authors themselves. Davin and Eddie are CCIEs that I had the pleasure of passing, and I eagerly await Frank's attempt in the near future.

I would also like to thank my wife, Sharon, and my one and only son, Simon, who turned eight years old while I was completing this book. I was always grateful to them both for their understanding and knowing when I needed time to complete this project. I treasure my time with my family and my growing little boy who makes me proud to be his dad. Simon, I love you to the sun and keep going around forever and ever.

This book would have never been written if my mum and dad had never told me to study. Thank you Dad. Thank you Mum.

Contents at a Glance

Table of Contents

Introduction

The Cisco Certified Network Professional (CCNP) certification on the Routing and Switching career track is becoming increasingly popular. CCNP certification builds on your foundation established from the Cisco Certified Network Associate (CCNA) certification. The Routing 2.0 exam is one of the exams that you must pass to become a CCNP. This book provides you with a practical way to prepare for the Routing examination and enables you to obtain some practical skills required to fully appreciate the power of routing in any environment. Professional-level certifications, such as CCNP, open the door to many career opportunities. CCNPs today are valuable compared to even CCIEs, based on the fact that a company can hire many CCNPs who are technically very sound and can provide quality technical skills without the burden of paying large amounts for a single individual who may have more expertise but whose vast expertise isn't necessary for that company's needs. By demonstrating the determination to prepare for and pass the extensive CCNP exam process, CCNPs also demonstrate a strong desire to succeed. CCNPs, through the examinations required, demonstrate a large knowledge base that can be built upon with almost any company running any technology.

Passing the Routing 2.0 exam means that you have mastered the concepts and implementation skills necessary to build a complex IP network of Cisco routers. This is a great skill and demonstrates to any employer that you are ready for any challenges that might be asked of you. *CCNP Practical Studies: Routing* is intended to help you move concepts and theories into practical experience on Cisco routers.

NOTE	The Routing 2.0 exam is a computer-based exam with multiple-choice, fill-in-the-blank, and list-in-order style questions. The exam can be taken at any Sylvan Prometric testing center (1-800-829-NETS, www.2test.com). The exam takes approximately 75 minutes and has approximately 60 questions. You should check with Sylvan Prometric for the exact length of the exam. The exam is constantly under review, so be sure to check the latest updates from Cisco at www.cisco.com/warp/public/10/wwtraining/.

Goals of This Book

The primary goal of this book is to ensure that a CCNP candidate has all the practical skills and knowledge required to pass the Routing 2.0 examination. Most Cisco certifications require practical skills, and the only way to provide you with those skills is to demonstrate them in a working environment that uses common Cisco-defined techniques. Having read many books, I know that technical content alone will probably not allow you to attain the skills necessary to pass a Cisco examination.

The second goal of this book is to provide you with comprehensive coverage of Routing 2.0 exam-related topics, without too much coverage of topics not on the exam. Ultimately, the goal of this book is to get you from where you are today to the point that you can confidently pass the Routing 2.0 exam. Therefore, all this book's features, which are outlined in this introduction, are geared toward helping you discover the IP routing challenges and configuration scenarios that are on the Routing exam, where you have a knowledge deficiency in these topics, and what you need to know to master those topics. The best method to accomplish this is to demonstrate these topics and provide a step-by-step practical studies guide.

Audience

CCNP Practical Studies: Routing is targeted to networking professionals, familiar with networking concepts and the principles of routing theory, who desire a hands-on approach to applying their knowledge. This book is designed to allow a reader, in a structured manner, to configure an entire network consisting of various topologies, technologies, and routing protocols from start to finish. You should have CCNA-level knowledge to use this book to its full extent.

Each chapter starts by briefly describing the technology that is covered in the practical portion of the chapter. This technology background is brief and assumes the reader has a strong technical background and now desires a practical environment to apply this knowledge.

The bulk of each chapter contains five scenarios, which provide you with an opportunity to apply the material at hand practically with the aid of complete explanations. A Practical Exercise, at the end of each chapter, lets you test yourself by applying your knowledge without the benefit of the inline explanations that are provided in the scenarios. You can assess your mastery of the subjects by looking over the Practical Exercise solution. Finally, each chapter ends with a series of review questions designed to allow you to further assess your knowledge of the technology covered. The final chapter in the book is a special chapter that reinforces all the concepts and technologies covered in this guide into one complex scenario. Chapter 9, "CCNP Routing Self-Study Lab," is designed to assist you in your final preparation for the Routing exam by providing you a lab scenario that incorporates many technologies and concepts. Detailed solutions and tips are provided to guide you through the configurations.

By working through these various elements, you will not only gain more confidence navigating within the Cisco IOS but also an understanding of how these various networking concepts relate. Various help tools and author experience are included to ensure that you are fully aware of any problematic configurations and challenges that face network designers in today's large networks.

The end result is that you will become a more complete network engineer ready to tackle and design any IP routing solution. *CCNP Practical Studies: Routing* is for individuals studying for the CCNP Routing 2.0 exam who would like to apply their knowledge while preparing themselves for the exam. Again, this book was written assuming you have CCNA-level experience and knowledge concerning Cisco routers and routing protocols.

Chapter Organization

This book has nine chapters. Each chapter (except Chapter 9) contains brief background information, five scenarios with detailed explanations and full Cisco IOS configurations, a Practical Exercise with solutions, and review questions. This book also contains four appendixes.

In each chapter, following the scenarios, one practical lab requires you to configure the network on your own. The solution contains the full configuration, so readers without network equipment can still follow the configuration requirements. A Review Questions section follows each Practical Exercise to ensure that you digest the fundamental terms and concepts presented in each chapter.

The following subsections briefly describe the subject of each chapter and appendix.

Chapter 1, "Internet Protocol"

Chapter 1 covers basic IP addressing, variable-length subnet masks, and subnetting topics.

IP concepts are reviewed and explained, followed by an explanation of the IP routing table on Cisco routers and instructions about how to minimize the IP routing table using summarization.

Chapter 2, "Routing Principles"

Chapter 2 covers the basic information required on Cisco routers to route IP data across an IP network. Topics include what a distance-vector protocol is and how to configure one on Cisco routers. Link-state routing protocols are described and configured. Finally, IP routing tables are covered in more detail using common IP routing algorithms, such as RIP and IGRP. This is followed by some common techniques used to ensure IP data is routing as correctly and efficiently as possible.

Chapter 3, "Basic Open Shortest Path First"

Chapter 3 covers basic OSPF routing principles and how OSPF routing is fundamental for any small or large network. Basic OSPF terminology is described and configured. The chapter briefly explains why OSPF is considered an improved routing protocol over RIP by explaining how OSPF discovers, chooses, and maintains routing tables. Nonbroadcast multiaccess (NBMA) is demonstrated using a common network topology. The issues and challenges facing network designers when configuring OSPF in larger networks are demonstrated with the practical scenarios.

Chapter 4, "Advanced OSPF and Integrated Intermediate System-to-Intermediate System"

Chapter 4 covers the more advanced topics in OSPF and another link-state routing protocol, IS-IS.

OSPF is explained in more detail, and the chapter explains how OSPF is used in large IP routing environments and how OSPF can be configured to reduce IP routing tables and CPU usage, and lower the memory requirements of access or edge routers. OSPF is a popular IP routing protocol, so most Cisco certifications, including CCNP and CCIE, heavily test on OSPF.

Chapter 5, "Enhanced Interior Gateway Routing Protocol"

Chapter 5 focuses on a protocol developed by Cisco Systems and used on Cisco IOS routers only, namely Enhanced Interior Gateway Routing Protocol (EIGRP). EIGRP is explained and configured on Cisco routers. You discover how EIGRP learns about new neighbors and how EIGRP operates in NMBA networks.

Chapter 6, "Basic Border Gateway Protocol"

Chapter 6 covers the most important routing protocol in use today, Border Gateway Protocol (BGP).

The basics terms and configuration options are described to help you appreciate the powerful nature of BGP. There are five practical scenarios to complete your understanding of BGP to help you appreciate its complexity.

Chapter 7, "Advanced BGP"

Chapter 7 describes BGP in greater detail; in particular, the chapter covers how BGP deals with large networks. Scalability issues are presented, and ways to overcome large BGP networks are covered and configured on Cisco routers.

Chapter 8, "Route Redistribution and Optimization"

Chapter 8 covers the issues and challenges facing networks when information from one routing algorithm is redistributed into another. This chapter also covers how information can be controlled to ensure that the network is routing IP as correctly and efficiently as possible.

Chapter 9, "CCNP Routing Self-Study Lab"

Chapter 9 is designed to assist you in your final preparation for the Routing 2.0 exam by providing you a lab scenario that incorporates many of the technologies and concepts covered in this book. The exercises presented are a combination of all the most critical topics found in this book into one scenario. Full working configurations and sample displays are presented.

Appendix A, "Study Tips"

Appendix A describes some useful study tips for CCNP candidates. Common exam techniques and the best study practices are provided to ensure that you are fully prepared on the day of the examination.

Appendix B, "What to Do After CCNP?"

Appendix B describes what a CCNP can achieve after becoming CCNP certified.

Appendix C, "Answers to Review Questions"

Appendix C provides answers to all of the review questions.

Appendix D, "CCIE Preparation—Sample Multiprotocol Lab"

Appendix D is a bonus aid designed to assist you in your final preparation for the most widely sought after certification in the world today, namely CCIE (Routing and Switching).

How Best to Use This Book

This book provides a practical approach to learning networking concepts. Having your own equipment or access to the equipment is the ideal way to use this book but is not required. Of course, most readers will appreciate that Cisco routers are not easy to come by, so full working solutions and sample displays are presented to ensure that you understand and fully appreciate all concepts. This gives you the opportunity to gain the hands-on experience of configuring each router according to the lab objectives without the need to have any physical equipment. Sample displays are provided to demonstrate the working solutions, and some great tips are provided in the explanations to show you how to ensure network connectivity.

Getting Equipment

You can obtain reasonably priced equipment from various places. If your place of employment has spare equipment that you can use, this may be your first option. If you want to purchase equipment, numerous places exist on the Internet; contact Cisco Systems for second-hand or used routers at very competitive prices. Alternatively, search Cisco partners or auction sites for cheap devices to help you. There are also simulators that offer a cheap solution to purchasing equipment. Cisco, for example, offers a product called Cisco Interactive Mentor (CIM) that enables candidates to simulate real-life networks. For more details on CIM, visit www.ciscopress.com.

NOTE   Visit the following web site for a number of quality tools and Internet links:

www.iponeverything.net

How to Use The Book if You Cannot Get Equipment

If you are unable to get equipment, do not despair; you can still profit from this book. The book is structured to walk you through each configuration task step by step. If you do not have the equipment, pay closer attention to the figures and examples within the chapter and observe the changes that are made to the network. Because each scenario includes thorough explanations, you will begin to understand how configuration tasks are applied and impact the network, even if you can't work along with the scenarios. You might find it handy to keep notes as you work through this book.

Because some experience and knowledge level has been assumed of the reader, you might run into concepts about which you want additional information. As a future CCNP, you should always strive to build upon your knowledge beyond a studying perspective so that you can proceed to a technical level far beyond the minimum required for Cisco-based certifications.

I recommend using the following resources as reference material while reading the book:

- *Routing TCP/IP*, Volumes I and II by Jeff Doyle and Jennifer DeHaven Carroll (Volume II only) (Cisco Press).
- *OSPF Network Design Solutions* by Thomas M. Thomas II (Cisco Press).
- *Routing in the Internet* by Christian Huitema (Prentice Hall PTR).
- *CCIE Routing and Switching Exam Cram: Exam: 350-001* by Henry Benjamin and Thomas M. Thomas II (The Coriolis Group).
- *Internet Routing Architectures,* Second Edition, by Sam Halabi (Cisco Press).
- *Building Cisco Multilayer Switched Networks* by Karen Webb (Cisco Press).
- *Building Scalable Cisco Networks* by Catherine Paquet and Diane Teare (Cisco Press).

In particular, I recommend the companion book to this guide from Cisco Press, *CCNP Routing Exam Certification Guide* by Clare Gough. As always, you will also find Cisco Connection Online (www.cisco.com) to be invaluable.

For more quality resources visit www.ciscopress.com and follow the links guiding you to certification materials. Cisco Press has plans to expand its line of Practical Studies books, so be on the lookout for Practical Studies books that will help you prepare for the other exams besides the Routing exam that you must pass to achieve CCNP status.

Command Syntax Conventions

The conventions used to present command syntax in this book are the same conventions used in the *Cisco IOS Command Reference*, as follows:

- **Boldface** indicates commands and keywords that are entered literally as shown. In examples (not syntax), boldface indicates user input (for example, a **show** command).
- *Italics* indicates arguments for which you supply values.
- Square brackets [and] indicate optional elements.
- Braces { and } contain a choice of required keywords.
- Vertical bars (|) separate alternative, mutually exclusive elements.

Conclusion

The CCNP certification has great value in the networking environment. It proves your competence and dedication. It is required for several other certifications, and it is a huge step in distinguishing yourself as someone who has proven knowledge of Cisco products and technology. *CCNP Practical Studies: Routing* is designed to help you attain CCNP certification. It is a CCNP certification book from the only Cisco-authorized publisher. The author and editors at Cisco Press believe that this book will help you achieve CCNP certification. The dedication required to achieve any success is up to you.

Having many Cisco certifications myself, the joy and success I have achieved has significantly changed my life and that of my family. There are always challenges facing network engineers; and no doubt, after you are a qualified Cisco professional, meeting those challenges will drive you to acquire skills you never thought you could master.

I sincerely hope you enjoy your time spent with this book; it took months and long nights to complete to ensure that you, as the reader, have the perfect companion through your journey to becoming a CCNP. And when you succeed in attaining your certification, please feel free to e-mail me at benjamin@cisco.com, so I too can enjoy your success and joy as well.

CHAPTER 1

Internet Protocol

This chapter focuses on a number of objectives falling under the CCNP routing principles. Understanding basic Internet Protocol (IP) networking not only applies to the CCNP certification but all Cisco-based certification. A concrete understanding of how IP is used in today's networking environments is one of the most important tools to have before taking on the more advanced chapters in this guide.

This chapter starts by covering basic IP concepts. It then briefly explains how to efficiently configure IP to ensure full use of address space. Next, this chapter covers when and how IP routing tables can be minimized using summarization techniques with various routing protocols.

Five practical scenarios complete your understanding of these topics and ensure you have all the basic IP networking knowledge to complement your knowledge of today's most widely used networking protocol, IP.

Basic Internet Protocol

IP is a term widely used in today's networking world to describe a Network layer protocol that logically defines a distinct host or end systems such as a PC or router with an IP address.

An IP address is configured on end systems to allow communication between hosts that are geographically dispersed. An IP address is 32 bits in length with the network mask or subnet mask (also 32 bits in length) defining the host and subnet portion. A subnet is a network that you, as network administrator, segment to allow a hierarchical routing topology. Routing allows communication between these subnets. The host address is a logical unique address that resides on a subnet.

The Internet Engineering Task Force (IETF) standards body, which is a task force consisting of over 80 working groups responsible for developing Internet standards, defined five classes of addresses and the appropriate address ranges. Table 1-1 displays the five ranges.

Table 1-1   *Class A, B, C, D, and E Ranges*

Class of Address	Starting Bit Pattern	Range	Default Subnet Mask
Class A	0	1–126, 127*	255.0.0.0
Class B	10	128–191	255.255.0.0
Class C	110	192–223	255.255.255.0
Class D	1110	224–239	255.255.255.240
Class E	1111	240–255	Reserved

*   127.0.0.0 is reserved for loopbacks purposes. Other reserved addresses for private use as defined by RFC 1918 are

10.0.0.0-10.255.255.255
172.16.0.0-172.16.255.255
192.168.0.0-192.168.255.255

Soon after these ranges were defined and the Internet's popularity extended beyond the Department of Defense in the United States, it became clear that to ensure that a larger community could connect to the World Wide Web there had to be a way to extend IP address space by using subnetting. Subnetting allows an administrator to extend the boundary for any given subnet.

To best illustrate an IP address and subnet portion, determine how many hosts are available on a particular subnet, or even how to best utilize an IP address space, consider the following example.

You are given the IP address 131.108.1.56 and the subnet mask is 255.255.255.0. This example helps you determine what the subnet is, how many hosts can reside on this subnet, and what the broadcast address is.

You can deduce the subnet for any IP address by performing a logical AND operation along with the subnet mask.

NOTE   A logical AND operation follows two basic rules. One is that positive and positive equal positive, and the second is that negative and positive or negative is negative. So, in binary (positive is 1 and negative is 0), 0 AND 0 is 0, 0 AND 1 is 0, 1 AND 1 is 1, 1 AND 0 is 0, and so forth.

Figure 1-1 displays the logical AND operation used to determine the subnet address.

Figure 1-1   *AND Logic Operation*

```
IP Address (131.108.1.56)        10000011.01101100.00000001.00111000
IP Subnet MASK (255.255.255.0)   11111111.11111111.11111111.00000000
Logical AND                      10000011.01101100.00000001.00000000
In Decimal                          131      108      1        0
```

The result of the logical AND operation reveals the subnet address is 131.108.1.0. The subnet address is reserved and cannot be assigned to end devices.

To determine the number of hosts available in any given subnet, you simply apply the formula $2^n - 2$ where n is the number of borrowed bits. This is best explained with examples. To determine the number of borrowed bits, you must examine the subnet mask in binary. For a default Class C network mask of 255.255.255.0, the last eight bits represent the borrowed bits. So, for a Class C network, the number of hosts that can reside are $2^8 - 2 = 256 - 2 = 254$ hosts. (You subtract two host addresses for the subnet address and the broadcast address, which are not permitted to be used by host devices.) In IP, a broadcast address consists of all binary 1s, so for this example, the broadcast address for the subnet 131.108.1.0 is 131.108.1.255. (255 in binary is 11111111.)

Now consider another example. Given the host address 171.224.10.67 and the subnet mask of 255.255.255.224, this example shows you how to determine the subnet and the number of hosts that can reside on this network.

To determine the subnet, perform a logical AND. Figure 1-2 displays the operation.

Figure 1-2   *Logical AND Operation*

```
IP Address (171.224.10.67)         10101011.11100000.00001010.01000011
IP Subnet MASK (255.255.255.224)   11111111.11111111.11111111.11100000
Logical AND                        10101011.11100000.00001010.01000000
In Decimal or subnet                  171      224      10       64
```

The subnet is 171.224.10.64. The number of hosts that can reside on this network with a subnet mask of 255.255.255.224 (or 11100000, 5 borrow bits) is $2^5 - 2 = 32 - 2 = 30$ hosts. You can apply the technique used in this simple example to any Class A, B, or C address, and applying a subnet mask that is not the default or classful kind enables you to extend IP address space and allow a larger number of devices to connect to the IP network.

Table 1-2 displays some common subnets used in today's network and the number of hosts available on those subnets.

Table 1-2   *Common Subnets in Today's Networks*

Decimal	Subnets	Hosts
252 (1111 1100)	64 subnets	2 hosts*
248 (1111 1000)	32 subnets	6 hosts
240 (1111 0000)	16 subnets	14 hosts
224 (1110 0000)	8 subnets	30 hosts
192 (1100 0000)	4 subnets	62 hosts
128 (1000 0000)	2 subnets	126 hosts
64 (0100 0000)		

*   Used commonly for WAN circuits when no more than 2 hosts reside.

Variable-Length Subnet Masks (VLSM)

A variable-length subnet mask (VLSM) is designed to allow more efficient use of IP address space by borrowing bits from the subnet mask and allocating them to host devices. To allow a greater number of devices to connect to the Internet and intranets, the standards body of various routing protocols designed an IP routing algorithm to cater to IP networks with a different subnet mask than the default used in classful networks.

NOTE   The following routing algorithms support VLSM: RIP Version 2, OSPF, IS-IS, EIGRP, and BGP4.

To demonstrate the use of VLSM, consider the example of connecting two Cisco routers through a wide-area link. Only two devices host systems are needed.

To use any IP address space effectively, it would be wise to use the lowest possible number of subnet bits and lowest possible number of host bits. You could use a Class C mask or a mask that allows for 254 hosts. For a link that never uses more than two hosts, this wastes a vast amount of space, 252 addresses in fact.

Apply the formula to determine the best subnet to use to cater to two hosts on any given subnet and class of address. Remember that you must subtract two host addresses for the subnet address and broadcast address.

Applying the formula, you get $2^n - 2 = 2$, or $2^n = 4$, or $n = 2$ borrowed bits. You need to borrow only two bits from the subnet mask to allow for two host addresses. The subnet mask is 30 bits in length or 255.255.255.252 in binary, which is represented as 11111111.11111111.11111111.111111100. The last two bits (00) are available for host addresses; the subnet is 00; the first host address is 01, the second is 10, and the broadcast address is 11.

NOTE	Loopback interfaces configured on Cisco routers are typically configured with a host address using a 32-bit subnet mask, which allows, for example, a Class C network with 255 hosts among 255 different routers and conserves valuable IP address space.

Summarization and How to Configure Summarization

Summarization, put simply, enables a given routing protocol to minimize IP routing tables by taking steps to advertise a smaller or lesser IP route destination for a large set of subnets or networks. IP routing entries consume bandwidth of expensive links between different geographic locations, take CPU cycles on routers, and, most importantly, require memory.

To give network designers the ability to manage large networks, summarization is important for limiting or reducing IP routing tables. The most important consideration to make when summarizing any IP address space is to ensure a hierarchical design.

In a hierarchical design, IP address space is configured across any given router so that it can be easily summarized. To illustrate the capabilities of summarization consider the following IP address ranges in Table 1-3.

Table 1-3   *IP Address Range*

IP Subnet	Binary Last Third Octet
131.108.1.0/24	0000 0001
131.108.2.0/24	0000 0010
131.108.3.0/24	0000 0011
131.108.4.0/24	0000 0100
131.108.5.0/24	0000 0101
131.108.6.0/24	0000 0110
131.107.7.0/24	0000 0111

A router would normally advertise each of the seven IP address ranges, from 131.108.1–7, as seven different IP route entries.

The binary examination of the subnets 1 to 7 in Table 1-3 displays that the first five bits (shaded) are unchanged. The most important fact is that these seven networks are contiguous or in a range that you can easily summarize. Because the high-order bits are common in Table 1-3 (0000 0) and all seven routes are contiguous (binary 001 to 111), you can perform summarization. Because the first five bits are the same, you can apply the mask 248 (11111 000) on the third octet and send an advertisement encompassing all seven routes. Before looking at how to complete this summarization using RIP, EIGRP, or OSPF, the following is a list of benefits when using summarization:

- Reduces routing table sizes
- Allows for network growth
- Simplifies routing algorithm recalculation when changes occur
- Reduces requirements for memory and CPU usage on routers significantly

The alternatives to network summarization are not easy to accomplish, and this includes renumbering an IP network or using secondary addressing on Cisco routers, which is not an ideal solution for management purposes and also provides extra overhead on a router. Also, it is important to understand that if a range of addresses is not contiguous (that is, they do not start from a range that can be easily summarized, such as the range of addresses 131.108.1.0/24 and 131.108.10.0/24), summarization is impossible. You could still summarize the first seven networks, for example, but they might reside in other parts of your network and cause IP routing problems. The best practice is to assign a group of addresses to a geographic area so that the distribution layer of any network enables summarization to be relatively easy to complete.

Depending on the routing protocols in use, summarization may be enabled by default. Automatic summarization simply announces a Class A network with an 8-bit mask, 255.0.0.0, Class B with 16-bit mask, and a Class C mask with a 24-bit mask, 255.255.255.0. With RIPv2, automatic summarization occurs. In other words, you must disable automatic summarization to allow the more specific routes to be advertised; otherwise a default mask is assumed.

To disable automatic summaries with RIPv2, use the following command:

```
router rip
 version 2
 no auto-summary
```

The command **no auto-summary** disables automatic summaries and allows subnets to be advertised.

EIGRP also applies automatic summaries but it also enables the manual configuration of summary addresses. The following example shows you how to summarize the networks in Table 1-3 using EIGRP.

To configure summarization with EIGRP, you must first disable automatic summarization with the following command:

```
router eigrp 1
 no auto-summary
```

Then, you apply the manual summarization on the interface to which you want to send the advertised summary. Example 1-1 displays the command you use to summarize the seven networks in Table 1-3.

Example 1-1 *Summary with EIGRP*

```
interface serial 0
 ip summary-address eigrp 1 131.108.1.0 255.255.248.0
```

Example 1-1 applies a summary on the serial interface. Also note that the EIGRP autonomous system number is 1, matching the configuration on the router because you can have more than one EIGRP process running. The actual summary is 131.108.1.0 255.255.248.0, which replaces the seven individual routers numbered 131.108.1-7.0/24 with one simple route.

OSPF allows summarization manually under the OSPF process ID. Now look at how to configure the seven networks in Table 1-3 with an OSPF summary. You use the following command in OSPF to summarize internal OSPF routes:

```
area area-id range address mask
```

Example 1-2 displays the configuration required to summarize the seven networks in Table 1-3. Assume the *area-id* for now is 1.

NOTE   With OSPF, you can correctly configure summarization only on area border routers (ABRs). An ABR resides in more than one OSPF area. For this example, assume the Cisco router is an ABR.

Example 1-2 *OSPF summary*

```
router ospf 1
area 1 range 131.108.1.0 255.255.248.0
```

NOTE   OSPF also enables you to summarize external OSPF routes redistributed from such protocols as IGRP or RIP.

BGP and IS-IS, covered in Chapters 4, "Advanced OSPF and Integrated Intermediate System-to-Intermediate System," 6, "Basic Border Gateway Protocol" and 7, "Advanced BGP," also provide complex summarization techniques.

IP Helper Address

As in any network, broadcasts are used to find and discover end systems. In a Layer 2 environment, you use broadcasts to find an end system's MAC address. Layer 3 of the TCP/IP model, IP also uses broadcasts for such services as sending IP datagrams to all hosts on a particular network. Broadcasts on any network consume CPU and bandwidth to reduce this even more. In an IP network, you use the IP helper address to change a broadcast into a more specific destination address so not all devices must view the IP data, which conserves bandwidth.

To save on bandwidth, all Cisco routers installed with Cisco Internet Operating System (IOS) software by default have an algorithm that dictates that not all broadcast packets be forwarded. So to allow the ability to forward packets wisely, you can use the IP helper address command to convert a broadcast into a more specific destination address. The command to enable an IP help address is as follows:

```
ip helper-address address
```

You can configure more than one helper address per interface on a Cisco router. The IP helper address forwards packets that are normally discarded by default to the following services:

- Trivial File Transfer Protocol (TFTP)
- Domain Name System (DNS)
- BOOTP server
- BOOTP client
- NetBIOS Name Server
- Dynamic Host Configuration Protocol (DHCP)

NOTE   The most common use for the helper address is for clients running DHCP, which remote servers assign IP addresses and subnet masks usually performed locally through a broadcast to be served remotely with a unicast (one) packet.

Scenarios

The following scenarios are designed to draw together some of the content described in this chapter and some of the content you have seen in your own networks or practice labs. There is no one right way to accomplish many of the tasks presented, and using good practice and defining your end goal are important in any real-life design or solution. The five scenarios presented in this chapter are based on simple IP technologies to introduce you to the configuration of IP on Cisco routers and give you the basic foundation required to complete the more advanced topics and scenarios found later in this book. Readers who are familiar with these basics may want to skip this chapter and move on to Chapter 2, "Routing Principles."

Scenario 1-1: Configuring a Cisco Router for IP

In this scenario, you see how to configure one Cisco router for IP routing using a Class B (/16) network 161.108.1.0 with a Class C subnet mask (255.255.255.0 or /24 mask).

Figure 1-3 displays the one router, named R1, with one Ethernet interface.

Figure 1-3   *IP Routing on Cisco Routers*

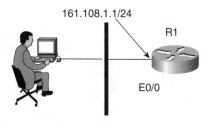

Example 1-3 displays the IP configuration performed on R1's Ethernet interface.

Example 1-3   *IP Configuration on R1*

```
R1(config)#int e 0/0
R1(config-if)#ip address 161.108.1.1 255.255.255.0
R1(config-if)#no shutdown
4w1d: %LINK-3-UPDOWN: Interface Ethernet0/0, changed state to up
4w1d: %LINEPROTO-5-UPDOWN: Line protocol on Interface Ethernet0/0,
    changed state to up
```

NOTE   When you enable the Ethernet interface with the command [**no**] **shutdown**, the IOS message tells you the Ethernet interface and the line protocol are up. To see these messages remotely, enable **terminal monitor** on any VTY lines. Also, by default, all Cisco routers are enabled for IP routing with the command **ip routing**. You can disable IP routing with the command [**no**] **ip routing**.

Example 1-4 displays the active Ethernet interface up and the current IP address configuration.

Example 1-4 **show interface ethernet e0/0** *on R1*

```
R1#show interfaces ethernet 0/0
Ethernet0/0 is up, line protocol is up  → Interface is up and active
   Hardware is AmdP2, address is 0001.9645.ff40 (bia 0001.9645.ff40)
   Internet address is 161.108.1.1/24 →configure IP address
   MTU 1500 bytes, BW 10000 Kbit, DLY 1000 usec, rely 255/255, load 1/255
   Encapsulation ARPA, loopback not set, keepalive set (10 sec)
   ARP type: ARPA, ARP Timeout 04:00:00
   Last input 00:00:21, output 00:00:02, output hang never
   Last clearing of "show interface" counters never
   Queueing strategy: fifo
   Output queue 0/40, 0 drops; input queue 0/75, 0 drops
   5 minute input rate 0 bits/sec, 0 packets/sec
   5 minute output rate 0 bits/sec, 0 packets/sec
      315871 packets input, 30894958 bytes, 0 no buffer
      Received 315628 broadcasts, 0 runts, 0 giants, 0 throttles
      0 input errors, 0 CRC, 0 frame, 0 overrun, 0 ignored, 0 abort
      0 input packets with dribble condition detected
      470705 packets output, 43588385 bytes, 0 underruns
      0 output errors, 3 collisions, 45 interface resets
      0 babbles, 0 late collision, 22 deferred
      0 lost carrier, 0 no carrier
      0 output buffer failures, 0 output buffers swapped out
```

Next, you see how to configure a secondary address on R1 using the IP address 131.108.1.1/24. Example 1-5 displays the secondary IP address assignment.

Example 1-5 *Secondary Address Configuration on R1*

```
R1(config)#interface ethernet 0/0
R1(config-if)#ip address 131.108.1.1 255.255.255.0 secondary
```

R1 now has two IP address assignments: 161.108.1.1/24 and 131.108.1.1/24. Confirm the IP address assignment by displaying the interface statistics with the command **show interfaces Ethernet 0/0**. Example 1-6 displays the Ethernet statistics on R1 and is truncated for clarity.

Example 1-6 **show interfaces ethernet 0/0**

```
R1#show interfaces ethernet 0/0
Ethernet0/0 is up, line protocol is up
   Hardware is AmdP2, address is 0001.9645.ff40 (bia 0001.9645.ff40)
   Internet address is 161.108.1.1/24
   MTU 1500 bytes, BW 10000 Kbit, DLY 1000 usec, rely 255/255, load 1/255
   Encapsulation ARPA, loopback not set, keepalive set (10 sec)
...truncated
```

Example 1-6 does not show the secondary addressing on R1. Unfortunately, the Cisco IOS does not display IP secondary addressing, and the only way to view any secondary addressing is to view the configuration. Example 1-7 displays the full working configuration on R1 along with the secondary IP address, 131.108.1.1.

Example 1-7 *Full working configuration on R1*

```
hostname R1
!
interface Ethernet0/0
 ip address 131.108.1.1 255.255.255.0 secondary
 ip address 161.108.1.1 255.255.255.0
 !
interface Serial0/0
shutdown
!
interface Serial0/1
shutdown
!
line con 0
line aux 0
line vty 0 4
!
end
```

Scenario 1-2: Efficiently Configuring a Network for IP

Suppose you have been asked by a network architect to break up the Class B address 131.108.1.0/24 into four equal subnets that can be used to allow at most 62 hosts per subnet. In addition to this, you must use the address space 131.108.2.0/24 for all wide-area network (WAN) connections that use no more than two hosts per subnet. The network architect has also asked you to document all WAN addresses for future use.

Figure 1-4 displays the network topology graphically.

Start by breaking up the subnet 131.108.1.0/24 into four equal subnets. To do this, examine the subnet in binary. The last eight bits are used for host addresses, so by default you have 254 IP address available. To allow at most 62 hosts, you use the formula $2^n - 2 = 62$, which becomes $2^n = 64$. n, which is the borrowed amount of bits, becomes six bits. So to allow at most 62 hosts, you must use the subnet mask of 255.255.255.192, where 192 in binary is 11000000. The host devices use the last six bits. This is only half the job; you must also configure the four different subnets on R1 in Figure 1-4. To determine the four subnets you must count in binary.

Figure 1-4   *IP Address Configuration Requirements*

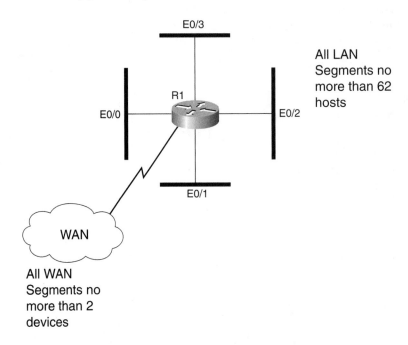

The first subnet starts from 131.108.1.0. You know the broadcast address ends in all 1s, so count from binary 0 to all 1s. Count only from the last octet. Table 1-4 displays the binary calculation.

Table 1-4   *Binary Addition 1*

Decimal	Binary	Comment
0	000000	Subnet (all zeros)
1	000001	First host address
2	000010	Second host address
3	000011	Third host address
...		
62	111110	Last host address
63	111111	Broadcast address (all 1s)

Table 1-4 counts in binary from 0 to 3 and so forth until 63, which in binary is 001111111. Notice that the last six bits are all 1s, which indicates the broadcast address, so the first subnet ranges from 131.108.1.0 to 131.108.1.63. The subnet is 131.108.1.0, and the broadcast address is 131.108.1.63.

Table 1-5 performs the same calculation in binary without the intermediate steps to demonstrate the broadcast address for the second subnet.

Table 1-5   *Binary Addition Subnet 2*

Decimal	Binary	Comment
64	1000000	Subnet all zeros
65	1000001	First host address
66	1000010	Second host address
...		
126	1111110	Last host address
127	1111111	Host address

Table 1-5 displays the second subnet with all zeros as 131.108.1.64 and the broadcast of 131.108.1.127.

Table 1-6 displays the third subnet calculation starting from the next available decimal number of 128.

Table 1-6   *Binary Addition Subnet 3*

Decimal	Binary	Comment
128	10000000	Subnet (all zeros)
129	10000001	First host address
130	10000010	Second host address
131	10000011	Third host address
...		
190	10111110	Last host address
191	10111111	Broadcast address (all 1s)

Table 1-6 displays the subnet as 131.108.1.128, and the broadcast address as 131.108.1.191.

Finally, you can deduce the last subnet available in exactly the same way. Table 1-7 displays the final binary addition.

Table 1-7 *Binary Addition Subnet 4*

Decimal	Binary	Comment
192	11000000	Subnet (all zeros)
193	11000001	First host address
194	11000010	Second host address
195	11000011	Third host address
...		
253	11111110	Last host address
255	11111111	Broadcast address (all 1s)

NOTE   If you are confused about how to convert binary from decimal, simply use a Windows-based calculator to perform the calculation to assist in your first few calculations. It is vital that you can perform these steps without much thought, so you can quickly break up any type of subnet in various design situations or examination scenarios.

Table 1-7 displays the subnet as 131.108.1.192 and the broadcast address for the final subnet as 131.108.1.255.

Now that you have the four broken subnets, configure the Router R1 in Figure 1-4 for IP routing. Example 1-8 displays the IP configuration on the four interfaces on R1.

Example 1-8 *IP Configuration on R1 with Four Subnets*

```
R1(config)#interface ethernet 0/0
R1(config-if)#ip address 131.108.1.1 255.255.255.192
R1(config)#interface ethernet 0/1
R1(config-if)#ip address 131.108.1.65 255.255.255.192
R1(config)#interface ethernet 0/2
R1(config-if)#ip address 131.108.1.129 255.255.255.192
R1(config)#interface ethernet 0/3
R1(config-if)#ip address 131.108.1.193 255.255.255.192
```

The mask is 255.255.255.192 in Example 1-8. The mask or subnet mask is derived from the six bits you borrowed to extend the Class B address 131.108.1.0. Binary 1100000 is 192.

To complete this scenario, you have to break up the network 131.108.2.0/24 into 30-bit sized subnets so that they can be used on WAN circuits that contain no more than two hosts.

Once more, use the simple formula $2^n - 2 = 2$, or $2^n = 4$, where n = 2. So, you need two bits per subnet, and you have already discovered that the mask is 255.255.255.252.

Table 1-8 displays the first four subnets available along with the subnet, broadcast address, and binary equivalent.

Table 1-8   *WAN Host Assignment*

Decimal	Binary	Comment
131.108.2.0	00000000	First subnet, last two bits all zeros
131.108.2.1	00000001	First host
131.108.2.2	00000010	Second host
131.108.2.3	00000011	Broadcast address, last two bits all 1s
131.108.2.4	00000100	Second subnet, last two bits all zeros
131.108.2.5	00000101	First host
131.108.2.6	00000110	Second Host
131.108.2.7	00000111	Broadcast address, last two bits all 1s
131.108.2.8	00001000	First subnet, last two bits all zeros
131.108.2.9	00001001	First host
131.108.2.10	00001010	Second host
131.108.2.11	00001011	Broadcast address, last two bits all 1s
131.108.2.12	00001100	Second subnet, last two bits all zeros
131.108.2.13	00001101	First host
131.108.2.14	00001110	Second host
131.108.2.15	00001111	Broadcast address, last two bits all 1s

As an exercise, you can try to complete the table on your own. Simply count in binary and the next available subnet is clearly evident to you. Notice that the subnets in decimal count in fours, so the first subnet is 131.108.2.0/30, then 131.108.2.4/30, 131.108.2.8/30, 131.108.2.12/30, and so forth.

Scenario 1-3: Configuring IP VLSM for a Large Network

This scenario is slightly more complex. Figure 1-5 displays a network requiring a core network with a large number of routers (assume around 20), a distribution network with three routers, and an access network initially containing only six routers. The access network should have a potential for at most 25 routers (commonly known as access-level routers) to be connected through the distribution routers. Figure 1-5 displays the core network surrounded by three distribution routers and the six access-level routers.

Figure 1-5 *VLSM in a Large Network*

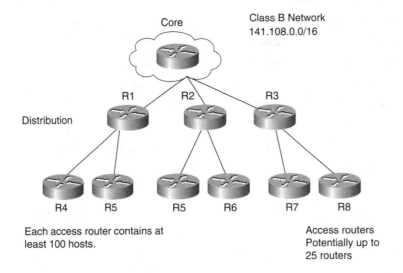

Core

Class B Network
141.108.0.0/16

R1   R2   R3

Distribution

R4   R5   R5   R6   R7   R8

Each access router contains at least 100 hosts.

Access routers
Potentially up to
25 routers

The Class B address 141.108.0.0 has been assigned to you for this task. You should ensure this address space is designed so that company growth allows you to use IP address space wisely to conserve it. Ensure summarization is possible with the three distribution routers.

It is important that the IP addressing scheme is correctly laid out in a hierarchical fashion so that you can use summarization IP routing tables to keep them to a minimum. Start with the core of the network with a possible 20 routers. The core network of any large organization typically grows at a slower pace than access routers, so assume that allowing for over 1500 hosts should suffice. Assign seven Class C networks for the core, and reserve another eight for future use. Using 15 subnets allows for easy summarization as well. Assign the range 141.108.1.0–141.108.15.255 to the core network. In binary, this is the range 00000001 to 00001111, so the first four bits are common.

The distribution routers generally perform all the summarization, so you can assign another seven subnets and reserve another eight Class C networks for future use. So now the distribution routers use the range 141.108.16.0–141.108.31.255.

The access-level routers, where the users generally reside, typically grow at a fast rate, and in this scenario, each site has over 100 users; it is also possible that over 30 (90 in total) remote sites will be added in the future. It is vital that the subnets used here are contiguous so that summarization can take place on the distribution Routers R1, R2, and R3. The following describes a sample solution:

- For access Routers R4 and R5 and possible new routers, use the range 141.108.32.0 to 141.100.63.255; in binary that ranges from 100000 (32) to 63(11111).

- For access Routers R6 and R7 and possible new routers, use the range 141.108.64.0 to 141.100.95.255; in binary that ranges from 1000000(64) to 1011111(95).

- For access Routers R8 and R9 and possible new routers, use the range 141.108.96.0 to 141.108.127.255; in binary that ranges from 1100000(96) to 1111111(127).

- You can reserve the remaining 128 subnets for future use.

This is by no means the only way you can accomplish the tasks in this scenario, but you need to apply these principles in any IP subnet addressing design.

NOTE   Cisco IOS gives you even more IP address space by allowing the use of subnet zero with the IOS command **ip subnet-zero**. Of course non-Cisco devices may not understand subnet zero. A good use for subnet zero would be for WAN links or loopback interfaces and conserving IP address space for real hosts, such as UNIX devices and user PCs. Subnet zero, for example, when using the Class B address 141.108.0.0 is 141.108.0.0, so a host address on a Cisco router could be 141.108.0.1/24.

When designing any IP network, you must answer the following core questions:

- How many subnets are available?
- What IP ranges will be used; will private address space be applied to conserve public addresses?
- How many hosts reside on the edge of the network?
- What are the expansion possibilities for the network?
- What are the geographic locations of remote sites?
- Is there a connection to the Internet or WWW?
- Is an IP address space currently being used?
- What are the current sizes of exiting IP routing tables?
- Are any non-IP protocols already in use? If so, can you tunnel these non-IP protocols?
- What routing protocols enable the use of VLSM?
- These are just some of the major questions that you need to look at carefully. Cisco Systems provides a comprehensive guide to subnets at the following URL:

    www.cisco.com/univercd/cc/td/doc/cisintwk/idg4/nd2003.htm

NOTE	Great resources for information on IP addressing and subnet calculators are also available on the Internet.

Scenario 1-4: Summarization with EIGRP and OSPF

In this scenario, given the address ranges in Table 1-9, you see how to configure summarization with EIGRP and OSPF.

Table 1-9 displays the IP address ranges to be summarized, as well as the binary representation of the third octet or the subnet port of the IP address space.

Table 1-9   *IP Address Ranges*

IP Subnet	Subnet Mask	Binary Representation of Third Octet
151.100.1.0	255.255.255.0	00000001
151.100.2.0	255.255.255.0	00000010
151.100.3.0	255.255.255.0	00000011
151.100.4.0	255.255.255.0	00000100
151.100.5.0	255.255.255.0	00000101
151.100.6.0	255.255.255.0	00000110
151.100.7.0	255.255.255.0	00000111
151.100.8.0	255.255.255.0	00001000
151.100.9.0	255.255.255.0	00001001
151.100.10.0	255.255.255.0	00001010
151.100.11.0	255.255.255.0	00001011
151.100.12.0	255.255.255.0	00001100
151.100.13.0	255.255.255.0	00001101
151.100.14.0	255.255.255.0	00001110
151.100.15.0	255.255.255.0	00001111
151.100.16.0	255.255.255.0	00010000

Before configuring EIGRP or OSPF summarization, you first need to decide whether summarization is possible at all. Table 1-9 displays 16 subnets, numbered from 1-16. The first 15 subnets all have one thing in common when viewed in binary: The first four bits or high-order bits are always 0. Therefore, you can summarize the first 15 networks using the subnet mask 255.255.255.240. (240 in binary is 1111000 where the first four bits are common.) The last four bits contains the networks 1 to 15 or in binary encompass all networks from 0000 to 1111.

The last remaining subnet 151.100.16.0 is the odd network out. Although it is contiguous, you cannot summarize it along with the first 15 network, because any summary address range encompasses networks beyond 151.100.16.0, which may reside in other parts of the network.

Configure EIGRP to summarize these routes out of a serial port (serial 0/0 in this example). Example 1-9 displays the configuration required to disable automatic summarization and the two required summary address commands on the serial 0/0 on a router named R1.

Example 1-9 *EIGRP Summary*

```
R1(config)#router eigrp 1
R1(config-router)#no auto-summary
R1(config)#interface serial 0/0
R1(config-if)#ip summary-address eigrp 1 151.100.1.0 255.255.255.240
R1(config-if)#ip summary-address eigrp 1 151.100.16.0 255.255.255.0
```

In Example 1-9, the router R1 sends only two updates: one for the networks ranging from 151.100.1.0 to 151.100.15.0 and another for 151.100.16.0. These two are instead of 16 separate IP route entries. Even in a small scenario like this, you saved 14 IP route entries. Reducing IP routing tables means when a router performs a routing table search, the time it takes to determine the outbound interface is reduced allowing end-user data to be sent faster over a given medium.

With OSPF, you do not need to disable automatic summarization, because OSPF does not automatically summarize IP subnets. Hence, to summarize the same block of addresses of a router (OSPF ABR), you apply two commands under the OSPF process. Example 1-10 displays the summary commands required.

Example 1-10 *OSPF Summary*

```
R1(config)#router ospf 1
R1(config-router)#no area 1 range 151.100.16.0 255.255.255.240
R1(config-router)#area 1 range 151.100.16.0 255.255.255.0
```

Scenario 1-5: Configuring IP Helper Address

The following scenario demonstrates the powerful use of the helper command and how broadcast traffic, which is dropped by default on Cisco routers, can be forwarded in a manageable fashion and enable IP connectivity across a WAN.

In this scenario, you have a group of users on one segment requiring IP address assignment. No local servers reside on the segment with this group of users.

Figure 1-6 displays the network topology.

Figure 1-6   *IP Helper Requirement*

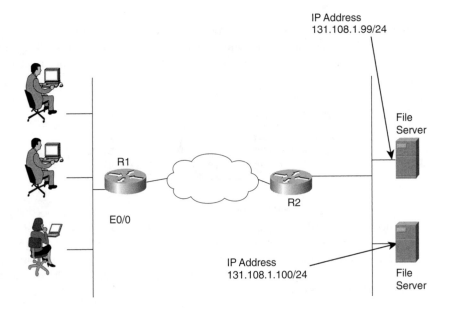

Now, when the users on the local-area network (LAN) segment attached to R1 send out a request for an IP address, this IP packet is sent to the broadcast address, which is dropped by default. Unless a local Dynamic Host Configuration Protocol (DHCP) server exists on this segment, the users' requests for an IP address aren't responded to. To alleviate this problem, you configure a helper address on R1 pointing to the remote file server(s)' address. In this case, two servers are available for redundancy, so you can configure two helper addresses on R1's Ethernet port.

NOTE   Remember, a helper address can forward many UDP-based protocols such as DNS and BOOTP requests. You can further restrict which protocols are sent by using the IOS command **ip forward-protocol** {**udp** [*port*]} or you can forward a packet based on a particular port number used by a certain application.

Example 1-11 displays the helper address configuration on R1.

Example 1-11 *IP Helper Address Configuration on R1*

```
R1(config)#interface ethernet 0/0
R1(config-if)#ip helper-address 131.108.1.99
R1(config-if)#ip helper-address 131.108.1.100
```

The five basic scenarios in this first chapter are aimed at addressing your basic knowledge or re-enforcing what you already know. The Practical Exercise that follows gives you an opportunity to test yourself on these concepts.

Practical Exercise: IP

NOTE   Practical Exercises are designed to test your knowledge of the topics covered in this chapter. The Practical Exercise begins by giving you some information about a situation and then asks you to work through the solution on your own. The solution can be found at the end.

Given the IP address ranges in Table 1-10 and using EIGRP as your routing algorithm, ensure that the least number of IP routing entries are sent out the Ethernet 0/0 port on a Cisco IOS-based router. Table 1-10 displays the IP subnet ranges.

Table 1-10   *IP Subnet Ranges*

IP Subnet	Subnet Mask	Binary Value of Third Octet
171.100.1.0	255.255.255.0	00000001
171.100.2.0	255.255.255.0	00000010
171.100.3.0	255.255.255.0	00000011
171.100.4.0	255.255.255.0	00000100
171.100.5.0	255.255.255.0	00000101
171.100.6.0	255.255.255.0	00000110
171.100.7.0	255.255.255.0	00000111

Practical Exercise Solution

You should notice that the first five bits are the same and the last three encompass the range 1-7, so you can apply the following summary command:

```
ip summary address eigrp 1 171.100.1.0 255.255.255.248
```

Example 1-12 displays the configuration required to summarize the networks from Table 1-10 on an Ethernet 0/0 port using the **?** tool to demonstrate the available options required by Cisco IOS.

Example 1-12 *Sample Configuration*

```
R1(config)#interface ethernet 0/0
R1(config-if)#ip summary-address ?
  eigrp  Enhanced Interior Gateway Routing Protocol (EIGRP)

R1(config-if)#ip summary-address eigrp 1 171.100.1.0 255.255.255.248
R1(config-if)#ip summary-address ?
  eigrp  Enhanced Interior Gateway Routing Protocol (EIGRP)
R1(config-if)#ip summary-address eigrp ?
  <1-65535>  Autonomous system number
R1(config-if)#ip summary-address eigrp 1 ?
  A.B.C.D  IP address

R1(config-if)#ip summary-address eigrp 1 171.100.1.0 255.255.255.248
```

NOTE   Example 1-12 displays the Cisco IOS prompts that appear when the user enters the question mark (**?**) to display the options or parameters the Cisco IOS requires next. They are illustrated here for your reference.

Review Questions

You can find the answers to these questions in Appendix C, "Answers to Review Questions."

1 Given the following host address and subnet mask combinations, determine the subnet address and broadcast addresses:

   - 131.108.1.24 255.255.255.0

   - 151.108.100.67 255.255.255.128

   - 171.199.100.10 255.255.255.224

   - 161.88.40.54 255.255.255.192

2 Given the network 141.56.80.0 and a subnet mask of 255.255.254.0, how many hosts are available on this subnet?

3 What is the broadcast address for the subnet 131.45.1.0/24?

4 What is the purpose of the broadcast address in any given subnet?

5 Given the subnet in binary notation 1111111.11111111.00000000.00000000, what is the decimal equivalent?

6 Which routing protocols support VLSM and why?

7 Which routing protocols do not support VLSM?

8 Which subnet mask provides approximately 1022 hosts?

9 What is the equivalent subnet mask for the notation 131.108.1.0/24?

10 Identify the private address ranges defined in RFC 1918.

Summary

You have successfully worked through five scenarios using common techniques in today's large IP networks. You can now begin to apply this knowledge to the chapters ahead and work through more complex scenarios. The basic information described in this chapter can be applied to any networking scenario you come across when designing and implementing a Cisco-powered network or any network for that matter.

Table 1-11 summarizes the commands used in this chapter.

Table 1-11 *Summary of IOS Commands Used in This Chapter*

Command	Purpose
area *area-id* **range** *network mask*	Summarizes OSPF network ranges between area border routers.
router ospf *process id*	Enables OSPF routing. The process ID is local to the router. You can have more than one OSPF running.
router eigrp *autonomous domain ID*	Enables EIGRP routing under a common administrative control known as the autonomous domain or AD.
no auto-summary	Disables automatic summarization.
show interfaces ethernet 0/0	Displays Ethernet statistics on port 0/0.
version 2	Enables RIPv2.
[no] shutdown	Enables or disables an interface. All hardware interfaces are shut down by default.

This chapter describes how to configure a Cisco Internet Operating System (IOS) router for IP routing and explains common troubleshooting techniques by covering the following:

- Internet Protocol (IP) routing tables
- Dynamic routing protocols
- Classful and classless routing
- Using **show**, **debug**, **ping**, and **trace** commands

CHAPTER 2

Routing Principles

This chapter focuses on a number of objectives relating to the CCNP routing principles. Understanding basic routing principles not only applies to the CCNP certification but to all Cisco-based certification. A concrete understanding of how to route traffic across the network is fundamental for the more advanced topics covered later in this book.

This chapter starts by covering the basic information a Cisco router requires to route traffic and then describes classful and classless routing protocols. The chapter then briefly covers distance vector and link-state protocols and examines IP routing tables and common testing techniques used to troubleshoot IP networks.

Five practical scenarios complete your understanding and ensure you have all the basic IP routing skills to complement your understanding of IP routing on Cisco IOS routers.

Routing IP on Cisco Routers

Routing is defined as a process whereby a path to a destination host is selected by either a dynamic routing protocol or static (manual) definition by a network administrator. A routing protocol is an algorithm that routes traffic or data across the network. Each router makes routing decisions from source to destination based on specific metrics used by the routing protocol in use. For example, Routing Information Protocol (RIP) uses hop count (commonly known as the network diameter) to determine which interface on a router sends the data. A lower hop count is always preferred. On the other hand, Open Shortest Path First (OSPF) uses a cost metric; the lower the cost of the path is the more preferred path to a destination.

NOTE   The method by which a routing algorithm, such as RIP/OSPF, determines that one route is better than another is based upon a metric. The metric value is stored in routing tables. Metrics can include bandwidth, communication cost, delay, hop count, load, MTU, path cost, and reliability.

For routing IP across a network, Cisco routers require IP address allocation to interfaces and then statically or dynamically advertise these networks to local or remote routers. After these networks are advertised, IP data can flow across the network. Routing occurs at Layer 3, or the network layer, of the Open System Interconnection (OSI) model.

By default, IP routing is enabled on Cisco routers. The command you use to start or disable it is [**no**] **ip routing**. However, because IP routing is enabled, you do not see this command by viewing the running configuration as displayed with the IOS command, **show running-config**. Consider a one-router network with two directly connected Ethernet interfaces as an introductory example, shown in Figure 2-1.

Figure 2-1   *Routing IP with Directly Connected Networks*

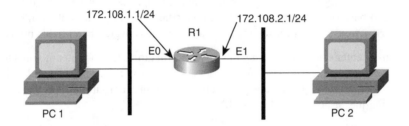

In Figure 2-1 router R1 has two interfaces: E0 (IP address 172.108.1.1/24) and E1 (172.108.2.1/24). Assume there are users on E0 and E1 with PCs labeled PC 1 and PC 2. By default, an IP packet from PC 1 to PC 2 is routed by R1 because both IP networks connect directly to R1. No routing algorithm is required on a single Cisco router (not attached to any other routers) when all interfaces are directly connected as described in this example. Example 2-1 displays R1's routing table.

Example 2-1   **show ip route** *Command on R1*

```
R1#show ip route
Codes: C - connected, S - static, I - IGRP, R - RIP, M - mobile, B - BGP
       D - EIGRP, EX - EIGRP external, O - OSPF, IA - OSPF inter area
       N1 - OSPF NSSA external type 1, N2 - OSPF NSSA external type 2
       E1 - OSPF external type 1, E2 - OSPF external type 2, E - EGP
       i - IS-IS, L1 - IS-IS level-1, L2 - IS-IS level-2, * - candidate default
       U - per-user static route, o - ODR

Gateway of last resort is not set

     172.108.0.0/24 is subnetted, 2 subnets
C       172.108.1.0 is directly connected, Ethernet0
C       172.108.2.0 is directly connected, Ethernet1
R1#
```

In Example 2-1, the C on the left side of the IP routing table denotes the two directly connected networks. Cisco IOS routers support many dynamic routing protocols as well as static (denoted by S) routes. Later chapters in this book cover the main dynamic routing protocols, such as the Open shortest Path First (OSPF) Protocol, RIP, Interior Gateway Routing Protocol (IGRP), and EIGRP. Scenario 2-1 covers all the fields used in an IP routing table.

NOTE   The IP address source and destination in an IP datagram does not change, but the Layer 2 Media Access Control (MAC) source and destination do. For example, when PC 1 sends a packet to PC 2, and because PC 2 resides on a different subnet, PC 1 automatically sends the IP packet to the default router using the destination MAC address of Router R1 (or E0 burnt in address) or the default gateway address of 172.108.1.1/24 (assuming a default gateway has been configured on PC 1 and PC 2). The router then strips the Layer 2 header and installs its own Layer 2 header when the packet enters the network where PC 2 resides. The Layer 2 header contains the source address of R1 E1 and the destination address of the PC 2 MAC address. The Layer 3 IP source and destination address do not change. Some exceptions exist, of course, and many new emerging technologies, because of IP address depletion, change the Layer 3 addressing to allow more hosts to connect to the Internet. Example technologies include Network Address Translation (NAT) or the implementation of Web proxies.

Cisco routers require only IP addressing and routing to allow hosts on different segments to communicate.

This chapter covers dynamic and static routing in the section "Classful and Classless Routing Protocols."

Cisco IOS-Based Routers

All Cisco routers support IP routing. Example 2-2 shows a full list of the protocols that Cisco IOS-based routers support.

Example 2-2   *Routing Protocols You Can Enable on a Cisco Router*

```
R1(config)#router ?
  bgp                Border Gateway Protocol (BGP)
  egp                Exterior Gateway Protocol (EGP)
  eigrp              Enhanced Interior Gateway Routing Protocol (EIGRP)
  igrp               Interior Gateway Routing Protocol (IGRP)
  isis               ISO IS-IS
  iso-igrp           IGRP for OSI networks
```

continues

Example 2-2   *Routing Protocols You Can Enable on a Cisco Router (Continued)*

```
    mobile                 Mobile routes
    odr                    On Demand stub Routes
    ospf                   Open Shortest Path First (OSPF)
    rip                    Routing Information Protocol (RIP)
    static                 Static routes
 traffic-engineering  Traffic engineered routes
```

Border Gateway Protocol (BGP), EIGRP, IGRP, Intermediate System-to-Intermediate
System (IS-IS) Protocol, OSPF, and RIP are dynamic routing protocols and are all covered
in this book. You can use static routing to minimize large routing tables and can manually
configure it to override dynamic information.

When you configure multiple routing algorithms on a Cisco router, deciding which path to
take is vital. To overcome this problem, you assign each routing method, whether dynamic
or static, an administrative distance (AD).

AD is important because routers cannot compare, for example, RIP's metric to OSPF's
metric because hop count means nothing in OSPF and cost means nothing in a RIP domain.
Using AD ensures that the Cisco routers can compare the remote destinations they learn
through various routing algorithms.

AD is defined as the trustworthiness of a routing information source. The higher the value
(between 0–255), the less trusted the source. Table 2-1 displays the default AD values on a
Cisco router.

Table 2-1   *Cisco AD Default Values*

Routing Method	Administrative Distance
Connected interface	0
Static route	1
Enhanced IGRP summary route	5
External BGP	20
Internal Enhanced IGRP	90
IGRP	100
OSPF	110
IS-IS	115
RIP	120
EGP	140
External Enhanced IGRP	170
Internal BGP	200
Unknown	255

For example, if a router has two paths to a destination and one is listed as OSPF (AD is 110) and another as IGRP (AD is 100), the router selects the IGRP path because of the lower AD. Cisco IOS enables the network designer to change the AD with the **distance** command.

Distance Vector and Link-State Routing Protocols

Now that you are aware of the routing methods available, this section looks at the two main types of routing methods that routers use to detect remote destinations dynamically.

Distance vector protocols (a vector contains both distance and direction), such as RIP, determine the path to remote networks using hop count as the metric. A hop count is defined as the number of times a packet needs to pass through a router to reach a remote destination. For IP RIP, the maximum hop is 15. A hop count of 16 indicates an unreachable network. Two versions of RIP exist: version 1 and version 2. IGRP is another example of a distance vector protocol with a higher hop count of 255 hops. A higher hop counts allows your network to scale larger. One of the drawbacks of protocols, such as RIP and IGRP, is convergence time, which is the time it takes for routing information changes to propagate through all your topology. Table 2-2 describes the characteristics of distance vector protocols.

Table 2-2   *Distance Vector Protocol Summary*

Characteristic	Description
Periodic updates	Periodic updates are sent at a set interval. For IP RIP, this interval is 30 seconds.
Broadcast updates	Updates are sent to the broadcast address 255.255.255.255. Only devices running routing algorithms listen to these updates.
Full table updates	When an update is sent, the entire routing table is sent.
Triggered updates	Also known as Flash updates, these are sent when a change occurs outside the update interval.
Split horizon	You use this method to stop routing loops. Updates are not sent out an outgoing interface from which the source network was received. This saves on bandwidth as well.
Count to infinity	This is the maximum hop count. For RIP, it is 15 and for IGRP, it is 255.
Algorithm	One algorithm example is Bellman-Ford for RIP.
Examples	RIP and IGRP are examples of distance vector protocols.

Link-state routing protocols, such as OSPF and IS-IS, create a topology of the network and place themselves at the root of the tree. Link-state protocols implement an algorithm called the shortest path first (SPF, also known as Dijkstra's Algorithm) to determine the path to a remote destination. There is no hop count limit. (For an IP datagram, the maximum time to live ensures that loops are avoided.)

NOTE Hello packets are used to discover neighboring routers, so when changes occur updates can be sent immediately. Hello packets are used to establish and maintain neighbors. OSPF uses the Class D multicast addresses in the range 224.0.0.0 through 239.255.255.255. The two most important reserved addresses are 224.0.0.5 for all OSPF routers and 224.0.0.6 for all DRs and BDRs. Any new OSPF-enabled routers immediately transmit a multicast Hello packet by using the OSPF routers multicast address of 224.0.0.5. DRs use the multicast address 224.0.0.6 to send updates to all other OSPF routers. Therefore, two reserved multicast addresses are vital for maintaining OSPF adjacencies across any broadcast media, such as Ethernet or Token Ring.

The OSPF database is populated with link-state advertisements (LSAs) from neighboring routers. The LSA packets contain information, such as cost and the advertising router or the router ID, which is the highest IP address configured on the local router. Typically, OSPF administrators configure loopback interfaces to ensure that the OSPF process is not prone to failures. (Loopback interfaces never fail unless you shut them down or manually delete them.) In the event that more than one loopback interface is configured on a Cisco router, the loopback interface with (numerically) the highest IP address is the router ID. Table 2-3 displays the characteristics of link-state protocols.

Table 2-3 *Link-State Protocol Summary*

Characteristic	Explanation
Periodic updates	Only when changes occur. OSPF, for example, also sends all summary information every 30 minutes by default.
Broadcast updates	Only devices running routing algorithms listen to these updates. Updates are sent to a multicast address.
Database	A database contains all topological information from which an IP routing table is assembled.
Algorithm	Dijkstra Algorithm for OSPF.
Convergence	Updates are faster and convergence times are reduced.
CPU/memory	Higher CPU and memory requirements to maintain link-state databases.
Examples	OSPF and IS-IS.

NOTE EIGRP is considered an advanced distance vector protocol because EIGRP sends out only incremental updates. BGP is considered a path vector protocol because autonomous system numbers are carried in all updates, and the vector indicates the direction and path to a remote network. Also note distance vector protocols are simpler to implement, and link-state protocols are more complex. BGP is considered the most complex routing protocol to configure, whereas RIP is considered the easiest.

Classful and Classless Routing Protocols

Routing protocols can also be described as classful and classless. Classful addressing is the use of Class A, Class B, and Class C addresses. (Class D is reserved for multicasts, and Class E is reserved for future use.) Class A, B, and C addresses define a set number of binary bits for the subnet portion. For example, a Class A network ranges from 1–127 and uses a subnet mask of 255.0.0.0. A Class B network uses the mask 255.255.0.0, and Class C uses 255.255.255.0. Classful routing protocols apply the same rules. If a router is configured with a Class A address 10.1.1.0, the default mask of 255.0.0.0 is applied and so forth. This method of routing does not scale well, and when designing networks, classless routing better utilizes address space. For example, you can use a Class B network, such as 131.108.0.0, and apply a Class C mask (255.255.255.0, or /24, mask).

NOTE	The following three blocks of IP address space for private networks have been reserved according to RFC 1597: • 10.0.0.0–10.255.255.255 • 172.16.0.0–172.31.255.255 • 192.168.0.0–192.168.255.255

Table 2-4 summarizes the addressing ranges in Class A, B, C, D, and E network.

Table 2-4   *IP Address Ranges*

IP Address Class	Typically Used By:	High-Order Bit(s)	Address Range	Maximum Hosts
A	Few large organizations	0	1.0.0.0–126.0.0.0	16,777,214
B	Medium-sized organizations	1, 0	128.1.0.0–191.254.0.0	65,543
C	Relatively small organizations	1, 1, 0	192.0.1.0–223.255.254.0	254
D	Multicast groups (RFC 1112)	1, 1, 1, 0	224.0.0.0–239.255.255.255	N/A
E	Experimental	1, 1, 1, 1	240.0.0.0–254.255.255.255	N/A

Examples of classful routing protocols are RIPv1 and IGRP. Examples of classless routing protocols are OSPF, IS-IS, EIGRP, and BGP. With classless routing, the ability to apply summarization techniques enables you to reduce the size of a routing table. At last count (October 2001), there are over 80,000 IP routing table entries on the Internet. Reducing the IP routing table size allows for faster delivery of IP packets and lower memory requirements.

Scenarios

The following scenarios and questions are designed to draw together some of the content described in this chapter and some of the content you have seen in your own networks or practice labs. There is not always one right way to accomplish the tasks presented here, and using good practice and defining your end goal are important in any real-life design or solution.

Scenario 2-1: Routing IP on Cisco Routers

In this scenario, you configure two Cisco routers for IP routing using a Class B (/16) network address, 131.108.0.0, with a Class C subnet mask (255.255.255.0, or /24). You learn how to build a small network up from the physical layer and build an IP routing table using one serial link between the two routers, R1 and R2. You also configure a number of loopback interfaces to populate the IP routing table.

NOTE	A *loopback interface* is a software interface. You can ping it and communicate with it. Most importantly, it never goes down, and you can use it as a tool to populate routing tables.

Figure 2-2 shows the network for this scenario.

Figure 2-2   *Routing IP with Directly Connected Networks*

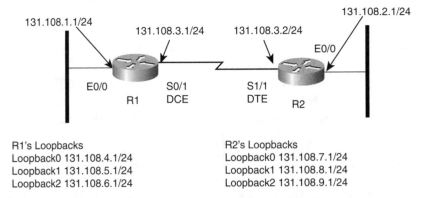

R1's Loopbacks
Loopback0 131.108.4.1/24
Loopback1 131.108.5.1/24
Loopback2 131.108.6.1/24

R2's Loopbacks
Loopback0 131.108.7.1/24
Loopback1 131.108.8.1/24
Loopback2 131.108.9.1/24

Routing IP with Cisco Routers

First, configure router R1 for IP routing. You need to start by configuring the loopbacks, Ethernet, and the serial interface.

A loopback interface is a software interface that can be numbered from 0-2147483647. Loopbacks are handy when you don't have access to a large number of routers and are vital tools when you are configuring IOS on Cisco routers.

Refer to Figure 2-2 for IP address assignments. R1 is directly connected to R2 with back-to-back serial cables. As with any wide-area network (WAN) connection, clocking is required to enable the two routers to communicate.

NOTE   To determine which router requires a clock to enable communication at Layer 2 of the OSI model, use the **show controller** command to determine which end of the network is the data circuit-terminating equipment (DCE). Typically, this is a modem.

Example 2-3 displays the hardware information on R1.

Example 2-3   **show controllers s0/1** *on R1*

```
R1#show controllers s0/1
Interface Serial0/1
Hardware is PowerQUICC MPC860
DCE V.35, no clock
...output omitted
```

Notice that R1 has the DCE connection so you need to configure a clock rate with the **clock rate** *speed* command.

Example 2-4 displays the hardware information on R2.

Example 2-4   **show controllers s0/1** *on R2*

```
R2#show controllers s1/0
CD2430 Slot 1, Port 0, Controller 0, Channel 0, Revision 15
Channel mode is synchronous serial
idb 0x61209474, buffer size 1524, V.35 DTE cable
    output omitted
```

NOTE	The output in Example 2-4 is different from that of Example 2-3 because this scenario uses different model routers for R1 (2600) and R2 (3600), and the cable types used on the routers are V.35. Router R2 has the data terminal equipment (DTE), so R2 requires a clocking source. In this case, R1, the DCE, supplies the clock.

To configure the loopbacks with an IP address, simply use the following command syntax:

```
interface loopback number
```

The value for *number* is a number within the range of 0-2147483647.

The Cisco IOS automatically enables the loopback interface if you have not previously created it. To configure the three loopbacks for this scenario, type the commands on R1 as displayed in Example 2-5.

Example 2-5 *IP Address Configuration on R1*

```
R1(config)#interface loopback 0
R1(config-if)#
2w1d: %LINK-3-UPDOWN: Interface Loopback0, changed state to up
2w1d: %LINEPROTO-5-UPDOWN: Line protocol on Interface Loopback0, changed state
     to up
R1(config-if)#ip address 131.108.4.1 255.255.255.0

R1(config-if)#interface loopback 1
2w1d: %LINK-3-UPDOWN: Interface Loopback1, changed state to up
2w1d: %LINEPROTO-5-UPDOWN: Line protocol on Interface Loopback1, changed state
     to up

R1(config-if)#ip address 131.108.5.1 255.255.255.0
R1(config-if)#interface loopback 2
2w1d: %LINK-3-UPDOWN: Interface Loopback2, changed state to up
2w1d: %LINEPROTO-5-UPDOWN: Line protocol on Interface Loopback2, changed state
     to up
R1(config-if)#ip address 131.108.6.1 255.255.255.0
```

In Example 2-5 when the first interface Loopback 0 is created, you get a message that indicates Loopback 0 is active. Similarly, this happens for loopbacks 1 and 2. You now simply configure the IP addresses for the Ethernet and serial link to R2, as demonstrated in Example 2-6.

Example 2-6 *IP Address Configuration on R1*

```
R1(config)#interface ethernet 0/0
R1(config-if)#ip address 131.108.1.1 255.255.255.0
R1(config-if)#interface s 0/1
R1(config-if)#ip address 131.108.3.1 255.255.255.0
R1(config-if)#clock rate 128000
```

This time you did not get any messages to indicate the link is active. The lack of such a message is because that all physical interfaces are shut down by default when you first configure a router from the default state. You need to enable the interfaces. You can assume that the Ethernet on R1 is connected to a Catalyst switch. Example 2-7 displays the Ethernet interface and serial interface on R1 being enabled.

NOTE   If you do not have access to any form of switch or hub, you can enable the Ethernet interface with the command **keepalive 0**, in which case hardware is unnecessary. Of course, no users can attach to your network, but for training purposes it is a great command to use. The Cisco IOS considers the interface active and includes the network in the IP routing table.

Example 2-7   **no shutdown** *Command on R1*

```
R1(config-if)#interface e0/0
R1(config-if)#no shutdown
R1(config-if)#
2w1d: %LINK-3-UPDOWN: Interface Ethernet0/0, changed state to up
2w1d: %LINEPROTO-5-UPDOWN: Line protocol on Interface Ethernet0/0, changed state
      to up
R1(config-if)#int s 0/1
R1(config-if)#no shutdown
```

The Ethernet interfaces is running, but you still have no active connection on R1 serial link because R1 S0/1 connects to R2, and you have yet to enable R2 serial interface to R1. Example 2-8 displays IP address configuration and the enabling of the hardware interfaces on R2.

Example 2-8   *Enabling E0/0 and S1/1 on R2*

```
R2(config)#interface e0/0
R2(config-if)#ip address 131.108.2.1 255.255.255.0
R2(config-if)#no shutdown
R2(config-if)#
2w1d: %LINK-3-UPDOWN: Interface Ethernet0/0, changed state to up
2w1d: %LINEPROTO-5-UPDOWN: Line protocol on Interface Ethernet0/0, changed state
      to up
R2(config-if)#int s 1/1
R2(config-if)#ip address 131.108.3.2 255.255.255.0
R2(config-if)#no shut
R2(config-if)#
2w1d: %LINK-3-UPDOWN: Interface Serial1/1, changed state to up
2w1d: %LINEPROTO-5-UPDOWN: Line protocol on Interface Serial1/1, changed state
      to up
```

On this occasion, notice both the Ethernet and serial connections are immediately active because R2 is connected to an Ethernet switch, and the link to R1 is active because R1 is enabled and supplying a clock source.

You have now configured two routers with IP addressing.

Viewing IP Routing Tables

Now view the routing tables on R1 and R2 in Scenario 2-1 to see what exactly is described in an IP routing table. Example 2-9 displays R1's routing table.

Example 2-9 **show ip route** *Command on R1*

```
R1#show ip route
Codes: C - connected, S - static, I - IGRP, R - RIP, M - mobile, B - BGP
       D - EIGRP, EX - EIGRP external, O - OSPF, IA - OSPF inter area
       N1 - OSPF NSSA external type 1, N2 - OSPF NSSA external type 2
       E1 - OSPF external type 1, E2 - OSPF external type 2, E - EGP
       i - IS-IS, L1 - IS-IS level-1, L2 - IS-IS level-2, * - candidate default
       U - per-user static route, o - ODR

Gateway of last resort is not set

     131.108.0.0/24 is subnetted, 5 subnets
C       131.108.6.0 is directly connected, Loopback2
C       131.108.5.0 is directly connected, Loopback1
C       131.108.4.0 is directly connected, Loopback0
C       131.108.3.0 is directly connected, Serial0/1
C       131.108.1.0 is directly connected, Ethernet0/0
R1#
```

Example 2-10 displays R2's IP routing table.

Example 2-10 show ip route *on R2*

```
R2#show ip route
Codes: C - connected, S - static, I - IGRP, R - RIP, M - mobile, B - BGP
       D - EIGRP, EX - EIGRP external, O - OSPF, IA - OSPF inter area
       N1 - OSPF NSSA external type 1, N2 - OSPF NSSA external type 2
       E1 - OSPF external type 1, E2 - OSPF external type 2, E - EGP
       i - IS-IS, L1 - IS-IS level-1, L2 - IS-IS level-2, * - candidate default
       U - per-user static route, o - ODR
Gateway of last resort is not set
     131.108.0.0/16 is variably subnetted, 9 subnets, 3 masks
C       131.108.9.0/24 is directly connected, Loopback2
C       131.108.8.0/25 is directly connected, Loopback1
C       131.108.7.0/24 is directly connected, Loopback0
C       131.108.3.0/30 is directly connected, Serial1/1
C       131.108.2.0/24 is directly connected, Ethernet0/0
R2#
```

Both of these cases show routing entries for only directly connected interfaces, which are denoted by the C on the left side of each routing table. Now, you take the R1 routing table and look at it in depth. In particular, look at the shaded portions in Example 2-9.

The first half of the display summarizes the abbreviations the Cisco IOS uses to denote how it learns or discovers routing entries. For example, entries that display C are directly connected networks; entries denoted by D are discovered by EIGRP, and so forth.

That the gateway of last resort is not set in this case means that if the router receives an IP packet, by default if the router doesn't know the destination, it drops the IP packet. If the router knows the gateway of last resort, which is typically represented by a next hop address, the router forwards the IP packets to that destination or next hop address.

The following entry describes the fact that R1 has the Class B network 131.108.0.0 subnetted with five individual networks, namely the three loopbacks, the Ethernet, and the serial link to R2:

```
131.108.0.0/24 is subnetted, 5 subnets
```

To make the routing table a little more interesting, configure R1/R2 with RIP and then OSPF. At this stage, R1 is not aware of any IP networks on R2 and vice versa.

To start, configure RIP on both R1 and R2. IP RIP is one of the easiest routing protocols to configure. To enable IP RIP, you need to perform the following steps:

Step 1   Enable the routing protocol with the command **router rip**.

Step 2   Specify the networks on which RIP will run. With RIP, you need to specify only the major network because RIP is a classful protocol. In this example, the Class B network is 131.108.0.0.

Example 2-11 and Example 2-12 display the configurations required on R1 and R2, respectively, to enable IP RIP.

Example 2-11 *Enable IP RIP on R1*

```
R1(config)#router rip
R1(config-router)#network 131.108.0.0
```

Example 2-12 *Enable IP RIP on R2*

```
R2(config)#router rip
R2(config-router)#network 131.108.0.0
```

Now enable debugging on R1 to view the routing updates on R1. Example 2-13 displays the debug commands enabled on R1.

Example 2-13 debug ip rip *Output on R1*

```
R1#debug ip rip
RIP protocol debugging is on
R1#debug ip rip events
RIP event debugging is on
2w1d: RIP: received v1 update from 131.108.3.2 on Serial0/1
2w1d:      131.108.2.0 in 1 hops
2w1d: RIP: Update contains 1 routes
2w1d: RIP: sending v1 update to 255.255.255.255 via Ethernet0/0 (131.108.1.1)
2w1d:      subnet  131.108.6.0, metric 1
2w1d:      subnet  131.108.5.0, metric 1
2w1d:      subnet  131.108.4.0, metric 1
2w1d:      subnet  131.108.3.0, metric 1
2w1d:      subnet  131.108.2.0, metric 2
2w1d: RIP: Update contains 5 routes
2w1d: RIP: Update queued
2w1d: RIP: sending v1 update to 255.255.255.255 via Serial0/1 (131.108.3.1)
2w1d:      subnet  131.108.6.0, metric 1
2w1d:      subnet  131.108.5.0, metric 1
2w1d:      subnet  131.108.4.0, metric 1
2w1d:      subnet  131.108.1.0, metric 1
2w1d: RIP: Update sent via Ethernet0/0
2w1d: RIP: Update contains 4 routes
2w1d: RIP: Update queued
2w1d: RIP: sending v1 update to 255.255.255.255 via Loopback0 (131.108.4.1)
2w1d:      subnet  131.108.6.0, metric 1
2w1d:      subnet  131.108.5.0, metric 1
2w1d:      subnet  131.108.3.0, metric 1
2w1d:      subnet  131.108.2.0, metric 2
2w1d:      subnet  131.108.1.0, metric 1
2w1d: RIP: Update sent via Serial0/1
2w1d: RIP: Update contains 5 routes
2w1d: RIP: Update queued
2w1d: RIP: sending v1 update to 255.255.255.255 via Loopback1 (131.108.5.1)
2w1d:      subnet  131.108.6.0, metric 1
2w1d:      subnet  131.108.4.0, metric 1
2w1d:      subnet  131.108.3.0, metric 1
2w1d:      subnet  131.108.2.0, metric 2
2w1d:      subnet  131.108.1.0, metric 1
2w1d: RIP: Update sent via Loopback0
2w1d: RIP: Update contains 5 routes
2w1d: RIP: Update queued
2w1d: RIP: sending v1 update to 255.255.255.255 via Loopback2 (131.108.6.1)
2w1d:      subnet  131.108.5.0, metric 1
2w1d:      subnet  131.108.4.0, metric 1
2w1d:      subnet  131.108.3.0, metric 1
2w1d:      subnet  131.108.2.0, metric 2
2w1d:      subnet  131.108.1.0, metric 1
2w1d: RIP: Update sent via Loopback1
2w1d: RIP: Update contains 5 routes
2w1d: RIP: Update queued
2w1d: RIP: Update sent via Loopback2
```

Example 2-13 displays routing updates sent (by default version 1 of RIP is sent and both versions 1 and 2 are accepted) and received by R1. Then R1 sends updates to loopbacks 0, 1, and 2, Ethernet 0/0, and most importantly to R2 through the serial link S0/1. R1 sends information about the local interfaces so that R2 can dynamically insert these entries into its own routing table. R2 performs the same routing function; that is, it sends updates to R1. Example 2-14 displays the IP routing table on R1.

Example 2-14 *R1's Ip Routing Table*

```
R1#show ip route

     131.108.0.0/24 is subnetted, 9 subnets
R       131.108.9.0 [120/1] via 131.108.3.2, 00:00:08, Serial0/1
R       131.108.8.0 [120/1] via 131.108.3.2, 00:00:08, Serial0/1
R       131.108.7.0 [120/1] via 131.108.3.2, 00:00:08, Serial0/1
C       131.108.6.0 is directly connected, Loopback2
C       131.108.5.0 is directly connected, Loopback1
C       131.108.4.0 is directly connected, Loopback0
C       131.108.3.0 is directly connected, Serial0/1
R       131.108.2.0 [120/1] via 131.108.3.2, 00:00:08, Serial0/1
C       131.108.1.0 is directly connected, Ethernet0/0
R1#
```

Example 2-15 shows just IP RIP routes using the command **show ip route rip**.

Example 2-15 *R1's RIP Entries Only*

```
R1#show ip route rip
     131.108.0.0/24 is subnetted, 9 subnets
R       131.108.9.0 [120/1] via 131.108.3.2, 00:00:20, Serial0/1
R       131.108.8.0 [120/1] via 131.108.3.2, 00:00:20, Serial0/1
R       131.108.7.0 [120/1] via 131.108.3.2, 00:00:20, Serial0/1
R       131.108.2.0 [120/1] via 131.108.3.2, 00:00:20, Serial0/1
R1#
```

As you can see in Example 2-15, R2 is advertising the Class B subnetted networks 131.108.2.0/24, 131.108.7.0/24, 131.108.8.0/24, and 131.108.108.9.0/24 through the next hop address 131.108.3.2. The outgoing interface is serial 0/1. RIP works in this environment because all the networks are Class C. Another important field described in the IP routing table is the administrative distance and the metric. In the case of IP RIP, the administrative distance is 120 and the metric is hop count. The hop count to all the remote networks in Example 2-15 is 1.

Now change the IP address on the serial link to the most commonly used subnet. To ensure the efficient use of IP address space when designing networks, you typically use a subnet that allows only two hosts. To allow two hosts, you must use the subnet mask 255.255.255.252. Example 2-16 displays the IP address change on R1 and R2 using the new subnet mask of 255.255.255.252.

Example 2-16 *IP Address Change on R1 and R2*

```
R1(config)#int s 0/1
R1(config-if)#ip address 131.108.3.1 255.255.255.252
R2(config)#int s 1/1
R2(config-if)#ip address 131.108.3.2 255.255.255.252
```

Look at the IP routing table on R1. Remember that RIP is classful so it applies the default subnet mask, or whatever mask is applied, to a directly attached interface. In the first RIP example, a /24 network was used on all interfaces. Example 2-17 now displays the new IP routing table on R1.

Example 2-17 **show ip route** *on R1*

```
R1#show ip route
     131.108.0.0/16 is variably subnetted, 5 subnets, 2 masks
C       131.108.6.0/24 is directly connected, Loopback2
C       131.108.5.0/24 is directly connected, Loopback1
C       131.108.4.0/24 is directly connected, Loopback0
C       131.108.3.0/30 is directly connected, Serial0/1
C       131.108.1.0/24 is directly connected, Ethernet0/0
R1#
```

Notice what happens to the IP RIP routes. Also notice that the serial link to R2 through Serial 0/1 is a /30 subnet, whereas all the other directly connected interfaces are /24.

Because you use a variable-length subnet mask (VLSM) across this network means you need a routing protocol that understands VLSM. IP RIP version 1 does not. Enable version 2 of IP RIP. To enable version 2, you type the command **version 2**. You can also use static routes to accomplish connectivity. Example 2-18 displays the enabling of RIP version 2.

Example 2-18 *Enabling RIPv 2 on R1 and R2*

```
R1(config)#router rip
R1(config-router)#version 2
R2(config)#router rip
R2(config-router)#version 2
```

IP RIPv2 understands VLSM. Example 2-19 displays the new IP routing table on R1.

Example 2-19 *R1's IP Route Table with RIPv2 Enabled*

```
R1#show ip route

     131.108.0.0/16 is variably subnetted, 9 subnets, 2 masks
R       131.108.9.0/24 [120/1] via 131.108.3.2, 00:00:00, Serial0/1
R       131.108.8.0/24 [120/1] via 131.108.3.2, 00:00:00, Serial0/1
R       131.108.7.0/24 [120/1] via 131.108.3.2, 00:00:00, Serial0/1
C       131.108.6.0/24 is directly connected, Loopback2
C       131.108.5.0/24 is directly connected, Loopback1
C       131.108.4.0/24 is directly connected, Loopback0
C       131.108.3.0/30 is directly connected, Serial0/1
R       131.108.2.0/24 [120/1] via 131.108.3.2, 00:00:00, Serial0/1
C       131.108.1.0/24 is directly connected, Ethernet0/0
```

The remote networks are now back in the routing table because RIPv2 understands VLSM. Another routing protocol that understands VLSM is OSPF. Before you learn how to configure OSPF, Example 2-20 and Example 2-21 display the full configurations for R1 and R2 using VLSM and RIPv2.

Example 2-20 *R1 Full Configuration*

```
version 12.0
!
!
hostname R1
!
enable password cisco
!
no ip domain-lookup
!
interface Loopback0
 ip address 131.108.4.1 255.255.255.0
 no ip directed-broadcast
!
interface Loopback1
 ip address 131.108.5.1 255.255.255.0
 no ip directed-broadcast
!
interface Loopback2
 ip address 131.108.6.1 255.255.255.0
 no ip directed-broadcast
!
interface Ethernet0/0
 ip address 131.108.1.1 255.255.255.0
 no ip directed-broadcast
```

continues

Example 2-20 *R1 Full Configuration (Continued)*

```
!
interface Serial0/0
 shutdown
!
interface Serial0/1
 ip address 131.108.3.1 255.255.255.252
 no ip directed-broadcast
 clockrate 128000
!
router rip
 version 2
 network 131.108.0.0
!
line con 0
 transport input none
line aux 0
line vty 0 4
end
```

Example 2-21 *R2 Full Configuration*

```
version 12.0
!
hostname R2
!
enable password cisco
no ip domain-lookup
!
interface Loopback0
 ip address 131.108.7.1 255.255.255.0
 no ip directed-broadcast
!
interface Loopback1
 ip address 131.108.8.1 255.255.255.0
 no ip directed-broadcast
!
interface Loopback2
 ip address 131.108.9.1 255.255.255.0
 no ip directed-broadcast
!
interface Ethernet0/0
 ip address 131.108.2.1 255.255.255.0
!
interface Serial1/0
shutdown
```

Example 2-21 *R2 Full Configuration (Continued)*

```
!
interface Serial1/1
 ip address 131.108.3.2 255.255.255.252
 ip directed-broadcast
!
interface Serial1/2
shutdown
!
interface Serial1/3
shutdown
!
router rip
 version 2
 network 131.108.0.0
!
line con 0
 exec-timeout 0 0
 transport input none
line aux 0
line vty 0 4
!
end
```

NOTE   In both cases, the command **no ip domain-lookup** is configured. This IOS command is a handy command to disable when you are studying on Cisco IOS routers. Every time you type an unknown command on a router in exec or priv mode, the router automatically queries the DNS server, which is time consuming and annoying. On R2, the extra serial interfaces are not configured and are in a shutdown state or are not enabled by default.

Scenario 2-2: Basic OSPF

In this scenario, you learn how to change the routing protocol to OSPF on both Routers R1 and R2. Figure 2-3 shows the network and areas you use for this scenario. You change the IP addresses as well to learn about VLSM. Leave the Ethernet segments with a Class C network to enable 254 hosts to attach to the router. Use a /30 mask on the serial link and host addressing or a /32 mask on all the loopbacks to conserve address space.

Figure 2-3   *Basic OSPF*

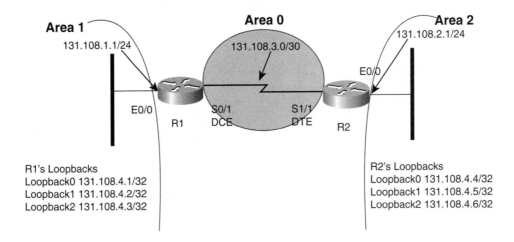

In this basic scenario, you configure three areas: 0, 1, and 2. Area 0 (or area 0.0.0.0) is the backbone; areas 1 and 2 cover the Ethernets on R1 and R2 and their respective loopbacks. As on all good OSPF networks, a backbone OSPF area 0 is configured. To enable OSPF, you need to perform the following steps:

Step 1   Enable the routing protocol with the command **router ospf** *process number*. The process number is significant to only the local router. You can run more than one process.

Step 2   Specify the networks on which OSPF will run and the area assignments. The IOS command to enable OSPF per interface is

   network *address wildcard-mask* **area** *area-id*

   The wildcard mask defines what networks are assigned; the area ID defines the OSPF area assignment.

Before you configure OSPF, renumber all interfaces and remove IP RIP with the command **no router rip**. Example 2-22 displays IP address changes and the removal of IP RIP.

Example 2-22   *IP Address Changes and Disabling IP RIP on R1*

```
R1(config)#int lo0
R1(config-if)#ip address 131.108.4.1 255.255.255.255
R1(config-if)#int lo1
R1(config-if)#ip address 131.108.4.2 255.255.255.255
R1(config-if)#int lo2
R1(config-if)#ip address 131.108.4.3 255.255.255.255
R1(config-if)#exit! it is not required to exit interface mode to remove RIP
R1(config)#no router rip
```

Example 2-23 displays the IP address changes and the removal of IP RIP on R2.

Example 2-23 *IP Address Change and Disabling IP RIP on R2*

```
R2(config)#int lo0
R2(config-if)#ip address 131.108.4.4 255.255.255.255
R2(config-if)#int lo1
R2(config-if)#ip address 131.108.4.5 255.255.255.255
R2(config-if)#int lo2
R2(config-if)#ip address 131.108.4.6 255.255.255.255
R2(config-if)#exit ! it is not required to exit interface mode to remove RIP
R2(config)#no router rip
```

Now that RIP is removed and the IP addressing is redone, configure R1 for OSPF by using the process number 1 and for R2 using process number 2. Example 2-24 and Example 2-25 display the new OSPF configurations on R1 and R2.

Example 2-24 *OSPF Configuration on R1*

```
R1(config)#router ospf 1
R1(config-router)#network 131.108.1.0 0.0.0.255 area 1
R1(config-router)#network 131.108.4.1 0.0.0.0 area 1
R1(config-router)#network 131.108.4.2 0.0.0.0 area 1
R1(config-router)#network 131.108.4.3 0.0.0.0 area 1
R1(config-router)#network 131.108.3.10 0.0.0.0 area 0
```

Example 2-25 *OSPF Configuration on R2*

```
R2(config)#router ospf 2
R2(config-router)#network 131.108.2.1 0.0.0.255 area 2
R2(config-router)#network 131.108.4.4 0.0.0.0 area 2
R2(config-router)#network 131.108.4.5 0.0.0.0 area 2
R2(config-router)#network 131.108.4.6 0.0.0.0 area 2
R2(config-router)#network 131.108.3.2 0.0.0.0 area 0
```

The wildcard mask 0.0.0.0 indicates an exact match. The wildcard mask 0.0.0.255 means the first three octets must match and the last octet does not matter. For example, the command **network 131.108.1.0 0.0.0.255** means 131.108.1.1 to 131.108.1.254 all match. In this case, you can configure any IP address in the range 131.108.1.1 to 131.108.1.254 to be in area 1 on R1 E0/0. Example 2-26 displays the IP routing table on R1.

Example 2-26 *IP Routing Table on R1*

```
       131.108.0.0/16 is variably subnetted, 9 subnets, 3 masks
C         131.108.4.3/32 is directly connected, Loopback2
C         131.108.4.2/32 is directly connected, Loopback1
C         131.108.4.1/32 is directly connected, Loopback0
```

continues

Example 2-26 *IP Routing Table on R1*

```
C       131.108.3.0/30 is directly connected, Serial0/1
O IA    131.108.4.6/32 [110/65] via 131.108.3.2, 00:01:29, Serial0/1
O IA    131.108.2.0/24 [110/74] via 131.108.3.2, 00:01:29, Serial0/1
O IA    131.108.4.5/32 [110/65] via 131.108.3.2, 00:01:29, Serial0/1
C       131.108.1.0/24 is directly connected, Ethernet0/0
O IA    131.108.4.4/32 [110/65] via 131.108.3.2, 00:01:29, Serial0/1
```

You can see from Example 2-26 that R1 discovers four remote networks (R2's Ethernet and three loopback interfaces) through OSPF. In addition, there are also the directly attached links.

R1 dynamically learns the remote networks on R2 through the next hop address of 131.108.3.2 and the outbound interface Serial 0/1. Notice once again the administrative distance and metric pairing. In the case of OSPF, the administrative distance is 110 (more trusted than RIP at 120) and the metric used by OSPF is cost. The left side indicates the routing type as O for OSPF. The IA (inter-area) indicates the remote network is part of another area, in this case area 2.

Example 2-27 uses the command **show ip route ospf** on Router R2 to display only the OSPF routes.

Example 2-27 *R2 OSPF Routing Table*

```
R2#show ip route ospf
     131.108.0.0/16 is variably subnetted, 9 subnets, 3 masks
O IA    131.108.4.3/32 [110/782] via 131.108.3.1, 00:43:09, Serial1/1
O IA    131.108.4.2/32 [110/782] via 131.108.3.1, 00:43:09, Serial1/1
O IA    131.108.4.1/32 [110/782] via 131.108.3.1, 00:43:09, Serial1/1
O IA    131.108.1.0/24 [110/791] via 131.108.3.1, 00:41:54, Serial1/1
R2#
```

Example 2-28 and Example 2-29 display the complete configurations for R1 and R2 for your reference.

Example 2-28 *28 R1 Full Configuration*

```
version 12.0
!
hostname R1
!
enable password cisco
!
ip subnet-zero
no ip domain-lookup
!
interface Loopback0
 ip address 131.108.4.1 255.255.255.255
 no ip directed-broadcast
```

Example 2-28 *28 R1 Full Configuration (Continued)*

```
!
interface Loopback1
 ip address 131.108.4.2 255.255.255.255
 no ip directed-broadcast
!
interface Loopback2
 ip address 131.108.4.3 255.255.255.255
 no ip directed-broadcast
!
interface Ethernet0/0
 ip address 131.108.1.1 255.255.255.0
 no ip directed-broadcast
!
interface Serial0/0
 shutdown
!
interface Serial0/1
 ip address 131.108.3.1 255.255.255.252
 clockrate 128000
!
router ospf 1
 network 131.108.1.0 0.0.0.255 area 1
 network 131.108.3.1 0.0.0.0 area 0
 network 131.108.4.1 0.0.0.0 area 1
 network 131.108.4.2 0.0.0.0 area 1
 network 131.108.4.3 0.0.0.0 area 1
!
router rip
 version 2
 network 131.108.0.0
!
ip classless
!
line con 0
line aux 0
line vty 0 4
end
```

Example 2-29 *R2 Full Configuration*

```
!
hostname R2
!
enable password cisco
!
no ip domain-lookup
interface Loopback0
 ip address 131.108.4.4 255.255.255.255
```

continues

Example 2-29 *R2 Full Configuration (Continued)*

```
!
interface Loopback1
 ip address 131.108.4.5 255.255.255.255
!
interface Loopback2
 ip address 131.108.4.6 255.255.255.255
!
interface Ethernet0/0
 ip address 131.108.2.1 255.255.255.0
!
interface Serial1/0
 shutdown
!
interface Serial1/1
 ip address 131.108.3.2 255.255.255.252
!
interface Serial1/2
shutdown
!
interface Serial1/3
shutdown
!
router ospf 2
 network 131.108.2.0 0.0.0.255 area 2
 network 131.108.3.2 0.0.0.0 area 0
 network 131.108.4.4 0.0.0.0 area 2
 network 131.108.4.5 0.0.0.0 area 2
 network 131.108.4.6 0.0.0.0 area 2
!
router rip
 version 2
 network 131.108.0.0
!
ip classless
!
line con 0
 exec-timeout 0 0
 transport input none
line aux 0
line vty 0 4
 no login
!
end
```

Scenario 2-3: Basic IGRP

This scenario is designed to introduce you to the basics of IGRP and EIGRP configurations.

Once more, revisit the two-router scenario. IGRP is a classful routing protocol, so you have to change the IP addressing back to a non-VLSM network. In this scenario, you use a different class address as well. Figure 2-4 displays the network topology and IP addressing scheme.

Figure 2-4 *Basic IGRP/EIGRP Network*

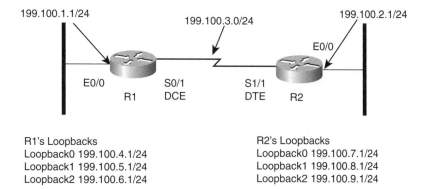

This scenario starts with IGRP and then changes the routing protocol to EIGRP.

In this basic scenario, you configure the two routers R1 and R2 for IGRP using the same administrative domain. To share information between routers in IGRP, you need to config-ure the same administrative domain. To enable IGRP, you need to perform the following steps:

Step 1   Use the command **router igrp** *administrative domain* to enable the routing protocol. The administrative domain must be the same for routers that are under a common administrative control or the same network.

Step 2   You then specify the networks on which IGRP runs. As with IP RIP, you need to specify only the major class network.

Use the Class C network 199.100.1.0/24 through to 199.100.9.0/24. Example 2-30 displays the IP address changes made to Router R1.

Example 2-30 *IP Addressing on R1*

```
R1(config)#int e 0/0
R1(config-if)#ip address 199.100.1.1 255.255.255.0
R1(config-if)#int lo0
```

continues

Example 2-30 *IP Addressing on R1 (Continued)*

```
R1(config-if)#ip address 199.100.4.1 255.255.255.0
R1(config-if)#int lo1
R1(config-if)#ip address 199.100.5.1 255.255.255.0
R1(config-if)#int lo2
R1(config-if)#ip address 199.100.6.1 255.255.255.0
R1(config-if)#int s0/1
R1(config-if)#ip address 199.100.3.1 255.255.255.0
```

Example 2-31 displays the IP address changes made to router R2.

Example 2-31 *IP Addressing on R2*

```
R2(config)#int e 0/0
R2(config-if)#ip address 199.100.2.1 255.255.255.0
R2(config-if)#int lo0
R2(config-if)#ip address 199.100.7.1 255.255.255.0
R2(config-if)#int lo1
R2(config-if)#ip address 199.100.8.1 255.255.255.0
R2(config-if)#int lo2
R2(config-if)#ip address 199.100.9.1 255.255.255.0
R2(config-if)#int s1/1
R2(config-if)#ip address 199.100.3.2 255.255.255.0
```

Example 2-32 displays the IOS commands required to enable IGRP in AS 1.

NOTE   When using a class C network with the default class C mask, you must specify each network in IGRP.

Example 2-32 *IP Addressing on R1*

```
R1(config)#router igrp 1
R1(config-router)#network 199.100.1.0
R1(config-router)#network 199.100.4.0
R1(config-router)#network 199.100.3.0
R1(config-router)#network 199.100.5.0
R1(config-router)#network 199.100.6.0
```

Example 2-33 similarly displays the IGRP commands configured on R2.

Example 2-33 *IP Addressing on R2*

```
R2(config)#router igrp 1
R2(config-router)#network 199.100.2.0
R2(config-router)#network 199.100.3.0
R2(config-router)#network 199.100.7.0
R2(config-router)#network 199.100.8.0
R2(config-router)#network 199.100.9.0
```

Example 2-34 now displays the IP routing table on R1.

Example 2-34 *R1 IP Routing Table*

```
R1#show ip route
Gateway of last resort is not set
I     199.100.9.0/24 [100/8976] via 199.100.3.2, 00:00:46, Serial0/1
I     199.100.8.0/24 [100/8976] via 199.100.3.2, 00:00:46, Serial0/1
C     199.100.3.0/24 is directly connected, Serial0/1
I     199.100.2.0/24 [100/8576] via 199.100.3.2, 00:00:46, Serial0/1
C     199.100.1.0/24 is directly connected, Ethernet0/0
I     199.100.7.0/24 [100/8976] via 199.100.3.2, 00:00:47, Serial0/1
C     199.100.6.0/24 is directly connected, Loopback2
C     199.100.5.0/24 is directly connected, Loopback1
C     199.100.4.0/24 is directly connected, Loopback0
```

On R1, you can see four remote IGRP networks learned through the next hop address 199.100.3.2 (R1's link to R2) and through the outbound interface Serial 0/1.

R1 dynamically learns the remote networks on R2 through the next hop address of 131.108.3.2 and the outbound interface Serial 0/1. Notice the administrative distance and metric pairing. In the case of IGRP, the administrative distance is 100 (more trusted than RIP at 120 and OSPF at 110) and the metric IGRP uses is called a composite metric. The left side indicates the routing type as I for IGRP.

NOTE   The calculation for a composite metric is as follows:

Composite metric = K1 x bandwidth + (K2 x bandwidth) / (256 – load) + K3 x delay

The values K1 through K5 are constants. If the defaults are used, K1 = K3 = 1 and K2 = K4 = K5 = 0.

Values K1 through K5 can be configured with nondefaults with the IOS command **metric weights** *tos k1 k2 k3 k4 k5*, where type of service must be zero.

If K5 is not zero, the formula is as follows:

$IGRP_{metric}$ = Metric x [K5 / (reliability + K4)].

Typically, the formula with K2 = K4 = K5 = 0, K1 = K3 = 1 is as follows:

IGRP composite metric = bandwidth + delay

Example 2-35 and Example 2-36 display the full configurations for R1 and R2, respectively.

Example 2-35 *Full Configuration for R1*

```
hostname R1
!
enable password cisco
!
ip subnet-zero
no ip domain-lookup
!
interface Loopback0
 ip address 199.100.4.1 255.255.255.0
 no ip directed-broadcast
!
interface Loopback1
 ip address 199.100.5.1 255.255.255.0
 no ip directed-broadcast
!
interface Loopback2
 ip address 199.100.6.1 255.255.255.0
 no ip directed-broadcast
!
interface Ethernet0/0
 ip address 199.100.1.1 255.255.255.0
 no ip directed-broadcast
!
interface Serial0/0
 shutdown
!
interface Serial0/1
 ip address 199.100.3.1 255.255.255.0
 clockrate 128000
!
router igrp 1
 network 199.100.1.0
 network 199.100.3.0
 network 199.100.4.0
 network 199.100.5.0
 network 199.100.6.0
```

Example 2-35 *Full Configuration for R1 (Continued)*

```
!
ip classless
!
line con 0
 transport input none
line aux 0
line vty 0 4
 no login
!
end
```

Example 2-36 *Full Configuration for R2*

```
Current configuration:
!
version 12.0
!
service timestamps log uptime
no service password-encryption
!
hostname R2
!
enable password c
!
ip subnet-zero
no ip domain-lookup
frame-relay switching
!
interface Loopback0
 ip address 199.100.7.1 255.255.255.0
 no ip directed-broadcast
!
interface Loopback1
 ip address 199.100.8.1 255.255.255.0
 no ip directed-broadcast
!
interface Loopback2
 ip address 199.100.9.1 255.255.255.0
 no ip directed-broadcast
!
interface Ethernet0/0
 ip address 199.100.2.1 255.255.255.0
 no ip directed-broadcast
 no cdp enable
```

continues

Example 2-36 *Full Configuration for R2 (Continued)*

```
!
interface TokenRing0/0
 no ip address
 no ip directed-broadcast
 shutdown
 ring-speed 16
 no cdp enable
!
interface Serial1/0
shutdown
!
interface Serial1/1
 ip address 199.100.3.2 255.255.255.0
 ip directed-broadcast
!
interface Serial1/2
shutdown
!
interface Serial1/3
shutdown
!
router igrp 1
 network 199.100.2.0
 network 199.100.3.0
 network 199.100.7.0
 network 199.100.8.0
 network 199.100.9.0
!
no ip classless
!
line con 0
 exec-timeout 0 0
 transport input none
line aux 0
line vty 0 4
end
```

Now remove IGRP and use EIGRP instead. To configure EIGRP, you simply enable the routing protocol and define the networks. EIGRP enables network summarization by default. That is, the default mask is assumed, or a classful network is assumed. Also, the metric EIGRP uses is the same as the metric IGRP uses, but it is multiplied by 256. You can use the command **no auto-summary** to disable automatic summarization. EIGRP also supports VLSM. Figure 2-5 shows the sample network for this EIGRP example.

Figure 2-5   *EIGRP Configuration*

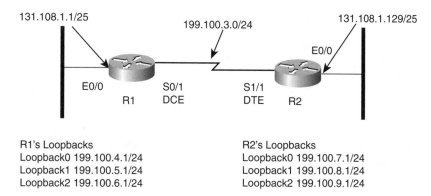

131.108.1.1/25   199.100.3.0/24   131.108.1.129/25

E0/0   S0/1   S1/1
R1   DCE   DTE   R2

E0/0

R1's Loopbacks
Loopback0 199.100.4.1/24
Loopback1 199.100.5.1/24
Loopback2 199.100.6.1/24

R2's Loopbacks
Loopback0 199.100.7.1/24
Loopback1 199.100.8.1/24
Loopback2 199.100.9.1/24

Modify the Ethernet segments on R1 and R2 to use a different class address of 131.108.1.0/25 and 131.108.1.128/25, respectively. Example 2-37 displays the removal of IGRP and the enabling of EIGRP in AS 1 on Router R1.

Example 2-37 *Configuring EIGRP on R1*

```
R1(config)#no router igrp 1
!remove igrp 1
R1(config)#router eigrp 1
!enable EIGRP in AS 1
R1(config-router)#network 131.108.1.0
!define network in eigrp
R1(config-router)#network 199.100.4.0
R1(config-router)#network  199.100.5.0
R1(config-router)#network 199.100.6.0
R2(config-router)#network 131.108.1.0
R1(config-router)#network 199.9.3.0
R1(config-router)#int e 0/0
! change IP address on R1 e0/0
R1(config-if)#ip address 131.108.1.1 255.255.255.128
```

Example 2-38 displays the removal of IGRP and the enabling of EIGRP in AS 1 on Router R2.

Example 2-38 *Configuring EIGRP on R2*

```
R2(config)#no router igrp 1
R2(config)#router eigrp 1
R2(config-router)#exit
R2(config)#int e 0/0
```

continues

Example 2-38 *Configuring EIGRP on R2*

```
R2(config-if)#ip address 131.108.1.129 255.255.255.128
R2(config-if)#router eigrp 1
R2(config-router)#network 199.100.7.0
R2(config-router)#network  199.100.8.0
R2(config-router)#network 199.100.9.0
R2(config-router)#network 131.108.1.0
R2(config-router)#network 199.9.3.0
```

Notice IGRP is removed first and the AS number is the same in R1 and R2 so that both routers can share information. You have not disabled automatic summarization yet. Now view R1's EIGRP routing table, as displayed in Example 2-39.

Example 2-39 *R1's IP Routing Table*

```
R1#show ip route eigrp
D      199.100.9.0/24 [90/2297856] via 199.100.3.2, 00:00:55, Serial0/1
D      199.100.8.0/24 [90/2297856] via 199.100.3.2, 00:00:55, Serial0/1
       131.108.0.0/16 is variably subnetted, 2 subnets, 2 masks
D         131.108.0.0/16 is a summary, 00:00:55, Null0
D      199.100.7.0/24 [90/2297856] via 199.100.3.2, 00:00:55, Serial0/1
R1#
```

On R1, you can see four remote EIGRP networks learned through the next hop address 199.100.3.2 (R1's link to R2) and through the outbound interface Serial 0/1. One of these routes is to null0. R1 dynamically learns the remote networks on R2 through the next hop address of 199.100.3.2 and the outbound interface Serial 0/1. Notice the administrative distance and metric pairing. In the case of EIGRP, the administrative distance is 90 (more trusted than RIP at 120, OSPF at 110, and IGRP at 100), and the metric EIGRP uses is 256 times that of IGRP. The left side indicates the routing type as D for EIGRP. You'll also see D EX, which means redistributed into an EIGRP domain.

The remote network 131.108.1.128/25 has no entry because R1 has a locally connected subnet 131.108.1.0/25. You can also see that all routes for 131.108.0.0/16 are sent to null0, short for the bit bucket, or discarded. Now, ping the remote network 131.108.1.129/25 from R1. Example 2-40 displays a sample ping from Router R1.

Example 2-40 *Ping Request from R1*

```
R1#ping 131.108.1.129

Type escape sequence to abort.
Sending 5, 100-byte ICMP Echos to 131.108.1.130, timeout is 2 seconds:
. . . . .
Success rate is 0 percent (0/5)
R1#
```

The response from the router in Example 2-40 is no reply (....) or, in this case, the packets are sent to null0. Packets sent to null0 are discarded.

To solve the problem of packets being discarded, you need to disable automatic summarization. Configure R1 and R2 to disable automatic summarization as in Example 2-41.

Example 2-41 *Disabling Automatic Summarization on R1 and R2*

```
R1(config)#router eigrp 1
R1(config-router)#no auto-summary

R2(config)#router eigrp 1
R2(config-router)#no auto-summary
```

Example 2-42 now displays R1's EIGRP routing table and a sample ping request to the remote network 131.108.1.129.

Example 2-42 **show ip route eigrp** *on R1*

```
R1#show ip route eigrp
D     199.100.9.0/24 [90/2297856] via 199.100.3.2, 00:00:01, Serial0/1
D     199.100.8.0/24 [90/2297856] via 199.100.3.2, 00:00:01, Serial0/1
      131.108.0.0/25 is subnetted, 2 subnets
D        131.108.1.128 [90/2195456] via 199.100.3.2, 00:00:01, Serial0/1
D     199.100.7.0/24 [90/2297856] via 199.100.3.2, 00:00:01, Serial0/1
R1#ping 131.108.1.129

Type escape sequence to abort.
Sending 5, 100-byte ICMP Echos to 131.108.1.129, timeout is 2 seconds:
!!!!!
Success rate is 100 percent (5/5), round-trip min/avg/max = 16/16/16 ms
R1#
```

Notice that the 131.108.1.128/25 is inserted and there is a successful ping from R1 to R2 Ethernet interface. It is vital you understand these simple topics, such as classful and classless, fixed-length variable subnet masks (FLSMs) and VLSM.

Example 2-43 and Example 2-44 display the full configurations for R1 and R2, respectively, using EIGRP.

Example 2-43 *R1 Full Configuration*

```
version 12.0
!
service timestamps log uptime
no service password-encryption
```

continues

Example 2-43 *R1 Full Configuration (Continued)*

```
!
hostname R1
!
enable password cisco
!
ip subnet-zero
no ip domain-lookup
!
interface Loopback0
 ip address 199.100.4.1 255.255.255.0
 no ip directed-broadcast
!
interface Loopback1
 ip address 199.100.5.1 255.255.255.0
 no ip directed-broadcast
!
interface Loopback2
 ip address 199.100.6.1 255.255.255.0
 no ip directed-broadcast
!
interface Ethernet0/0
 ip address 131.108.1.1 255.255.255.128
 no ip directed-broadcast
!
interface Serial0/0
 shutdown
!
interface Serial0/1
 ip address 199.100.3.1 255.255.255.0
 no ip directed-broadcast
 clockrate 128000
!
router eigrp 1
 network 131.108.0.0
 network 199.100.3.0
 network 199.100.4.0
 network 199.100.5.0
 network 199.100.6.0
 no auto-summary
!
ip classless
!
line con 0
 transport input none
line aux 0
line vty 0 4
 no login
!
end
```

Example 2-44 *R2 Full Configuration*

```
version 12.0
!
service timestamps log uptime
no service password-encryption
!
hostname R2
!
enable password cisco
!
no ip domain-lookup
interface Loopback0
 ip address 199.100.7.1 255.255.255.0
 no ip directed-broadcast
!
interface Loopback1
 ip address 199.100.8.1 255.255.255.0
 no ip directed-broadcast
!
interface Loopback2
 ip address 199.100.9.1 255.255.255.0
 no ip directed-broadcast
!
interface Ethernet0/0
 ip address 131.108.1.129 255.255.255.128
 no ip directed-broadcast
 no cdp enable
!
interface Serial1/0
shutdown
!
interface Serial1/1
 ip address 199.100.3.2 255.255.255.0
 ip directed-broadcast
!
interface Serial1/2
shutdown
!
interface Serial1/3
shutdown
!
router eigrp 1
 network 131.108.0.0
 network 199.100.3.0
 network 199.100.7.0
 network 199.100.8.0
 network 199.100.9.0
 no auto-summary
```

continues

Example 2-44 *R2 Full Configuration (Continued)*

```
!
no ip classless
!
line con 0
line aux 0
line vty 0 4
!
end
```

Scenario 2-4: Basic EIGRP

This scenario covers another simple example of routing between classless and classful networks. Here, you need to perform redistribution from one routing protocol to another. This simple two-router example uses the same class network and IGRP and OSPF. It is easier to understand this scenario if you use the same Class B address 131.108.0.0.

Figure 2-6 displays the OSPF/IGRP topology and the IP addressing scheme in place between R1 and R2.

Figure 2-6   *IGRP/OSPF Topology*

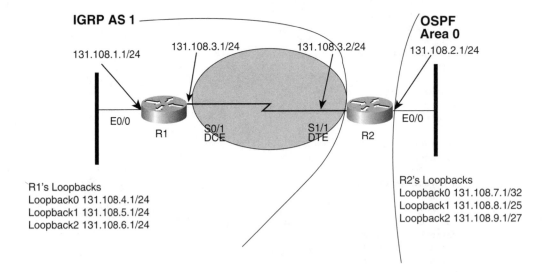

Example 2-45 and Example 2-46 display the IP addressing changes to R1 and R2, respectively.

Example 2-45 *R1 IP Address Changes*

```
R1(config)#int lo0
R1(config-if)#ip address 131.108.4.1 255.255.255.0
R1(config-if)#int lo1
R1(config-if)#ip address 131.108.5.1 255.255.255.0
R1(config-if)#int lo2
R1(config-if)#ip address 131.108.6.1 255.255.255.0
R1(config-if)#int e 0/0
R1(config-if)#ip address 131.108.1.1 255.255.255.0
R1(config-if)#int s 0/1
R1(config-if)#ip address 131.108.3.1 255.255.255.0
```

Example 2-46 *R2 IP Address Changes*

```
R2(config)#int lo0
R2(config-if)#ip address 131.108.7.1 255.255.255.255
R2(config-if)#int lo1
R2(config-if)#ip address 131.108.8.1 255.255.255.128
R2(config-if)#int lo2
R2(config-if)#ip address 131.108.9.1 255.255.255.224
R2(config-if)#int e 0/0
R2(config-if)#ip address 131.108.8.129 255.255.255.128
R2(config-if)#int s 0/0
R2(config-if)#ip address 131.108.3.2 255.255.255.0
```

On R1, configure IGRP; again IGRP is classful, so you need to enable IGRP only in AS 1. R2 runs both IGRP and OSPF; hence redistribution is required. Example 2-47 enables IGRP in AS 1 on R1.

Example 2-47 *Enabling IGRP on R1*

```
R1(config)#router igrp 1
R1(config-router)#network 131.108.0.0
```

On R2, configure IGRP and OSPF. Example 2-48 enables IGRP in AS 1 and OSPF with a process ID of 1.

Example 2-48 *Enabling IGRP on R1*

```
R2(config)#router igrp 1
R2(config-router)#network 131.108.0.0
```

continues

Example 2-48 *Enabling IGRP on R1 (Continued)*

```
R2(config)#router ospf 1
R2(config-router)#network 131.108.8.0 0.0.0.255 area 0
R2(config-router)#network 131.108.7.1 0.0.0.0 area 0
R2(config-router)#network 131.108.9.1 0.0.0.0 area 0
R2(config-router)#no network 131.108.8.0 0.0.0.255 area 0
R2(config-router)#network 131.108.8.1 0.0.0.0 area 0
R2(config-router)#network 131.108.8.129 0.0.0.0 area 0
```

You also need to configure redistribution on R2 so that R1 discovers the OSPF interfaces through IGRP. (R1 is running only IGRP.)

On R2, configure IGRP to redistribute the OSPF interfaces into IGRP. As with any form of redistribution, you must use the metric that the routing protocol you are redistributing into uses. IGRP does not use OSPF cost but uses a composite metric. Therefore, you need to define values so that IGRP has a valid metric. Follow the prompts, as in Example 2-49, using the **?** character to discover which metric IGRP requires. You need to advise R1 of the bandwidth (128 kbps), delay (20000 ms), reliability (1 is low, 255 is 100 percent loaded), loading (1 out of 255, 255 being 100 percent loaded), and finally the MTU (1500 bytes). Example 2-49 displays the redistribution and also displays the various options the Cisco IOS Software requires.

Example 2-49 *Enabling Redistribution on R2*

```
R2(config-router)#router igrp 1

R2(config-router)#redistribute ospf 1 metric ?
  <1-4294967295>  Bandwidth metric in Kbits per second

R2(config-router)#redistribute ospf 1 metric 128 ?
  <0-4294967295>  IGRP delay metric, in 10 microsecond units

R2(config-router)#redistribute ospf 1 metric 128 20000 ?
  <0-255>  IGRP reliability metric where 255 is 100% reliable

R2(config-router)#redistribute ospf 1 metric 128 20000 255 ?
  <1-255>  IGRP Effective bandwidth metric (Loading) where 255 is 100% loaded

R2(config-router)#redistribute ospf 1 metric 128 20000 255 1 ?
  <1-4294967295>  IGRP MTU of the path
R2(config-router)#redistribute ospf 1 metric 128 20000 255 1 150
```

Look on R1 and R2 to find which IP networks have been discovered. Example 2-50 displays R1's IP routing table.

Example 2-50 *IP Routing Table on R1*

```
R1#show ip route
     131.108.0.0/24 is subnetted, 5 subnets
C       131.108.6.0 is directly connected, Loopback2
C       131.108.5.0 is directly connected, Loopback1
C       131.108.4.0 is directly connected, Loopback0
C       131.108.3.0 is directly connected, Serial0/1
C       131.108.1.0 is directly connected, Ethernet0/0
```

Example 2-51 displays R2's IP routing table.

Example 2-51 *IP Routing Table on R2*

```
R2#show ip route
C    199.100.8.0/24 is directly connected, Loopback1
     131.108.0.0/16 is variably subnetted, 8 subnets, 4 masks
C       131.108.8.128/25 is directly connected, Ethernet0/0
C       131.108.8.0/27 is directly connected, Loopback2
I       131.108.6.0/24 [100/80625] via 131.108.3.1, 00:00:52, Serial1/1
C       131.108.7.1/32 is directly connected, Loopback0
I       131.108.5.0/24 [100/80625] via 131.108.3.1, 00:00:52, Serial1/1
I       131.108.4.0/24 [100/80625] via 131.108.3.1, 00:00:52, Serial1/1
C       131.108.3.0/24 is directly connected, Serial1/1
I       131.108.1.0/24 [100/80225] via 131.108.3.1, 00:00:53, Serial1/1
R2#
```

On R1 in Example 2-50, you only see the directly connected routes, but on R2, you see the remote routes from R1. Why is this so? This scenario is a typical routing problem caused by the lack of understanding between VLSM and FLSM. IGRP on R1 is configured using a /24 bit subnet in all interfaces. On R2, you have applied a number of non-/24 subnets. You need to trick R1 into believing that all these networks are indeed /24 bit subnets by using summarization techniques on R2.

To perform summarization from OSPF to IGRP, use the following command:

```
summary-address address mask
```

For example, to summarize the loopbacks and Ethernet on R2 as /24 bits to R1, perform the commands in Example 2-52 under the OSPF process. Example 2-52 displays the IOS configuration to enable the summary of the three networks on R2.

Example 2-52 *Enabling Redistribution on R2*

```
R2(config)#router ospf 1
R2(config-router)#summary-address 131.108.7.0 255.255.255.0
R2(config-router)#summary-address 131.108.8.0 255.255.255.0
R2(config-router)#summary-address 131.108.9.0 255.255.255.0
```

Look at R1's routing table now. Example 2-53 displays the IP routing table on R1.

Example 2-53 *R1's IP Routing Table*

```
R1#show ip route

     131.108.0.0/24 is subnetted, 5 subnets
C       131.108.6.0 is directly connected, Loopback2
C       131.108.5.0 is directly connected, Loopback1
C       131.108.4.0 is directly connected, Loopback0
C       131.108.3.0 is directly connected, Serial0/1
C       131.108.1.0 is directly connected, Ethernet0/0
```

Still there are no routing entries. Can you think why IGRP on R1 is still not aware of the remote networks on R2? The problem is that OSPF assumes that only a nonsubnetted network will be sent. For example, in this case, you are using the Class B network 131.108.0.0. You also need to use the command **redistributed connected subnets** to advise OSPF to send subnetted networks.

NOTE   An alternative to using summarization in this scenario is static or default routes.

Example 2-54 displays the configuration required so that OSPF redistributes the Class B subnetted networks.

Example 2-54 *Redistribution on R2*

```
R2(config)#router ospf 1
R2(config-router)#redistribute connected subnets
```

Example 2-55 now displays R1's routing table.

Example 2-55 *R1's IP Routing Table*

```
R1#show ip route
      131.108.0.0/24 is subnetted, 8 subnets
I        131.108.9.0 [100/100125] via 131.108.3.2, 00:00:23, Serial0/1
I        131.108.8.0 [100/100125] via 131.108.3.2, 00:00:23, Serial0/1
I        131.108.7.0 [100/100125] via 131.108.3.2, 00:00:23, Serial0/1
C        131.108.6.0 is directly connected, Loopback2
C        131.108.5.0 is directly connected, Loopback1
C        131.108.4.0 is directly connected, Loopback0
C        131.108.3.0 is directly connected, Serial0/1
C        131.108.1.0 is directly connected, Ethernet0/0
R1#
```

The remote subnets 131.108.7–9 now appear on R1 (shaded in Example 2-55).

Example 2-56 and Example 2-57 display the full configurations on Routers R1 and R2.

Example 2-56 *R1 Full Configuration*

```
version 12.0
!
service timestamps log uptime
no service password-encryption
!
hostname R1
!
enable password cisco
!
ip subnet-zero
no ip domain-lookup
!
interface Loopback0
 ip address 131.108.4.1 255.255.255.0
 no ip directed-broadcast
!
interface Loopback1
 ip address 131.108.5.1 255.255.255.0
 no ip directed-broadcast
!
interface Loopback2
 ip address 131.108.6.1 255.255.255.0
 no ip directed-broadcast
!
interface Ethernet0/0
 ip address 131.108.1.1 255.255.255.0
!
interface Serial0/0
 shutdown
```

continues

Example 2-56 *R1 Full Configuration (Continued)*

```
!
interface Serial0/1
 ip address 131.108.3.1 255.255.255.0
 no ip directed-broadcast
 clockrate 128000
!
router igrp 1
 network 131.108.0.0
!
ip classless
!
line con 0
 transport input none
line aux 0
line vty 0 4

end
```

Example 2-57 *R2 Full Configuration*

```
version 12.0
!
service timestamps log uptime
no service password-encryption
!
hostname R2
!
enable password cisco
!
no ip domain-lookup
interface Loopback0
 ip address 131.108.7.1 255.255.255.255
!
interface Loopback1
 ip address 131.108.8.1 255.255.255.128
interface Loopback2
 ip address 131.108.9.1 255.255.255.224
!
interface Ethernet0/0
 ip address 131.108.8.129 255.255.255.128
!
interface Serial1/0
shutdown
!
interface Serial1/1
 ip address 131.108.3.2 255.255.255.0
 ip directed-broadcast
!
interface Serial1/2
shutdown
```

Example 2-57 *R2 Full Configuration (Continued)*

```
!
interface Serial1/3
shutdown
!
router ospf 1
redistribute connected subnets
 summary-address 131.108.8.0 255.255.255.0
 summary-address 131.108.7.0 255.255.255.0
 summary-address 131.108.9.0 255.255.255.0
 redistribute igrp 1 metric 1 subnets
 network 131.108.7.1 0.0.0.0 area 0
 network 131.108.8.1 0.0.0.0 area 0
 network 131.108.8.129 0.0.0.0 area 0
 network 131.108.9.1 0.0.0.0 area 0
!
router igrp 1
 redistribute ospf 1 metric 128 20000 255 1 1500
 passive-interface Ethernet0/0
!Stop IGRP sending out updates to E0/0 and similarly lo0/1/2 because we are running
!OSPF on these interfaces.
 passive-interface Loopback0
 passive-interface Loopback1
 passive-interface Loopback2
 network 131.108.0.0
!
ip classless
!
line con 0
 exec-timeout 0 0
 transport input none
line aux 0
line vty 0 4
end
```

The R2 routing table is more complicated. Example 2-58 shows R2's routing table.

Example 2-58 *show ip route* *on R2*

```
     131.108.0.0/16 is variably subnetted, 12 subnets, 4 masks
C       131.108.8.128/25 is directly connected, Ethernet0/0
O       131.108.9.0/24 is a summary, 00:04:59, Null0
C       131.108.9.0/27 is directly connected, Loopback2
O       131.108.8.0/24 is a summary, 00:04:59, Null0
C       131.108.8.0/25 is directly connected, Loopback1
O       131.108.7.0/24 is a summary, 00:04:59, Null0
I       131.108.6.0/24 [100/80625] via 131.108.3.1, 00:00:38, Serial1/1
C       131.108.7.1/32 is directly connected, Loopback0
I       131.108.5.0/24 [100/80625] via 131.108.3.1, 00:00:38, Serial1/1
I       131.108.4.0/24 [100/80625] via 131.108.3.1, 00:00:39, Serial1/1
C       131.108.3.0/24 is directly connected, Serial1/1
I       131.108.1.0/24 [100/80225] via 131.108.3.1, 00:00:39, Serial1/1
```

Notice the two entries for the same network sent to null0, or the bit bucket. The longest match rule applies on all routers; so for example, when an IP packet arrives for the network 131.108.8.129, the IP routing entry sends that to the directly connected interface E0/0. Similarly, if a pack arrives for network 131.108.8.0/25, the packet is sent to the directly connected loopback 1 interface. This is commonly known as the longest match rule.

Scenario 2-5: Using the show, ping, trace, and debug Commands

The previous four scenarios covered four relatively easy networks. This scenario shows you how to use common show and debug techniques and **ping** and **trace** commands to determine why routing entries are missing, for example, or why some networks are unreachable. To see a real-life scenario using two routers, refer to Scenario 2-3 and view some of the output from the **show** and **debug** commands. This scenario also displays some simple ping and trace tests. All **show**, **ping**, **trace**, and **debug** commands are taken from Figure 2-6 in the previous scenario.

You are familiar with the command **show ip route** from the previous scenarios, so start with that command on R1 from Figure 2-6. Here, you are only interested in IGRP learned routes. Example 2-59 displays only IGRP routes.

Example 2-59 *R1's IGRP Routes*

```
R1#show ip route igrp
     131.108.0.0/24 is subnetted, 8 subnets
I       131.108.9.0 [100/100125] via 131.108.3.2, 00:01:01, Serial0/1
I       131.108.8.0 [100/100125] via 131.108.3.2, 00:01:01, Serial0/1
I       131.108.7.0 [100/100125] via 131.108.3.2, 00:01:01, Serial0/1
```

Almost all troubleshooting techniques involve the **ping** command. Ping is a simple tool that sends an ICMP-request packet to the remote network and back. A successful ping receives an ICMP-reply. Example 2-60 displays a sample ping from R1 to R2 and the three remote networks: 131.108.7.1, 131.108.8.1, and 131.108.9.1.

Example 2-60 *Ping Tests from R1 to R2*

```
R1#ping 131.108.7.1
Type escape sequence to abort.
Sending 5, 100-byte ICMP Echos to 131.108.7.1, timeout is 2 seconds:
!!!!!
Success rate is 100 percent (5/5), round-trip min/avg/max = 16/16/16 ms
R1#ping 131.108.8.1
Type escape sequence to abort.
Sending 5, 100-byte ICMP Echos to 131.108.8.1, timeout is 2 seconds:
!!!!!
Success rate is 100 percent (5/5), round-trip min/avg/max = 16/16/16 ms
```

Example 2-60 *Ping Tests from R1 to R2 (Continued)*

```
R1#ping 131.108.1.1
Type escape sequence to abort.
Sending 5, 100-byte ICMP Echos to 131.108.1.1, timeout is 2 seconds:
!!!!!
Success rate is 100 percent (5/5), round-trip min/avg/max = 1/1/4 ms
R1#
```

This is an example of the standard **ping** command. At times, an extended **ping** is required. The extended **ping** enables you to provide the Cisco IOS with more parameters, such as the source address, the number of packets to send, the size of the datagram, and the timeout. The extended **ping** is a useful tool when users are complaining, for example, that when they FTP large files, the data is not transferred or a particular network of users cannot reach a remote destination.

Example 2-61 is an example of an extended **ping** using the source address 131.108.1.1/24 (the Ethernet address of R1), a modified repeat count of 10, a default datagram size of 100 bytes, and a timeout of 2 seconds. To use the extended **ping** command, simply type **ping**, press **Return**, and the options appear. Example 2-61 also displays the options in an extended **ping**.

Example 2-61 *Extended **ping** Request on R1*

```
R1#ping
Protocol [ip]:
Target IP address: 131.108.8.129
Repeat count [5]: 10
Datagram size [100]:
Timeout in seconds [2]:
Extended commands [n]: y
Source address or interface: 131.108.1.1
Type of service [0]:
Set DF bit in IP header? [no]:
Validate reply data? [no]:
Data pattern [0xABCD]:
Loose, Strict, Record, Timestamp, Verbose[none]:
Sweep range of sizes [n]:
Type escape sequence to abort.
Sending 10, 100-byte ICMP Echos to 131.108.8.129, timeout is 2 seconds:
!!!!!!!!!!
Success rate is 100 percent (10/10), round-trip min/avg/max = 16/16/16 ms
R1#
```

Table 2-5 describes the possible output of a ping.

Table 2-5   *Ping Output Symbols*

Output	Description
!	Each exclamation point indicates receipt of a reply.
.	Each period indicates the network server timed out while waiting for a reply.
U	A destination unreachable error was received.
C	A congestion-experienced packet was received.
I	User interrupted test.
?	Unknown packet type.
&	Packet lifetime exceeded.

Table 2-6 describes the parameters of the extended **ping** command.

Table 2-6   *Extended Ping Parameters*

Parameter	Description
Protocol [ip]:	Supports the following protocols (not just **ip**): **appletalk**, **clns**, **ip**, **novell**, **apollo**, **vines**, **decnet**, or **xns**. The default parameter is **ip** so you can simply press **Return**.
Target IP address:	Prompts for the IP address or host name of the destination node you plan to ping. The default value is **none**.
Repeat count [5]:	Number of ping packets sent to the destination address. The default value is **5**. The maximum is **2147483647**.
Datagram size [100]:	Size of the ping packet (in bytes). The default is **100** bytes. The range of values allowed is between **1** and **2147483647** bytes.
Timeout in seconds [2]:	Timeout interval. The default is **2** (seconds). The range is between **0** and **3600**.
Extended commands [n]:	Specifies whether a series of additional commands appears. If you enter **y** for yes, you are prompted for the following information. (The default is **no**.)
Sweep range of sizes [n]:	Enables you to vary the sizes of the echo packets being sent. This parameter determines the minimum MTU size configured along the network path from source to destination. This is typically used to determine whether packet fragmentation is causing network problems.

NOTE	To terminate a large ping test, within a few seconds, type the escape sequence, which is **Ctrl+Shift-^** followed by **x**.

Look at a simulated network failure to determine what's wrong with a remote network. View R1 IGRP routing table when the remote network 131.108.10.0/24 is down. Example 2-62 displays R1's IP routing table.

Example 2-62 *R1's IP Routing Table*

```
R1#show ip route igrp
        131.108.0.0/24 is subnetted, 9 subnets
I        131.108.10.0/24 is possibly down,
           routing via 131.108.3.2, Serial0/1
I        131.108.9.0 [100/100125] via 131.108.3.2, 00:00:03, Serial0/1
I        131.108.8.0 [100/100125] via 131.108.3.2, 00:00:03, Serial0/1
I        131.108.7.0 [100/100125] via 131.108.3.2, 00:00:03, Serial0/1
```

You can see from Example 2-62 that the remote network 131.108.10.0/24 is possibly down. Use the command **debug ip routing** to see whether you can see the problem. This debug displays routing entries added or deleted into the IP routing table. Use the command on R1. Example 2-63 displays a command used to debug the IP routing table and displays how to force the IP routing algorithm, in this case IGRP, to add and delete remote routes by using the command **clear ip route** *.

Example 2-63 debug ip routing *and* **clear ip route** * *Commands*

```
R1#debug ip routing
IP routing debugging is on
R1#clear ip route *
R1#
02:03:45: RT: add 131.108.1.0/24 via 0.0.0.0, connected metric [0/0]
02:03:45: RT: add 131.108.3.0/24 via 0.0.0.0, connected metric [0/0]
02:03:45: RT: add 131.108.4.0/24 via 0.0.0.0, connected metric [0/0]
02:03:45: RT: add 131.108.5.0/24 via 0.0.0.0, connected metric [0/0]
02:03:45: RT: add 131.108.6.0/24 via 0.0.0.0, connected metric [0/0]
02:03:45: RT: add 131.108.9.0/24 via 131.108.3.2, igrp metric [100/100125]
02:03:45: RT: add 131.108.8.0/24 via 131.108.3.2, igrp metric [100/100125]
02:03:45: RT: add 131.108.7.0/24 via 131.108.3.2, igrp metric [100/100125]
```

Example 2-64 displays another **clear ip route** * after the network 131.108.10.0/24 is restored.

Example 2-64 **clear ip route** * *on R1*

```
R1#clear ip route *
02:07:25: RT: add 131.108.1.0/24 via 0.0.0.0, connected metric [0/0]
02:07:25: RT: add 131.108.3.0/24 via 0.0.0.0, connected metric [0/0]
02:07:25: RT: add 131.108.4.0/24 via 0.0.0.0, connected metric [0/0]
02:07:25: RT: add 131.108.5.0/24 via 0.0.0.0, connected metric [0/0]
02:07:25: RT: add 131.108.6.0/24 via 0.0.0.0, connected metric [0/0]
02:07:25: RT: add 131.108.10.0/24 via 131.108.3.2, igrp metric [100/8539]
02:07:25: RT: add 131.108.9.0/24 via 131.108.3.2, igrp metric [100/100125]
02:07:25: RT: add 131.108.8.0/24 via 131.108.3.2, igrp metric [100/100125]
02:07:25: RT: add 131.108.7.0/24 via 131.108.3.2, igrp metric [100/100125]
02:08:03: RT: delete route to 131.108.10.0 via 131.108.3.2, igrp metric [100/85]
02:08:03: RT: no routes to 131.108.10.0, entering holddown
```

This time, you see the route added, but it enters the holddown state, which means the remote network 131.108.10.0 is not accepted and inserted into the IP routing table during the holddown interval. This prevents routing loops. Now view the IP route table on R1. Example 2-65 displays the IP routing table (IGRP) on R1.

Example 2-65 *R1 IP Route IGRP-Only Table*

```
R1#show ip route igrp
     131.108.0.0/24 is subnetted, 9 subnets
I       131.108.10.0/24 is possibly down,
          routing via 131.108.3.2, Serial0/1
I       131.108.9.0 [100/100125] via 131.108.3.2, 00:00:09, Serial0/1
I       131.108.8.0 [100/100125] via 131.108.3.2, 00:00:09, Serial0/1
I       131.108.7.0 [100/100125] via 131.108.3.2, 00:00:09, Serial0/1
```

When the IP network 131.108.10.0 goes into holddown mode, the entry in the IP routing table is displayed as possibly down during holddown. After a set interval, known as the flush timer, the entry is completely removed. Example 2-66 displays the IP routing table on R1 after this happens.

Example 2-66 *R1's IGRP Routing Table*

```
R1#show ip route igrp
     131.108.0.0/24 is subnetted, 8 subnets
I       131.108.9.0 [100/100125] via 131.108.3.2, 00:00:29, Serial0/1
I       131.108.8.0 [100/100125] via 131.108.3.2, 00:00:29, Serial0/1
I       131.108.7.0 [100/100125] via 131.108.3.2, 00:00:29, Serial0/1
```

If the remote entry is re-advertised as a valid route after the holddown interval, the network 131.108.1.0/24 is re-inserted into the IP routing table.

The command **show ip protocol** is a useful command that displays the characteristic of the protocols in use on a Cisco router. Perform this command on R1. Example 2-67 displays a sample output of the **show ip protocol** command on R1.

Example 2-67 **show ip protocol** *Command*

```
R1#show ip protocol
Routing Protocol is "igrp 1"
  Sending updates every 90 seconds, next due in 32 seconds
  Invalid after 270 seconds, hold down 280, flushed after 630
  Outgoing update filter list for all interfaces is
  Incoming update filter list for all interfaces is
  Default networks flagged in outgoing updates
  Default networks accepted from incoming updates
  IGRP metric weight K1=1, K2=0, K3=1, K4=0, K5=0
  IGRP maximum hopcount 100
  IGRP maximum metric variance 1
  Redistributing: igrp 1
  Routing for Networks:
    131.108.0.0
  Routing Information Sources:
    Gateway         Distance      Last Update
    131.108.3.2          100      00:00:06
  Distance: (default is 100)

R1#
```

After 270 seconds, the route is marked as invalid, and after 630 seconds, the route is deleted. The holddown interval for IGRP is 280 seconds. Also notice that the default hop count is 100; you can set this to 255. The default constants are always displayed as their default values K1 = K3 = 1 and K2 = K4 = K5 = 0.

Finally, the other most widely used command in today's networks is the **trace** command. The **trace** command makes use of the Time to Live (TTL). The TTL field is used to stop routing loops. Perform a **trace** route command over the World Wide Web. Example 2-68 describes the route hops from the source to destination for the site www.cnn.com.

Example 2-68 *Trace Route to www.cnn.com*

```
ccie-term#trace www.cnn.com
Type escape sequence to abort.
Tracing the route to cnn.com (207.25.71.26)
  1 sydney-c6k-1-vlan333.abc.com (100.64.205.2) 0 msec
  2 sydney-c6k-1-vlan150.abc.com (100.64.177.2) 4 msec 4 msec
  3 telstra-c6k-bbn1-msfc-vlan51.abc.com (100.64.176.2) 4 msec
```

continues

Example 2-68 *Trace Route to www.cnn.com (Continued)*

```
   4 telstra-gw.abc.com (103.41.198.241) 8 msec
     sydney-1.abc.com (64.104.192.196) 4 msec
     telstra-gateway.abc.com (213.41.198.241) 4 msec
   5 telstra-gw.abc.com (213.41.198.241) 4 msec
     213.41.198.233 8 msec 4 msec
   6 213.41.198.233 4 msec 4 msec
     213.41.198.234 4 msec
   7  FastEthernet6-1-0.chw12.Sydney.telstra.net (139.130.185.53) 8 msec
   8 FastEthernet6-1-0.chw12.Sydney.telstra.net (139.130.185.53) 4 msec
     GigabitEthernet4-2.chw-core2.Sydney.telstra.net (203.50.6.205) 8 msec
     FastEthernet6-1-0.chw12.Sydney.telstra.net (139.130.185.53) 4 msec
   9 Pos4-0.exi-core1.Melbourne.telstra.net (203.50.6.18) 20 msec
     GigabitEthernet4-2.chw-core2.Sydney.telstra.net (203.50.6.205) 4 msec
     Pos4-0.exi-core1.Melbourne.telstra.net (203.50.6.18) 16 msec
  10 Pos4-0.exi-core1.Melbourne.telstra.net (203.50.6.18) 16 msec
     Pos5-0.way-core4.Adelaide.telstra.net (203.50.6.162) 32 msec
     Pos4-0.exi-core1.Melbourne.telstra.net (203.50.6.18) 16 msec
  11 Pos6-0.wel-core3.Perth.telstra.net (203.50.6.194) 64 msec
     Pos5-0.way-core4.Adelaide.telstra.net (203.50.6.162) 32 msec
     Pos6-0.wel-core3.Perth.telstra.net (203.50.6.194) 60 msec
  12 Pos6-0.wel-core3.Perth.telstra.net (203.50.6.194) 60 msec
     GigabitEthernet4-0.wel-gw1.Perth.telstra.net (203.50.113.18) 64 msec
     Pos6-0.wel-core3.Perth.telstra.net (203.50.6.194) 60 msec
  13 Pos1-0.paix1.PaloAlto.net.reach.com (203.50.126.30) 288 msec
     GigabitEthernet4-0.wel-gw1.Perth.telstra.net (203.50.113.18) 60 msec
     Pos1-0.paix1.PaloAlto.net.reach.com (203.50.126.30) 288 msec
  14 Pos1-0.paix1.PaloAlto.net.reach.com (203.50.126.30) 288 msec
     sjo-brdr-02.inet.qwest.net (205.171.4.105) 296 msec 292 msec
  15 sjo-brdr-02.inet.qwest.net (205.171.4.105) 292 msec
     sjo-core-02.inet.qwest.net (205.171.22.69) 308 msec 304 msec
  16 sjo-core-02.inet.qwest.net (205.171.22.69) 312 msec
     iah-core-01.inet.qwest.net (205.171.5.145) 344 msec 344 msec
  17 iah-core-01.inet.qwest.net (205.171.5.145) 344 msec
     iah-core-03.inet.qwest.net (205.171.31.6) 332 msec 328 msec
  18 iah-core-03.inet.qwest.net (205.171.31.6) 332 msec
     atl-core-01.inet.qwest.net (205.171.8.146) 364 msec 360 msec
  19 atl-core-01.inet.qwest.net (205.171.8.146) 360 msec *  364 msec
  20    atl-edge-05.inet.qwest.net (205.171.21.22) 364 msec 364 msec
  21 208.47.124.130
ccie-term#
```

The **trace** command displays the route taken from the source to destination. From
Example 2-68, you can determine the next hop, the time taken, and whether multiple
hops exist.

NOTE	The **trace** command works by first sending three packets with a TTL of 1. The first router sees these packets and returns an error message. Now the source of the first hop is known. The next three packets are sent with a TTL of 2 and this process is repeated until the final destination is reached.

Practical Exercise: RIP Version 2

NOTE	Practical Exercises are designed to test your knowledge of the topics covered in this chapter. The Practical Exercise begins by giving you some information about a situation and then asks you to work through the solution on your own. The solution can be found at the end.

Configure the network in Figure 2-7 for IP routing using the IP addressing scheme provided. Ensure that both Routers R1 and R2 have full connectivity to each other. Use the **ping** command to ensure all networks are reachable. You must use IP RIP as your dynamic routing protocol.

Figure 2-7 *Practical Exercise: Routing RIP*

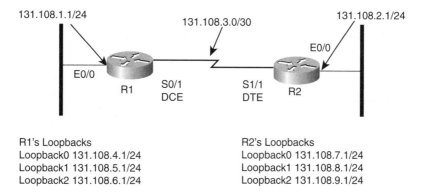

Practical Exercise Solution

You will notice that the entire IP addressing scheme is /24 except for the serial link between R1 and R2. The serial link contains a mask that is 255.255.255.252, or /30. Because you have /24 and /30, the only way RIP can understand variable-length subnet mask is with

RIPv2 or with the use of static routes. The configurations in Example 2-69 and Example 2-70 answer these issues using RIPv2. Static routes are fine to configure, but you must be aware that static routes have an AD of 1, which means if you use any dynamic routing protocols, static information is more trusted, even though you may have a dynamic routing protocol such as RIPv2 advertising the network's reachability and next hop details dynamically. In a changing network, static routes can be cumbersome to document and administrate. If you do have access to two routers, experiment with RIPv1 and static routes. Another major disadvantage of static routes is that they do not scale well in large networks and can lead to routing loops or black holes (discarded packets) if configured incorrectly. In that case, you should change the protocols to RIPv2, OSPF, IGRP, or EIGRP and apply the skills you learned in this chapter to test connectivity. Configure loopbacks with VLSM and experiment with **debug** commands to discover why IP entries are added or not advertised. Examples 2-69 and 2-70 display the full working configuration on R1 and R2.

Example 2-69 *R1's Full Configuration*

```
version 12.0
!
hostname R1
!
enable password cisco
!
ip subnet-zero
no ip domain-lookup
!
interface Loopback0
 ip address 131.108.4.1 255.255.255.0
 no ip directed-broadcast
!
interface Loopback1
 ip address 131.108.5.1 255.255.255.0
 no ip directed-broadcast
!
interface Loopback2
 ip address 131.108.6.1 255.255.255.0
 no ip directed-broadcast
!
interface Ethernet0/0
 ip address 131.108.1.1 255.255.255.0
!
interface Serial0/0
 shutdown
!
interface Serial0/1
 ip address 131.108.3.1 255.255.255.252
 clockrate 128000
!
router rip
 version 2
 network 131.108.0.0
```

Example 2-69 *R1's Full Configuration (Continued)*

```
!
line con 0
 transport input none
line aux 0
line vty 0 4
!
end
```

Example 2-70 *R2's Full Configuration*

```
!
service timestamps log uptime
no service password-encryption
!
hostname R2
!
enable password cisco
!
ip subnet-zero
no ip domain-lookup
!
interface Loopback0
 ip address 131.108.7.1 255.255.255.0
 no ip directed-broadcast
!
interface Loopback1
 ip address 131.108.8.1 255.255.255.0
 no ip directed-broadcast
!
interface Loopback2
 ip address 131.108.9.1 255.255.255.0
 no ip directed-broadcast
!
interface Ethernet0/0
 ip address 131.108.2.1 255.255.255.0
!
interface Serial1/0
shutdown
!
interface Serial1/1
 ip address 131.108.3.2 255.255.255.252
 ip directed-broadcast
!
interface Serial1/2
shutdown
!
interface Serial1/3
shutdown
```

continues

Example 2-70 *R2's Full Configuration (Continued)*

```
!
router rip
 version 2
 network 131.108.0.0
!
ip classless
!
line con 0
 exec-timeout 0 0
 transport input none
line aux 0
line vty 0 4
!
end
```

Review Questions

These review questions are based on the Practical Exercise. Use the router displays taken from R1 from the preceding Practical Exercise to answer the following questions. View Example 2-71 for sample output taken from R1; this output includes the IP routing table and sample pings to the router R2.

You can find the answers to these questions in Appendix C, "Answers to Review Questions."

Example 2-71 **show ip route** *on R1*

```
R1#show ip route
Gateway of last resort is not set
     131.108.0.0/16 is variably subnetted, 9 subnets, 2 masks
R       131.108.9.0/24 [120/1] via 131.108.3.2, 00:00:05, Serial0/1
R       131.108.8.0/24 [120/1] via 131.108.3.2, 00:00:05, Serial0/1
R       131.108.7.0/24 [120/1] via 131.108.3.2, 00:00:05, Serial0/1
C       131.108.6.0/24 is directly connected, Loopback2
C       131.108.5.0/24 is directly connected, Loopback1
C       131.108.4.0/24 is directly connected, Loopback0
C       131.108.3.0/30 is directly connected, Serial0/1
R       131.108.2.0/24 [120/1] via 131.108.3.2, 00:00:05, Serial0/1
C       131.108.1.0/24 is directly connected, Ethernet0/0

R1#ping 131.108.7.1

Type escape sequence to abort.
Sending 5, 100-byte ICMP Echos to 131.108.7.1, timeout is 2 seconds:
!!!!!
Success rate is 100 percent (5/5), round-trip min/avg/max = 16/16/16 ms
R1#ping 131.108.8.1

Type escape sequence to abort.
Sending 5, 100-byte ICMP Echos to 131.108.8.1, timeout is 2 seconds:
```

Example 2-71 **show ip route** *on R1 (Continued)*

```
!!!!!
Success rate is 100 percent (5/5), round-trip min/avg/max = 16/16/16 ms
R1#ping 131.108.9.1

Type escape sequence to abort.
Sending 5, 100-byte ICMP Echos to 131.108.9.1, timeout is 2 seconds:
!!!!!
Success rate is 100 percent (5/5), round-trip min/avg/max = 12/15/16 ms

R1#show ip route rip
     131.108.0.0/16 is variably subnetted, 9 subnets, 2 masks
R       131.108.9.0/24 [120/1] via 131.108.3.2, 00:00:15, Serial0/1
R       131.108.8.0/24 [120/1] via 131.108.3.2, 00:00:15, Serial0/1
R       131.108.7.0/24 [120/1] via 131.108.3.2, 00:00:15, Serial0/1
R       131.108.2.0/24 [120/1] via 131.108.3.2, 00:00:15, Serial0/1
```

1 What information is stored in an IP routing table as seen by R1?

2 Which command do you use to view only RIP routes?

3 Which command do you use to view only connected routes?

4 How many subnets are known by R1 using the Class B network 131.108.0.0/16?

5 From R1, a ping test is sent to three remote networks. Is the ping test successful or not? Explain why or why not?

6 Why is the command **version 2** configured on each router?

7 Each remote routing entry is labeled with the following information: [120/1]. What does the 120 represent and what does the 1 represent?

8 Besides a ping test, what other methods could you use to ensure connectivity to the remote networks?

Summary

You have now successfully worked through five routing principles scenarios using different routing protocols and have configured IP addressing across a sample two-router network. You should have a strong knowledge base of routing principles to apply to the remainder of this book. Table 2-7 summarizes the commands used in this chapter.

Table 2-7   *Summary of Commands Used in This Chapter*

Command	Purpose
show ip route	Displays IP routing table in full.
router rip	Enables RIP routing protocol.
router igrp *autonomous system*	Enables IGRP routing in a particular autonomous system.
router eigrp *autonomous system*	Enables EIGRP routing in a particular autonomous system.
router ospf *process id*	Enables OSPF routing. The process ID is local to the router. You can have more than one OSPF process running.
network	Enables network advertisements from a particular interface and also the routing of the same interface through a dynamic routing protocol.
passive-interface *interface*	Stops the router sending routing updates on an interface.
show controllers	Displays hardware information about a particular interface.
Ctrl-Shift-6, x	Escape sequence to escape from the current session and return to terminal server.
interface loopback *number*	Creates a loopback interface.
interface ethernet	In configuration mode, enables you to modify Ethernet parameters.
interface serial	In configuration mode, enables you to modify serial interface parameters.
ip domain-lookup	Enables automatic DNS lookup. The IOS command **no ip domain-lookup** disables automatic DNS lookups.
ip subnet-zero	Enables you to use subnet zero on a Cisco router.
ping	Enables you to send ICMP packets to local and remote destinations to test network connectivity.
trace	Enables you to find the path taken from source to destination.
show ip protocol	Displays all routing protocols in use on a Cisco router.
debug	Troubleshooting command used to display messages received and sent by a Cisco router.
hostname *name*	Configures a name on a router.
[no] shutdown	Enables or disables an interface. All hardware interfaces are shut down by default.

CHAPTER 3

Basic Open Shortest Path First

This chapter focuses on a number of objectives falling under the CCNP routing principles. Understanding basic Open Shortest Path First (OSPF) routing principles not only applies to the CCNP certification but to all Cisco-based certifications. A concrete understanding of how OSPF routing works is fundamental for any small or large network. OSPF is commonly used in large service provider networks or large financial institutions. This chapter assumes knowledge of the previous chapter, which deals conceptually with IP routing principles and in particular link-state routing protocols.

The chapter starts by covering the basic OSPF concepts. It then briefly explains why OSPF is considered an improved routing protocol over Routing Information Protocol (RIP) by covering how OSPF discovers, chooses, and maintains routing tables.

Nonbroadcast multiaccess (NBMA) is a particular challenge in any network environment. This chapter covers how OSPF overcomes any limitations imposed by NBMA networks.

Five practical scenarios, included in the chapter, help you complete your understanding and ensure you have all the basic OSPF routing skills to complement your understanding of how to configure and maintain OSPF on Cisco Internet Operating System (IOS) routers.

Basic OSPF

OSPF is a link-state routing protocol. Link-state protocols use the shortest path first (SPF) algorithm to populate the routing table. OSPF shares information with every router in the network.

OSPF is considered a difficult protocol to configure and requires a thorough understanding of terms that are commonly used. Table 3-1 explains briefly the common OSPF terminology used throughout this chapter.

Table 3-1   *Common OSPF Terms*

Term	Description
Link state	Information is shared between directly connected routers. This information propagates throughout the network unchanged and is also used to create a shortest path first (SPF) tree.
Area	A group of routers that share the same area ID. All OSPF routers require area assignments.
Autonomous system (AS)	A network under a common network administration.
Cost	The routing metric used by OSPF. Lower costs are always preferred. You can manually configure the cost with the **ip ospf cost** command. By default, the cost is calculated by using the formula cost = 10^8 / bandwidth.
Router ID	Each OSPF router requires a unique router ID, which is the highest IP address configured on a Cisco router or the highest numbered loopback address. You can manually assign the router ID.
Adjacency	When two OSPF routers have exchanged information between each other and have the same topology table. An adjacency can have the following different states or exchange states:
	1. **Init state**—When Hello packets have been sent and are awaiting a reply to establish two-way communication.
	2. **Establish bi-directional (two-way) communication**—Accomplished by the discovery of the Hello protocol routers and the election of a DR.
	3. **Exstart**—Two neighbor routers form a master/slave relationship and agree upon a starting sequence to be incremented to ensure LSAs are acknowledged.
	4. **Exchange state**—Database Description (DD) packets continue to flow as the slave router acknowledges the master's packets. OSPF is operational because the routers can send and receive LSAs between each other. DD packets contain information, such as the router ID, area ID, checksum, if authentication is used, link-state type, and the advertising router. LSA packets contain information, such as router ID also but in addition include MTU sizes, DD sequence numbering, and any options.
	5. **Loading state**—Link-state requests are sent to neighbors asking for recent advertisements that have not yet been discovered.
	6. **Full state**—Neighbor routers are fully adjacent because their link-state databases are fully synchronized. Routing tables begin to be populated.
Topology table	Also called the link-state table. This table contains every link in the whole network.

Table 3-1 *Common OSPF Terms (Continued)*

Term	Description
Designated router (DR)	This router is responsible for ensuring adjacencies between all neighbors on a multiaccess network (such as Ethernet). This ensures all routers do not need to maintain full adjacencies with each other.
	The DR is selected based on the router priority. In a tie, the router with the highest router ID is selected.
Backup DR	A backup router designed to perform the same functions in case the DR fails.
Link-state advertisement (LSA)	A packet that contains all relevant information regarding a router's links and the state of those links.
Priority	Sets the router's priority so a DR or BDR can be correctly elected.
Router links	Describe the state and cost of the router's interfaces to the area. Router links use LSA type 1.
Summary links	Originated by area border routers (ABRs) and describe networks in the AS. Summary links use LSA types 3 and 4.
Network links	Originated by DRs. Network links use LSA type 2.
External links	Originated by autonomous system boundary routers (ASBRs) and describe external or default routes to the outside (that is, non-OSPF) devices for use with redistribution. External Links use the LSA type 5.
Area border router (ABR)	Router located on the border of one or more OSPF areas that connects those areas to the backbone network.
Autonomous system boundary router (ASBR)	ABR located between an OSPF autonomous system and a non-OSPF network.

OSPF has so many features that the most efficient way to appreciate them is to enable OSPF on routers and observe how the routers dynamically discover IP networks.

Before covering various OSPF scenarios, this chapter covers how OSPF is configured in single and multiple OSPF areas.

Configuring OSPF in a Single Area

When configuring any OSPF router, you must establish which area assignment to enable the interface for. OSPF has some basic rules when it comes to area assignment. OSPF must be configured with areas. The backbone area 0, or 0.0.0.0, must be configured if you use more than one area assignment. You can configure OSPF in one area; you can choose any area, although good OSPF design dictates that you configure area 0.

To enable OSPF on a Cisco router and advertise interfaces, the following tasks are required:

Step 1   Use the command **router ospf** *process ID* to start OSPF.

Step 2   Use the **network** command to enable the interfaces.

Step 3   Identify area assignments.

Step 4   (Optional) Assign the router ID.

Example 3-1 displays OSPF with a process ID of 1 and places all interfaces configured with an IP address in area 0. The network command **network 0.0.0.0 255.255.255.255 area 0** dictates that you do not care (255.255.255.255) what the IP address is, but if an IP address is enabled on any interface, place it in area 0.

Example 3-1 *Configuring OSPF in a Single Area*

```
router ospf 1
network 0.0.0.0 255.255.255.255 area 0
```

The following is a list of reasons OSPF is considered a better routing protocol than RIP:

- OSPF has no hop count limitations. (RIP has 15 hops only.)
- OSPF understands variable-length subnet masks (VLSMs) and allows for summarization.
- OSPF uses multicasts (not broadcasts) to send updates.
- OSPF converges much faster than RIP, because OSPF propagates changes immediately.
- OSPF allows for load balancing with up to six equal-cost paths.
- OSPF has authentication available. (RIPv2 does also, but RIPv1 does not.)
- OSPF allows for tagging of external routes injected by other autonomous systems.
- OSPF configuration, monitoring, and troubleshooting have a far greater IOS tool base than RIP.

NOTE   OSPF does have some disadvantages, including the level of difficulty and understanding required to configure, monitor, and troubleshoot it. The other two factors are the memory and Central Processing Unit (CPU) requirements that can affect even high-end router performance. You can configure more than one OSPF process, but you must be mindful that the SPF calculations associated with multiple OSPF processes can consume a considerable amount of CPU and memory.

OSPF and Nonbroadcast Multiaccess Environments

A nonbroadcast multiaccess (NBMA) environment presents the OSPF designer a number of challenges. The main challenge is that NBMA environments do not carry broadcast traffic but have the added characteristics that multiple destinations may be present. In a normal broadcast environment, this is not a challenge because a packet can be sent to a broadcast or multicast address and be received by all recipients.

To overcome these problems, OSPF, and in particular Cisco IOS, allows you to define the networks types and also allows static OSPF neighbor configurations.

Cisco IOS enables you to configure five main network types as displayed in Table 3-2. These five possible solutions available with Cisco IOS are listed for your reference.

Table 3-2   *OSPF over NBMA Using Cisco IOS*

Method	Description
Point-to-point nonbroadcast	Used typically for Frame Relay interfaces.
Point-to-point	This is the default mode for subinterfaces.
Point-to-multipoint	Used for multiple destinations.
Nonbroadcast	NBMA mode.
Broadcast	Used in Ethernet and broadcast environments in which the election of DR/BDR takes place.

Scenario 3-4 illustrates the behavior of OSPF in an NBMA environment.

Scenarios

The following scenarios are designed to draw together and further explore the content described earlier in this chapter and some of the content you have seen in your own networks or practice labs. There is not always one right way to accomplish the tasks presented, and using good practice and defining your end goal are important in any real-life design or solution.

Scenario 3-1: Configuring OSPF in a Single Area

In this scenario, you configure two Cisco routers for OSPF routing using a Class B (/16) network (131.108.0.0) with a Class C subnet mask (255.255.255.0, or /24 mask). You build a small network and an OSPF routing table.

You must also configure a number of loopback interfaces to populate the IP routing table. Figure 3-1 displays two routers named R1 and R2 connected through Ethernet. Configure the routers of OSPF area 1 and place the loopbacks in area 1 also.

Figure 3-1 displays the IP addressing and area assignments for Routers R1 and R2.

Figure 3-1   *Basic OSPF*

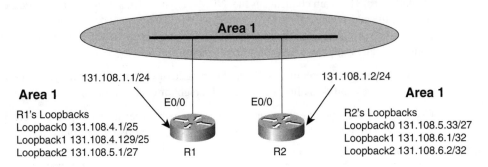

Configure R1 for OSPF first. Assign all interfaces with the area assignment 1. Also note that this scenario uses VLSM. Use the **network** command and match the IP subnet exactly. Example 3-2 displays the OSPF configuration performed on R1.

NOTE   Routers R1 and R2 reside in one area; so, in fact, you could apply the one IOS command to enable all interfaces configured with an IP address in the range 131.108.0.0 through 131.108.255.255 with the command **network 131.108.0.0 0.0.255.255 area 1**.

Example 3-2   *R1 OSPF Configuration*

```
router ospf 1
 network 131.108.1.0 0.0.0.255 area 1
 network 131.108.4.0 0.0.0.127 area 1
 network 131.108.4.128 0.0.0.127 area 1
 network 131.108.5.0 0.0.0.31 area 1
```

Example 3-3 displays the OSPF configuration performed on R2.

Example 3-3   *R2 OSPF Configuration*

```
router ospf 2
 network 131.108.1.0 0.0.0.255 area 1
 network 131.108.5.32 0.0.0.31 area 1
 network 131.108.6.1 0.0.0.0 area 1
 network 131.108.6.2 0.0.0.0 area 1
```

NOTE   R1 has a process ID of 1 and R2 has a process ID of 2. The process ID is locally significant only and doesn't need to match between routers. The process ID can be any number between 1–65535. Also, because R2 has host (or /32 subnets) masks on loopbacks 2 and 3, the inverse mask is 0.0.0.0, or an exact match.

Example 3-4 displays the three remote networks reachable through OSPF with a cost metric of 11 for all three. The next hop address is 131.108.1.2 through Ethernet 0/0. You might ask yourself why some of the remote networks are displayed as a /32 route when you used a /27 mask.

To discover why loopbacks appear as /32 host routers, examine Example 3-4, which displays the IP routing table on R1.

Example 3-4   *R1's IP Routing Table*

```
R1#show ip route
     131.108.0.0/16 is variably subnetted, 7 subnets, 4 masks
C       131.108.4.128/25 is directly connected, Loopback1
O       131.108.5.33/32 [110/11] via 131.108.1.2, 00:02:22, Ethernet0/0
O       131.108.6.1/32 [110/11] via 131.108.1.2, 00:02:22, Ethernet0/0
C       131.108.5.0/27 is directly connected, Loopback2
O       131.108.6.2/32 [110/11] via 131.108.1.2, 00:02:22, Ethernet0/0
C       131.108.4.0/25 is directly connected, Loopback0
C       131.108.1.0/24 is directly connected, Ethernet0/0
R1#
```

The remote network is displayed as a /32 route when a /27 mask is used because, by default, OSPF advertises loopbacks as host addresses, or as /32 routes. Change this default configuration and make the routes appear as /27 with the configuration on R2, as displayed in Example 3-5. To make things a little more interesting, modify the cost as well to 1000.

Example 3-5   *Advertising Loopbacks as /27 on R2 and Changing the Default Cost to 1000*

```
R2#conf t
Enter configuration commands, one per line.  End with CNTL/Z.
R2(config)#int loopback0
R2(config-if)#ip ospf cost 1000
R2(config-if)#ip ospf network point-to-point
```

The command **ip ospf cost 1000** changes the cost to 1000. The command **ip ospf network point-to-point** changes the route advertisement to /27. Example 3-6 displays R1's routing table after these changes.

Example 3-6 *R1 Routing Table*

```
R1#show ip route
     131.108.0.0/16 is variably subnetted, 7 subnets, 4 masks
C       131.108.4.128/25 is directly connected, Loopback1
O       131.108.5.32/27 [110/1010] via 131.108.1.2, 00:01:19, Ethernet0/0
O       131.108.6.1/32 [110/11] via 131.108.1.2, 00:01:19, Ethernet0/0
C       131.108.5.0/27 is directly connected, Loopback2
O       131.108.6.2/32 [110/11] via 131.108.1.2, 00:01:19, Ethernet0/0
C       131.108.4.0/25 is directly connected, Loopback0
C       131.108.1.0/24 is directly connected, Ethernet0/0
R1#
```

In Example 3-6, the subnet 131.108.5.32 displayed is 27 bits. The remaining loopbacks are still /32, so you need to modify them also.

The associated cost of the remote network 131.108.5.32/27 is 1010. To figure out why, remember that OSPF calculates the total cost from source to destination. The 1000 is the cost R2 assigns and advertises to R1. When R1 receives the update, it makes a calculation on total cost. The path taken to the remote network 131.108.5.32 is through Ethernet 0/0. Find out the cost associated with R1 Ethernet 0/0 by using the **show ip ospf interface ethernet 0/0** command as displayed in Example 3-7.

Example 3-7 **show ip ospf interface ethernet 0/0** *on R1*

```
R1#show ip ospf interface ethernet 0/0
Ethernet0/0 is up, line protocol is up
  Internet Address 131.108.1.1/24, Area 1
  Process ID 1, Router ID 131.108.5.1, Network Type BROADCAST, Cost: 10
  Transmit Delay is 1 sec, State DR, Priority 1
  Designated Router (ID) 131.108.5.1, Interface address 131.108.1.1
  Backup Designated router (ID) 131.108.1.2, Interface address 131.108.1.2
  Timer intervals configured, Hello 10, Dead 40, Wait 40, Retransmit 5
    Hello due in 00:00:06
  Neighbor Count is 1, Adjacent neighbor count is 1
    Adjacent with neighbor 131.108.1.2  (Backup Designated Router)
  Suppress hello for 0 neighbor(s)
R1#
```

The cost associated with the path on the Ethernet segment is 10. Therefore, the total cost is 1000 (as advertised by R2) plus 10, which equals 1010. Another method you can use to determine the cost with an Ethernet segment is to use the cost calculation, cost = 10^8 / Bandwidth = 10^8 / 10^7 = 10. Example 3-8 displays the full routing configuration on R1.

Example 3-8 *R1 Full Configuration*

```
version 12.0
!
hostname R1
!
enable password cisco
!
no ip domain-lookup
interface Loopback0
 ip address 131.108.4.1 255.255.255.128
!
interface Loopback1
 ip address 131.108.4.129 255.255.255.128
!
interface Loopback2
 ip address 131.108.5.1 255.255.255.224
!
interface Ethernet0/0
 ip address 131.108.1.1 255.255.255.0
!
interface Serial0/0
 shutdown
!
interface Serial0/1
 shutdown
router ospf 1
 network 131.108.1.0 0.0.0.255 area 1
 network 131.108.4.0 0.0.0.127 area 1
 network 131.108.4.128 0.0.0.127 area 1
 network 131.108.5.0 0.0.0.31 area 1
!
line con 0
line aux 0
line vty 0 4
!
end
```

Example 3-9 displays the full routing configuration on R2.

Example 3-9 *R2 Full Configuration*

```
version 12.0
!
hostname R2
!
enable password cisco
```

continues

Example 3-9 *R2 Full Configuration (Continued)*

```
!
no ip domain-lookup
!
interface Loopback0
 ip address 131.108.5.33 255.255.255.224
 ip ospf network point-to-point
 ip ospf cost 1000
!
interface Loopback1
 ip address 131.108.6.1 255.255.255.255
!
interface Loopback2
 ip address 131.108.6.2 255.255.255.255
!
interface Ethernet0/0
 ip address 131.108.1.2 255.255.255.0
!
interface Serial1/0
 shutdown
!
interface Serial1/1
 shutdown
!
interface Serial1/2

 shutdown
!
interface Serial1/3
 shutdown
!
router ospf 2
 network 131.108.1.0 0.0.0.255 area 1
 network 131.108.5.32 0.0.0.31 area 1
 network 131.108.6.1 0.0.0.0 area 1
 network 131.108.6.2 0.0.0.0 area 1
!
line con 0
line aux 0
line vty 0 4
end
```

Now, apply the OSPF principles to a larger, more complex network in Scenario 3-2.

Scenario 3-2: Configuring OSPF in Multiple Areas

Turn your attention to a far more complex OSPF scenario and apply some of the advanced features in OSPF.

This scenario uses four routers: R1 and R2 from scenario 3-1 and two new routers named R6 and R3. Figure 3-2 displays the routers in this scenario.

Figure 3-2 *OSPF Topology and IP Addressing*

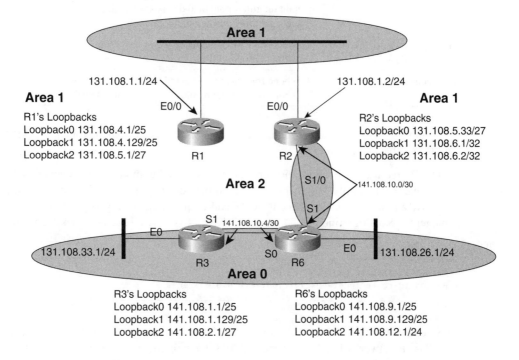

In this scenario, you add two new routers, R3 and R6, and create an additional two new areas: Area 0 and Area 2. That makes a total of three areas: the backbone Area 0 between R3 and R6, Area 2 covering the link between R6 and R2, and Area 1 covering the Ethernets between R1 and R2.

Routers R2 and R6 in this case are referred to area border routers (ABRs) because more than one area is configured on each router. OSPF includes a number of different router types. Table 3-3 displays all the possible routers types.

Table 3-3 *OSPF Router Types*

Router type	Description
Internal router	This router is within a specific area only. Internal router functions include maintaining the OSPF database and forwarding data to other networks. All interfaces on internal routers are in the same area.

continues

Table 3-3   *OSPF Router Types (Continued)*

Router type	Description
Area border router (ABR)	ABRs are responsible for connecting two or more areas. ABRs contain the full topological database of each area they are connected to and send this information to other areas.
Autonomous system border router (ASBR)	ASBRs connect to the outside world or perform some form of redistribution into OSPF.
Backbone router	Backbone routers are connected to area 0, also know as area 0.0.0.0. Backbone routers can be internal routers and ASBRs.

In Figure 3-2, R1 is an internal router; R2 is an ABR; R6 is a backbone router and ABR, and R3 is a backbone router.

Router R1 requires no configuration change, but you need to modify R2 and enable OSPF on R3 and R6. Example 3-10 displays the modifications required on R2. Remember that you have a link to R6, so you need to set IP addressing and clocking as you did in the Chapter 2, "Routing Principles." Example 3-5 uses Cisco serial back-to-back V.35 cables.

Example 3-10 *Configuration of R2 as ABR*

```
R2(config)#router ospf 2
R2(config-router)#network 141.108.10.0 0.0.0.3 area 2
```

Now, enable OSPF on R3 and R6. Notice the IP addressing in Figure 3-2 has a mixture of the Class B networks 131.108.0.0 and 141.108.0.0 with different subnets. Hence, this scenario uses VLSM extensively to illustrate the capability of OSPF to handle VLSM.

To enable OSPF on R6, start the OSPF process with the process ID 6 and enable the interfaces to advertise the networks as displayed by Example 3-11.

Example 3-11 *Enable OSPF on R6 with Process ID 6*

```
r6(config)#router ospf 6
r6(config-router)# network 141.108.9.0 0.0.0.127 area 0
r6(config-router)# network 141.108.9.128 0.0.0.127 area 0
r6(config-router)# network 141.108.10.0 0.0.0.3 area 2
r6(config-router)# network 141.108.10.4 0.0.0.3 area 0
r6(config-router)# network 141.108.12.0 0.0.0.255 area 0
r6(config-router)# network 141.108.12.26 0.0.0.255 area 0
```

Similarly, Example 3-12 displays the OSPF configuration required on R3.

Example 3-12 *Enable OSPF on R3*

```
R3(config)#router ospf 3
R3(config-router)#network 141.108.10.4 0.0.0.3 area 0
R3(config-router)#network 141.108.1.0 0.0.0.127 area 0
R3(config-router)#network 141.108.1.128 0.0.0.127 area 0
R3(config-router)#network 141.108.2.0 0.0.0.31 area 0
R3(config-router)#network 131.108.33.0 0.0.0.255 area 0
```

Now that OSPF is configured on all four routers, examine the routing table on the backbone network to ensure that all networks are routable. Example 3-13 displays the IP routing table on R6.

Example 3-13 *IP Routing Table on R6*

```
r6#show ip route
     141.108.0.0/16 is variably subnetted, 7 subnets, 3 masks
O        141.108.1.128/25 [110/65] via 141.108.10.5, 00:00:32, Serial0
C        141.108.9.128/25 is directly connected, Loopback1
O        141.108.1.0/25 [110/65] via 141.108.10.5, 00:00:32, Serial0
C        141.108.9.0/25 is directly connected, Loopback0
C        141.108.10.0/30 is directly connected, Serial1
C        141.108.12.0/24 is directly connected, Loopback2
C        141.108.10.4/30 is directly connected, Serial0
     131.108.0.0/24 is subnetted, 2 subnets
O        131.108.33.0 [110/74] via 141.108.10.5, 00:00:32, Serial0
C        131.108.26.0 is directly connected, Ethernet0
r6#
```

Example 3-13 displays the remote networks on Router R3, but not the networks from R1 or R2. For example, the Ethernet network 131.108.1.0/24 in area 1 is not routable from R6. Examine R3's routing table. Example 3-14 displays R3's IP routing table.

Example 3-14 *R3's IP Routing Table*

```
R3>show ip route
     141.108.0.0/16 is variably subnetted, 8 subnets, 4 masks
C        141.108.1.128/25 is directly connected, Loopback1
O        141.108.9.128/25 [110/65] via 141.108.10.6, 00:23:42, Serial1
C        141.108.1.0/25 is directly connected, Loopback0
C        141.108.2.0/27 is directly connected, Loopback2
O        141.108.9.0/25 [110/65] via 141.108.10.6, 00:23:42, Serial1
O IA     141.108.10.0/30 [110/128] via 141.108.10.6, 00:23:42, Serial1
O        141.108.12.0/24 [110/65] via 141.108.10.6, 00:23:42, Serial1
C        141.108.10.4/30 is directly connected, Serial1
     131.108.0.0/24 is subnetted, 1 subnets
C        131.108.33.0 is directly connected, Ethernet0
```

Once more, Example 3-14 doesn't display the networks in area 1 on Routers R1 and R2. Example 3-15 displays R2's IP routing table.

Example 3-15 *R2's IP Routing Table*

```
R2>show ip route
     141.108.0.0/16 is variably subnetted, 7 subnets, 3 masks
O IA    141.108.1.128/25 [110/846] via 141.108.10.2, 00:08:05, Serial1/0
O IA    141.108.9.128/25 [110/782] via 141.108.10.2, 00:26:20, Serial1/0
O IA    141.108.1.0/25 [110/846] via 141.108.10.2, 00:08:15, Serial1/0
O IA    141.108.9.0/25 [110/782] via 141.108.10.2, 00:26:20, Serial1/0
C       141.108.10.0/30 is directly connected, Serial1/0
O IA    141.108.12.0/24 [110/782] via 141.108.10.2, 00:26:20, Serial1/0
O IA    141.108.10.4/30 [110/845] via 141.108.10.2, 00:26:20, Serial1/0
     131.108.0.0/16 is variably subnetted, 8 subnets, 3 masks
O       131.108.4.129/32 [110/11] via 131.108.1.1, 00:46:09, Ethernet0/0
C       131.108.5.32/27 is directly connected, Loopback0
O IA    131.108.33.0/24 [110/855] via 141.108.10.2, 00:09:06, Serial1/0
C       131.108.6.1/32 is directly connected, Loopback1
O       131.108.4.1/32 [110/11] via 131.108.1.1, 00:46:09, Ethernet0/0
O       131.108.5.1/32 [110/11] via 131.108.1.1, 00:46:09, Ethernet0/0
C       131.108.6.2/32 is directly connected, Loopback2
C       131.108.1.0/24 is directly connected, Ethernet0/0
R2>
```

Notice, however, that R2 has access to the remote networks in area 0 or on the backbone, but not vice versa, because Router R2 is connected to area 2.

Area 2 is not partitioned from the backbone. In fact, area 2 is directly connected to the backbone through Router R6.

Area 1 is not directly connected to the backbone. Therefore, Router R1 is missing IP networks.

The golden rule in any OSPF network is that all areas must be contiguous or all areas must be connected to the backbone. Scenario 3-2 includes three areas. If an area cannot be assigned to the backbone or is partitioned from the backbone, a virtual link is required. When designing a network, you use a virtual link to attach areas that do not have a physical connection to the backbone or in cases in which the backbone is partitioned, as in the example shown in Figure 3-2.

Figure 3-3 displays the areas and the requirement for a virtual link.

Figure 3-3 *Area Assignments and the Virtual Link Requirement*

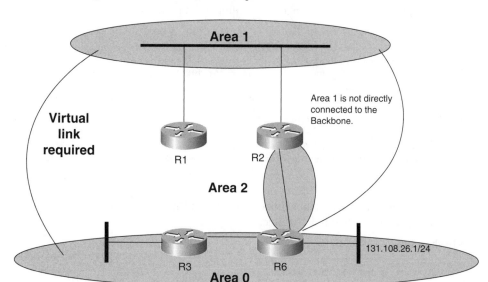

The virtual link in this scenario is required from R2 to R6. The virtual link allows information about area 1 to be sent to the backbone. Another solution to this problem is to change the area 1 assignment to area 2 or to connect a physical link from area 1 to the backbone. In this scenario, configure a virtual link between R2 and R6.

To create a virtual link, you use the following command:

```
[no] area area-id virtual-link router-id [hello-interval seconds]
    [retransmit-interval seconds] [transmit-delay seconds]
    [dead-interval seconds] [[authentication-key key] |
    [message-digest-key keyid md5 key]]
```

As you can see, this command has many options. The following is a simplification:

```
area area-id virtual-link router-id
```

The *area-id* is the transit network between the two partitioned areas, in this case area 2. You can find the *router-id* by using the **show ip ospf database** command, which displays the complete OSPF database. Example 3-16 shows you how to discover the router IDs on R2 and R6. Note that the extensive amount of information typically supplied by the **show ip ospf database** command is not all displayed in Example 3-16.

Example 3-16 show ip ospf database *Command on R2 and R6*

```
R2>show ip ospf database
        OSPF Router with ID (131.108.6.2) (Process ID 2)
r6>show ip ospf database
        OSPF Router with ID (141.108.12.1) (Process ID 6)
```

You now have the information required to configure a virtual link between R3 and R6.
Examples 3-17 and 3-18 display the configuration performed on Routers R2 and R6.

Example 3-17 *Configuring a Virtual Link on R2*

```
R2(config)#router ospf 2
R2(config-router)#area 2 virtual-link 141.108.12.1
```

Example 3-18 *Configuring a Virtual Link on R6*

```
R6(config)#router ospf 6
r6(config-router)#area 2 virtual-link 131.108.6.2
```

Use the **show ip ospf virtual-links** command on R2, demonstrated in Example 3-19, to
ensure that the virtual link is active.

Example 3-19 **show ip ospf virtual-links**

```
R2#show ip ospf virtual-links
Virtual Link OSPF_VL0 to router 141.108.12.1 is up
  Run as demand circuit
  DoNotAge LSA allowed.
  Transit area 2, via interface Serial1/0, Cost of using 781
  Transmit Delay is 1 sec, State POINT_TO_POINT,
  Timer intervals configured, Hello 10, Dead 40, Wait 40, Retransmit 5
    Hello due in 00:00:07
    Adjacency State FULL (Hello suppressed)
```

Example 3-19 displays an active link to the remote OSPF router with the ID 141.108.12.1.
Now, view the routing tables on R3 to determine whether the area 1 networks have been
inserted into the IP routing table, as demonstrated in Example 3-20.

Example 3-20 **show ip route** *on R3*

```
R3#show ip route
     141.108.0.0/16 is variably subnetted, 8 subnets, 4 masks
C       141.108.1.128/25 is directly connected, Loopback1
O       141.108.9.128/25 [110/65] via 141.108.10.6, 00:01:43, Serial1
C       141.108.1.0/25 is directly connected, Loopback0
C       141.108.2.0/27 is directly connected, Loopback2
O       141.108.9.0/25 [110/65] via 141.108.10.6, 00:01:43, Serial1
O IA    141.108.10.0/30 [110/128] via 141.108.10.6, 00:01:43, Serial1
O       141.108.12.0/24 [110/65] via 141.108.10.6, 00:01:43, Serial1
C       141.108.10.4/30 is directly connected, Serial1
     131.108.0.0/16 is variably subnetted, 9 subnets, 3 masks
O IA    131.108.4.129/32 [110/139] via 141.108.10.6, 00:01:43, Serial1
O IA    131.108.5.32/27 [110/1128] via 141.108.10.6, 00:01:43, Serial1
C       131.108.33.0/24 is directly connected, Ethernet0
```

Example 3-20 show ip route *on R3 (Continued)*

```
O IA     131.108.6.1/32 [110/129] via 141.108.10.6, 00:01:43, Serial1
O IA     131.108.4.1/32 [110/139] via 141.108.10.6, 00:01:43, Serial1
O IA     131.108.6.2/32 [110/129] via 141.108.10.6, 00:01:43, Serial1
O IA     131.108.5.1/32 [110/139] via 141.108.10.6, 00:01:43, Serial1
O IA     131.108.1.0/24 [110/138] via 141.108.10.6, 00:01:43, Serial1
O        131.108.26.0/24 [110/74] via 141.108.10.6, 00:01:44, Serial1
```

Router R3 discovers the remote networks from the partitioned area 1 through the virtual link between the routers R2 and R6 as demonstrated by the IP routing table in Example 3-20.

Examples 3-21, 3-22, and 3-23 show the three configurations of routers R2, R3, and R6, respectively. R1's configuration is unchanged from Scenario 3-1.

Example 3-21 *Full Configuration on R2*

```
Current configuration:
!
version 12.0
service timestamps debug uptime
service timestamps log uptime
no service password-encryption
!
hostname R2
!
enable password cisco
!
no ip domain-lookup
!
interface Loopback0
 ip address 131.108.5.33 255.255.255.224

 ip ospf network point-to-point
 ip ospf cost 1000
!
interface Loopback1
 ip address 131.108.6.1 255.255.255.255
!
interface Loopback2
 ip address 131.108.6.2 255.255.255.255
!
interface Ethernet0/0
 ip address 131.108.1.2 255.255.255.0
!
interface TokenRing0/0
 shutdown
!
interface Serial1/0
 ip address 141.108.10.1 255.255.255.252
```

continues

Example 3-21 *Full Configuration on R2 (Continued)*

```
!
interface Serial1/1
 shutdown
!
interface Serial1/2
shutdown
!
interface Serial1/3
 shutdown
!
router ospf 2
 area 2 virtual-link 141.108.12.1
 network 131.108.1.0 0.0.0.255 area 1
 network 131.108.5.32 0.0.0.31 area 1
 network 131.108.6.1 0.0.0.0 area 1
 network 131.108.6.2 0.0.0.0 area 1
 network 141.108.10.0 0.0.0.3 area 2
!
line con 0
line aux 0
line vty 0 4
 login
!
end
```

Example 3-22 displays R3's full configuration.

Example 3-22 *Full Configuration on R3*

```
version 12.0
!
hostname R3
!
enable password cisco
!
interface Loopback0
ip address 141.108.1.1 255.255.255.128
ip ospf network point-to-point
!
interface Loopback1
ip address 141.108.1.129 255.255.255.128
ip ospf network point-to-point
!
interface Loopback2
ip address 141.108.2.1 255.255.255.224
ip ospf network point-to-point
!
interface Ethernet0
ip address 131.108.33.1 255.255.255.0
```

Example 3-22 *Full Configuration on R3 (Continued)*

```
!
interface Ethernet1
shutdown
!
interface Serial0
shutdown
!
interface Serial1
ip address 141.108.10.5 255.255.255.252
!
router ospf 3
network 131.108.33.0 0.0.0.255 area 0
network 141.108.1.0 0.0.0.127 area 0
network 141.108.1.128 0.0.0.127 area 0
network 141.108.2.0 0.0.0.31  area 0
network 141.108.10.4 0.0.0.3 area 0
line con 0
line aux 0
line vty 0 4
!
end
```

Example 3-23 displays R6's full configuration.

Example 3-23 *Full Configuration on R6*

```
!
version 12.0
!
hostname r6
!
enable password cisco
!
interface Loopback0
 ip address 141.108.9.1 255.255.255.128
 ip ospf network point-to-point
!
interface Loopback1
 ip address 141.108.9.129 255.255.255.128
  ip ospf network point-to-point
!
interface Loopback2
 ip address 141.108.12.1 255.255.255.0
 ip ospf network point-to-point
!
interface Ethernet0
 ip address 131.108.26.1 255.255.255.0
 media-type 10BaseT
```

continues

Example 3-23 *Full Configuration on R6 (Continued)*

```
!
interface Ethernet1
shutdown
!
interface Serial0
 ip address 141.108.10.6 255.255.255.252
 clockrate 125000
!
interface Serial1
 ip address 141.108.10.2 255.255.255.252
 clockrate 125000
!
interface Serial2
 shutdown
!
interface Serial3
 shutdown
!
interface TokenRing0
 shutdown
!
interface TokenRing1
 shutdown
!
router ospf 6
 area 2 virtual-link 131.108.6.2
 network 141.108.9.0 0.0.0.127 area 0
 network 141.108.9.128 0.0.0.127 area 0
 network 141.108.10.0 0.0.0.3 area 2
 network 141.108.10.4 0.0.0.3 area 0
 network 131.108.26.0 0.0.0.255 area 0
!
line con 0
line aux 0
line vty 0 4
end
```

Now, you move on to learn about some common OSPF commands you can use to ensure that remote networks are reachable.

Scenario 3-3: How OSPF Monitors, Manages, and Maintains Routes

In this scenario, you re-examine in detail the network in Figure 3-2 and discover some of the common OSPF commands for monitoring, managing, and maintaining IP routing tables. This scenario also looks at ways to configure OSPF to modify IP routing table entries, such as cost metrics and DR/BDR election.

Table 3-4 displays a summary of the commands executed in this scenario.

Table 3-4   *OSPF Commands for Monitoring, Managing, and Maintaining IP Routing Tables*

Command	Description
show ip ospf	Displays the OSPF process and details such as OSPF process ID and router ID.
show ip ospf database	Displays routers topological database.
show ip ospf neighbor	Displays OSPF neighbors.
show ip ospf neighbor detail	Displays OSPF neighbors in detail, providing parameters, such as neighbor address, hello interval, and dead interval.
show ip ospf interface	Displays information on how OSPF has been configured for a given interface.
ip ospf priority	Interface command used to change the DR/BDR election process.
ip ospf cost	Interface command used to change the cost of an OSPF interface.

Example 3-24 shows the output of the command **show ip ospf** taken from the backbone Router R3 in Figure 3-2. Table 3-5 explains how to read the most important information contained within the output.

NOTE   Scenario 3-2, and thus this scenario, have four routers with the following router IDs:

- R1—131.108.5.1

- R2—131.108.6.2

- R3—141.108.12.1

- R6—141.108.2.1

This information is shown in the examples that follow.

Example 3-24 show ip ospf *Output*

```
R3>show ip ospf
 Routing Process "ospf 3" with ID 141.108.2.1
 Supports only single TOS(TOS0) routes
 SPF schedule delay 5 secs, Hold time between two SPFs 10 secs
 Minimum LSA interval 5 secs. Minimum LSA arrival 1 secs
 Number of external LSA 0. Checksum Sum 0x0
 Number of DCbitless external LSA 0
 Number of DoNotAge external LSA 0
```

continues

Example 3-24 **show ip ospf** *Output (Continued)*

```
Number of areas in this router is 1. 1 normal 0 stub 0 nssa
   Area BACKBONE(0)
        Number of interfaces in this area is 4
        Area has no authentication
        SPF algorithm executed 3 times
        Area ranges are
        Number of LSA 13. Checksum Sum 0x54D76
        Number of DCbitless LSA 0
        Number of indication LSA 0
        Number of DoNotAge LSA 9
```

Table 3-5   *Explanation of the* **show ip ospf** *Command Output Taken from R3*

Field	Explanation
Routing process ID	Displays the process ID. In this case 141.108.2.1.
Minimum LSA interval 5 secs Minimum LSA arrival 1 sec	The amount of time that the IOS waits before the SPF calculation is completed after receiving an update. The minimum LSA interval is five seconds and the minimum LSA arrival is one second on R3.
Number of areas in this router is 1	Displays the number of areas configured on the local router. In this example, R3 has all interfaces in the backbone, or area 0. So only one area is displayed by this command.
Area BACKBONE(0)	Displays the area the router is configured for. R3 is a backbone router, so this output advises the area in backbone 0.
Number of interfaces in this area is 4	Displays the number of interfaces in area 0. R3 has four interfaces in area 0.
Area has no authentication	Displays the fact that no authentication is used on R3.

Example 3-25 shows the output of the command **show ip ospf database** taken from the backbone R3 in Figure 3-2. Table 3-6 explains how to read the most important information contained within the output.

Example 3-25 **show ip ospf database** *Output*

```
R3>show ip ospf database
        OSPF Router with ID (141.108.2.1) (Process ID 3)
                   Router Link States (Area 0)
Link ID         ADV Router      Age          Seq#        Checksum Link count
131.108.6.2     131.108.6.2     7     (DNA)  0x80000002 0x38EB    1
141.108.2.1     141.108.2.1     559          0x80000003 0xCC2     5
141.108.10.5    141.108.10.5    3110         0x8000000B 0x1AC     5
141.108.12.1    141.108.12.1    153          0x80000010 0xC3A     7
```

Example 3-25 show ip ospf database *Output (Continued)*

```
              Summary Net Link States (Area 0)
Link ID         ADV Router      Age        Seq#       Checksum
131.108.1.0     131.108.6.2     82    (DNA) 0x80000001 0xE663
131.108.4.1     131.108.6.2     82    (DNA) 0x80000001 0xC57F
131.108.4.129   131.108.6.2     82    (DNA) 0x80000001 0xC004
131.108.5.1     131.108.6.2     82    (DNA) 0x80000001 0xBA89
131.108.5.32    131.108.6.2     82    (DNA) 0x80000001 0x8ED4
131.108.6.1     131.108.6.2     82    (DNA) 0x80000001 0x4B02
131.108.6.2     131.108.6.2     82    (DNA) 0x80000001 0x410B
141.108.10.0    131.108.6.2     82    (DNA) 0x80000001 0x280C
141.108.10.0    141.108.12.1    1958        0x80000006 0x846B
```

Table 3-6   *Explanation of the* **show ip ospf database** *Command*

Field	Explanation
OSPF Router with ID (141.108.2.1) (Process ID 3)	The router ID and process ID on the router configured by the network administrator.
Router Link States (Area 0)	Displays the link-state advertisements from connected neighbors discovered by the Hello protocol.
Summary Net Link States (Area 0)	Information displayed by ABRs.

To show you some different output, look at two more examples from Scenario 3-2: one from R2 and one from R6. Example 3-26 displays the **show ip ospf neighbor** command from R2.

Example 3-26 show ip ospf neighbor *from R2*

```
R2>show ip ospf neighbor
Neighbor ID     Pri   State        Dead Time   Address        Interface
131.108.5.1      1    FULL/DR      00:00:39    131.108.1.1    Ethernet0/0
141.108.12.1     1    FULL/  -     00:00:34    141.108.10.2   Serial1/0
```

Router R2 has two neighbors: one across the Ethernet segment and another through the serial connection to R6. The **show ip ospf neighbor** command displays the neighbor router ID and the priority of the neighbor (both 1 in this example) as well as the DR. Notice that the DR is R1 as seen by R2. The state of the adjacency (Full) and the dead time are displayed. The dead time is the amount of time before the adjacency is declared dead or inactive if a Hello packet is not received. The dead time must be the same of the adjacent router. The dead time is four times the hello interval. The address field displays the remote router's IP address. In this case, the IP address assigned to R1 is 131.108.1.1. The interface field describes the outbound interface from which the neighbor was discovered. Example 3-27 displays the neighbors on R6 in more detail by adding the **detail** parameter to the **show ip ospf neighbor** command.

Example 3-27 **show ip ospf neighbor detail** *from R6*

```
r6#show ip ospf neighbor detail
 Neighbor 141.108.2.1, interface address 141.108.10.5
    In the area 0 via interface Serial0
    Neighbor priority is 1, State is FULL, 6 state changes
    DR is 0.0.0.0 BDR is 0.0.0.0
    Options 2
    Dead timer due in 00:00:35
 Neighbor 131.108.6.2, interface address 141.108.10.1
    In the area 2 via interface Serial1
    Neighbor priority is 1, State is FULL, 6 state changes
    DR is 0.0.0.0 BDR is 0.0.0.0
    Options 2
    Dead timer due in 00:00:33
```

Router R6 has no adjacency across any broadcast media, such as Ethernet. Therefore, the neighbors are all in a Full state but no DR or BDR is elected across the wide-area network (WAN) link, because the WAN link is considered a point-to-point link. To determine what type of OSPF network the given interface is, use the **show ip ospf interface** command. Example 3-28 displays this command in its most basic form taken from R6. You can provide more parameters, such as **interface serial** *number.*

Example 3-28 **show ip ospf interface** *from R6*

```
r6#show ip ospf interface
Ethernet0 is up, line protocol is up
  Internet Address 131.108.26.1/24, Area 0
  Process ID 6, Router ID 141.108.12.1, Network Type BROADCAST, Cost: 10
  Transmit Delay is 1 sec, State WAITING, Priority 1
  No designated router on this network
  No backup designated router on this network
  Timer intervals configured, Hello 10, Dead 40, Wait 40, Retransmit 5
    Hello due in 00:00:01
    Wait time before Designated router selection 00:00:11
  Neighbor Count is 0, Adjacent neighbor count is 0
  Suppress hello for 0 neighbor(s)
Loopback0 is up, line protocol is up
  Internet Address 141.108.9.1/25, Area 0
  Process ID 6, Router ID 141.108.12.1, Network Type POINT_TO_POINT, Cost: 1
  Transmit Delay is 1 sec, State POINT_TO_POINT,
  Timer intervals configured, Hello 10, Dead 40, Wait 40, Retransmit 5
    Hello due in 00:00:00
  Neighbor Count is 0, Adjacent neighbor count is 0
  Suppress hello for 0 neighbor(s)
Loopback1 is up, line protocol is up
  Internet Address 141.108.9.129/25, Area 0
```

Example 3-28 show ip ospf interface *from R6 (Continued)*

```
     Process ID 6, Router ID 141.108.12.1, Network Type POINT_TO_POINT, Cost: 1
     Transmit Delay is 1 sec, State POINT_TO_POINT,
     Timer intervals configured, Hello 10, Dead 40, Wait 40, Retransmit 5
       Hello due in 00:00:00
     Neighbor Count is 0, Adjacent neighbor count is 0
     Suppress hello for 0 neighbor(s)
   Loopback2 is up, line protocol is up
     Internet Address 141.108.12.1/24, Area 0
     Process ID 6, Router ID 141.108.12.1, Network Type POINT_TO_POINT, Cost: 1
     Transmit Delay is 1 sec, State POINT_TO_POINT,
     Timer intervals configured, Hello 10, Dead 40, Wait 40, Retransmit 5
       Hello due in 00:00:00
     Neighbor Count is 0, Adjacent neighbor count is 0
     Suppress hello for 0 neighbor(s)
   Serial0 is up, line protocol is up
     Internet Address 141.108.10.6/30, Area 0
     Process ID 6, Router ID 141.108.12.1, Network Type POINT_TO_POINT, Cost: 64
     Transmit Delay is 1 sec, State POINT_TO_POINT,
     Timer intervals configured, Hello 10, Dead 40, Wait 40, Retransmit 5
       Hello due in 00:00:06
     Neighbor Count is 1, Adjacent neighbor count is 1
       Adjacent with neighbor 141.108.2.1
     Suppress hello for 0 neighbor(s)
   Serial1 is up, line protocol is up
     Internet Address 141.108.10.2/30, Area 2
     Process ID 6, Router ID 141.108.12.1, Network Type POINT_TO_POINT, Cost: 64
     Transmit Delay is 1 sec, State POINT_TO_POINT,
     Timer intervals configured, Hello 10, Dead 40, Wait 40, Retransmit 5
       Hello due in 00:00:06
     Neighbor Count is 1, Adjacent neighbor count is 1
       Adjacent with neighbor 131.108.6.2
     Suppress hello for 0 neighbor(s)
   r6#
```

Router R6 has six interfaces configured with OSPF, so you should expect details about those interfaces. Example 3-28 displays all interface network types as point-to-point (loopbacks by default are configured as loopback, but the IOS command **ip ospf network point-to-point** configures the loopback as point-to-point networks) except the Ethernet segment, because Ethernet is a broadcast medium. Also notice that because R6 has no neighbors over the Ethernet network, no DR/BDR is elected, because there is no need. The dead interval is four times the hello interval on all interfaces.

Now use some interface commands on the Figure 3-2 network to modify the behavior of the DR/BDR election process. Start by changing the designated router in area 1 and ensure that Router R2 becomes the DR. Example 3-29 displays the current DR and the configuration change on R2 to make the priority higher than R1 by setting the priority to 255.

Example 3-29 *Changing the IP OSPF Priority on R2*

```
R2#show ip ospf neighbor
Neighbor ID     Pri   State       Dead Time   Address       Interface
131.108.5.1      1    FULL/DR     00:00:35    131.108.1.1   Ethernet0/0
141.108.12.1     1    FULL/  -    00:00:37    141.108.10.2  Serial1/0
R2#configure term
Enter configuration commands, one per line.  End with CNTL/Z.
R2(config)#interface e 0/0
R2(config-if)#ip ospf priority 255
R2# show ip ospf neighbor
Neighbor ID     Pri   State       Dead Time   Address       Interface
131.108.5.1      1    FULL/DR     00:00:33    131.108.1.1   Ethernet0/0
141.108.12.1     1    FULL/  -    00:00:34    141.108.10.2  Serial1/0
R2# show ip ospf neighbor
Neighbor ID     Pri   State       Dead Time   Address       Interface
131.108.5.1      1    FULL/DR     00:00:31    131.108.1.1   Ethernet0/0
141.108.12.1     1    FULL/  -    00:00:32    141.108.10.2  Serial1/0
```

Example 3-29 stills displays the DR as R1 and not R2 even after the configuration setting changes the priority to 255, because the election process has already taken place and R1 is still the DR. Example 3-30 simulates a network outage by shutting down R1 E0/0. Now look at the OSPF neighbor on R1, as displayed by Example 3-30.

Example 3-30 *Shutting Down R1 E0/0 and* **show ip ospf neighbor** *Commands*

```
R1(config)#interface e 0/0
R1(config-if)#shutdown
1w6d: %LINEPROTO-5-UPDOWN: Line protocol on Interface Ethernet0/0, changed state
 to down
1w6d: %LINK-3-UPDOWN: Interface Ethernet0/0, changed state to up
1w6d: %LINEPROTO-5-UPDOWN: Line protocol on Interface Ethernet0/0, changed state
 to up
R1(config-if)#no shutdown
1w6d: %LINK-3-UPDOWN: Interface Ethernet0/0, changed state to up
1w6d: %LINEPROTO-5-UPDOWN: Line protocol on Interface Ethernet0/0, changed state
 to up
R1#show ip ospf neighbor
Neighbor ID     Pri   State       Dead Time   Address       Interface
131.108.6.2     255   INIT/-      00:00:39    131.108.1.2   Ethernet0/0
R1#show ip ospf neighbor
Neighbor ID     Pri   State       Dead Time   Address       Interface
131.108.6.2     255   EXCHANGE/-  0:39        131.108.1.2   Ethernet0/0
R1#show ip ospf neighbor
Neighbor ID     Pri   State       Dead Time   Address       Interface
131.108.6.2     255   EXSTART/DR  00:00:39    131.108.1.2   Ethernet0/0
R1#show ip ospf neighbor
Neighbor ID     Pri   State       Dead Time   Address       Interface
```

Example 3-30 *Shutting Down R1 E0/0 and* **show ip ospf neighbor** *Commands (Continued)*

```
131.108.6.2      255    LOADING/DR    0:00:39    131.108.1.2    Ethernet0/0
R1#show ip ospf nei
Neighbor ID      Pri    State         Dead Time  Address        Interface
131.108.6.2      255    FULL/DR       00:00:39   131.108.1.2    Ethernet0/0
```

Example 3-30 displays some interesting facts. The first is that when you shut down the interface and enable the Ethernet port E0/0 on R1, IOS displays messages to advise you of the changed state. Second, the first neighbor state is INIT, which means R1 sent Hello packets, which are awaiting R2's reply. The state of EXSTART/DR means the two routers have formed a master relationship. The LOADING state indicates that link-state requests have been sent. The FULL state indicates the two routers are fully adjacent or share the same OSPF database.

The DR indicates that the designated router is the neighbor with the IP address 131.108.1.2, which is Router R2. Example 3-31 displays the neighbor state as seen by R2, which is now the backup designated router (BDR).

Example 3-31 **show ip ospf neighbor** *on R2*

```
R2#show ip ospf neighbor
Neighbor ID      Pri    State         Dead Time  Address        Interface
131.108.5.1      1      FULL/BDR      00:00:34   131.108.1.1    Ethernet0/0
141.108.12.1     1      FULL/  -      00:00:35   141.108.10.2   Serial1/0
```

The final command in this scenario is the **ip ospf cost** command. You use this command to change the cost Cisco routers assign by default by using the formula OSPF cost = 10^8 / bandwidth. This command is not the only method you can use to change the cost. You can also use the **bandwidth** command on a particular interface and let the Cisco IOS use the bandwidth portion of the cost formula to calculate the new cost.

NOTE   You can also use the command **auto-cost reference-bandwidth** *reference-bandwidth* during the OSPF process to change the bandwidth portion of the cost calculation. You should set this command equally across all your routers if you choose to use it. The *reference-bandwidth* is set to 10^8 by default.

Assume you have a request from the network administrator that all loopbacks on R1 being advertised to R2 have a total cost of 100. Example 3-32 displays the current cost on R2.

Example 3-32 *R2's OSPF Routing Table*

```
R2#show ip route ospf
     141.108.0.0/16 is variably subnetted, 7 subnets, 3 masks
O       141.108.1.128/25 [110/846] via 141.108.10.2, 3d03h, Serial1/0
O       141.108.9.128/25 [110/782] via 141.108.10.2, 3d03h, Serial1/0
O       141.108.1.0/25 [110/846] via 141.108.10.2, 3d03h, Serial1/0
O       141.108.9.0/25 [110/782] via 141.108.10.2, 3d03h, Serial1/0
O       141.108.12.0/24 [110/782] via 141.108.10.2, 3d03h, Serial1/0
O       141.108.10.4/30 [110/845] via 141.108.10.2, 3d03h, Serial1/0
     131.108.0.0/16 is variably subnetted, 9 subnets, 3 masks
O       131.108.4.129/32 [110/11] via 131.108.1.1, 00:02:03, Ethernet0/0
O       131.108.33.0/24 [110/855] via 141.108.10.2, 3d03h, Serial1/0
O       131.108.4.1/32 [110/11] via 131.108.1.1, 00:02:03, Ethernet0/0
O       131.108.5.1/32 [110/11] via 131.108.1.1, 00:02:03, Ethernet0/0
O       131.108.26.0/24 [110/791] via 141.108.10.2, 3d03h, Serial1/0
```

The three loopbacks display a cost of 11. To increase this to 100, you can increase the cost per interface. Example 3-33 displays the cost change on R1 loopback interfaces from the default of 1 to 90. Remember that by default, the cost of a 10MB Ethernet interface is 10.

Example 3-33 *Changing the Default Cost on R1 E0/0*

```
R1(config)#interface loopback 0
R1(config-if)#ip ospf cost 90
R1(config-if)#interface loopback 1
R1(config-if)#ip ospf cost 90
R1(config-if)#interface loopback 2
R1(config-if)#ip ospf cost 90
```

Changing the default cost from 1 to 90 means that the total cost R2 sees is 10, which is the default cost on an Ethernet interface plus the 90 you configured. Example 3-34 now displays the new OSPF routing table with the loopbacks from R1 with a new cost of 100.

Example 3-34 *R2's OSPF Routing Table After the Cost Change*

```
R2#show ip route ospf
     141.108.0.0/16 is variably subnetted, 7 subnets, 3 masks
O       141.108.1.128/25 [110/846] via 141.108.10.2, 3d03h, Serial1/0
O       141.108.9.128/25 [110/782] via 141.108.10.2, 3d03h, Serial1/0
O       141.108.1.0/25 [110/846] via 141.108.10.2, 3d03h, Serial1/0
O       141.108.9.0/25 [110/782] via 141.108.10.2, 3d03h, Serial1/0
O       141.108.12.0/24 [110/782] via 141.108.10.2, 3d03h, Serial1/0
O       141.108.10.4/30 [110/845] via 141.108.10.2, 3d03h, Serial1/0
```

Example 3-34 *R2's OSPF Routing Table After the Cost Change (Continued)*

```
        131.108.0.0/16 is variably subnetted, 9 subnets, 3 masks
O       131.108.4.129/32 [110/100] via 131.108.1.1, 00:00:35, Ethernet0/0
O       131.108.33.0/24 [110/855] via 141.108.10.2, 3d03h, Serial1/0
O       131.108.4.1/32 [110/100] via 131.108.1.1, 00:00:35, Ethernet0/0
O       131.108.5.1/32 [110/100] via 131.108.1.1, 00:00:35, Ethernet0/0
O       131.108.26.0/24 [110/791] via 141.108.10.2, 3d03h, Serial1/0
```

Example 3-34 displays the cost to the remote networks on R1 as 100.

The next scenario shows you how to configure an advanced OSPF network using a three-router network over Frame Relay.

Scenario 3-4: OSPF over Frame Relay in an NBMA Environment

This scenario covers configuring OSPF over Frame Relay in an NBMA environment. This scenario helps you discover some of the advanced features of OSPF, such as DR election in an NBMA environment.

Figure 3-4 displays the three-router network over Frame Relay used in this scenario. Included in Figure 3-4 are the IP addressing scheme, Frame Relay DLCI numbering, and OSPF area assignments.

Figure 3-4   *OSPF over Frame Relay*

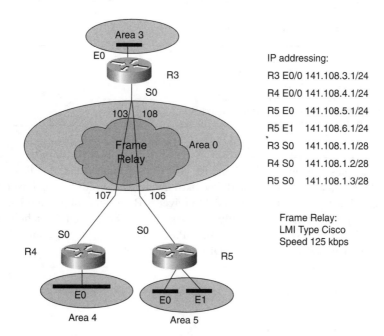

IP addressing:

R3 E0/0 141.108.3.1/24

R4 E0/0 141.108.4.1/24

R5 E0   141.108.5.1/24

R5 E1   141.108.6.1/24

R3 S0   141.108.1.1/28

R4 S0   141.108.1.2/28

R5 S0   141.108.1.3/28

Frame Relay:
LMI Type Cisco
Speed 125 kbps

This scenario involves three routers running OSPF over Frame Relay. Start by configuring the Frame Relay parameters. Figure 3-4 displays the Frame Relay DLCIs and Local Management Interface (LMI) types. Example 3-35 displays R3's Frame Relay configuration. You do not use subinterfaces in this scenario to demonstrate an NBMA environment.

Example 3-35 *R3's Frame Relay Configuration*

```
R3(config)#interface serial 0
R3(config-if)#ip address 141.108.1.1 255.255.255.248
R3(config-if)# encapsulation frame-relay
R3(config-if)# frame-relay interface-dlci 103
R3(config-fr-dlci)# frame-relay interface-dlci 108
```

Example 3-35 shows you how to configure the IP address and how to enable Frame Relay encapsulation. R3 also requires the DLCI information, as displayed in Figure 3-4. The specific DLCIs are 103, which is the path to R4, and 108, which is the path to R5.

Example 3-36 and Example 3-37 show the configurations of R4 and R5, respectively.

Example 3-36 *The Frame Relay Configuration on R4*

```
interface Serial0
 ip address 141.108.1.2 255.255.255.248
 encapsulation frame-relay
 frame-relay interface-dlci 107
 frame-relay map ip 141.108.1.1 107 broadcast
```

Example 3-37 *The Frame Relay Configuration on R5*

```
interface Serial0
 ip address 141.108.1.3 255.255.255.248
 encapsulation frame-relay
 frame-relay interface-dlci 106
 frame-relay map ip 141.108.1.1 106 broadcast
```

NOTE   In Examples 3-36 and 3-37, R4 and R5 map IP over Frame Relay, but this is not the case on R3 in Example 3-35. Frame Relay, like any protocol, needs to map Layer 2 of the Open System Interconnection (OSI) model to Layer 3. R3 is not configured for static mapping, because Frame Relay dynamically discovers the maps because R3 is a hub router using Frame Relay inverse Address resolution Protocol (ARP) protocol. Frame Relay inverse ARP automatically discovers the DLCI and next hop IP address.

Now that you have enabled Frame Relay, you can start the OSPF configuration. Example 3-38 displays the OSPF configuration on R3 along with the IP address assignment to E0.

Example 3-38 *OSPF and IP Address Configuration on R3*

```
R3(config)#interface ethernet 0
R3(config-if)#ip address 141.108.3.1 255.255.255.0
R3(config-if)#router ospf 3
R3(config-router)#network 141.108.3.0 0.0.0.255 area 3
R3(config-router)#network 141.108.1.0 0.0.0.7 area 0
```

You must also enable OSPF on Routers R4 and R5. Example 3-39 displays the OSPF configuration on R4 along with the IP address assignment to E0.

Example 3-39 *OSPF and IP Address Configuration on R4*

```
R4(config)#interface ethernet 0
R4(config-if)#ip address 141.108.4.1 255.255.255.0
R4(config)#router ospf 4
R4(config-router)#network 141.108.4.0 0.0.0.255 area
R4(config-router)#network 141.108.1.0 0.0.0.7 area 0
```

Example 3-40 displays the OSPF configuration on R5 along with the IP address assignment to E0.

Example 3-40 *OSPF and IP Address Configuration on R5*

```
R5(config-if)#ip address 141.108.5.1 255.255.255.0
R5(config-if)#interface ethernet 1
R5(config-if)#ip address 141.108.6.1 255.255.255.0
R5(config-if)#router ospf 5
R5(config-router)#network 141.108.5.0 0.0.3.255 area 5
R5(config-router)#network 141.108.1.0 0.0.0.7 area 0
```

NOTE   Example 3-40 places the two Ethernet networks with the one OSPF statement.

Ensure that OSPF adjacencies are up and in a FULL state on R3. Example 3-41 displays the OSPF neighbor state on router R3.

Example 3-41 **show ip ospf neighbor** *Command on R3*

```
R3>show ip ospf neighbor
R3>
```

As you can see from the lack of output in Example 3-41, Router R3 has no adjacencies. The IOS on R3 in Example 3-41 tells you there are no OSPF relationships to R4 and R5. That lack of relationships is because OSPF Hello packets (using multicast address, of course) are not sent over a nonbroadcast OSPF network type.

Figure 3-4 shows a classic example of OSPF over NBMA. In an NBMA environment, broadcasts or multicasts do not propagate over the Frame Relay. Example 3-42 displays the OSPF network type on R3 link to R4 and R5.

Example 3-42 show ip ospf interface serial 0 *Command on R3*

```
R3>show ip ospf int s 0
Serial0 is up, line protocol is up
  Internet Address 141.108.1.1/29, Area 0
  Process ID 3, Router ID 141.108.10.5, Network Type NON_BROADCAST, Cost: 64
  Transmit Delay is 1 sec, State DR, Priority 1
  Designated Router (ID) 141.108.10.5, Interface address 141.108.1.1
  No backup designated router on this network
  Timer intervals configured, Hello 30, Dead 120, Wait 120, Retransmit 5
    Hello due in 00:00:00
  Neighbor Count is 0, Adjacent neighbor count is 0
  Suppress hello for 0 neighbor(s)
```

Example 3-42 displays no neighbor and the main fact that the link is considered a nonbroadcast link. OSPF can be configured a variety of ways to accomplish this. To demonstrate OSPF over NBMA in this scenario, you do not modify the network type, but rather you statically configure a neighbor relationship from R3 to R4 and R5. To enable a static OSPF neighbor relationship, enter the following command:

neighbor *ip address of neighbor*

Example 3-43 displays the configuration on R3 to remote routers R4 and R5.

Example 3-43 *Static Neighbor Configuration on R3*

```
R3(config)#router ospf 3
R3(config-router)#neighbor 141.108.1.2
R3(config-router)#neighbor 141.108.1.3
```

The command **neighbor 141.108.1.2** configures the neighbor to R4. The command **neighbor 141.108.1.3** configures the neighbor to R5.

Example 3-43 overcomes the need to change the network environment from nonbroadcast and allows a static configuration of remote OSPF routers. One more important task is required. Router R4 and R5 are spoke, or edge, routers. The hub router, R3, must become the DR, because R3 has links to both R4 and R5 and information will be sent from R4 to R5, for example, through R3. The easiest way to make R3 the DR is to disable R4 and R5 from ever becoming the DR by applying a 0 priority on R4 and R5. Example 3-44 demonstrates how to set the priority to 0, in effect disabling any chance for R4 or R5 to become the DR.

Example 3-44 *IP OSPF Priority Set to 0 on R4 and R5*

```
R4(config)#interface serial 0
R4(config-if)#ip ospf priority 0
R5(config)#interface serial 0
R5(config-if)#ip ospf priority 0
```

Examples 3-45 displays the OSPF neighbors on R3.

Example 3-45 **show ip ospf neighbor** *Command on R3*

```
R3#show ip ospf nei
Neighbor ID     Pri   State        Dead Time   Address       Interface
141.108.5.1      0    FULL/DROTHER  00:01:54    141.108.1.3   Serial0
141.108.1.2      0    FULL/DROTHER  00:01:44    141.108.1.2   Serial0
```

The state shown in Example 3-45 displays a FULL adjacency and a state known as DROTHER, which indicates that the neighbor was not chosen as the DR or BDR and cannot be because the priority has been set to zero. Example 3-46 displays the full working configuration of R3.

Example 3-46 *R3's Full Configuration*

```
version 12.0
!
hostname R3
!
enable password cisco
!
ip subnet-zero
!
interface Ethernet0
 ip address 141.108.3.1 255.255.255.0
!
interface Ethernet1
 no ip address
 shutdown
!
interface Serial0
 ip address 141.108.1.1 255.255.255.248
 encapsulation frame-relay
 frame-relay interface-dlci 103
 frame-relay interface-dlci 108
!
interface Serial1
 ip address 141.108.10.5 255.255.255.252
```

continues

Example 3-46 *(Continued)R3's Full Configuration (Continued)*

```
!
router ospf 3
 network 141.108.1.0 0.0.0.7 area 0
 network 141.108.3.0 0.0.0.255 area 3
 neighbor 141.108.1.3
 neighbor 141.108.1.2
!
line con 0
line aux 0
line vty 0 4
end
```

Example 3-47 displays the full working configuration of R4.

Example 3-47 *R4's Full Configuration*

```
version 12.0
!
hostname R4
!
enable password cisco
!
ip subnet-zero
!
interface Ethernet0
 ip address 141.108.4.1 255.255.255.0
interface Serial0
 ip address 141.108.1.2 255.255.255.248
 encapsulation frame-relay
 ip ospf priority 0
 frame-relay map ip 141.108.1.1 107 broadcast
 frame-relay interface-dlci 107
 frame-relay lmi-type cisco
!
interface Serial1
 shutdown
!
router ospf 4
 network 141.108.1.0 0.0.0.7 area 0
 network 141.108.4.0 0.0.0.255 area 4
!
line con 0
line aux 0
line vty 0 4
!
end
```

Example 3-48 displays the full working configuration of R5.

Example 3-48 *R5's Full Configuration*

```
version 12.0
!
hostname R5
!
enable password cisco
!
ip subnet-zero
!
interface Ethernet0
 ip address 141.108.5.1 255.255.255.0
!
interface Ethernet1
 ip address 141.108.6.1 255.255.255.0
!
interface Serial0
 ip address 141.108.1.3 255.255.255.248
 encapsulation frame-relay
 ip ospf priority 0
 frame-relay map ip 141.108.1.1 106 broadcast
 frame-relay interface-dlci 106
!
interface Serial1
 shutdown
!
router ospf 5
 network 141.108.1.0 0.0.0.7 area 0
 network 141.108.4.0 0.0.3.255 area 5
!
line con 0
line aux 0
line vty 0 4
!
end
```

The final scenario covers common **show** and **debug** commands used to verify correct OSPF implementation.

Scenario 3-5: Verifying OSPF Routing

This scenario covers common techniques used in OSPF networks to verify correct configuration in a single OSPF area. In this scenario, the configurations supplied are not the full working solutions to demonstrate the power of OSPF.

Figure 3-5 displays a simple two-router topology. The two routers are named SanFran and Chicago. Figure 3-5 displays the correct IP address assignment and OSPF area assignment.

The network administrator of R1 has told you that a number of remote networks on R2 are not reachable by R1.

Figure 3-5   *Sample Network for Verifying OSPF Routing*

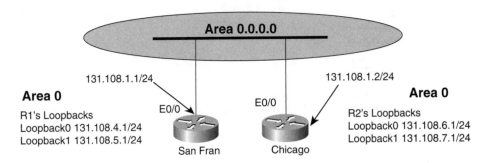

Figure 3-5 displays two routers with the names SanFran and Chicago. To change the name of a router, you use the **hostname** *name* command. Also, notice that the backbone segment is displayed as 0.0.0.0. The backbone can be configured on Cisco routers as 0 or 0.0.0.0.

Example 3-49 displays SanFran's IP routing table.

Example 3-49 *SanFran's IP Routing Table*

```
SanFran#show ip route
     131.108.0.0/24 is subnetted, 3 subnets
C       131.108.5.0 is directly connected, Loopback1
C       131.108.4.0 is directly connected, Loopback0
C       131.108.1.0 is directly connected, Ethernet0/0
R1#
```

Example 3-49 displays no remote entries on R1. Start by ensuring that OSPF is correctly configured on R1 by using the **show ip ospf interface** command. Example 3-50 displays a sample output taken from the router SanFran.

Example 3-50 show ip ospf interface *Command on SanFran*

```
SanFran#show ip ospf interface
Ethernet0/0 is up, line protocol is up
  Internet Address 131.108.1.1/24, Area 0.0.0.0
  Process ID 1, Router ID 131.108.5.1, Network Type BROADCAST, Cost: 10
  Transmit Delay is 1 sec, State DR, Priority 1
  Designated Router (ID) 131.108.5.1, Interface address 131.108.1.1
```

Example 3-50 **show ip ospf interface** *Command on SanFran (Continued)*

```
  No backup designated router on this network
  Timer intervals configured, Hello 30, Dead 120, Wait 120, Retransmit 5
    Hello due in 00:00:00
  Neighbor Count is 0, Adjacent neighbor count is 0
  Suppress hello for 0 neighbor(s)
Loopback0 is up, line protocol is up
  Internet Address 131.108.4.1/24, Area 0.0.0.0
  Process ID 1, Router ID 131.108.5.1, Network Type LOOPBACK, Cost: 90
  Loopback interface is treated as a stub Host
Loopback1 is up, line protocol is up
  Internet Address 131.108.5.1/24, Area 0.0.0.0
  Process ID 1, Router ID 131.108.5.1, Network Type LOOPBACK, Cost: 90
  Loopback interface is treated as a stub Host
```

Example 3-50 displays a number of important details, such as the Ethernet interface on R1 resides in area 0.0.0.0, or the backbone; the network type over the Ethernet interface is broadcast; and the router SanFran is the elected DR. The loopbacks on Chicago and SanFran are active (software interfaces, like loopbacks, are active as long as they are not administratively shutdown), so OSPF looks like it is correctly configured on R1. Take the same steps on Chicago. Example 3-51 displays a sample output from the **show ip ospf interface** command.

Example 3-51 **show ip ospf interface** *Command on Chicago*

```
Chicago#show ip ospf interface
Loopback0 is up, line protocol is up
  Internet Address 131.108.6.1/24, Area 0.0.0.0
  Process ID 2, Router ID 131.108.7.1, Network Type POINT_TO_POINT, Cost: 1
  Transmit Delay is 1 sec, State POINT_TO_POINT,
  Timer intervals configured, Hello 10, Dead 40, Wait 40, Retransmit 5
    Hello due in 00:00:00
  Neighbor Count is 0, Adjacent neighbor count is 0
  Suppress hello for 0 neighbor(s)
Loopback1 is up, line protocol is up
  Internet Address 131.108.7.1/24, Area 0.0.0.0
  Process ID 2, Router ID 131.108.7.1, Network Type LOOPBACK, Cost: 1
  Loopback interface is treated as a stub Host
```

Example 3-51 displays the loopbacks in OSPF process 2, but the Ethernet interface is not enabled. Example 3-52 displays the OSPF configuration on Chicago.

Example 3-52 *OSPF Configuration on Chicago*

```
router ospf 2
 network 131.108.1.0 0.0.0.0 area 0.0.0.0
 network 131.108.6.0 0.0.0.255 area 0.0.0.0
 network 131.108.7.0 0.0.0.255 area 0.0.0.0
```

Example 3-52 displays the fault with the router Chicago. The command **network 131.108.1.0 0.0.0.0** causes the router to enable OSPF for the interface configured with the IP address 131.108.1.0. This address is a reserved address for the subnet 131.108.1.0/24; hence OSPF cannot run. Remove this command and install the correct network and mask command. Example 3-53 displays the removal of the incorrect command and insertion of the correct network statement.

Example 3-53 *Modifying the OSPF Configuration on Chicago*

```
Chicago(config)#router ospf 2
Chicago (config-router)#no network 131.108.1.0 0.0.0.0 area 0.0.0.0
Chicago (config-router)#network 131.108.1.2 0.0.0.0 area 0.0.0.0
```

Make sure that OSPF is enabled on Chicago's Ethernet interface. Example 3-54 displays a sample output with the **show ip ospf interface** command.

Example 3-54 show ip ospf interface *Command on Chicago*

```
Ethernet0/0 is up, line protocol is up
  Internet Address 131.108.1.2/24, Area 0.0.0.0
  Process ID 2, Router ID 131.108.7.1, Network Type BROADCAST, Cost: 10
  Transmit Delay is 1 sec, State WAITING, Priority 1
  No designated router on this network
  No backup designated router on this network
  Timer intervals configured, Hello 10, Dead 40, Wait 120, Retransmit 5
    Hello due in 00:00:16
    Wait time before Designated router selection 00:01:46
  Neighbor Count is 0, Adjacent neighbor count is 0
  Suppress hello for 0 neighbor(s)
Loopback0 is up, line protocol is up
  Internet Address 131.108.6.1/24, Area 0.0.0.0
  Process ID 2, Router ID 131.108.7.1, Network Type POINT_TO_POINT, Cost: 1
  Transmit Delay is 1 sec, State POINT_TO_POINT,
  Timer intervals configured, Hello 10, Dead 40, Wait 40, Retransmit 5
    Hello due in 00:00:00
  Neighbor Count is 0, Adjacent neighbor count is 0
  Suppress hello for 0 neighbor(s)
Loopback1 is up, line protocol is up
  Internet Address 131.108.7.1/24, Area 0.0.0.0
  Process ID 2, Router ID 131.108.7.1, Network Type LOOPBACK, Cost: 1
  Loopback interface is treated as a stub Host
```

Example 3-54 displays that the Ethernet interface is now, in fact, enabled in OSPF area 0.0.0.0. The fact that no adjacent neighbor is present still represents a problem.

Move back to the router named SanFran, and check for OSPF adjacency. Example 3-55 displays the OSPF characteristic of the Router SanFran.

Example 3-55 **show ip ospf interface ethernet 0/0** *Command on SanFran*

```
SanFran#show ip ospf interface ethernet 0/0
Ethernet0/0 is up, line protocol is up
  Internet Address 131.108.1.1/24, Area 0.0.0.0
  Process ID 1, Router ID 131.108.5.1, Network Type BROADCAST, Cost: 10
  Transmit Delay is 1 sec, State DR, Priority 1
  Designated Router (ID) 131.108.5.1, Interface address 131.108.1.1
  No backup designated router on this network
  Timer intervals configured, Hello 30, Dead 120, Wait 120, Retransmit 5
    Hello due in 00:00:11
  Neighbor Count is 0, Adjacent neighbor count is 0
  Suppress hello for 0 neighbor(s)
```

No neighbor exists on this segment. Now introduce a new command using the **debug** command set:

```
debug ip ospf adj
```

This command enables IOS output of all events relating to adjacencies. Example 3-56 displays the command being enabled and a sample output taken from the router SanFran.

Example 3-56 **debug ip ospf adj** *and Sample IOS Display*

```
SanFran#debug ip ospf adj
OSPF adjacency events debugging is on
SanFran#
2w5d: OSPF: Rcv hello from 131.108.7.1 area 0.0.0.0 from Ethernet0/0 131.108.1.2
2w5d: OSPF: Mismatched hello parameters from 131.108.1.2
2w5d: Dead R 40 C 120, Hello R 10 C 30  Mask R 255.255.255.0 C 255.255.255.0
```

The error message displayed by the IOS in Example 3-56 clearly states you have a mismatch in the hello interval. In other words, the hello interval the Router SanFran uses (local router where the display is taken from) is different from the router sending out a Hello packet with the router ID 131.108.7.1, through the IP address 131.108.1.2.

Remember that hello and dead intervals must match before neighboring routers can become fully adjacent.

Example 3-56 displays **Dead R 40 C 120, Hello R 10 C 30**. The first information tells you that the dead interval (displayed as Dead in the debug output) received from the router Chicago (Dead R 40) is set to 40 seconds, whereas the configured (displayed as C from the debug output) dead interval (Dead C 120) on SanFran is 120 seconds. Therefore, there is a mismatch error. Similarly, the hello interval Chicago receives is set to 10 seconds; whereas the configured hello interval on SanFran is 30, another mismatch. The sample debug output, as displayed in Example 3-56, advises you that the hello and dead interval should be correctly set on both routers: SanFran and Chicago.

OSPF routers never become adjacent (in other words, never exchange OSPF databases) unless all OSPF parameters, such as the hello interval or dead interval, are the same.

Example 3-56 advises you that the Chicago dead interval is 40 seconds, whereas the configured interval on SanFran is 120 seconds.

Example 3-56 advises you that Chicago's hello interval is 10 seconds, whereas the configured hello interval on SanFran is 30 seconds. These two clearly do not match.

Example 3-57 displays the configuration change on SanFran to ensure hello and dead intervals are configured the same way. The hello interval is set to 10 seconds.

NOTE   The dead interval, by default, is four times the hello interval. Hence, Router SanFran is configured with a hello interval of 10 seconds, which automatically configures the dead interval to 40 seconds thereby matching the hello and dead intervals set on the router named Chicago.

Example 3-57 *Changing Hello Interval to 10 Seconds on SanFran*

```
SanFran(config)#interface ethernet 0/0
SanFran(config-if)#ip ospf hello-interval 10
SanFran(config-if)#^Z
SanFran#
2w5d: %SYS-5-CONFIG_I: Configured from console by console
SanFran#
2w5d: OSPF: Rcv hello from 131.108.7.1 area 0.0.0.0 from Ethernet0/0 131.108.1.2
2w5d: OSPF: End of hello processing
2w5d: OSPF: Rcv DBD from 131.108.7.1 on Ethernet0/0 seq 0x1235 opt 0x2 flag 0x7
len 32  mtu 1500 state INIT
2w5d: OSPF: 2 Way Communication to 131.108.7.1 on Ethernet0/0, state 2WAY
2w5d: OSPF: Neighbor change Event on interface Ethernet0/0
2w5d: OSPF: DR/BDR election on Ethernet0/0
2w5d: OSPF: Elect BDR 0.0.0.0
2w5d: OSPF: Elect DR 131.108.7.1
2w5d: OSPF: Elect BDR 131.108.5.1
2w5d: OSPF: Elect DR 131.108.7.1
2w5d:         DR: 131.108.7.1 (Id)    BDR: 131.108.5.1 (Id)
2w5d: OSPF: Send DBD to 131.108.7.1 on Ethernet0/0 seq 0x11C4 opt 0x2 flag 0x7 l
en 32
2w5d: OSPF: Set Ethernet0/0 flush timer
2w5d: OSPF: Remember old DR 131.108.5.1 (id)
2w5d: OSPF: NBR Negotiation Done. We are the SLAVE
2w5d: OSPF: Send DBD to 131.108.7.1 on Ethernet0/0 seq 0x1235 opt 0x2 flag 0x2 l
en 72
```

Example 3-57 *Changing Hello Interval to 10 Seconds on SanFran (Continued)*

```
2w5d: OSPF: Rcv DBD from 131.108.7.1 on Ethernet0/0 seq 0x1236 opt 0x2 flag 0x3
len 92  mtu 1500 state EXCHANGE
2w5d: OSPF: Send DBD to 131.108.7.1 on Ethernet0/0 seq 0x1236 opt 0x2 flag 0x0 l
en 32
2w5d: OSPF: Database request to 131.108.7.1
2w5d: OSPF: sent LS REQ packet to 131.108.1.2, length 24
2w5d: OSPF: Rcv DBD from 131.108.7.1 on Ethernet0/0 seq 0x1237 opt 0x2 flag 0x1
len 32  mtu 1500 state EXCHANGE
2w5d: OSPF: Exchange Done with 131.108.7.1 on Ethernet0/0
2w5d: OSPF: Send DBD to 131.108.7.1 on Ethernet0/0 seq 0x1237 opt 0x2 flag 0x0 l
en 32
2w5d: OSPF: We are not DR to build Net Lsa for interface Ethernet0/0
2w5d: OSPF: Synchronized with 131.108.7.1 on Ethernet0/0, state FULL
2w5d: OSPF: Include link to old DR on Ethernet0/0
2w5d: OSPF: Build router LSA for area 0.0.0.0, router ID 131.108.5.1, seq 0x8000
0004
2w5d: OSPF: Rcv hello from 131.108.7.1 area 0.0.0.0 from Ethernet0/0 131.108.1.2
2w5d: OSPF: End of hello processing
```

As soon as you correct the problem, you see the hello process completed, and an OSPF database exchange occurs. In other words, Routers Chicago and SanFran are now OSPF neighbors. Example 3-57 highlights the OSPF neighbor state from the initial INIT state to the FULL state. Example 3-58 now displays SanFran's IP routing table.

Example 3-58 *SanFran IP Routing Table*

```
SanFran#show ip route
     131.108.0.0/16 is variably subnetted, 5 subnets, 2 masks
O       131.108.7.1/32 [110/11] via 131.108.1.2, 00:01:25, Ethernet0/0
O       131.108.6.1/32 [110/11] via 131.108.1.2, 00:01:25, Ethernet0/0
C       131.108.5.0/24 is directly connected, Loopback1
C       131.108.4.0/24 is directly connected, Loopback0
C       131.108.1.0/24 is directly connected, Ethernet0/0
```

The Router SanFran now discovers the remote networks 131.108.7.1/32 and 131.108.6.0/32 through OSPF.

This scenario has introduced you to some powerful OSPF commands that you can use to discover why OSPF is not functioning correctly. Cisco IOS is updated almost daily, so you need to reference the IOS documentation for new and ever-expanding commands. Example 3-59 displays the **debug** and **show** commands possible on a Cisco router running IOS release 12.0.10.

Example 3-59 *Possible* **show** *and* **debug** *OSPF Commands*

```
SanFran#show ip ospf ?
  <1-4294967295>       Process ID number
  border-routers       Border and Boundary Router Information
  database             Database summary
  interface            Interface information
  neighbor             Neighbor list
  request-list         Link state request list
  retransmission-list  Link state retransmission list
  summary-address      Summary-address redistribution Information
  virtual-links        Virtual link information
  <cr>
SanFran#debug ip ospf ?
  adj              OSPF adjacency events
  database-timer   OSPF database timer
  events           OSPF events
  flood            OSPF flooding
  lsa-generation   OSPF lsa generation
  packet           OSPF packets
  retransmission   OSPF retransmission events
  spf              OSPF spf
  tree             OSPF database tree
```

NOTE   Using the **?** character on the command-line interface displays a list of commands available to the user. Example 3-59 takes advantage of this tool to display commands available to the network administrator.

Example 3-60 displays the full working configuration on SanFran.

Example 3-60 *The Full Working Configuration on SanFran*

```
version 12.0
hostname SanFran
!
enable password cisco
!
ip subnet-zero
no ip domain-lookup
interface Loopback0
 ip address 131.108.4.1 255.255.255.0
!
interface Loopback1
 ip address 131.108.5.1 255.255.255.0
!
interface Ethernet0/0
 ip address 131.108.1.1 255.255.255.0
```

Example 3-60 *The Full Working Configuration on SanFran (Continued)*

```
!
interface Serial0/0
shutdown
!
interface Serial0/1
shutdown
!
router ospf 1
 network 0.0.0.0 255.255.255.255 area 0.0.0.0
!
ip classless
line con 0
line aux 0
line vty 0 4
!
end
```

Example 3-61 displays the full working configuration on Chicago.

Example 3-61 *The Full Working Configuration on Chicago*

```
version 12.0
!
hostname Chicago
!
enable password cisco
!
ip subnet-zero
no ip domain-lookup
interface Loopback0
 ip address 131.108.6.1 255.255.255.0
!
interface Loopback1
 ip address 131.108.7.1 255.255.255.0
interface Ethernet0/0
 ip address 131.108.1.2 255.255.255.0
!
interface Serial1/0
 shutdown
!
interface Serial1/1
 shutdown
!
router ospf 2
 network 131.108.1.2 0.0.0.0 area 0.0.0.0
 network 131.108.6.0 0.0.0.255 area 0.0.0.0
 network 131.108.7.0 0.0.0.255 area 0.0.0.0
```

continues

Example 3-61 *The Full Working Configuration on Chicago (Continued)*

```
line con 0
line aux 0
line vty 0 4
!
end
```

Practical Exercise: Routing OSPF

NOTE   Practical Exercises are designed to test your knowledge of the topics covered in this chapter. The Practical Exercise begins by giving you some information about a situation and then asks you to work through the solution on your own. The solution can be found at the end.

Configure the network in Figure 3-6 for OSPF routing using the IP addressing scheme provided. Ensure that both routers R1 and R2 have full connectivity to Routers R3 and R6 in the backbone. Use the **ping** command to ensure all networks are reachable. You must use OSPF as your only dynamic routing protocol.

Figure 3-6   *Practical Exercise: Routing OSPF*

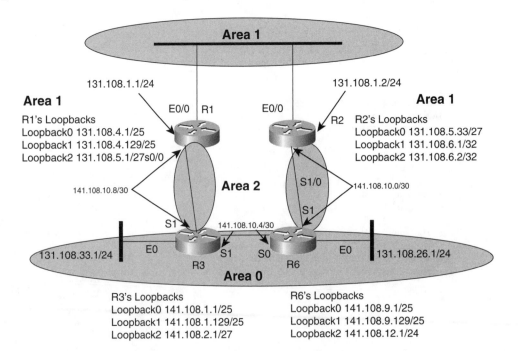

Practical Exercise Solution

You will notice that the IP addressing scheme uses VLSM and the serial links use the subnet 141.108.10.0.

The serial link contains a mask that is 255.255.255.252, or /30.

The following example configurations provide a solution using OSPF. This practical example is similar to Scenario 2-2 with the extra link between area 1 and area 0. This means that you need to configure two virtual links: one from router R2 to R6 and another between R1 and R3. This second virtual link is required in case of link failure or hardware failure from the Routers R1 and R2.

Configure the loopbacks with VLSM and experiment with **debug** commands to discover why IP entries are added or not advertised. Remove the second virtual link from R1 to R3, and see how OSPF behaves when the link between R2 and R6 fails.

You will find that because the areas are partitioned, you actually do need two virtual links to ensure full connectivity in any network failure situation. Example 3-62 displays R1's full working configuration.

Example 3-62 *R1's Full Configuration*

```
version 12.0
!
hostname R1
!
enable password cisco
!
ip subnet-zero
no ip domain-lookup
interface Loopback0
 ip address 131.108.4.1 255.255.255.128
 ip ospf cost 90
!
interface Loopback1
 ip address 131.108.4.129 255.255.255.128
 ip ospf cost 90
!
interface Loopback2
 ip address 131.108.5.1 255.255.255.224
 ip ospf cost 90
!
interface Ethernet0/0
 ip address 131.108.1.1 255.255.255.0
!
interface Serial0/0
 ip address 141.108.10.9 255.255.255.252
 clockrate 125000
```

continues

Example 3-62 *R1's Full Configuration (Continued)*

```
!
interface Serial0/1
 no ip address
 shutdown
 clockrate 128000
!
router ospf 1
 area 2 virtual-link 141.108.2.1
 network 131.108.1.0 0.0.0.255 area 1
 network 131.108.4.0 0.0.0.127 area 1
 network 131.108.4.128 0.0.0.127 area 1
 network 131.108.5.0 0.0.0.31 area 1
 network 141.108.10.8 0.0.0.3 area 2
!
line con 0
line aux 0
line vty 0 4
!
end
```

Example 3-63 displays R2's full working configuration.

Example 3-63 *R2's Full Configuration*

```
version 12.0
service timestamps debug uptime
service timestamps log uptime
no service password-encryption
!
hostname R2
!
enable password cisco
!
ip subnet-zero
no ip domain-lookup
!
interface Loopback0
 ip address 131.108.5.33 255.255.255.224
 ip ospf network point-to-point
 ip ospf cost 1000
!
interface Loopback1
 ip address 131.108.6.1 255.255.255.255
!
interface Loopback2
 ip address 131.108.6.2 255.255.255.255
!
interface Ethernet0/0
 ip address 131.108.1.2 255.255.255.0
 ip ospf priority 255
```

Example 3-63 *R2's Full Configuration (Continued)*

```
interface Serial1/0
 ip address 141.108.10.1 255.255.255.252
!
interface Serial1/1
 no ip address
shutdown
!
interface Serial1/2
 no ip address
 shutdown
!
interface Serial1/3
 no ip address
 shutdown
!
router ospf 2
 area 2 virtual-link 141.108.12.1
 network 131.108.1.0 0.0.0.255 area 1
 network 131.108.5.32 0.0.0.31 area 1
 network 131.108.6.1 0.0.0.0 area 1
 network 131.108.6.2 0.0.0.0 area 1
 network 141.108.10.0 0.0.0.3 area 2
!
line con 0
line aux 0
line vty 0 4
!
end
```

Example 3-64 displays R3's working configuration.

Example 3-64 *R3's Full Configuration*

```
version 12.0
hostname R3
!
enable password cisco
!
ip subnet-zero
interface Loopback0
 ip address 141.108.1.1 255.255.255.128
 ip ospf network point-to-point
!
interface Loopback1
 ip address 141.108.1.129 255.255.255.128
 ip ospf network point-to-point
!
interface Loopback2
 ip address 141.108.2.1 255.255.255.224
 ip ospf network point-to-point
```

continues

Example 3-64 *R3's Full Configuration (Continued)*

```
!
interface Ethernet0
 ip address 131.108.33.1 255.255.255.0
!
interface Serial0
 ip address 141.108.10.10 255.255.255.252
!
interface Serial1
 ip address 141.108.10.5 255.255.255.252
!
router ospf 3
 area 2 virtual-link 131.108.5.1
 network 131.108.33.0 0.0.0.255 area 0
 network 141.108.1.0 0.0.0.127 area 0
 network 141.108.1.128 0.0.0.127 area 0
 network 141.108.2.0 0.0.0.31 area 0
 network 141.108.10.4 0.0.0.3 area 0
 network 141.108.10.8 0.0.0.3 area 2
!
line con 0
line aux 0
line vty 0 4
!
end
```

Finally, Example 3-65 displays R6's working configuration.

Example 3-65 *R6's Full Configuration*

```
version 12.0
hostname r6
!
enable password cisco
ip subnet-zero
!
interface Loopback0
 ip address 141.108.9.1 255.255.255.128
 ip ospf network point-to-point
interface Loopback1
 ip address 141.108.9.129 255.255.255.128
 ip ospf network point-to-point
interface Loopback2
 ip address 141.108.12.1 255.255.255.0
 ip ospf network point-to-point
interface Ethernet0
 ip address 131.108.26.1 255.255.255.0
 media-type 10BaseT
```

Example 3-65 *R6's Full Configuration (Continued)*

```
!
interface Serial0
 ip address 141.108.10.6 255.255.255.252
 clockrate 125000
!
interface Serial1
 ip address 141.108.10.2 255.255.255.252
 clockrate 125000
!
interface Serial2
 shutdown
!
interface Serial3
 shutdown
!
router ospf 6
 area 2 virtual-link 131.108.6.2
 network 131.108.26.0 0.0.0.255 area 0
 network 141.108.9.0 0.0.0.127 area 0
 network 141.108.9.128 0.0.0.127 area 0
 network 141.108.10.0 0.0.0.3 area 2
 network 141.108.10.4 0.0.0.3 area 0
 network 141.108.12.0 0.0.0.255 area 0
!
line con 0
line aux 0
line vty 0 4
end
```

Review Questions

Use router output taken from R1 from the previous Practical Exercise to answer the following questions. Example 3-66 shows this sample output taken from R1 and includes the IP routing table and sample pings to area 1.

Example 3-66 *R1's IP Routing Table and Ping Requests to Area 1*

```
R1>show ip route
Gateway of last resort is not set
     141.108.0.0/16 is variably subnetted, 8 subnets, 3 masks
O       141.108.1.128/25 [110/65] via 141.108.10.10, 00:15:28, Serial0/0
O       141.108.9.128/25 [110/129] via 141.108.10.10, 00:15:28, Serial0/0
O       141.108.1.0/25 [110/65] via 141.108.10.10, 00:15:28, Serial0/0
C       141.108.10.8/30 is directly connected, Serial0/0
O       141.108.9.0/25 [110/129] via 141.108.10.10, 00:15:28, Serial0/0
O IA    141.108.10.0/30 [110/192] via 141.108.10.10, 00:15:28, Serial0/0
O       141.108.12.0/24 [110/129] via 141.108.10.10, 00:15:28, Serial0/0
O       141.108.10.4/30 [110/128] via 141.108.10.10, 00:15:29, Serial0/0
```

continues

Example 3-66 *R1's IP Routing Table and Ping Requests to Area 1 (Continued)*

```
        131.108.0.0/16 is variably subnetted, 9 subnets, 4 masks
C       131.108.4.128/25 is directly connected, Loopback1
O       131.108.5.32/27 [110/1010] via 131.108.1.2, 00:16:04, Ethernet0/0
O       131.108.33.0/24 [110/74] via 141.108.10.10, 00:15:29, Serial0/0
O       131.108.6.1/32 [110/11] via 131.108.1.2, 00:16:04, Ethernet0/0
C       131.108.5.0/27 is directly connected, Loopback2
O       131.108.6.2/32 [110/11] via 131.108.1.2, 00:16:06, Ethernet0/0
C       131.108.4.0/25 is directly connected, Loopback0
C       131.108.1.0/24 is directly connected, Ethernet0/0
O       131.108.26.0/24 [110/138] via 141.108.10.10, 00:15:31, Serial0/0
R1#ping 131.108.4.1
Type escape sequence to abort.
Sending 5, 100-byte ICMP Echos to 131.108.4.1, timeout is 2 seconds:
!!!!!
Success rate is 100 percent (5/5), round-trip min/avg/max = 1/2/4 ms
R1#ping 131.108.4.129
Type escape sequence to abort.
Sending 5, 100-byte ICMP Echos to 131.108.4.129, timeout is 2 seconds:
!!!!!
Success rate is 100 percent (5/5), round-trip min/avg/max = 1/1/4 ms
R1#ping 131.108.5.1
Type escape sequence to abort.
Sending 5, 100-byte ICMP Echos to 131.108.5.1, timeout is 2 seconds:
!!!!!
Success rate is 100 percent (5/5), round-trip min/avg/max = 1/1/4 ms
R1#ping 131.108.5.33
Type escape sequence to abort.
Sending 5, 100-byte ICMP Echos to 131.108.5.33, timeout is 2 seconds:
!!!!!
Success rate is 100 percent (5/5), round-trip min/avg/max = 1/2/4 ms
R1#ping 131.108.6.1
Type escape sequence to abort.
Sending 5, 100-byte ICMP Echos to 131.108.6.1, timeout is 2 seconds:
!!!!!
Success rate is 100 percent (5/5), round-trip min/avg/max = 1/2/4 ms
R1#ping 131.108.6.2
Type escape sequence to abort.
Sending 5, 100-byte ICMP Echos to 131.108.6.2, timeout is 2 seconds:
!!!!!
Success rate is 100 percent (5/5), round-trip min/avg/max = 1/2/4 ms
R1#
```

View Example 3-66 to answer the following review questions.

The answers to these question can be found in Appendix C, "Answers to Review Questions."

1 Which information is stored in an IP routing table as seen by R1?

2 Which command do you use to view only OSPF routes?

3 How many subnets are known by R1 using the Class B networks 131.108.0.0/16 and 141.108.0.0/16?

4 What path is taken to the remote network 141.108.100.1/24?

5 Why is the remote network 141.108.6.0/32 displayed as learned through the denotation: O IA?

6 What is the cost associated with the remote network 131.108.33.0/24 [110/74]?

Summary

You have now completed some basic and challenging OSPF scenarios and discovered how powerful OSPF is when enabled on Cisco IOS routers.

OSPF can be configured in single or multiple areas. You saw that all OSPF areas must be connected to the backbone for proper and correct operation. Standard techniques using Cisco IOS **show** commands were demonstrated to ensure that you have all the required knowledge to monitor and maintain small or large OSPF networks.

Table 3-7 summarizes the commands used in this chapter.

Table 3-7   *Summary of IOS Commands used in this Chapter*

Command	Purpose
show ip route	Displays IP routing tables.
router ospf *process id*	Enables OSPF routing. The process ID is local to the router. You can have more than one OSPF running.
network mask	Enables network advertisements out of a particular interface and also the routing of the same interface through OSPF.
show ip ospf	Displays the OSPF process and details, such as OSPF process ID and router ID.
show ip ospf database	Displays router's topological database.
show ip ospf neighbor	Displays OSPF neighbors.
show ip ospf neighbor detail	Displays OSPF neighbors in detail, providing such parameters as neighbor address, hello interval, and dead interval.
show ip ospf interface	Displays information on how OSPF has been configured for a given interface.
ip ospf cost	Interface command that changes the cost of an OSPF interface.
ip ospf priority	Interface command that changes the DR/BDR election process.
ip ospf network	Interface command that changes the network type.
interface loopback *number*	Creates a loopback interface.

Table 3-7   *Summary of IOS Commands used in this Chapter (Continued)*

interface Ethernet *mod/num*	In configuration mode, enables you modify an interface number, for example **interface E0/0**.
interface serial *mod/num*	In configuration mode, enables you to modify serial interface parameters by module and interface number. For example, **interface S0/0**.
no ip domain-lookup	Disables automatic DNS lookup.
ip subnet-zero	Enables you to use subnet zero on a Cisco router.
show ip protocol	Displays all routing protocols in use on a Cisco router.
debug ip ospf adj	Troubleshooting command that displays messages, such as the state of the adjacency, received and sent by a Cisco router from or to neighboring OSPF routers.
hostname *name*	Configures a name on a router.
[no] shutdown	Enables or disables an interface. All hardware interfaces are shut down by default.

CHAPTER 4

Advanced OSPF and Integrated Intermediate System-to-Intermediate System

This chapter focuses on a number of objectives falling under the CCNP routing principles. Understanding advanced OSPF routing principles not only applies to the CCNP Routing certification but to all Cisco-based certifications, and it lays the foundations for future certifications in any field of networking.

Chapter 3, "Basic Open Shortest Path First," started by covering some of the basic Open Shortest Path First (OSPF) concepts. This chapter covers some of the ways OSPF deals with large Internet Protocol (IP) routing environments and how you can configure OSPF to reduce IP routing tables and the CPU and memory requirements of access or edge routers. OSPF is a popular IP routing protocol; therefore, most Cisco certification exams test heavily on OSPF.

This chapter contains five practical scenarios to complete your understanding and ensure you have all the OSPF routing skills to complement your understanding of how to configure and maintain OSPF in large IP networks. Integrated Intermediate System-to-Intermediate System (IS-IS) is another link-state protocol common in today's networks used to route IP. Integrated IS-IS is covered in detail in Scenarios 4-3 and 4-4.

Advanced OSPF

OSPF is an industry-standard routing protocol developed by the Internet Engineering Taskforce (IETF) as a replacement for legacy routing protocols that did not scale well in large environments. OSPF supports the following features:

- Variable-length subnet masks (VLSM).

- The use of areas to minimize Central Processing Unit (CPU) and memory requirements.

- A simple cost metric that you can manipulate to support up to six equal cost paths. The number of paths is limited only by the Internet Operating System (IOS).

- The use of authentication to ensure OSPF updates are secure and the use of multicast updates to conserve bandwidth.

- Faster convergence times ensuring updates and changes are propagated across the network.

- No limitation of network diameter or hop count. Limiting factors include only CPU and memory resources.

- The ability to tag OSPF information injected from any autonomous systems.

The following topics are covered in this section:

- Connecting multiple OSPF areas

- VLSM and summarization with OSPF

- OSPF over multiarea NBMA

Connecting Multiple OSPF Areas

An OSPF area is defined as a logical grouping of routers by a network administrator. OSPF routers in any area share the same topological view (also known as the OSPF database) of the network. The core reason that OSPF is configured in multiple areas is to reduce routing table sizes, which in turn reduces the topological database and CPU/memory requirements on a router.

OSPF is not just configured in one large area, so all routers share the same topological database. The use of multiple areas ensures that the flooding and database management required in large OSPF networks is reduced within each area so that the process of flooding the full database and maintaining full network connectivity does not consume a large portion of the CPU processing power. Every time a network change occurs, the CPU on a router is interrupted and a new OSPF tree is calculated. Running the shortest path first (SPF) algorithm itself is not CPU intensive, but sending and flooding the network with new topological information is extremely CPU intensive.

Routing tables become very large even with only 50 routers. The OSPF database is exchanged every 30 minutes in full, and if this database is too large, every time the exchange occurs, the amount of bandwidth used over the network increases, which can cause severe delays in sending user-based traffic because convergence times increase.

Considering the demands on CPU and memory along with reduced IP routing tables, you should now have a good understanding of why OSPF requires more than one area. In Scenario 3-2 in Chapter 3, you saw how to configure an OSPF network that is partitioned from the backbone. All OSPF areas must be connected to the backbone in case of network failure. When an area cannot reside physically or logically on the backbone, a virtual link is required. For partitioned areas, OSPF treats the area as a separate area, and no routing information flows to the backbone; therefore, you do not have IP connectivity.

Virtual links add a layer of complexity and might cause additional problems when applied to large IP networks. It is best to avoid virtual links in the real world.

When configuring a virtual link, you must be aware of the following design restrictions:

- Virtual links must be configured between two area border routers (ABRs).
- The transit area cannot be a stub area.
- The transit area must have full routing knowledge of both partitioned areas.

NOTE   Stub areas are covered later in this chapter. Remember that all routers must be connected to the backbone logically or you must use a virtual link. To understand why logical links are required in today's networks, consider the case were Company XYZ buys Company ACME. Both companies use OSPF and have their own individual backbones. Rather than re-address the networks, a virtual link can provide immediate IP connectivity.

Table 4-1 summarizes the four OSPF area types and their functions.

Table 4-1   *OSPF Router Types*

Router Type	Description
Internal router	This router is within a specific area only. Internal router functions include maintaining the OSPF database and forwarding data to other networks. All interfaces on internal routers are in the same area.
Area border router (ABR)	ABRs are responsible for connecting two or more areas. An ABR contains the full topological database for each area it is connected to and sends this information to other areas.
Autonomous system boundary router (ASBR)	ASBRs connect to the outside world or perform some form of redistribution into OSPF.
Backbone router	Backbone routers are connected to area 0, which is also represented as area 0.0.0.0. Backbone routers can be internal routers or ASBRs.

Figure 4-1 displays a typical OSPF area assignment and the function of these routers.

In Figure 4-1, the routers residing in the backbone (area 0) are called backbone routers. A backbone router connecting to another area can also be an ABR. Routers that connect to, for example, the Internet and redistribute external IP routing tables from such protocols as Border Gateway Protocol (BGP) are termed autonomous system boundary routers (ASBRs). So, you can have a backbone router perform ASBR functions as well as ABR functions.

Each router, depending on its function, sends out a link-state advertisement (LSA). An LSA is a packet used by such routing protocols as OSPF (that is, link-state routing protocols) to send information to neighboring routers describing networks and path costs.

Figure 4-1 *Typical OSPF Area Assignment and OSPF Routers*

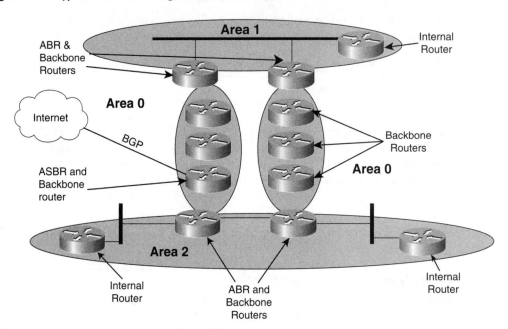

TIP

Before flooding any neighboring routers with LSAs, Cisco IOS routers must first undergo the following:

Step 1 Ensure the neighboring router is in a state of adjacency.

Step 2 The interface cannot be a stub area (LSA type 5. Stub areas are discussed later in this chapter.)

Step 3 The interface cannot be connected to a totally stubby area. (LSA type 3, 4, or 5 will not be sent. Totally stubby areas are discussed later in this chapter.)

For a detailed summary of OSPF and the packet types, the Cisco Press titles *Routing TCP/IP*, Volumes I and II, by Jeff Doyle and Jennifer DeHaven Carroll (Volume II only) explain all the advanced concepts you could ever need.

OSPF supports a number of LSA types as well as three other area types: a stub area, a totally stubby area, and a not-so-stubby area (NSSA). These additional areas provide even more functionality in OSPF. Before covering these new areas in detail, this section first goes over the link-state advertisement types and when to use them in an OSPF environment.

The OSPF standard defines a number of LSAs types. Unlike distance vector protocols (for example, RIP), OSPF does not actually send its routing table to other routers. Instead, OSPF sends the LSA database and derives the IP routing table from LSAs. Table 4-2 describes the six most common LSAs and their functions.

Table 4-2 *Six Common Supported LSA Types on Cisco IOS Routers*

LSA Packet Type	Name	Function
1	Router link advertisements	Describes the state and cost of the router's own interfaces.
2	Network link advertisements	Used on multiaccess networks. These are originated by the designated router (DR).
3	Summary link advertisements (ABRs)	Originated by ABRs only. This LSA type sends out information into the autonomous system (AS) but outside of the area (interarea routes).
4	Summary link advertisements (ASBRs)	Originated by ASBRs describing IP networks external to the AS.
5	Autonomous system (AS) external link advertisements	An LSA sent to a router that connects to the Internet, for example. An advertisement sent from ABR to the ASBR.
6	Not-so-stubby areas (NSSA)	An advertisement bound to an NSSA area.

A stub area is defined as an area that contains a single exit point from the area. A stub in the English dictionary means a dead end, and that is exactly what it means in OSPF. Areas that reside on the edge of the network with no exit point except one path can be termed a stub area. Stubs come in three types.

Table 4-3 summarizes the functions of these new areas, called stubby areas, total stubby areas, and not-so-stubby areas. Take important note of the LSA type allowed or not allowed to fully appreciate the value of a stub area.

Table 4-3 *Additional Area Types*

Area Type	Function
Stub area	This area does not accept LSA types 4 and 5, which are summary links and external link advertisements, respectively. The only way to achieve a route to unknown destinations is, thereby, a default route injected by the ABR.
Totally stubby area	This area blocks LSA types 3, 4, and 5. Although similar to a stub area, a totally stubby area blocks LSAs of type 3 as well. This solution is Cisco-proprietary and is used to further reduce a topological database.

continues

Table 4-3   *Additional Area Types (Continued)*

Area Type	Function
Not-so-stubby area	This area is used primarily for connections to an ISP. This area is designed to allow LSAs of type 7 only. All advertised routes can be flooded through the NSSA but are blocked by the ABR. Basically, a type 7 LSA (if the P bit is set to one) will be convert to a type 5 LSA and flooded throughout the rest of the network. If the P bit is set to zero, no translation takes place. Type 4 or 5 LSAs are not permitted. This advertisement will not be propagated to the rest of the network. Typically used to provide a default route.

The only way to appreciate these new areas is to configure them and view the OSPF database. The scenarios that follow cover stub, totally stubby, and not-so-stubby areas in more detail.

NOTE   A stub area cannot be a transit for a virtual link. This is a design limitation by the protocol itself. When a router is defined as a stub area, a bit, called the E bit, in the Hello packet is set to 0. All routers that form any OSPF neighbor relationship must have the E bit set to 0 as well; otherwise, no adjacency is formed.

Also a stub (does not permit LSA types 4 and 5) area or totally stubby (does not permit LSA types 3, 4, and 5) area does not allow external routes. Nor is redistribution allowed. Those functions must be performed by ABRs or ASBRs.

Table 4-4 summarizes the LSA types by area and indicates which LSAs are permitted or disallowed in certain areas.

Table 4-4   *LSA Types and Area Restrictions*

	LSA Type Permitted?			
Area	**1/2**	**3/4**	**6**	**7**
NSSA	Yes	Yes	No	Yes
Totally stubby	Yes	No	No	No
Stub	Yes	Yes	No	No

TIP   All OSPF packets are sent using IP protocol port number 89. OSPF runs over the IP layer (also called the Network layer) of the Open System Interconnection (OSI) model.

VLSM and Summarization with OSPF

OSPF supports a number of features. The two main features that interest most network designers are that it supports VLSM and provides the ability to summarize networks.

When an LSA packet or routing update is received or sent, the packet includes the following information:

- LSA type
- Router ID (unique IP address, no other router can share the same router ID)
- Subnet mask
- Attached router
- Metric

Because the subnet mask is carried along with the update, OSPF can support VLSM. Without a mechanism that sends the subnet mask, there can be no support for VLSM. Routing Information Protocol (RIPv1) and Interior Gateway Routing Protocol (IGRP), for example, do not carry the subnet mask when they send out updates.

Summarization occurs using the LSA type 4 packet or by the ASBR.

You configure OSPF in two ways to summarize networks using Cisco IOS routers:

- Interarea summarization creating type 3 or 4 LSAs
- External summarization with type 5 LSAs

Consider an OSPF network containing two routers across an Ethernet segment. Figure 4-2 displays this two-router topology with the routers named R1 and R2.

Figure 4-2 *Sample Network for OSPF Summarization Example*

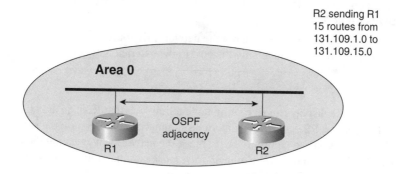

R2 is sending R1 15 OSPF routes ranging from 131.109.1.0 to 131.109.15.0. Instead of populating R1's routing table with 15 IP route entries, you can use summarization. Example 4-1 displays R1's routing table.

Example 4-1 *R1's OSPF Routing Table*

```
R1>show ip route ospf
     131.109.0.0/24 is subnetted, 14 subnets
O IA    131.109.14.0 [110/11] via 131.108.2.2, 00:00:48, Ethernet0/0
O IA    131.109.15.0 [110/11] via 131.108.2.2, 00:00:48, Ethernet0/0
O IA    131.109.12.0 [110/11] via 131.108.2.2, 00:00:48, Ethernet0/0
O IA    131.109.13.0 [110/11] via 131.108.2.2, 00:00:48, Ethernet0/0
O IA    131.109.10.0 [110/11] via 131.108.2.2, 00:00:58, Ethernet0/0
O IA    131.109.11.0 [110/11] via 131.108.2.2, 00:00:58, Ethernet0/0
O IA    131.109.8.0 [110/11] via 131.108.2.2, 00:00:58, Ethernet0/0
O IA    131.109.9.0 [110/11] via 131.108.2.2, 00:00:58, Ethernet0/0
O IA    131.109.6.0 [110/11] via 131.108.2.2, 00:00:00, Ethernet0/0
O IA    131.109.7.0 [110/11] via 131.108.2.2, 00:00:58, Ethernet0/0
O IA    131.109.4.0 [110/11] via 131.108.2.2, 00:00:58, Ethernet0/0
O IA    131.109.5.0 [110/11] via 131.108.2.2, 00:00:58, Ethernet0/0
O IA    131.109.2.0 [110/11] via 131.108.2.2, 00:01:08, Ethernet0/0
O IA    131.109.3.0 [110/11] via 131.108.2.2, 00:00:58, Ethernet0/0
O IA    131.109.1.0 [110/11] via 131.108.2.2, 00:02:54, Ethernet0/0
```

The remote networks are indicated by O IA, which indicates interarea routes. Intra-area routes are indicated by O.

NOTE   Two more types of OSPF routes exist: external type 1 routes, indicated by Cisco IOS as O E1, and external type 2 routes, indicated by Cisco IOS as O E2. External OSPF routes are routing entries in OSPF route tables injected by an external routing protocol, such as BGP or IGRP.

When calculating the cost to a remote network, E1 routes add the total cost to destination; whereas E2 routes include only the cost to the external network.

Example 4-1 displays an IP routing table telling you that R2 is in area 0 and another area (ABR); hence, R2 can perform interarea summarization. Because the networks 1 to 15 are contiguous, you can configure R2 to mask the networks by masking the first 15 networks with the IOS **area** *area ID* **range** *address mask* command. Example 4-2 displays the summary applied to R2 under the OSPF router process ID of 1.

Example 4-2 *Summary of R2*

```
R2(config)#router ospf 1
R2(config-router)#area 1 range 131.109.0.0 255.255.240.0
```

Example 4-3 displays R1's routing table now. Remember that previously there were 15 IP routing entries.

Example 4-3   *OSPF Route Table on R1 After Summarization*

```
R1#sh ip route ospf
     131.109.0.0/20 is subnetted, 1 subnets
O IA    131.109.0.0 [110/11] via 131.108.2.2, 00:02:33, Ethernet0/0
R1#
```

By using OSPF summarization techniques, you can summarize a simple network with 15 IP networks by using 1 IP routing entry.

In OSPF, you can also externally summarize IP routes by using the **summary** *ip-address mask* command.

OSPF summarization examples are included among the five scenarios in this chapter.

OSPF over Multiarea NBMA

OSPF over a multiple-area NBMA network presents some challenges to a network designer as you discovered in Chapter 3.

Typically, in a large NBMA environment, the backbone (area 0) assignment encompasses the NBMA connections themselves, because all remote or edge sites need to transit the NBMA network. The same commands that applied in Chapter 3 are used in large NBMA environments.

To summarize the command set used in large NBMA environments, the following commands and steps are required to configure OSPF in a multiarea OSPF Network:

- The **network** command enables OSPF across interfaces.
- Summarization enables networks to reduce IP routing table sizes by using **area range** on ABRs and the **summary** *address subnet mask* command for an ASBR.
- Any stubby configurations to reduce memory and CPU requirements.
- Any virtual links that may be required.
- Any command that manipulates the OSPF cost metrics for equal costs path load balancing.

Next, this chapter describes another common link-state routing protocol used in large IP routing environments, namely Intermediate System-to-Intermediate System (IS-IS).

Integrated Intermediate System-to-Intermediate System

Integrated IS-IS is a link-state routing protocol, but few people consider it an alternative to OSPF. Even so, IS-IS is a common routing protocol typically used in large ISP environments. IS-IS was developed at the same time OSPF was being developed. In brief, IS-IS was designed to provide two routing mechanisms (in competition with OSPF forum, which could only route IP) at the same time: one for IP and another for Decnet Phase V. This chapter covers integrated IS-IS IP routing capabilities only.

As with any new protocol, you need to be familiar with some new terms and definitions to fully understand IS-IS. Instead of using areas as OSPF does, IS-IS has routers perform Level 1 (L1) and Level 2 (L2) functions.

Routers that have no direct connectivity to any other area are called L1 routers. Routers that connect areas are called L2 routers.

In Figure 4-3, Routers R1 and R2 are Level 1/Level 2 (L1/L2) routers, and the edge routers R3 and R4, which are each in only one area, are L2 routers. An L1 router performs the functions similar to those an OSPF internal router performs. A L1/L2 router performs similar functions to an ABR in OSPF. Both L1 and L2 routers maintain link-state databases.

Figure 4-3   *IS-IS Terminology Diagram*

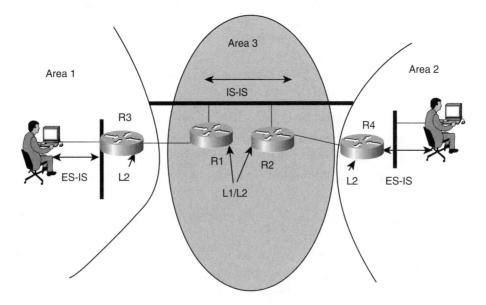

NOTE	IS-IS is the protocol between two IS-IS-enabled routers.
	IS-ES is the protocol—Connectionless Network Protocol (CLNP)—between an end system, such as a PC, and an IS-IS enabled router.

IS-IS has many similarities to OSPF, including the following characteristics:

- IS-IS maintains a link-state database.
- IS-IS uses hello packets to form neighbor relations with other IS-IS enabled routers.
- IS-IS uses areas to form a hierarchy.
- IS-IS supports VLSM.
- IS-IS support routing authentication mechanisms.
- IS-IS on broadcast networks elects a designated router (DR).

To configure IS-IS on a Cisco IOS router, you must perform the following configurations and tasks:

- Enable IS-IS with the command **router isis**.
- Configure any IS-IS interface parameters, such as hello interfaces, and enable IS-IS to send out updates from an interface.
- Configure area parameters.

Scenarios

The following scenarios are designed to draw together some of the content described in this chapter and some of the content you have seen in your own networks or practice labs. There is no one right way to accomplish many of the tasks presented, and using good practice and defining your end goal are important in any real-life design or solution. You start by building an OSPF network and then use the methods described in this chapter to help reduce the size of IP routing tables.

Scenario 4-1: Configuring OSPF with Multiple Areas

In this scenario, you configure an eight-router, three-area network with OSPF. Figure 4-4 displays the OSPF topology and area assignment.

Figure 4-4 *OSPF Topology and Area Assignment*

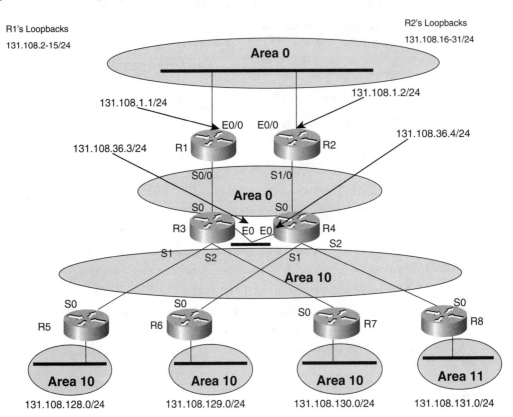

This scenario represents a typical OSPF network with semi-redundancy and a hierarchical address assignment. To simulate a large network environment, you configure several loopback address assignments on R1 and R2. Typically in an environment like this, the hosts (devices, such as mainframes, large computer hosts, or printers) reside in the backbone and the end users are connected to the remote sites. Assume all IP traffic is between the edge, or access, routers and the backbone network in area 0.

Table 4-5 displays the IP address assignment used in Figure 4-4.

Table 4-5 *IP Address and Area Assignments*

Router	IP Address Range	Area
R1	131.108.2.0–15/32	0
R2	131.108.16.0–31/32	0
R3	131.108.32–33/32	0

Table 4-5   *IP Address and Area Assignments (Continued)*

Router	IP Address Range	Area
R4	131.108.34–35/32	0
R5	131.108.128.0/24	10
R6	131.108.129.0/24	10
R7	131.108.130.0/24	10
R8	131.108.131.0/24	11
WAN links	131.108.255.0	30-bit subnet masks applied to all WAN links
LAN link between R3 and R4	131.108.36.0	0

To start OSPF on the eight routers, you must first enable the OSPF process by using the command **router ospf** *process ID*. In this scenario, use the same process ID of 1 on all routers, and remember that the process ID is locally significant only. To send and receive LSAs per interface, use the **network** command.

From Figure 4-4, the remote network on Router R8, with the IP subnet 131.108.131.0/24, resides in area 11. Area 11 is partitioned from the backbone and hence requires a virtual link so that all OSPF routers have a routing entry for the subnet 131.108.131.0/24. Example 4-4 displays the IP routing table on R1 after OSPF has been configured on all the routers in this network.

Example 4-4   *R1 Routing Table*

```
R1#show ip route
Codes: C - connected, O - OSPF, IA - OSPF inter area
       N1 - OSPF NSSA external type 1, N2 - OSPF NSSA external type 2
       E1 - OSPF external type 1, E2 - OSPF external type 2,
     131.108.0.0/16 is variably subnetted, 39 subnets, 2 masks
O IA   131.108.255.16/30 [110/855] via 131.108.1.2, 00:08:21, Ethernet0/0
O IA   131.108.255.20/30 [110/855] via 131.108.1.2, 00:05:29, Ethernet0/0
C      131.108.255.0/30 is directly connected, Serial0/0
O      131.108.255.4/30 [110/791] via 131.108.1.2, 00:12:44, Ethernet0/0
O IA   131.108.255.8/30 [110/128] via 131.108.255.2, 00:10:15, Serial0/0
O IA   131.108.255.12/30 [110/128] via 131.108.255.2, 00:07:02, Serial0/0
O IA   131.108.129.0/24 [110/865] via 131.108.1.2, 00:07:51, Ethernet0/0 - To R6
O IA   131.108.128.0/24 [110/138] via 131.108.255.2, 00:09:16, Serial0/0 - To R5
O IA   131.108.130.0/24 [110/138] via 131.108.255.2, 00:00:18, Serial0/0 - To R7
C      131.108.15.0/24 is directly connected, Loopback13
C      131.108.14.0/24 is directly connected, Loopback12
C      131.108.13.0/24 is directly connected, Loopback11
C      131.108.12.0/24 is directly connected, Loopback10
C      131.108.11.0/24 is directly connected, Loopback9
C      131.108.10.0/24 is directly connected, Loopback8
```

continues

Example 4-4 *R1 Routing Table (Continued)*

```
C       131.108.9.0/24 is directly connected, Loopback7
C       131.108.8.0/24 is directly connected, Loopback6
C       131.108.7.0/24 is directly connected, Loopback5
C       131.108.6.0/24 is directly connected, Loopback4
C       131.108.5.0/24 is directly connected, Loopback3
C       131.108.4.0/24 is directly connected, Loopback2
C       131.108.3.0/24 is directly connected, Loopback1
C       131.108.2.0/24 is directly connected, Loopback0
C       131.108.1.0/24 is directly connected, Ethernet0/0
O       131.108.31.0/24 [110/11] via 131.108.1.2, 00:12:47, Ethernet0/0
O       131.108.30.0/24 [110/11] via 131.108.1.2, 00:12:47, Ethernet0/0
O       131.108.29.0/24 [110/11] via 131.108.1.2, 00:12:47, Ethernet0/0
O       131.108.28.0/24 [110/11] via 131.108.1.2, 00:12:47, Ethernet0/0
O       131.108.27.0/24 [110/11] via 131.108.1.2, 00:12:47, Ethernet0/0
O       131.108.26.0/24 [110/11] via 131.108.1.2, 00:12:47, Ethernet0/0
O       131.108.25.0/24 [110/11] via 131.108.1.2, 00:12:47, Ethernet0/0
O       131.108.24.0/24 [110/11] via 131.108.1.2, 00:12:47, Ethernet0/0
O       131.108.23.0/24 [110/11] via 131.108.1.2, 00:12:47, Ethernet0/0
O       131.108.22.0/24 [110/11] via 131.108.1.2, 00:12:47, Ethernet0/0
O       131.108.21.0/24 [110/11] via 131.108.1.2, 00:12:47, Ethernet0/0
O       131.108.20.0/24 [110/11] via 131.108.1.2, 00:12:47, Ethernet0/0
O       131.108.19.0/24 [110/11] via 131.108.1.2, 00:12:47, Ethernet0/0
O       131.108.18.0/24 [110/11] via 131.108.1.2, 00:17:10, Ethernet0/0
O       131.108.17.0/24 [110/11] via 131.108.1.2, 00:17:10, Ethernet0/0
O       131.108.16.0/24 [110/11] via 131.108.1.2, 00:17:10, Ethernet0/0
O       131.108.36.0/24 [110/11] via 131.108.1.2, 00:17:10, Ethernet0/0
```

Example 4-4 displays the remote routers learned through Ethernet interface and the next hop address of 131.108.1.2, which is R2. There is, of course, another path on R1 through the serial link to R2. Because the cost is lower through the Ethernet LAN segment, R1 chooses the path to R2 as the preferred path.

The three remote networks on the access Routers R5, R6, and R7 are listed in Example 4-4, but the network on R8 is not. Configure a virtual link between R4 and R8. Before you can configure a virtual link, you must know the router ID on R4 and R8. The **show ip ospf database** command displays the local router ID, which is typically a loopback address or the highest IP address assignment. Loopbacks are always preferred because a loopback interface is logically never going to become unavailable unless the network administrator removes it. A router ID that is a physical interface is prone to network failure and OSPF recalculations, which lead to network downtimes.

To configure a virtual link, use the IOS command **area** *transit area router-id*. The transit area in this example is area 10, and the router ID is the IP address of the remote router. Example 4-5 displays the router ID on Routers R4 and R8.

Example 4-5 *Router ID on R4 and R8*

```
R4#show ip ospf database
        OSPF Router with ID (131.108.255.6  (Process ID 1)
R8#show ip ospf database
            OSPF Router with ID (131.108.255.22) (Process ID 1)
```

Example 4-6 displays the virtual link configuration on R4.

Example 4-6 *Virtual Link Configuration on R4*

```
R4(config-router)#router ospf 1
R4(config-router)#area 10 virtual-link 131.108.255.22
```

Example 4-7 displays the virtual link configuration on R8 along with the IOS ? command
to display the available options.

Example 4-7 *Virtual Link Configuration and Options on R8*

```
R8(config-router)#area 10 ?
  authentication  Enable authentication
  default-cost    Set the summary default-cost of a NSSA/stub area
  nssa            Specify a NSSA area
  range           Summarize routes matching address/mask (border routers only)
  stub            Specify a stub area
  virtual-link    Define a virtual link and its parameters
R8(config-router)#area 10 virtual-link ?
  A.B.C.D  ID (IP addr) associated with virtual link neighbor
R8(config-router)#area 10 virtual-link 131.108.255.6
```

Example 4-8 displays the IP routing table on the core router, R1, along with the remote
network 131.108.131.0 because of the virtual link configuration.

Example 4-8 **show ip router ospf** *Command on R1*

```
R1#show ip route ospf
     131.108.0.0/16 is variably subnetted, 41 subnets, 2 masks
O IA    131.108.255.16/30 [110/855] via 131.108.1.2, 00:00:47, Ethernet0/0
O IA    131.108.255.20/30 [110/855] via 131.108.1.2, 00:00:47, Ethernet0/0
O       131.108.255.4/30 [110/791] via 131.108.1.2, 00:00:47, Ethernet0/0
O IA    131.108.255.8/30 [110/128] via 131.108.255.2, 00:00:47, Serial0/0
O IA    131.108.255.12/30 [110/128] via 131.108.255.2, 00:00:47, Serial0/0
O IA    131.108.131.0/24 [110/865] via 131.108.1.2, 00:00:47, Ethernet0/0
O IA    131.108.130.0/24 [110/138] via 131.108.255.2, 00:00:48, Serial0/0
O IA    131.108.129.0/24 [110/865] via 131.108.1.2, 00:00:48, Ethernet0/0
O IA    131.108.128.0/24 [110/138] via 131.108.255.2, 00:00:48, Serial0/0
O       131.108.31.0/24 [110/11] via 131.108.1.2, 00:00:48, Ethernet0/0
```

continues

Example 4-8   **show ip router ospf** *Command on R1 (Continued)*

```
O        131.108.30.0/24 [110/11] via 131.108.1.2, 00:00:48, Ethernet0/0
O        131.108.29.0/24 [110/11] via 131.108.1.2, 00:00:48, Ethernet0/0
O        131.108.28.0/24 [110/11] via 131.108.1.2, 00:00:48, Ethernet0/0
O        131.108.27.0/24 [110/11] via 131.108.1.2, 00:00:48, Ethernet0/0
O        131.108.26.0/24 [110/11] via 131.108.1.2, 00:00:48, Ethernet0/0
O        131.108.25.0/24 [110/11] via 131.108.1.2, 00:00:48, Ethernet0/0
O        131.108.24.0/24 [110/11] via 131.108.1.2, 00:00:48, Ethernet0/0
O        131.108.23.0/24 [110/11] via 131.108.1.2, 00:00:48, Ethernet0/0
O        131.108.22.0/24 [110/11] via 131.108.1.2, 00:00:48, Ethernet0/0
O        131.108.21.0/24 [110/11] via 131.108.1.2, 00:00:48, Ethernet0/0
O        131.108.20.0/24 [110/11] via 131.108.1.2, 00:00:49, Ethernet0/0
O        131.108.19.0/24 [110/11] via 131.108.1.2, 00:00:49, Ethernet0/0
O        131.108.18.0/24 [110/11] via 131.108.1.2, 00:00:50, Ethernet0/0
O        131.108.17.0/24 [110/11] via 131.108.1.2, 00:00:50, Ethernet0/0
O        131.108.16.0/24 [110/11] via 131.108.1.2, 00:00:50, Ethernet0/0
O        131.108.36.0/24 [110/11] via 131.108.1.2, 00:17:10, Ethernet0/0
```

To view the status of the virtual link, use the **show ip ospf virtual-links** command. Example 4-9 displays sample output from this command used on R4.

Example 4-9   **show ip ospf virtual-links** *on R4*

```
R4#sh ip ospf virtual-links
Virtual Link OSPF_VL0 to router 131.108.255.22 is up
  Run as demand circuit
  DoNotAge LSA allowed.
  Transit area 10, via interface Serial2, Cost of using 64
  Transmit Delay is 1 sec, State POINT_TO_POINT,
  Timer intervals configured, Hello 10, Dead 40, Wait 40, Retransmit 5
    Hello due in 00:00:09
    Adjacency State FULL (Hello suppressed)
    Index 2/4, retransmission queue length 0, number of retransmission 1
    First 0x0(0)/0x0(0) Next 0x0(0)/0x0(0)
    Last retransmission scan length is 1, maximum is 1
    Last retransmission scan time is 0 msec, maximum is 0 msec
```

You have successfully configured a complex network with eight Cisco routers in multiple areas. The routing table, even with only eight routers, has over 20 IP route entries.

Before using summarization on this network to reduce the IP routing table size, look at the full working configurations on all routers. Pay particular attention to the shaded sections and the router functions within the OSPF network. Also note how the **clockrate** command is used to enable back-to-back serial high-level data link control (HDLC) connections among Cisco routers. Example 4-10 displays R1's full working configuration. R1 is a backbone router.

Example 4-10 *R1's Full Configuration*

```
hostname R1
!
logging buffered 64000 debugging
enable password cisco
!
ip subnet-zero
no ip domain-lookup
!
interface Loopback0
 ip address 131.108.2.1 255.255.255.0
 ip ospf network point-to-point
!
interface Loopback1
 ip address 131.108.3.1 255.255.255.0
 ip ospf network point-to-point
!
interface Loopback2
 ip address 131.108.4.1 255.255.255.0
 ip ospf network point-to-point
!
interface Loopback3
 ip address 131.108.5.1 255.255.255.0
 ip ospf network point-to-point
!
interface Loopback4
 ip address 131.108.6.1 255.255.255.0
 ip ospf network point-to-point
!
interface Loopback5
 ip address 131.108.7.1 255.255.255.0
 ip ospf network point-to-point
!
interface Loopback6
 ip address 131.108.8.1 255.255.255.0
 ip ospf network point-to-point
!
interface Loopback7
 ip address 131.108.9.1 255.255.255.0
 ip ospf network point-to-point
!
interface Loopback8
 ip address 131.108.10.1 255.255.255.0
 ip ospf network point-to-point
!
interface Loopback9
 ip address 131.108.11.1 255.255.255.0
 ip ospf network point-to-point
```

continues

Example 4-10 *R1's Full Configuration (Continued)*

```
!
interface Loopback10
 ip address 131.108.12.1 255.255.255.0
 ip ospf network point-to-point
!
interface Loopback11
 ip address 131.108.13.1 255.255.255.0
 ip ospf network point-to-point
!
interface Loopback12
 ip address 131.108.14.1 255.255.255.0
 ip ospf network point-to-point
!
interface Loopback13
 ip address 131.108.15.1 255.255.255.0
 ip ospf network point-to-point
!
interface Ethernet0/0
 ip address 131.108.1.1 255.255.255.0
!
interface Serial0/0
 ip address 131.108.255.1 255.255.255.252
  clockrate 125000
!
interface Serial0/1
 shutdown
!
router ospf 1
 network 131.108.0.0 0.0.255.255 area 0
!
line con 0
line aux 0
line vty 0 4
end
```

Example 4-11 displays R2's full working configuration.

Example 4-11 *R2's Full Configuration*

```
hostname R2
!
enable password cisco
!
ip subnet-zero
no ip domain-lookup
!
interface Loopback0
 ip address 131.108.16.1 255.255.255.0
 ip ospf network point-to-point
```

Example 4-11 *R2's Full Configuration (Continued)*

```
!
interface Loopback1
 ip address 131.108.17.1 255.255.255.0
 ip ospf network point-to-point
!
interface Loopback2
 ip address 131.108.18.1 255.255.255.0
 ip ospf network point-to-point
!
interface Loopback3
 ip address 131.108.19.1 255.255.255.0
 ip ospf network point-to-point
!
interface Loopback4
 ip address 131.108.20.1 255.255.255.0
 ip ospf network point-to-point
!
interface Loopback5
 ip address 131.108.21.1 255.255.255.0
 ip ospf network point-to-point
!
interface Loopback6
 ip address 131.108.22.1 255.255.255.0
 ip ospf network point-to-point
!
interface Loopback7
 ip address 131.108.23.1 255.255.255.0
 ip ospf network point-to-point
!
interface Loopback8
 ip address 131.108.24.1 255.255.255.0
 ip ospf network point-to-point
!
interface Loopback9
 ip address 131.108.25.1 255.255.255.0
 ip ospf network point-to-point
!
interface Loopback10
 ip address 131.108.26.1 255.255.255.0
 ip ospf network point-to-point
!
interface Loopback11
 ip address 131.108.27.1 255.255.255.0
 ip ospf network point-to-point
!
interface Loopback13
 ip address 131.108.28.1 255.255.255.0
 ip ospf network point-to-point
!
```

continues

Example 4-11 *R2's Full Configuration (Continued)*

```
interface Loopback14
 ip address 131.108.29.1 255.255.255.0
 ip ospf network point-to-point
!
interface Loopback15
 ip address 131.108.30.1 255.255.255.0
 ip ospf network point-to-point
!
interface Loopback16
 ip address 131.108.31.1 255.255.255.0
 ip ospf network point-to-point
!
interface Ethernet0/0
 ip address 131.108.1.2 255.255.255.0
!
interface Serial1/0
 ip address 131.108.255.5 255.255.255.252
 clockrate 128000
!
interface Serial1/1
 shutdown
!
interface Serial1/2
 shutdown
!
interface Serial1/3
 shutdown
!
router ospf 1
 network 131.108.0.0 0.0.255.255 area 0
!
ip classless
!
line con 0
line aux 0
line vty 0 4
!
end
```

Example 4-12 displays R3's full working configuration. R3 is an ABR.

Example 4-12 *R3's Full Configuration*

```
hostname R3
!
enable password cisco
!
no ip domain-lookup
!
interface Ethernet0
```

Example 4-12 *R3's Full Configuration (Continued)*

```
ip address 131.108.36.3 255.255.255.0
!
interface Serial0
 ip address 131.108.255.2 255.255.255.252
!
interface Serial1
 ip address 131.108.255.9 255.255.255.252
 clockrate 128000
!
interface Serial2
 ip address 131.108.255.13 255.255.255.252
 clockrate  128000
!
interface Serial3
 shutdown
!
router ospf 1
 network 131.108.255.0 0.0.0.3 area 0
 network 131.108.36.0 0.0.0.255 area 10
 network 131.108.255.8 0.0.0.3 area 10
 network 131.108.255.12 0.0.0.3 area 10
!
line con 0
line aux 0
line vty 0 4
!
end
```

Example 4-13 displays R4's full working configuration. R4 is an ABR.

Example 4-13 *R4's Full Configuration*

```
hostname R4
!
enable password cisco
!
ip subnet-zero
no ip domain-lookup
!
interface Ethernet 0
ip address 131.108.36.4 255.255.255.0
!
interface Serial0
 ip address 131.108.255.6 255.255.255.252
!
interface Serial1
 ip address 131.108.255.17 255.255.255.252
  clockrate 128000
```

continues

Example 4-13 *R4's Full Configuration (Continued)*

```
!
interface Serial2
 ip address 131.108.255.21 255.255.255.252
  clockrate 128000
!
interface Serial3
 shutdown
!
router ospf 1
 area 10 virtual-link 131.108.255.22
 network 131.108.255.4 0.0.0.3 area 0
network 131.108.36.0 0.0.0.255 area 10
 network 131.108.255.16 0.0.0.3 area 10
 network 131.108.255.20 0.0.0.3 area 10
!
line con 0
line aux 0
line vty 0 4
!
end
```

Example 4-14 displays R5's full working configuration. R5 is an internal OSPF area.

Example 4-14 *R5's Full Configuration*

```
hostname R5
!
enable password cisco
!
interface Ethernet0
 ip address 131.108.128.1 255.255.255.0
!
interface Serial0
 ip address 131.108.255.10 255.255.255.252
!
interface Serial1
  shutdown
!
router ospf 1
 network 131.108.128.0 0.0.0.255 area 10
 network 131.108.255.8 0.0.0.3 area 10
!
line con 0
line aux 0
line vty 0 4
end
```

Example 4-15 displays R6's full working configuration. R6 is an internal OSPF router.

Example 4-15 *R6's Full Configuration*

```
hostname R6
!
enable password cisco
!
ip subnet-zero
!
interface Ethernet0
 ip address 131.108.129.1 255.255.255.0
 !
interface Serial0
 ip address 131.108.255.18 255.255.255.252
interface Serial1
 shutdown
 !
router ospf 1
 network 131.108.129.0 0.0.0.255 area 10
 network 131.108.255.16 0.0.0.3 area 10
 !
line con 0
line aux 0
line vty 0 4
 !
end
```

Example 4-16 displays R7's full working configuration. R7 is an internal OSPF area.

Example 4-16 *R7's Full Configuration*

```
hostname R7
!
enable password cisco
!
ip subnet-zero
no ip domain-lookup
interface Ethernet0
 ip address 131.108.130.1 255.255.255.0
interface Serial0
 ip address 131.108.255.14 255.255.255.252
 !
interface Serial1
 shutdown
 !
router ospf 1
 network 131.108.130.0 0.0.0.255 area 10
 network 131.108.255.12 0.0.0.3 area 10
 !
```

continues

Example 4-16 *R7's Full Configuration (Continued)*

```
line con 0
line aux 0
line vty 0 4
!
end
```

Example 4-17 displays R8's full working configuration. R8 is an internal OSPF area, requiring a virtual link because area 11 is not connected to area 0.

Example 4-17 *R8's Full Configuration*

```
hostname R8
enable password cisco
!
no ip domain-lookup
!
interface Ethernet0
 ip address 131.108.131.1 255.255.255.0
!
interface Serial0
 ip address 131.108.255.22 255.255.255.252
interface Serial1
 shutdown
!
router ospf 1
 area 10 virtual-link 131.108.255.6
 network 131.108.131.0 0.0.0.255 area 11
 network 131.108.255.20 0.0.0.3 area 10
!
line con 0
line aux 0
line vty 0 4
!
end
```

Scenario 4-2: Configuring OSPF Summarization

This scenario covers the same network topology shown in Figure 4-4. The aim of any network designer is to use summarization wherever possible. OSPF, as you have seen, has some advanced features to allow summarization. The first method you can apply is intra-area summarization on the backbone Routers R1 and R2. A total of 30 networks (contiguous) exist from 131.108.1.0 to 131.108.31.255.

For the core routers in area 0, namely R1, R2, R3, and R4, which pass on routing information to other core or remote routers, you need to have a more detailed view of the network. This detail is required so you do not perform any summarization on the core network and maintain a full IP routing topology in the core (or backbone) network.

The access-level routers, R5, R6, R7, and R8, do not typically require an IP routing entry for every network in the core because they require access to only the core network in area 0, the backbone. Therefore, these routers are perfect examples of how you can use summarization to reduce the size of routing tables. Only a single exit point to the core of the network exists, so you can configure stubby networks. First, use some summary commands. Example 4-18 displays R5's IP routing table.

Example 4-18 *R5's Current IP Routing Table*

```
R5#show ip route
Codes: C - connected, O - OSPF, IA - OSPF inter area
       N1 - OSPF NSSA external type 1, N2 - OSPF NSSA external type 2
       E1 - OSPF external type 1, E2 - OSPF external type 2, E - EGP
    131.108.0.0/16 is variably subnetted, 41 subnets, 2 masks
O IA    131.108.255.16/30 [110/983] via 131.108.255.9, 04:14:50, Serial0
O IA    131.108.255.20/30 [110/983] via 131.108.255.9, 04:14:50, Serial0
O IA    131.108.255.0/30 [110/128] via 131.108.255.9, 04:14:51, Serial0
O IA    131.108.255.4/30 [110/919] via 131.108.255.9, 04:14:51, Serial0
C       131.108.255.8/30 is directly connected, Serial0
O       131.108.255.12/30 [110/128] via 131.108.255.9, 04:14:51, Serial0
O IA    131.108.131.0/24 [110/993] via 131.108.255.9, 04:05:58, Serial0
O       131.108.130.0/24 [110/138] via 131.108.255.9, 04:14:51, Serial0
O IA    131.108.129.0/24 [110/993] via 131.108.255.9, 04:14:51, Serial0
C       131.108.128.0/24 is directly connected, Ethernet0
O IA    131.108.15.0/24 [110/129] via 131.108.255.9, 03:51:04, Serial0
O IA    131.108.14.0/24 [110/129] via 131.108.255.9, 03:51:04, Serial0
O IA    131.108.13.0/24 [110/129] via 131.108.255.9, 03:51:14, Serial0
O IA    131.108.12.0/24 [110/129] via 131.108.255.9, 03:51:14, Serial0
O IA    131.108.11.0/24 [110/129] via 131.108.255.9, 03:51:14, Serial0
O IA    131.108.10.0/24 [110/129] via 131.108.255.9, 03:51:14, Serial0
O IA    131.108.9.0/24 [110/129] via 131.108.255.9, 03:51:15, Serial0
O IA    131.108.8.0/24 [110/129] via 131.108.255.9, 03:51:25, Serial0
O IA    131.108.7.0/24 [110/129] via 131.108.255.9, 03:51:25, Serial0
O IA    131.108.6.0/24 [110/129] via 131.108.255.9, 03:51:25, Serial0
O IA    131.108.5.0/24 [110/129] via 131.108.255.9, 03:51:25, Serial0
O IA    131.108.4.0/24 [110/129] via 131.108.255.9, 03:51:25, Serial0
O IA    131.108.3.0/24 [110/129] via 131.108.255.9, 03:51:25, Serial0
O IA    131.108.2.0/24 [110/129] via 131.108.255.9, 03:51:35, Serial0
O IA    131.108.1.0/24 [110/138] via 131.108.255.9, 04:14:52, Serial0
O IA    131.108.31.0/24 [110/139] via 131.108.255.9, 04:14:52, Serial0
O IA    131.108.30.0/24 [110/139] via 131.108.255.9, 04:14:52, Serial0
O IA    131.108.29.0/24 [110/139] via 131.108.255.9, 04:14:52, Serial0
O IA    131.108.28.0/24 [110/139] via 131.108.255.9, 04:14:52, Serial0
O IA    131.108.27.0/24 [110/139] via 131.108.255.9, 04:14:52, Serial0
O IA    131.108.26.0/24 [110/139] via 131.108.255.9, 04:14:52, Serial0
O IA    131.108.25.0/24 [110/139] via 131.108.255.9, 04:14:53, Serial0
O IA    131.108.24.0/24 [110/139] via 131.108.255.9, 04:14:53, Serial0
O IA    131.108.23.0/24 [110/139] via 131.108.255.9, 04:14:53, Serial0
O IA    131.108.22.0/24 [110/139] via 131.108.255.9, 04:14:53, Serial0
O IA    131.108.21.0/24 [110/139] via 131.108.255.9, 04:14:53, Serial0
O IA    131.108.20.0/24 [110/139] via 131.108.255.9, 04:14:53, Serial0
```

continues

Example 4-18 *R5's Current IP Routing Table (Continued)*

```
O IA    131.108.19.0/24 [110/139] via 131.108.255.9, 04:14:53, Serial0
O IA    131.108.18.0/24 [110/139] via 131.108.255.9, 04:14:53, Serial0
O IA    131.108.17.0/24 [110/139] via 131.108.255.9, 04:14:53, Serial0
O IA    131.108.16.0/24 [110/139] via 131.108.255.9, 04:14:53, Serial0
O       131.108.36.0/24 [110/11] via 131.108.255.9, 04:14:53, Serial0
```

Use OSPF summarization for the core IP networks ranging from 131.108.1.0 to
131.108.31.255 on Routers R3 and R4. Example 4-19 displays the use of the IOS **area** *area
ID* **range** *mask* command on R3.

Example 4-19 *Summary on R3*

```
R3(config)#router ospf 1
R3(config-router)#area 0 ?
  authentication  Enable authentication
  default-cost    Set the summary default-cost of a NSSA/stub area
  nssa            Specify a NSSA area
  range           Summarize routes matching address/mask (border routers only)
  stub            Specify a stub area
  virtual-link    Define a virtual link and its parameters
R3(config-router)#area 0 range 131.108.0.0 ?
  A.B.C.D  IP mask for address

R3(config-router)#area 0 range 131.108.0.0 255.255.224.0
```

The IOS tells you only ABRs can perform OSPF summarization. Routers R3 and R4 are
ABRs; hence, you can perform network summarization on R3 and R4.

Example 4-20 displays the OSPF summary on R4.

Example 4-20 *Summary on R4*

```
R4(config)#router ospf 1
R4(config-router)#area 0 range 131.108.1.0 255.255.224.0
```

View the IP routing table on R5. Example 4-21 displays R5's routing table after network
summarization is configured on R3 and R4. Also displayed in Example 4-21 are a few ping
requests to IP networks covered in the summary range 131.108.0.0/19, which are networks
covering the range 131.108.1.0 to 131.108.31.255.

Example 4-21 *Summary on R5*

```
R5#show ip route
Codes: C - connected, O - OSPF, IA - OSPF inter area
       N1 - OSPF NSSA external type 1, N2 - OSPF NSSA external type 2
       E1 - OSPF external type 1, E2 - OSPF external type 2
    131.108.0.0/16 is variably subnetted, 11 subnets, 3 masks
```

Example 4-21 *Summary on R5 (Continued)*

```
O IA    131.108.255.16/30 [110/983] via 131.108.255.9, 05:09:00, Serial0
O IA    131.108.255.20/30 [110/983] via 131.108.255.9, 05:09:00, Serial0
O IA    131.108.255.0/30 [110/128] via 131.108.255.9, 05:09:00, Serial0
O IA    131.108.255.4/30 [110/919] via 131.108.255.9, 05:09:00, Serial0
C       131.108.255.8/30 is directly connected, Serial0
O       131.108.255.12/30 [110/128] via 131.108.255.9, 05:09:00, Serial0
O       131.108.36.0/24 [110/11] via 131.108.255.9, 05:14:53, Serial0
O IA    131.108.131.0/24 [110/993] via 131.108.255.9, 05:00:08, Serial0
O       131.108.130.0/24 [110/138] via 131.108.255.9, 05:09:00, Serial0
O IA    131.108.129.0/24 [110/993] via 131.108.255.9, 05:09:01, Serial0
C       131.108.128.0/24 is directly connected, Ethernet0
O IA    131.108.0.0/19 [110/129] via 131.108.255.9, 00:46:25, Serial0
R5#ping 131.108.1.1

Type escape sequence to abort.
Sending 5, 100-byte ICMP Echos to 131.108.1.1, timeout is 2 seconds:
!!!!! (R1 Ethernet e0/0 address)
Success rate is 100 percent (5/5), round-trip min/avg/max = 32/32/32 ms
R5#ping 131.108.2.1
Type escape sequence to abort.
Sending 5, 100-byte ICMP Echos to 131.108.2.1, timeout is 2 seconds:
!!!!!
Success rate is 100 percent (5/5), round-trip min/avg/max = 28/31/32 ms
R5#ping 131.108.3.1
Type escape sequence to abort.
Sending 5, 100-byte ICMP Echos to 131.108.3.1, timeout is 2 seconds:
!!!!!
Success rate is 100 percent (5/5), round-trip min/avg/max = 32/32/32 ms
R5#ping 131.108.31.1
Type escape sequence to abort.
Sending 5, 100-byte ICMP Echos to 131.108.31.1, timeout is 2 seconds:
!!!!!
Success rate is 100 percent (5/5), round-trip min/avg/max = 32/32/36 ms
```

By using a simple command on the ABRs, you have significantly reduced the IP routing table size on R5 to nine remote OSPF entries. The same occurs on Routers R6, R7, and R8.

Also because R5 and R7 have single exit points to the core, you can configure a stub network. You cannot configure a stub network on R8 because you have a virtual link. To create a stub network, use the **area** *area id* **stub** command. Create a stub network between Routers R3 (the ABR) and R5. Example 4-22 displays the stub configuration on R3.

Example 4-22 *Stub Configuration on R3*

```
R3(config)#router ospf  1
R3(config-router)#area 10 stub
```

If you attempt to configure a stub network on R4, Cisco's IOS displays the message in Example 4-23.

Example 4-23 *Configuring a Stub Area*

```
R4(config)#router ospf 1
R4(config-router)#area 10 stub
% OSPF: Area cannot be a stub as it contains a virtual link
R4(config-router)#
```

You cannot create a stub between R4 and R8 because of the virtual link. So, change the area assignments on R8 to area 10 so you can create a stub.

Figure 4-5 displays the change of area assignments to remove the necessity of a virtual link between R8 and R4. To change the area assignment on R8 from 11 to 10, configure the following commands on R8:

```
no network 131.108.131.0 0.0.0.255 area 11
network 131.108.131.0 0.0.0.255 area 10
```

Figure 4-5 *OSPF Sample Network After R8 Area Change*

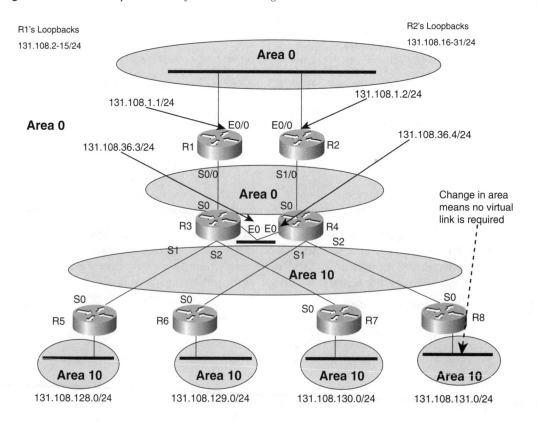

Because a change has been made to OSPF area assignment, you must ensure that OSPF is still active on R5. Example 4-24 displays R5's OSPF neighbor state after you configure the ABR R3 as a stub network in area 10.

Example 4-24 show ip ospf neighbor *Command on R5*

```
R5#show ip ospf neighbor

Neighbor ID      Pri   State           Dead Time   Address          Interface
131.108.255.13    1   DOWN/  -             -        131.108.255.9    Serial0
```

The OSPF relationship between R3 and R5 is down because if one router is configured as a stub, the neighboring router must also be configured as a stub, and in this case, R5 has not yet been configured as a stub. Example 4-25 displays the configuration of a stub network on R5 and the OSPF relationship change to full adjacency.

Example 4-25 *Stub Configuration on R5*

```
R5(config)#router ospf 1
R5(config-router)#area 10 stub
R5#sh ip ospf neighbor

Neighbor ID      Pri   State           Dead Time   Address          Interface
131.108.255.13    1   FULL/  -          00:00:38    131.108.255.9    Serial0
```

Now, view the IP routing table on R5. Example 4-26 displays the new IP routing table after the stub configuration is completed on both Routers R3 and R5.

Example 4-26 *R5's Routing Table*

```
R5#sh ip route
Gateway of last resort is 131.108.255.9 to network 0.0.0.0
      131.108.0.0/16 is variably subnetted, 10 subnets, 3 masks
O IA    131.108.255.16/30 [110/983] via 131.108.255.9, 00:01:22, Serial0
O IA    131.108.255.20/30 [110/983] via 131.108.255.9, 00:01:22, Serial0
O IA    131.108.255.0/30 [110/128] via 131.108.255.9, 00:01:22, Serial0
O IA    131.108.255.4/30 [110/919] via 131.108.255.9, 00:01:22, Serial0
C       131.108.255.8/30 is directly connected, Serial0
O       131.108.255.12/30 [110/128] via 131.108.255.9, 00:01:22, Serial0
O       131.108.36.0/24 [110/11] via 131.108.255.9, 00:01:22, Serial0
O       131.108.131.0/24 [110/128] via 131.108.255.9, 00:01:22, Serial0
O IA    131.108.131.0/24 [110/993] via 131.108.255.9, 00:01:22, Serial0
O IA    131.108.129.0/24 [110/993] via 131.108.255.9, 00:01:22, Serial0
C       131.108.128.0/24 is directly connected, Ethernet0
O IA    131.108.0.0/19 [110/129] via 131.108.255.9, 00:01:23, Serial0
O*IA 0.0.0.0/0 [110/65] via 131.108.255.9, 00:01:23, Serial0
```

You now have on R5 a default route labeled 0.0.0.0 through the next hop address 131.108.255.9 (R3). You have a gateway of last resort, which effectively means any packets to unknown destinations are sent to the next hop address 131.108.255.9 (R3). Configuring a stub network performs exactly this function; it provides a default route.

Now, you can assume that all IP traffic from the edge routers is destined for the core network, so there is no reason for R5 or R6 to have network entries for every individual IP route in the core. All IP traffic is destined for the core anyway. To further reduce the IP routing table, you can configure OSPF to stop the entries labeled as O IA (interarea routes) from populating the edge routers by configuring a stubby network with the **no-summary** option by applying the IOS **area** *area id* **stub no-summary** command.

This option prevents the ABR from sending summary link advertisements from other areas except the area that connects R5, area 10 in this case. To ensure OSPF full adjacency is achieved between R3, R4, R5, R6, R7, and R8, you must configure both the core and edge routers. Example 4-27 displays the configuration of the core router, R3, with the **no-summary** option.

Example 4-27 *Preventing Summary LSAs from Other Areas*

```
R3(config)#router ospf 1
R3(config-router)#area 10 stub no-summary
```

You also complete the **area 10 stub no-summary** on the remaining routers. Example 4-28 displays the **no-summary** option configured on R5.

Example 4-28 **no-summary** *Command Option on R5*

```
R5(config)#router ospf 1
R5(config-router)#area 10 stub no-summary
```

R5's routing table should now contain even fewer entries. Example 4-29 displays R5 IP routing table. View the IP routing table on R5 in Example 4-29 and compare it to Example 4-26.

Example 4-29 *R5's IP Routing Table*

```
R5#show ip route
Gateway of last resort is 131.108.255.9 to network 0.0.0.0
     131.108.0.0/16 is variably subnetted, 9 subnets, 2 masks
O        131.108.255.16/30 [110/138] via 131.108.255.9, 00:01:04, Serial0
O        131.108.255.20/30 [110/138] via 131.108.255.9, 00:01:04, Serial0
C        131.108.255.8/30 is directly connected, Serial0
O        131.108.255.12/30 [110/128] via 131.108.255.9, 00:01:04, Serial0
O        131.108.131.0/24 [110/148] via 131.108.255.9, 00:01:04, Serial0
O        131.108.130.0/24 [110/138] via 131.108.255.9, 00:01:04, Serial0
```

Example 4-29 *R5's IP Routing Table (Continued)*

```
O       131.108.129.0/24 [110/148] via 131.108.255.9, 00:01:04, Serial0
C       131.108.128.0/24 is directly connected, Ethernet0
O       131.108.36.0/24 [110/74] via 131.108.255.9, 00:01:04, Serial0
O*IA 0.0.0.0/0 [110/65] via 131.108.255.9, 00:01:04, Serial0
```

The only networks displayed now are the default network and networks residing in the same area as Router R5, which is area 10. You now have only 8 remote entries instead of over 30, as shown in Example 4-18. The use of the stub configuration is effective in this type of network topology.

List the full OSPF working configurations of the ABR Routers R3 and R4 and the edge routers that are configured as stubby networks. Example 4-30 displays R3's OSPF configuration. The shaded portion highlights the configuration required for the stub network.

NOTE   The configuration in Example 4-30 contains only the message in Example 4-23; the OSPF routing process changes because the remaining configuration is identical to that in Examples 4-10 to 4-17.

Example 4-30 *R3's OSPF Working Configuration*

```
router ospf 1
 network 131.108.255.0 0.0.0.3 area 0
 network 131.108.255.8 0.0.0.3 area 10
 network 131.108.255.12 0.0.0.3 area 10
 network 131.108.36.0 0.0.0.255 area 10
 area 0 range 131.108.0.0 255.255.224.0
 area 10 stub no-summary
```

Example 4-31 displays R4's full OSPF working configuration. The shaded portion highlights the configuration required for the stub network.

Example 4-31 *R4's OSPF Working Configuration*

```
router ospf 1
 area 0 range 131.108.0.0 255.255.224.0
 area 10 stub no-summary
 network 131.108.36.0 0.0.0.255 area 10
 network 131.108.255.4 0.0.0.3 area 0
 network 131.108.255.16 0.0.0.3 area 10
 network 131.108.255.20 0.0.0.3 area 10
```

Example 4-32 displays R5's OSPF working configuration. The shaded portion highlights the configuration required for the stub network.

Example 4-32 *R5's OSPF Working Configuration*

```
router ospf 1
 area 10 stub no-summary
 network 131.108.128.0 0.0.0.255 area 10
 network 131.108.255.4 0.0.0.3 area 10
!
```

Example 4-33 displays R6's OSPF working configuration. The shaded portion highlights the configuration required for the stub network.

Example 4-33 *R6's OSPF Working Configuration*

```
router ospf 1
 area 10 stub no-summary
 network 131.108.129.0 0.0.0.255 area 10
 network 131.108.255.8 0.0.0.3 area 10
```

Example 4-34 displays R7's OSPF working configuration. The shaded portion highlights the configuration required for the stub network.

Example 4-34 *R7's OSPF Working Configuration*

```
router ospf 1
 area 10 stub no-summary
 network 131.108.130.0 0.0.0.255 area 10
 network 131.108.255.12 0.0.0.3 area 10
```

Example 4-35 displays R8's OSPF working configuration. The shaded portion highlights the configuration required for the stub network.

Example 4-35 *R8's OSPF Working Configuration*

```
router ospf 1
 area 10 stub no-summary
 network 131.108.131.0 0.0.0.255 area 10
 network 131.108.255.20 0.0.0.3 area 10
```

TIP   To best appreciate OSPF and the features covered here, you can configure a simple two-router network with loopback address and follow the steps completed here on a smaller scale and continually view the IP routing table to see the benefits of summarization and stubby networks.

Scenario 4-3: Configuring Integrated IS-IS

This scenario shows you how to configure another link-state protocol, IS-IS, in a three-router topology. The topology for this scenario is displayed in Figure 4-6, with the routers named R4, R8, and R9.

Figure 4-6   *IS-IS with VLSM*

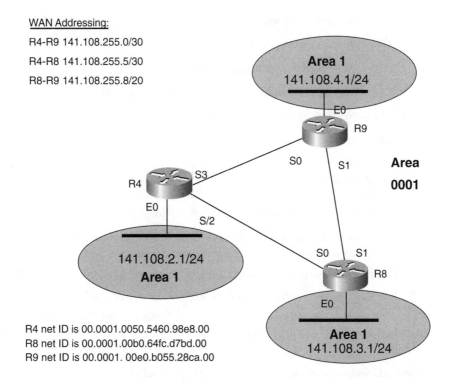

WAN Addressing:
R4-R9 141.108.255.0/30
R4-R8 141.108.255.5/30
R8-R9 141.108.255.8/20

R4 net ID is 00.0001.0050.5460.98e8.00
R8 net ID is 00.0001.00b0.64fc.d7bd.00
R9 net ID is 00.0001. 00e0.b055.28ca.00

Where this scenario covers redistribution, you use these routers to connect to an OSPF router.

The IP addressing scheme is displayed in Figure 4-6. Note that VLSM is in use. IS-IS supports VLSM, and you configure the three routers to be in domain 1 using the network entity known as the simple format, which describes the area and system ID.

NOTE   Three methods (referred to as network entities) can define the area: simple format, OSI format, and Government OSI Profile (GOSIP) format as described in the following list:

Simple format:

Area→System ID→SEL

OSI format:

Domain→Area→System ID→SEL

GOSIP format:

AFI→ICD→DFI→AAI→Reserved→RDI→Area System ID→SEL

These fields are defined as follows:

- AFI—Authority and format identifier (47 for Cisco routers)

- ICD—International code designator

- DFI—Domain specific part

- AAI—Administrative authority identifier

- RDI—Routing domain identifier (autonomous system number)

- SEL—Network Service Access Port (NSAP)

- Area—Used by L2 routers

- System ID—Used by L1 routers; typically an interface Media Access Control (MAC) address

Each IS-IS routers must be configured with the following:

- Enable IS-IS with the command **router isis** *optional area tag*. The tag groups routers in one domain. You must also enter the global command **clns routing**.

- Configure the network interfaces with the command **net** *network-entity-title*.

- Enable IS-IS per interface with the command **ip router isis**.

Figure 4-6 shows a small three-router network. All routers reside in one area. The areas are encoded as 00.0001, and the system IDs are the MAC addresses from the local Ethernet interface.

The MAC addresses of the respective routers are as follows:

- R4—0050.5460.98e8, net ID is 00.0001.0050.5460.98e8.00

- R8—00b0.64fc.d7bd, net ID is 00.0001.00b0.64fc.d7bd.00

- R9—00e0.b055.28ca, net ID is 00.0001.00e0.b055.28ca.00

Now, configure the first router, R4, for IS-IS. Example 4-36 displays the configuration required to enable IS-IS on Router R4.

Example 4-36 *Configuration on R4*

```
R4(config)#router isis
R4(config-router)#net 00.0001.0050.5460.98e8.00
R4(config-router)#exit
R4(config)#clns routing
```

Example 4-36 *Configuration on R4*

```
R4(config)#int ethernet 0
R4(config-if)#ip router isis
R4(config-if)#inter serial 3
R4(config-if)#ip router isis
R4(config-if)#int serial  2
R4(config-if)#ip router isis
```

The first configuration completed on R4 enables the IP routing and then enables Connectionless Network Service (CLNS) and interface configuration on all participating IS-IS interfaces. Example 4-37 displays the configuration of IS-IS on R8.

Example 4-37 *Configuration on R8*

```
R8(config)#router isis
R8(config-router)#net 00.0001.00b0.64fc.d7bd.00
R8(config-router)#exit
R8(config)#clns routing
R8(config)#int ethernet 0
R8(config-if)#ip router isis
R8(config)#interface serial 0
R8(config-if)#ip router isis
R8(config-if)#interface serial 1
R8(config-if)#ip router isis
```

Example 4-38 displays the configuration completed on R9.

Example 4-38 *Configuration on R9*

```
R9(config)#router isis
R9(config-router)#net 00.0001.00e0.b055.28ca.00
R9(config-router)#exit
R9(config)#clns routing
R9(config)#int ethernet 0
R9(config-if)#ip router isis
R9(config-if)#interface serial 0
R9(config-if)#ip router isis
R9(config-if)#interface serial 1
R9(config-if)#ip router isis
```

Now that IS-IS is configured on all three routers, examine the IP routing tables for IP connectivity. Example 4-39 displays R4's IP routing table.

Example 4-39 *R4's IP Routing Table*

```
R4#sh ip route
 Codes     i - IS-IS, L1 - IS-IS level-1, L2 - IS-IS level-2, ia - IS-IS inter area

       141.108.0.0/16 is variably subnetted, 6 subnets, 2 masks
C        141.108.255.4/30 is directly connected, Serial2
C        141.108.255.0/30 is directly connected, Serial3
C        141.108.2.0/24 is directly connected, Ethernet0
i L1     141.108.4.0/24 [115/20] via 141.108.255.2, Serial3
i L1     141.108.3.0/24 [115/20] via 141.108.255.5, Serial2
i L1     141.108.255.8/30 [115/20] via 141.108.255.5, Serial2
                          [115/20] via 141.108.255.2, Serial3
```

R4's routing table has four remote entries, all of which are labeled L1 (level 1 route) because all three routers reside in area 1 as configured by the **net** command. The administrative distance for IS-IS is 115 and is followed by the metric. The IS-IS metric is between 0 and 63. The default metric is set to 10, and the total metric is calculated from source to destination. Notice the path to the remote network 141.108.255.8/30 is calculated with two paths: one path through Serial 2 and the other through Serial 3. In other words, IS-IS supports equal cost path load balancing, as does OSPF.

As with OSPF, the command set for monitoring IS-IS is large. Now look at a few examples of the most commonly used **show** commands. Example 4-40 displays the IS-IS neighbor states with the **show clns isis-neighbor** command.

Example 4-40 *Sample Output of* **show clns isis-neighbor** *Command from R4*

```
R4#sh clns is-neighbors

System Id      Interface    State  Type Priority  Circuit Id        Format
R8             Se2          Up     L1L2 0 /0       00             Phase V
R9             Se3          Up     L1L2 0 /0       00             Phase V
```

R4 has two CLNS neighbors, namely Routers R8 and R9. This means all routers share the same IS-IS link-state database. To view the link-state database on an IS-IS router, use the command **show isis database**, which is displayed in Example 4-41.

Example 4-41 *Sample Output of* **show isis database** *Command from R4*

```
R4#sh isis database
IS-IS Level-1 Link State Database:
LSPID               LSP Seq Num  LSP Checksum  LSP Holdtime     ATT/P/OL
R4.00-00          * 0x00000007   0xE25D        921              0/0/0
R8.00-00            0x00000007   0xFE0A        788              0/0/0
```

Example 4-41 *Sample Output of* **show isis database** *Command from R4 (Continued)*

```
00E0.B055.28CA.00-00  0x00000007   0x3A8A        475           0/0/0
00E0.B055.28CA.01-00  0x00000002   0x87A6        517           0/0/0
IS-IS Level-2 Link State Database:
LSPID                 LSP Seq Num  LSP Checksum  LSP Holdtime  ATT/P/OL
R4.00-00            * 0x00000009   0xA3ED        928           0/0/0
R8.00-00              0x0000000A   0x49DC        794           0/0/0
00E0.B055.28CA.00-00  0x0000000B   0x0C26        926           0/0/0
```

Table 4-6 summarizes the output in Example 4-41.

Table 4-6   *Field Descriptions of* **show isis database** *Command*

Field	Description
LSPID	The link-state protocol data unit (PDU) ID.
LSP Seq Num	Link-state packet (LSP) Sequence number for the LSP that allows other systems to determine whether they have received the latest information from the source.
LSP Checksum	Checksum of the entire LSP packet.
LSP Holdtime	Amount of time the LSP remains valid, in seconds.
ATT	Attach bit. This indicates that the router is also a Level 2 router and it can reach other areas.
P	P bit. Detects whether the area is partition-repair capable.
OL	Overload bit.

IS-IS, as OSPF, is an advanced link-state routing protocol that you can use in large environments to route IP. Before you look at redistributing IS-IS with OSPF, here are the full working configurations of the three routers in this IS-IS topology. Example 4-42 displays R4's full working configuration.

Example 4-42 *R4's Full Configuration*

```
hostname R4
!
enable password cisco
ip subnet-zero
no ip domain-lookup
!
clns routing
!
interface Ethernet0
 ip address 141.108.2.1 255.255.255.0
 ip router isis
```

continues

Example 4-42 *R4's Full Configuration (Continued)*

```
!
interface Serial0
shutdown
!
interface Serial1
 ip address 131.108.255.17 255.255.255.252
 clockrate  128000
!
interface Serial2
 ip address 141.108.255.6 255.255.255.252
 ip router isis
 clockrate 128000!
interface Serial3
 ip address 141.108.255.1 255.255.255.252
 ip router isis
 clockrate  128000
!
router isis
 net 00.0001.0050.5460.98e8.00
!
line con 0
line aux 0
line vty 0 4
!
end
```

Example 4-43 displays R8's full working configuration.

Example 4-43 *R8's Full Configuration*

```
hostname R8
!
enable password cisco
!
ip subnet-zero
no ip domain-lookup
clns routing
!
interface Ethernet0
 ip address 141.108.3.1 255.255.255.0
 ip router isis
!
interface Serial0
 ip address 141.108.255.5 255.255.255.252
 ip router isis
```

Example 4-43 *R8's Full Configuration (Continued)*

```
!
interface Serial1
 ip address 141.108.255.10 255.255.255.252
 ip router isis
!
router isis
 net 00.0001.00b0.64fc.d7bd.00
line con 0
line 1 8
line aux 0
line vty 0 4
!
end
```

Example 4-44 displays R9's full working configuration.

Example 4-44 *R9's Full Configuration*

```
hostname R9
!
clns routing
!
interface Ethernet0
 ip address 141.108.4.1 255.255.255.0
 ip router isis
!
interface Serial0
 ip address 141.108.255.2 255.255.255.252
 ip router isis
!
interface Serial1
 ip address 141.108.255.9 255.255.255.252
 ip router isis
 clockrate  128000
!
router isis
 net 00.0001.00e0.b055.28ca.00
!
line con 0
line 1 8
line aux 0
line vty 0 4
!
end
```

Example 4-45 displays some sample ping requests and replies to the remote network to demonstrate IP connectivity among all three routers.

Example 4-45 *Sample Ping Requests from R4*

```
R4#ping 141.108.3.1
Type escape sequence to abort.
Sending 5, 100-byte ICMP Echos to 141.108.3.1, timeout is 2 seconds:
!!!!!
Success rate is 100 percent (5/5), round-trip min/avg/max = 28/36/60 ms
R4#ping 141.108.4.1
Type escape sequence to abort.
Sending 5, 100-byte ICMP Echos to 141.108.4.1, timeout is 2 seconds:
!!!!!
Success rate is 100 percent (5/5), round-trip min/avg/max = 16/17/20 ms
R4#ping 141.108.255.9
Type escape sequence to abort.
Sending 5, 100-byte ICMP Echos to 141.108.255.9, timeout is 2 seconds:
!!!!!
Success rate is 100 percent (5/5), round-trip min/avg/max = 16/16/20 ms
R4#ping 141.108.255.10
Type escape sequence to abort.
Sending 5, 100-byte ICMP Echos to 141.108.255.10, timeout is 2 seconds:
!!!!!
Success rate is 100 percent (5/5), round-trip min/avg/max = 28/46/104 ms
R4#
```

The IS-IS IOS command set is comprehensive. Table 4-7 summarizes the most common IS-IS configuration and **show** commands.

Table 4-7   *IS-IS Command Summary*

Command	Description
area-password *password*	Configures IS-IS Level 1 authentication
domain-password *password*	Configures the domain password for L2 routers
isis password *password*	Configures authentication between two IS-IS routers
ip router isis [*tag*]	Enables IS-IS per interface
clns routing	Enables routing of CLNS packets
default-information-originate	Generates a default route inside the IS-IS domain
show isis database	Displays the link-state database
summary-address *address mask*	Configures address summarization
show isis spf-log	Displays the number of times the SPF calculation has been completed

Scenario 4-4: OSPF and Integrated IS-IS Redistribution

In this scenario, you integrate the IS-IS network you configured in Scenario 4-3 with an OSPF network. Figure 4-7 displays the OSPF network and IS-IS. Router R1 has loopbacks ranging from 131.108.2.0 to 131.108.15.255.

Figure 4-7   *OSPF and Integrated IS-IS Network Topology*

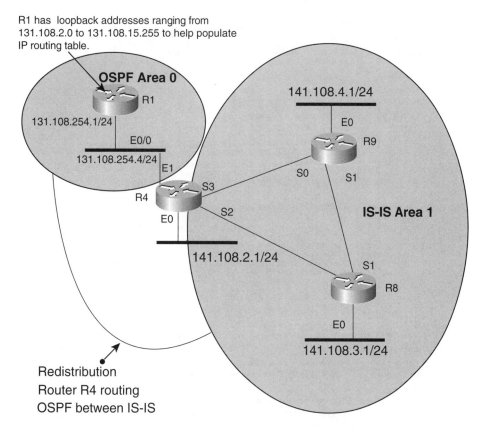

Because R4 is within both the OSPF and IS-IS domain, you can configure redistribution between OSPF and IS-IS.

To configure redistribution between any IP routing protocols, you must configure a metric that is used within the IP dynamic routing protocol. For OSPF, you must define a cost metric, for example.

Example 4-46 displays the configuration of OSPF redistribution from OSPF to IS-IS on R4 and the step-by-step process required to ensure that all the OSPF routes are advertised as IS-IS routes in the IS-IS domain. The **?** tool is used to bring up the available options.

Example 4-46 *Routing OSPF to IS-IS on R4*

```
R4(config)#router isis
R4(config-router)#redistribute ?
  bgp          Border Gateway Protocol (BGP)
  connected    Connected
  egp          Exterior Gateway Protocol (EGP)
  eigrp        Enhanced Interior Gateway Routing Protocol (EIGRP)
  igrp         Interior Gateway Routing Protocol (IGRP)
  isis         ISO IS-IS
  iso-igrp     IGRP for OSI networks
  level-1      IS-IS level-1 routes only
  level-1-2    IS-IS level-1 and level-2 routes
  level-2      IS-IS level-2 routes only
  metric       Metric for redistributed routes
  metric-type  OSPF/IS-IS exterior metric type for redistributed routes
  mobile       Mobile routes
  odr          On Demand stub Routes
  ospf         Open Shortest Path First (OSPF)
  rip          Routing Information Protocol (RIP)
  route-map    Route map reference
  static       Static routes
  <cr>
R4(config-router)#redistribute ospf ?
  <1-65535>  Process ID
R4(config-router)#redistribute ospf 1 ?
  level-1      IS-IS level-1 routes only
  level-1-2    IS-IS level-1 and level-2 routes
  level-2      IS-IS level-2 routes only
  match        Redistribution of OSPF routes
  metric       Metric for redistributed routes
  metric-type  OSPF/IS-IS exterior metric type for redistributed routes
  route-map    Route map reference
  vrf          VPN Routing/Forwarding Instance
  <cr>
R4(config-router)#redistribute ospf 1 level-2 ?
  match        Redistribution of OSPF routes
  metric       Metric for redistributed routes
  metric-type  OSPF/IS-IS exterior metric type for redistributed routes
  route-map    Route map reference
  <cr>
R4(config-router)#redistribute ospf 1 level-2 metric ?
  <0-63>  ISIS default metric

R4(config-router)#redistribute ospf 1 level-2 metric 10
```

When redistributing from OSPF to IS-IS, you need to define the OSPF process ID from which the OSPF routes will be injected. The OSPF process ID is 1.

Because OSPF uses cost as the metric for making routing decisions and IS-IS uses L1 or L2, you must define the IS-IS router type. (The router type along with IS-IS metric is between 0–63.)

Three options are available when you are redistributing from OSPF to IS-IS: L1, L2, and L1/2.

In this scenario, you configure L2 routes. Finally, you need to define an IS-IS metric; the chosen value of 10 is used. Any value between 0 and 63 is a valid metric.

View the IP routing table inside in IS-IS network. Example 4-47 displays the IP routing table on R8.

Example 4-47 *R8's IP Routing Table*

```
R8#show ip route
Codes: C - connected, i - IS-IS, L1 - IS-IS level-1, L2 - IS-IS level-2, ia - IS-IS
inter area
       141.108.0.0/16 is variably subnetted, 6 subnets, 2 masks
C        141.108.255.8/30 is directly connected, Serial1
C        141.108.255.4/30 is directly connected, Serial0
i L1     141.108.255.0/30 [115/20] via 141.108.255.9, Serial1
C        141.108.3.0/24 is directly connected, Ethernet0
i L1     141.108.2.0/24 [115/30] via 141.108.255.9, Serial1
i L1     141.108.4.0/24 [115/20] via 141.108.255.9, Serial1
       131.108.0.0/24 is subnetted, 15 subnets
i L2     131.108.254.0 [115/30] via 141.108.255.9, Serial1
i L2     131.108.15.0 [115/30] via 141.108.255.9, Serial1
i L2     131.108.14.0 [115/30] via 141.108.255.9, Serial1
i L2     131.108.13.0 [115/30] via 141.108.255.9, Serial1
i L2     131.108.12.0 [115/30] via 141.108.255.9, Serial1
i L2     131.108.11.0 [115/30] via 141.108.255.9, Serial1
i L2     131.108.10.0 [115/30] via 141.108.255.9, Serial1
i L2     131.108.9.0 [115/30] via 141.108.255.9, Serial1
i L2     131.108.8.0 [115/30] via 141.108.255.9, Serial1
i L2     131.108.7.0 [115/30] via 141.108.255.9, Serial1
i L2     131.108.6.0 [115/30] via 141.108.255.9, Serial1
i L2     131.108.5.0 [115/30] via 141.108.255.9, Serial1
i L2     131.108.4.0 [115/30] via 141.108.255.9, Serial1
i L2     131.108.3.0 [115/30] via 141.108.255.9, Serial1
i L2     131.108.2.0 [115/30] via 141.108.255.9, Serial1
```

Example 4-47 displays the remote OSPF routes redistributed from the OSPF backbone on R1 into IS-IS as L2 routes, and a metric of 30, which comes from the addition of the 10 used in redistribution and the two hop counts between R4 to R9 and R9 to R8. Try to ping the remote address. Example 4-48 displays a sample ping request from R8 to the L2 IS-IS route 131.108.2.1 (R2's loopback address).

Example 4-48 *Sample Ping Request to 131.108.2.1 from R8*

```
R8#ping 131.108.2.1

Type escape sequence to abort.
Sending 5, 100-byte ICMP Echos to 131.108.2.1, timeout is 2 seconds:
.....
Success rate is 0 percent (0/5)
R8#
```

The ping request receives no replies. R8 has a routing entry for this network. The reason the ping request receives no replies is because R8 sends the request to the next hop address of 141.108.255.9 (R9) and R9 sends the request to R4. Example 4-49 displays R9's IP routing table confirming the next hop address.

Example 4-49 *IP Routing Table on R9*

```
R9#sh ip route
Codes: C - connected, i - IS-IS, L1 - IS-IS level-1, L2 - IS-IS level-2, * - candidate
default
       141.108.0.0/16 is variably subnetted, 6 subnets, 2 masks
C       141.108.255.8/30 is directly connected, Serial1
i L1    141.108.255.4/30 [115/50] via 141.108.255.1, Serial0
                         [115/50] via 141.108.255.10, Serial1
C       141.108.255.0/30 is directly connected, Serial0
i L1    141.108.3.0/24 [115/20] via 141.108.255.10, Serial1
i L1    141.108.2.0/24 [115/20] via 141.108.255.1, Serial0
C       141.108.4.0/24 is directly connected, Ethernet0
       131.108.0.0/24 is subnetted, 15 subnets
i L2    131.108.254.0 [115/20] via 141.108.255.1, Serial0
i L2    131.108.15.0 [115/20] via 141.108.255.1, Serial0
i L2    131.108.14.0 [115/20] via 141.108.255.1, Serial0
i L2    131.108.13.0 [115/20] via 141.108.255.1, Serial0
i L2    131.108.12.0 [115/20] via 141.108.255.1, Serial0
i L2    131.108.11.0 [115/20] via 141.108.255.1, Serial0
i L2    131.108.10.0 [115/20] via 141.108.255.1, Serial0
i L2    131.108.9.0 [115/20] via 141.108.255.1, Serial0
i L2    131.108.8.0 [115/20] via 141.108.255.1, Serial0
i L2    131.108.7.0 [115/20] via 141.108.255.1, Serial0
i L2    131.108.6.0 [115/20] via 141.108.255.1, Serial0
i L2    131.108.5.0 [115/20] via 141.108.255.1, Serial0
i L2    131.108.4.0 [115/20] via 141.108.255.1, Serial0
i L2    131.108.3.0 [115/20] via 141.108.255.1, Serial0
i L2    131.108.2.0 [115/20] via 141.108.255.1, Serial0
```

Example 4-49 displays the next hop address of 141.108.255.1 (R4). Now, R4 can ping the remote address as confirmed by Example 4-50.

Example 4-50 *Sample Ping from R4 to 131.108.2.1*

```
R4>ping 131.108.2.1
Type escape sequence to abort.
Sending 5, 100-byte ICMP Echos to 131.108.2.1, timeout is 2 seconds:
!!!!!
Success rate is 100 percent (5/5), round-trip min/avg/max = 1/2/4 ms
R4>
```

The last hop you need to look at is R1. Example 4-51 displays R1's OSPF routing table. Remember that R1 is configured for OSPF only.

Example 4-51 *R1's OSPF Routing Table*

```
R1#sh ip route ospf
R1#
```

NOTE   R4's routing table contains all the OSPF network entries advertised by R1, and because R1 and R4 are maintaining a full OSPF adjacency and the next hop address is a directly connected LAN, ping requests are replied to when R4 pings the address 131.108.2.1.

The reason that R1 has no remote OSPF entries and hence has no return path to the remote routers R8 or R9 in the IS-IS domain is that you have not redistributed from IS-IS to OSPF. So far you have only configured one-way redistribution; you must also advise the OSPF domain of the IS-IS routes. Once more, configure redistribution on R4, but this time, configure IS-IS to OSPF redistribution. Example 4-52 displays the configuration options when redistributing from IS-IS to OSPF.

Example 4-52 *Configuring IS-IS to OSPF Redistribution*

```
R4(config)#router ospf 1
R4(config-router)#redistribute isis ?
  level-1        IS-IS level-1 routes only
  level-1-2      IS-IS level-1 and level-2 routes
  level-2        IS-IS level-2 routes only
  metric         Metric for redistributed routes
  metric-type    OSPF/IS-IS exterior metric type for redistributed routes
  route-map      Route map reference
  subnets        Consider subnets for redistribution into OSPF
  tag            Set tag for routes redistributed into OSPF
  <cr>
```

continues

Example 4-52 *Configuring IS-IS to OSPF Redistribution (Continued)*

```
    WORD          ISO routing area tag
  R4(config-router)#redistribute isis level-1-2 ?
    metric        Metric for redistributed routes
    metric-type   OSPF/IS-IS exterior metric type for redistributed routes
    route-map     Route map reference
    subnets       Consider subnets for redistribution into OSPF
    tag           Set tag for routes redistributed into OSPF
    <cr>
  R4(config-router)#redistribute isis level-1-2 metric 100 ?
    metric        Metric for redistributed routes
    metric-type   OSPF/IS-IS exterior metric type for redistributed routes
    route-map     Route map reference
    subnets       Consider subnets for redistribution into OSPF
    tag           Set tag for routes redistributed into OSPF
    <cr>
  R4(config-router)#redistribute isis level-2 metric 100 metric?
  metric  metric-type
  R4(config-router)#redistribute isis level-2 metric 100 metric-type ?
    1  Set OSPF External Type 1 metrics
    2  Set OSPF External Type 2 metrics
  R4(config-router)#redistribute isis level-1-2 metric 100 metric-type 1 subnets
```

NOTE The keyword **subnets** is required here because 141.108.0.0 is subnetted using a Class C address, which is required whenever redistribution is configured to a classless domain and a 30-bit mask on serial connections.

Now, view R1's IP routing table. Example 4-53 displays R1's OSPF routing table.

Example 4-53 *R1's OSPF Routing Table*

```
R1>sh ip route ospf
     141.108.0.0/16 is variably subnetted, 3 subnets, 2 masks
O E2    141.108.255.8/30 [110/100] via 131.108.254.2, 00:00:00, Ethernet0/0
O E2    141.108.3.0/24 [110/100] via 131.108.254.2, 00:00:00, Ethernet0/0
O E2    141.108.4.0/24 [110/100] via 131.108.254.2, 00:00:00, Ethernet0/0
```

Three remote networks are present, but none of the directly connected links on R4 are present. You also need to redistribute any locally connected routers on R4. Configure this and use type 1 OSPF routes this time. Example 4-54 displays the configuration of locally connected routes to be injected into IS-IS on R4.

Example 4-54 *Redistribute Connected on R4*

```
R4(config-router)#router ospf 1
R4(config-router)# redistribute connected subnets metric 100 metric-type 1
```

Example 4-55 now displays the full IP network present in the IS-IS domain.

Example 4-55 **show ip route ospf** *Command on R1*

```
R1>sh ip route ospf
     141.108.0.0/16 is variably subnetted, 6 subnets, 2 masks
O E2    141.108.255.8/30 [110/100] via 131.108.254.2, 00:07:39, Ethernet0/0
O E2    141.108.3.0/24 [110/100] via 131.108.254.2, 00:07:39, Ethernet0/0
O E2    141.108.4.0/24 [110/100] via 131.108.254.2, 00:07:39, Ethernet0/0
O E1    141.108.2.0/24 [110/110] via 131.108.254.2, 00:07:29, Ethernet0/0
O E1    141.108.255.4/30 [110/110] via 131.108.254.2, 00:07:29, Ethernet0/0
O E1    141.108.255.0/30 [110/110] via 131.108.254.2, 00:07:29, Ethernet0/0
```

You have seen the power of the command **redistribute**. By simply using keywords, you can redistribute routes with the appropriate metric and route type (1 or 2 in OSPF or L1/L2 in IS-IS). You can now provide connectivity between the two different routing domains. Confirm connectivity by pinging from R8 to R1 loopback addresses 131.108.2.1/24 through 131.108.10.1/24, as displayed in Example 4-56.

Example 4-56 *Sample Pings from R8 to R1*

```
R8#ping 131.108.2.1
Type escape sequence to abort.
Sending 5, 100-byte ICMP Echos to 131.108.2.1, timeout is 2 seconds:
!!!!!
Success rate is 100 percent (5/5), round-trip min/avg/max = 16/17/20 ms
R8#ping 131.108.3.1
Type escape sequence to abort.
Sending 5, 100-byte ICMP Echos to 131.108.3.1, timeout is 2 seconds:
!!!!!
Success rate is 100 percent (5/5), round-trip min/avg/max = 16/17/20 ms
R8#ping 131.108.4.1
Type escape sequence to abort.
Sending 5, 100-byte ICMP Echos to 131.108.4.1, timeout is 2 seconds:
!!!!!
Success rate is 100 percent (5/5), round-trip min/avg/max = 16/17/20 ms
R8#ping 131.108.5.1
Type escape sequence to abort.
Sending 5, 100-byte ICMP Echos to 131.108.5.1, timeout is 2 seconds:
```

continues

Example 4-56 *Sample Pings from R8 to R1 (Continued)*

```
!!!!!
Success rate is 100 percent (5/5), round-trip min/avg/max = 16/17/20 ms
R8#ping 131.108.6.1
Type escape sequence to abort.
Sending 5, 100-byte ICMP Echos to 131.108.6.1, timeout is 2 seconds:
!!!!!
Success rate is 100 percent (5/5), round-trip min/avg/max = 16/17/20 ms
R8#ping 131.108.7.1
Type escape sequence to abort.
Sending 5, 100-byte ICMP Echos to 131.108.7.1, timeout is 2 seconds:
!!!!!
Success rate is 100 percent (5/5), round-trip min/avg/max = 16/18/20 ms
R8#ping 131.108.8.1
Type escape sequence to abort.
Sending 5, 100-byte ICMP Echos to 131.108.8.1, timeout is 2 seconds:
!!!!!
Success rate is 100 percent (5/5), round-trip min/avg/max = 16/18/20 ms
R8#ping 131.108.9.1
Type escape sequence to abort.
Sending 5, 100-byte ICMP Echos to 131.108.9.1, timeout is 2 seconds:
!!!!!
Success rate is 100 percent (5/5), round-trip min/avg/max = 16/17/20 ms
R8#ping 131.108.10.1
Type escape sequence to abort.
Sending 5, 100-byte ICMP Echos to 131.108.10.1, timeout is 2 seconds:
!!!!!
Success rate is 100 percent (5/5), round-trip min/avg/max = 16/18/20 ms
R8#
```

A sample trace from R9 to R1 displays the route path taken to the network 131.108.2.1/24, as displayed in Example 4-57.

Example 4-57 *Trace Route to 131.108.2.1 from R9*

```
R9#trace 131.108.2.1

Type escape sequence to abort.
Tracing the route to 131.108.2.1

 1 141.108.255.1 8 msec 8 msec 12 msec
 2 131.108.254.1 12 msec 8 msec *
```

Assume the link between R9 and R4 fails, so the only path to the OSPF backbone is through R8. Example 4-58 displays a sample trace when the primary path fails.

Example 4-58 *Trace on R9 Through R8*

```
R9# trace 131.108.2.1
Type escape sequence to abort.
Tracing the route to 131.108.2.1
  1 141.108.255.10 8 msec 8 msec 12 msec
  2 141.108.255.6 20 msec 16 msec 16 msec
  3 131.108.254.1 16 msec 16 msec *
```

The new IP routing table on R9 contains a path to all OSPF routes through the Serial connection to R8. Example 4-59 displays R9's IS-IS routing table when the link failure to R4 occurs.

Example 4-59 show ip route isis *Command on R9*

```
R9#sh ip route isis
      141.108.0.0/16 is variably subnetted, 5 subnets, 2 masks
i L1    141.108.255.4/30 [115/20] via 141.108.255.10, Serial1
i L1    141.108.3.0/24 [115/20] via 141.108.255.10, Serial1
i L1    141.108.2.0/24 [115/30] via 141.108.255.10, Serial1
      131.108.0.0/24 is subnetted, 15 subnets
i L2    131.108.254.0 [115/158] via 141.108.255.10, Serial1
i L2    131.108.15.0 [115/158] via 141.108.255.10, Serial1
i L2    131.108.14.0 [115/158] via 141.108.255.10, Serial1
i L2    131.108.13.0 [115/158] via 141.108.255.10, Serial1
i L2    131.108.12.0 [115/158] via 141.108.255.10, Serial1
i L2    131.108.11.0 [115/158] via 141.108.255.10, Serial1
i L2    131.108.10.0 [115/158] via 141.108.255.10, Serial1
i L2    131.108.9.0 [115/158] via 141.108.255.10, Serial1
i L2    131.108.8.0 [115/158] via 141.108.255.10, Serial1
i L2    131.108.7.0 [115/158] via 141.108.255.10, Serial1
i L2    131.108.6.0 [115/158] via 141.108.255.10, Serial1
i L2    131.108.5.0 [115/158] via 141.108.255.10, Serial1
i L2    131.108.4.0 [115/158] via 141.108.255.10, Serial1
i L2    131.108.3.0 [115/158] via 141.108.255.10, Serial1
i L2    131.108.2.0 [115/158] via 141.108.255.10, Serial1
```

Scenario 4-5: Recommendations for Designing OSPF Networks

This scenario presents some of the design recommendations found in common literature. This is not a practical scenario but rather a presentation of some design guidelines to help you in real-life network situations you might come across in designing today's complex IP networks.

By no means are these rules standard, and they are provided here for reference so you can easily refer to a sample network design and the common rules experts adhere to in large OSPF networks.

When architecting a network, you should try to accomplish five basic goals with dynamic routing protocols:

- **Functionality**—The network works; that is, no matter what failure or scenario, the network must always be functioning.

- **Scalability**—As the network grows in size, your initial topology or design must be able to cope with growth and new challenges, such as new acquisitions.

- **Adaptability**—With ever-increasing new technologies, such as Voice over IP, your network should cope with and embrace new features.

- **Manageability**—This point refers to proactive management. Any large network should be able to foresee new challenges before the network grinds to a halt.

- **Cost effectiveness**—In reality, cost drives most network designers. The bigger your budget, the better able you are to provide users the ability to work around network failures.

You can manage and configure OSPF so that the preceding five criteria are fully supported.

Implementing a hierarchical IP addressing scheme and performing summarization wherever possible are two key points in any large OSPF network.

The following are some general guidelines when designing a large OSPF network.

Determine the number of routers in each area. Anything between 40–50 is an acceptable number. The number of calculations any given router must perform given m LSAs is mlogm. For example, 100 routers require 100log 100 or $100 \times 2 = 200$. Keeping these calculations to a minimum means the CPU/memory requirements are also kept low. The IETF standards committee provides the following sample design guidelines:

- The minimum number of routers per domain is 20; the maximum is 1000.

- The minimum routers per single area is 20; the maximum is 350.

- The number of areas per domain is 1; the maximum is 60.

TIP   OSPF is such a large topic that many books have been written about it. For a concise guide to OSPF and a more detailed guide, you cannot invest in anything better than the following two quality Cisco Press titles: *Routing TCP/IP* by Jeff Doyle and *OSPF Network Design Solutions* by Tom Thomas.

Practical Exercise: OSPF and RIP Redistribution

NOTE   Practical Exercises are designed to test your knowledge of the topics covered in this chapter.
The Practical Exercise begins by giving you some information about a situation and then asks
you to work through the solution on your own. The solution can be found at the end.

Configure the network in Figure 4-8 for OSPF between the three routers named SanFran,
Mel, and Simon. Configure the edge router named Sydney for RIP and ensure IP connectivity
among all four routers. You must use only RIPv1 and OSPF as your IP routing protocols.
Ensure that a default route appears on all routers so users can connect to the Internet. Configure summarization wherever possible to minimize IP routing tables.

Figure 4-8   *RIP-to-OSPF Redistribution*

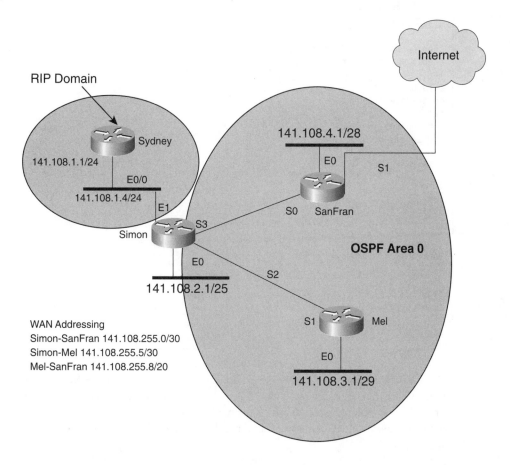

Practical Exercise Solution

The router named Simon is configured in the OSPF area 0 (backbone) and the RIP domain and needs to run redistribution between OSPF and OSPF. Also, because you are using RIPv1, you must also provide summary addresses for all networks, but not /24 because RIPv1 does not carry subnet mask information in routing updates. (RIPv2 does).

Router SanFran is connected to the Internet, so you need to configure SanFran to provide a default route to the rest of the internal network by using the OSPF command **default-information originate always**. This IOS command injects a default route into the OSPF domain and Router Simon because redistribution also injects a default route into the RIP domain.

The following are the full working configurations of all four routers with the shaded portions highlighting critical configuration commands. Example 4-60 displays the full working configuration of Router Sydney. Sydney is running RIP only.

Example 4-60 *Full Working Configuration of Router Sydney*

```
hostname Sydney
!
logging buffered 64000 debugging
enable password cisco
!
ip subnet-zero
no ip domain-lookup
interface Ethernet0/0
 ip address 141.108.1.1 255.255.255.0
 no ip directed-broadcast
!
interface Serial0/0
 shutdown
!
interface Serial0/1
 shutdown
!
router rip
 network 141.108.0.0
!
line con 0
line aux 0
line vty 0 4
!
end
```

Example 4-61 displays the full working configuration of Router Simon. Simon is running OSPF and RIP. You must always be careful when redistributing information from one routing domain into another. Simon advertises the non /24 subnets as Class C networks so the RIP domain (Sydney router) can inject them into the routing table. Because RIPv1 is classless and the subnet 141.108.1.0/24 is configured locally, all interfaces in this Class B network (141.108.0.0) are assumed to be Class C.

Example 4-61 *Full Working Configuration of Router Simon*

```
Building configuration...

Current configuration:
!
version 12.0
service timestamps debug uptime
service timestamps log uptime
no service password-encryption
!
hostname Simon
!
enable password cisco
!
ip subnet-zero
no ip domain-lookup
!
cns event-service server
!
interface Ethernet0
 ip address 141.108.2.1 255.255.255.128
!
interface Ethernet1
 ip address 141.108.1.4 255.255.255.0
!
interface Serial0
 shutdown
!
interface Serial1
 shutdown
!
interface Serial2
 ip address 141.108.255.5 255.255.255.252
 clockrate  128000
!
interface Serial3
 ip address 141.108.255.1 255.255.255.252
 clockrate  128000
!
router ospf 1
 summary-address 141.108.2.0 255.255.255.0
 summary-address 141.108.255.0 255.255.255.0
 summary-address 141.108.3.0 255.255.255.0
 summary-address 141.108.4.0 255.255.255.0
 redistribute connected subnets
 redistribute rip metric 10 subnets
 network 141.108.2.0 0.0.0.127 area 0
 network 141.108.255.0 0.0.0.255 area 0
```

continues

Example 4-61 *Full Working Configuration of Router Simon (Continued)*

```
!
router rip
 redistribute ospf 1 metric 2
 passive-interface Ethernet0 -> Stops RIP updates on OSPF interfaces
 passive-interface Serial2
 passive-interface Serial3
 network 141.108.0.0
 !
 =
ip route 141.108.3.0 255.255.255.0 Null0
ip route 141.108.4.0 255.255.255.0 Null0
 !
line con 0
line aux 0
line vty 0 4
 !
end
```

Example 4-62 displays the full working configuration of Router Mel. Mel is running OSPF only.

Example 4-62 *Full Working Configuration of Router Mel*

```
hostname Mel
enable password cisco
!
ip subnet-zero
no ip domain-lookup
!
interface Ethernet0
 ip address 141.108.3.1 255.255.255.248
!
interface Serial0
 ip address 141.108.255.6 255.255.255.252
!
interface Serial1
  shutdown
!
router ospf 1
network 141.108.0.0 0.0.255.255 area 0
 !
line con 0
line 1 8
line aux 0
line vty 0 4
 !
 end
```

Example 4-63 displays the full working configuration of Router SanFran. SanFran has a default static route pointing to Serial 1, which is the Internet connection. Under the routing OSPF process, this default route is injected by using the **default-information originate always** command.

Example 4-63 *Full Working Configuration of Router SanFran*

```
hostname SanFran
!
no ip domain-lookup
!
interface Ethernet0
 ip address 141.108.4.1 255.255.255.240
!
interface Serial0
 ip address 141.108.255.2 255.255.255.252
!
interface Serial1
 shutdown
!
router ospf 1
 network 141.108.0.0 0.0.255.255 area 0
 default-information originate always
!
ip route 0.0.0.0 0.0.0.0 Serial1
!
line con 0
line aux 0
line vty 0 4
!
end
```

Review Questions

Based on the following IP routing table, answer the following questions relating to the preceding Practical Exercise on OSPF/RIP routing. Example 4-64 displays the IP routing table of Router Sydney.

Example 4-64 *Sydney IP Routing Table*

```
Sydney#show ip route

Gateway of last resort is 141.108.1.4 to network 0.0.0.0

     141.108.0.0/24 is subnetted, 5 subnets
R       141.108.255.0 [120/2] via 141.108.1.4, 00:00:05, Ethernet0/0
C       141.108.1.0 is directly connected, Ethernet0/0
R       141.108.3.0 [120/1] via 141.108.1.4, 00:00:05, Ethernet0/0
```

continues

Example 4-64 *Sydney IP Routing Table*

```
R       141.108.2.0 [120/2] via 141.108.1.4, 00:00:05, Ethernet0/0
R       141.108.4.0 [120/1] via 141.108.1.4, 00:00:05, Ethernet0/0
R*   0.0.0.0/0 [120/2] via 141.108.1.4, 00:00:05, Ethernet0/0
```

The answers to these question can be found in Appendix C, "Answers to Review Questions."

1   What does the routing entry shaded in Example 4-64 display?

2   In Example 4-64, what is the hop count or metric to the remote network 141.108.2.0/24?

3   What path does the packet sent to the IP subnet 171.108.255.0/24 take?

4   What type of OSPF routers are the Routers Simon, Mel, and SanFran.

5   Why are static routes injected into the router named Simon?

6   How many OSPF neighbor adjacencies do you expect to see on the router named Simon?

7   Two methods are used in OSPF to summarize IP networks. What are they and what IOS command is used to provide summarization?

8   Why does creating areas reduce the size of the OSPF database?

Summary

OSPF and integrated IS-IS have the advantage of being an industry-wide standard and have a long-term success rate of routing IP in large IP networks. The capabilities of link-state routing protocols are demonstrated in this chapter along with some challenging scenarios. Although only one solution per scenario is presented, there are many alternative ways to enable OSPF and Integrated IS-IS to meet the needs of any network in today's large networking environments.

Table 4-8 summarizes the OSPF commands used in this chapter.

Table 4-8   *Summary of IOS Commands Used in This Chapter*

Command	Purpose
show ip route	Displays IP routing tables.
router ospf *process id*	Enables OSPF routing. The process ID is local to the router. You can have more than one OSPF running.
network mask	Enables network advertisements from a particular interface and also the routing of the same interface through OSPF.

Table 4-8 *Summary of IOS Commands Used in This Chapter (Continued)*

Command	Purpose
show ip ospf	Displays the OSPF process and details, such as OSPF process ID and router ID.
show ip ospf database	Displays a router's topological database.
show ip ospf neighbor	Displays OSPF neighbors.
show ip ospf virtual-links	Displays OSPF virtual links, if any.
show ip ospf interface	Displays information about how OSPF is configured for a given interface.
interface loopback *number*	Creates a loopback interface.
ip ospf network point-to-point	Enables a more specific route on loopback interfaces.
interface ethernet *mod/num*	In configuration mode, enables you modify the Ethernet, for example, **interface Ethernet0/0**.
interface serial *mod/num*	In configuration mode, enables you to modify serial interface parameters by module and interface number, for example, **interface S0/0**.
no ip domain-lookup	Disables automatic DNS lookup.
ip subnet-zero	Enables you to use subnet zero on a Cisco router.
ip ospf name-lookup	Enables OSPF DNS lookup.
hostname *name*	Configures a name on a router.
summary *network mask*	Enables summarization of external routes in OSPF.
area *area id* **range** *mask*	Enables interarea summarization in OSPF.
redistribute	Redistributes from one IP routing protocol to another.
[no] shutdown	Enables or disables an interface. All hardware interfaces are shut down by default.

CHAPTER 5

Enhanced Interior Gateway Routing Protocol

Now that you have learned about and practiced with some basic and advanced routing protocols, this chapter covers a protocol developed by Cisco Systems used on Cisco IOS routers only.

The chapter starts by covering the basic Enhanced Interior Gateway Routing Protocol (EIGRP) concepts. It then explains of how EIGRP can be configured and monitored.

You discover how EIGRP learns about new neighbors and how EIGRP operates in NBMA networks. The five scenarios in this chapter help to complete your understanding of EIGRP and ensure that you have all the basic IP networking knowledge to complement your understanding of today's most widely used networking protocol, IP.

Introduction to Enhanced Interior Gateway Routing Protocol (EIGRP)

Cisco Systems followed the development of IGRP with Enhanced IGRP. Enhanced IGRP combines the characteristics of distance-vector protocols and link-state protocols. EIGRP is commonly referred to as a hybrid routing protocol or an advanced distance-vector routing protocol. EIGRP can be used to route IP, IPX, and AppleTalk traffic. This chapter concentrates on IP routing with EIGRP.

EIGRP uses distance-vector properties to determine the best path to a network, but it uses link-state properties when changes occur or when detecting new neighbors. Like OSPF, EIGRP sends hello packets to find new neighbors and maintain neighbor adjacencies.

Some of the main features of EIGRP when used to route IP data are as follows:

- The metric is based on a composite that considers delay, bandwidth, and MTU sizes to ensure the best possible path to any destinations containing dual paths.
- Periodic updates are not sent; only network changes are sent.
- EIGRP can load share up to six paths. (The default is four paths, as with OSPF.)

- By default, EIGRP uses up to 50 percent of the bandwidth of an interface and can be configured to go lower or higher.
- EIGRP includes support for VLSM.
- EIGRP supports authentication of routing updates.

EIGRP was developed by Cisco to provide enhancements to IGRP and, in particular, to provide support for large IP networks and reduce the convergence time for IP routing updates.

To achieve this goal, EIGRP has been designed with the following features:

- **Diffusing Update Algorithm (DUAL)**—Like any routing protocol, EIGRP uses DUAL to maintain a loop-free topology.
- **Incremental updates**—Instead of sending the complete IP routing table, EIGRP sends incremental updates when network changes occur.
- **Hello protocol**—EIGRP uses hello packets to discover neighboring routers.

Table 5-1 defines some of the common terminology used when discussing EIGRP networks.

Table 5-1   *EIGRP Terms*

Term	Meaning
Neighbor	A router in the same autonomous system (AS) running EIGRP
Hello	A packet used to monitor and maintain EIGRP neighbor relationships
Query	A query packet that is sent to neighboring routers when a network path is lost
Reply	A reply packet to a query packet
ACK	Acknowledgment of a packet, typically a hello packet with no data
Holdtime	The length of time a router waits for a hello packet before tearing down a neighbor adjacency
Smooth Route Trip Time (SSRT)	The amount of time required to send a packet reliably to an acknowledgment
Retransmission Timeout (RTO)	The amount of time required to respond to an acknowledge packet
Feasible distance	Metric to remote network; lowest is preferred
Feasible successor	A neighboring router with a lower AD
Successor	A neighboring router that meets the feasibility condition

Table 5-1   *EIGRP Terms (Continued)*

Term	Meaning
Stuck in Active (SIA)	An EIGRP router waiting for an acknowledgment from a neighboring router
Active	The time during which a router is querying neighboring routers about a network path
Passive	Normal operation of a route to a remote destination

You have already configured IGRP and EIGRP in Chapter 2, "Routing Principles." This chapter covers EIGRP in greater detail using a simple two-router topology.

Discovering and Maintaining Routes in EIGRP

EIGRP uses hello packets to discover new neighboring routes, and after it finds a neighbor, the Cisco routers advertise all IP network entries.

Figure 5-1 displays a simple two-router EIGRP network in Autonomous System 1. This section shows you how to enable EIGRP on both routers in Figure 5-1.

Figure 5-1   *Two-Router EIGRP Network*

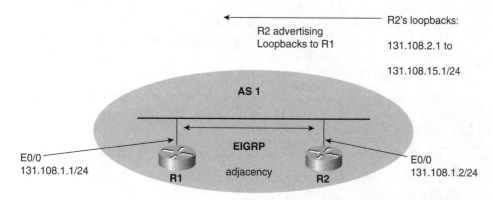

To start EIGRP on a Cisco router, you must first enable EIGRP with the command **router eigrp** *autonomous system* while in global configuration mode.

For routers sharing the same IP domain, the AS needs to be the same. Example 5-1 displays the configuration of EIGRP on R1.

Example 5-1   *R1 EIGRP Configuration*

```
R1(config)#router eigrp 1
R1(config-router)#network 131.108.1.0
```

Notice that 131.108.1.0 is, by default, a Class B network. Next, view the configuration after you enter the **network 131.108.1.0** command.

Example 5-2 displays the running configuration of R1, truncated for clarity.

Example 5-2   *R1 EIGRP Configuration*

```
...
router eigrp 1
 network 131.108.0.0
...
```

NOTE   IOS version 12.0.4(T) supports the use of the wildcard mask, which works as the OSPF wildcard mask does. For example, the **network 131.108.1.1 0.0.0.0** command places the Ethernet interface of R1 in EIGRP 1. Consult the latest command reference on the Cisco Web site at www.cisco.com/univercd/home/home.htm for more information. This URL can be accessed for free and contains every command available on Cisco routers and switches.

EIGRP needs only the major network boundary when using the **network** command. For example, you can configure the Class B network, 131.108.0.0, instead of entering the address 131.108.1.0.

EIGRP supports summarization and VLSM, which are covered in this chapter.

Example 5-3 displays the same EIGRP configuration on R2. The AS is set to 1 on both routers to enable both routers to share IP routing information.

Example 5-3   *R2 EIGRP Configuration*

```
R2(config)#router eigrp 1
R2(config-router)#network 131.108.0.0
```

R2 has a number of loopbacks to populate the IP routing tables ranging from 131.108.2.0 to 131.108.15.0/24. To view EIGRP neighbor relations between two Cisco routers, use the **show ip eigrp neighbors** command.

Example 5-4 displays the EIGRP neighbors on R1.

Example 5-4 *EIGRP Neighbors on R1*

```
R1#show ip eigrp neighbors
IP-EIGRP neighbors for process 1
H    Address                 Interface     Hold Uptime    SRTT    RTO   Q  Seq
                                           (sec)          (ms)         Cnt Num
0    131.108.1.2             Et0/0          12 00:00:34      4    200   0  1
```

Example 5-4 displays the neighbor R2 with the IP address 131.108.1.2, and the outbound interface the EIGRP neighbor (in this case R2) was discovered. R1 discovered a remote EIGRP neighbor through the Ethernet interface (displayed as Et0/0). The holdtime indicates the length of time, in seconds, that the Cisco IOS Software waits to hear from the peer before declaring it down. Smooth Round Trip Time (SRTT) is the number of milliseconds it takes for an EIGRP packet to be sent to this neighbor and for the local router to receive an acknowledgment of that packet. Retransmission timeout (RTO) indicates the amount of time the IOS software waits before resending a packet from the local retransmission queue. Q Cnt indicates the number of update, query, or reply packets that the IOS software is waiting to send to the neighbor. Sequence number (SEQ NUM) is the last sequenced number used in an update, query, or reply packet that was received from this neighbor.

To maintain EIGRP between R1 and R2, you use hello packets to ensure that both routers are active and running. Any updates or changes are sent immediately and both routers maintain topology tables. A topology table is created from updates received from all EIGRP neighbors. The EIGRP topology table is used to maintain IP routing entries in the IP routing table.

Example 5-5 displays the EIGRP topology table on R1 using the IOS **show ip eigrp topology** command.

Example 5-5 *R1's EIGRP Topology Table*

```
R1#show ip eigrp  ?
  interfaces   IP-EIGRP interfaces
  neighbors    IP-EIGRP neighbors
  topology     IP-EIGRP Topology Table
  traffic      IP-EIGRP Traffic Statistics
R1#show ip eigrp topology
IP-EIGRP Topology Table for process 1
Codes: P - Passive, A - Active, U - Update, Q - Query, R - Reply,
       r - Reply status
P 131.108.15.0/24, 1 successors, FD is 409600
         via 131.108.1.2 (409600/128256), Ethernet0/0
P 131.108.14.0/24, 1 successors, FD is 409600
         via 131.108.1.2 (409600/128256), Ethernet0/0
```

continues

Example 5-5   *R1's EIGRP Topology Table (Continued)*

```
P 131.108.13.0/24, 1 successors, FD is 409600
        via 131.108.1.2 (409600/128256), Ethernet0/0
P 131.108.12.0/24, 1 successors, FD is 409600
        via 131.108.1.2 (409600/128256), Ethernet0/0
P 131.108.11.0/24, 1 successors, FD is 409600
        via 131.108.1.2 (409600/128256), Ethernet0/0
P 131.108.10.0/24, 1 successors, FD is 409600
        via 131.108.1.2 (409600/128256), Ethernet0/0
P 131.108.9.0/24, 1 successors, FD is 409600
        via 131.108.1.2 (409600/128256), Ethernet0/0
P 131.108.8.0/24, 1 successors, FD is 409600
        via 131.108.1.2 (409600/128256), Ethernet0/0
P 131.108.7.0/24, 1 successors, FD is 409600
        via 131.108.1.2 (409600/128256), Ethernet0/0
P 131.108.6.0/24, 1 successors, FD is 409600
        via 131.108.1.2 (409600/128256), Ethernet0/0
P 131.108.5.0/24, 1 successors, FD is 409600
        via 131.108.1.2 (409600/128256), Ethernet0/0
P 131.108.4.0/24, 1 successors, FD is 409600
        via 131.108.1.2 (409600/128256), Ethernet0/0
P 131.108.3.0/24, 1 successors, FD is 409600
        via 131.108.1.2 (409600/128256), Ethernet0/0
P 131.108.2.0/24, 1 successors, FD is 409600
        via 131.108.1.2 (409600/128256), Ethernet0/0
P 131.108.1.0/24, 1 successors, FD is 281600 via Connected, Ethernet0/0
```

Example 5-5 displays a wealth of information about all the remote entries EIGRP discovers. Also, notice the number of different IOS **show** commands possible. Entries in this topology table can be updated by changes in the network or interface failures. For example, if a network failure does occur, the topology table receives an update to recalculate the path to the remote entry using the algorithm called Diffusing Update Algorithm (DUAL). DUAL is an algorithm developed by Cisco that performs the calculations on the topology table. DUAL is based on detecting a network change within a finite amount of time. Any changes sent among neighboring routers are sent reliably (using sequence packets and ensuring packet delivery). Because the algorithm is calculated almost instantaneously, in order, and with a finite time, updates are sent and received quickly, which increases convergence time.

Table 5-2 summarizes the contents of the topology table in Example 5-5.

Table 5-2 *EIGRP Topology Table Definitions*

Term	Definition
Codes	State of this topology table entry.
P	Passive. No Enhanced IGRP computations are being performed for this destination.
A	Active. Enhanced IGRP computations are being performed for this destination.
U	Update. Indicates that an update packet was sent to this destination.
Q	Query. Indicates that a query packet was sent to this destination.
R	Reply. Indicates that a reply packet was sent to this destination.
r	Reply status. Flag that is set after the software has sent a query and is waiting for a reply.
131.108.15.0/24 and so on	These indicate the destination IP network number and mask, in this case 255.255.255.0.
successors	Number of successors. This number corresponds to the number of next hops in the IP routing table. R1 has only one path, hence only one successor.
FD	Feasible distance. This value is used in the feasibility condition check. If the neighbor's reported distance (the metric after the slash) is less than the feasible distance, the feasibility condition is met, and that path is a feasible successor. After the software determines it has a feasible successor, it does not have to send a query for that destination.
Replies	Number of replies that are still outstanding (have not been received) with respect to this destination. This information appears only when the destination is in active state. R1's next hop address is 131.108.1.2.
State	Exact enhanced IGRP state that this destination is in. It can be the number 0, 1, 2, or 3. This information appears only when the destination is active.
Via	IP address of the peer that tells the software about this destination. The first N of these entries, where N is the number of successors, are the current successors. The remaining entries on the list are feasible successors.
(409600/128256)	The first number is the Enhanced IGRP metric that represents the cost to the destination. The second number is the Enhanced IGRP metric that this peer advertises.
Ethernet0/0	Interface from which this information was learned.

Now that R1 has established a relationship with R2, by maintaining a topology table, with all entries in a passive state, you can expect to see remote IP routing entries. (Active means the remote entry is being recalculated.) Example 5-6 displays R1's IP routing table.

Example 5-6 *R1's IP Routing Table*

```
R1#show ip route
Codes:      D - EIGRP, EX - EIGRP external
        131.108.0.0/24 is subnetted, 15 subnets
D       131.108.15.0 [90/409600] via 131.108.1.2, 00:31:02, Ethernet0/0
D       131.108.14.0 [90/409600] via 131.108.1.2, 00:31:02, Ethernet0/0
D       131.108.13.0 [90/409600] via 131.108.1.2, 00:31:02, Ethernet0/0
D       131.108.12.0 [90/409600] via 131.108.1.2, 00:31:02, Ethernet0/0
D       131.108.11.0 [90/409600] via 131.108.1.2, 00:31:02, Ethernet0/0
D       131.108.10.0 [90/409600] via 131.108.1.2, 00:31:02, Ethernet0/0
D       131.108.9.0 [90/409600] via 131.108.1.2, 00:31:02, Ethernet0/0
D       131.108.8.0 [90/409600] via 131.108.1.2, 00:31:02, Ethernet0/0
D       131.108.7.0 [90/409600] via 131.108.1.2, 00:31:02, Ethernet0/0
D       131.108.6.0 [90/409600] via 131.108.1.2, 00:31:02, Ethernet0/0
D       131.108.5.0 [90/409600] via 131.108.1.2, 00:31:02, Ethernet0/0
D       131.108.4.0 [90/409600] via 131.108.1.2, 00:31:02, Ethernet0/0
D       131.108.3.0 [90/409600] via 131.108.1.2, 00:31:02, Ethernet0/0
D       131.108.2.0 [90/409600] via 131.108.1.2, 00:31:04, Ethernet0/0
C       131.108.1.0 is directly connected, Ethernet0/0
```

If you simulate a network failure by shutting down the network 131.108.15.0 on R2, Example 5-7 displays R1's new topology table.

Example 5-7 *R1's Topology Table*

```
R1#show ip eigrp topology
IP-EIGRP Topology Table for process 1
P 131.108.14.0/24, 1 successors, FD is 409600
        via 131.108.1.2 (409600/128256), Ethernet0/0
P 131.108.13.0/24, 1 successors, FD is 409600
        via 131.108.1.2 (409600/128256), Ethernet0/0
P 131.108.12.0/24, 1 successors, FD is 409600
        via 131.108.1.2 (409600/128256), Ethernet0/0
P 131.108.11.0/24, 1 successors, FD is 409600
        via 131.108.1.2 (409600/128256), Ethernet0/0
P 131.108.10.0/24, 1 successors, FD is 409600
        via 131.108.1.2 (409600/128256), Ethernet0/0
P 131.108.9.0/24, 1 successors, FD is 409600
        via 131.108.1.2 (409600/128256), Ethernet0/0
P 131.108.8.0/24, 1 successors, FD is 409600
        via 131.108.1.2 (409600/128256), Ethernet0/0
P 131.108.7.0/24, 1 successors, FD is 409600
        via 131.108.1.2 (409600/128256), Ethernet0/0
P 131.108.6.0/24, 1 successors, FD is 409600
        via 131.108.1.2 (409600/128256), Ethernet0/0
```

Example 5-7 *R1's Topology Table (Continued)*

```
P 131.108.5.0/24, 1 successors, FD is 409600
        via 131.108.1.2 (409600/128256), Ethernet0/0
P 131.108.4.0/24, 1 successors, FD is 409600
        via 131.108.1.2 (409600/128256), Ethernet0/0
P 131.108.3.0/24, 1 successors, FD is 409600
        via 131.108.1.2 (409600/128256), Ethernet0/0
P 131.108.2.0/24, 1 successors, FD is 409600
        via 131.108.1.2 (409600/128256), Ethernet0/0
P 131.108.1.0/24, 1 successors, FD is 281600
        via Connected, Ethernet0/0
```

Example 5-7 does not display the remote entry 131.108.15.0/24, and, therefore, it is not present in the IP routing table. EIGRP maintains IP routes by using DUAL and maintaining an EIGRP topology table. For remote entries with multiple routes, EIGRP uses the feasible condition (FC) to determine the best path.

The EIGRP routing algorithm always chooses the path to a remote destination with the lowest metric. The topology table maintains all paths to remote networks, so by simply viewing the topology table, you can discover the number of paths available and why EIGRP chooses a certain path.

EIGRP supports the use of VLSM; all updates contain an entry for the subnet mask. To demonstrate this, modify the IP networks on R2, and look at R1's topology table after you alter all the networks from Class C networks to a range of variable-length subnet masks (VLSM).

Example 5-8 displays R1's topology table after the networks on R2 have been changed.

Example 5-8 *R1's Topology Table*

```
R1#show ip eigrp topology
IP-EIGRP Topology Table for process 1
P 131.108.15.0/24, 1 successors, FD is 409600
        via 131.108.1.2 (409600/128256), Ethernet0/0
P 131.108.14.0/24, 1 successors, FD is 409600
        via 131.108.1.2 (409600/128256), Ethernet0/0
P 131.108.13.0/29, 1 successors, FD is 409600
        via 131.108.1.2 (409600/128256), Ethernet0/0
P 131.108.12.0/30, 1 successors, FD is 409600
        via 131.108.1.2 (409600/128256), Ethernet0/0
P 131.108.11.0/30, 1 successors, FD is 409600
        via 131.108.1.2 (409600/128256), Ethernet0/0
P 131.108.10.0/27, 1 successors, FD is 409600
        via 131.108.1.2 (409600/128256), Ethernet0/0
P 131.108.9.0/25, 1 successors, FD is 409600
        via 131.108.1.2 (409600/128256), Ethernet0/0
```

continues

Example 5-8 *R1's Topology Table (Continued)*

```
P 131.108.8.0/25, 1 successors, FD is 409600
        via 131.108.1.2 (409600/128256), Ethernet0/0
P 131.108.7.0/26, 1 successors, FD is 409600
        via 131.108.1.2 (409600/128256), Ethernet0/0
P 131.108.6.0/27, 1 successors, FD is 409600
        via 131.108.1.2 (409600/128256), Ethernet0/0
P 131.108.5.0/28, 1 successors, FD is 409600
        via 131.108.1.2 (409600/128256), Ethernet0/0
P 131.108.4.0/29, 1 successors, FD is 409600
        via 131.108.1.2 (409600/128256), Ethernet0/0
P 131.108.3.0/30, 1 successors, FD is 409600
        via 131.108.1.2 (409600/128256), Ethernet0/0
P 131.108.2.0/27, 1 successors, FD is 409600
        via 131.108.1.2 (409600/128256), Ethernet0/0
P 131.108.1.0/24, 1 successors, FD is 281600
        via Connected, Ethernet0/0
```

Example 5-8 displays a range of non-Class C networks, demonstrating the powerful use of VLSM with EIGRP. Example 5-9 displays the new IP routing table for completeness.

Example 5-9 *R1's EIGRP Routing Table*

```
R1#show ip route eigrp
     131.108.0.0/16 is variably subnetted, 15 subnets, 7 masks
D       131.108.15.0/24 [90/409600] via 131.108.1.2, 00:20:15, Ethernet0/0
D       131.108.14.0/24 [90/409600] via 131.108.1.2, 00:58:15, Ethernet0/0
D       131.108.13.0/29 [90/409600] via 131.108.1.2, 00:02:20, Ethernet0/0
D       131.108.12.0/30 [90/409600] via 131.108.1.2, 00:02:22, Ethernet0/0
D       131.108.11.0/30 [90/409600] via 131.108.1.2, 00:02:24, Ethernet0/0
D       131.108.10.0/27 [90/409600] via 131.108.1.2, 00:02:25, Ethernet0/0
D       131.108.9.0/25 [90/409600] via 131.108.1.2, 00:02:27, Ethernet0/0
D       131.108.8.0/25 [90/409600] via 131.108.1.2, 00:02:29, Ethernet0/0
D       131.108.7.0/26 [90/409600] via 131.108.1.2, 00:02:30, Ethernet0/0
D       131.108.6.0/27 [90/409600] via 131.108.1.2, 00:02:32, Ethernet0/0
D       131.108.5.0/28 [90/409600] via 131.108.1.2, 00:02:34, Ethernet0/0
D       131.108.4.0/29 [90/409600] via 131.108.1.2, 00:02:35, Ethernet0/0
D       131.108.3.0/30 [90/409600] via 131.108.1.2, 00:02:37, Ethernet0/0
D       131.108.2.0/27 [90/409600] via 131.108.1.2, 00:02:39, Ethernet0/0
```

EIGRP in NBMA Environments

You can successfully configure EIGRP over NBMA networks if you apply the following rules:

- EIGRP traffic should not exceed the committed information rate (CIR).

- EIGRP aggregated traffic over all virtual circuits should not exceed the access line speed.

- The allocated bandwidth for EIGRP must be the same on each virtual circuit between two remote routers.

The use of the **bandwidth** command should reflect the true speed of any interface. The **bandwidth** command is used in EIGRP metric calculation and defines the amount of bandwidth. (By default, up to 50 percent of any link can be consumed by EIGRP; this is also configurable using the ip **bandwidth-percent eigrp** *AS percent* command.) EIGRP does not have any way of statically defined neighboring, so you must ensure that EIGRP packets or updates are sent over a nonbroadcast network. The **bandwidth** command does not always have to reflect the actual bandwidth of the interface. In fact, you can use the **bandwidth** command to adjust the composite EIGRP metric so that you can perform equal-cost load balancing on unequal speed links. The IOS **variance** command provides another method for achieving unequal load balancing.

Setting a variance value lets the Cisco IOS Software determine the feasibility of a potential route, even though the path might be over a slower wide-area network (WAN) link.

The following two conditions are required before load balancing over unequal paths can take place:

- The local best metric must be greater than the metric learned from the next router.
- The multiplier times the local best metric for the destination must be greater than or equal to the metric through the next router.

EIGRP Route Summarization and Large IP Network Support

EIGRP supports the use of summarization to conserve IP routing table size. Summarization in EIGRP can be configured on any router in the same AS. By default, EIGRP automatically summarizes at the major network boundaries. To perform static summarization, you must disable this feature with the **no auto-summary** IOS command, under the routing process.

To manually summarize networks, you must advertise the supernet, for example, on an interface level with the **ip summary address eigrp** *autonomous system mask* command.

Re-examine Figure 5-1 and summarize the networks 131.108.8.0 to 131.108.15.255. First, you must disable automatic summarization on R2. Example 5-10 displays the disabling of automatic summarization on R2.

Example 5-10 *Disabling Automatic Summarization on R2*

```
R2(config)#router eigrp 1
R2(config-router)#no auto-summary
```

Because the networks 131.108.8.0–131.108.15.0 are contiguous, you can apply the mask 255.255.248.0 to incorporate the range of networks from 131.108.8.255–131.108.15.255.

Example 5-11 displays the summary command completed on R2's link to R1.

Example 5-11 *Summary on R2*

```
R2(config)#interface ethernet 0/0
R2(config-if)#ip summary-address eigrp 1 131.108.8.0 255.255.248.0
```

R1 should now have only one remote routing entry for the networks 131.108.8.255–131.108.15.255 as displayed in Example 5-12.

Example 5-12 *R1's EIGRP Routing Table*

```
R1#show ip route eigrp
     131.108.0.0/16 is variably subnetted, 8 subnets, 2 masks
D       131.108.8.0/21 [90/409600] via 131.108.1.2, 00:01:13, Ethernet0/0
D       131.108.7.0/24 [90/409600] via 131.108.1.2, 00:01:13, Ethernet0/0
D       131.108.6.0/24 [90/409600] via 131.108.1.2, 00:01:13, Ethernet0/0
D       131.108.5.0/24 [90/409600] via 131.108.1.2, 00:01:13, Ethernet0/0
D       131.108.4.0/24 [90/409600] via 131.108.1.2, 00:01:13, Ethernet0/0
D       131.108.3.0/24 [90/409600] via 131.108.1.2, 00:01:13, Ethernet0/0
D       131.108.2.0/24 [90/409600] via 131.108.1.2, 00:01:14, Ethernet0/0
```

To support large IP networks, you can use several Cisco IOS enhancements, such as network summarization, load balancing, and reducing the load on WAN links with the **bandwidth** command, to fine-tune EIGRP. Several factors can contribute to a poorly designed network, such as the amount of routing information exchanged between routers, the number of routers in your network, the network diameter of your network (hop count in EIGRP is still 255), and the number of alternative paths between routers.

EIGRP can scale in a well-designed IP network, and with proper configuration, it can be well-maintained.

As with any legacy protocol, the used-by date of EIGRP is fast approaching, especially in today's large IP-based network. Open Shortest Path First (OSPF), Intermediate System-to-Intermediate System (IS-IS), and Border Gateway Protocol (BGP) are far more common routing protocols.

In the following five scenarios, you configure and monitor some sample EIGRP networks and apply the knowledge you have gained.

Scenarios

The following scenarios are designed to draw together some of the content described in this chapter and some of the content you have seen in your own networks or practice labs. There is no one right way to accomplish many of the tasks presented, and the abilities to use good practice and define your end goal are important in any real-life design or solution.

Scenario 5-1: Configuring EIGRP

In this scenario, you configure eight Cisco routers for IP routing using a Class B (/16) network 131.108.0.0 with a Class C subnet mask (255.255.255.0 or /24). The serial links will use a two-host subnet to demonstrate the use of VLSM with EIGRP.

Assume the core backbone network resides on the Ethernet between R1 and R2.

Figure 5-2 displays a network with seven routers in AS1 and one remote router in AS2.

Figure 5-2 *EIGRP in AS 1 and AS 2*

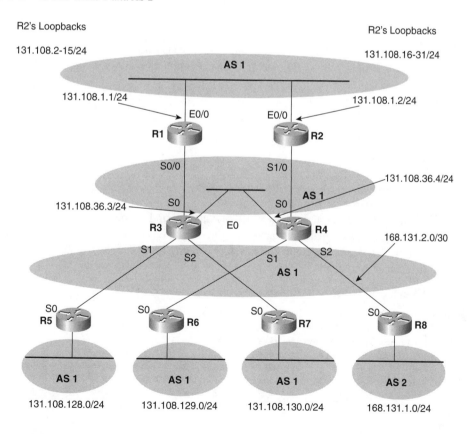

The IP address assignment for the WAN links is described in Table 5-3. Note the use of VLSM across the WAN Links.

Table 5-3 *IP Address Assignments*

Router	IP Address Range
R1	131.108.2.1-15.1/24
R2	131.108.16.1-31.1/24
R3	131.108.32.1-33.1./24
R4	131.108.34.1-35.1/24
R5	131.108.128.0/24
R6	131.108.129.0/24
R7	131.108.130.0/24
R8	168.131.1.0/24
WAN links	131.108.255.0/30
LAN link	131.108.36.0/24

Start by enabling EIGRP on all the routers in AS 1. Example 5-13 displays enabling EIGRP on R1. The same configuration commands are applied to all routers in AS 1 because the same Class B network, 131.108.0.0, is in use.

Example 5-13 *Enabling EIGRP on R1*

```
R1(config)#router eigrp ?
  <1-65535>  Autonomous system number
R1(config)#router eigrp 1
R1(config-router)#network 131.108.0.0
```

Example 5-13 configures R1 with EIGRP in AS 1 and enables EIGRP updates to be sent and received on all interfaces configured with an address in the range 131.108.0.0– 131.108.255.255. To display the interface running EIGRP, issue the **show ip eigrp interfaces** command.

Example 5-14 displays the interfaces running EIGRP on R1.

Example 5-14 *Sample Output of* **show ip eigrp interfaces** *on R1*

```
R1#show ip eigrp interfaces
IP-EIGRP interfaces for process 1
                 Xmit Queue   Mean   Pacing Time   Multicast    Pending
Interface  Peers Un/Reliable  SRTT   Un/Reliable   Flow Timer   Routes
Et0/0        1      0/0         2       0/10          50          0
Se0/0        1      0/0        57       0/15          50          0
```

Example 5-14 *Sample Output of* **show ip eigrp interfaces** *on R1 (Continued)*

```
Lo0        0        0/0        0        0/10        0        0
Lo1        0        0/0        0        0/10        0        0
Lo2        0        0/0        0        0/10        0        0
Lo3        0        0/0        0        0/10        0        0
Lo4        0        0/0        0        0/10        0        0
Lo5        0        0/0        0        0/10        0        0
Lo6        0        0/0        0        0/10        0        0
Lo7        0        0/0        0        0/10        0        0
Lo8        0        0/0        0        0/10        0        0
Lo9        0        0/0        0        0/10        0        0
Lo10       0        0/0        0        0/10        0        0
Lo11       0        0/0        0        0/10        0        0
Lo12       0        0/0        0        0/10        0        0
Lo13       0        0/0        0        0/10        0        0
```

Example 5-14 displays a number of physical (E0/0 and Se0/0) interfaces running EIGRP and a number of loopbacks numbered from 0 to 13. Also, note that you have EIGRP neighbors through E0/0 and S0/0. In other words, R1 has established a neighbor relationship to R2 through Ethernet 0/0 and R3 through S0/0.

Next, display the neighbors on R1 by using the **show ip eigrp neighbors** command on R1.

Example 5-15 displays the sample output taken from R1.

Example 5-15 **show ip eigrp neighbors** *Command on R1*

```
R1#show ip eigrp neighbors
IP-EIGRP neighbors for process 1
H   Address                 Interface    Hold Uptime    SRTT    RTO   Q   Seq
                                         (sec)          (ms)          Cnt Num
1   131.108.255.2           Se0/0        14 03:41:45    57      342   0   3
0   131.108.1.2             Et0/0        10 03:43:42    2       200   0   4
```

Two neighbors are formed with R1, namely R2 (131.108.1.2) and R3 (131.108.1.2).

Example 5-16 displays R1's EIGRP IP routing table.

Example 5-16 **show ip route eigrp** *on R1*

```
R1#show ip route eigrp
     131.108.0.0/16 is variably subnetted, 41 subnets, 2 masks
D        131.108.255.16/30 [90/21529600] via 131.108.255.2, 00:00:15, Serial0/0
                           [90/21529600] via 131.108.1.2, 00:00:15, Ethernet0/0
D        131.108.255.20/30 [90/21529600] via 131.108.1.2, 00:04:14, Ethernet0/0
                           [90/21529600] via 131.108.255.2, 00:04:14, Serial0/0
D        131.108.255.4/30 [90/20537600] via 131.108.1.2, 00:04:16, Ethernet0/0
D        131.108.255.8/30 [90/21504000] via 131.108.255.2, 00:04:15, Serial0/0
```

continues

Example 5-16 show ip route eigrp *on R1 (Continued)*

```
D       131.108.255.12/30 [90/21504000] via 131.108.255.2, 00:04:16, Serial0/0
D       131.108.130.0/24 [90/21529600] via 131.108.255.2, 00:04:14, Serial0/0
D       131.108.129.0/24 [90/21555200] via 131.108.255.2, 00:00:10, Serial0/0
                         [90/21555200] via 131.108.1.2, 00:00:10, Ethernet0/0
D       131.108.128.0/24 [90/21529600] via 131.108.255.2, 00:04:14, Serial0/0
D       131.108.36.0/24 [90/20537600] via 131.108.255.2, 00:04:16, Serial0/0
D       131.108.31.0/24 [90/409600] via 131.108.1.2, 00:04:15, Ethernet0/0
D       131.108.30.0/24 [90/409600] via 131.108.1.2, 00:04:15, Ethernet0/0
D       131.108.29.0/24 [90/409600] via 131.108.1.2, 00:04:15, Ethernet0/0
D       131.108.28.0/24 [90/409600] via 131.108.1.2, 00:04:15, Ethernet0/0
D       131.108.27.0/24 [90/409600] via 131.108.1.2, 00:04:15, Ethernet0/0
D       131.108.26.0/24 [90/409600] via 131.108.1.2, 00:04:15, Ethernet0/0
D       131.108.25.0/24 [90/409600] via 131.108.1.2, 00:04:15, Ethernet0/0
D       131.108.24.0/24 [90/409600] via 131.108.1.2, 00:04:15, Ethernet0/0
D       131.108.23.0/24 [90/409600] via 131.108.1.2, 00:04:15, Ethernet0/0
D       131.108.22.0/24 [90/409600] via 131.108.1.2, 00:04:15, Ethernet0/0
D       131.108.21.0/24 [90/409600] via 131.108.1.2, 00:04:15, Ethernet0/0
D       131.108.20.0/24 [90/409600] via 131.108.1.2, 00:04:15, Ethernet0/0
D       131.108.19.0/24 [90/409600] via 131.108.1.2, 00:04:15, Ethernet0/0
D       131.108.18.0/24 [90/409600] via 131.108.1.2, 00:04:16, Ethernet0/0
D       131.108.17.0/24 [90/409600] via 131.108.1.2, 00:04:16, Ethernet0/0
D       131.108.16.0/24 [90/409600] via 131.108.1.2, 00:04:16, Ethernet0/0
```

R1 has a dual path to three remote networks because the composite metric is the same. R1 has no path to the remote network on R8 in EIGRP AS 2.

Next, configure EIGRP on R4 and R8 in AS 2. R4 resides in two autonomous systems: 1 and 2. The serial link between R4 and R8 contains the network 168.131.2.0/30.

Example 5-17 displays the EIGRP configuration on R4 in AS 2 (network 168.131.0.0).

Example 5-17 *EIGRP in AS 2 on R4*

```
R4(config)#router eigrp 2
R4(config-router)#network 168.131.0.0
```

Example 5-18 displays the EIGRP configuration on R8 in AS 2 (network 168.131.0.0).

Example 5-18 *EIGRP in AS 2 on R8*

```
R8(config)#router eigrp 2
R8(config-router)#network 168.131.0.0
```

You should expect to see a neighbor between R4 and R8. Example 5-19 displays the EIGRP neighbors on R4.

Example 5-19 **show ip eigrp neighbors** *on R4*

```
R4#show ip eigrp neighbors
IP-EIGRP neighbors for process 1
H   Address                  Interface    Hold Uptime    SRTT   RTO   Q   Seq Type
                                          (sec)          (ms)         Cnt Num
2   131.108.255.18           Se1            14 00:09:02   640   3840   0   4
0   131.108.255.5            Se0            11 00:14:09    15   1164   0   92
1   131.108.36.3             Et0            12 00:18:22     1    200   0   157
IP-EIGRP neighbors for process 2
H   Address                  Interface    Hold Uptime    SRTT   RTO   Q   Seq Type
                                          (sec)          (ms)         Cnt Num
0   168.131.2.2              Se2            12 00:04:04   239   1434   0   3
```

Router R4 resides in two different autonomous systems: 1 and 2. Hence, R4 has established EIGRP neighbors with routers in AS 1 and AS 2. Display the IP routing table on R8, and ensure connectivity to the rest of the network. Example 5-20 displays the IP routing table on R8.

Example 5-20 **show ip route neighbors** *on R8*

```
R8#show ip route
     168.131.0.0/16 is variably subnetted, 2 subnets, 2 masks
C       168.131.2.0/30 is directly connected, Serial0
C       168.131.1.0/24 is directly connected, Ethernet0
```

R8 has no remote EIGRP entries because R4 is not redistributing IP networks from EIGRP AS 1 into 2. R4 must be configured for redistribution because EIGRP does not automatically redistribute among different autonomous systems. (EIGRP and IGRP automatic redistribution occurs only if the AS is the same.) If the routers in AS 1 want to send data to AS 2, R4 must provide two-way redistribution.

Example 5-21 displays the configuration of two-way redistribution between AS 1 and 2. The **?** tool is used here to highlight the parameters the Cisco IOS requires.

TIP   You must be careful when performing any redistribution to ensure that networks residing in one domain do not contain routes or subnets in the redistributed domain. Route maps or distributed lists should always be applied to ensure routing loops do not occur.

Example 5-21 *Redistribution on R4 Between AS 1 and 2*

```
R4(config)#router eigrp 1
R4(config-router)#redistribute eigrp ?
  <1-65535>  Autonomous system number
R4(config-router)#redistribute eigrp 2 ?
  metric     Metric for redistributed routes
  route-map  Route map reference
  <cr>
R4(config-router)#redistribute eigrp 2 metric ?
  <1-4294967295>  Bandwidth metric in Kbits per second

R4(config-router)#redistribute eigrp 2 metric 125 ?
  <0-4294967295>  IGRP delay metric, in 10 microsecond units

R4(config-router)#redistribute eigrp 2 metric 125 20000 ?
  <0-255>  IGRP reliability metric where 255 is 100% reliable

R4(config-router)#redistribute eigrp 2 metric 125 20000 255 ?
  <1-255>  IGRP Effective bandwidth metric (Loading) where 255 is 100% loaded

R4(config-router)#redistribute eigrp 2 metric 125 20000 255 1 ?
  <1-4294967295>  IGRP MTU of the path

R4(config-router)#redistribute eigrp 2 metric 125 20000 255 1 1500
R4(config-router)#router eigrp 2
R4(config-router)#redistribute eigrp 1  metric 125 20000 255 1 1500
```

After you configure redistribution on R4, you can expect to see R8 with IP routing information from AS 1.

Example 5-22 displays R8's IP routing table.

Example 5-22 *show ip route Command on R8*

```
R8#show ip route
Codes: C - connected, D - EIGRP, EX - EIGRP external
       168.131.0.0/16 is variably subnetted, 2 subnets, 2 masks
C        168.131.2.0/30 is directly connected, Serial0
C        168.131.1.0/24 is directly connected, Ethernet0
       131.108.0.0/16 is variably subnetted, 41 subnets, 3 masks
D EX     131.108.255.16/30 [170/26112000] via 168.131.2.1, 00:02:57, Serial0
D EX     131.108.255.0/30 [170/26112000] via 168.131.2.1, 00:02:57, Serial0
D EX     131.108.255.4/30 [170/26112000] via 168.131.2.1, 00:02:57, Serial0
D EX     131.108.255.8/30 [170/26112000] via 168.131.2.1, 00:02:58, Serial0
D EX     131.108.255.12/30 [170/26112000] via 168.131.2.1, 00:02:58, Serial0
D EX     131.108.130.0/24 [170/26112000] via 168.131.2.1, 00:02:58, Serial0
D EX     131.108.129.0/24 [170/26112000] via 168.131.2.1, 00:02:58, Serial0
D EX     131.108.128.0/24 [170/26112000] via 168.131.2.1, 00:02:58, Serial0
D EX     131.108.36.0/24 [170/26112000] via 168.131.2.1, 00:02:58, Serial0
```

Example 5-22 show ip route *Command on R8 (Continued)*

```
D EX    131.108.15.0/24 [170/26112000] via 168.131.2.1, 00:02:58, Serial0
D EX    131.108.14.0/24 [170/26112000] via 168.131.2.1, 00:02:58, Serial0
D EX    131.108.13.0/24 [170/26112000] via 168.131.2.1, 00:02:58, Serial0
D EX    131.108.12.0/24 [170/26112000] via 168.131.2.1, 00:02:58, Serial0
D EX    131.108.11.0/24 [170/26112000] via 168.131.2.1, 00:02:58, Serial0
D EX    131.108.10.0/24 [170/26112000] via 168.131.2.1, 00:02:58, Serial0
D EX    131.108.9.0/24 [170/26112000] via 168.131.2.1, 00:02:58, Serial0
D EX    131.108.8.0/24 [170/26112000] via 168.131.2.1, 00:02:58, Serial0
D EX    131.108.7.0/24 [170/26112000] via 168.131.2.1, 00:02:58, Serial0
D EX    131.108.6.0/24 [170/26112000] via 168.131.2.1, 00:02:59, Serial0
D EX    131.108.5.0/24 [170/26112000] via 168.131.2.1, 00:02:59, Serial0
D EX    131.108.4.0/24 [170/26112000] via 168.131.2.1, 00:02:59, Serial0
D EX    131.108.3.0/24 [170/26112000] via 168.131.2.1, 00:02:59, Serial0
D EX    131.108.2.0/24 [170/26112000] via 168.131.2.1, 00:02:59, Serial0
D EX    131.108.1.0/24 [170/26112000] via 168.131.2.1, 00:02:59, Serial0
D EX    131.108.0.0/16 [170/26112000] via 168.131.2.1, 00:02:59, Serial0
D EX    131.108.31.0/24 [170/26112000] via 168.131.2.1, 00:02:59, Serial0
D EX    131.108.30.0/24 [170/26112000] via 168.131.2.1, 00:02:59, Serial0
D EX    131.108.29.0/24 [170/26112000] via 168.131.2.1, 00:02:59, Serial0
D EX    131.108.28.0/24 [170/26112000] via 168.131.2.1, 00:02:59, Serial0
D EX    131.108.27.0/24 [170/26112000] via 168.131.2.1, 00:02:59, Serial0
D EX    131.108.26.0/24 [170/26112000] via 168.131.2.1, 00:02:59, Serial0
D EX    131.108.25.0/24 [170/26112000] via 168.131.2.1, 00:02:59, Serial0
D EX    131.108.24.0/24 [170/26112000] via 168.131.2.1, 00:02:59, Serial0
D EX    131.108.23.0/24 [170/26112000] via 168.131.2.1, 00:03:00, Serial0
D EX    131.108.22.0/24 [170/26112000] via 168.131.2.1, 00:03:00, Serial0
D EX    131.108.21.0/24 [170/26112000] via 168.131.2.1, 00:03:00, Serial0
D EX    131.108.20.0/24 [170/26112000] via 168.131.2.1, 00:03:00, Serial0
D EX    131.108.19.0/24 [170/26112000] via 168.131.2.1, 00:03:00, Serial0
D EX    131.108.18.0/24 [170/26112000] via 168.131.2.1, 00:03:00, Serial0
D EX    131.108.17.0/24 [170/26112000] via 168.131.2.1, 00:03:00, Serial0
D EX    131.108.16.0/24 [170/26112000] via 168.131.2.1, 00:03:00, Serial0
```

R8 has an expanded IP routing table. Notice that all the networks from AS 1 are tagged as D EX, or external EIGRP, and the AD distance is 170 (or less trusted than Internal EIGRP set at 90). Before you configure EIGRP to summarize wherever possible in Figure 5-2, here are the full working configurations of all eight Cisco routers running EIGRP.

Take particular note of the shaded sections, such as the **bandwidth** statement used to match the wire speed between routers. The **bandwidth** statement ensures proper calculation of the EIGRP composite metric and also ensures that EIGRP does not consume more than 50 percent of the bandwidth. By default, Cisco IOS routers set the bandwidth to 1544 kbps.

Example 5-23 displays R1's full working configuration.

Example 5-23 *R1's Full Working Configuration*

```
hostname R1
!
enable password cisco
!
ip subnet-zero
no ip domain-lookup
interface Loopback0
 ip address 131.108.2.1 255.255.255.0
!
interface Loopback1
 ip address 131.108.3.1 255.255.255.0
!
interface Loopback2
 ip address 131.108.4.1 255.255.255.0
!
interface Loopback3
 ip address 131.108.5.1 255.255.255.0
!
interface Loopback4
 ip address 131.108.6.1 255.255.255.0
!
interface Loopback5
 ip address 131.108.7.1 255.255.255.0
!
interface Loopback6
 ip address 131.108.8.1 255.255.255.0
!
interface Loopback7
 ip address 131.108.9.1 255.255.255.0
!
interface Loopback8
 ip address 131.108.10.1 255.255.255.0
!
interface Loopback9
 ip address 131.108.11.1 255.255.255.0
!
interface Loopback10
 ip address 131.108.12.1 255.255.255.0
!
interface Loopback11
 ip address 131.108.13.1 255.255.255.0
!
interface Loopback12
 ip address 131.108.14.1 255.255.255.0
!
interface Loopback13
 ip address 131.108.15.1 255.255.255.0
```

Example 5-23 *R1's Full Working Configuration (Continued)*

```
 !
 interface Ethernet0/0
  ip address 131.108.1.1 255.255.255.0
 !
 interface Serial0/0
  bandwidth 128
  ip address 131.108.255.1 255.255.255.252
  clockrate 128000
 !
 interface Serial0/1
  shutdown
 !
 router eigrp 1
  network 131.108.0.0
 !
 line con 0
 line aux 0
 line vty 0 4
 !
 end
```

Example 5-24 displays R2's full working configuration.

Example 5-24 *R2's Full Working Configuration*

```
 hostname R2
 !
 enable password cisco
 !
 ip subnet-zero
 no ip domain-lookup
 !
 interface Loopback0
  ip address 131.108.16.1 255.255.255.0
 !
 interface Loopback1
  ip address 131.108.17.1 255.255.255.0
 !
 interface Loopback2
  ip address 131.108.18.1 255.255.255.0
 !
 interface Loopback3
  ip address 131.108.19.1 255.255.255.0
 !
 interface Loopback4
  ip address 131.108.20.1 255.255.255.0
 !
 interface Loopback5
  ip address 131.108.21.1 255.255.255.0
```

continues

Example 5-24 *R2's Full Working Configuration (Continued)*

```
 !
 interface Loopback6
  ip address 131.108.22.1 255.255.255.0
 !
 interface Loopback7
  ip address 131.108.23.1 255.255.255.0
 !
 interface Loopback8
  ip address 131.108.24.1 255.255.255.0
 !
 interface Loopback9
  ip address 131.108.25.1 255.255.255.0
 !
 interface Loopback10
  ip address 131.108.26.1 255.255.255.0
 !
 interface Loopback11
  ip address 131.108.27.1 255.255.255.0
 !
 interface Loopback13
  ip address 131.108.28.1 255.255.255.0
 !
 interface Loopback14
  ip address 131.108.29.1 255.255.255.0
 !
 interface Loopback15
  ip address 131.108.30.1 255.255.255.0
 !
 interface Loopback16
  ip address 131.108.31.1 255.255.255.0

 !
 interface Ethernet0/0
  ip address 131.108.1.2 255.255.255.0
 !
 interface Serial1/0
  bandwidth 128
  ip address 131.108.255.5 255.255.255.252

  clockrate 128000
 !
 interface Serial1/1

  shutdown

 router eigrp 1
  network 131.108.0.0
 !
 ip classless
```

Example 5-24 *R2's Full Working Configuration (Continued)*

```
!
line con 0
line aux 0
line vty 0 4
end
```

Example 5-25 displays R3's full working configuration.

Example 5-25 *R3's Full Working Configuration*

```
hostname R3
!
enable password cisco
!
no ip domain-lookup
!
interface Ethernet0
 ip address 131.108.36.3 255.255.255.0
 media-type 10BaseT
!
interface Serial0
 ip address 131.108.255.2 255.255.255.252
 bandwidth 125
!
interface Serial1
 ip address 131.108.255.9 255.255.255.252
 bandwidth 125
 clockrate 125000
!
interface Serial2
 ip address 131.108.255.13 255.255.255.252
 bandwidth 125
 clockrate 125000
!
interface Serial3
 no ip address
 shutdown
!
router eigrp 1
 network 131.108.0.0
!
line con 0
line aux 0
line vty 0 4
end
```

Example 5-26 displays R4's full working configuration. R4 is redistributing between the two EIGRP autonomous systems, 1 and 2.

Example 5-26 *R4's Full Working Configuration*

```
hostname R4
!
enable password cisco
ip subnet-zero
no ip domain-lookup
interface Ethernet0
 ip address 131.108.36.4 255.255.255.0
 !
interface Serial0
 bandwidth 125
 ip address 131.108.255.6 255.255.255.252
 !
interface Serial1
 bandwidth 125
 ip address 131.108.255.17 255.255.255.252
 clockrate 125000
 !
interface Serial2
 bandwidth 125
 ip address 168.131.2.1 255.255.255.252
 clockrate 125000
 !
interface Serial3
 ip address 141.108.255.1 255.255.255.252
 clockrate 125000
 !
router eigrp 1
 redistribute eigrp 2 metric 125 20000 255 1 1500
 network 131.108.0.0
 !
router eigrp 2
 redistribute eigrp 1 metric 125 20000 255 1 1500
 network 168.131.0.0
 !
line con 0
line aux 0
line vty 0 4
end
```

Example 5-27 displays R5's full working configuration.

Example 5-27 *R5's Full Working Configuration*

```
hostname R5
!
enable password cisco
!
ip subnet-zero
interface Ethernet0
 ip address 131.108.128.1 255.255.255.0
!
interface Serial0
 bandwidth 125
 ip address 131.108.255.10 255.255.255.252
!
interface Serial1
 shutdown
!
router eigrp 1
 network 131.108.0.0
!
line con 0
line aux 0
line vty 0 4
end
```

Example 5-28 displays R6's full working configuration.

Example 5-28 *R6's Full Working Configuration*

```
hostname R6
!
enable password cisco
!
ip subnet-zero
interface Ethernet0
 ip address 131.108.129.1 255.255.255.0
!
interface Serial0
 bandwidth 125
 ip address 131.108.255.18 255.255.255.252
!
interface Serial1
 shutdown
!
router eigrp 1
 network 131.108.0.0
!
line con 0
line aux 0
line vty 0 4!
end
```

Example 5-29 displays R7's full working configuration.

Example 5-29 *R7's Full Working Configuration*

```
hostname R7
!
enable password cisco
!
ip subnet-zero
no ip domain-lookup
!
interface Ethernet0
 ip address 131.108.130.1 255.255.255.0
!
interface Serial0
 bandwidth 125
 ip address 131.108.255.14 255.255.255.252
!
interface Serial1
 shutdown
!
router eigrp 1
 network 131.108.0.0
!
line con 0
line aux 0
line vty 0 4
end
```

Example 5-30 displays R8's full working configuration. R8 is running EIGRP in AS 2 only.

Example 5-30 *R8's Full Working Configuration*

```
hostname R8
enable password cisco
!
ip subnet-zero
no ip domain-lookup
!
interface Ethernet0
 ip address 168.131.1.1 255.255.255.0
!
interface Serial0
 bandwidth 125
 ip address 168.131.2.2 255.255.255.252
!
interface Serial1
 shutdown
!
router eigrp 2
 network 168.131.0.0
```

Example 5-30 *R8's Full Working Configuration (Continued)*

```
!
line con 0
line aux 0
line vty 0 4
!
end
```

Scenario 5-2: Summarization with EIGRP

In this scenario, you use summarization with the network configured for EIGRP in Scenario 5-1 and reduce the IP routing table size within an AS and external to the AS.

Figure 5-3 displays the connected routes being advertised by R1 and R2.

Figure 5-3 *R1 and R2 Connected Networks*

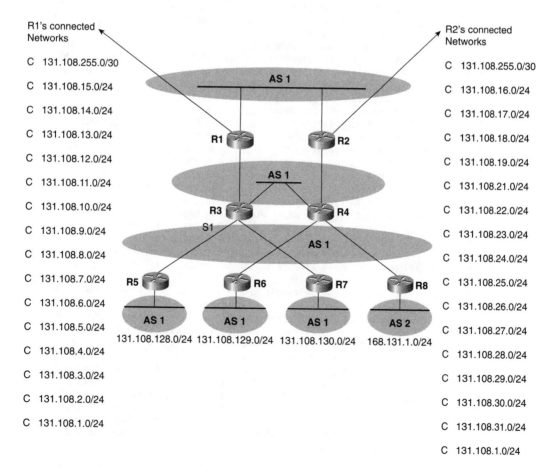

R1's connected
Networks

C 131.108.255.0/30

C 131.108.15.0/24

C 131.108.14.0/24

C 131.108.13.0/24

C 131.108.12.0/24

C 131.108.11.0/24

C 131.108.10.0/24

C 131.108.9.0/24

C 131.108.8.0/24

C 131.108.7.0/24

C 131.108.6.0/24

C 131.108.5.0/24

C 131.108.4.0/24

C 131.108.3.0/24

C 131.108.2.0/24

C 131.108.1.0/24

R2's connected
Networks

C 131.108.255.0/30

C 131.108.16.0/24

C 131.108.17.0/24

C 131.108.18.0/24

C 131.108.19.0/24

C 131.108.21.0/24

C 131.108.22.0/24

C 131.108.23.0/24

C 131.108.24.0/24

C 131.108.25.0/24

C 131.108.26.0/24

C 131.108.27.0/24

C 131.108.28.0/24

C 131.108.29.0/24

C 131.108.30.0/24

C 131.108.31.0/24

C 131.108.1.0/24

AS 1

R1   R2

AS 1

R3   R4

S1

AS 1

R5   R6   R7   R8

AS 1   AS 1   AS 1   AS 2
131.108.128.0/24   131.108.129.0/24   131.108.130.0/24   168.131.1.0/24

The networks ranging from 131.108.1.0 to 131.108.31.255 reside on two routers; in other words, 31 subnets or IP routing entries populate the routing tables in AS 1 and AS 2.

Example 5-31 displays the IP routing table on R3.

Example 5-31 *R3's IP Routing Table*

```
R3#show ip route
      168.131.0.0/16 is variably subnetted, 3 subnets, 3 masks
D EX    168.131.2.0/30 [170/25625600] via 131.108.36.4, 10:54:34, Ethernet0
D EX    168.131.1.0/24 [170/25625600] via 131.108.36.4, 10:54:34, Ethernet0
D EX    168.131.0.0/16 [170/25625600] via 131.108.36.4, 10:54:34, Ethernet0
      131.108.0.0/16 is variably subnetted, 40 subnets, 2 masks
D       131.108.255.16/30 [90/21017600] via 131.108.36.4, 11:13:47, Ethernet0
C       131.108.255.0/30 is directly connected, Serial0
D       131.108.255.4/30 [90/21017600] via 131.108.36.4, 11:17:45, Ethernet0
C       131.108.255.8/30 is directly connected, Serial1
C       131.108.255.12/30 is directly connected, Serial2
D       131.108.130.0/24 [90/21017600] via 131.108.255.14, 11:17:46, Serial2
D       131.108.129.0/24 [90/21043200] via 131.108.36.4, 11:13:41, Ethernet0
D       131.108.128.0/24 [90/21017600] via 131.108.255.10, 11:17:46, Serial1
C       131.108.36.0/24 is directly connected, Ethernet0
D       131.108.15.0/24 [90/21120000] via 131.108.255.1, 11:17:47, Serial0
D       131.108.14.0/24 [90/21120000] via 131.108.255.1, 11:17:47, Serial0
D       131.108.13.0/24 [90/21120000] via 131.108.255.1, 11:17:47, Serial0
D       131.108.12.0/24 [90/21120000] via 131.108.255.1, 11:17:47, Serial0
D       131.108.11.0/24 [90/21120000] via 131.108.255.1, 11:17:47, Serial0
D       131.108.10.0/24 [90/21120000] via 131.108.255.1, 11:17:47, Serial0
D       131.108.9.0/24 [90/21120000] via 131.108.255.1, 11:17:47, Serial0
D       131.108.8.0/24 [90/21120000] via 131.108.255.1, 11:17:47, Serial0
D       131.108.7.0/24 [90/21120000] via 131.108.255.1, 11:17:47, Serial0
D       131.108.6.0/24 [90/21120000] via 131.108.255.1, 11:17:47, Serial0
D       131.108.5.0/24 [90/21120000] via 131.108.255.1, 11:17:48, Serial0
D       131.108.4.0/24 [90/21120000] via 131.108.255.1, 11:17:48, Serial0
D       131.108.3.0/24 [90/21120000] via 131.108.255.1, 11:17:48, Serial0
D       131.108.2.0/24 [90/21120000] via 131.108.255.1, 11:17:48, Serial0
D       131.108.1.0/24 [90/21017600] via 131.108.255.1, 11:17:48, Serial0
D       131.108.31.0/24 [90/21145600] via 131.108.36.4, 11:17:48, Ethernet0
                       [90/21145600] via 131.108.255.1, 11:17:48, Serial0
D       131.108.30.0/24 [90/21145600] via 131.108.36.4, 11:17:48, Ethernet0
                       [90/21145600] via 131.108.255.1, 11:17:48, Serial0
D       131.108.29.0/24 [90/21145600] via 131.108.36.4, 11:17:48, Ethernet0
                       [90/21145600] via 131.108.255.1, 11:17:49, Serial0
D       131.108.28.0/24 [90/21145600] via 131.108.36.4, 11:17:49, Ethernet0
                       [90/21145600] via 131.108.255.1, 11:17:49, Serial0
D       131.108.27.0/24 [90/21145600] via 131.108.36.4, 11:17:49, Ethernet0
                       [90/21145600] via 131.108.255.1, 11:17:49, Serial0
D       131.108.26.0/24 [90/21145600] via 131.108.36.4, 11:17:49, Ethernet0
                       [90/21145600] via 131.108.255.1, 11:17:49, Serial0
D       131.108.25.0/24 [90/21145600] via 131.108.36.4, 11:17:49, Ethernet0
                       [90/21145600] via 131.108.255.1, 11:17:49, Serial0
D       131.108.24.0/24 [90/21145600] via 131.108.36.4, 11:17:49, Ethernet0
                       [90/21145600] via 131.108.255.1, 11:17:50, Serial0
```

Example 5-31 *R3's IP Routing Table (Continued)*

```
D        131.108.23.0/24 [90/21145600] via 131.108.36.4, 11:17:50, Ethernet0
                         [90/21145600] via 131.108.255.1, 11:17:50, Serial0
D        131.108.22.0/24 [90/21145600] via 131.108.36.4, 11:17:50, Ethernet0
                         [90/21145600] via 131.108.255.1, 11:17:50, Serial0
D        131.108.21.0/24 [90/21145600] via 131.108.36.4, 11:17:50, Ethernet0
                         [90/21145600] via 131.108.255.1, 11:17:50, Serial0
D        131.108.20.0/24 [90/21145600] via 131.108.36.4, 11:17:50, Ethernet0
                         [90/21145600] via 131.108.255.1, 11:17:50, Serial0
D        131.108.19.0/24 [90/21145600] via 131.108.36.4, 11:17:50, Ethernet0
                         [90/21145600] via 131.108.255.1, 11:17:50, Serial0
D        131.108.18.0/24 [90/21145600] via 131.108.36.4, 11:17:50, Ethernet0
                         [90/21145600] via 131.108.255.1, 11:17:50, Serial0
D        131.108.17.0/24 [90/21145600] via 131.108.36.4, 11:17:51, Ethernet0
                         [90/21145600] via 131.108.255.1, 11:17:51, Serial0
D        131.108.16.0/24 [90/21145600] via 131.108.36.4, 11:17:51, Ethernet0
                         [90/21145600] via 131.108.255.1, 11:17:51, Serial0
```

R3 has 31 separate network entries for the ranges 131.108.1.0–131.108.31.255. You can clearly summarize the networks on R1 and R2 to reduce the IP routing table. To summarize the EIGRP network, you apply the **ip summary-address eigrp** *AS IP address mask* command.

Apply summarization on R1 for its directly connected links.

Example 5-32 displays the interface configuration required for summarizing the networks ranging 131.108.1.0–131.108.15.255. The subnet mask covering this range is 255.255.240.0.

Example 5-32 *Summary Configuration on R1 with* **?** *Tool*

```
R1(config)#interface serial 0/0
R1(config-if)#ip summary-address ?
  eigrp  Enhanced Interior Gateway Routing Protocol (EIGRP)
R1(config-if)#ip summary-address eigrp ?
  <1-65535>  Autonomous system number
R1(config-if)#ip summary-address eigrp 1 ?
  A.B.C.D  IP address
R1(config-if)#ip summary-address eigrp 1 131.108.1.0 255.255.240.0
```

Next, display the IP routing table on R3. Example 5-33 displays the IP routing table on R3 after summarization is configured on R1.

Example 5-33 *R3's IP Routing Table*

```
R3#show ip route eigrp
        168.131.0.0/16 is variably subnetted, 3 subnets, 3 masks
D EX    168.131.2.0/30 [170/25625600] via 131.108.36.4, 00:02:45, Ethernet0
D EX    168.131.1.0/24 [170/25625600] via 131.108.36.4, 00:02:45, Ethernet0
D EX    168.131.0.0/16 [170/25625600] via 131.108.36.4, 00:02:45, Ethernet0
        131.108.0.0/16 is variably subnetted, 41 subnets, 3 masks
D       131.108.255.16/30 [90/21017600] via 131.108.36.4, 00:02:45, Ethernet0
D       131.108.255.4/30 [90/21017600] via 131.108.36.4, 00:02:45, Ethernet0
D       131.108.130.0/24 [90/21017600] via 131.108.255.14, 00:02:46, Serial2
D       131.108.129.0/24 [90/21043200] via 131.108.36.4, 00:02:46, Ethernet0
D       131.108.128.0/24 [90/21017600] via 131.108.255.10, 00:02:46, Serial1
D       131.108.15.0/24 [90/21171200] via 131.108.36.4, 00:02:51, Ethernet0
D       131.108.14.0/24 [90/21171200] via 131.108.36.4, 00:02:51, Ethernet0
D       131.108.13.0/24 [90/21171200] via 131.108.36.4, 00:02:51, Ethernet0
D       131.108.12.0/24 [90/21171200] via 131.108.36.4, 00:02:51, Ethernet0
D       131.108.11.0/24 [90/21171200] via 131.108.36.4, 00:02:51, Ethernet0
D       131.108.10.0/24 [90/21171200] via 131.108.36.4, 00:02:51, Ethernet0
D       131.108.9.0/24 [90/21171200] via 131.108.36.4, 00:02:51, Ethernet0
D       131.108.8.0/24 [90/21171200] via 131.108.36.4, 00:02:51, Ethernet0
D       131.108.7.0/24 [90/21171200] via 131.108.36.4, 00:02:51, Ethernet0
D       131.108.6.0/24 [90/21171200] via 131.108.36.4, 00:02:51, Ethernet0
D       131.108.5.0/24 [90/21171200] via 131.108.36.4, 00:02:52, Ethernet0
D       131.108.4.0/24 [90/21171200] via 131.108.36.4, 00:02:52, Ethernet0
D       131.108.3.0/24 [90/21171200] via 131.108.36.4, 00:02:52, Ethernet0
D       131.108.2.0/24 [90/21171200] via 131.108.36.4, 00:02:53, Ethernet0
D       131.108.1.0/24 [90/21043200] via 131.108.36.4, 00:02:53, Ethernet0
D       131.108.0.0/20 [90/21120000] via 131.108.255.1, 00:02:48, Serial0
D       131.108.31.0/24 [90/21145600] via 131.108.36.4, 00:02:48, Ethernet0
                        [90/21145600] via 131.108.255.1, 00:02:48, Serial0
D       131.108.30.0/24 [90/21145600] via 131.108.36.4, 00:02:48, Ethernet0
                        [90/21145600] via 131.108.255.1, 00:02:48, Serial0
D       131.108.29.0/24 [90/21145600] via 131.108.36.4, 00:02:49, Ethernet0
                        [90/21145600] via 131.108.255.1, 00:02:49, Serial0
D       131.108.28.0/24 [90/21145600] via 131.108.36.4, 00:02:49, Ethernet0
                        [90/21145600] via 131.108.255.1, 00:02:49, Serial0
D       131.108.27.0/24 [90/21145600] via 131.108.36.4, 00:02:49, Ethernet0
                        [90/21145600] via 131.108.255.1, 00:02:49, Serial0
D       131.108.26.0/24 [90/21145600] via 131.108.36.4, 00:02:49, Ethernet0
                        [90/21145600] via 131.108.255.1, 00:02:49, Serial0
D       131.108.25.0/24 [90/21145600] via 131.108.36.4, 00:02:49, Ethernet0
                        [90/21145600] via 131.108.255.1, 00:02:49, Serial0
D       131.108.24.0/24 [90/21145600] via 131.108.36.4, 00:02:49, Ethernet0
                        [90/21145600] via 131.108.255.1, 00:02:49, Serial0
D       131.108.23.0/24 [90/21145600] via 131.108.36.4, 00:02:49, Ethernet0
                        [90/21145600] via 131.108.255.1, 00:02:50, Serial0
D       131.108.22.0/24 [90/21145600] via 131.108.36.4, 00:02:50, Ethernet0
                        [90/21145600] via 131.108.255.1, 00:02:50, Serial0
D       131.108.21.0/24 [90/21145600] via 131.108.36.4, 00:02:50, Ethernet0
                        [90/21145600] via 131.108.255.1, 00:02:50, Serial0
D       131.108.20.0/24 [90/21145600] via 131.108.36.4, 00:02:50, Ethernet0
                        [90/21145600] via 131.108.255.1, 00:02:50, Serial0
```

Example 5-33 *R3's IP Routing Table (Continued)*

```
D       131.108.19.0/24 [90/21145600] via 131.108.36.4, 00:02:50, Ethernet0
                        [90/21145600] via 131.108.255.1, 00:02:50, Serial0
D       131.108.18.0/24 [90/21145600] via 131.108.36.4, 00:02:50, Ethernet0
                        [90/21145600] via 131.108.255.1, 00:02:51, Serial0
D       131.108.17.0/24 [90/21145600] via 131.108.36.4, 00:02:51, Ethernet0
                        [90/21145600] via 131.108.255.1, 00:02:51, Serial0
D       131.108.16.0/24 [90/21145600] via 131.108.36.4, 00:02:51, Ethernet0
                        [90/21145600] via 131.108.255.1, 00:02:51, Serial0
```

R3 still has the 15 network entries advertised through the next hop address 131.108.36.4, or R4, as well as the summary address 131.108.0.0/20. (This encompasses the range 131.108.1.0–131.108.15.255.) R3 has two paths to the remote router R1. Cisco EIGRP-enabled routers always accept an incoming route with a more specific destination.

When you performed summarization, you configured only R1 to summarize to R3; you must also provide the same summary address to R2. Example 5-34 configures summarization on R1 pointing to R2. The interface that R1 and R2 are adjacent to, namely Ethernet 0/0, is where you need to apply the same summary command used in Example 5-32.

Example 5-34 *Summary on R1 Pointing to R2*

```
R1(config)#interface ethernet 0/0
R1(config-if)#ip summary-address eigrp  1 131.108.1.0 255.255.240.0
```

Before you look at R3's IP routing table, you must perform the same summary configuration on R2 because R2 has 15 directly contiguous networks ranging from 131.108.16.0 to 131.108.31.255.

Example 5-35 displays the summary configuration on R2. Two summary commands are required: one to R1 through Ethernet 0/0 and another to R4 through Serial 1/0.

Example 5-35 *Summary on R2*

```
R2(config)#interface ethernet 0/0
R2(config-if)#ip summary-address eigrp 1 131.108.16.0 255.255.240.0
R2(config-if)#interface serial1/0
R2(config-if)#ip summary-address eigrp 1 131.108.16.0 255.255.240.0
```

Example 5-36 displays the IP routing table on R3.

Example 5-36 show ip route eigrp *on R3*

```
R3#show ip route eigrp
     168.131.0.0/16 is variably subnetted, 3 subnets, 3 masks
D EX    168.131.2.0/30 [170/25625600] via 131.108.36.4, 00:02:17, Ethernet0
D EX    168.131.1.0/24 [170/25625600] via 131.108.36.4, 00:02:17, Ethernet0
D EX    168.131.0.0/16 [170/25625600] via 131.108.36.4, 00:02:17, Ethernet0
     131.108.0.0/16 is variably subnetted, 12 subnets, 3 masks
D       131.108.255.16/30 [90/21017600] via 131.108.36.4, 00:02:17, Ethernet0
D       131.108.255.4/30 [90/21017600] via 131.108.36.4, 00:02:22, Ethernet0
D       131.108.130.0/24 [90/21017600] via 131.108.255.14, 00:12:20, Serial2
D       131.108.129.0/24 [90/21043200] via 131.108.36.4, 00:02:17, Ethernet0
D       131.108.128.0/24 [90/21017600] via 131.108.255.10, 00:12:20, Serial1
D       131.108.1.0/24 [90/21043200] via 131.108.36.4, 00:02:14, Ethernet0
D       131.108.0.0/20 [90/21120000] via 131.108.255.1, 00:02:14, Serial0
D       131.108.16.0/20 [90/21145600] via 131.108.255.1, 00:02:14, Serial0
                        [90/21145600] via 131.108.36.4, 00:02:14, Ethernet0
```

R3's IP routing table has been significantly reduced from 31 network entries for the subnets ranging from 1 to 31 to two network entries. Prior to summarization, there were 41 subnets; now only 12 subnets are present in the Class B network 131.108.0.0 in R3's routing table.

Also, note that load balancing is in place to R2's directly connected loopbacks because the EIGRP metrics are the same through serial 0 and Ethernet 0. Also, in turn, summarization reduces the EIGRP topology table. The added benefit of summarization is that a network failure on any one network is not propagated to remote networks to which a summary route is sent.

Example 5-37 displays R4's IP routing table to demonstrate similar benefits.

Example 5-37 show ip route eigrp *Command on R4*

```
R4>sh ip route eigrp
     168.131.0.0/16 is variably subnetted, 3 subnets, 3 masks
D       168.131.1.0/24 [90/21017600] via 168.131.2.2, 11:29:38, Serial2
D       168.131.0.0/16 is a summary, 11:29:40, Null0
     131.108.0.0/16 is variably subnetted, 13 subnets, 4 masks
D       131.108.255.0/30 [90/21017600] via 131.108.36.3, 00:06:27, Ethernet0
D       131.108.255.8/30 [90/21017600] via 131.108.36.3, 11:30:01, Ethernet0
D       131.108.255.12/30 [90/21017600] via 131.108.36.3, 11:30:01, Ethernet0
D       131.108.130.0/24 [90/21043200] via 131.108.36.3, 11:30:01, Ethernet0
D       131.108.129.0/24 [90/21017600] via 131.108.255.18, 11:30:01, Serial1
D       131.108.128.0/24 [90/21043200] via 131.108.36.3, 11:30:01, Ethernet0
D       131.108.1.0/24 [90/21017600] via 131.108.255.5, 00:06:28, Serial0
D       131.108.0.0/20 [90/21145600] via 131.108.36.3, 00:06:28, Ethernet0
                        [90/21145600] via 131.108.255.5, 00:06:28, Serial0
D       131.108.16.0/20 [90/21120000] via 131.108.255.5, 00:06:29, Serial0
```

Because R4 is directly connected to R2, there is only one path (lower metric) taken to R2's directly connected interfaces, while load balancing is taking place for R1's directly connected networks.

Example 5-38 displays the summary EIGRP configuration on R1.

Example 5-38 *Summary EIGRP Configuration on R1*

```
interface Ethernet0/0
 ip address 131.108.1.1 255.255.255.0
 ip summary-address eigrp 1 131.108.0.0 255.255.240.0
!
interface Serial0/0
 bandwidth 128
 ip address 131.108.255.1 255.255.255.252
 ip summary-address eigrp 1 131.108.0.0 255.255.240.0
 clockrate 125000
```

Example 5-39 displays the summary EIGRP configuration on R2.

Example 5-39 *Summary EIGRP Configuration on R2*

```
interface Ethernet0/0
 ip address 131.108.1.2 255.255.255.0
 ip summary-address eigrp 1 131.108.16.0 255.255.240.0
!
interface Serial1/0
 bandwidth 128
 ip address 131.108.255.5 255.255.255.252
 ip summary-address eigrp 1 131.108.16.0 255.255.240.0
 clockrate 128000
```

Scenario 5-3: EIGRP and VLSM

This scenario demonstrates the capability of EIGRP to handle VLSM with a simple four-router topology.

Figure 5-4 displays the four-router topology along with the IP addressing scheme.

Four routers in Figure 5-4 reside in the same AS, so you do not need to configure any redistribution. Also, the Class A addresses, 10.1.1.0/25 and 10.1.1.128/25, are configured on the Ethernet interfaces on R3 and R4, respectively. VLSM is used on all four routers.

The Class A address, 10.0.0.0/8, is reserved for private use and not routable in the Internet.

Figure 5-4 *VLSM and EIGRP Topology*

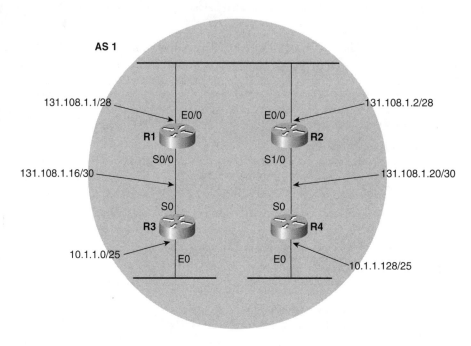

Enable EIGRP in AS 1 on all four routers. Example 5-40 displays the EIGRP configuration on routers R1 and R2. Both routers reside in AS 1 and are connected to only the network 131.108.1.0, so the EIGRP configuration is the same on R1 and R2.

Example 5-40 *EIGRP Configuration on R1 and R2*

```
router eigrp 1
 network 131.108.0.0
```

R3 and R4 require both 131.108.0.0 and 10.0.0.0 **network** statements, as displayed by Example 5-41.

Example 5-41 *EIGRP Configuration on R3 and R4*

```
router eigrp 1
 network 131.108.0.0
 network 10.0.0.0
```

View the IP routing table on R1 to ensure that all subnets are routable through R1.
Example 5-42 displays R1's routing table.

Example 5-42 *R1's IP Routing Table*

```
R1#show ip route
D     10.0.0.0/8 [90/20537600] via 131.108.1.18, 00:06:19, Serial0/0
      131.108.0.0/16 is variably subnetted, 4 subnets, 3 masks
C        131.108.1.0/28 is directly connected, Ethernet0/0
D        131.108.1.20/30 [90/20537600] via 131.108.1.2, 00:08:55, Ethernet0/0
C        131.108.1.16/30 is directly connected, Serial0/0
```

R1's IP routing tables display a total of two dynamically learned EIGRP routers: one route
to the network 131.108.1.20/30 (the serial link between R2 and R4) and one to network
remote network 10.0.0.0 through R3. Take a closer look at the remote IP network on R3.
R3 is configured with the network 10.1.1.0/25, yet R1 assumes that the entire Class A
network is available through Serial 0/0, or R3. Example 5-43 displays R2's IP routing table.

Example 5-43 *R2's IP Routing Table*

```
R2#show ip route
D     10.0.0.0/8 [90/20537600] via 131.108.1.22, 00:02:15, Serial1/0
      131.108.0.0/16 is variably subnetted, 3 subnets, 2 masks
C        131.108.1.0/28 is directly connected, Ethernet0/0
C        131.108.1.20/30 is directly connected, Serial1/0
D        131.108.1.16/30 [90/20537600] via 131.108.1.1, 00:02:16, Ethernet0/0
```

R2 also has two remote EIGRP routes: one pointing to the remote network 131.108.1.20/30
(the serial link between R1 and R3) and the entire Class A network 10.0.0.0 through R4.
Therefore, Routers R1 and R2 do not contain more specific routing entries for the 10.0.0.0
network.

EIGRP, by default, automatically summarizes at the network boundary for any IP networks
not locally configured. Because R1 and R2 do not have any interfaces configured in the
Class A address 10.0.0.0, both routers assume the default Class A mask of 255.0.0.0.

You can turn this feature off with the **no auto-summary** command under the EIGRP
routing process. Disable automatic summarization on R1 and R2. Example 5-44 displays
the disabling of automatic summarization on R1 and R2.

Example 5-44 *Disabling Auto Summary on R1 and R2*

```
R1(config)#router eigrp 1
R1(config-router)#no auto-summary

R2(config)#router eigrp 1
R2(config-router)#no auto-summary
```

Example 5-45 displays the IP routing table on R1.

Example 5-45 *R1's EIGRP IP Routing Table*

```
R1#show ip route eigrp
D     10.0.0.0/8 [90/20537600] via 131.108.1.18, 00:00:24, Serial0/0
      131.108.0.0/16 is variably subnetted, 3 subnets, 2 masks
D        131.108.1.20/30 [90/20537600] via 131.108.1.2, 00:00:24, Ethernet0/0
```

R1 still assumes the entire Class A network is through R3 because even after you disable automatic summarization, you must still summarize on the edge routers: R3 and R4.

Summarize 10.1.1.0/25 on R3 and 10.1.1.128/25 on R4.

Example 5-46 displays the summary on R3.

Example 5-46 *Summary Configuration on R3*

```
R3(config)#interface serial 0
R3(config-if)#ip summary-address eigrp 1 10.1.1.0 255.255.255.128
```

Example 5-47 displays the summary on R4.

Example 5-47 *Summary Configuration on R4*

```
R4(config)#interface serial 0
R4(config-if)#ip summary-address eigrp 1 10.1.1.128 255.255.255.128
```

R3 and R4 send an update to R1 and R2.

Example 5-48 displays R1's IP routing table.

Example 5-48 *R1's IP Routing Table*

```
R1#show ip route
      10.0.0.0/8 is variably subnetted, 2 subnets, 2 masks
D        10.1.1.0/0 [90/20537600] via 131.108.1.18, 00:01:29, Serial0/0
D        10.1.1.128/25 [90/20563200] via 131.108.1.2, 00:02:07, Ethernet0/0
      131.108.0.0/16 is variably subnetted, 3 subnets, 2 masks
C        131.108.1.0/28 is directly connected, Ethernet0/0
D        131.108.1.20/30 [90/20537600] via 131.108.1.2, 00:04:46, Ethernet0/0
C        131.108.1.16/30 is directly connected, Serial0/0
```

Example 5-49, for completeness, displays R2's IP routing table.

Example 5-49 *R2's IP Routing Table*

```
R2#show ip route
     10.0.0.0/8 is variably subnetted, 2 subnets, 2 masks
D        10.1.1.0/0 [90/20537600] via 131.108.1.1, 00:02:00, Ethernet0/0
D        10.1.1.128/25 [90/20537600] via 131.108.1.22, 00:03:17, Serial1/0
     131.108.0.0/16 is variably subnetted, 3 subnets, 2 masks
C        131.108.1.0/28 is directly connected, Ethernet0/0
C        131.108.1.20/30 is directly connected, Serial1/0
D        131.108.1.16/30 [90/20537600] via 131.108.1.1, 00:06:06, Ethernet0/0
```

EIGRP supports VLSM, and you have just seen how careful you must be when using EIGRP as your IP routing protocol. EIGRP supports VLSM as all IP routing updates do, when configured appropriately, and sends the subnet mask along with the network information.

Example 5-50 displays R1's full working configuration.

Example 5-50 *R1's Full Working Configuration*

```
hostname R1
!
logging buffered 64000 debugging
enable password cisco
!
ip subnet-zero
no ip domain-lookup
interface Ethernet0/0
 ip address 131.108.1.1 255.255.255.240
!
interface Serial0/0
 bandwidth 128
 ip address 131.108.1.17 255.255.255.252
 clockrate 125000
!
interface Serial0/1
 shutdown
!
router eigrp 1
 network 131.108.0.0
 no auto-summary
!
line con 0
line aux 0
line vty 0 4
end
```

Example 5-51 displays R2's full working configuration.

Example 5-51 *R2's Full Working Configuration*

```
hostname R2
!
enable password cisco
!
ip subnet-zero
no ip domain-lookup
!
interface Ethernet0/0
 ip address 131.108.1.2 255.255.255.240
!
interface Serial1/0
 bandwidth 128
 ip address 131.108.1.21 255.255.255.252
 clockrate 128000
!
interface Serial1/1
shutdown
!
interface Serial1/2
 shutdown!
interface Serial1/3
 shutdown
!
router eigrp 1
 network 131.108.0.0
 no auto-summary
line con 0
line aux 0
line vty 0 4
!
end
```

Example 5-52 displays R3's full working configuration.

Example 5-52 *R3's Full Working Configuration*

```
hostname R3
!
enable password cisco
!
no ip domain-lookup
!
interface Ethernet0
 ip address 10.1.1.1 255.255.255.128
!
interface Serial0
 ip address 131.108.1.18 255.255.255.252
```

Example 5-52 *R3's Full Working Configuration*

```
 ip summary-address eigrp 1 10.1.1.0 255.255.255.128
 bandwidth 125
!
interface Serial1
 shutdown
interface Serial2
shutdown
interface Serial3
 shutdown
!
router eigrp 1
 network 131.108.0.0
 network 10.0.0.0
!
line con 0
line aux 0
line vty 0 4
!
end
```

Example 5-53 displays R4's full working configuration.

Example 5-53 *R4's Full Working Configuration*

```
hostname R4
!
enable password cisco
!
ip subnet-zero
no ip domain-lookup
interface Ethernet0
 ip address 10.1.1.129 255.255.255.128
interface Serial0
 bandwidth 125
 ip address 131.108.1.22 255.255.255.252
 ip summary-address eigrp 1 10.1.1.128 255.255.255.128
!
interface Serial1
shutdown
interface Serial2
shutdown
interface Serial3
shutdown
!
router eigrp 1
 network 10.0.0.0
 network 131.108.0.0
```

continues

Example 5-53 *R4's Full Working Configuration*

```
!
line con 0
line aux 0
line vty 0 4
end
```

Scenario 5-4: Configuring Advanced EIGRP and Redistribution

In this scenario, you configure a network composed of six Cisco routers running a combination of IP routing protocols, namely EIGRP in AS 1, IGRP in AS 10, and OSPF, as displayed in Figure 5-5.

Figure 5-5   *IP Routing Topology Using EIGRP, IGRP, and OSPF*

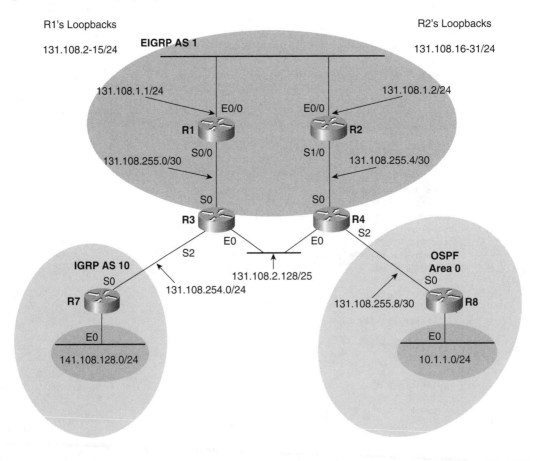

NOTE	The IGRP domain is configured with a Class C mask everywhere because IGRP does not support VLSM.

The Class B network, 131.108.0.0, is present on all routers. The Class A network resides in OSPF area 0. Finally, the Class B address, 141.108.0.0, is located in IGRP AS 10. R3 and R4 need to have redistribution configured among the different routing domains.

Router R3 needs to run EIGRP in AS 1 and IGRP 10. R3 must ensure that EIGRP updates are sent to interfaces E0 and Serial 0 only, and because you are using the same Class B address, you must make the interfaces not in IGRP AS 10 passive. The same condition applies to the IGRP process; you should also make interfaces not in IGRP 10 passive. There is no reason to send EIGRP updates, for example, to R7 and waste CPU and WAN bandwidth because R7 is configured for IGRP only. The classful behavior of IGRP and EIGRP means you must be careful when using the same class network among different routing domains.

Start by configuring R3.

Example 5-54 displays the EIGRP and IGRP configuration on R3.

Example 5-54 *EIGRP and IGRP Configuration on R3*

```
R3(config)#router eigrp 1
R3(config-router)#network 131.108.0.0
R3(config-router)#passive-interface serial 2

R3(config)#router igrp 10
R3(config-router)#network 131.108.0.0
R3(config-router)#passive-interface ethernet 0
R3(config-router)#passive-interface serial 0
```

As yet, you have not configured any redistribution on R3. Configure redistribution between EIGRP and IGRP (both ways) on R3.

Example 5-55 displays how to configure redistribution from IGRP to EIGRP. Even though the metric used by IGRP and EIGRP is the same, you must still advise EIGRP of the metric values because the AS numbers are different.

Example 5-55 *Redistribution on R3*

```
R3(config)#router igrp 10
R3(config-router)#redistribute eigrp 1 ?
  metric     Metric for redistributed routes
  route-map  Route map reference
  <cr>
```

continues

Example 5-55 *Redistribution on R3 (Continued)*

```
R3(config-router)#redistribute eigrp 1 metric ?
  <1-4294967295>  IGRP bandwidth metric in kilobits per second
R3(config-router)#redistribute eigrp 1 metric 128 ?
  <0-4294967295>  IGRP delay metric, in 10 microsecond units
R3(config-router)#redistribute eigrp 1 metric 128 20000 ?
  <0-255>  IGRP reliability metric where 255 is 100% reliable
R3(config-router)#redistribute eigrp 1 metric 128 20000 255 ?
  <1-255>  IGRP Effective bandwidth metric (Loading) where 255 is 100% loaded
R3(config-router)#redistribute eigrp 1 metric 128 20000 255 1 255
```

Example 5-56 displays redistribution from EIGRP to IGRP.

Example 5-56 *Redistributing EIGRP into IGRP on R3*

```
R3(config-router)#redistribute eigrp 1 ?
  metric     Metric for redistributed routes
  route-map  Route map reference
  <cr>
R3(config-router)#redistribute eigrp 1 metric ?
  <1-4294967295>  IGRP bandwidth metric in kilobits per second
R3(config-router)#redistribute eigrp 1 metric 128 ?
  <0-4294967295>  IGRP delay metric, in 10 microsecond units
R3(config-router)#redistribute eigrp 1 metric 128 20000 ?
  <0-255>  IGRP reliability metric where 255 is 100% reliable
R3(config-router)#redistribute eigrp 1 metric 128 20000 255 ?
  <1-255>  IGRP Effective bandwidth metric (Loading) where 255 is 100% loaded
R3(config-router)#redistribute eigrp 1 metric 128 20000 255 1 ?
  <1-4294967295>  IGRP MTU of the path
R3(config-router)#redistribute eigrp 1 metric 128 20000 255 1 1500
```

Next, examine R7's IP routing table to see whether the EIGRP networks are installed.

Example 5-57 displays R7's IP routing table.

Example 5-57 show ip route *on R7*

```
R7#show ip route
     141.108.0.0/24 is subnetted, 1 subnets
C       141.108.128.0 is directly connected, Ethernet0
     131.108.0.0/24 is subnetted, 2 subnets
C       131.108.254.0 is directly connected, Serial0
I       131.108.1.0 [100/84100] via 131.108.254.1, 00:00:05, Serial0
```

R7 IGRP entries are only those networks that are classful or Class C because the directly connected serial interface to R3 is a Class C mask. Those networks in the EIGRP domain that are not Class C networks, such as the Serial link between R1 and R2 (/30) or the Ethernet segment between R3 and R4 (/25), are not present in R7's routing table.

You can use static routes on R7 to correctly identify the networks in the EIGRP domain. (You have yet to learn how to configure static routes; static routes are covered in Chapters 6, "Basic Border Gateway Protocol.") Example 5-58 displays the static IP routing configuration on R7 pointing to the remote networks 131.108.2.128/25 and 131.108.255.0/30 networks. The variably subnetted network, 131.108.2.128/25, is not present on R7's IP (IGRP) routing table because IGRP does not support VLSM. You can use static routes to overcome this limitation because static router have a more trusted administrative distance of 1.

Example 5-58 *Static Route Configuration on R7*

```
R7(config)#ip route 131.108.2.128 255.255.255.128 Serial0
R7(config)#ip route 131.108.255.0 255.255.255.252 Serial0
R7(config)#ip route 131.108.255.4 255.255.255.252 Serial0
R7(config)#ip route 131.108.255.8 255.255.255.252 Serial0
```

Example 5-59 displays R7's routing table along with some successful pings to the non-Class C networks.

Example 5-59 *R7's IP Routing Table and Ping Requests*

```
R7#show ip route
     141.108.0.0/24 is subnetted, 1 subnets
C       141.108.128.0 is directly connected, Ethernet0
     131.108.0.0/16 is variably subnetted, 6 subnets, 3 masks
S       131.108.255.0/30 is directly connected, Serial0
C       131.108.254.0/24 is directly connected, Serial0
S       131.108.255.4/30 is directly connected, Serial0
S       131.108.255.8/30 is directly connected, Serial0
S       131.108.2.128/25 is directly connected, Serial0
I       131.108.1.0/24 [100/84100] via 131.108.254.1, 00:00:57, Serial0
R7#ping 131.108.255.5
Type escape sequence to abort.
Sending 5, 100-byte ICMP Echos to 131.108.255.5, timeout is 2 seconds:
!!!!!
Success rate is 100 percent (5/5), round-trip min/avg/max = 28/32/36 ms
R7#ping 131.108.255.6
Type escape sequence to abort.
Sending 5, 100-byte ICMP Echos to 131.108.255.6, timeout is 2 seconds:
!!!!!
Success rate is 100 percent (5/5), round-trip min/avg/max = 16/16/20 ms
R7#ping 131.108.255.9
Type escape sequence to abort.
Sending 5, 100-byte ICMP Echos to 131.108.255.9, timeout is 2 seconds:
!!!!!
```

Configure R4 for redistribution because R4 is attached to the EIGRP 1 domain and OSPF. Once more, you need to make any interfaces not required in the EIGRP domain passive. Example 5-60 displays the redistribution from OSPF into EIGRP 1.

Example 5-60 *Redistribution on R4 from OSPF to EIGRP*

```
R4(config)#router eigrp 1
R4(config-router)#passive-interface s2
R4(config-router)#redistribute ospf 1 metric ?
  <1-4294967295>  Bandwidth metric in Kbits per second
R4(config-router)#redistribute ospf 1 metric 128 ?
  <0-4294967295>  IGRP delay metric, in 10 microsecond units
R4(config-router)#redistribute ospf 1 metric 128 20000 ?
  <0-255>  IGRP reliability metric where 255 is 100% reliable
R4(config-router)#redistribute ospf 1 metric 128 20000 255 ?
  <1-255>  IGRP Effective bandwidth metric (Loading) where 255 is 100% loaded
R4(config-router)#redistribute ospf 1 metric 128 20000 255 1 ?
  <1-4294967295>  IGRP MTU of the path
R4(config-router)#redistribute ospf 1 metric 128 20000 255 1 1500
```

Example 5-61 displays the redistribution from EIGRP into OSPF. Remember, EIGRP domains have subnetted networks, so you must apply the keyword **subnets** when redistributing from EIGRP to OSPF.

Example 5-61 *Redistribution from EIGRP to OSPF on R4*

```
R4(config-router)#router ospf 1
R4(config-router)#redistribute eigrp ?
  <1-65535>  Autonomous system number
R4(config-router)#redistribute eigrp 1 ?
  metric       Metric for redistributed routes
  metric-type  OSPF/IS-IS exterior metric type for redistributed routes
  route-map    Route map reference
  subnets      Consider subnets for redistribution into OSPF
  tag          Set tag for routes redistributed into OSPF
  <cr>
R4(config-router)#redistribute eigrp 1 metric 100 ?
  metric       Metric for redistributed routes
  metric-type  OSPF/IS-IS exterior metric type for redistributed routes
  route-map    Route map reference
  subnets      Consider subnets for redistribution into OSPF
  tag          Set tag for routes redistributed into OSPF
  <cr>
R4(config-router)#redistribute eigrp 1 metric 100 subnets
```

View the IP routing table on R1 in EIGRP 1 to ensure that R1 has a path to every network in this topology.

Example 5-62 displays R1's IP routing table.

Example 5-62 *R1's IP Routing Table*

```
R1>sh ip route
Codes: C - connected      D - EIGRP, EX - EIGRP external,
D EX 141.108.0.0/16 [170/21529600] via 131.108.255.2, 00:19:05, Serial0/0
D    10.0.0.0/8 [90/25657600] via 131.108.255.2, 00:08:30, Serial0/0
                [90/25657600] via 131.108.1.2, 00:08:30, Ethernet0/0
     131.108.0.0/16 is variably subnetted, 6 subnets, 3 masks
D       131.108.254.0/24 [90/21504000] via 131.108.255.2, 00:19:06, Serial0/0
D       131.108.255.4/30 [90/20537600] via 131.108.1.2, 00:19:06, Ethernet0/0
D       131.108.255.8/30 [90/21529600] via 131.108.1.2, 00:19:06, Ethernet0/0
                         [90/21529600] via 131.108.255.2, 00:19:06, Serial0/0
D       131.108.2.128/25 [90/20537600] via 131.108.255.2, 00:19:06, Serial0/0
C       131.108.1.0/24 is directly connected, Ethernet0/0
C       131.108.255.0/30 is directly connected, Serial0/0
```

R1 has an IP routing entry for all EIGRP networks in AS 1, as well as the external EIGRP network routing from OSPF and IGRP.

To confirm network connectivity, ping from R1 to all the remote networks.

Example 5-63 displays a ping request and reply from R1 to all the remote networks in Figure 5-5.

Example 5-63 *Sample Ping Request from R1*

```
R1>ping 141.108.128.1
Type escape sequence to abort.
Sending 5, 100-byte ICMP Echos to 141.108.128.1, timeout is 2 seconds:
!!!!!
Success rate is 100 percent (5/5), round-trip min/avg/max = 28/31/32 ms
R1>ping 10.1.1.1
Type escape sequence to abort.
Sending 5, 100-byte ICMP Echos to 10.1.1.1, timeout is 2 seconds:
!!!!!
Success rate is 100 percent (5/5), round-trip min/avg/max = 32/33/36 ms
R1>ping 131.108.255.1
Type escape sequence to abort.
Sending 5, 100-byte ICMP Echos to 131.108.255.1, timeout is 2 seconds:
!!!!!
Success rate is 100 percent (5/5), round-trip min/avg/max = 28/30/32 ms
R1>ping 131.108.255.9
Type escape sequence to abort.
Sending 5, 100-byte ICMP Echos to 131.108.255.9, timeout is 2 seconds:
```

continues

Example 5-63 *Sample Ping Request from R1 (Continued)*

```
!!!!!
Success rate is 100 percent (5/5), round-trip min/avg/max = 16/16/16 ms
R1>ping 131.108.2.129
Type escape sequence to abort.
Sending 5, 100-byte ICMP Echos to 131.108.2.129, timeout is 2 seconds:
!!!!!
Success rate is 100 percent (5/5), round-trip min/avg/max = 16/16/16 ms
```

You have just configured a complex network with three different IP routing protocols and have successfully enabled network IP connectivity among all routers.

Example 5-64 provides the full working configuration of R1.

Example 5-64 **show running-config** *on R1*

```
hostname R1
!
logging buffered 64000 debugging
enable password cisco
!
ip subnet-zero
no ip domain-lookup
!
interface Ethernet0/0
 ip address 131.108.1.1 255.255.255.0
!
interface Serial0/0
 bandwidth 125
 ip address 131.108.255.1 255.255.255.252
 clockrate 125000
!
interface Serial0/1
 shutdown
!
router eigrp 1
 network 131.108.0.0
line con 0
line aux 0
line vty 0 4
!
end
```

Example 5-65 provides the full working configuration of R2.

Example 5-65 show running-config *on R2*

```
hostname R2
!
enable password cisco
!
ip subnet-zero
no ip domain-lookup
interface Ethernet0/0
 ip address 131.108.1.2 255.255.255.0
!
interface Serial1/0
 bandwidth 128
 ip address 131.108.255.5 255.255.255.252
 clockrate 128000
!
interface Serial1/1
 shutdown
!
router eigrp 1
 network 131.108.0.0
line con 0
line aux 0
line vty 0 4
end
```

Example 5-66 provides the full working configuration of R3.

Example 5-66 show running-config *on R3*

```
hostname R3
!
enable password cisco
!
no ip domain-lookup
!
interface Ethernet0
 ip address 131.108.2.129 255.255.255.128
!
interface Serial0
 ip address 131.108.255.2 255.255.255.252
 bandwidth 125
!
interface Serial1
shutdown
```

continues

Example 5-66 show running-config *on R3 (Continued)*

```
!
interface Serial2
 ip address 131.108.254.1 255.255.255.0
 bandwidth 125
 clockrate 125000
!
interface Serial3
 shutdown
!
router eigrp 1
 redistribute igrp 10 metric 128 20000 255 1 255
 passive-interface Serial2
 network 131.108.0.0
!
router igrp 10
 redistribute eigrp 1 metric 128 20000 255 1 1500
 passive-interface Ethernet0
 passive-interface Serial0
 network 131.108.0.0
!
line con 0
line aux 0
line vty 0 4
end
```

Example 5-67 provides the full working configuration of R4.

Example 5-67 show running-config *on R4*

```
hostname R4
!
enable password cisco
ip subnet-zero
no ip domain-lookup
interface Ethernet0
 ip address 131.108.2.130 255.255.255.128
interface Serial0
shutdown
!
interface Serial1
shutdown
!
interface Serial2
 bandwidth 125
 ip address 131.108.255.9 255.255.255.252
 clockrate 125000
!
interface Serial3
 shutdown
```

Example 5-67 show running-config *on R4 (Continued)*

```
!
router eigrp 1
  redistribute ospf 1 metric 128 20000 255 1 1500
  passive-interface Serial2
  network 131.108.0.0
!
router ospf 1
  redistribute eigrp 1 metric 100 subnets
  network 131.108.255.8 0.0.0.3 area 0
line con 0
line aux 0
line vty 0 4
end
```

Example 5-68 provides the full working configuration of R7.

Example 5-68 show running-config *on R7*

```
hostname R7
!
enable password cisco
!
ip subnet-zero
no ip domain-lookup
!
interface Ethernet0
  ip address 141.108.128.1 255.255.255.0
!
interface Serial0
  bandwidth 125
  ip address 131.108.254.2 255.255.255.0
!
interface Serial1
  shutdown
!
router igrp 10
  network 131.108.0.0
  network 141.108.0.0
!
ip route 131.108.2.128 255.255.255.128 Serial0
ip route 131.108.255.0 255.255.255.252 Serial0
ip route 131.108.255.4 255.255.255.252 Serial0
ip route 131.108.255.8 255.255.255.252 Serial0
!
line con 0
line aux 0
line vty 0 4
end
```

Example 5-69 provides the full working configuration of R8.

Example 5-69 **show running-config** *on R8*

```
hostname R8
enable password cisco
!
ip subnet-zero
no ip domain-lookup
!
interface Ethernet0
 ip address 10.1.1.1 255.255.255.0
!
interface Serial0
 bandwidth 125
 ip address 131.108.255.10 255.255.255.252
interface Serial1
 shutdown
!
router ospf 1
 network 10.1.1.0 0.0.0.255 area 0
 network 131.108.255.8 0.0.0.3 area 0
!
line con 0
line aux 0
line vty 0 4
!
end
```

Scenario 5-5: Verifying EIGRP Configuration

This final scenario looks at ways the Cisco IOS enables you to monitor and verify EIGRP IP routing within a Cisco router network.

This scenario uses the network in Figure 5-5 to demonstrate some common **show** commands that verify that EIGRP is operating correctly.

Properly using **show** and **debug** commands can be valuable, not only in the real-life networks you will come across but also on your certification exams—particularly when you take the next step in your career and try for CCIE certification.

This scenario covers the following **show** commands:

- **show ip eigrp neighbors**—Displays EIGRP neighbors
- **show ip eigrp topology**—Displays the topology table
- **show ip eigrp interfaces**—Displays interfaces in which EIGRP is sent and received
- **show ip eigrp traffic**—Displays the number of EIGRP packets sent and received

Example 5-70 displays the use of the **show ip eigrp neighbor** taken from R1.

NOTE	This scenario uses the network in Figure 5-5 (the one you configured in Scenario 5-4) to demonstrate these commands.

Example 5-70 show ip eigrp neighbors *Command on R1*

```
R1>show ip eigrp neighbors
IP-EIGRP neighbors for process 1
H   Address             Interface   Hold Uptime   SRTT   RTO   Q   Seq
                                    (sec)         (ms)         Cnt Num
1   131.108.255.2       Se0/0         14 00:48:21   14  1140   0   558
0   131.108.1.2         Et0/0         10 01:22:13    1   200   0   337
```

Example 5-70 shows that R1 has two remote EIGRP neighbors: one through Serial 0/0 and another through Ethernet 0/0. The EIGRP process is also identified as 1.

Example 5-71 displays the topology table with the **show ip eigrp topology** command.

Example 5-71 show ip eigrp topology *Command on R1*

```
R1>sh ip eigrp topology
IP-EIGRP Topology Table for process 1
Codes: P - Passive, A - Active, U - Update, Q - Query, R - Reply,
       r - Reply status
P 10.0.0.0/8, 2 successors, FD is 25657600
        via 131.108.255.2 (25657600/25145600), Serial0/0
        via 131.108.1.2 (25657600/25632000), Ethernet0/0
P 131.108.255.0/30, 1 successors, FD is 20512000
        via Connected, Serial0/0
P 131.108.254.0/24, 1 successors, FD is 21504000
        via 131.108.255.2 (21504000/20992000), Serial0/0
P 131.108.255.4/30, 1 successors, FD is 20537600
        via 131.108.1.2 (20537600/20512000), Ethernet0/0
P 131.108.255.8/30, 2 successors, FD is 21529600
        via 131.108.255.2 (21529600/21017600), Serial0/0
        via 131.108.1.2 (21529600/21504000), Ethernet0/0
P 131.108.2.128/25, 1 successors, FD is 20537600
        via 131.108.255.2 (20537600/281600), Serial0/0
P 141.108.0.0/16, 1 successors, FD is 21529600
        via 131.108.255.2 (21529600/21017600), Serial0/0
P 131.108.1.0/24, 1 successors, FD is 281600
        via Connected, Ethernet0/0
```

The table in Example 5-71 contains a wealth of information. The P on the left side indicates that remote networks are passive and routable. Any active entry (displayed as A) should concern you if any entries remain active or stuck in active (SIA). A remote entry in an active state (SIA) results in a loss of network connectivity because EIGRP is querying the remote EIGRP neighbors about the path to the remote network in question. Because a reply has not been received, the EIGRP topology table installs the remote network in an active state.

Example 5-72 displays sample output from R1 with the **show ip eigrp interfaces** command.

Example 5-72 **show ip eigrp interfaces** *Command*

```
R1>show ip eigrp interfaces
IP-EIGRP interfaces for process 1
                    Xmit Queue   Mean   Pacing Time   Multicast    Pending
Interface   Peers  Un/Reliable  SRTT   Un/Reliable   Flow Timer   Routes
Et0/0         1       0/0         1        0/10          50          0
Se0/0         1       0/0        14        5/190        250          0
```

This command is extremely useful when you are trying to explain why neighbors are not adjacent. The output in Example 5-72 displays two interfaces running EIGRP in AS 1 and one peer per interface, namely to R2 through Ethernet 0/0 and R3 through Serial 0/0.

Example 5-73 displays the output from the **show ip eigrp traffic** command.

Example 5-73 **show ip eigrp traffic** *Command*

```
R1>show ip eigrp traffic
IP-EIGRP Traffic Statistics for process 1
  Hellos sent/received: 387565/387575
  Updates sent/received: 545/219
  Queries sent/received: 98/47
  Replies sent/received: 47/84
  Acks sent/received: 283/265
```

The **traffic** commands summarize the number of hello packets R1 receives and sends. **Traffic** commands show how many updates, queries, replies, and acknowledges R1 uses to ensure that EIGRP is running correctly and with adjacent EIGRP routers. With every version of IOS, there are always new commands and changes in IOS displays. Use the **?** tool to view all your options. Example 5-74 displays the **debug** commands possible with EIGRP on Cisco IOS running version 12-0.10-enterprise code. You must be in privilege mode to view the **debug** command set.

Example 5-74 **debug ip eigrp ?** *Command on R1*

```
R1#debug ip eigrp ?
  <1-65535>     AS number
  neighbor      IP-EIGRP neighbor debugging
  notifications IP-EIGRP event notifications
  summary       IP-EIGRP summary route processing
  <cr>
```

For a comprehensive list of EIGRP commands, visit the Cisco web site for free information at www.cisco.com/univercd/home/home.htm.

Practical Exercise: EIGRP

NOTE   Practical Exercises are designed to test your knowledge of the topics covered in this chapter. The Practical Exercise begins by giving you some information about a situation and then asks you to work through the solution on your own. The solution can be found at the end.

Configure the network in Figure 5-6 for EIGRP in autonomous system 1. Ensure that SanFran has all the remote entries being advertised by Router Sydney and the router in the RIP domain. Summarize wherever possible to reduce the IP routing table on the Router SanFran.

Figure 5-6   *EIGRP Network*

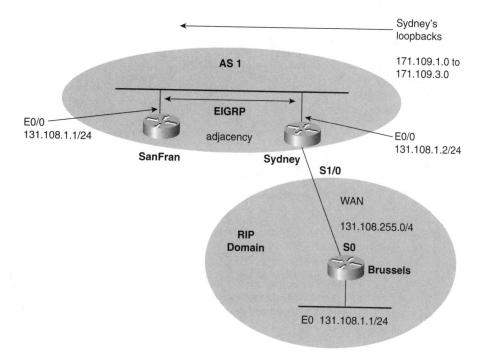

Practical Exercise Solution

All routers in this practical exercise use the same Class B network, namely 131.108.0.0/24.

The RIP network attached to Brussels shares the identical subnet in the EIGRP 1 domain. Therefore, to avoid a routing loop, any redistribution you configure on the Router Sydney has to ensure that these networks are not propagated. To stop EIGRP updates from being sent to the RIP domain, you must also use passive interfaces on Router Sydney. Likewise for RIP, you should make sure passive interfaces are not running RIP. You use route maps to ensure that networks are not advertised incorrectly. You can also use distribute lists.

For summarization, you can provide a summary in EIGRP AS 1 covering the networks 171.109.1.0–171.108.3.0 with the following command:

```
ip summary-address eigrp 1 171.109.0.0 255.255.252.0
```

Example 5-75 displays the configuration required on Router SanFran.

Example 5-75 *SanFran's Full Working Configuration*

```
hostname SanFran
!
ip subnet-zero
no ip domain-lookup
!
interface Ethernet0/0
 ip address 131.108.1.1 255.255.255.0
!
interface Serial0/0
shutdown
!
interface Serial0/1
shutdown
router eigrp 1
 network 131.108.0.0
 no auto-summary
!
line con 0
 line aux 0
line vty 0 4
end
```

Example 5-76 displays the configuration required on Router Sydney. To make the configuration a little more interesting, route maps have been applied to redistribution on Router Sydney. Route maps are covered in more detail in Chapters 6 and 7, "Advanced BGP."

Example 5-76 *Sydney's Full Working Configuration*

```
hostname Sydney
!
enable password cisco
!
ip subnet-zero
no ip domain-lookup
interface Loopback0
 ip address 171.109.1.1 255.255.255.0
!
interface Loopback1
 ip address 171.109.2.1 255.255.255.0
!
interface Loopback2
 ip address 171.109.3.1 255.255.255.0
interface Ethernet0/0
 ip address 131.108.1.2 255.255.255.0
 no ip directed-broadcast
 ip summary-address eigrp 1 171.109.0.0 255.255.252.0
!
interface Serial1/0
 bandwidth 128
 ip address 131.108.255.1 255.255.255.0
 clockrate 128000
!
router eigrp 1
 redistribute rip metric 128 20000 255 1 1500 route-map riptoeigrp
 passive-interface Serial1/0
 network 131.108.0.0
 network 171.109.0.0
 no auto-summary
!
router rip
 redistribute eigrp 1 metric 2 route-map eigrptorip
 passive-interface Ethernet0/0
 network 131.108.0.0
!
access-list 1 deny   131.108.1.0 0.0.0.255
access-list 1 permit any
route-map riptoeigrp permit 10
 match ip address 1
!
route-map eigrptorip permit 10
 match ip address 1
line con 0
line aux 0
line vty 0 4
end
```

Example 5-77 displays the configuration required on Router Brussels.

Example 5-77 *Brussels' Full Working Configuration*

```
hostname Brussels
!
enable password cisco
ip subnet-zero
no ip domain-lookup
interface Ethernet0
 ip address 131.108.1.1 255.255.255.0
 !
interface Serial0
 bandwidth 125
 ip address 131.108.255.2 255.255.255.0
router rip
 network 131.108.0.0
 !
line con 0
line aux 0
line vty 0 4
end
```

Example 5-78 displays SanFran's IP routing table, which shows the remote RIP link and the summary address advertised by Router Sydney.

Example 5-78 show ip route *Command on SanFran*

```
SanFran#show ip route

     171.109.0.0/22 is subnetted, 1 subnets
D       171.109.0.0 [90/409600] via 131.108.1.2, 00:05:41, Ethernet0/0
     131.108.0.0/24 is subnetted, 2 subnets
D       131.108.255.0 [90/20537600] via 131.108.1.2, 00:05:41, Ethernet0/0
C       131.108.1.0 is directly connected, Ethernet0/0
```

Review Questions

The following questions are based on material covered in this chapter. Examples 5-79 and 5-80 are from the previous Practical Exercise. Refer to the examples to answer the first question.

The answers to these questions can be found in Appendix C, "Answers to Review Questions."

Example 5-79 displays the detailed paths to the three remote networks, 171.109.1.0, 171.109.2.0 and 171.109.3.0/24, as seen by Router SanFran along with a successful **ping** to the remote networks.

Example 5-79 show ip route *and* ping *on SanFran*

```
SanFran#show ip route 171.109.1.0
Routing entry for 171.109.0.0/22
  Known via "eigrp 1", distance 90, metric 409600, type internal
  Redistributing via eigrp 1
  Last update from 131.108.1.2 on Ethernet0/0, 00:13:26 ago
  Routing Descriptor Blocks:
  * 131.108.1.2, from 131.108.1.2, 00:13:26 ago, via Ethernet0/0
      Route metric is 409600, traffic share count is 1
      Total delay is 6000 microseconds, minimum bandwidth is 10000 Kbit
      Reliability 255/255, minimum MTU 1500 bytes
      Loading 1/255, Hops 1
SanFran#ping 171.109.1.1
Type escape sequence to abort.
Sending 5, 100-byte ICMP Echos to 171.109.1.1, timeout is 2 seconds:
!!!!!
Success rate is 100 percent (5/5), round-trip min/avg/max = 1/2/4 ms
SanFran#show ip route 171.109.2.0
Routing entry for 171.109.0.0/22
  Known via "eigrp 1", distance 90, metric 409600, type internal
  Redistributing via eigrp 1
  Last update from 131.108.1.2 on Ethernet0/0, 00:13:32 ago
  Routing Descriptor Blocks:
  * 131.108.1.2, from 131.108.1.2, 00:13:32 ago, via Ethernet0/0
      Route metric is 409600, traffic share count is 1
      Total delay is 6000 microseconds, minimum bandwidth is 10000 Kbit
      Reliability 255/255, minimum MTU 1500 bytes
      Loading 1/255, Hops 1
SanFran#ping 171.109.2.1
Type escape sequence to abort.
Sending 5, 100-byte ICMP Echos to 171.109.2.1, timeout is 2 seconds:
!!!!!
Success rate is 100 percent (5/5), round-trip min/avg/max = 1/2/4 ms
SanFran#show ip route 171.109.3.0
Routing entry for 171.109.0.0/22
  Known via "eigrp 1", distance 90, metric 409600, type internal
  Redistributing via eigrp 1
  Last update from 131.108.1.2 on Ethernet0/0, 00:13:38 ago
  Routing Descriptor Blocks:
  * 131.108.1.2, from 131.108.1.2, 00:13:38 ago, via Ethernet0/0
      Route metric is 409600, traffic share count is 1
      Total delay is 6000 microseconds, minimum bandwidth is 10000 Kbit
      Reliability 255/255, minimum MTU 1500 bytes
      Loading 1/255, Hops 1
SanFran#ping 171.109.3.1
Type escape sequence to abort.
Sending 5, 100-byte ICMP Echos to 171.109.3.1, timeout is 2 seconds:
!!!!!
Success rate is 100 percent (5/5), round-trip min/avg/max = 1/3/4 ms
```

If you perform a **show ip route** to the network 171.109.4.0/24 on SanFran, you see the output displayed in Example 5-80.

Example 5-80 **show ip route 171.109.4.0** *on SanFran*

```
SanFran#show ip route 171.109.4.0
% Subnet not in table
```

The reason that subnet 4 is not included in the IP routing table is that the summary address configured on Router Sydney includes only the subnets 1, 2, and 3.

1 Example 5-79 displays the IP routing table of the Router SanFran. Which networks does the entry 171.109.0.0/22 embrace?

2 What is the default administrative distance for EIGRP internal routes?

3 Which IOS command is used to display the output in Example 5-81?

Example 5-81 *Neighbors Output*

```
IP-EIGRP neighbors for process 1
H   Address            Interface    Hold Uptime   SRTT   RTO  Q  Seq
                                    (sec)         (ms)       Cnt Num
0   131.108.1.2        Et0/0          11 00:18:37    4   200  0  353
```

4 Why does EIGRP need to be manually configured to redistribute into another autonomous system?

5 When is the EIGRP topology table updated?

6 What is the purpose of the command **no auto-summary**?

7 What is the **variance** command used for?

8 What does the term Stuck in Active mean?

Summary

Although EIGRP is not an industry standard across routing vendors, it is a potentially useful protocol for routing IP.

EIGRP terminology and the fundamental operation of EIGRP is covered in this chapter, along with some detailed configurations, showing how EIGRP interacts with other classful and classless routing algorithms. Summarization is described to demonstrate the powerful nature of EIGRP and its capability to take advantage of VLSM to optimize IP address space usage across small or large IP networks.

Table 5-4 summarizes the most useful commands from this chapter.

Table 5-4 *Summary of IOS Commands*

Command	Purpose
router eigrp *autonomous system*	Enables EIGRP routing under a common administrative control known as the autonomous domain (AD)
network *network*	Enables EIGRP on a router interface
no auto-summary	Disables automatic network summarization
ip summary-address eigrp *AS address mask*	Manual network summary command
bandwidth *link speed*	Configures actual bandwidth on a WAN interface
variance *multiplier*	Allows EIGRP to load balance across unequal paths
show ip eigrp neighbors	Displays EIGRP neighbors
show ip eigrp topology	Displays the EIGRP topology table
show ip eigrp traffic	Shows EIGRP traffic on the router

CHAPTER 6

Basic Border Gateway Protocol

This chapter focuses on Border Gateway Protocol Version 4 (BGP4). BGP4 is covered only slightly in the CCNP routing examination. However, this chapter covers BGP4 in a little more detail to ensure that you have a good appreciation of the way networks connect to the Internet or in large organizations.

This chapter covers the basics of Border Gateway Protocol (BGP). Chapter 7, "Advanced BGP," covers more advanced BGP topics and scenarios. This chapter contains five practical scenarios to complete your understanding of basic BGP and to help you appreciate the complexity of BGP.

Basic Border Gateway Protocol (BGP4) Defined

The different versions of BGP range from 1–4; the industry standard is Version 4. You can, however, configure BGP Versions 2, 3, and 4 on a Cisco IOS router. The default standard is BGP Version 4 and is referred to as BGP4.

BGP4 is defined in industry standard RFC 1771. BGP enables you to create an IP network free of routing loops among different *autonomous systems*. An AS is a set of routers under the same administrative control.

BGP is called a *path-vector protocol* because BGP carries a sequence of AS numbers that indicate the path taken to a remote network. This information is stored so that routing loops can be avoided.

BGP uses *Transmission Control Protocol (TCP)* as its Layer 4 protocol (TCP port number 179). No other routing protocol in use today relies on TCP. This allows TCP to ensure that updates are sent reliably, leaving the routing protocol to concentrate on gathering information about remote networks and ensuring a loop-free topology.

Routers configured for BGP are typically called *BGP speakers*, and any two BGP routers that form a BGP TCP sessions are called *BGP peers* or *BGP neighbors*.

BGP peers exchange full BGP routing tables initially. After that, only BGP updates are sent between peers, ensuring that only useful data is sent, unless a change occurs.

BGP4 uses the following four message types to ensure that peers are active and updates are sent:

- **Open messages**—These messages are used when establishing BGP peers.
- **Keepalives**—These messages are sent periodically to ensure that connections are still active or established.
- **Update messages**—Any change that occurs, such as a loss of network availability, results in an update message.
- **Notification**—These messages are used only to notify BGP peers of receiving errors.

The key characteristics of BGP include the following:

- BGP is termed a path vector protocol.
- BGP uses TCP as the transport layer protocol.
- Full routing tables are exchanged only during the initial BGP session.
- Updates are sent over TCP port 179.
- BGP sessions are maintained by keepalive messages.
- Any network changes result in update messages.
- BGP has its own BGP table. Any network entry must reside in the BGP table first.
- BGP has a complex array of metrics, called attributes, which include the next hop address and origin.
- BGP supports variable-length subnet masking (VLSM) and summarization (sometimes called classless interdomain routing [CIDR]).

The capability of BGP4 to guarantee routing delivery and the complexity of the routing decision process ensure that BGP will be widely used in any large IP routing environment, such as the Internet. The Internet consists of over 80,000 BGP network entries, and there is no doubt that only BGP can handle such a complex routing table.

Before you look at some simple examples, the following section describes the BGP attributes.

BGP Attributes

BGP has a number of complex attributes used to determine a path to a remote network. These attributes allow greater flexibility and enable a complex routing decision to ensure that the path to a remote network is the best possible path.

The network designer can also manipulate these attributes. BGP, when supplied with multiple paths to a remote network, always chooses a single path to a specific destination. (Load balancing is possible with static routes.) BGP always propagates the best path to any peers.

BGP attributes are carried in update packets.

Table 6-1 describes the well-known and optional attributes used in BGP4.

Table 6-1   *Well-Known and Optional BGP Attributes*

Attribute	Description
Origin	This attribute is mandatory and defines the origin of the path and can have three different values: <ul><li>IGP indicates the remote path originated from within the AS. Typically, when the **network** command or redistribution is configured, BGP installs the network with an origin set to IGP.</li><li>EBG means learned through an External Gateway Protocol.</li><li>Incomplete means the BGP route was discovered using redistribution or static routers.</li></ul>
AS_Path	This attribute describes the sequence of autonomous systems that the packet has traversed.
Next Hop	This attribute describes the next hop address taken to a remote path, typically the BGP peer.
Local Preference	This attribute indicates to the AS the preferred path to exit the AS. A higher local preference is always preferred.
MED	Multiexit Discriminator informs BGP peers in other autonomous systems which path to take to a remote network. A lower MED is always preferred.
Weight	This Cisco-only attribute is used in local router selection. Weight is not sent to other BGP peers, and a higher weight value is always preferred. The weight value is between 0–294967295.
Atomic	This attribute advises BGP routers that aggregation has taken place and is not used in the router-selection process.
Aggregator	This is the router ID responsible for aggregation and is not used in the router-selection process.
Community	Communities allow routes to be tagged for use with a group of routers sharing the same characteristics.
Originator ID	This attribute is used to prevent routing loops. This information is not used for router selection.
Cluster-List	This attribute is used in route-reflector environments. This information is not used for router selection.

Internal BGP (IBGP) and *External BGP (EBGP)* are the two types of BGP sessions. IBGP is a connection between two BGP speakers in the same AS. EBGP is a connection between two BGP speakers in different autonomous systems.

Figure 6-1 displays a simple three-router BGP topology and the different BGP connection types: IBGP and EBGP.

Figure 6-1   *IBGP and EBGP*

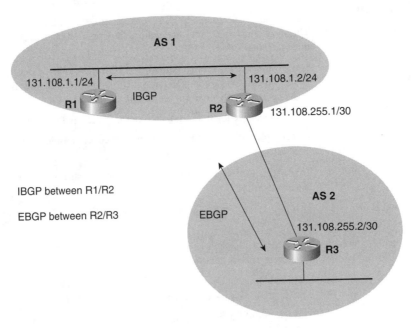

IBGP peers also make certain that routing loops cannot occur by ensuring that any routes sent to another AS are known through an interior routing protocol, such as Open Shortest Path First (OSPF), before sending the route information. In other words, the routers must be synchronized. The benefit of this additional rule in IBGP TCP sessions is that information is not sent unless the remote path is reachable, which reduces any unnecessary traffic, and, therefore, saves bandwidth. You can disable this feature with the **no synchronization** command, which is covered later in this chapter.

The BGP routing decision is quite complex and takes into account the attributes listed in Table 6-1.

The process a Cisco router running BGP4 takes is as follows:

Step 1   If the next hop address is reachable, consider it.

Step 2   Prefer the route with the highest weight (Cisco IOS routers only).

Step 3 If the weight is the same, prefer the largest local preference attribute.

Step 4 If the local preference is the same, prefer the route this local router originated.

Step 5 Prefer the route with the shortest AS path.

Step 6 If this is equal, prefer the route with the origin set to originated (through BGP); IGP is preferred to EGP followed by incomplete.

Step 7 If the origin codes are the same, prefer the route with the lowest MED.

Step 8 If the MED is the same, prefer EBGP over IBGP.

Step 9 Prefer the closest path.

Step 10 Finally, if all paths are equal, prefer the path with lowest BGP router ID.

Configuring BGP

To start BGP on a Cisco router, the following command is required:

```
router bgp autonomous system number
```

To define networks to be advertised, apply the following command:

```
network network-number mask network-mask
```

You must be aware that the **network** command is not used in the same way you use it when you apply networks in OSPF or EIGRP. With BGP, you use the **network** command to advertise networks that originate from the router and need to be advertised through BGP.

To identify peer routers, apply the following command:

```
neighbor ip-address | peer-group name remote-as autonomous system number
```

Next, you see how to configure IBGP and EBGP among the three routers in Figure 6-1. Example 6-1 displays the IBGP configuration on R1 to R2.

Example 6-1 *IBGP on R1*

```
R1(config)#router bgp ?
  <1-65535>  Autonomous system number
R1(config)#router bgp 1
R1(config-router)#neighbor 131.108.1.2 remote 1
```

Example 6-2 displays the IBGP configuration to R1 and EBGP configuration to R3.

Example 6-2 *IBGP/EBGP on R2*

```
R2(config)#router bgp 1
R2(config-router)#neighbor 131.108.1.1  remote-as 1
R2(config-router)#neighbor 131.108.255.2 remote-as 2
```

Finally, Example 6-3 displays the EBGP connection from R3 to R2.

Example 6-3 *EBGP on R3*

```
R3(config)#router bgp ?
  <1-65535>  Autonomous system number
R3(config)#router bgp 2
R3(config-router)#neighbor 131.108.255.1 remote-as 1
```

At this stage, because no **network** statements have been applied, no BGP entries are on any routers. Use some loopback interfaces on R1 and advertise them through BGP to R2 and R3.

Example 6-4 displays the three new loopback addresses on R1, ranging from 131.108.2.0 to 131.108.4.0.

Example 6-4 *Loopback Configuration on R1*

```
R1(config)#interface loopback 0
R1(config-if)#ip address 131.108.2.1 255.255.255.0
R1(config-if)#interface loopback 1
R1(config-if)#ip address 131.108.3.1 255.255.255.0
R1(config-if)#interface loopback 2
R1(config-if)#ip address 131.108.4.1 255.255.255.0
```

You must next advertise these loopbacks with the **network** command. Because these networks are local to R1 and present in R1's IP routing table as connected routes, you can apply the **network** command as displayed in Example 6-5.

Example 6-5 **network** *Command on R1*

```
R1(config)#router bgp 1
R1(config-router)#network 131.108.2.0 mask 255.255.255.0
R1(config-router)#network 131.108.3.0 mask 255.255.255.0
R1(config-router)#network 131.108.4.0 mask 255.255.255.0
```

Example 6-6 displays the BGP table on R1, using the command **show ip bgp**.

Example 6-6 **show ip bgp** *on R1*

```
R1#show ip bgp
BGP table version is 4, local router ID is 131.108.1.1
Status codes: s suppressed, d damped, h history, * valid, > best, i - internal
Origin codes: i - IGP, e - EGP, ? - incomplete

   Network          Next Hop         Metric LocPrf Weight Path
*> 131.108.2.0/24   0.0.0.0               0         32768 i
*> 131.108.3.0/24   0.0.0.0               0         32768 i
*> 131.108.4.0/24   0.0.0.0               0         32768 i
```

The BGP table on R1 displays three local networks (next hop is 0.0.0.0 or local interfaces). Example 6-6 also displays the path as i, or advertised through BGP. The local router ID is 131.108.1.1.

Example 6-7 displays the BGP table on R2.

Example 6-7   show ip bgp *on R2*

```
R2#show ip bgp
BGP table version is 7, local router ID is 171.109.3.1
Status codes: s suppressed, d damped, h history, * valid, > best, i - internal
Origin codes: i - IGP, e - EGP, ? - incomplete

   Network          Next Hop          Metric LocPrf Weight Path
*  i131.108.2.0/24  131.108.1.1            0    100      0 i
*  i131.108.3.0/24  131.108.1.1            0    100      0 i
*  i131.108.4.0/24  131.108.1.1            0    100      0 i
```

R2's local router is 131.108.1.2, and it learns the remote loopbacks on R1 through the next hop address 131.108.1.1, or R1's Ethernet interface. Notice that R2 has set the local preference to 100 (default value); the origin attribute is set to i or IGP.

Because R1 and R2 are running only IBGP and no other interior gateway protocol, R2's IP routing table does not have the BGP entries inserted because of synchronization. Example 6-8 confirms this with only the locally connected routes visible on R2.

Example 6-8   show ip route *on R2*

```
R2#show ip route
     131.108.0.0/24 is subnetted, 2 subnets
C       131.108.255.0 is directly connected, Serial1/0
C       131.108.1.0 is directly connected, Ethernet0/0
```

To enable BGP to insert the routes, you must disable synchronization or configure an IGP routing protocol. R2, in turn, does not propagate the loopbacks to R3; therefore, R3 does not have any entries at all, either in the BGP table or IP routing table.

Disable synchronization on R1 and R2. Example 6-9 displays the **no synchronization** command on R1 and R2.

Example 6-9   *Disabling Synchronization on R1/R2*

```
R1(config)#router bgp 1
R1(config-router)#no synchronization

R2(config)#router bgp 1
R2(config-router)#no synchronization
```

Example 6-10 displays R2's routing table.

Example 6-10 *R2's Routing Table*

```
R2#sh ip route
     131.108.0.0/24 is subnetted, 5 subnets
C       131.108.255.0 is directly connected, Serial1/0
B       131.108.4.0 [200/0] via 131.108.1.1, 00:00:43
B       131.108.3.0 [200/0] via 131.108.1.1, 00:00:43
B       131.108.2.0 [200/0] via 131.108.1.1, 00:00:43
C       131.108.1.0 is directly connected, Ethernet0/0
```

The three remote networks are inserted into the IP routing tables as BGP-learned networks.

Example 6-11 displays R3's BGP and IP routing table.

Example 6-11 *R3's BGP and IP Tables*

```
R3>show ip bgp
BGP table version is 10, local router ID is 131.108.255.2
Status codes: s suppressed, d damped, h history, * valid, > best, i - internal
Origin codes: i - IGP, e - EGP, ? - incomplete
   Network          Next Hop            Metric LocPrf Weight Path
*> 131.108.2.0/24   131.108.255.1                        0 1 i
*> 131.108.3.0/24   131.108.255.1                        0 1 i
*> 131.108.4.0/24   131.108.255.1                        0 1 i
R3>show ip route
     131.108.0.0/24 is subnetted, 5 subnets
C       131.108.255.0 is directly connected, Serial0
B       131.108.4.0 [20/0] via 131.108.255.1, 00:02:09
B       131.108.3.0 [20/0] via 131.108.255.1, 00:02:09
B       131.108.2.0 [20/0] via 131.108.255.1, 00:02:09
C       131.108.1.0 is directly connected, Ethernet0
```

Notice that the next hop address on R3 is R2. The AS path on R3 indicates that the remote networks, 131.108.2.0 to 131.108.4.0/24, transverse autonomous system number 1, as displayed in the BGP table in Example 6-11.

The following five scenarios examine how BGP is configured and monitored and how BGP can use policy-based routing to change the routing decision of any IP network using powerful tools, such as route maps and the changing the BGP attributes.

Scenarios

The following scenarios are designed to draw together some of the content described in this chapter and some of the content you have seen in your own networks or practice labs. There is no one right way to accomplish many of the tasks presented, and the abilities to use good practice and define your end goal are important in any real-life design or solution. Again, use loopback interfaces to help populate BGP tables, and use back-to-back serial connections among Cisco routers.

Scenario 6-1: EBGP and IBGP

Configure the four-router topology in Figure 6-2 for IBGP and EBGP. OSPF is configured between R1 and R2, and to ensure a loop-free topology, do not disable synchronization on any router. Ensure that the loopback addresses on R1 (131.108.2.0–131.108.5.0/24) and R2 (131.108.5.0–131.108.7.0) are reachable from R3 and R4.

Figure 6-2 *IBGP/EBGP*

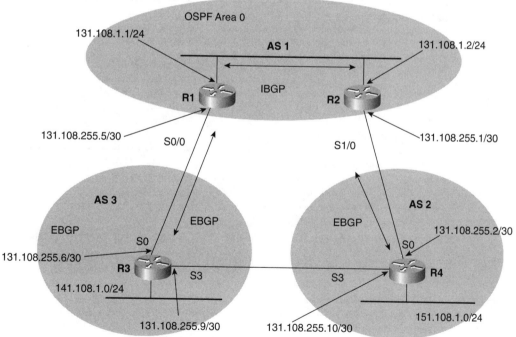

In this scenario, you configure BGP on four routers and ensure that all BGP peers have remote IP routing entries. R1 and R2 are running OSPF across the Ethernet subnet 131.108.1.0/24. Also, notice that this network contains a potential routing loop, so you discover how BGP helps you avoid loops.

Example 6-12 displays the OSPF configuration on R1; the loopbacks are placed in area 0.

Example 6-12 *R1 OSPF Configuration*

```
R1(config)#router ospf 1
R1(config-router)# network 131.108.1.0 0.0.0.255 area 0
R1(config-router)# network 131.108.2.0 0.0.0.255 area 0
R1(config-router)# network 131.108.3.0 0.0.0.255 area 0
R1(config-router)# network 131.108.4.0 0.0.0.255 area 0
```

Example 6-13 displays the OSPF configuration on R2.

Example 6-13 *R2 OSPF Configuration*

```
R2(config)#router ospf 1
R2(config-router)#network 131.108.1.0 0.0.0.255 area 0
R2(config-router)#network 131.108.5.0 0.0.0.255 area 0
R2(config-router)#network 131.108.6.0 0.0.0.255 area 0
R2(config-router)#network 131.108.7.0 0.0.0.255 area 0
```

Example 6-14 confirms that OSPF neighbors are active to R2.

Example 6-14 **show ip ospf neighbor** *on R1*

```
R1#show ip ospf neighbor
Neighbor ID     Pri   State        Dead Time   Address        Interface
131.108.7.1       1   FULL/BDR     00:00:36    131.108.1.2    Ethernet0/0
```

Next, enable IBGP between R1 and R2 and EBGP connections between R1/R3 and R2/R4.

Example 6-15 displays the IBGP configuration to R2 and the EBGP configuration to R3, both on R1.

Example 6-15 *IBGP/EBGP Configuration on R1*

```
R1(config-router)#router bgp 1
R1(config-router)# neighbor 131.108.1.2 remote-as 1
R1(config-router)# neighbor 131.108.255.6 remote-as 3
```

Now that you have configured BGP4 (by default, BGP Version 4 is enabled on Cisco IOS routers), Example 6-16 displays R1's BGP table.

Example 6-16 *R1's BGP Table*

```
R1#show ip bgp
BGP table version is 1, local router ID is 131.108.4.1
Status codes: s suppressed, d damped, h history, * valid, > best, i - internal
Origin codes: i - IGP, e - EGP, ? - incomplete

   Network          Next Hop            Metric LocPrf Weight Path
*i131.108.0.0       131.108.1.2              0    100     0 ?
```

R1's BGP table has no information about the locally connected loopbacks 131.108.2.0, 131.108.3.0, or 131.108.4.0, and the only network in the BGP table is the remote network 131.108.0.0 through R2.

You need to use the **network** command to configure the local interfaces. Example 6-17 displays the network configuration on R1.

Example 6-17 *Inserting Local Loopback on R1*

```
R1(config)#router bgp 1
R1(config-router)#network 131.108.2.0 mask 255.255.255.0
R1(config-router)#network 131.108.3.0 mask 255.255.255.0
R1(config-router)#network 131.108.4.0 mask 255.255.255.0
```

The same network configuration is required on R2. Example 6-18 displays the network configuration on R2.

Example 6-18 *Inserting Local Loopback on R2*

```
R2(config)#router bgp 1
R2(config-router)#network 131.108.5.0 mask 255.255.255.0
R2(config-router)#network 131.108.6.0 mask 255.255.255.0
R2(config-router)#network 131.108.7.0 mask 255.255.255.0
```

NOTE   Whenever you make BGP configuration changes on Cisco IOS routers, you must use the **clear ip bgp *** command to clear the TCP sessions (* for all BGP TCP peers). You use the **clear ip bgp** *ip–address-of-peer* command to clear a specific BGP peer.

Example 6-19 displays the BGP table on R1 after the loopbacks on R1 and R2 are advertised through BGP.

Example 6-19 *R1's BGP Table*

```
R1#show ip bgp
BGP table version is 4, local router ID is 131.108.4.1
Status codes: s suppressed, d damped, h history, * valid, > best, i - internal
Origin codes: i - IGP, e - EGP, ? - incomplete

   Network          Next Hop         Metric LocPrf Weight Path
* i131.108.0.0      131.108.1.2           0    100      0 ?
*> 131.108.2.0/24   0.0.0.0               0         32768 i
*> 131.108.3.0/24   0.0.0.0               0         32768 i
*> 131.108.4.0/24   0.0.0.0               0         32768 i
* i131.108.5.0/24   131.108.1.2           0    100      0 i
* i131.108.6.0/24   131.108.1.2           0    100      0 i
* i131.108.7.0/24   131.108.1.2           0    100      0 i
```

R1 has three local interfaces in BGP and three remote networks advertised by R2 (next hop address is 131.108.1.2). Also, notice that the default weight on R1 is set to 32768 (for local networks), and the local preference is 100 for the remote networks. These settings are set by default. You can change any BGP attribute, as you discover shortly.

The first entry in Example 6-19 displays the remote network 131.108.0.0 reachable through R2 (131.108.1.2). By default, BGP automatically summarizes at the network boundary. To turn off this behavior, you apply the **no auto-summary** command. Example 6-20 displays this configuration completed on R1 and R2.

Example 6-20 *Disabling Automatic Summarization on R1 and R2*

```
R1(config)#router bgp 1
R1(config-router)#no auto-summary
R2(config)#router bgp 1
R2(config-router)#no auto-summary
```

After clearing the BGP session to R2 with the **clear ip bgp 131.108.1.2** command, you can expect the BGP table on R1 to contain only specific network entries. Example 6-21 displays R1's BGP table.

Example 6-21 *R1's BGP Table*

```
R1#show ip bgp
BGP table version is 5, local router ID is 131.108.4.1
Status codes: s suppressed, d damped, h history, * valid, > best, i - internal
Origin codes: i - IGP, e - EGP, ? - incomplete
   Network          Next Hop         Metric LocPrf Weight Path
*>i131.108.1.0/24   131.108.1.2           0    100      0 ?
```

Example 6-21 *R1's BGP Table (Continued)*

```
*> 131.108.2.0/24    0.0.0.0              0         32768 i
*> 131.108.3.0/24    0.0.0.0              0         32768 i
*> 131.108.4.0/24    0.0.0.0              0         32768 i
* i131.108.5.0/24    131.108.1.2          0    100      0 i
* i131.108.6.0/24    131.108.1.2          0    100      0 i
* i131.108.7.0/24    131.108.1.2          0    100      0 i
```

One of the most important commands used in BGP networks is the IOS **show ip bgp neighbor** command, which displays the remote BGP peers and their states. Example 6-22 displays the remote BGP peers on R1. Note that the information relates to the BGP peer to R2 and R3.

Example 6-22 **show ip bgp neighbors** *on R1*

```
R1#sh ip bgp neighbors
BGP neighbor is 131.108.1.2,  remote AS 1, internal link
  Index 1, Offset 0, Mask 0x2
    BGP version 4, remote router ID 131.108.255.1
    BGP state = Established, table version = 5, up for 00:04:30
    Last read 00:00:30, hold time is 180, keepalive interval is 60 seconds
    Minimum time between advertisement runs is 5 seconds
    Received 1297 messages, 0 notifications, 0 in queue
    Sent 1290 messages, 0 notifications, 0 in queue
    Prefix advertised 14, suppressed 0, withdrawn 0
    Connections established 7; dropped 6
    Last reset 00:04:39, due to User reset
    4 accepted prefixes consume 128 bytes
    0 history paths consume 0 bytes
Connection state is ESTAB, I/O status: 1, unread input bytes: 0
Local host: 131.108.1.1, Local port: 11632
Foreign host: 131.108.1.2, Foreign port: 179

Enqueued packets for retransmit: 0, input: 0  mis-ordered: 0 (0 bytes)

Event Timers (current time is 0x190F313B):
Timer         Starts    Wakeups         Next
Retrans            9         0           0x0
TimeWait           0         0           0x0
AckHold           10         3           0x0
SendWnd            0         0           0x0
KeepAlive          0         0           0x0
GiveUp             0         0           0x0
PmtuAger           0         0           0x0
DeadWait           0         0           0x0

iss:  249485567  snduna:  249485774  sndnxt:  249485774    sndwnd:  16178
irs: 3880799333  rcvnxt: 3880799843  rcvwnd:       15875  delrcvwnd:   509
```

continues

Example 6-22 *show ip bgp neighbors on R1 (Continued)*

```
SRTT: 510 ms, RTTO: 3547 ms, RTV: 1263 ms, KRTT: 0 ms
minRTT: 0 ms, maxRTT: 300 ms, ACK hold: 200 ms
Flags: higher precedence, nagle

Datagrams (max data segment is 1460 bytes):
Rcvd: 16 (out of order: 0), with data: 10, total data bytes: 509
Sent: 13 (retransmit: 0), with data: 8, total data bytes: 206
BGP neighbor is 131.108.255.6,  remote AS 3, external link
 Index 2, Offset 0, Mask 0x4
  BGP version 4, remote router ID 0.0.0.0
  BGP state = Active, table version = 0
  Last read 00:17:54, hold time is 180, keepalive interval is 60 seconds
  Minimum time between advertisement runs is 5 seconds
  Received 0 messages, 0 notifications, 0 in queue
  Sent 0 messages, 0 notifications, 0 in queue
  Prefix advertised 0, suppressed 0, withdrawn 0
  Connections established 0; dropped 0
  Last reset 00:17:55, due to User reset
  0 accepted prefixes consume 0 bytes
  0 history paths consume 0 bytes
  No active TCP connection
```

The BGP neighbors on R1 are established to R2, but not to R3. You have yet to configure BGP on R3. Anything other than the keyword established between two BGP indicates a problem. The possible BGP states are as follows:

- **Idle**—BGP is waiting for a starting event, which is initiated by an operator of BGP, such as clearing the BGP peers.

- **Connect**—BGP is waiting for the TCP connection to be completed.

- **Active**—BGP is trying to acquire a remote peer by initiating a new TCP connection.

- **OpenSent**—BGP is waiting for an open message from the remote peer.

- **OpenConfirm**—BGP is waiting for a keepalive message.

- **Established**—After a keepalive message is sent, this is the final stage of BGP peer negotiation during which both peers exchange their BGP tables.

Next, you enable EBGP between R1 and R3. Example 6-23 displays the BGP configuration on R3, along with the **network** statement, so that R3 advertises the network 141.108.1.0/24 as originating from AS 3. Also, note the EBGP connection between R3 (AS 3) and R4 (AS 2).

Example 6-23 *EBGP Configuration on R3*

```
R3(config)#router bgp 3
R3(config-router)#network 141.108.1.0 mask 255.255.255.0
R3(config-router)#neighbor 131.108.255.5 remote-as 1
```

The BGP peers on R1 are displayed in Example 6-24 (truncated for clarity).

Example 6-24 show ip bgp neighbors *on R1 (Truncated)*

```
R1>show ip bgp neighbors
BGP neighbor is 131.108.1.2,  remote AS 1, internal link
 Index 1, Offset 0, Mask 0x2
  BGP version 4, remote router ID 131.108.255.1
  BGP state = Established, table version = 8, up for 00:58:56
  Last read 00:00:56, hold time is 180, keepalive interval is 60 seconds
  Minimum time between advertisement runs is 5 seconds
  Received 1351 messages, 0 notifications, 0 in queue
  Sent 1347 messages, 0 notifications, 0 in queue
  Prefix advertised 16, suppressed 0, withdrawn 1
  Connections established 7; dropped 6
  Last reset 00:59:05, due to User reset
  4 accepted prefixes consume 128 bytes
  0 history paths consume 0 bytes
Connection state is ESTAB, I/O status: 1, unread input bytes: 0
Local host: 131.108.1.1, Local port: 11632
Foreign host: 131.108.1.2, Foreign port: 179
...
BGP neighbor is 131.108.255.6,  remote AS 3, external link
 Index 2, Offset 0, Mask 0x4
  BGP version 4, remote router ID 141.108.1.1
  BGP state = Established, table version = 8, up for 00:38:16
  Last read 00:00:16, hold time is 180, keepalive interval is 60 seconds
  Minimum time between advertisement runs is 30 seconds
  Received 46 messages, 0 notifications, 0 in queue
  Sent 48 messages, 0 notifications, 0 in queue
  Prefix advertised 8, suppressed 0, withdrawn 0
  Connections established 2; dropped 1
  Last reset 00:38:38, due to Peer closed the session
  1 accepted prefixes consume 32 bytes
  0 history paths consume 0 bytes
Connection state is ESTAB, I/O status: 1, unread input bytes: 0
Local host: 131.108.255.5, Local port: 179
Foreign host: 131.108.255.6, Foreign port: 11001
...
R1>
```

R1 has two established peers: one IBGP peer to R2, and an EBGP peer to R3.

Example 6-25 enables EBGP between R4 and R2.

Example 6-25 *Configuring BGP on R4*

```
R4(config)#router bgp 2
R4(config-router)#neighbor 131.108.255.1 remote-as 1
R4(config-router)#neighbor 131.108.255.9 remote 3
R4(config-router)#network 151.108.1.0 mask 255.255.255.0
```

The **show ip bgp summary** command is a useful command that summarizes all BGP peers. Example 6-26 displays the BGP peers on R4 in a summarized format.

Example 6-26 **show ip bgp summary** *on R4*

```
R4#show ip bgp ?
  A.B.C.D           IP prefix <network>/<length>, e.g., 35.0.0.0/8
  A.B.C.D           Network in the BGP routing table to display
  cidr-only         Display only routes with non-natural netmasks
  community         Display routes matching the communities
  community-list    Display routes matching the community-list
  dampened-paths    Display paths suppressed due to dampening
  filter-list       Display routes conforming to the filter-list
  flap-statistics   Display flap statistics of routes
  inconsistent-as   Display only routes with inconsistent origin ASs
  ipv4              Address family
  neighbors         Detailed information on TCP and BGP neighbor connections
  paths             Path information
  peer-group        Display information on peer-groups
  quote-regexp      Display routes matching the AS path "regular expression"
  regexp            Display routes matching the AS path regular expression
  summary           Summary of BGP neighbor status
  vpnv4             Display VPNv4 NLRI specific information
  |                 Output modifiers
  <cr>
R4#show ip bgp summary
BGP router identifier 151.108.1.1, local AS number 2
BGP table version is 9, main routing table version 9
8 network entries and 8 paths using 1064 bytes of memory
4 BGP path attribute entries using 208 bytes of memory
1 BGP AS-PATH entries using 24 bytes of memory
0 BGP route-map cache entries using 0 bytes of memory
0 BGP filter-list cache entries using 0 bytes of memory
BGP activity 8/0 prefixes, 8/0 paths, scan interval 15 secs
Neighbor        V    AS MsgRcvd MsgSent   TblVer  InQ OutQ Up/Down  State/PfxRcd
131.108.255.1   4     1      32      22       13    0    0 00:01:21         7
131.108.255.9   4     3       7       8       13    0    0 00:01:15         5
```

Table 6-2 summarizes the descriptions and field definition, as displayed by the IOS **show ip bgp summary** command.

Table 6-2 *Field Summary for* **show ip bgp summary**

Field	Description
BGP router identifier	In order of precedence and availability, router identifier specified by the **bgp router-id** command, loopback address, or lowest IP address. For Example, in Example 6-26, the router ID of R4 is 151.108.1.1/24.
BGP table version	Internal version number of BGP database.

Table 6-2   *Field Summary for* **show ip bgp summary** *(Continued)*

Field	Description
main routing table version	Last version of BGP database injected into main routing table.
Neighbor	IP address of a neighbor.
V	BGP version number spoken to that neighbor. Typically you see only version 4.
AS	Peer autonomous system.
MsgRcvd	BGP messages received from that neighbor.
MsgSent	BGP messages sent to that neighbor.
TblVer	Last version of the BGP database sent to that neighbor.
InQ	Number of messages from that neighbor waiting to be processed.
OutQ	Number of messages waiting to be sent to that neighbor.
Up/Down	The length of time that the BGP session has been in the Established state, or the current state, if the state is not Established.
State/PfxRcd	Current state of the BGP session/the number of prefixes the router has received from a neighbor or peer group. When the maximum number (as set by the **neighbor maximum-prefix** command) is reached, the string, PfxRcd, appears in the entry, the neighbor is shut down, and the connection is idle. No information below the state indicates an active peer, as displayed in Example 6-26.

Next, view some IP routing tables to ensure that you are routing IP. Example 6-27 displays R3's IP routing table.

Example 6-27 *R3's IP Routing Table*

```
R3#show ip route
      141.108.0.0/24 is subnetted, 1 subnets
C        141.108.1.0 is directly connected, Ethernet0
      131.108.0.0/16 is variably subnetted, 12 subnets, 3 masks
C        131.108.255.4/30 is directly connected, Serial0
C        131.108.255.8/30 is directly connected, Serial3
B        131.108.7.0/24 [20/0] via 131.108.255.10, 00:06:10
B        131.108.6.0/24 [20/0] via 131.108.255.10, 00:06:10
B        131.108.5.0/24 [20/0] via 131.108.255.10, 00:06:10
B        131.108.4.1/32 [20/0] via 131.108.255.10, 00:06:10
B        131.108.4.0/24 [20/0] via 131.108.255.5, 00:56:22
B        131.108.2.1/32 [20/0] via 131.108.255.10, 00:06:11
B        131.108.3.0/24 [20/0] via 131.108.255.5, 00:56:23
B        131.108.3.1/32 [20/0] via 131.108.255.10, 00:06:11
B        131.108.2.0/24 [20/0] via 131.108.255.5, 00:56:23
B        131.108.1.0/24 [20/0] via 131.108.255.5, 00:56:24
      151.108.0.0/24 is subnetted, 1 subnets
B        151.108.1.0 [20/0] via 131.108.255.10, 00:05:46
```

R3 has a full set of BGP routes for all BGP AS networks. To view more information about how the BGP entries were learned, view the BGP table with the **show ip bgp** command. Example 6-28 displays R3's BGP table.

Example 6-28 *R3's BGP Table*

```
R3#show ip bgp
BGP table version is 16, local router ID is 141.108.1.1
Status codes: s suppressed, d damped, h history, * valid, > best, i - internal
Origin codes: i - IGP, e - EGP, ? - incomplete
   Network          Next Hop         Metric LocPrf Weight Path
*  131.108.1.0/24   131.108.255.10                    0 2 1 ?
*>                  131.108.255.5                     0 1 ?
*> 131.108.2.0/24   131.108.255.5         0           0 1 i
*> 131.108.2.1/32   131.108.255.10                    0 2 1 ?
*> 131.108.3.0/24   131.108.255.5         0           0 1 i
*> 131.108.3.1/32   131.108.255.10                    0 2 1 ?
*> 131.108.4.0/24   131.108.255.5         0           0 1 i
*> 131.108.4.1/32   131.108.255.10                    0 2 1 ?
*> 131.108.5.0/24   131.108.255.10                    0 2 1 i
*> 131.108.6.0/24   131.108.255.10                    0 2 1 i
*> 131.108.7.0/24   131.108.255.10                    0 2 1 i
*> 141.108.1.0/24   0.0.0.0               0       32768 i
*> 151.108.1.0/24   131.108.255.10        0           0 2 i
```

A lot of information is stored here. Start by analyzing why the remote network 131.108.1.0 has a dual path and why the next hop address 13.108.255.5, or the link to R1, is preferred as the path through R4. BGP does not load balance and always chooses one path. (Static routes can be used to change this behavior.) R3 chooses the path through the serial link to R1 because the BGP algorithm decision is based on 10 parameters and because the first four are the same (next hop reachable, weight equal, local preference the same, not originated by local router). The next decision is based on the path with the shortest AS path. The path to R1 is through one AS path only as opposed by two AS paths to R4. Because weight has a higher preference than AS path, change the weight on R3 to prefer the path through R4.

Example 6-29 displays how to use the **neighbor** command to set all entries advertised through R4 to a weight value of 1 so that the network advertised by R4 has a higher weight value for the network 131.108.1.0/24 only. (There are many ways to accomplish this task.)

Example 6-29 *Changing the Weight on R3*

```
R3(config)#router bgp 3
R3(config-router)#neighbor 131.108.255.10 weight 1
```

Example 6-30 displays the BGP table on R3 after the configuration change.

Example 6-30 show ip bgp *on R3*

```
R3#show ip bgp
BGP table version is 16, local router ID is 141.108.1.1
Status codes: s suppressed, d damped, h history, * valid, > best, i - internal
Origin codes: i - IGP, e - EGP, ? - incomplete
   Network          Next Hop          Metric LocPrf Weight Path
*  131.108.1.0/24   131.108.255.10                      0 2 1 ?
*>                  131.108.255.5               1        0 1 ?
*> 131.108.2.0/24   131.108.255.5          0            0 1 i
*> 131.108.2.1/32   131.108.255.10                      0 2 1 ?
*> 131.108.3.0/24   131.108.255.5          0            0 1 i
*> 131.108.3.1/32   131.108.255.10                      0 2 1 ?
*> 131.108.4.0/24   131.108.255.5          0            0 1 i
*> 131.108.4.1/32   131.108.255.10                      0 2 1 ?
*> 131.108.5.0/24   131.108.255.10                      0 2 1 i
*> 131.108.6.0/24   131.108.255.10                      0 2 1 i
*> 131.108.7.0/24   131.108.255.10                      0 2 1 i
*> 141.108.1.0/24   0.0.0.0                0        32768 i
*> 151.108.1.0/24   131.108.255.10         0            0 2 i
```

The change is not implemented because you must first clear the BGP peer session. Clear the BGP TCP peer session on R3 to R4 with the **clear ip bgp 131.108.255.10** command. Example 6-31 displays the BGP table on R3 after the BGP TCP peer is established again.

Example 6-31 show ip bgp *on R3*

```
R3#show ip bgp
BGP table version is 32, local router ID is 141.108.1.1
Status codes: s suppressed, d damped, h history, * valid, > best, i - internal
Origin codes: i - IGP, e - EGP, ? - incomplete
   Network          Next Hop          Metric LocPrf Weight Path
R3#show ip bgp
BGP table version is 16, local router ID is 141.108.1.1
Status codes: s suppressed, d damped, h history, * valid, > best, i - internal
Origin codes: i - IGP, e - EGP, ? - incomplete
   Network          Next Hop          Metric LocPrf Weight Path
*> 131.108.1.0/24   131.108.255.10                      1 2 1 ?
*                   131.108.255.5        100            0 1 ?
*> 131.108.2.0/24   131.108.255.5        100            0 1 i
*> 131.108.2.1/32   131.108.255.10                      1 2 1 ?
*> 131.108.3.0/24   131.108.255.5        100            0 1 i
*> 131.108.3.1/32   131.108.255.10                      1 2 1 ?
*> 131.108.4.0/24   131.108.255.5        100            0 1 i
*> 131.108.4.1/32   131.108.255.10                      1 2 1 ?
*> 131.108.5.0/24   131.108.255.10                      1 2 1 i
*> 131.108.6.0/24   131.108.255.10                      1 2 1 i
*> 131.108.7.0/24   131.108.255.10                      1 2 1 i
*> 141.108.1.0/24   0.0.0.0                0        32768 i
*> 151.108.1.0/24   131.108.255.10         0            1 2 i
```

Even though the path to the remote network 131.108.1.0/24 through R1 has a shorter AS path (through AS 1 only) because weight has a higher preference than AS path in the BGP routing decision, the path to 131.108.1.0/24 is now preferred through R4 (weight is 1) as opposed to the link through R1. All entries advertised through the next hop address 131.108.255.10, or R4, have the weight value set to 1.

You have successfully configured a four-router topology with BGP4. Provided here for your reference are the four configurations on the Routers R1 through R4.

Example 6-32 display R1's full working configuration.

Example 6-32 *R1's Full Working Configuration*

```
hostname R1
enable password cisco
!
ip subnet-zero
no ip domain-lookup
!
interface Loopback0
 ip address 131.108.2.1 255.255.255.0
!
interface Loopback1
 ip address 131.108.3.1 255.255.255.0
!
interface Loopback2
 ip address 131.108.4.1 255.255.255.0
!
interface Ethernet0/0
 ip address 131.108.1.1 255.255.255.0
!
interface Serial0/0
 ip address 131.108.255.5 255.255.255.252
 clockrate 125000
!
router ospf 1
 network 131.108.1.0 0.0.0.255 area 0
 network 131.108.2.0 0.0.0.255 area 0
 network 131.108.3.0 0.0.0.255 area 0
 network 131.108.4.0 0.0.0.255 area 0
!
router bgp 1
 network 131.108.2.0 mask 255.255.255.0
 network 131.108.3.0 mask 255.255.255.0
 network 131.108.4.0 mask 255.255.255.0
 neighbor 131.108.1.2 remote-as 1
 neighbor 131.108.255.6 remote-as 3
 no auto-summary
line con 0
line aux 0
line vty 0 4
end
```

Example 6-33 display R2's full working configuration.

Example 6-33 *R2's Full Working Configuration*

```
hostname R2
!
enable password cisco
!
no ip domain-lookup
interface Loopback0
 ip address 131.108.5.1 255.255.255.0
interface Loopback1
 ip address 131.108.6.1 255.255.255.0
!
interface Loopback2
 ip address 131.108.7.1 255.255.255.0
!
interface Ethernet0/0
 ip address 131.108.1.2 255.255.255.0
!
interface Serial1/0
 ip address 131.108.255.1 255.255.255.0
 clockrate 128000
!
router ospf 1
 network 131.108.1.0 0.0.0.255 area 0
 network 131.108.5.0 0.0.0.255 area 0
 network 131.108.6.0 0.0.0.255 area 0
 network 131.108.7.0 0.0.0.255 area 0
!
router bgp 1
 network 131.108.5.0 mask 255.255.255.0
 network 131.108.6.0 mask 255.255.255.0
 network 131.108.7.0 mask 255.255.255.0
 redistribute ospf 1 metric 100
 neighbor 131.108.1.1 remote-as 1
 neighbor 131.108.255.2 remote-as 2
 no auto-summary
!
line con 0
line aux 0
line vty 0 4
end
```

Example 6-34 display R3's full working configuration.

Example 6-34 *R3's Full Working Configuration*

```
hostname R3
!
enable password cisco
!
no ip domain-lookup
!
interface Ethernet0
 ip address 141.108.1.1 255.255.255.0
 media-type 10BaseT
!
interface Serial0
 ip address 131.108.255.6 255.255.255.252
 bandwidth 125
!
interface Serial1
shutdown
!
interface Serial2
shutdown
!
interface Serial3
 ip address 131.108.255.9 255.255.255.252
 !
router bgp 3
 network 141.108.1.0 mask 255.255.255.0
 neighbor 131.108.255.5 remote-as 1
 neighbor 131.108.255.10 remote-as 2
 neighbor 131.108.255.10 weight 1
!
line con 0
line aux 0
line vty 0 4
!
end
```

Example 6-35 display R4's full working configuration.

Example 6-35 *R4's Full Working Configuration*

```
hostname R4
!
enable password cisco
no ip domain-lookup
interface Ethernet0
 ip address 151.108.1.1 255.255.255.0
interface Serial0
 ip address 131.108.255.2 255.255.255.252
 !
interface Serial1
shutdown
```

Example 6-35 *R4's Full Working Configuration (Continued)*

```
!
router bgp 2
 network 151.108.1.0 mask 255.255.255.0
 neighbor 131.108.255.1 remote-as 1
 neighbor 131.108.255.9 remote-as 3
!
line con 0
line aux 0
line vty 0 4
end
```

Scenario 6-2: BGP and Static Routes

In this scenario, you use static routes to load balance BGP over a dual-path connection between two routers.

BGP chooses only one path to a remote network. To achieve any form of load balancing of two or more network paths, you can use static routes to the remote peer address.

Figure 6-3 displays a simple two-router BGP topology.

Figure 6-3   *BGP Topology*

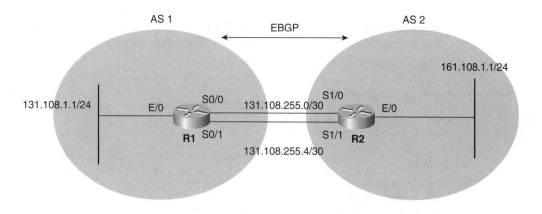

Enable BGP on R1 and configure the **network** command to advertise the Ethernet IP network 131.108.1.0/24. Because you are running EBGP, synchronization is not an issue in this network. Also, to achieve load balancing, you need to peer the BGP neighbors using the Ethernet IP addresses. In the case of R1, the next hop peer address is 161.108.1.1/24, and in the case of R2, the peer address is 131.108.1.1/24.

With BGP, if the next hop address in EBGP is not used, such as in this scenario in which you want to achieve load balancing, you must enable EBGP multihop so that the EBGP peer is established. The IOS command to enable EBGP multihop is **neighbor** *peer address* **ebgp-multihop**. Also, because the next hop address is not a directly connected address, BGP needs to advertise the update source IP address to EBGP. In the case of R1, it is 131.108.1.1 (Ethernet 0/0), and in the case of R2, it is 161.108.1.0/24 (Ethernet 0/0).

Example 6-36 displays the EBGP configuration (with multihop) on R1.

Example 6-36 *EBGP Configuration on R1*

```
R1(config)#router bgp 1
R1(config-router)#network 131.108.1.0 mask 255.255.255.0
R1(config-router)#neighbor 161.108.1.1 remote-as 2
R1(config-router)#neighbor 161.108.1.1 ebgp-multihop
R1(config-router)#neighbor 161.108.1.1 update-source Ethernet0/0
```

Example 6-37 displays the EBGP configuration on R2.

Example 6-37 *EBGP Configuration on R2*

```
R2(config)#router bgp 2
R2(config-router)#network 161.108.1.0 mask 255.255.255.0
R2(config-router)#neighbor 131.108.1.1 remote-as 1
R2(config-router)#neighbor 131.108.1.1 ebgp-multihop
R2(config-router)#neighbor 131.108.1.1 update-source Ethernet0/0
```

Now that R1 and R2 are configured with EBGP, ensure that BGP peer sessions are up with the **show ip bgp neighbor** command. Example 6-38 displays the peers on R1.

Example 6-38 **show ip bgp neighbors** *on R1*

```
R1#show ip bgp neighbors
BGP neighbor is 161.108.1.1,  remote AS 2, external link
 Index 1, Offset 0, Mask 0x2
  BGP version 4, remote router ID 0.0.0.0
  BGP state = Active  table version = 0
  Last read 00:03:37, hold time is 180, keepalive interval is 60 seconds
  Minimum time between advertisement runs is 30 seconds
  Received 0 messages, 0 notifications, 0 in queue
  Sent 0 messages, 0 notifications, 0 in queue
  Prefix advertised 0, suppressed 0, withdrawn 0
  Connections established 0; dropped 0
  Last reset never
  0 accepted prefixes consume 0 bytes
  0 history paths consume 0 bytes
  External BGP neighbor may be up to 255 hops away.
  No active TCP connection
```

R1 has no peer relationship to R2. To discover why, display the IP routing table on R1. Example 6-39 displays R1's IP routing table.

Example 6-39 **show ip route** *on R1*

```
R1#show ip route
     131.108.0.0/16 is variably subnetted, 2 subnets, 2 masks
C       131.108.255.0/30 is directly connected, Serial0/0
C       131.108.255.4/30 is directly connected, Serial0/1
C       131.108.1.0/24 is directly connected, Ethernet0/0
```

R1 does not have any entries for the remote network 161.108.1.0/24 and thereby cannot establish a TCP session to R2. Configure two static routes on R1 pointing to the remote network through Serial 0/0 and Serial 0/1.

Example 6-40 displays the IP static route configuration on R1.

Example 6-40 *Static Route Configuration on R1*

```
R1(config)#ip route 161.108.1.0 255.255.255.0 serial 0/0
R1(config)#ip route 161.108.1.0 255.255.255.0 serial 0/1
```

To ensure that R2 can route to the remote network 131.108.1.0, install two static routes pointing to R1 over Serial 1/0 and Serial 1/1. Example 6-41 displays the IP static route configuration on R2.

Example 6-41 *Static Route Configuration on R2*

```
R2(config)#ip route 131.108.1.0 255.255.255.0 serial 1/0
R2(config)#ip route 131.108.1.0 255.255.255.0 serial 1/1
```

The BGP peers on R1 display the established peer to R1. Example 6-42 shows a truncated display of the peer with R2.

Example 6-42 **show ip bgp neighbors** *on R1*

```
R1#show ip bgp neighbors
BGP neighbor is 161.108.1.1,  remote AS 2, external link
 Index 1, Offset 0, Mask 0x2
  BGP version 4, remote router ID 161.108.1.1
  BGP state = Established  table version = 3, up for 00:03:51
  Last read 00:00:51, hold time is 180, keepalive interval is 60 seconds
  Minimum time between advertisement runs is 30 seconds
  Received 7 messages, 0 notifications, 0 in queue
  Sent 7 messages, 0 notifications, 0 in queue
  Prefix advertised 1, suppressed 0, withdrawn 0
```

continues

Example 6-42 **show ip bgp neighbors** *on R1 (Continued)*

```
Connections established 1; dropped 0
Last reset 00:04:21, due to User reset
1 accepted prefixes consume 32 bytes
0 history paths consume 0 bytes
External BGP neighbor may be up to 255 hops away.
..[truncated display]
```

Ensure that load balancing is taking place by pinging the remote network 161.108.1.1/24 from R1. Turn on **debug ip packet**, so you can see on which outbound interface the ping request is sent. Example 6-43 shows the ping request after the **debug ip packet** command is enabled. This command enables you to view where IP packets are sent to and received from.

Example 6-43 *Debug Output on R1*

```
R1#debug ip packet
IP packet debugging is on
R1#ping 161.108.1.1
Type escape sequence to abort.
Sending 5, 100-byte ICMP Echos to 161.108.1.1, timeout is 2 seconds:
!!!!!
Success rate is 100 percent (5/5), round-trip min/avg/max = 16/17/20 ms
00:09:27: IP: s=131.108.255.1 (local), d=161.108.1.1 (Serial0/0), len 100,
   sending
00:09:27: IP: s=161.108.1.1 (Serial0/0), d=131.108.255.1 (Serial0/0), len 100,
   rcvd 3
00:09:27: IP: s=131.108.255.5 (local), d=161.108.1.1 (Serial0/1), len 100,
   sending
00:09:27: IP: s=161.108.1.1 (Serial0/1), d=131.108.255.5 (Serial0/1), len 100,
   rcvd 3
00:09:27: IP: s=131.108.255.1 (local), d=161.108.1.1 (Serial0/0), len 100,
   sending
00:09:27: IP: s=161.108.1.1 (Serial0/0), d=131.108.255.1 (Serial0/0), len 100,
   rcvd 3
00:09:27: IP: s=131.108.255.5 (local), d=161.108.1.1 (Serial0/1), len 100,
   sending
00:09:27: IP: s=161.108.1.1 (Serial0/1), d=131.108.255.5 (Serial0/1), len 100,
   rcvd 3
00:09:27: IP: s=131.108.255.1 (local), d=161.108.1.1 (Serial0/0), len 100,
   sending
00:09:27: IP: s=161.108.1.1 (Serial0/0), d=131.108.255.1 (Serial0/0), len 100,
   rcvd 3
```

You can see from Example 6-43 that the first ping request is sent through Serial 0/0 and the reply is received through Serial 0/0. The second ping request is sent through Serial 0/1, and the reply is received through Serial 0/1; therefore, load balancing is occurring. It is important to note that BGP still only sends packets through one path, but because IP at Layer 3 is load balancing, in effect you are load balancing BGP by using static routes.

Example 6-44 displays the full working configuration of R1. Take note of the shaded sections, which contain the critical commands used to achieve load balancing between R1 and R2.

Example 6-44 *R1's Full Working Configuration*

```
hostname R1
enable password cisco
!
ip subnet-zero
no ip domain-lookup
!
interface Ethernet0/0
 ip address 131.108.1.1 255.255.255.0
 no ip directed-broadcast
!
interface Serial0/0
 ip address 131.108.255.1 255.255.255.252
 clockrate 125000
!
interface Serial0/1
 ip address 131.108.255.5 255.255.255.252
 clockrate 125000
!
router bgp 1
 network 131.108.1.0 mask 255.255.255.0
 neighbor 161.108.1.1 remote-as 2
 neighbor 161.108.1.1 ebgp-multihop 255
 neighbor 161.108.1.1 update-source Ethernet0/0
!
ip route 161.108.1.0 255.255.255.0 Serial0/0
ip route 161.108.1.0 255.255.255.0 Serial0/1
!
line con 0
line aux 0
line vty 0 4
end
```

Example 6-45 displays R2's full working configuration.

Example 6-45 *R2's Full Working Configuration*

```
hostname R2
!
enable password cisco
!
ip subnet-zero
no ip domain-lookup
```

Example 6-45 *R2's Full Working Configuration (Continued)*

```
 !
 interface Ethernet0/0
  ip address 161.108.1.1 255.255.255.0
  !
 interface Serial1/0
 ip address 131.108.255.2 255.255.255.252
 interface Serial1/1
  ip address 131.108.255.6 255.255.255.252
  !
 router bgp 2
  network 161.108.1.0 mask 255.255.255.0
  neighbor 131.108.1.1 remote-as 1
  neighbor 131.108.1.1 ebgp-multihop 255
  neighbor 131.108.1.1 update-source Ethernet0/0
  !
 ip route 131.108.1.0 255.255.255.0 Serial1/0
 ip route 131.108.1.0 255.255.255.0 Serial1/1
  !
 line con 0
 line aux 0
 line vty 0 4
 end
```

Scenario 6-3: BGP with Policy-Based Routing

In this scenario, you configure EBGP using the next hop addresses and use policy-based routing to allow certain network design policies to affect IP routing decisions.

Policy-based routing is used for the following main reasons:

- To control traffic flow direction either by source or destination address
- To change the next hop address
- To change the way traffic is sent to a neighboring router

The advantages of using policy routing is the ability to load share to provide high-quality service and cost saving, based on data traffic, for expensive links.

Figure 6-4 displays the same two-router network used in Scenario 6-3, except this time you configure two EBGP sessions between R1 and R2 and use BGP to route dynamically without static routing.

Figure 6-4   *Two-EBGP Session Topology*

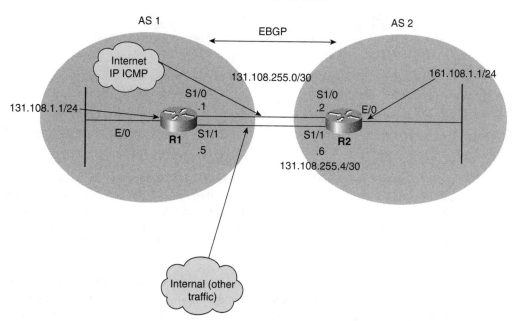

Configure two EBGP TCP sessions between R1 and R2. Example 6-46 displays the EBGP configuration on R1. (Notice, you don't need EBGP multihop because you are using a directly connected peer.)

Example 6-46   *EBGP on R1*

```
R1(config)#router bgp 1
R1(config-router)#network 131.108.1.0 mask 255.255.255.0
R1(config-router)#neighbor 131.108.255.2 remote-as 2
R1(config-router)#neighbor 131.108.255.6 remote-as 2
```

Example 6-47 displays the two EBGP sessions configured on R2.

Example 6-47   *EBGP on R2*

```
R2(config)#router bgp 2
R2(config-router)#network 161.108.1.0 mask 255.255.255.0
R2(config-router)#neighbor 131.108.255.1 remote-as 1
R2(config-router)#neighbor 131.108.255.5 remote-as 1
```

Example 6-48 displays the IP BGP table on R1 after the two BGP sessions are established.

Example 6-48 *BGP Table on R1*

```
R1#show ip bgp
BGP table version is 3, local router ID is 131.108.255.5
Status codes: s suppressed, d damped, h history, * valid, > best, i - internal
Origin codes: i - IGP, e - EGP, ? - incomplete

   Network          Next Hop          Metric LocPrf Weight Path
*> 131.108.1.0/24   0.0.0.0                0          32768 i
*  161.108.1.0/24   131.108.255.6          0              0 2 i
*>                  131.108.255.2          0              0 2 i
```

Example 6-48 displays R1 choosing the path through the next hop address. 131.108.255.2.
to reach the remote network 161.108.1.0/24 because BGP does not load balance as you
discovered in Scenario 6-2. The path is chosen through 131.108.255.2 because of its lower
IP addresses; all other parameters that BGP bases decisions on are equal in this case. Assume
that all traffic from the Ethernet segment on R1 bound for 161.108.1.0 must be sent through
the next hop address 131.108.255.6, or Serial 1/1, and all traffic destined for the Internet is
sent through Serial 1/0.

You can force BGP to complete this task by using policy-based routing or changing BGP
attributes. But, suppose you want to send internal traffic through one path and all Internet
traffic through the second link. Next, you learn to configure policy-based routing to illustrate
how you can use route maps to achieve this.

To illustrate policy-based routing, configure R1 to choose a different next hop address for
IP ICMP packets destined for the remote network 161.108.1.0 (Serial 1/1) than for all other
destinations (for example, Internet-based traffic), which will be through the second link
(Serial 1/0).

Policy routing is based on incoming packets only, so you need to apply the **policy** command
on the Ethernet interface on R1.

First, configure R2 to advertise a default route to R1.

Example 6-49 displays the configuration on R2 so that it sends a default BGP route to R1.
Two default statements are configured for redundancy purposes.

Example 6-49 *Default Route Configuration on R2*

```
R2(config)#router bgp 2
R2(config-router)#neighbor 131.108.255.1 default-originate
R2(config-router)#neighbor 131.108.255.5 default-originate
```

Example 6-50 displays the BGP default route in R1's BGP table.

Example 6-50 show ip bgp *Command on R1*

```
R1>show ip bgp
BGP table version is 4, local router ID is 131.108.255.5
Status codes: s suppressed, d damped, h history, * valid, > best, i - internal
Origin codes: i - IGP, e - EGP, ? - incomplete

   Network          Next Hop          Metric LocPrf Weight Path
*  0.0.0.0          131.108.255.6                      0 2 i
*>                  131.108.255.2                      0 2 i
*> 131.108.1.0/24   0.0.0.0                0        32768 i
*  161.108.1.0/24   131.108.255.6          0           0 2 i
*>                  131.108.255.2          0           0 2 i
```

Example 6-50 tells you that R1 is choosing all traffic through the next hop address 131.108.255.2. Example 6-51 confirms this when you view the IP routing table on R1.

Example 6-51 show ip route *Command on R1*

```
R1>show ip route
Gateway of last resort is 131.108.255.2 to network 0.0.0.0
     131.108.0.0/16 is variably subnetted, 3 subnets, 2 masks
C       131.108.255.0/30 is directly connected, Serial1/0
C       131.108.255.4/30 is directly connected, Serial1/1
C       131.108.1.0/24 is directly connected, Ethernet0/0
     161.108.0.0/24 is subnetted, 1 subnets
B       161.108.1.0 [20/0] via 131.108.255.2, 00:23:11
B*   0.0.0.0/0 [20/0] via 131.108.255.2, 00:13:58
```

Policy routing needs to be configured on R1 to ensure that IP ICMP packets destined for the remote network 161.108.1.0/24 are sent through the next hop address 131.108.255.6 and all other traffic is sent through 131.108.1.1 (Serial 1/0 to R2).

To configure policy routing, you apply the **policy** statement on the outbound interface and reference a route map. The IOS command is **ip policy route-map** *route-map-name*.

Example 6-52 displays the policy routing interface configuration on R1. The route map name is an arbitrary name you can assign. This example assigns a route map called *nondefault*.

Example 6-52 *Policy Configuration on R1*

```
R1(config)#interface E0/0
R1(config-if)#ip policy route
R1(config-if)#ip policy route-map ?
  WORD  Route map name

R1(config-if)#ip policy route-map nondefault
```

Next, you must set the conditions on R1 so that policy routing can occur. Example 6-53 sets all IP ICMP traffic from the Ethernet segment on R1 destined for 161.108.1.0/24 through Serial 1/1 (next hop address 131.108.255.6) and all default traffic through Serial 1/0 (next hop address 131.108.255.1). Remember that BGP, as displayed in Example 6-50, is sending all traffic through Serial 1/0 on R1. Example 6-52 uses the **?** tool to illustrate the options available to you.

Example 6-53 *Route Map Configuration on R1*

```
route-map default permit 10
 match ip address 100
 set ip next-hop 131.108.255.6
access-list 100 permit icmp 131.108.1.0 0.0.0.255 161.108.1.0 0.0.0.255
```

The route map on R1 policy routes any IP ICMP packets with a source address in the range 131.108.1.1–131.108.1.255 through the next hop address 131.108.255.6.

Unfortunately, you cannot verify policy routing with the IP routing table. Example 6-54 displays R1's IP routing table.

Example 6-54 **show ip route** *on R1*

```
R1#show ip route
     131.108.0.0/16 is variably subnetted, 3 subnets, 2 masks
C       131.108.255.0/30 is directly connected, Serial1/0
C       131.108.255.4/30 is directly connected, Serial1/1
C       131.108.1.0/24 is directly connected, Ethernet0/0
     161.108.0.0/24 is subnetted, 1 subnets
B       161.108.1.0 [20/0] via 131.108.255.2, 00:22:52
B*  0.0.0.0/0 [20/0] via 131.108.255.2, 00:22:52
```

Example 6-54 stills displays that all remote networks are routed through 131.108.255.2, or Serial 1/0.

An extended ping request along with a **debug ip policy** on R1 displays any policy routing.

Example 6-55 displays an extended ping using the source address 131.108.1.1 (R1's Ethernet interface) to the remote network 161.108.1.0/4.

Example 6-55 *Extended Ping on R1*

```
R1#debug ip policy
Policy routing debugging is on
R1#ping
Protocol [ip]:
Target IP address: 161.108.1.1
Repeat count [5]:
Datagram size [100]:
```

Example 6-55 *Extended Ping on R1 (Continued)*

```
Timeout in seconds [2]:
Extended commands [n]: y
Source address or interface: 131.108.1.1
Type of service [0]:
Set DF bit in IP header? [no]:
Validate reply data? [no]:
Data pattern [0xABCD]:
Loose, Strict, Record, Timestamp, Verbose[none]:
Sweep range of sizes [n]:
Type escape sequence to abort.
Sending 5, 100-byte ICMP Echos to 161.108.1.1, timeout is 2 seconds:
!!!!!
Success rate is 100 percent (5/5), round-trip min/avg/max = 16/18/20 ms
00:26:57: IP: s=131.108.1.1 (local), d=161.108.1.1, len 100, policy match
00:26:57: IP: route map default, item 10, permit
00:26:57: IP: s=131.108.1.1 (local), d=161.108.1.1 (Serial1/1), len 100, policy
    routed
00:26:57: IP: local to Serial1/1 131.108.255.6
00:26:57: IP: s=131.108.1.1 (local), d=161.108.1.1, len 100, policy match
00:26:57: IP: route map default, item 10, permit
00:26:57: IP: s=131.108.1.1 (local), d=161.108.1.1 (Serial1/1), len 100, policy
    routed
00:26:57: IP: local to Serial1/1 131.108.255.6
00:26:57: IP: s=131.108.1.1 (local), d=161.108.1.1, len 100, policy match
00:26:57: IP: route map default, item 10, permit
00:26:57: IP: s=131.108.1.1 (local), d=161.108.1.1 (Serial1/1), len 100, policy
    routed
00:26:57: IP: local to Serial1/1 131.108.255.6
00:26:57: IP: s=131.108.1.1 (local), d=161.108.1.1, len 100, policy match
00:26:57: IP: route map default, item 10, permit
00:26:57: IP: s=131.108.1.1 (local), d=161.108.1.1 (Serial1/1), len 100, policy
    routed
00:26:57: IP: local to Serial1/1 131.108.255.6
00:26:57: IP: s=131.108.1.1 (local), d=161.108.1.1, len 100, policy match
00:26:57: IP: route map default, item 10, permit
00:26:57: IP: s=131.108.1.1 (local), d=161.108.1.1 (Serial1/1), len 100, policy
    routed
00:26:57: IP: local to Serial1/1 131.108.255.6
```

Example 6-55 displays the five ping requests successfully policy routed through Serial 1/1, or the next hop address 131.108.255.6.

Example 6-56 displays a ping request to the unknown network 141.108.1.1 on R1 and the subsequent policy debug output.

Example 6-56 *ping 141.108.1.1 on R1*

```
R1#ping 141.108.1.1
Type escape sequence to abort.
Sending 5, 100-byte ICMP Echos to 141.108.1.1, timeout is 2 seconds:
!!!!!
Success rate is 100 percent (5/5), round-trip min/avg/max = 16/16/20 ms
00:30:35: IP: s=131.108.255.1 (local), d=141.108.1.1, len 100, policy rejected -
- normal forwarding
00:30:35: IP: s=131.108.255.1 (local), d=141.108.1.1, len 100, policy rejected -
- normal forwarding
00:30:35: IP: s=131.108.255.1 (local), d=141.108.1.1, len 100, policy rejected -
- normal forwarding
00:30:35: IP: s=131.108.255.1 (local), d=141.108.1.1, len 100, policy rejected -
- normal forwarding
00:30:35: IP: s=131.108.255.1 (local), d=141.108.1.1, len 100, policy rejected -
- normal forwarding
00:30:37: IP: s=131.108.255.1 (local), d=131.108.255.2, len 59, policy rejected
-- normal forwarding
00:30:39: IP: s=131.108.255.5 (local), d=131.108.255.6, len 59, policy rejected
-- normal forwarding
```

R1 sends all packets to an unknown destination through normal forwarding through Serial 1/0. The debug output in Example 6-56 displays a nonmatching policy; hence, the IP datagram is forwarded through the normal outbound interface.

This simple scenario demonstrates the powerful use of policy-based routing on source and destination addresses. With the use of extended access lists, you can also base routing on port numbers. For example, you can do this if you want Telnet sessions to go through one interface or another.

Configure R1 to send all Telnet traffic originated from the network 131.108.1.0/24 through the next hop interface 131.108.255.6.

Example 6-57 displays the access-list configuration to allow Telnet sessions through Serial 1/1.

Example 6-57 *Allowing Telnet to Be Policy Routed on R1*

```
access-list 100 permit tcp 131.108.1.0 0.0.0.255 161.108.1.0 0.0.0.255 eq telnet
```

Example 6-58 *Sample* **debug ip policy** *Output on R1*

```
R1#debug ip policy
Policy routing debugging is on
R1#telnet 161.108.1.1 /source-interface ethernet 0/0
Trying 161.108.1.1 ... Open
R2>
01:04:00: IP: s=131.108.1.1 (local), d=161.108.1.1, len 44, policy match
```

Example 6-58 *Sample* **debug ip policy** *Output on R1*

```
01:04:00: IP: route map default, item 10, permit
01:04:00: IP: s=131.108.1.1 (local), d=161.108.1.1 (Serial1/1), len 44, policy
   routed
01:04:00: IP: local to Serial1/1 131.108.255.6
01:04:00: IP: s=131.108.1.1 (local), d=161.108.1.1, len 40, policy match
01:04:00: IP: route map default, item 10, permit
01:04:00: IP: s=131.108.1.1 (local), d=161.108.1.1 (Serial1/1), len 40, policy
   routed
01:04:00: IP: local to Serial1/1 131.108.255.6
01:04:00: IP: s=131.108.1.1 (local), d=161.108.1.1, len 52, policy match
01:04:00: IP: route map default, item 10, permit
01:04:00: IP: s=131.108.1.1 (local), d=161.108.1.1 (Serial1/1), len 52, policy
   routed
01:04:00: IP: local to Serial1/1 131.108.255.6
01:04:00: IP: s=131.108.1.1 (local), d=161.108.1.1, len 40, policy match
01:04:00: IP: route map default, item 10, permit
01:04:00: IP: s=131.108.1.1 (local), d=161.108.1.1 (Serial1/1), len 40, policy
   routed
01:04:00: IP: local to Serial1/1 131.108.255.6
01:04:00: IP: s=131.108.1.1 (local), d=161.108.1.1, len 43, policy match
01:04:00: IP: route map default, item 10, permit
01:04:00: IP: s=131.108.1.1 (local), d=161.108.1.1 (Serial1/1), len 43, policy
   routed
01:04:00: IP: local to Serial1/1 131.108.255.6
01:04:00: IP: s=131.108.1.1 (local), d=161.108.1.1, len 43, policy match
01:04:00: IP: route map default, item 10, permit
01:04:00: IP: s=131.108.1.1 (local), d=161.108.1.1 (Serial1/1), len 43, policy
   routed
01:04:00: IP: local to Serial1/1 131.108.255.6
01:04:00: IP: s=131.108.1.1 (local), d=161.108.1.1, len 49, policy match
01:04:00: IP: route map default, item 10, permit
01:04:00: IP: s=131.108.1.1 (local), d=161.108.1.1 (Serial1/1), len 49, policy
   routed
01:04:00: IP: local to Serial1/1 131.108.255.6
01:04:00: IP: s=131.108.1.1 (local), d=161.108.1.1, len 43, policy match
01:04:00: IP: route map default, item 10, permit
01:04:00: IP: s=131.108.1.1 (local), d=161.108.1.1 (Serial1/1), len 43, policy
   routed
01:04:00: IP: local to Serial1/1 131.108.255.6
01:04:00: IP: s=131.108.1.1 (local), d=161.108.1.1, len 40, policy match
01:04:00: IP: route map default, item 10, permit
01:04:00: IP: s=131.108.1.1 (local), d=161.108.1.1 (Serial1/1), len 40, policy
   routed
01:04:00: IP: local to Serial1/1 131.108.255.6
```

Example 6-58 displays a sample debug output when you telnet to 161.108.1.1 from R1 using the source address of 131.108.1.1. R2 has no login on vty 0 4 lines; therefore, when you telnet from R1 to R2, you are immediately placed at the R2 prompt.

Because a policy is matched on access list 100, R1 sends all Telnet traffic through Serial 1/1.

Example 6-59 displays R1's full working configuration.

Example 6-59 *R1's Full Working Configuration*

```
hostname R1
!
enable password cisco
!
interface Ethernet0/0
 ip address 131.108.1.1 255.255.255.0
 ip route-cache policy
 ip policy route-map default
!
interface Serial1/0
 ip address 131.108.255.1 255.255.255.252
 clockrate 128000
!
interface Serial1/1
 ip address 131.108.255.5 255.255.255.252
 clockrate 128000
!
router bgp 1
 network 131.108.1.0 mask 255.255.255.0
 neighbor 131.108.255.2 remote-as 2
 neighbor 131.108.255.6 remote-as 2
!
ip local policy route-map default
access-list 100 permit icmp 131.108.1.0 0.0.0.255 161.108.1.0 0.0.0.255
access-list 100 permit tcp 131.108.1.0 0.0.0.255 161.108.1.0 0.0.0.255 eq telnet
route-map default permit 10
 match ip address 100
 set ip next-hop 131.108.255.6
line con 0
line aux 0
line vty 0 4
 no login
!
end
```

Example 6-60 displays R2's full working configuration.

Example 6-60 *R2's Full Working Configuration*

```
hostname R2
!
enable password cisco
!
interface Loopback0
 ip address 141.108.1.1 255.255.255.255
```

Example 6-60 *R2's Full Working Configuration (Continued)*

```
!
interface Ethernet0/0
 ip address 161.108.1.1 255.255.255.0
!
interface Serial1/0
 ip address 131.108.255.2 255.255.255.252
interface Serial1/1
 ip address 131.108.255.6 255.255.255.252
router bgp 2
 network 161.108.1.0 mask 255.255.255.0
 neighbor 131.108.255.1 remote-as 1
 neighbor 131.108.255.1 default-originate
 neighbor 131.108.255.5 remote-as 1
 neighbor 131.108.255.5 default-originate
!
line con 0
line aux 0
line vty 0 4
 no login
!
end
```

Scenario 6-4: BGP with Communities and Peer Groups

BGP deals with large BGP peers by using many different scalable solutions, such as the community attribute and peer groups. In this scenario, you discover how BGP uses the community attribute along with a peer group to ensure that IBGP is scalable in a large network environment. A community is a group of routers sharing the same property. A peer group is a group of BGP neighbors sharing the same update policies.

In this scenario, you configure a well-known BGP community and discover the advantages of peer groups.

NOTE

The community attribute is a number defined in the range 1 to 4,294,967,200. The IOS **set community** *community-number* [**additive**] command is used to define a value. Some well-known community attributes, such as **no-export** (do not advertise to EBGP peers) and **no-advertise** (do not advertise this route to any peer), can substitute for *community-number*.

The no export community attribute advises a BGP router carrying this attribute that the route advertised should not be advertised to any peers outside the AS.

The no advertise community attribute advises a BGP router carrying this attribute that the route advertised should not be advertised to any peers.

To apply the community attribute to a remote BGP neighbor, use the **neighbor** command:

```
neighbor {ip address | peer group} send-community
```

Figure 6-5 displays a simple four-router topology, including an Internet connection on R1 and R2. R1 peers to an EBGP peer with the IP address 141.199.1.1 (Remote AS 1001), and R2 peers to an EBGP peer with the IP address 151.100.1.1 (Remote AS 1002). Typically, large companies have more than one Internet connection, so to ensure that R1 and R2 are not the transit paths for any ISP-based traffic, you set the community attribute (well-known) **no-export** on R1 and R2.

Figure 6-5 *IBGP*

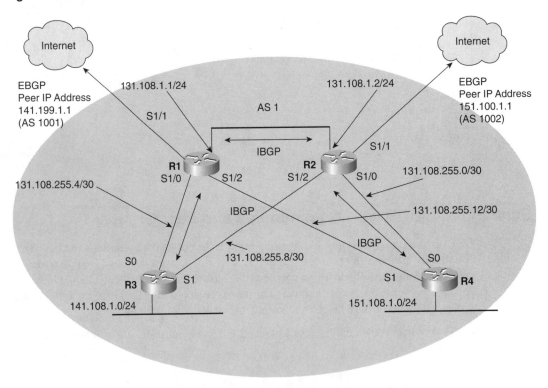

Example 6-61 displays the community attribute setting on R1.

Example 6-61 *BGP Configuration on R1*

```
R1(config)#router bgp 1
R1(config-router)#neighbor 141.199.1.1 remote-as 1001
R1(config-router)#neighbor 141.199.1.1 send-community
R1(config-router)#neighbor 141.199.1.1 route-map setcommunity ?
  in   Apply map to incoming routes
  out  Apply map to outbound routes
R1(config-router)#neighbor 141.199.1.1 route-map setcommunity out
```

R1 is configured for EBGP and IBGP. The EBGP connection to the remote peer address, 141.199.1.1, is the Internet gateway. Therefore, you must send the community to the remote peer and apply an outbound route map, so the Internet routers do not use R1 as a transit path. You have yet to apply the route map named setcommunity (arbitrary name). Example 6-62 displays the route map configuration on R1. Apply the well-known community **no-export**, which informs the neighboring router not to use R1 for any traffic not destined for the network 131.108.0.0/16.

Example 6-62 *Route Map Configuration on R1*

```
R1(config)#route-map setcommunity
R1(config-route-map)#set community ?
  <1-4294967295>  community number
  aa:nn           community number in aa:nn format
  additive        Add to the existing community
  local-AS        Do not send outside local AS (well-known community)
  no-advertise    Do not advertise to any peer (well-known community)
  no-export       Do not export to next AS (well-known community)
  none            No community attribute
  <cr>
R1(config-route-map)#set community no-export
```

Notice that the **?** tool displays all the community variations, including a community number and the two other well-known community values: **local-AS** and **no-advertise**.

You must ensure that the ISP connected to R2 does not use R2 as a transit path. Example 6-63 configures R2 to ensure that the ISP is not using the network of Routers R1–R4 as a transit path.

Example 6-63 *Community Configuration on R2*

```
R2(config)#router bgp 1
R2(config-router)#neighbor 151.100.1.1  remote-as 1002
R2(config-router)#neighbor 151.100.1.1  remote-as 1002
R2(config-router)#neighbor 151.100.1.1  se
R2(config-router)#neighbor 151.100.1.1  send-community
R2(config-router)#neighbor 151.100.1.1  route-map setcommunity out
R2(config-router)#exit
R2(config)#route-map setcommunity
R2(config-route-map)#set community no-export
```

The route map name is the same as the name used on R1 because route map names are locally significant on Cisco routers.

Next, configure the four routers, R1–R4, for IBGP, and set the same policies on all four routers. Assume the network designer has asked you to ensure that R1 does not receive any default routes from R2, R3, or R4. Also set the **next-hop-self** attribute on all IBGP peer sessions. Ensure that R1 sets the community to the value 2000.

For a small network such as this, the configuration on R1 can grow quite large. Take advantage of peer groups and configure one policy, and apply that policy on R1 to all three remote routers (R2, R3, and R4).

First, to demonstrate the power of peer groups, configure IBGP on R1.

Example 6-64 configures R1 for IBGP to R2 only, sets the **next-hop-self** attribute (no defaults routes permitted), sends the community value of 2000, and sets the weight to 1000.

Example 6-64 *R1's IBGP Configuration to R2*

```
R1(config-router)#neighbor 131.108.1.2 route-map setattributes in
R1(config-router)#neighbor 131.108.1.2 next-hop-self
R1(config-router)#neighbor 131.108.1.2 distribute-list 1 in
R1(config-router)#neighbor 131.108.1.2 send-community
R1(config-router)#neighbor 131.108.1.2 weight 1000
R1(config)#route-map setattributes
R1(config-route-map)#set community 2000
R1(config)#access-list 1 deny    0.0.0.0
```

To configure R1 to set the same attributes and conditions to R3 and R4, you need to complete the same set of IOS commands (seven IOS commands in total) and have different route maps and access lists. Clearly with a large network, this is not scalable.

To create a BGP peer group, use the **neighbor peer-group** command, beginning in router configuration mode. Example 6-65 creates a peer group on R1 named internal; again, the name is an arbitrary name.

Example 6-65 *Peer Group Command on R1*

```
R1(config)#router bgp 1
R1(config-router)#neighbor internal peer-group
```

You must then assign the options, such as the weight and community value, to the peer groups. Example 6-66 displays all the available options you can assign to a peer group.

Example 6-66 *Peer Groups Options*

```
R1(config-router)#neighbor internal ?
  advertise-map            specify route-map for conditional advertisement
  advertisement-interval   Minimum interval between sending EBGP routing updates
  default-originate        Originate default route to this neighbor
  description              Neighbor specific description
  distribute-list          Filter updates to/from this neighbor
  ebgp-multihop            Allow EBGP neighbors not on directly connected
                           networks
  filter-list              Establish BGP filters
  maximum-prefix           Maximum number of prefix accept from this peer
  next-hop-self            Disable the next hop calculation for this neighbor
```

Example 6-66 *Peer Groups Options (Continued)*

```
password                 Set a password
peer-group               Configure peer-group
prefix-list              Filter updates to/from this neighbor
remote-as                Specify a BGP neighbor
remove-private-AS        Remove private AS number from outbound updates
route-map                Apply route map to neighbor
route-reflector-client   Configure a neighbor as Route Reflector client
send-community           Send Community attribute to this neighbor
shutdown                 Administratively shut down this neighbor
soft-reconfiguration     Per neighbor soft reconfiguration
timers                   BGP per neighbor timers
unsuppress-map           Route-map to selectively unsuppress suppressed routes
```

The shaded sections in Example 6-66 contain the options you set. Example 6-67 displays the setting of a distribution list to stop a default route from being accepted on R1, advertising the **next-hop-self** attribute, setting the remote AS number to 1 (same on all IBGP peers), and ensuring that community 2000 is sent to R2, R3, and R4.

Example 6-67 *Peer Group Definitions*

```
R1(config-router)#neighbor internal  distribute-list 1 in
R1(config-router)#neighbor internal  next-hop-self
R1(config-router)#neighbor internal  remote-as 1
R1(config-router)#neighbor internal route-map setattributes in
```

Finally, apply these settings to all the remote peers. Example 6-68 shows how to make R2, R3, and R4 members of the peer group called internal.

Example 6-68 *Making R2, R3, and R4 Members of the Peer Group Internal*

```
router bgp 1
 neighbor 131.108.1.2 peer-group internal
 neighbor 131.108.255.6 peer-group internal
 neighbor 131.108.255.14 peer-group internal
```

R1 has defined three remote IBGP peers with one statement that sets all the parameters defined by the peer group internal. You can configure BGP peers to override configuration options if required. The beauty of using peer groups is that you can add more BGP peers by using only one command. This scales much better than configuring a multitude of IOS commands on several routers. Chapter 7 describes two other main methods used in BGP networks to scale in large networks, namely route reflectors (you might notice this network is fully meshed, that is, every BGP routers has a peer to each other) and confederations.

Example 6-69 displays the full working configuration on R1. Take note of the shaded sections that configure R1 to set local-based policies to all three IBGP peers. Peer groups can also be applied to EBGP peers and are commonly used in large ISP networks in which many thousands of customers might have Internet connections.

Example 6-69 *R1's Full Working Configuration*

```
hostname R1
!
enable password cisco
!
interface Ethernet0/0
 ip address 131.108.1.1 255.255.255.0
!
interface Serial1/0
 ip address 131.108.255.5 255.255.255.252
 clockrate 128000
!
interface Serial1/1
 Description Link to Internet
 ip address 141.199.2.1 255.255.255.252
!
interface Serial1/2
 ip address 131.108.255.13 255.255.255.252
 no ip directed-broadcast
!
router bgp 1
 no synchronization
 network 131.108.255.4 mask 255.255.255.252
 network 131.108.255.12 mask 255.255.255.252
 neighbor internal peer-group
 neighbor internal remote-as 1
 neighbor internal distribute-list 1 in
 neighbor internal route-map setattributes in
 neighbor 131.108.1.2 peer-group internal
 neighbor 131.108.255.6 peer-group internal
 neighbor 131.108.255.14 peer-group internal
 neighbor 141.199.1.1 remote-as 1001
 neighbor 141.199.1.1 send-community
 neighbor 141.199.1.1 route-map setcommunity out
access-list 1 deny   0.0.0.0
access-list 1 permit any
route-map setcommuntiy permit 10
 set community no-export
!
route-map setattributes permit 10
 match ip address 2
 set weight 1000
 set community 1000
line con 0
line aux 0
line vty 0 4
end
```

Example 6-70 displays the full working configuration on R2. Notice R2 is not configured for peer groups.

Example 6-70 *R2's Full Working Configuration*

```
hostname R2
!
enable password cisco
!
interface Ethernet0/0
 ip address 131.108.1.2 255.255.255.0
interface Serial1/0
 bandwidth 128
 ip address 131.108.255.1 255.255.255.252
 no ip directed-broadcast
 no ip mroute-cache
!
interface Serial1/1
Description Link to Internet
ip address 151.100.2.1 255.255.255.252
!
interface Serial1/2
 ip address 131.108.255.9 255.255.255.252
 clockrate 128000
!
router bgp 1
 no synchronization
 network 131.108.255.0 mask 255.255.255.252
 network 131.108.255.8 mask 255.255.255.252
 neighbor 131.108.1.1 remote-as 1
 neighbor 131.108.255.2 remote-as 1
 neighbor 131.108.255.10 remote-as 1
 neighbor 151.100.1.1 remote-as 1002
 neighbor 151.100.1.1 send-community
 neighbor 151.100.1.1 route-map setcommunity out
!
route-map setcommunity permit 10
 set community no-export
!
line con 0
line aux 0
line vty 0 4
!
end
```

Example 6-71 displays the full working configuration on R3. Notice R3 is not configured for peer groups.

Example 6-71 *R3's Full Working Configuration*

```
hostname R3
!
enable password cisco
!
interface Ethernet0
 ip address 141.108.1.1 255.255.255.0
!
interface Serial0
 ip address 131.108.255.6 255.255.255.252
!
interface Serial1
 ip address 131.108.255.10 255.255.255.252
!
router bgp 1
 no synchronization
 network 141.108.1.0 mask 255.255.255.0
 network 131.108.255.4 mask 255.255.255.252
 network 131.108.255.8 mask 255.255.255.252
 neighbor 131.108.255.5 remote-as 1
 neighbor 131.108.255.9 remote-as 1
!
no ip classless
route-map setweight permit 10
 match ip address 1
 set weight 1
!
route-map setweight permit 20
 match ip address 2
!
line con 0
line aux 0
line vty 0 4
end
```

Example 6-72 displays the full working configuration on R4. Notice R4 is not configured for peer groups.

Example 6-72 *R4's Full Working Configuration*

```
hostname R4
!
enable password cisco
!
interface Ethernet0
 ip address 151.108.1.1 255.255.255.0
```

Example 6-72 *R4's Full Working Configuration (Continued)*

```
!
interface Serial0
 ip address 131.108.255.2 255.255.255.252
 clockrate 125000
!
interface Serial1
 ip address 131.108.255.14 255.255.255.252
  clockrate 125000
!
interface Serial3
 ip address 131.108.255.10 255.255.255.252
 clockrate 125000
!
router bgp 1
 no synchronization
 network 131.108.255.0 mask 255.255.255.252
 network 131.108.255.12 mask 255.255.255.252
 network 151.108.1.0 mask 255.255.255.0
 neighbor 131.108.255.1 remote-as 1
 neighbor 131.108.255.13 remote-as 1
!
line con 0
line aux 0
line vty 0 4
end
```

Scenario 6-5: Verifying BGP Operation

This final scenario looks at Cisco IOS mechanisms for monitoring and verifying BGP routing within a Cisco router network.

Refer to Figure 6-4 and the BGP topology to see how to use some common **show** commands to verify that BGP is operating correctly.

Show and **debug** commands can be valuable, not only in the real-life networks you come across, but also during your certification exams.

This scenario covers the following commands:

- **show ip bgp** summary—Displays BGP neighbors in summary mode
- **show ip bgp**—Displays the BGP topology table
- **clear ip bgp** *—Clears all BGP TCP sessions
- **show tcp brief**—Displays all TCP sessions (BGP uses TCP)
- **debug ip bgp events**—Displays any BGP events, such as neighbor state changes

Example 6-73 displays a sample output taken from R1 in Figure 6-4 using the IOS **show ip bgp summary** command.

Example 6-73 **show ip bgp summary** *on R1*

```
R1#show ip bgp summary
BGP router identifier 131.108.255.13, local AS number 1
BGP table version is 11, main routing table version 11
6 network entries and 10 paths using 854 bytes of memory
3 BGP path attribute entries using 280 bytes of memory
BGP activity 50/44 prefixes, 73/63 paths
Neighbor        V    AS MsgRcvd MsgSent    TblVer  InQ OutQ Up/Down   State/PfxRcd
131.108.1.2     4     1    194     195        11    0    0 00:03:22          2
131.108.255.6   4     1     84      83        11    0    0 00:03:23          3
131.108.255.14  4     1    152     152        11    0    0 00:03:23          3
141.199.1.1     4  1001      0       0         0    0    0 never     Idle
```

Example 6-73 displays a lot of useful information, including the local router identifier 131.108.255.13, the local AS of 1, and the BGP table version of 11. (An increasing version number indicates a network change is occurring; if no changes occur, this number remains the same.) It also shows six network paths on R1, using 854 bytes of memory.

Memory is important in BGP because in a large network, such as the Internet, memory can be a limiting factor. As more BGP entries populate the IP routing table, more memory is required. Example 6-73 displays four configured remote peers: the first three are IBGP (because the AS is 1 and the same as the local AS) and one remote peer that has never been active. (The output indicates an idle session, and the up/down time displays this connection was never established.)

The BGP table is one that confuses most people. Most engineers are familiar with a standard Cisco IOS IP routing table and mistakenly apply the same principles to the BGP table. The BGP table is *not* an IP routing table. The BGP table displays information, such as remote and local network entries, BGP attributes, and selected paths. Entries are then inserted into the IP routing table.

Example 6-74 displays the BGP table on R1 in Figure 6-4. Notice the **show ip bgp** command can be performed in executive mode.

Example 6-74 **show ip bgp**

```
R1>show ip bgp
BGP table version is 11, local router ID is 131.108.255.13
Status codes: s suppressed, d damped, h history, * valid, > best, i - internal
Origin codes: i - IGP, e - EGP, ? - incomplete
    Network          Next Hop            Metric LocPrf Weight Path
*>i131.108.255.0/30  131.108.1.2              0    100   1000 i
* i                  131.108.255.14           0    100   1000 i
*>  131.108.255.4/30 0.0.0.0                  0          32768 i
* i                  131.108.255.6            0    100   1000 i
```

Example 6-74 show ip bgp *(Continued)*

```
*>i131.108.255.8/30 131.108.1.2          0    100    1000 i
* i                  131.108.255.6       0    100    1000 i
*> 131.108.255.12/30 0.0.0.0             0           32768 i
* i                  131.108.255.14      0    100    1000 i
*>i141.108.1.0/24    131.108.255.6       0    100    1000 i
*>i151.108.1.0/24    131.108.255.14      0    100    1000 i
```

Again, the BGP table version is displayed as 11 and the local router ID is 131.108.255.13. The various networks are listed along with the next hop address, metric (MED), local preference (Locpref), weight, and the path. The i on the left side (part of the status codes) indicates an internal BGP route and the i on the right side of Example 6-74 indicates the origin. (i is for IGP, part of the origin codes.)

If a BGP configuration change is completed on Cisco IOS routers, the BGP peer session must be cleared. The command to clear all sessions is **clear ip bgp ***. To clear a single peer router, use the **clear ip bgp** *peer-ip-address* command.

Example 6-75 clears all BGP sessions on R1 after a configuration change to set all IBGP peer **localpref** attributes to 1000, instead of the default value of 100.

Example 6-75 displays the BGP table after the change is configured and you clear all BGP peers sessions on R1.

Example 6-75 clear ip bgp * *and* show ip bgp *on R1*

```
R1#clear ip bgp ?
  *                 Clear all connections
  <1-65535>         AS number of the peers
  A.B.C.D           BGP neighbor address to clear
  dampening         Clear route flap dampening information
  flap-statistics   Clear route flap statistics
  peer-group        Clear BGP connections of peer-group
R1#clear ip bgp *
R1#show ip bgp
BGP table version is 11, local router ID is 131.108.255.13
Status codes: s suppressed, d damped, h history, * valid, > best, i - internal
Origin codes: i - IGP, e - EGP, ? - incomplete
   Network          Next Hop        Metric LocPrf Weight Path
*>i131.108.255.0/30 131.108.1.2          0   1000   1000 i
* i                 131.108.255.14       0   1000   1000 i
*> 131.108.255.4/30 0.0.0.0              0          32768 i
* i                 131.108.255.6        0   1000   1000 i
*>i131.108.255.8/30 131.108.1.2          0   1000   1000 i
* i                 131.108.255.6        0   1000   1000 i
*> 131.108.255.12/30 0.0.0.0             0          32768 i
* i                 131.108.255.14       0   1000   1000 i
*>i141.108.1.0/24   131.108.255.6        0   1000   1000 i
*>i151.108.1.0/24   131.108.255.14       0    100   1000 i
```

The **?** tool displays a number of options, including clearing BGP sessions based on AS numbers or remote peer address. On Cisco IOS routers, you must clear the BGP sessions if you want a change to take place because BGP does not update changes after a BGP session is established. You can, however, configure soft configurations with the **neighbor** *peer address* **soft-reconfiguration inbound** command, which enables you to make changes and not have to clear the TCP peer, resulting in no downtime.

Example 6-76 displays the output from the **show tcp brief** command on R1.

Example 6-76 show tcp brief

```
R1#show tcp brief
TCB        Local Address         Foreign Address       (state)
812CC228   131.108.255.5.11040   131.108.255.6.179     ESTAB
812CF508   131.108.1.1.11039     131.108.1.2.179       ESTAB
812D0054   131.108.255.13.11041  131.108.255.14.179    ESTAB
```

Router R1, as displayed in Example 6-76, has three TCP sessions in an established state. The TCP port numbers are also listed. This command is useful because you need to be certain that TCP is active at Layer 4 of the OSI model when troubleshooting to discover why two BGP peers are not sending updates, for example. The foreign addresses list the TCP port as 179, and the local address is a number TCP generates. This tells you that R1 has three TCP sessions active, and you can expect BGP to send updates and keepalives across each TCP session.

Debugging BGP is useful. The most widely used tool when establishing why BGP is or is not peering is the **debug ip bgp events** command. Next, clear all BGP sessions on R1 with this **debug** command turned on to discover the session you activated.

Example 6-77 displays the sample output taken from R1 when the BGP sessions are cleared for demonstration purposes. You would never use this command during normal working hours, because BGP loses peering to any remote peers. Also, notice that the **clear** and **debug** commands are performed in privileged mode.

Example 6-77 debug ip bgp events *and* clear ip bgp *on R1*

```
R1#debug ip bgp events
BGP events debugging is on
R1#clear ip bgp *
4d01h: BGP: reset all neighbors due to User reset
4d01h: BGP: 131.108.1.2 went from Established to Idle
4d01h: BGP: 131.108.255.6 went from Established to Idle
4d01h: BGP: 131.108.255.14 went from Established to Idle
4d01h: BGP: 131.108.1.2 went from Idle to Active
4d01h: BGP: 131.108.255.6 went from Idle to Active
4d01h: BGP: 131.108.255.14 went from Idle to Active
4d01h: BGP: 131.108.255.6 went from Active to OpenSent
```

Example 6-77 debug ip bgp events *and* clear ip bgp *on R1 (Continued)*

```
4d01h: BGP: 131.108.255.6 went from OpenSent to OpenConfirm
4d01h: BGP: 131.108.255.6 went from OpenConfirm to Established
4d01h: BGP: 131.108.255.6 computing updates, neighbor version 0, table version 1,
   starting at 0.0.0.0
4d01h: BGP: 131.108.255.6 update run completed, ran for 0ms, neighbor version 0,
   start version 1, throttled to 1, check point net 0.0.0.0
4d01h: BGP: 131.108.255.14 went from Active to OpenSent
4d01h: BGP: 131.108.255.14 went from OpenSent to OpenConfirm
4d01h: BGP: 131.108.255.14 went from OpenConfirm to Established
4d01h: BGP: 131.108.255.14 computing updates, neighbor version 0, table version 1,
   starting at 0.0.0.0
4d01h: BGP: 131.108.255.14 update run completed, ran for 0ms, neighbor version 0,
   start version 1, throttled to 1, check point net 0.0.0.0
4d01h: BGP: 131.108.1.2 went from Active to OpenSent
4d01h: BGP: 131.108.1.2 went from OpenSent to OpenConfirm
4d01h: BGP: 131.108.1.2 went from OpenConfirm to Established
4d01h: BGP: 131.108.1.2 computing updates, neighbor version 0, table version 1,
   starting at 0.0.0.0
4d01h: BGP: 131.108.1.2 update run completed, ran for 0ms, neighbor version 0,
   start version 1, throttled to 1, check point net 0.0.0.0
4d01h: BGP: 131.108.255.6 computing updates, neighbor version 1, table version 9,
   starting at 0.0.0.0
4d01h: BGP: 131.108.255.6 update run completed, ran for 0ms, neighbor version 1,
   start version 9, throttled to 9, check point net 0.0.0.0
4d01h: BGP: scanning routing tables
4d01h: BGP: scanning routing tables
4d01h: BGP: scanning routing tables
```

The sample output from Example 6-77 displays the BGP session's teardown state (reset by user) and the re-establishing of TCP sessions to the three peers: 131.108.255.14, 131.108.255.14, and 131.108.1.2. After the sessions are active, only changes are sent across the TCP peers. You can view keepalives with the **debug ip bgp keepalives** command. Example 6-78 displays a sample output taken from R1 after the TCP peers are established.

Example 6-78 debug ip bgp keepalives *on R1*

```
R1#debug ip bgp keepalives
BGP keepalives debugging is on
4d01h: BGP: 131.108.255.6 sending KEEPALIVE
4d01h: BGP: 131.108.255.6 KEEPALIVE rcvd
4d01h: BGP: 131.108.255.14 sending KEEPALIVE
4d01h: BGP: 131.108.255.14 KEEPALIVE rcvd
4d01h: BGP: 131.108.1.2 sending KEEPALIVE
4d01h: BGP: 131.108.1.2 KEEPALIVE rcvd
```

R1 is sending and receiving keepalives to the three remote peers to ensure that the remote routers are still active. Assume that R1 is reloaded.

If you display the TCP sessions now, you will discover three TCP sessions using a new local TCP port number because the sessions have been re-established and a new random local TCP port number has been chosen by TCP.

Example 6-79 displays the TCP sessions on R1.

Example 6-79 **show tcp brief** *on R1*

```
R1#sh tcp brief
TCB         Local Address         Foreign Address       (state)
812CF984    131.108.255.5.11042   131.108.255.6.179     ESTAB
812CCB20    131.108.1.1.11044     131.108.1.2.179       ESTAB
812CC6A4    131.108.255.13.11043  131.108.255.14.179    ESTAB
```

Practical Exercise: EBGP and Attributes

NOTE   Practical Exercises are designed to test your knowledge of the topics covered in this chapter. The Practical Exercise begins by giving you some information about a situation and then asks you to work through the solution on your own. The solution can be found at the end.

Using the IP addressing scheme provided and BGP4 as your routing protocol, configure the network in Figure 6-6 for IP routing. Ensure that both Routers R1 and R2 have full connectivity to each other. Use the **ping** command to ensure that all networks are reachable. You must use BGP4 as your dynamic routing protocol. Ensure that all routes received by R2 are tagged as follows:

- All even routes have weight set to 100.
- All odd routes have weight set to 200.
- All even routes have MED set to 100.
- All odd routes have MED set to 200.

Figure 6-6   *EBGP Topology*

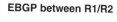

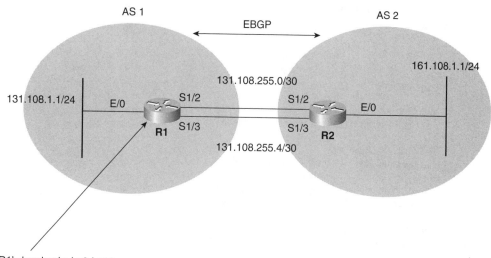

R1's loopbacks Lo0-Lo16

131.108.100.0-
131.108.116.255/24

Practical Exercise Solution

You will notice that all the IP addressing schemes are /24, except for the serial link between R1 and R2. The serial link contains a mask, 255.255.255.252 or /30. BGP has no issues with VLSM. The 16 loopbacks on R1 are advertised to R2 using the **redistribute connected** command. The **no-auto summary** command ensures that R2 sees all 16 individual routes. The access list on R2 must be set with a mask of 0.0.254.255, or all even networks match these criteria. The dual-path connections between R1 and R2 allow redundancy. There are two EBGP sessions between R1 and R2; therefore, the route map on R2 is applied to both EBGP peers in case of link failure.

Examples 6-80 and 6-81 display the full working configuration on R1 and R2, respectively. Take note of the shaded sections, as they contain critical IOS commands that ensure the desired solution is achieved.

Example 6-80 *R1's Full Working Configuration*

```
hostname R1
!
enable password cisco
!
ip subnet-zero
no ip domain-lookup
!
interface Loopback0
 ip address 131.108.110.1 255.255.255.0
!
interface Loopback1
 ip address 131.108.101.1 255.255.255.0
!
interface Loopback2
 ip address 131.108.102.1 255.255.255.0
!
interface Loopback3
 ip address 131.108.103.1 255.255.255.0
!
interface Loopback4
 ip address 131.108.104.1 255.255.255.0
!
interface Loopback5
 ip address 131.108.105.1 255.255.255.0
!
interface Loopback6
 ip address 131.108.106.1 255.255.255.0
!
interface Loopback7
 ip address 131.108.107.1 255.255.255.0
!
interface Loopback8
 ip address 131.108.108.1 255.255.255.0
!
interface Loopback9
 ip address 131.108.109.1 255.255.255.0
!
interface Loopback10
 ip address 131.108.111.1 255.255.255.0
!
interface Loopback11
 ip address 131.108.112.1 255.255.255.0
!
interface Loopback12
 ip address 131.108.113.1 255.255.255.0
!
interface Loopback13
 ip address 131.108.114.1 255.255.255.0
!
interface Loopback14
 ip address 131.108.115.1 255.255.255.0
```

Example 6-80 *R1's Full Working Configuration (Continued)*

```
!
interface Loopback15
 ip address 131.108.116.1 255.255.255.0
!
interface Ethernet0/0
 ip address 131.108.1.1 255.255.255.0
!
interface Serial1/0
shutdown
!
interface Serial1/1
shutdown
!
interface Serial1/2
 ip address 131.108.255.1 255.255.255.252
!
interface Serial1/3
 ip address 131.108.255.5 255.255.255.252
!
router bgp 1
 redistribute connected metric 100
 neighbor 131.108.255.2 remote-as 2
 neighbor 131.108.255.6 remote-as 2
 no auto-summary
line con 0
line aux 0
line vty 0 4
!
end
```

Example 6-81 shows the R2's full working configuration.

Example 6-81 *R2's Full Working Configuration*

```
hostname R2
!
enable password cisco
!
ip subnet-zero
no ip domain-lookup
interface Ethernet0/0
 ip address 161.108.1.1 255.255.255.0
interface Serial1/0
 shutdown
!
interface Serial1/1
 shutdown
```

continues

Example 6-81 *R2's Full Working Configuration (Continued)*

```
!
interface Serial1/2
 ip address 131.108.255.2 255.255.255.252
  clockrate 128000
!
interface Serial1/3
 ip address 131.108.255.6 255.255.255.252
  clockrate 128000
!
router bgp 2
 network 161.108.1.0 mask 255.255.255.0
 neighbor 131.108.255.1 remote-as 1
 neighbor 131.108.255.1 route-map setweight in
 neighbor 131.108.255.5 remote-as 1
 neighbor 131.108.255.5 route-map setweight in
 no auto-summary
!
access-list 1 permit 131.108.0.0 0.0.254.0
!
route-map setweight permit 10
 match ip address 1
 set local-preference 100
 set weight 100
!
route-map setweight permit 20
 set local-preference 200
 set weight 200
!
line con 0
line aux 0
line vty 0 4
!
end
```

Review Questions

The following questions are based on material covered in this chapter. The answers to these question can be found in Appendix C, "Answers to Review Questions."

1   Which IOS command clears all BGP sessions on a Cisco router?

2   Which IOS command is used to enable BGP4 on a Cisco router?

3   Example 6-82 displays the output from the **show tcp brief** command. How many BGP sessions are in use?

Example 6-82 show tcp brief

```
R2>show tcp brief
TCB        Local Address           Foreign Address        (state)
613EE508   131.108.255.6.11009     131.108.255.5.179      ESTAB
613ED584   131.108.255.2.11008     131.108.255.1.179      ESTAB
611654BC   161.108.1.1.23          131.108.255.1.11051    ESTAB
```

4 Which path is chosen to the remote network 131.108.1.0/24 in Example 6-83?

Use Example 6-83 to answer questions 4-6. Example 6-83 displays the BGP table on a Cisco BGP router.

Example 6-83 show ip bgp

```
R2>show ip bgp
BGP table version is 21, local router ID is 161.108.1.1
Status codes: s suppressed, d damped, h history, * valid, > best, i - internal
Origin codes: i - IGP, e - EGP, ? - incomplete
   Network          Next Hop        Metric LocPrf Weight Path
*  131.108.1.0/24   131.108.255.5      100    200    200 1 ?
*>                  131.108.255.1      100    200    200 1 ?
*  131.108.101.0/24 131.108.255.5      100    200    200 1 ?
*>                  131.108.255.1      100    200    200 1 ?
*> 161.108.1.0/24   0.0.0.0              0           32768 i
```

5 Which autonomous system does the network 131.108.101.0/24 originate from?

6 What is the metric and local preference for the remote network 131.108.101.0/24?

7 Example 6-84 displays the output from the **show ip bgp summary** command for a Cisco BGP-enabled router. What is the BGP autonomous system that R2 resides in? How many BGP sessions are active, and what version of BGP is configured on the router named R2?

Example 6-84 show ip bgp summary *on R2*

```
R2>show ip bgp summary
BGP router identifier 161.108.1.1, local AS number 2
BGP table version is 21, main routing table version 21
20 network entries and 39 paths using 3028 bytes of memory
4 BGP path attribute entries using 432 bytes of memory
BGP activity 61/41 prefixes, 119/80 paths
Neighbor        V    AS MsgRcvd MsgSent   TblVer  InQ OutQ Up/Down  State/PfxRcd
131.108.255.1   4     1    2755    2699       21    0    0 1d20h          19
131.108.255.5   4     1    2755    2699       21    0    0 1d20h          19
```

8 On a Cisco router, what value is preferred, higher or lower weight, and what is the range of values for weight?

9 What are the terms *peer* or *neighbor* used to describe in BGP?

10 What is the BGP table?

Summary

You can now begin to apply this knowledge to the more complex scenarios found in the next chapter. You learned how to successfully configure IBGP and EBGP, along with techniques used to load balance BGP using static routes. The BGP principles presented in this chapter's Practical Exercise will benefit you in the next chapter's advanced BGP scenarios.

Table 6-3 summarizes the BGP commands used in this chapter.

Table 6-3   *Summary of IOS Commands*

Command	Purpose
router bgp *number*	Enables BGP routing protocol
neighbor *remote IP address* **remote-as** *as*	Configures a BGP TCP peer
show ip bgp	Displays BGP table
{**no**} **synchronization**	Enables or disables (**no**) BGP synchronization
show ip bgp neighbors	Displays the status of BGP TCP peer sessions
show ip bgp summary	Displays status of BGP TCP peer sessions in summary format

CHAPTER 7

Advanced BGP

This chapter focuses on the advanced features of Border Gateway Protocol Version 4 (BGP4) and builds on the material presented in Chapter 6, "Basic Border Gateway Protocol." This chapter covers BGP4 in even greater detail than the CCNP Routing Exam does in order to ensure that you have a good appreciation for how networks are connected to the Internet.

BGP is a routing protocol designed for use in large IP networks. The five practical scenarios in this chapter complete your understanding and ensure that you have advanced BGP networking knowledge to complement your understanding of today's most widely used networking protocol, IP.

Scalability with Border Gateway Protocol (BGP4)

BGP is a complex routing protocol that requires that all routers be fully meshed in an Internal BGP (IBGP) network. To maintain accurate and up-to-date information in IBGP networks, all routers must peer to one another.

Consider a network consisting of 100 routers. Having this many routers leads to a large number of TCP BGP peers. In fact, you can easily calculate the number of peers by using the formula n(n-1)/2, where n is the number of BGP routers.

NOTE   To avoid routing loops, BGP only propagates updates learned from IBGP connections to other IBGP sessions that are fully meshed. Fully meshed networks contain a BGP peer to every BGP speaker in the network.

For a 100-router network, there are 100(100-1)/2 = 100(99)/2 = 4950 TCP peers.

IBGP works well in small networks, and as the network grows even to just 100 routers, the scalability and administration of BGP becomes a task you must carefully consider.

BGP deals with large BGP networks using two methods:

- Route reflectors
- Confederations (advanced form of route reflectors; confederations are beyond the scope of this chapter.)

Route reflectors are used to address the scalability issues in large IBGP networks. A route reflector is a BGP router configured to forward routing updates to BGP peers within the same autonomous system (AS). Route reflectors are not used in External BGP (EBGP) sessions.

Figure 7-1 displays a simple four-router network running IBGP.

Figure 7-1   *Four-Router IBGP Network*

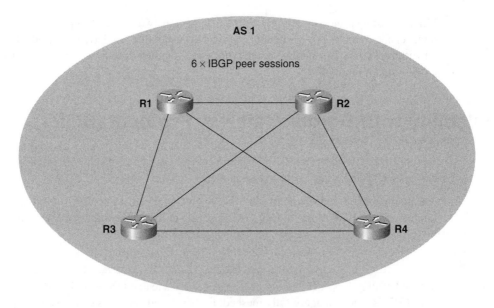

The number of IBGP sessions required to maintain full connectivity in the network in Figure 7-1 is 4(3)/2 = 6 IBGP sessions.

By using route reflectors, you can reduce the number of IBGP sessions from six to three (a 50 percent reduction). Figure 7-2 displays R1 reflecting (route reflector) BGP routing information to R2, R3, and R4.

Figure 7-2   *R1 Configured as Route Reflector*

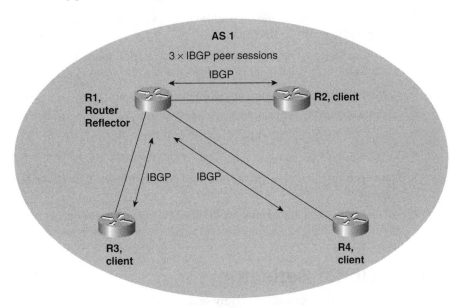

Similarly, for a network consisting of 100 routers, instead of 4950 IBGP TCP sessions (fully meshed), using route reflectors can reduce this number to 99 IBGP sessions (a 98 percent reduction).

In reality, what happens is that a router or routers running BGP become the focal point for disseminating routing information, and these routers are called route reflectors. The routers on the edge are termed the router reflector clients (or just clients).

The level of complexity, manageability, and scalability concerns in a large BGP network can be overcome by specifying a core router(s), also known as a route reflector, to perform core routing functions, such as routing updates to all edge routers. Route reflectors reduce the need to configure IBGP (full-mesh) large networks.

TIP   *Cluster* is a term used to describe a route reflector and the clients. For example, the four routers in Figure 7-2 form a BGP cluster. Confederations are another way of dealing with the explosion of an IBGP network and are typically used in networks that contain thousands of IBGP peers. The concept of confederations is based on multiple subautonomous systems.

The following are the characteristics of router reflectors:

- Route reflector configuration is enabled only on the route reflector; clients are configured normally as IBGP peers.

- The usual BGP routing algorithm is applied to all BGP routes to ensure a loop-free topology.

- Route reflectors preserve all BGP attributes.

- Updates are sent from the route reflector to all clients.

- Clients receive all updates from the route reflector only.

- In any cluster, there must be at least one route reflector.

- Nonclients (not part of a cluster) must still be fully meshed to maintain full connectivity.

- All updates contain the **originator-ID** attribute, which ensures a loop-free topology, in which the route reflector ignores any update it receives with its own originator-ID.

Configuring Route Reflectors

Configuring route reflectors is a relatively straightforward exercise. On the route reflector, apply the following IOS command to all IBGP peers:

```
neighbor ip-address route-reflector-client
```

Next, configure the four routers in Figure 7-2 for route reflectors with R1 configured as the route reflector.

Example 7-1 displays the configuration on R1, which is configured as the route reflector, to R2 (peer address 131.108.2.2), R3 (peer address (131.108.3.2), and R4 (peer address 131.108.4.2).

Example 7-1 *Configuration on R1 for Route Reflection*

```
router bgp 1
! Connection to R2
 neighbor 131.108.2.2 remote-as 1
 neighbor 131.108.2.2 route-reflector-client
! connection to R3
 neighbor 131.108.3.2 remote-as 1
 neighbor 131.108.3.2 route-reflector-client
! Connection to R4
 neighbor 131.108.4.2 remote-as 1
 neighbor 131.108.4.2 route-reflector-client
```

Example 7-1 displays the route reflector IOS command pointing to R2, R3, and R4. Also, whenever you configure route reflectors, you must still configure the IBGP session indicating the IBGP peer to R2, R3, and R4. Hence, R1 is configured as an IBGP peer to all clients, as you would normally configure an IBGP network.

The benefits of using route reflectors include the following:

- Addressing of scalability issues
- Enables a hierarchical design
- Reduces the number of TCP peers and, therefore, the amount of traffic across WAN circuits
- Fast convergence in propagation of information
- Provides easier troubleshooting as the information is typically sent from one source

Filtering is vital to any large BGP network, and to allow the network designer flexibility, BGP can be filtered using the following methods:

- **Access lists**—Used when configuring route maps and filtering networks based on IP networks using filter-based lists
- **Distribute lists**—Filter incoming or outgoing IP networks
- **Prefix lists**— Filter information based on the prefix of any address, for example, all networks starting with 131.108.0.0

Prefix lists are a new and a more efficient way of identifying routes for matching and filtering BGP information. Prefix lists are efficient because BGP routers perform lookups on only the prefix (beginning) address and can make faster routing decisions. For example, you might want to accept all networks in the range 4.0.0.0 to 4.255.255.255 and reject all other networks. In this case, a prefix list accomplishes this task efficiently and easily.

Use the following IOS command to enable a prefix list:

```
ip prefix-list list-name [seq seq value] {deny | permit} network | len
    [ge ge-value] [le le-value]
```

To apply a prefix list to a BGP peer, the following IOS command syntax is required:

```
neighbor {ip address | peer-group} prefix-list prefix-list-name {in | out}
```

To verify prefix list configuration, use the **show ip prefix-list** command in exec mode.

Table 7-1 displays some common prefix list examples used in today's large BGP networks.

Table 7-1   *Prefix List Examples Using the Prefix Name CCNP*

Filtering required	Example IOS command
Deny default routes	**ip prefix-list ccnp deny 0.0.0.0/0**
Permit a default route	**ip prefix-list ccnp permit 0.0.0.0/0**
Permit exact prefix 30.0.0.0/8	**ip prefix-list ccnp permit 30.0.0.0/8**
Deny mask lengths greater than 25 bits in routes with a prefix of 131/8	**ip prefix-list ccnp deny 131.0.0.0/8 ge 25**
Permit mask lengths from 8 to 24 bits in all address spaces	**ip prefix-list ccnp permit 0.0.0.0/0 ge 8 le 24**

Multihoming Connections to the Internet

Today, most organizations have one or more connections to the Internet. When a company connects two or more connections to the Internet, the BGP connection between the company and the ISP is termed a multihomed connection. Connections can be to the same ISP; however, typically, for redundancy, they are connected to two different ISPs.

This presents a problem because, in practice, two or more connections provide the same BGP routing information, and the BGP network designer must ensure that the ISPs do not use the company's network as a transit, specific routing information is not received through their Internet connection, and only a default route is accepted. Remember, routing involves knowing only the next hop and not the full path to a remote destination; as long as a next hop router exists, traffic transverses the Internet.

It is not uncommon to accept a full BGP routing table, but in practice, this has little or no value because all traffic to a default route is sent through the ISP connection.

Another primary concern of a multihomed connection is redistributing interior routing protocols into BGP. You can use three basic methods to accomplish this task:

- **network command**—As you saw in Chapter 6, the **network** command enables you to advertise networks to other BGP routers.

- **redistribution command**—To avoid routing loops, you must be careful when you configure redistribution from one interior protocol to and from BGP . Route maps are typically used to ensure that only the correct networks are sent to the ISP and vice versa.

- **Static routes**—Typically, static routes are used to send all traffic to unknown destinations through the ISP connection. The ISP, on the other hand, has the network in the BGP table, so traffic from the Internet can be directed to the correct outgoing interface.

Scenarios

The following scenarios are designed to draw together some of the content described in this chapter and some of the content you have seen in your own networks or practice labs. There is no one right way to accomplish many of the tasks presented, and the ability to use good practice and define your end goal are important in any real-life design or solution.

The five scenarios presented in this chapter are based on complex BGP technologies so that you become fully aware of the powerful nature of BGP in large IP networks.

Scenario 7-1: Configuring Route Reflectors

Configure the four-router topology in Figure 7-3 for IBGP using route reflectors with R1 as the route reflector and R2, R3, and R4 as the clients. To reduce TCP traffic among all BGP-speaking routers, ensure that the minimum number of peers exist.

Figure 7-3 *Four-Router Topology with Route Reflectors*

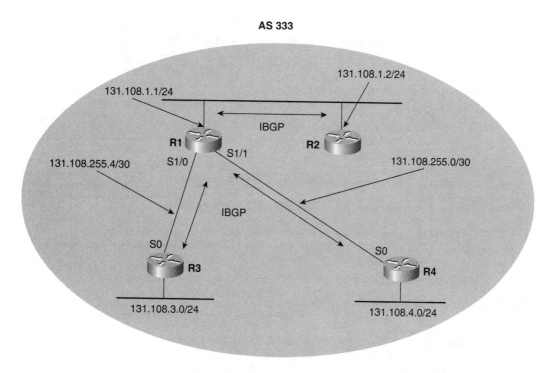

Figure 7-3 displays a simple four-router topology in AS 333. Also, notice that the Class B address 131.1.08.0.0 is used throughout this network. Typically, in a well-designed IP network, the designer applies a hierarchical IP address design to ensure that all IP address space is used efficiently. The WAN links between R1 and R2, for example, use a 30-bit subnet mask, allowing for only two hosts. R1 is configured as the route reflector, and R2, R3, and R4 are the clients.

First, you must configure IBGP on Router R1. Example 7-2 displays the IBGP configuration on R1.

Example 7-2 *R1 IBGP Configuration*

```
R1(config)#router bgp 333
! Peer to R2
R1(config-router)#neighbor 131.108.1.2 remote-as 333
! Peer to R3
R1(config-router)#neighbor 131.108.255.6 remote-as 333
! Peer to R4
R1(config-router)#neighbor 131.108.255.2 remote-as 333
```

R1 is the route reflector, so you must configure R1 to reflect BGP information to R2, R3, and R4. Example 7-3 displays the configuration with R1 as a route reflector.

Example 7-3 *R1 Route Reflector Configuration*

```
R1(config)#router bgp 333
! RR to R2
R1(config-router)#neighbor 131.108.1.2 route-reflector-client
! RR to R3
R1(config-router)#neighbor 131.108.255.6 route-reflector-client
! RR to R4
R1(config-router)#neighbor 131.108.255.2 route-reflector-client
```

Example 7-4 displays the BGP neighbors on R1 in summary format.

Example 7-4 **show ip bgp summary** *Command on R1*

```
R1#show ip bgp summary
BGP router identifier 131.108.255.5, local AS number 333
BGP table version is 3, main routing table version 3
3 network entries and 3 paths using 363 bytes of memory
1 BGP path attribute entries using 92 bytes of memory
BGP activity 6/3 prefixes, 7/4 paths
Neighbor        V    AS MsgRcvd MsgSent   TblVer  InQ OutQ Up/Down  State/PfxRcd
131.108.1.2     4   333      15      13        1    0    0 00:00:03            1
131.108.255.2   4   333      10      12        3    0    2 00:00:00            0
131.108.255.6   4   333      13      13        2    0    0 00:00:01            2
```

Example 7-4 shows that three remote peers, to R2 (131.108.1.2), R3 (131.108.255.6), and R4 (131.108.255.2), are established.

Example 7-5 displays the BGP table on R1.

Example 7-5 **show ip bgp** *Command on R1*

```
R1#show ip bgp
BGP table version is 5, local router ID is 131.108.255.5
Status codes: s suppressed, d damped, h history, * valid, > best, i - internal
Origin codes: i - IGP, e - EGP, ? - incomplete
   Network          Next Hop          Metric LocPrf Weight Path
*> 131.108.1.0/24   0.0.0.0                0          32768 i
* i                 131.108.1.2            0    100      0 i
* i131.108.3.0/24   131.108.255.6          0    100      0 i
* i131.108.4.0/24   131.108.255.2          0    100      0 i
*>i131.108.255.0/30 131.108.255.2          0    100      0 i
*>i131.108.255.4/30 131.108.255.6          0    100      0 i
```

R1 dynamically learns the remote networks 131.108.3.0/24 and 131.108.4.0/24. The IP table on R1, however, displays something quite different. Example 7-6 displays the IP routing table on R1.

Example 7-6 **show ip route** *on R1*

```
R1>show ip route
     131.108.0.0/16 is variably subnetted, 3 subnets, 2 masks
C       131.108.255.0/30 is directly connected, Serial1/1
C       131.108.255.4/30 is directly connected, Serial1/0
C       131.108.1.0/24 is directly connected, Ethernet0/0
```

The R1 routing table contains no BGP entries because, with route reflectors, IBGP does not insert any network into the IP routing table due to synchronization. In this simple case, you have no other IGP configured, so you must disable synchronization. Disable synchronization on R1, R2, R3, and R4. Example 7-7 displays disabling synchronization on Router R1; the same command should be completed on all four routers in Figure 7-3.

Example 7-7 *Disabling Synchronization on R1*

```
R1(config)#router bgp 333
R1(config-router)#no synchronization
```

The IP routing table on R1 is displayed in Example 7-8.

Example 7-8 **show ip route** *on R1*

```
R1#show ip route
Codes: C - connected, B - BGP
     131.108.0.0/16 is variably subnetted, 5 subnets, 2 masks
C       131.108.255.0/30 is directly connected, Serial1/1
```

continues

Example 7-8 show ip route *on R1 (Continued)*

```
C       131.108.255.4/30 is directly connected, Serial1/0
B       131.108.4.0/24 [200/0] via 131.108.255.2, 00:00:32
B       131.108.3.0/24 [200/0] via 131.108.255.6, 00:00:32
C       131.108.1.0/24 is directly connected, Ethernet0/0
```

R1 can now reach the two remote networks: 131.108.3.0/24 (R3) and 131.108.4.0/24 (R4). Verify that R2 can also reach these networks because R2 is a route reflector client. Example 7-9 displays the IP routing table on R2.

Example 7-9 show ip route *on R2*

```
R2#show ip route
C       131.108.1.0 is directly connected, Ethernet0/0
```

R2, even though synchronization is disabled, has no remote BGP entries. To discover why, view the BGP table on R2. Example 7-10 displays the BGP table on R2.

Example 7-10 show ip bgp *and* show ip route *on R2*

```
R2#show ip bgp
BGP table version is 3, local router ID is 131.108.7.1
Status codes: s suppressed, d damped, h history, * valid, > best, i - internal
Origin codes: i - IGP, e - EGP, ? - incomplete

   Network          Next Hop        Metric LocPrf Weight Path
*> 131.108.1.0/24   0.0.0.0              0          32768 i
* i                 131.108.1.1          0    100      0 i
* i131.108.3.0/24   131.108.255.6        0    100      0 i
* i131.108.4.0/24   131.108.255.2        0    100      0 i
* i131.108.255.0/30 131.108.255.2        0    100      0 i
* i131.108.255.4/30 131.108.255.6        0    100      0 i
R2#show ip route 131.108.255.6
% Subnet not in table
R2#show ip route 131.108.255.2
% Subnet not in table
```

Example 7-10 displays the remote entries present in R2's BGP table with a next hop address that is not routable. In other words, BGP does not insert any remote network when the next hop address is not routable. To fix this, configure R1 to advertise the WAN links to R2 and R3.

Example 7-11 displays the configuration on R1.

Example 7-11 *Advertising WAN links on R1*

```
R1(config)#router bgp 333
R1(config-router)#network 131.108.255.0 mask 255.255.255.252
R1(config-router)#network 131.108.255.4 mask 255.255.255.252
```

After you clear all the BGP sessions on R1 with the **clear ip bgp *** command, the BGP table on R2 displays the remote BGP entries in its IP routing table.

Example 7-12 displays the IP routing table on R2 and some successful ping requests to R3 E0 (131.108.3.1/24) and R4 E0 (131.108.4.1/24).

Example 7-12 show ip bgp *on R2 and* ping *on R2*

```
R2#show ip route
     131.108.0.0/16 is variably subnetted, 5 subnets, 2 masks
B       131.108.255.0/30 [200/0] via 131.108.1.1, 00:02:58
B       131.108.255.4/30 [200/0] via 131.108.1.1, 00:02:58
B       131.108.4.0/24 [200/0] via 131.108.255.2, 00:03:25
B       131.108.3.0/24 [200/0] via 131.108.255.6, 00:03:20
C       131.108.1.0/24 is directly connected, Ethernet0/0
R2#ping 131.108.3.1
Type escape sequence to abort.
Sending 5, 100-byte ICMP Echos to 131.108.3.1, timeout is 2 seconds:
!!!!!
Success rate is 100 percent (5/5), round-trip min/avg/max = 16/16/20 ms
R2#ping 131.108.4.1
Type escape sequence to abort.
Sending 5, 100-byte ICMP Echos to 131.108.4.1, timeout is 2 seconds:
!!!!!
Success rate is 100 percent (5/5), round-trip min/avg/max = 16/16/20 ms
```

Example 7-12 displays the remote BGP entries on R2, a successful ping request, and a reply to the remote networks attached to R3 and R4.

Before you consider a more complex route reflector scenario, here are the full working configurations on all four routers. Take particular note of the shaded sections, which contain critical commands, especially on R1, the route reflector.

Example 7-13 displays R1's full working configuration.

Example 7-13 *R1's Full Working Configuration*

```
hostname R1
!
enable password cisco
!
ip subnet-zero
no ip domain-lookup
interface Ethernet0/0
 ip address 131.108.1.1 255.255.255.0
!
interface Serial1/0
 ip address 131.108.255.5 255.255.255.252
 clockrate 128000
```

continues

Example 7-13 *R1's Full Working Configuration (Continued)*

```
!
interface Serial1/1
 ip address 131.108.255.1 255.255.255.252
 !
router bgp 333
 no synchronization
 network 131.108.1.0 mask 255.255.255.0
 network 131.108.255.0 mask 255.255.255.252
 network 131.108.255.4 mask 255.255.255.252
 neighbor 131.108.1.2 remote-as 333
 neighbor 131.108.1.2 route-reflector-client
 neighbor 131.108.255.2 remote-as 333
 neighbor 131.108.255.2 route-reflector-client
 neighbor 131.108.255.6 remote-as 333
 neighbor 131.108.255.6 route-reflector-client
line con 0
line aux 0
line vty 0 4
end
```

Example 7-14 displays R2's full working configuration.

Example 7-14 *R2's Full Working Configuration*

```
hostname R2
!
enable password cisco
!
ip subnet-zero
no ip domain-lookup
!
interface Ethernet0/0
 ip address 131.108.1.2 255.255.255.0
! R2 is a RR client to R1
router bgp 333
 no synchronization
 network 131.108.1.0 mask 255.255.255.0
 neighbor 131.108.1.1 remote-as 333
line con 0
line aux 0
line vty 0 4
end
```

Example 7-15 displays R3's full working configuration.

Example 7-15 *R3's Full Working Configuration*

```
hostname R3
!
enable password cisco
```

Example 7-15 *R3's Full Working Configuration (Continued)*

```
!
no ip domain-lookup
!
interface Ethernet0
 ip address 131.108.3.1 255.255.255.0
!
interface Serial0
 ip address 131.108.255.6 255.255.255.252
 bandwidth 125
!
interface Serial1
 shutdown
router bgp 333
 no synchronization
 network 131.108.3.0 mask 255.255.255.0
 network 131.108.255.4 mask 255.255.255.252
 neighbor 131.108.255.5 remote-as 333
!
line con 0
line aux 0
line vty 0 4
end
```

Example 7-16 displays R4's full working configuration.

Example 7-16 *R4's Full Working Configuration*

```
hostname R4
!
enable password cisco
!
ip subnet-zero
no ip domain-lookup
interface Ethernet0
 ip address 131.108.4.1 255.255.255.0
!
interface Serial0
 bandwidth 125
 ip address 131.108.255.2 255.255.255.252
 clockrate 125000
!
interface Serial1
shutdown
!
router bgp 333
 no synchronization
 network 131.108.4.0 mask 255.255.255.0
 network 131.108.255.0 mask 255.255.255.252
 neighbor 131.108.255.1 remote-as 333
```

continues

Example 7-16 *R4's Full Working Configuration (Continued)*

```
line con 0
line aux 0
line vty 0 4
!
end
```

Scenario 7-2: Configuring Advanced BGP Route Reflectors

Figure 7-4 displays a typical dual-homed BGP network and expands upon the network in Scenario 7-1. OSPF is the interior routing protocol used on routers R1–R5, and each router is assigned a loopback address of the form 131.108.254.1 for R1, 131.108.254.2 for R2, 131.108.253.3 for R3, 131.108.254.4 for R4, and 131.108.254.5 for R5.

Ensure that as long as there is IP connectivity, the IBGP sessions are established to R1 and R2.

The two routers, R1 and R2, have one connection to the Internet through Serial 1/0. Figure 7-4 displays the physical topology.

Figure 7-4   *Scenario 7-2 Physical Topology*

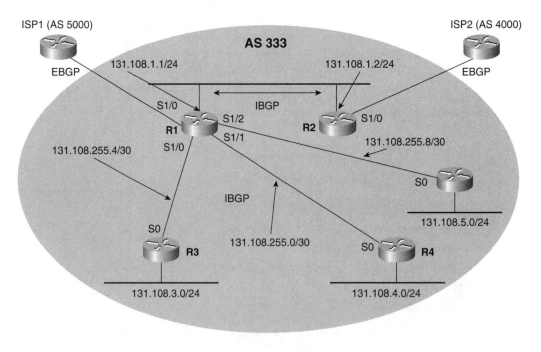

Assume the Routers R1–R5 are part of a large company and route reflectors are configured on R1 and R2 for redundancy purposes.

Figure 7-5 displays the IBGP and EBGP connections logically.

Figure 7-5   *BGP Logical Connections*

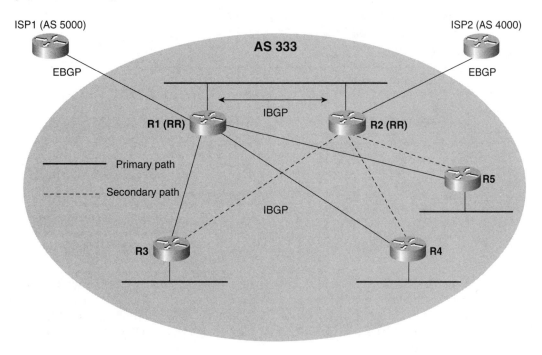

The primary path for the edge routers R3, R4, and R5 is through R1; if R1 fails, the primary path is through R2. Hence, R1 and R2 are both configured as router reflectors to provide redundancy.

Enable OSPF on the IGP routers by enabling all interfaces in area 0, so you can take advantage of loopbacks for the source and destination address for all IBGP peer sessions.

Example 7-17 configures all IP-enabled interfaces on R1 in area 0.

Example 7-17 *R1 OSPF Configuration*

```
R1(config)#router ospf 1
R1(config-router)# network 0.0.0.0 255.255.255.255 area 0
```

Configure the same two commands on R2–R5 to enable OSPF as the IGP.

Next, configure IBGP on R1 and use the loopback addresses as the next hop addresses because as long as you have IP connectivity, BGP should remain active. In fact, good IBGP design always uses loopbacks so that one routing failure does not result in loss (TCP fails) of IBGP connectivity.

Example 7-18 configures IBGP on R1 to act as a route reflector to R3, R4, and R5 using the loopback interfaces as the source and peer addresses. OSPF is used as the IGP to ensure IP connectivity among all loopback interfaces.

Example 7-18 *IBGP on R1*

```
router bgp 333
 network 131.108.1.0 mask 255.255.255.0
 neighbor 131.108.254.2 remote-as 333
 neighbor 131.108.254.2 update-source Loopback0
 neighbor 131.108.254.3 remote-as 333
 neighbor 131.108.254.3 update-source Loopback0
 neighbor 131.108.254.3 route-reflector-client
 neighbor 131.108.254.4 remote-as 333
 neighbor 131.108.254.4 update-source Loopback0
 neighbor 131.108.254.4 route-reflector-client
 neighbor 131.108.254.5 remote-as 333
 neighbor 131.108.254.5 update-source Loopback0
 neighbor 131.108.254.5 route-reflector-client
```

Example 7-18 displays the local advertisement of the network 131.108.1.0 on R1 and displays the enabling of R1 to reflect BGP information to R3, R4, and R5. For redundancy purposes, R1 is configured to peer to R2 but not as a route reflector. R1 is configured to peer to the loopback interfaces to ensure that as long as there is IP connectivity, BGP is established.

Example 7-19 displays the configuration of R2 as a backup route reflector to R3, R4, and R5.

Example 7-19 *IBGP on R2*

```
router bgp 333
 network 131.108.1.0 mask 255.255.255.0
 neighbor 131.108.254.1 remote-as 333
 neighbor 131.108.254.1 update-source Loopback0
 neighbor 131.108.254.3 remote-as 333
 neighbor 131.108.254.3 update-source Loopback0
 neighbor 131.108.254.3 route-reflector-client
 neighbor 131.108.254.4 remote-as 333
 neighbor 131.108.254.4 update-source Loopback0
 neighbor 131.108.254.4 route-reflector-client
 neighbor 131.108.254.5 remote-as 333
 neighbor 131.108.254.5 update-source Loopback0
 neighbor 131.108.254.5 route-reflector-client
 neighbor 131.108.255.2 remote-as 333
 neighbor 131.108.255.2 update-source Loopback0
```

Example 7-19 displays the local advertisement of the network 131.108.1.0 on R2 and the enabling of R2 to reflect BGP information to R3, R4, and R5. R2 is configured to peer to the loopback interfaces to ensure that as long as there is IP connectivity, IBGP is established.

Next, configure one of the edge routers, R3, for IBGP.

Example 7-20 displays the IBGP configuration on R3 pointing to R1 and R2. Because R3 is locally connected to 131.108.3.0, use the **network** command to advertise this network to R1 and R2.

Example 7-20 *IBGP on R3*

```
router bgp 333
 network 131.108.3.0 mask 255.255.255.0
 neighbor 131.108.254.1 remote-as 333
 neighbor 131.108.254.1 update-source Loopback0
 neighbor 131.108.254.2 remote-as 333
 neighbor 131.108.254.2 update-source Loopback0
```

R3 is configured normally for IBGP to R1 and R2. After the BGP peer sessions are established on routers R4 and R5, you can take a look at the BGP tables.

Example 7-21 and Example 7-22 display the IBGP configuration on R4 and R5, respectively.

Example 7-21 *IBGP on R4*

```
router bgp 333
 network 131.108.4.0 mask 255.255.255.0
 neighbor 131.108.254.1 remote-as 333
 neighbor 131.108.254.1 update-source Loopback0
 neighbor 131.108.254.2 remote-as 333
 neighbor 131.108.254.2 update-source Loopback0
```

Example 7-22 *IBGP on R5*

```
router bgp 333
 network 131.108.5.0 mask 255.255.255.0
 neighbor 131.108.254.1 remote-as 333
 neighbor 131.108.254.1 update-source Loopback0
 neighbor 131.108.254.2 remote-as 333
 neighbor 131.108.254.2 update-source Loopback0
```

All the routers in Figure 7-5 have IBGP peers configured. Example 7-23 displays the BGP table on the client router R3.

Example 7-23 show ip bgp *on R3*

```
R3#show ip bgp
   Network          Next Hop          Metric LocPrf Weight Path
*>i131.108.1.0/24   131.108.254.2          0    100      0 i
* i                 131.108.254.1          0    100      0 i
*> 131.108.3.0/24   0.0.0.0                0          32768 i
*>i131.108.4.0/24   131.108.254.4          0    100      0 i
* i                 131.108.254.4          0    100      0 i
*>i131.108.5.0/24   131.108.254.5          0    100      0 i
* i                 131.108.254.5          0    100      0 i
```

R3's BGP table has the local network 131.108.3.0/24 (indicated with the next of 0.0.0.0). Also present in the BGP table is the remote network, 131.108.1.0/24, advertised by R1 and R2. R4 advertises 131.108.4.0/24, and R5 advertises 131.108.5.0. To confirm IP connectivity, view the IP routing table on R3. Example 7-24 displays the IP routing table on R3; remember that you have OSPF configured as the IGP.

Example 7-24 show ip route *on R3*

```
R3#show ip route
Codes: C - connected, B - BGP, O - OSPF
       131.108.0.0/16 is variably subnetted, 12 subnets, 3 masks
O        131.108.255.0/30 [110/1581] via 131.108.255.5, 00:29:59, Serial0
O        131.108.254.1/32 [110/801] via 131.108.255.5, 00:29:59, Serial0
C        131.108.254.3/32 is directly connected, Loopback0
O        131.108.254.2/32 [110/811] via 131.108.255.5, 00:29:59, Serial0
O        131.108.254.5/32 [110/1582] via 131.108.255.5, 00:29:59, Serial0
C        131.108.255.4/30 is directly connected, Serial0
O        131.108.254.4/32 [110/1582] via 131.108.255.5, 00:29:59, Serial0
O        131.108.255.8/30 [110/1581] via 131.108.255.5, 00:29:59, Serial0
O        131.108.5.0/24 [110/1591] via 131.108.255.5, 00:04:22, Serial0
O        131.108.4.0/24 [110/1591] via 131.108.255.5, 00:04:22, Serial0
C        131.108.3.0/24 is directly connected, Ethernet0
O        131.108.1.0/24 [110/810] via 131.108.255.5, 00:04:10, Serial0
```

R3's IP routing table displays the remote networks 131.108.4.0/24 and 131.108.5.0/24 discovered by OSPF (indicated by the O on the left side of the IP routing table).

Even though BGP (view the BGP table in Example 7-23) has inserted the remote networks, 131.108.1.0/24, 131.108.4.0/24, and 131.108.5.0/24, as OSPF discovered routes, you need to disable synchronization on all the IBGP routers so that BGP entries are inserted into the IP routing table to see whether this solves the problem.

Example 7-25 displays the disabling of synchronization on all five routers.

Example 7-25 *Disabling Synchronization on R1–R5*

```
R1(config)#router bgp 333
R1(config-router)#no synchronization
R2(config)#router bgp 333
R2(config-router)#no synchronization
R3(config)#router bgp 333
R3(config-router)#no synchronization
R4(config)#router bgp 333
R4(config-router)#no synchronization
R5(config)#router bgp 333
R5(config-router)#no synchronization
```

After you clear all IBGP sessions on R1 and R2 with the **clear ip bgp** * command, you can expect to see BGP routing entries in the IP routing table on R3. Example 7-26 displays the IP routing table on R3.

Example 7-26 **show ip route** *on R3*

```
R3#show ip route
     131.108.0.0/16 is variably subnetted, 12 subnets, 3 masks
O       131.108.255.0/30 [110/1581] via 131.108.255.5, 01:04:33, Serial0
O       131.108.254.1/32 [110/801] via 131.108.255.5, 01:04:33, Serial0
C       131.108.254.3/32 is directly connected, Loopback0
O       131.108.254.2/32 [110/811] via 131.108.255.5, 01:04:33, Serial0
O       131.108.254.5/32 [110/1582] via 131.108.255.5, 01:04:33, Serial0
C       131.108.255.4/30 is directly connected, Serial0
O       131.108.254.4/32 [110/1582] via 131.108.255.5, 01:04:33, Serial0
O       131.108.255.8/30 [110/1581] via 131.108.255.5, 01:04:33, Serial0
O       131.108.5.0/24 [110/1591] via 131.108.255.5, 00:21:51, Serial0
O       131.108.4.0/24 [110/1591] via 131.108.255.5, 00:21:53, Serial0
C       131.108.3.0/24 is directly connected, Ethernet0
O       131.108.1.0/24 [110/810] via 131.108.255.5, 00:38:44, Serial0
```

The reason that OSPF is chosen for the preferred path is that OSPF has a lower administrative distance of 110, compared to 200 for IBGP. Change the default administrative distance on all five routers so that internal BGP is the preferred path in this five-router network.

| NOTE | The same scenario can be duplicated using EBGP, in which case, you use the concept of a backdoor to ensure that your IGP is the preferred routing method. For example, if EBGP is configured between two routers and OSPF is the interior routing protocol, EBGP administrative distance is 20, far lower than OSPF (AD is 110). By default, a lower AD is always preferred; therefore, the next hop address is the EBGP connection. To change this default |

behavior without the changing AD values, use the **network** <*network subnet-mask*> **back-door** command. Specifying the network allows the router to choose OSPF as the preferred path rather than the EBGP discovered path.

Changing the administrative distance is not always the most desirable method because all routers typically need modification, as in this scenario.

The IOS command to change the default BGP distance is as follows:

```
distance bgp external-distance internal-distance local-distance
```

The external distance is for EBGP routes (default is 20); the internal distance is for IBGP routes (default is 200), and the local distance defines the AD for locally connected routes (default is 200).

Example 7-27 displays the distance configuration on R1 and is configured on all five routers. You use the **?** tool to display the options as you enter the values.

Example 7-27 *Changing Default Distance*

```
R1(config)#router bgp 333
R1(config-router)#distance ?
  <1-255>  Administrative distance
  bgp      BGP distance
R1(config-router)#distance bgp ?
  <1-255>  Distance for routes external to the AS
R1(config-router)#distance bgp 20 ?
  <1-255>  Distance for routes internal to the AS
R1(config-router)#distance bgp 20 109 ?
  <1-255>  Distance for local routes
R1(config-router)#distance bgp 20 109 109
```

The internal distance is set to 109 (less than OSPF 110); the external distance is unchanged at 20, and the local distance is also changed to 109. Example 7-28 displays the IP routing table on R3 after the TCP peers are cleared.

Example 7-28 show ip route *on R3*

```
R3#sh ip route
     131.108.0.0/16 is variably subnetted, 12 subnets, 3 masks
O       131.108.255.0/30 [110/1581] via 131.108.255.5, 01:18:33, Serial0
O       131.108.254.1/32 [110/801] via 131.108.255.5, 01:18:33, Serial0
C       131.108.254.3/32 is directly connected, Loopback0
O       131.108.254.2/32 [110/811] via 131.108.255.5, 01:18:33, Serial0
O       131.108.254.5/32 [110/1582] via 131.108.255.5, 01:18:33, Serial0
C       131.108.255.4/30 is directly connected, Serial0
O       131.108.254.4/32 [110/1582] via 131.108.255.5, 01:18:33, Serial0
O       131.108.255.8/30 [110/1581] via 131.108.255.5, 01:18:33, Serial0
```

Example 7-28 show ip route *on R3 (Continued)*

```
B        131.108.5.0/24 [109/0] via 131.108.254.5, 00:01:38
B        131.108.4.0/24 [109/0] via 131.108.255.2, 00:01:37
C        131.108.3.0/24 is directly connected, Ethernet0
B        131.108.1.0/24 [109/0] via 131.108.254.1, 00:00:50
```

R1 now uses BGP with an AD of 109 as the preferred path to the remote networks connected to R1/R2, R4, and R5.

This scenario built a redundant IBGP network. Next, simulate a routing BGP failure to R1 and ensure that R2 becomes the preferred path on all route reflector clients.

Example 7-29 displays the current BGP table on R3.

Example 7-29 show ip bgp *on R3*

```
R3#show ip bgp
BGP table version is 84, local router ID is 131.108.254.3
Status codes: s suppressed, d damped, h history, * valid, > best, i - internal
Origin codes: i - IGP, e - EGP, ? - incomplete

   Network          Next Hop         Metric LocPrf Weight Path
* i131.108.1.0/24   131.108.254.2         0    100      0 i
*>i                 131.108.254.1         0    100      0 i
*> 131.108.3.0/24   0.0.0.0               0            32768 i
*>i131.108.4.0/24   131.108.254.4         0    100      0 i
* i                 131.108.254.4         0    100      0 i
*>i131.108.5.0/24   131.108.254.5         0    100      0 i
* i                 131.108.254.5         0    100      0 i
```

The preferred path on R3 to 131.108.1.0/24 is through R1; the peer address is 131.108.254.1 (R1's loopback address). When the TCP peer to R1 fails on R3, the preferred path is through R2 (a route reflector).

Example 7-30 displays the BGP table on R3 after the BGP failure.

Example 7-30 show ip bgp *on R3 after R1 Failure*

```
R3#show ip bgp
BGP table version is 86, local router ID is 131.108.254.3
Status codes: s suppressed, d damped, h history, * valid, > best, i - internal
Origin codes: i - IGP, e - EGP, ? - incomplete
   Network          Next Hop         Metric LocPrf Weight Path
*>i131.108.1.0/24   131.108.254.2         0    100      0 i
*> 131.108.3.0/24   0.0.0.0               0            32768 i
*>i131.108.4.0/24   131.108.254.4         0    100      0 i
*>i131.108.5.0/24   131.108.254.5         0    100      0 i
```

The path to 131.108.1.0/24 is now through R2.

Before you build upon this scenario and add the EBGP connections to the two different ISP routers, view the full working configurations of R1–R5.

Example 7-31 displays R1's full working configuration.

Example 7-31 *R1's Full Working Configuration*

```
hostname R1
!
enable password cisco
!
ip subnet-zero
no ip domain-lookup
!
interface Loopback0
 ip address 131.108.254.1 255.255.255.255
!
interface Ethernet0/0
 ip address 131.108.1.1 255.255.255.0
!
interface Serial1/0
 ip address 131.108.255.5 255.255.255.252
 clockrate 128000
!
interface Serial1/1
 ip address 131.108.255.1 255.255.255.252
!
interface Serial1/2
 ip address 131.108.255.9 255.255.255.252
clockrate 128000
!
interface Serial1/3
 shutdown
!
router ospf 1
 network 0.0.0.0 255.255.255.255 area 0
!
router bgp 333
 no synchronization
 network 131.108.1.0 mask 255.255.255.0
 neighbor 131.108.254.2 remote-as 333
 neighbor 131.108.254.2 update-source Loopback0
 neighbor 131.108.254.3 remote-as 333
 neighbor 131.108.254.3 update-source Loopback0
 neighbor 131.108.254.3 route-reflector-client
 neighbor 131.108.254.4 remote-as 333
 neighbor 131.108.254.4 update-source Loopback0
 neighbor 131.108.254.4 route-reflector-client
 neighbor 131.108.254.5 remote-as 333
 neighbor 131.108.254.5 update-source Loopback0
 neighbor 131.108.254.5 route-reflector-client
 distance bgp 20 109 109
```

Example 7-31 *R1's Full Working Configuration (Continued)*

```
!
line con 0
line aux 0
line vty 0 4
end
```

Example 7-32 displays R2's full working configuration.

Example 7-32 *R2's Full Working Configuration*

```
hostname R2
!
enable password cisco
!
ip subnet-zero
no ip domain-lookup
interface Loopback0
 ip address 131.108.254.2 255.255.255.255
!
interface Ethernet0/0
 ip address 131.108.1.2 255.255.255.0
!
router ospf 1
 network 0.0.0.0 255.255.255.255 area 0
!
router bgp 333
 no synchronization
 network 131.108.1.0 mask 255.255.255.0
 neighbor 131.108.254.1 remote-as 333
 neighbor 131.108.254.1 update-source Loopback0
 neighbor 131.108.254.3 remote-as 333
 neighbor 131.108.254.3 update-source Loopback0
 neighbor 131.108.254.3 route-reflector-client
 neighbor 131.108.254.4 remote-as 333
 neighbor 131.108.254.4 update-source Loopback0
 neighbor 131.108.254.4 route-reflector-client
 neighbor 131.108.254.5 remote-as 333
 neighbor 131.108.254.5 update-source Loopback0
 neighbor 131.108.254.5 route-reflector-client
 neighbor 131.108.255.2 remote-as 333
 neighbor 131.108.255.2 update-source Loopback0
 distance bgp 20 109 109
!
line con 0
line aux 0
line vty 0 4
!
end
```

Example 7-33 displays R3's full working configuration.

Example 7-33 *R3's Full Working Configuration*

```
hostname R3
!
enable password cisco
!
no ip domain-lookup
!
interface Loopback0
 ip address 131.108.254.3 255.255.255.255
!
interface Ethernet0
 ip address 131.108.3.1 255.255.255.0
!
interface Serial0
 ip address 131.108.255.6 255.255.255.252
 bandwidth 125
!
interface Serial1
  shutdown
!
router ospf 1
 network 0.0.0.0 255.255.255.255 area 0
!
router bgp 333
 no synchronization
 network 131.108.3.0 mask 255.255.255.0
 neighbor 131.108.254.1 remote-as 333
 neighbor 131.108.254.1 update-source Loopback0
 neighbor 131.108.254.2 remote-as 333
 neighbor 131.108.254.2 update-source Loopback0
 distance bgp 20 109 109
!
line con 0
line aux 0
line vty 0 4
!
end
```

Example 7-34 displays R4's full working configuration.

Example 7-34 *R4's Full Working Configuration*

```
hostname R4
!
enable password cisco
!
ip subnet-zero
no ip domain-lookup
```

Example 7-34 *R4's Full Working Configuration (Continued)*

```
interface Loopback0
 ip address 131.108.254.4 255.255.255.255
!
interface Ethernet0
 ip address 131.108.4.1 255.255.255.0
!
interface Serial0
 ip address 131.108.255.2 255.255.255.252
 clockrate 125000
!
interface Serial1
 shutdown
!
router ospf 1
 network 0.0.0.0 255.255.255.255 area 0
!
router bgp 333
 no synchronization
 network 131.108.4.0 mask 255.255.255.0
 neighbor 131.108.254.1 remote-as 333
 neighbor 131.108.254.1 update-source Loopback0
 neighbor 131.108.254.2 remote-as 333
 neighbor 131.108.254.2 update-source Loopback0
 distance bgp 20 109 109
line con 0
line aux 0
line vty 0 4
!
end
```

Example 7-35 displays R5's full working configuration.

Example 7-35 *R5's Full Working Configuration*

```
hostname R5
!
enable password cisco
!
ip subnet-zero
interface Loopback0
 ip address 131.108.254.5 255.255.255.255
!
interface Ethernet0
 ip address 131.108.5.1 255.255.255.0
!
interface Serial0
 ip address 131.108.255.10 255.255.255.252
!
interface Serial1
 shutdown
```

continues

Example 7-35 *R5's Full Working Configuration (Continued)*

```
!
router ospf 1
 network 0.0.0.0 255.255.255.255 area 0
!
router bgp 333
 no synchronization
 network 131.108.5.0 mask 255.255.255.0
 neighbor 131.108.254.1 remote-as 333
 neighbor 131.108.254.1 update-source Loopback0
 neighbor 131.108.254.2 remote-as 333
 neighbor 131.108.254.2 update-source Loopback0
 distance bgp 20 109 109
line con 0
line aux 0
line vty 0 4
 !
end
```

Scenario 7-3: Configuring Dual-Homing ISP Connections

In this scenario, you build upon the IBGP network in Figure 7-4 and configure EBGP on R1 and R2 and simulate a dual-homing ISP connection.

Because most CCNP candidates do not have two ISP connections to configure in a lab environment, you configure two routers and inject default routes along with a large IP routing table to simulate an ISP router.

Figure 7-6 displays the EBGP connections on R1 and R2 and the IP addressing.

Configure the routers ISP1 and ISP2 for EBGP and advertise a default route to the internal BGP network along with some routes that simulate an Internet environment.

Example 7-36 configures ISP1 for EBGP and allows a default route to be advertised to the EBGP peer to R1.

Example 7-36 *EBGP on ISP1*

```
router bgp 50001
 neighbor 171.108.1.2 remote-as 333
 neighbor 171.108.1.2 default-originate
```

Figure 7-6   *EBGP Connections*

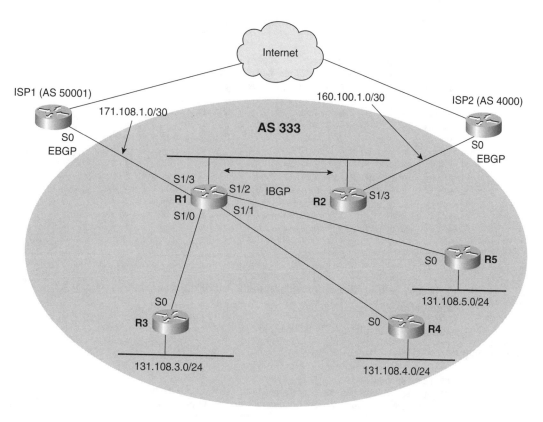

Example 7-37 displays the EBGP configuration on ISP2. Remember that both Internet routers, ISP1 and ISP2, are providing default routes to R1 and R2, respectively.

Example 7-37 *EBGP on ISP2*

```
router bgp 4000
 neighbor 160.100.1.2 remote-as 333
 neighbor 160.100.1.2 default-originate
```

View the BGP tables on R1 and R2 and ensure that the BGP table contains a default route.

Example 7-38 displays R1's BGP table.

Example 7-38 *R1's BGP table*

```
R1#show ip bgp
BGP table version is 8, local router ID is 131.108.254.1
Status codes: s suppressed, d damped, h history, * valid, > best, i - internal
Origin codes: i - IGP, e - EGP, ? - incomplete

   Network          Next Hop         Metric LocPrf Weight Path
*> 0.0.0.0          171.108.1.1                        0 50001 i
* i                 160.100.1.1              100        0 4000 i
*> 131.108.1.0/24   0.0.0.0              0            32768 i
* i                 131.108.254.2        0      100    0 i
* i131.108.3.0/24   131.108.254.3        0      100    0 i
*>i                 131.108.254.3        0      100    0 i
* i131.108.4.0/24   131.108.254.4        0      100    0 i
*>i                 131.108.254.4        0      100    0 i
* i131.108.5.0/24   131.108.254.5        0      100    0 i
*>i                 131.108.254.5        0      100    0 i
```

R1, because it has a direct connection to the EBGP peer to ISP1, selects ISP1 for default-based traffic.

Example 7-39 displays R2's BGP table.

Example 7-39 *R2's BGP table*

```
R2#show ip bgp
BGP table version is 12, local router ID is 131.108.254.2
Status codes: s suppressed, d damped, h history, * valid, > best, i - internal
Origin codes: i - IGP, e - EGP, ? - incomplete

   Network          Next Hop         Metric LocPrf Weight Path
* i0.0.0.0          171.108.1.1              100        0 50001 i
*>                  160.100.1.1                         0 4000 i
* i131.108.1.0/24   131.108.254.1        0      100    0 i
*>                  0.0.0.0              0            32768 i
* i131.108.3.0/24   131.108.254.3        0      100    0 i
*>i                 131.108.254.3        0      100    0 i
* i131.108.4.0/24   131.108.254.4        0      100    0 i
*>i                 131.108.254.4        0      100    0 i
* i131.108.5.0/24   131.108.254.5        0      100    0 i
*>i                 131.108.254.5        0      100    0 i
```

Similarly, because R2 has a direct connection to the EBGP peer to ISP2, R2 selects ISP2 for all default-based traffic. This means that traffic is sent to different ISP routers for any traffic to the Internet. This traffic pattern is undesirable because IP packets might take different paths and not reach the destination in a timely manner, resulting in loss or slow user-data transfer, such as HTTP traffic.

Ideally, a dual-home connection is for redundancy purposes only. Configure R2 to send all default traffic through the connection on R1 to ISP1, unless R1 loses the connection to ISP1.

To accomplish this task, you modify the MED value on R2 to ensure that all default traffic is sent through R1. Lower MED values are preferred, and MED influences only EBGP connections.

Example 7-40 displays the MED configuration on R2. To demonstrate another method, an example using AS_Path manipulation follows.

Example 7-40 *MED Modification on R2*

```
R2(config)#router bgp 333
R2(config-router)#neighbor 131.108.254.1 route-map setmedr1 in
R2(config-router)#neighbor 160.100.1.1 route-map setmedisp2 in
R2(config)#route-map setmedr1
R2(config-route-map)#match ip address 1
R2(config-route-map)#set metric 100
R2(config-route-map)#exit
R2(config)#route-map setmedisp2
R2(config-route-map)#match ip address 1
R2(config-route-map)#set metric 200
```

After you clear the BGP sessions to R1 and ISP2 on R2, the BGP table on R2 is displayed, as shown in Example 7-41.

Example 7-41 **show ip bgp** *on R2*

```
R2#show ip bgp
BGP table version is 9, local router ID is 131.108.254.2
Status codes: s suppressed, d damped, h history, * valid, > best, i - internal
Origin codes: i - IGP, e - EGP, ? - incomplete
   Network          Next Hop            Metric LocPrf Weight Path
*> 0.0.0.0          160.100.1.1           200          0 4000 i
*  i                171.108.1.1           100    100    0 50001 i
*  i131.108.1.0/24  131.108.254.1         100    100    0 i
*>                  0.0.0.0                 0         32768 i
*>i131.108.3.0/24   131.108.254.3           0    100    0 i
*  i                131.108.254.3         100    100    0 i
*>i131.108.4.0/24   131.108.254.4           0    100    0 i
*  i                131.108.254.4         100    100    0 i
*  i131.108.5.0/24  131.108.254.5         100    100    0 i
*>i                 131.108.254.5           0    100    0 i
```

As displayed in Example 7-41, the preferred path to the next hop 160.100.1.1, even though the MED is lower, is through ISP2. The MED attribute is compared only for paths from neighbors in the same AS.

R1 (in AS 333) and ISP2 (in AS 4000) are in different autonomous systems, so to enable BGP to compare MED in different autonomous systems, you must enable the **bgp always-compare-med** command. The **bgp always-compare-med** command allows the MED values to be compared, and BGP decisions are even though the two routers, R1 and R2, are in different autonomous systems.

Example 7-42 displays the configuration on R2 to allow MED to be compared between R1 and ISP2.

Example 7-42 **bgp always-compare-med** *Command on R2*

```
R2(config)#router bgp 333
R2(config-router)#bgp always-compare-med
```

After you clear the BGP sessions on R2, the BGP table on R2 displays the preferred default route 0.0.0.0/0 through R1.

Example 7-43 displays the BGP table on R2.

Example 7-43 **show ip bgp** *on R2*

```
R2#show ip bgp
BGP table version is 9, local router ID is 131.108.254.2
Status codes: s suppressed, d damped, h history, * valid, > best, i - internal
Origin codes: i - IGP, e - EGP, ? - incomplete
   Network          Next Hop          Metric LocPrf Weight Path
*  0.0.0.0          160.100.1.1          200            0 4000 i
*>i                 171.108.1.1          100    100     0 50001 i
*  i131.108.1.0/24  131.108.254.1        100    100     0 i
*>                  0.0.0.0                0          32768 i
*>i131.108.3.0/24   131.108.254.3          0    100     0 i
*  i                131.108.254.3        100    100     0 i
*>i131.108.4.0/24   131.108.254.4          0    100     0 i
*  i                131.108.254.4        100    100     0 i
*>i131.108.5.0/24   131.108.254.5          0    100     0 i
*  i                131.108.254.5        100    100     0 i
```

Example 7-43 shows that the new preferred path is through R1 because the MED is lower.

Before removing the configuration comparing MED on R2 and demonstrating how the AS_Path attribute can also be used to accomplish the task, Example 7-44 displays R2's full working configuration.

Example 7-44 *R2's Full Working Configuration Using MED*

```
hostname R2
!
enable password cisco
!
ip subnet-zero
no ip domain-lookup
!
interface Loopback0
 ip address 131.108.254.2 255.255.255.255
 no ip directed-broadcast
!
interface Ethernet0/0
 ip address 131.108.1.2 255.255.255.0
!
interface Serial1/3
 ip address 160.100.1.2 255.255.255.252
 clockrate 128000
!
router ospf 1
 network 0.0.0.0 255.255.255.255 area 0
!
router bgp 333
 no synchronization
 bgp always-compare-med
 network 131.108.1.0 mask 255.255.255.0
 neighbor 131.108.254.1 remote-as 333
 neighbor 131.108.254.1 update-source Loopback0
 neighbor 131.108.254.1 route-map setmedr1 in
 neighbor 131.108.254.3 remote-as 333
 neighbor 131.108.254.3 update-source Loopback0
 neighbor 131.108.254.3 route-reflector-client
 neighbor 131.108.254.4 remote-as 333
 neighbor 131.108.254.4 update-source Loopback0
 neighbor 131.108.254.4 route-reflector-client
 neighbor 131.108.254.5 remote-as 333
 neighbor 131.108.254.5 update-source Loopback0
 neighbor 131.108.254.5 route-reflector-client
 neighbor 160.100.1.1 remote-as 4000
 neighbor 160.100.1.1 route-map setmedisp2 in
 distance bgp 20 109 109
access-list 1 permit 0.0.0.0
!
route-map setmedr1 permit 10
 match ip address 1
 set metric 100
```

continues

Example 7-44 *R2's Full Working Configuration Using MED (Continued)*

```
!
route-map setmedisp2 permit 10
 match ip address 1
 set metric 200
 !
line con 0
line aux 0
line vty 0 4
 !
end
```

In Chapter 6, you learned the BGP routing decisions and one of the decisions are based on shortest AS_Path. Configure R2 to prepend AS_Paths (add AS_Paths) from ISP2 so that R1's connection to ISP1 is the preferred path for default routing.

Example 7-45 *AS_Path Manipulation of R2*

```
R2(config)#router bgp 333
R2(config-router)#no neighbor 160.100.1.1 route-map setmedisp2 in
R2(config-router)#no neighbor 131.108.254.1 route-map setmedr1 in
R2(config-router)#neighbor 160.100.1.1 route-map aspath in
R2(config)#route-map aspath
R2(config-route-map)#set ?
  as-path            Prepend string for a BGP AS-path attribute
  automatic-tag      Automatically compute TAG value
  clns               OSI summary address
  comm-list          set BGP community list (for deletion)
  community          BGP community attribute
  dampening          Set BGP route flap dampening parameters
  default            Set default information
  interface          Output interface
  ip                 IP specific information
  level              Where to import route
  local-preference   BGP local preference path attribute
  metric             Metric value for destination routing protocol
  metric-type        Type of metric for destination routing protocol
  origin             BGP origin code
  tag                Tag value for destination routing protocol
  weight             BGP weight for routing table
R2(config-route-map)#set as-path ?
  prepend  Prepend to the as-path
  tag      Set the tag as an AS-path attribute
R2(config-route-map)#set as-path prepend 4000 3999 3998
```

The? tool in Example 7-45 displays the options for prepending AS_Paths on R2. Next, configure the AS_Path to 4000 3999 3998 on R2 for all incoming routes from ISP2. Example 7-46 displays the BGP table on R2.

Example 7-46 show ip bgp *on R2*

```
R2#show ip bgp
BGP table version is 7, local router ID is 131.108.254.2
Status codes: s suppressed, d damped, h history, * valid, > best, i - internal
Origin codes: i - IGP, e - EGP, ? - incomplete
   Network          Next Hop         Metric LocPrf Weight Path
*  0.0.0.0          160.100.1.1                        0 4000 3999 3998 4000 i
*>i                 171.108.1.1                 100     0 50001 i
*> 131.108.1.0/24   0.0.0.0               0         32768 i
*  i                131.108.254.1         0      100     0 i
*  i131.108.3.0/24  131.108.254.3         0      100     0 i
*>i                 131.108.254.3         0      100     0 i
*  i131.108.4.0/24  131.108.254.4         0      100     0 i
*>i                 131.108.254.4         0      100     0 i
*  i131.108.5.0/24  131.108.254.5         0      100     0 i
*>i                 131.108.254.5         0      100     0 i
```

R2 now prefers the path through the next hop address 171.108.1.1 (R1's link to ISP1) because the AS_Path is only 50001 (one hop), or a lower hop count away compared to 4000 3999 3998 (three hops).

You have seen two methods used on R2 and discovered how powerful BGP can be in allowing the network administrator to manipulate BGP and achieve any routing path desired.

Some other common configurations completed on routers connected to the Internet include the following:

- Ensuring that only a default route is accepted
- Ensuring that you are not a transit path for any Internet traffic

Next, configure R1 and R2 to accept only a default route and ensure that the service providers, ISP1 and ISP2, do not use the network between R1 and R2 as a transit path.

Example 7-47 displays the configuration on R1 to allow only default routes and displays setting the **no-export** community to ISP1. You can use a filter list along with a route map to permit a default route.

Example 7-47 *R1 Allowing Only Default Routes (Filter List) and Setting Community*

```
R1(config)#router bgp 333
R1(config-router)#neighbor 171.108.1.1 filter
R1(config-router)#neighbor 171.108.1.1 filter-list 1
R1(config-router)#neighbor 171.108.1.1 filter-list 1 in
R1(config-router)#neighbor 171.108.1.1 send-community
```

continues

Example 7-47 *R1 Allowing Only Default Routes (Filter List) and Setting Community (Continued)*

```
R1(config-router)#neighbor 171.108.1.1 route-map noexport ?
R1(config-router)#neighbor 171.108.1.1 route-map noexport out
R1(config)#route-map no-export
R1(config-route-map)#set community no-export
R1(config)#access-list 1 permit 0.0.0.0
```

Example 7-47 displays the configuration on R2 to allow only default routes and setting the no export community to ISP1.

Example 7-48 also shows the use of a well-known community value: **no-export**. The **no-export** community attribute advises a BGP router carrying this attribute that the route advertised should not be advertised to any peers outside the AS.

Example 7-48 configures R2 (because R2 is also connected to an ISP router) using a route map to set the community and allowing only a default route using a filter list on inbound updates. In the next scenario, you use prefix lists to accomplish the same task.

Example 7-48 *R2 Allowing Only Default Routes (Filter List) and Setting Community*

```
R2(config)#router bgp 333
R2(config-router)#neighbor 160.100.1.1 route-map setcommuntiy out
R2(config-router)#neighbor 160.100.1.1 send-community
R2(config-router)#neighbor 160.100.1.1 filter-list 1 in
R2(config)#access 1 permit 0.0.0.0
R2(config)#route-map setcommuntiy
R2(config-route-map)#set community no-export
```

Before looking at how to use prefix lists to achieve complex routing filters, view the full working configurations of the four main routers in this scenario.

Example 7-49 displays ISP1's full working configuration.

Example 7-49 *ISP1's Full Working Configuration*

```
hostname ISP1
!
enable password cisco
!
ip subnet-zero
!
interface Serial0
 ip address 171.108.1.1 255.255.255.252
interface Serial1
 shutdown
!
router bgp 50001
 neighbor 171.108.1.2 remote-as 333
 neighbor 171.108.1.2 default-originate
```

Example 7-49 *ISP1's Full Working Configuration (Continued)*

```
!
line con 0
line aux 0
line vty 0 4
!
end
```

Example 7-50 displays ISP2's full working configuration.

Example 7-50 *ISP2's Full Working Configuration*

```
hostname ISP2
!
enable password cisco
!
ip subnet-zero
no ip domain-lookup
!
interface Serial0
 ip address 160.100.1.1 255.255.255.252
!
interface Serial1
 shutdown
!
router bgp 4000
 neighbor 160.100.1.2 remote-as 333
 neighbor 160.100.1.2 default-originate
line con 0
line aux 0
line vty 0 4
!
end
```

Example 7-51 displays R1's full working configuration.

Example 7-51 *R1's Full Working Configuration*

```
hostname R1
!
enable password cisco
!
ip subnet-zero
no ip domain-lookup
!
interface Loopback0
 ip address 131.108.254.1 255.255.255.255
 no ip directed-broadcast
```

continues

Example 7-51 *R1's Full Working Configuration (Continued)*

```
!
interface Ethernet0/0
 ip address 131.108.1.1 255.255.255.0
 no ip directed-broadcast
!
interface Serial1/0
 ip address 131.108.255.5 255.255.255.252
 clockrate 128000
!
interface Serial1/1
 ip address 131.108.255.1 255.255.255.252
!
interface Serial1/2
 ip address 131.108.255.9 255.255.255.252
 clockrate 128000
!
interface Serial1/3
 ip address 171.108.1.2 255.255.255.252
 clockrate 128000
!
router ospf 1
 network 0.0.0.0 255.255.255.255 area 0
!
router bgp 333
 no synchronization
 network 131.108.1.0 mask 255.255.255.0
 neighbor 131.108.254.2 remote-as 333
 neighbor 131.108.254.2 update-source Loopback0
 neighbor 131.108.254.3 remote-as 333
 neighbor 131.108.254.3 update-source Loopback0
 neighbor 131.108.254.3 route-reflector-client
 neighbor 131.108.254.4 remote-as 333
 neighbor 131.108.254.4 update-source Loopback0
 neighbor 131.108.254.4 route-reflector-client
 neighbor 131.108.254.5 remote-as 333
 neighbor 131.108.254.5 update-source Loopback0
 neighbor 131.108.254.5 route-reflector-client
 neighbor 171.108.1.1 remote-as 50001
 neighbor 171.108.1.1 send-community
 neighbor 171.108.1.1 route-map noexport out
 neighbor 171.108.1.1 filter-list 1 in
 distance bgp 20 109 109
!
route-map noexport permit 10
 set community no-export
!
line con 0
line aux 0
line vty 0 4
end
```

Example 7-52 displays R2's full working configuration.

Example 7-52 *R2's Full Working Configuration*

```
hostname R2
!
enable password cisco
!
ip subnet-zero
no ip domain-lookup
interface Loopback0
 ip address 131.108.254.2 255.255.255.255
 no ip directed-broadcast
!
interface Ethernet0/0
 ip address 131.108.1.2 255.255.255.0
!
interface Serial1/3
 ip address 160.100.1.2 255.255.255.252
 clockrate 128000
!
router ospf 1
 network 0.0.0.0 255.255.255.255 area 0
!
router bgp 333
 no synchronization
 bgp always-compare-med
 network 131.108.1.0 mask 255.255.255.0
 neighbor 131.108.254.1 remote-as 333
 neighbor 131.108.254.1 update-source Loopback0
 neighbor 131.108.254.3 remote-as 333
 neighbor 131.108.254.3 update-source Loopback0
 neighbor 131.108.254.3 route-reflector-client
 neighbor 131.108.254.4 remote-as 333
 neighbor 131.108.254.4 update-source Loopback0
 neighbor 131.108.254.4 route-reflector-client
 neighbor 131.108.254.5 remote-as 333
 neighbor 131.108.254.5 update-source Loopback0
 neighbor 131.108.254.5 route-reflector-client
 neighbor 160.100.1.1 remote-as 4000
 neighbor 160.100.1.1 send-community
 neighbor 160.100.1.1 route-map aspath in
 neighbor 160.100.1.1 route-map setcommuntiy out
 neighbor 160.100.1.1 filter-list 1 in
 distance bgp 20 109 109
!
access-list 1 permit 0.0.0.0
route-map setcommunity permit 10
 set community no-export
!
route-map setcommuntiy permit 10
 set community no-export
```

continues

Example 7-52 *R2's Full Working Configuration (Continued)*

```
!
route-map aspath permit 10
 set as-path prepend 4000 3999 3998
!
route-map setmedr1 permit 10
 match ip address 1
 set metric 100
!
route-map setmedisp2 permit 10
 match ip address 1
 set metric 200
!
line con 0
line aux 0
line vty 0 4
!
end
```

Scenario 7-4: Configuring Prefix Lists

In this scenario, you build upon the network in Figure 7-6. You use some handy configuration tips to simulate an ISP environment and use prefix lists on R1 to ensure that you receive only necessary information to save bandwidth and IP and BGP table sizes. This scenario encompasses only two routers to demonstrate the power of BGP. Figure 7-7 displays the two-router topology with the router named ISP1 simulating an ISP environment.

First, configure some routes on ISP1 pointing to Null0 (a bit bucket, commonly used in BGP to advertise routes statically for entries in the IP routing table). You use the **redistribute static** command to inject networks into R1. To make things simpler, you remove all the IBGP sessions on R1 and advertise these static routes to R1.

NOTE   All filtering, route maps, and IBGP peers configured in the previous scenario have been removed from Router R1 for clarity.

Figure 7-7   *Two-Router ISP Simulation*

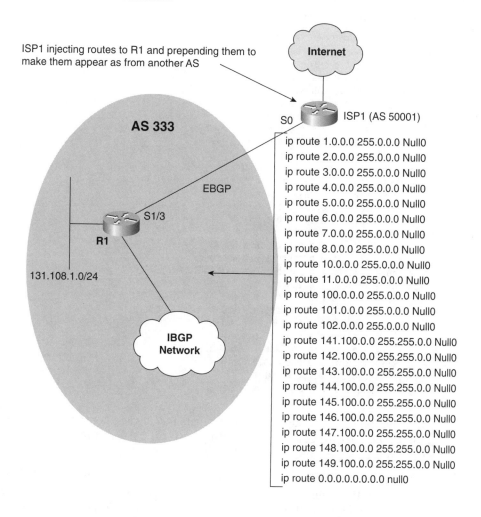

ISP1 injecting routes to R1 and prepending them to
make them appear as from another AS

Internet

AS 333

S0   ISP1 (AS 50001)

ip route 1.0.0.0 255.0.0.0 Null0
ip route 2.0.0.0 255.0.0.0 Null0
ip route 3.0.0.0 255.0.0.0 Null0
ip route 4.0.0.0 255.0.0.0 Null0
ip route 5.0.0.0 255.0.0.0 Null0
ip route 6.0.0.0 255.0.0.0 Null0
ip route 7.0.0.0 255.0.0.0 Null0
ip route 8.0.0.0 255.0.0.0 Null0
ip route 10.0.0.0 255.0.0.0 Null0
ip route 11.0.0.0 255.0.0.0 Null0
ip route 100.0.0.0 255.0.0.0 Null0
ip route 101.0.0.0 255.0.0.0 Null0
ip route 102.0.0.0 255.0.0.0 Null0
ip route 141.100.0.0 255.255.0.0 Null0
ip route 142.100.0.0 255.255.0.0 Null0
ip route 143.100.0.0 255.255.0.0 Null0
ip route 144.100.0.0 255.255.0.0 Null0
ip route 145.100.0.0 255.255.0.0 Null0
ip route 146.100.0.0 255.255.0.0 Null0
ip route 147.100.0.0 255.255.0.0 Null0
ip route 148.100.0.0 255.255.0.0 Null0
ip route 149.100.0.0 255.255.0.0 Null0
ip route 0.0.0.0 0.0.0.0 null0

EBGP

S1/3

R1

131.108.1.0/24

IBGP
Network

Example 7-53 displays the static route configuration of 25 networks on ISP1 and the advertisement of these static routes to R1.

Example 7-53 *Static Route Configuration on ISP1*

```
ip route 1.0.0.0 255.0.0.0 Null0
ip route 2.0.0.0 255.0.0.0 Null0
ip route 3.0.0.0 255.0.0.0 Null0
ip route 4.0.0.0 255.0.0.0 Null0
ip route 5.0.0.0 255.0.0.0 Null0
ip route 6.0.0.0 255.0.0.0 Null0
ip route 7.0.0.0 255.0.0.0 Null0
ip route 8.0.0.0 255.0.0.0 Null0
ip route 10.0.0.0 255.0.0.0 Null0
ip route 11.0.0.0 255.0.0.0 Null0
ip route 100.0.0.0 255.0.0.0 Null0
ip route 101.0.0.0 255.0.0.0 Null0
ip route 102.0.0.0 255.0.0.0 Null0
ip route 141.100.0.0 255.255.0.0 Null0
ip route 142.100.0.0 255.255.0.0 Null0
ip route 143.100.0.0 255.255.0.0 Null0
ip route 144.100.0.0 255.255.0.0 Null0
ip route 145.100.0.0 255.255.0.0 Null0
ip route 146.100.0.0 255.255.0.0 Null0
ip route 147.100.0.0 255.255.0.0 Null0
ip route 148.100.0.0 255.255.0.0 Null0
ip route 149.100.0.0 255.255.0.0 Null0
ip route 150.100.1.0 255.255.255.0 Null0
ip route 141.108.0.0 255.255.0.0 Null0
ip route 0.0.0.0 0.0.0.0 null0
```

Example 7-53 displays the static route configuration of Class A networks ranging from 1.0.0.0–11.0.0.0; the Class A networks 100.0.0.0, 101.0.0.0, and 102.0.0.0; and finally the Class B networks ranging from 141.100.0.0–150.100.0.0/16.

The last entry, 0.0.0.0/0, is a default route advertisement. In a real-world BGP environment, the router ISP1 would have more specific entries to all these networks, and a static route would be configured so that information can be sent over the EBGP peers without the need for dynamic routing advertisements. Null routes and loopbacks are great learning tools. To simulate a real environment, configure ISP1 to prepend some of the static routes with varying autonomous systems. Example 7-54 configures all networks in the range 1.0.0.0–11.0.0.0. The origin AS is 1000, with the path through 998 999. All other networks are prepended with the autonomous systems 400, 300, and 200. The route map name is set to prepend.

Example 7-54 *Prepending Routes on ISP1*

```
router bgp 50001
neighbor 171.108.1.2 route-map prepend out
access-list 1 permit 1.0.0.0 0.255.255.255
access-list 1 permit 2.0.0.0 0.255.255.255
access-list 1 permit 3.0.0.0 0.255.255.255
access-list 1 permit 4.0.0.0 0.255.255.255
access-list 1 permit 5.0.0.0 0.255.255.255
access-list 1 permit 6.0.0.0 0.255.255.255
access-list 1 permit 7.0.0.0 0.255.255.255
access-list 1 permit 8.0.0.0 0.255.255.255
access-list 1 permit 9.0.0.0 0.255.255.255
access-list 1 permit 10.0.0.0 0.255.255.255
access-list 1 permit 11.0.0.0 0.255.255.255
access-list 2 permit any
route-map prepend permit 10
 match ip address 1
 set origin igp
 set as-path prepend 998 999
!
route-map prepend permit 20
 match ip address 2
 set origin igp
 set as-path prepend 400 300 200
```

The route map also configures the BGP **origin** attribute to IGP (as advertised by the **network** command). All subnets allowed by access list 1 prepend all networks to 998 999 and set the origin to IGP.

Similarly, line 20 in the route map (**route-map prepend permit 20**) statement configures all networks in access list 2 with an IGP **origin** attribute. The networks defined in access list 2 are prepended with an AS of 400, 300, and 200 or {400 300 200}.

Example 7-55 confirms that the attributes are set correctly, by viewing the BGP table on R1.

Example 7-55 **show ip bgp** *on R1*

```
R1#show ip bgp
BGP table version is 25, local router ID is 131.108.254.1
Status codes: s suppressed, d damped, h history, * valid, > best, i - internal
Origin codes: i - IGP, e - EGP, ? - incomplete

   Network          Next Hop            Metric LocPrf Weight Path
*> 1.0.0.0          171.108.1.1              0             0 50001 998 999 i
*> 2.0.0.0          171.108.1.1              0             0 50001 998 999 i
*> 3.0.0.0          171.108.1.1              0             0 50001 998 999 i
*> 4.0.0.0          171.108.1.1              0             0 50001 998 999 i
*> 5.0.0.0          171.108.1.1              0             0 50001 998 999 i
*> 6.0.0.0          171.108.1.1              0             0 50001 998 999 i
```

continues

Example 7-55 show ip bgp *on R1 (Continued)*

```
*> 7.0.0.0          171.108.1.1            0              0 50001 998 999 i
*> 8.0.0.0          171.108.1.1            0              0 50001 998 999 i
*> 10.0.0.0         171.108.1.1            0              0 50001 998 999 i
*> 11.0.0.0         171.108.1.1            0              0 50001 998 999 i
*> 100.0.0.0        171.108.1.1            0              0 50001 400 300 200 i
*> 101.0.0.0        171.108.1.1            0              0 50001 400 300 200 i
*> 102.0.0.0        171.108.1.1            0              0 50001 400 300 200 i
*> 131.108.1.0/24   0.0.0.0                0          32768 i
*> 141.100.0.0      171.108.1.1            0              0 50001 400 300 200 i
*> 141.108.0.0      171.108.1.1            0              0 50001 400 300 200 i
*> 142.100.0.0      171.108.1.1            0              0 50001 400 300 200 i
*> 143.100.0.0      171.108.1.1            0              0 50001 400 300 200 i
*> 144.100.0.0      171.108.1.1            0              0 50001 400 300 200 i
*> 145.100.0.0      171.108.1.1            0              0 50001 400 300 200 i
*> 146.100.0.0      171.108.1.1            0              0 50001 400 300 200 i
*> 147.100.0.0      171.108.1.1            0              0 50001 400 300 200 i
*> 148.100.0.0      171.108.1.1            0              0 50001 400 300 200 i
*> 149.100.0.0      171.108.1.1            0              0 50001 400 300 200 i
```

The first eleven networks in Example 7-55 match access list 1 configured on ISP1.

To demonstrate full IP connectivity, view the IP routing table on R1.

Example 7-56 displays the IP (BGP routes only) routing table on R1.

Example 7-56 show ip route bgp *on R1*

```
R1#show ip route bgp
B    102.0.0.0/8 [20/0] via 171.108.1.1, 00:04:02
B    1.0.0.0/8 [20/0] via 171.108.1.1, 00:04:02
B    2.0.0.0/8 [20/0] via 171.108.1.1, 00:04:02
B    100.0.0.0/8 [20/0] via 171.108.1.1, 00:04:02
B    3.0.0.0/8 [20/0] via 171.108.1.1, 00:04:02
B    101.0.0.0/8 [20/0] via 171.108.1.1, 00:04:02
B    4.0.0.0/8 [20/0] via 171.108.1.1, 00:04:02
B    5.0.0.0/8 [20/0] via 171.108.1.1, 00:04:02
B    141.100.0.0/16 [20/0] via 171.108.1.1, 00:04:02
B    141.108.0.0/16 [20/0] via 171.108.1.1, 00:04:02
B    6.0.0.0/8 [20/0] via 171.108.1.1, 00:04:03
B    142.100.0.0/16 [20/0] via 171.108.1.1, 00:04:03
B    7.0.0.0/8 [20/0] via 171.108.1.1, 00:04:03
B    143.100.0.0/16 [20/0] via 171.108.1.1, 00:04:03
B    145.100.0.0/16 [20/0] via 171.108.1.1, 00:04:03
B    8.0.0.0/8 [20/0] via 171.108.1.1, 00:04:03
B    144.100.0.0/16 [20/0] via 171.108.1.1, 00:04:03
B    147.100.0.0/16 [20/0] via 171.108.1.1, 00:04:03
B    10.0.0.0/8 [20/0] via 171.108.1.1, 00:04:03
B    146.100.0.0/16 [20/0] via 171.108.1.1, 00:04:03
B    11.0.0.0/8 [20/0] via 171.108.1.1, 00:04:03
B    149.100.0.0/16 [20/0] via 171.108.1.1, 00:04:03
B    148.100.0.0/16 [20/0] via 171.108.1.1, 00:04:03
```

Example 7-56 displays all the networks advertised through ISP1. (Next hop address is 171.108.1.1, the EBGP peer address of ISP1.)

NOTE

If you try to ping any of these networks from R1, the ping request reaches ISP1, but because you have configured a null0 route, the packets are dropped on ISP1. For the purposes of this exercise, all you need to be interested in is generating routes. There are other methods to generate BGP routes, such as BGP generators. Cisco IOS (internal only) allows a router to generate as many routes as you could ever need to simulate the Internet. Alternatively, you could peer to your corporate Internet gateway and receive the full BGP table, although this is not a recommended exercise.

Manually generating routes to null0 using static routes is a great learning tool to deploy in any practice lab.

As you can determine, Example 7-56 shows many BGP entries. There is no need for R1, or the IBGP network, to be fully aware of all the entries advertised from ISP1 because you already have a default route. This is especially true because ISP1 is advertising the nonroutable 10.0.0.0 network, which might be in use on Router R1, or an internal network running an IGP, such as OSPF. Configure a prefix list on R1 to stop unnecessary routing traffic.

Next, you configure a prefix list on R1 to stop any BGP routes, matching the following criteria:

- Permit the default route 0.0.0.0.
- Allow any routes in the range 1.0.0.0–11.0.0.0, but not 10.0.0.0/24.
- Allow all routes 141.1.0.0/16 only. (This might be a network, for example, where a virtual private network might be configured for extranets, so you might want specific routing information such as this.)
- Deny all other routes.

NOTE

Prefix lists follow sequence numbers just as route maps do. You do not need to specify the sequence; the initial number is 5 and is incremented by 5 each time. When you view the final configuration, you will discover the IOS has inserted the sequence numbers for you.

Configure a prefix list on R1 to obtain the preceding objectives. Example 7-57 uses the **?** to guide you through the various options. First, configure a prefix list on inbound traffic from ISP1 on R1. Example 7-57 displays the filter list configuration in BGP configuration mode.

Example 7-57 *Initial Prefix List Configuration on R1 Pointing to ISP1*

```
R1(config-router)#neighbor 171.108.1.1 prefix-list ?
  WORD  Name of a prefix list
R1(config-router)#neighbor 171.108.1.1 prefix-list ccnp ?
  in   Filter incoming updates
  out  Filter outgoing updates
R1(config-router)#neighbor 171.108.1.1 prefix-list ccnp in
```

R1 is configured to apply a prefix list to all inbound traffic from the router ISP1. As yet, you have not defined the prefix list. As with an access list, you need to configure the options for the prefix list to perform any filtering.

Example 7-58 displays the prefix list configuration in global configuration mode.

Example 7-58 *Prefix List Configuration on R1*

```
R1(config)#ip prefix-list ?
  WORD             Name of a prefix list
  sequence-number  Include/exclude sequence numbers in NVGEN
R1(config)#ip prefix-list ccnp ?
  deny         Specify packets to reject
  description  Prefix-list specific descriptin
  permit       Specify packets to forward
  seq          sequence number of an entry
R1(config)#ip prefix-list ccnp permit ?
  A.B.C.D  IP prefix <network>/<length>, e.g., 35.0.0.0/8
R1(config)#ip prefix-list ccnp permit 0.0.0.0/0
R1(config)#ip prefix-list ccnp permit ?
  A.B.C.D  IP prefix <network>/<length>, e.g., 35.0.0.0/8
R1(config)#ip prefix-list ccnp permit 1.0.0.0/8
R1(config)#ip prefix-list ccnp permit 2.0.0.0/8
R1(config)#ip prefix-list ccnp permit 2.0.0.0/8
R1(config)#ip prefix-list ccnp permit 3.0.0.0/8
R1(config)#ip prefix-list ccnp permit 45.0.0.0/8
R1(config)#no ip prefix-list ccnp permit 45.0.0.0/8
R1(config)#ip prefix-list ccnp permit 4.0.0.0/8
R1(config)#ip prefix-list ccnp permit 5.0.0.0/8
R1(config)#ip prefix-list ccnp permit 6.0.0.0/8
R1(config)#ip prefix-list ccnp permit 7.0.0.0/8
R1(config)#ip prefix-list ccnp permit 8.0.0.0/8
R1(config)#ip prefix-list ccnp permit 9.0.0.0/8
R1(config)#ip prefix-list ccnp permit 11.0.0.0/8
R1(config)#ip prefix-list ccnp permit 141.1.0.0/16
```

Prefix lists, by default, implicitly deny all other networks. You do not need to deny any other networks because the Cisco IOS automatically denies all networks not specifically permitted in the prefix list, named ccnp in Example 7-58.

Example 7-59 displays the configuration on R1 when the **show running-config** command is entered in privilege mode on R1 (truncated).

Example 7-59 **show running-config** *on R1*

```
R1#show running-config
Building configuration...
Current configuration:
!...truncated
!
router bgp 333
 network 131.108.1.0 mask 255.255.255.0
 neighbor 171.108.1.1 remote-as 50001
 neighbor 171.108.1.1 prefix-list ccnp in
!
ip prefix-list ccnp seq 5 permit 0.0.0.0/0
ip prefix-list ccnp seq 10 permit 1.0.0.0/8
ip prefix-list ccnp seq 15 permit 2.0.0.0/8
ip prefix-list ccnp seq 20 permit 3.0.0.0/8
ip prefix-list ccnp seq 25 permit 4.0.0.0/8
ip prefix-list ccnp seq 30 permit 5.0.0.0/8
ip prefix-list ccnp seq 35 permit 6.0.0.0/8
ip prefix-list ccnp seq 40 permit 7.0.0.0/8
ip prefix-list ccnp seq 45 permit 8.0.0.0/8
ip prefix-list ccnp seq 50 permit 9.0.0.0/8
ip prefix-list ccnp seq 55 permit 11.0.0.0/8
ip prefix-list ccnp seq 60 permit 141.1.0.0/16
```

The Cisco IOS automatically configures sequence numbering starting from 5–60.

NOTE   The examples of prefix lists are practically endless. For more great examples, visit www.cisco.com/univercd/cc/td/doc/product/software/ios122/122cgcr/fipr_c/ipcprt2/1cfbgp.htm#xtocid798074.

Cisco recommends that prefix lists be used in preference to route maps because prefix lists are hard coded in software (complied in code terms) and take less time to process.

Example 7-60 displays the BGP table on R1 after the BGP peer is cleared and re-established on R1.

Example 7-60 show ip bgp *on R1*

```
R1#show ip bgp
BGP table version is 12, local router ID is 171.108.1.2
Status codes: s suppressed, d damped, h history, * valid, > best, i - internal
Origin codes: i - IGP, e - EGP, ? - incomplete
   Network          Next Hop          Metric LocPrf Weight Path
*> 0.0.0.0          171.108.1.1                        0 50001 i
*> 1.0.0.0          171.108.1.1            0            0 50001 998 999 i
*> 2.0.0.0          171.108.1.1            0            0 50001 998 999 i
*> 3.0.0.0          171.108.1.1            0            0 50001 998 999 i
*> 4.0.0.0          171.108.1.1            0            0 50001 998 999 i
*> 5.0.0.0          171.108.1.1            0            0 50001 998 999 i
*> 6.0.0.0          171.108.1.1            0            0 50001 998 999 i
*> 7.0.0.0          171.108.1.1            0            0 50001 998 999 i
*> 8.0.0.0          171.108.1.1            0            0 50001 998 999 i
*> 11.0.0.0         171.108.1.1            0            0 50001 998 999 i
*> 131.108.1.0/24   0.0.0.0                0        32768 i
```

R1 defines only the networks in the prefix list named ccnp.

Typically, prefix lists are used by large ISPs networks and are used to ensure that only routes permitted into an ISP are routed into the Internet. Some ISPs, for example, use the Class A 10.0.0.0 private address for network-layer addressing on all network devices and, therefore, block this network from all BGP sessions using prefix lists.

The best method you can apply to fully appreciate prefix lists is to set up a simple two-router topology and configure prefix lists to see the effect on the BGP table.

Example 7-61 displays R1's full working configuration.

Example 7-61 *R1's Full Working Configuration*

```
hostname R1
!
enable password cisco
!
ip subnet-zero
no ip domain-lookup
!
interface Ethernet0/0
 ip address 131.108.1.1 255.255.255.0
!
interface Serial1/3
 ip address 171.108.1.2 255.255.255.252
 clockrate 128000
!
router bgp 333
```

Example 7-61 *R1's Full Working Configuration (Continued)*

```
 network 131.108.1.0 mask 255.255.255.0
 neighbor 171.108.1.1 remote-as 50001
 neighbor 171.108.1.1 prefix-list ccnp in
!
ip prefix-list ccnp seq 5 permit 0.0.0.0/0
ip prefix-list ccnp seq 10 permit 1.0.0.0/8
ip prefix-list ccnp seq 15 permit 2.0.0.0/8
ip prefix-list ccnp seq 20 permit 3.0.0.0/8
ip prefix-list ccnp seq 25 permit 4.0.0.0/8
ip prefix-list ccnp seq 30 permit 5.0.0.0/8
ip prefix-list ccnp seq 35 permit 6.0.0.0/8
ip prefix-list ccnp seq 40 permit 7.0.0.0/8
ip prefix-list ccnp seq 45 permit 8.0.0.0/8
ip prefix-list ccnp seq 50 permit 9.0.0.0/8
ip prefix-list ccnp seq 55 permit 11.0.0.0/8
ip prefix-list ccnp seq 60 permit 141.1.0.0/16
!
line con 0
line aux 0
line vty 0 4
end
```

Example 7-62 displays ISP1's full working configuration.

Example 7-62 *ISP1's Full Working Configuration*

```
hostname ISP1
!
enable password cisco
!
interface Serial0
 ip address 171.108.1.1 255.255.255.252
!
router bgp 50001
 redistribute static
 neighbor 171.108.1.2 remote-as 333
 neighbor 171.108.1.2 default-originate
 neighbor 171.108.1.2 route-map prepend out
!
ip classless
ip route 0.0.0.0 0.0.0.0 Null0
ip route 1.0.0.0 255.0.0.0 Null0
ip route 2.0.0.0 255.0.0.0 Null0
ip route 3.0.0.0 255.0.0.0 Null0
ip route 4.0.0.0 255.0.0.0 Null0
ip route 5.0.0.0 255.0.0.0 Null0
ip route 6.0.0.0 255.0.0.0 Null0
ip route 7.0.0.0 255.0.0.0 Null0
ip route 8.0.0.0 255.0.0.0 Null0
```

continues

Example 7-62 *ISP1's Full Working Configuration (Continued)*

```
ip route 10.0.0.0 255.0.0.0 Null0
ip route 11.0.0.0 255.0.0.0 Null0
ip route 100.0.0.0 255.0.0.0 Null0
ip route 101.0.0.0 255.0.0.0 Null0
ip route 102.0.0.0 255.0.0.0 Null0
ip route 141.100.0.0 255.255.0.0 Null0
ip route 141.108.0.0 255.255.0.0 Null0
ip route 142.100.0.0 255.255.0.0 Null0
ip route 143.100.0.0 255.255.0.0 Null0
ip route 144.100.0.0 255.255.0.0 Null0
ip route 145.100.0.0 255.255.0.0 Null0
ip route 146.100.0.0 255.255.0.0 Null0
ip route 147.100.0.0 255.255.0.0 Null0
ip route 148.100.0.0 255.255.0.0 Null0
ip route 149.100.0.0 255.255.0.0 Null0
!
access-list 1 permit 1.0.0.0 0.255.255.255
access-list 1 permit 2.0.0.0 0.255.255.255
access-list 1 permit 3.0.0.0 0.255.255.255
access-list 1 permit 4.0.0.0 0.255.255.255
access-list 1 permit 5.0.0.0 0.255.255.255
access-list 1 permit 6.0.0.0 0.255.255.255
access-list 1 permit 7.0.0.0 0.255.255.255
access-list 1 permit 8.0.0.0 0.255.255.255
access-list 1 permit 9.0.0.0 0.255.255.255
access-list 1 permit 10.0.0.0 0.255.255.255
access-list 1 permit 11.0.0.0 0.255.255.255
access-list 2 permit any
route-map prepend permit 10
 match ip address 1
 set origin igp
 set as-path prepend 998 999
!
route-map prepend permit 20
 match ip address 2
 set origin igp
 set as-path prepend 400 300 200
!
line con 0
line aux 0
line vty 0 4
end
```

Scenario 7-5: Monitoring BGP and Verifying Correct Operation

Chapter 6 covered common BGP **show** commands. This scenario covers some of the more advanced BGP monitoring commands.

The full list of available **show** commands used in BGP is displayed in Example 7-63.

Example 7-63 *Full* **show ip bgp** *Command List*

```
R1#show ip bgp ?
  A.B.C.D          IP prefix <network>/<length>, e.g., 35.0.0.0/8
  A.B.C.D          Network in the BGP routing table to display
  cidr-only        Display only routes with non-natural netmasks
  community        Display routes matching the communities
  community-list   Display routes matching the community-list
  dampened-paths   Display paths suppressed due to dampening
  filter-list      Display routes conforming to the filter-list
  flap-statistics  Display flap statistics of routes
  inconsistent-as  Display only routes with inconsistent origin ASs
  neighbors        Detailed information on TCP and BGP neighbor connections
  paths            Path information
  peer-group       Display information on peer-groups
  regexp           Display routes matching the AS path regular expression
  summary          Summary of BGP neighbor status
  <cr>
```

This scenario covers the highlighted options in Example 7-63.

NOTE   The following sample IOS displays are taken from the two-router topology in Figure 7-7. For more examples of the full IOS command set, visit www.cisco.com/univercd/cc/td/doc/ product/software/ios122/122cgcr/fiprrp_r/bgp_r/1rfbgp2.htm.

Suppose you want Router R1 to detail information about the remote network 1.0.0.0/8. Example 7-64 displays the output of the IOS **show ip bgp 1.0.0.0/8** command.

Example 7-64 **show ip bgp 1.0.0.0/8**

```
R1#show ip bgp 1.0.0.0/8
BGP routing table entry for 1.0.0.0/8, version 3
Paths: (1 available, best #1)
  Not advertised to any peer
  50001 998 999
    171.108.1.1 from 171.108.1.1 (171.108.1.1)
      Origin IGP, metric 0, localpref 100, valid, external, best, ref 2
```

Example 7-64 shows that the remote entry is reachable through the next hop address 171.108.1.1 (ISP1). The network 1.0.0.0/8 is not advertised to any peer because R1 has only one EBGP peer to ISP1. The path traversed to reach 1.0.0.0/8 is through the AS paths 50001 (ISP1), then 998, and finally originates from 999; the **origin** attribute is set to IGP (meaning that BGP advertised this network through the **network** command). This IOS command is typically used to determine which AS path is taken to reach a remote network and the advertised peer.

Table 7-2 summarizes all the fields from Example 7-64.

Table 7-2   **show ip bgp 1.0.0.0/8** *Explained*

Field	Description
BGP table version	Internal version number of the table. This number is incremented whenever the table changes.
	Every network change results in a new table version number incremented by 1 for every change.
Status codes	Status of the table entry. The status is displayed at the beginning of each line in the table. It can be one of the following values:
	s—Entry suppressed.
	*—Entry is valid.
	>—Entry is the best entry.
	i—Entry was learned through an internal BGP (IBGP).
Origin codes	Origin of the entry. The origin code is placed at the end of each line in the table. It can be one of the following values:
	i—Entry originated from Interior Gateway Protocol (IGP) and was advertised with a **network** router configuration command.
	e—Entry originated from Exterior Gateway Protocol (EGP).
	?—Origin of the path is not clear. Usually, this is a router that is redistributed into BGP from an IGP.
Network	IP address of a network entity, 1.0.0.0/8, for example.
Next Hop	IP address of the next system that is used when forwarding a packet to the destination network.
Metric	MED.
LocPrf	Local preference value as set with the **set local-preference** *route-map* configuration command. The default value is 100.
Weight	Weight of the route, Cisco-specific only.
Path	Autonomous system paths to the destination network. In Example 7-66, the AS path is 50001 998 999.

To display routes with unnatural network masks (that is, classless interdomain routing [CIDR]), use the **show ip bgp cidr-only** command. Example 7-65 displays the output from the **show ip bgp cidr-only** command on R1. You should expect the network 131.108.1.0 (Class B subnetted or /24 network mask).

Example 7-65 **show ip bgp cidr-only** *on R1*

```
R1#show ip bgp cidr-only
BGP table version is 12, local router ID is 171.108.1.2
Status codes: s suppressed, d damped, h history, * valid, > best, i - internal
Origin codes: i - IGP, e - EGP, ? - incomplete

   Network          Next Hop          Metric LocPrf Weight Path
*> 131.108.1.0/24   0.0.0.0                0          32768 i
```

Table 7-3 displays the field descriptions for the **show ip bgp cidr-only** command.

Table 7-3   **show ip bgp cidr-only** *Descriptions*

Field	Description
BGP table version is 12	Internal version number for the table. This number is incremented whenever the table changes.
local router ID 171.108.1.2	IP address of the router.
Status codes	Status of the table entry. The status is displayed at the beginning of each line in the table. It can be one of the following values: s—The table entry is suppressed. *—The table entry is valid. >—The table entry is the best entry to use for that network. i—The table entry was learned through an internal BGP (IBGP) session.
Origin codes (131.108.1.0 is advertised using the **network** command. Hence, I is displayed.)	Origin of the entry. The origin code is placed at the end of each line in the table. It can be one of the following values: i—Entry originated from Interior Gateway Protocol (IGP) and was advertised with a **network** router configuration command. e—Entry originated from Exterior Gateway Protocol (EGP). ?—Origin of the path is not clear. Usually, this is a router that is redistributed into BGP from an IGP.

continues

Table 7-3 show ip bgp cidr-only *Descriptions (Continued)*

Field	Description
Network (131.108.1.0/24)	Internet address of the network the entry describes.
Next Hop (171.108.1.1)	IP address of the next system to use when forwarding a packet to the destination network.
Metric	MED.
LocPrf	Local preference value, as set with the **set local-preference** *route-map* configuration command.
Weight	Weight of the route, as set through autonomous system filters.
Path	Autonomous system paths to the destination network. There can be one entry in this field for each autonomous system in the path. At the end of the path is the origin code for the path: i—The entry was originated with the IGP and advertised with a **network** router configuration command. e—The route originated with EGP. ?—The origin of the path is not clear. Usually this is a path that is redistributed into BGP from an IGP

The final command most network designers use is the **show ip bgp regexp** command. This IOS command is used to match networks meeting certain path descriptions. For example, if you want to discover all the paths originating locally, you would use the **show ip bgp regexp ^$** command. This command is used to discover which networks match certain paths. Example 7-66 displays the output taken from R1 matching all networks originating locally.

Example 7-66 show ip bgp regexp ^$

```
R1#show ip bgp regexp ^$
BGP table version is 12, local router ID is 171.108.1.2
Status codes: s suppressed, d damped, h history, * valid, > best, i - internal
```

Example 7-66 show ip bgp regexp ^$ *(Continued)*

```
Origin codes: i - IGP, e - EGP, ? - incomplete

   Network          Next Hop          Metric LocPrf Weight Path
*> 131.108.1.0/24   0.0.0.0                0            32768 i
```

Because R1 is advertising the network 131.108.1.0 (connected to E0), the output from the **show ip bgp regexp ^$** command displays all locally connected originating routes.

Example 7-67 displays all networks coming through AS 998, as seen on R1.

Example 7-67 show ip bgp regexp _998_

```
R1#show ip bgp regexp _998_
BGP table version is 12, local router ID is 171.108.1.2
Status codes: s suppressed, d damped, h history, * valid, > best, i - internal
Origin codes: i - IGP, e - EGP, ? - incomplete

   Network          Next Hop          Metric LocPrf Weight Path
*> 1.0.0.0          171.108.1.1            0         0 50001 998 999 i
*> 2.0.0.0          171.108.1.1            0         0 50001 998 999 i
*> 3.0.0.0          171.108.1.1            0         0 50001 998 999 i
*> 4.0.0.0          171.108.1.1            0         0 50001 998 999 i
*> 5.0.0.0          171.108.1.1            0         0 50001 998 999 i
*> 6.0.0.0          171.108.1.1            0         0 50001 998 999 i
*> 7.0.0.0          171.108.1.1            0         0 50001 998 999 i
*> 8.0.0.0          171.108.1.1            0         0 50001 998 999 i
*> 11.0.0.0         171.108.1.1            0         0 50001 998 999 i
```

After you ascertain which networks are encompassed in path AS 998, you might want to implement a route map. For example, you could implement a route map that sets the MED to 100 and weight to 1000 for only those paths passing through 998. REGEXPs are used prior to making changes to BGP neighbors to ensure that the correct networks are tagged for further processing. You can easily discover the power of BGP—even by using only the most basic show commands described in this book.

Practical Exercise: Advanced BGP

NOTE Practical Exercises are designed to test your knowledge of the topics covered in this chapter. The Practical Exercise begins by giving you some information about a situation and then asks you to work through the solution on your own. The solution can be found at the end.

Configure the five-router topology in Figure 7-8 for IP routing. R3 runs only OSPF. R1 and R2 run BGP and OSPF.

Figure 7-8 *Five-Router Topology*

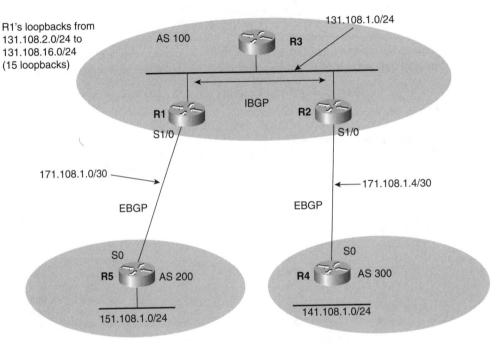

R1 has an EBGP peer to R5 and an IBGP peer to R2.

R2 has an EBGP peer to R4 and IBGP peer to R1.

Ensure that the 15 loopbacks on R1 (131.108.2.0–131.108.16.0/24) are advertised to R5 and that R5 modifies all even networks with a local weight to 1000 and metric (MED) to 100. For all odd networks, set the weight to 2000 and the metric (MED) to 200.

Ensure that R1 advertises a default route to R5 and that R2 advertises a default route to R4. Use a prefix list to accomplish this task.

Ensure that R4 does not accept any networks in the range 131.108.0.0 but does accept a default route only. All other networks must be denied on R4.

Ensure that R3 can reach all BGP-advertised networks using OSPF as the only routing protocol. (That is, redistribution is required on R1/R2).

Practical Exercise Solution

You have a lot to accomplish and you should begin by ensuring Layer 1, or the physical layer between all routers, is running. Ensure that IP addressing is accurate.

Then, perform some simple pings, for example, from R1 to R5 and R2 to R4. After Layer 1 is up, start by configuring OSPF between R1/R2 and R3. Then configure IBGP between R1 and R2, followed by EBGP between R1/R5 and R2/R4. Redistribution is required on R1/R2 so that R3 can dynamically learn the remote BGP networks on R4/R5 through OSPF (external routes Type 2).

Example 7-68 displays the full working configuration on R1. The shaded portions call your attention to critical commands required for full IP connectivity. R1 has OSPF and BGP enabled. Synchronization is disabled, and the next hop self-attribute is set to R5 so that R5 is able to reach R4's Ethernet network, 141.108.1.0/24.

Example 7-68 *R1's Full Working Configuration*

```
hostname R1
!
enable password cisco
!
ip subnet-zero
no ip domain-lookup
!
interface Loopback0
 ip address 131.108.2.1 255.255.255.0
!
interface Loopback1
 ip address 131.108.3.1 255.255.255.0
!
interface Loopback2
 ip address 131.108.4.1 255.255.255.0
!
interface Loopback3
 ip address 131.108.5.1 255.255.255.0
!
interface Loopback4
 ip address 131.108.6.1 255.255.255.0
!
interface Loopback5
 ip address 131.108.7.1 255.255.255.0
!
interface Loopback6
 ip address 131.108.8.1 255.255.255.0
!
interface Loopback7
 ip address 131.108.9.1 255.255.255.0
!
interface Loopback8
 ip address 131.108.10.1 255.255.255.0
```

continues

Example 7-68 *R1's Full Working Configuration (Continued)*

```
!
interface Loopback9
 ip address 131.108.11.1 255.255.255.0
!
interface Loopback10
 ip address 131.108.12.1 255.255.255.0
!
interface Loopback11
 ip address 131.108.13.1 255.255.255.0
!
interface Loopback12
 ip address 131.108.14.1 255.255.255.0
!
interface Loopback13
 ip address 131.108.15.1 255.255.255.0
!
interface Loopback14
 ip address 131.108.16.1 255.255.255.0
!
interface Ethernet0/0
 ip address 131.108.1.1 255.255.255.0
!
interface Serial1/0
 ip address 171.108.1.1 255.255.255.252
!
 clockrate 128000
!
router ospf 1
 redistribute connected metric 100 subnets
 redistribute bgp 100 metric 100 subnets
 network 0.0.0.0 255.255.255.255 area 0
!
router bgp 100
 no synchronization
 network 131.108.1.0 mask 255.255.255.0
 network 131.108.2.0 mask 255.255.255.0
 network 131.108.3.0 mask 255.255.255.0
 network 131.108.4.0 mask 255.255.255.0
 network 131.108.5.0 mask 255.255.255.0
 network 131.108.6.0 mask 255.255.255.0
 network 131.108.7.0 mask 255.255.255.0
 network 131.108.8.0 mask 255.255.255.0
 network 131.108.9.0 mask 255.255.255.0
 network 131.108.10.0 mask 255.255.255.0
 network 131.108.11.0 mask 255.255.255.0
 network 131.108.12.0 mask 255.255.255.0
 network 131.108.13.0 mask 255.255.255.0
 network 131.108.14.0 mask 255.255.255.0
 network 131.108.15.0 mask 255.255.255.0
 network 131.108.16.0 mask 255.255.255.0
```

Example 7-68 *R1's Full Working Configuration (Continued)*

```
 neighbor 131.108.1.2 remote-as 100
 neighbor 171.108.1.2 remote-as 200
 neighbor 171.108.1.2 next-hop-self
 neighbor 171.108.1.2 default-originate
!
ip classless
ip route 0.0.0.0 0.0.0.0 Null0
!
line con 0
line aux 0
line vty 0 4
end
```

Example 7-69 displays the full working configuration on R2. The shaded portions call your attention to critical commands required for full IP connectivity. R2 has OSPF and BGP enabled. Synchronization is disabled, and the **next-hop-self** attribute is set to R4 so that R4 can reach R5's Ethernet network, 151.108.1.0/24.

Example 7-69 *R2's Full Working Configuration*

```
hostname R2
!
enable password cisco
!
ip subnet-zero
no ip domain-lookup
!
interface Ethernet0/0
 ip address 131.108.1.2 255.255.255.0
!
interface Serial1/0
 ip address 171.108.1.5 255.255.255.252
 clockrate 128000
!
router ospf 1
 redistribute connected metric 100 subnets
 redistribute bgp 100 metric 100 subnets
 network 0.0.0.0 255.255.255.255 area 0
!
router bgp 100
 no synchronization
 network 131.108.1.0 mask 255.255.255.0
 redistribute ospf 1 metric 100
 neighbor 131.108.1.1 remote-as 100
 neighbor 171.108.1.6 remote-as 300
 neighbor 171.108.1.6 next-hop-self
 neighbor 171.108.1.6 default-originate
```

continues

Example 7-69 *R2's Full Working Configuration (Continued)*

```
!
ip classless
ip route 0.0.0.0 0.0.0.0 Null0
line con 0
line aux 0
line vty 0 4
!
end
```

Example 7-70 displays the full working configuration on R3. The shaded portions call your attention to critical commands required for full IP connectivity. R3 is running only OSPF.

Example 7-70 *R3's Full Working Configuration*

```
hostname R3
!
enable password cisco
!
no ip domain-lookup
!
interface Ethernet0
 ip address 131.108.1.3 255.255.255.0
! Places all interfaces in OSPPD area 0
router ospf 1
 network 0.0.0.0 255.255.255.255 area 0
!
line con 0
line aux 0
line vty 0 4
end
```

Example 7-71 displays the full working configuration on R4. The shaded portions call your attention to critical commands required for full IP connectivity.

Example 7-71 *R4's Full Working Configuration R4*

```
hostname R4
!
enable password cisco
!
ip subnet-zero
no ip domain-lookup
!
cns event-service server
!
interface Loopback0
 ip address 131.108.254.4 255.255.255.255
 no ip directed-broadcast
```

Example 7-71 *R4's Full Working Configuration R4 (Continued)*

```
!
interface Ethernet0
 ip address 141.108.1.1 255.255.255.0
!
interface Serial0
 ip address 171.108.1.6 255.255.255.252
router bgp 300
 network 141.108.1.0 mask 255.255.255.0
 neighbor 171.108.1.5 remote-as 100
 neighbor 171.108.1.5 prefix-list default in
ip prefix-list default seq 5 permit 0.0.0.0/0
!
line con 0
line aux 0
line vty 0 4
end
```

Example 7-72 displays the full working configuration on R5. The shaded portions call your attention to critical commands required for full IP connectivity.

Example 7-72 *R5's Full Working Configuration*

```
hostname R5
!
enable password cisco
!
ip subnet-zero
interface Ethernet0
 ip address 151.108.1.1 255.255.255.0
!
interface Serial0
 ip address 171.108.1.2 255.255.255.252
!
router bgp 200
 network 151.108.1.0 mask 255.255.255.0
 neighbor 171.108.1.1 remote-as 100
 neighbor 171.108.1.1 route-map changeattributes in
 no auto-summary
!
ip classless
!This ACL permits all even networks
access-list 1 permit 131.108.0.0 0.0.254.255
route-map changeattributes permit 10
 match ip address 1
 set metric 100
 set weight 1000
```

continues

Example 7-72 *R5's Full Working Configuration (Continued)*

```
! This statement matches all odd statements as ACL matches even networks
route-map changeattributes permit 20
 set metric 200
 set weight 2000
!
line con 0
line aux 0
line vty 0 4
!
end
```

Review Questions

The answers to these question can be found in Appendix C, "Answers to Review Questions."

1 What does a route reflector do to nonclient IBGP peer?

2 What is a BGP cluster?

3 How is a route reflector client configured for IBGP?

4 Which IOS command is used to display the following output?

```
BGP table version is 61, local router ID is 131.108.254.4
Status codes: s suppressed, d damped, h history, * valid, > best, i - internal
Origin codes: i - IGP, e - EGP, ? - incomplete

   Network          Next Hop          Metric LocPrf Weight Path
*> 0.0.0.0          171.108.1.5                        0 100 i
*> 141.108.1.0/24   0.0.0.0                0        32768 i
```

5 How many TCP peers are required in a 1000 IBGP network?

6 Provide the IOS command syntax to enable a default route to be sent to a remote peer.

7 To display route reflector clients, which **show** command(s) can you use, if any?

8 View the following BGP table. What is the originating AS for the remote preferred path to the remote network 141.108.1.0/24?

```
R5#show ip bgp
BGP table version is 22, local router ID is 171.108.1.2
Status codes: s suppressed, d damped, h history, * valid, > best, i - internal
Origin codes: i - IGP, e - EGP, ? - incomplete

   Network          Next Hop          Metric LocPrf Weight Path
*> 141.108.1.0/24   171.108.1.1          200        2000 100 300 i
*> 151.108.1.0/24   0.0.0.0                0        32768 i
*> 171.108.0.0      171.108.1.1          200        2000 100 ?
```

9 Using a route map, which IOS command sets the weight and local preference attribute to 100.

10 Can you set the BGP attribute **next-hop-self** to both EBGP and IBGP peers?

Summary

After configuring many of the advanced features deployed in today's large IP environments and the Internet community, you can now understand and appreciate the level of complexity of BGP.

You discovered how BGP is enabled efficiently in large IBGP networks, how BGP can be modified using BGP attributes, and the resulting routing decisions that are made based on the configuration. The alternative methods used to change the routing decision made by BGP were also configured, and you saw how to monitor BGP.

BGP is a favorite topic on many Cisco certification examinations.

Table 7-4 summarizes the BGP commands used in this chapter.

Table 7-4   *Summary of IOS BGP Commands*

Command	Purpose
router bgp *number*	Enables BGP routing protocol
neighbor *remote IP address* **remote-as** *as*	Configures a BGP TCP peer
show ip bgp	Displays a BGP table
[no] synchronization	Enables or disables (**no**) BGP synchronization
show ip bgp neighbors	Displays status of BGP TCP peer sessions
show ip bgp summary	Displays status of BGP TCP peer sessions in summary format
neighbor *ip-address* **route-reflector-client**	Configures a remote router as a route reflector client
ip prefix-list *name* **permit	deny**	Configures a prefix list in global configuration mode.
show ip bgp route	Displays the BGP table
show ip bgp cidr-only	Displays CIDR networks (classless networks)
show ip bgp regexp *word*	Finds matching networks based on a regular expression

CHAPTER 8

Route Redistribution and Optimization

This chapter covers the issues and challenges facing networks when information from one routing algorithm is redistributed into another. In such a situation, information can be controlled to ensure that the network is routing Internet Protocol (IP) as correctly and efficiently as possible. Routing with one particular algorithm is difficult enough, and managing and controlling many different routing algorithms that might be used in a network is a considerable challenge.

The CCNP Routing exam devotes approximately 25 percent of its test questions to route optimization. A thorough knowledge of how routing information can be shared across different routing domains not only aids you on the CCNP Routing exam but also in the more difficult scenarios you might experience in real-life networks.

This chapter contains five practical scenarios to complete your understanding of route redistribution and optimization and ensure that you have all the practical knowledge you need for understanding routing optimization.

Controlling Routing Updates

By now, you have discovered that minimizing routing table size and simplifying how routers choose the next hop destination path are critical for a well-tuned IP network. When routing information from one routing protocol, such as Open shortest Path First (OSPF), is redistributed into Internet Gateway Routing Protocol (IGRP), for example, you must always be mindful of possible routing loops.

A *routing loop* is a path to a remote network that alternates between two routers, each of which assumes the path is reachable through the other. Hence, the time to live present in every IP packet expires, and the packet or user data is dropped, resulting in the loss of network connectivity.

Routing using a single routing algorithm is usually more desirable than running multiple IP and non-IP routing protocols, especially from a configuration and troubleshooting perspective. However, with today's changing networks, mergers, department politics, and acquisitions, more than one IP routing protocol is often in use.

You can use several methods to control information sent from one protocol to another to ensure that you avoid a routing loop.

Cisco IOS Software allows the following methods to control route filtering:

- **Passive interfaces**—A passive interface is a Cisco interface configured for routing, but it does not send any routing information on the outbound interface. Routing information (if any exists) is still received and processed normally.

- **Distribution lists**—Distribution lists define which networks are permitted or denied when receiving or sending routing updates. Distribution lists require that you configure access lists to define which networks are permitted or denied.

- **Route maps**—Route maps can also be used to define which networks are permitted or denied. Route maps can also be used along with access lists to define which networks are permitted or denied when applying match statements under any route map configuration options.

Along with passive interfaces and filtering, you can also use static routes, policy routing, default routes, or routes to null0 (routing black hole or bit bucket) to ensure that network paths to nonexisting destinations are dropped.

Redistribution Defined

Redistribution is defined as the exchange of routing updates from one routing protocol to another. Every routing protocol in use today can support redistribution. Because protocols, such as OSPF or RIP, have defined metrics, when you perform any redistribution you must convert the metric. For example, when redistributing from RIP to OSPF, you must convert the metric from hop count (RIP) to OSPF cost.

NOTE   The Cisco IOS Software automatically redistributes between IGRP and Extended Internet Gateway Routing Protocol (EIGRP) when the same autonomous system (AS) is defined. This is the only form of automatic redistribution that the Cisco IOS Software performs. All other methods must be manually configured, as you discover in this chapter.

The reasons that multiple IP routing protocols might be configured in any one network are numerous. Here are some reasons why a network administrator might configure more than one routing algorithm:

- An organization might have purchased another company that runs another routing protocol. Instead of reconfiguring potentially thousands of routers, it is easier to configure redistribution on one router and allow immediate communication.

- An organization might be transitioning from one protocol to another, for example, from legacy RIP to OSPF.

- Some business units within an organization might have host-based routing and require RIP, for example, to be configured on the edge of the network. RIP is fine for a LAN-based network.

- Political reasons within an organization or department can impact routing algorithm decisions. For example, payroll might have specific needs or an engineer might prefer a different routing algorithm to ensure that only certain networks are propagated between each other.

The number of reasons is countless. What is definite is that you need to understand redistribution and how it is configured and controlled on Cisco IOS-based routers.

There are two primary concerns when redistributing from one protocol to another:

- Metric conversion
- Administrative distances

You have seen already in this guide the various metrics used by OSPF or RIP. Cisco IOS routers always choose administrative distance over any metric; hence, you must be careful when changing administrative distances.

Table 8-1 displays the administrative distances Cisco routers use by default.

Table 8-1   *Cisco Default Administrative Distances*

Default Administrative Distances Route Source	Default Distance
Connected interface	0
Static route	1
Enhanced IGRP summary route	5
External BGP	20
Internal Enhanced IGRP	90
IGRP	100
OSPF	110

continues

Table 8-1   *Cisco Default Administrative Distances (Continued)*

Default Administrative Distances Route Source	Default Distance
IS-IS	115
RIP	120
EGP	140
External Enhanced IGRP	170
Internal BGP	200
Unknown	255

Table 8-1 shows that a Cisco router always prefers an EIGRP route (AD is 100) over an OSPF (AD is 110) or RIP (AD is 120), for example.

Redistributing from Classless to Classful Protocols

Any form of redistribution from classless or classful IP routing protocols must be carefully configured. To understand, consider the simple design rules when configuring between classless protocols and classful protocols.

TIP   Classful protocols do not understand variable-length subnet masks (VLSM), nor do they send updates with the subnet mask. Examples of classful protocols are IGRP and RIP.

Classless protocols understand VLSM and examples include IS-IS, OSPF, and BGP.

For every router configured in a classful network, the following rules apply:

- The router configured as a classless router has one or more interfaces attached to a major network, such as a Class A, B, or C network. For example, the local router might have the Class A network 9.1.1.1/8 configured locally and assumes the same Class A mask on any networks received on any given interface.

- The router does not have any interfaces attached to the major network being advertised, and hence, assumes the subnet mask is at the bit boundary: 8 bits for Class A (255.0.0.0), 16 bits for Class B (255.255.0.0), and 24 bits for Class C (255.255.255.0).

Consider the example in Figure 8-1.

Figure 8-1   *R1 Is Redistributing OSPF Routes to RIP (to R2)*

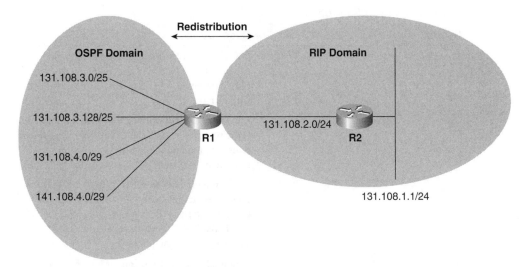

Figure 8-1 displays R1 configured for redistribution to R2. R1 has a number of local interfaces subnetted using the Class B network 131.108.0.0. R2, on the other hand, is running RIP and has two local interfaces configured in the Class B network with Class C routers: 131.108.1.0/24 and 131.108.2.0/24.

The RIP process on R2 assumes all networks in the Class B network 131.108.0.0 have a 24-bit subnet mask because of the local attached interfaces. Hence, the subnetted routes on R1 are not passed to R2. The 141.108.0.0 network on R1 is advertised to R2 as a Class B network. In other words, R2 assumes the entire Class B network, 141.108.0.0, is reachable through R1 for networks not locally connected.

To solve this problem and others you encounter, this chapter covers the Cisco IOS command required for enabling redistribution.

Cisco IOS Command Syntax for Redistribution

To configure redistribution among routing protocols, the following command is used under the routing process configuration:

```
redistribute protocol [process-id] {level-1 | level-1-2 | level-2} [as-number]
    [metric metric-value] [metric-type type-value] [match {internal |
    external 1 | external 2}] [tag tag-value] [route-map map-tag]
    [weight number-value] [subnets]
```

The redistribution command syntax is further explained in Table 8-2.

Table 8-2   *Command Syntax for Redistribution*

Syntax	Description
Protocol	Source protocol from which routes are being redistributed. It can be one of the following keywords: **bgp**, **connected**, **egp**, **igrp**, **isis**, **mobile**, **ospf**, **static** [**ip**], or **rip**.
	The **static** [**ip**] keyword is used to redistribute IP static routes. The optional **ip** keyword is used when redistributing into the Intermediate System-to-Intermediate System (IS-IS) protocol.
	The **connected** keyword refers to routes that are established automatically by virtue of having enabled IP on an interface. For routing protocols, such as OSPF and IS-IS, these routes are redistributed as external to the autonomous system (AS).
process-id	(Optional) For the **bgp**, **egp**, or **igrp** keyword, this is an autonomous system number, which is a 16-bit decimal number.
	For the **ospf** keyword, this is an appropriate OSPF process ID from which routes are to be redistributed.
level-1	Specifies that for IS-IS, level 1 routes are redistributed into other IP routing protocols independently.
level-1-2	Specifies that for IS-IS, both level 1 and level 2 routes are redistributed into other IP routing protocols.
level-2	Specifies that for IS-IS, level 2 routes are redistributed into other IP routing protocols independently.
as-number	AS number for the redistributed route.
metric *metric-value*	(Optional) Metric used for the redistributed route. If a value is not specified for this option, and no value is specified using the **default-metric** command, the default metric value is 0. Use a value consistent with the destination protocol.

Table 8-2   *Command Syntax for Redistribution (Continued)*

Syntax	Description
metric-type *type-value*	(Optional) For OSPF, the external link type associated with the default route advertised into the OSPF routing domain. It can be one of two values: **1**—Type 1 external route **2**—Type 2 external route If a **metric-type** is not specified, the Cisco IOS software adopts a Type 2 external route. For IS-IS, it can be one of two values: **internal**—IS-IS metric that is < 63 **external**—IS-IS metric that is > 64 < 128 The default is **internal**.
match {**internal** I **external 1** I **external 2**}	(Optional) For the criteria by which OSPF routes are redistributed into other routing domains. It can be one of the following: **internal**—Routes that are internal to a specific autonomous system. **external 1**—Routes that are external to the autonomous system, but are imported into OSPF as Type 1 external routes. **external 2**—Routes that are external to the autonomous system, but are imported into OSPF as Type 2 external routes.
tag *tag-value*	(Optional) 32-bit decimal value attached to each external route. This is not used by OSPF itself. It can be used to communicate information between autonomous system boundary routers (ASBRs). If none is specified, the remote AS number is used for routes from Border Gateway Protocol (BGP) and Exterior Gateway Protocol (EGP); for other protocols, zero (0) is used.
route-map	(Optional) Allows you to indicate a route map that should be interrogated to filter the importation of routes from this source routing protocol to the current routing protocol. If not specified, all routes are redistributed. If this keyword is specified, but no route map tags are listed, no routes are imported.

continues

Table 8-2   *Command Syntax for Redistribution (Continued)*

Syntax	Description
map-tag	(Optional) Identifier of a configured route map.
weight *number-value*	(Optional) Network weight when redistributing into BGP. An integer from 0 to 65,535.
subnets	(Optional) For redistributing routes into OSPF, the scope of redistribution for the specified protocol.

Routing redistribution is best described by examples, so the five practical scenarios in this chapter concentrate on how redistribution is configured on Cisco IOS routers. You have already encountered some redistribution in previous scenarios, and the following five scenarios are designed to enhance your knowledge of why, when, and how to successfully and efficiently redistribute routing protocols.

Scenarios

The following scenarios are designed to draw together some of the content described in this chapter and some of the content you have seen in your own networks or practice labs. There is no one right way to accomplish many of the tasks presented, and the abilities to use good practice and define your end goal are important in any real-life design or solution.

The five scenarios presented in this chapter are based on complex redistribution technologies so that you become fully aware of the powerful nature of redistribution in large IP networks.

Scenario 8-1: Redistributing Between RIP and IGRP

In this scenario, you configure three routers running RIP and IGRP. Router R1 is running both RIP and IGRP, and you configure it for redistribution.

Figure 8-2 displays the three-router topology with the Router R1 running RIP and IGRP.

Figure 8-2 displays a simple scenario with the Class A network 9.0.0.0 subnetted with a Class C mask. Notice that R2 has the Class 10.1.1.0/24 network configured locally on the Ethernet interface.

Start by configuring the edge devices for IGRP on R3 and RIP on R2.

Figure 8-2 *RIP/IGRP Redistribution*

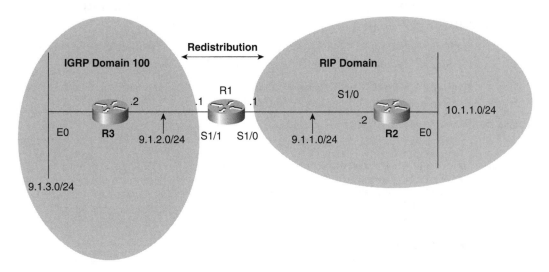

Example 8-1 displays the IP address configuration on R1 and the enabling of IGRP in AS 100.

Example 8-1 *IP Address Configuration and Enabling IGRP on R3*

```
R3(config)#interface ethernet 0
R3(config-if)#ip address 9.1.3.1 255.255.255.0
R3(config-if)#interface serial0
R3(config-if)#ip address 9.1.2.2 255.255.255.0
R3(config-if)#exit
R3(config)#router igrp 10
R3(config-router)#network 9.0.0.0
```

Notice, on R3, when enabling IGRP in AS 10, the **network** command used is **network 9.0.0.0** because IGRP is classful and automatically summarizes at the Class A network boundary.

Example 8-2 configures R2 for IP addressing and enables RIP.

Example 8-2 *IP Address Configuration and Enabling RIP*

```
R2(config)#interface ethernet 0/0
R2(config-if)#ip address 10.1.1.2 255.255.255.0
R2(config-if)#interface serial 1/0
R2(config-if)#ip address 9.1.1.2 255.255.255.0
R2(config)#router rip
R2(config-router)#network 9.0.0.0
R2(config-router)#network 10.0.0.0
```

R2 is running another classful IP routing protocol: RIP. Therefore, when defining networks under the RIP process, you need to identify only the major network boundary, in this case 9.0.0.0 and 10.0.0.0.

R2 is configured for RIP and IGRP, and hence, requires redistribution, and you must ensure the metrics are converted from RIP (hop count) to IGRP (composite metric).

Example 8-3 displays the IP address configuration on R1 along with enabling IGRP and RIP. No redistribution is configured at this time.

Example 8-3   *Enable IP and RIP/IGRP on R1*

```
R1(config)#interface S1/0
R1(config-if)#ip address 9.1.1.1 255.255.255.0
R1(config-if)#interface S1/1
R1(config-if)#ip address 9.1.2.1 255.255.255.0
R1(config-if)#exit
R1(config)#router rip
R1(config-router)#network 9.0.0.0
R1(config-router)#exit
R1(config)#router igrp 10
R1(config-router)#network 9.0.0.0
```

R1 is configured locally for the Class A subnet network 9.0.0.0 for both RIP and IGRP. Therefore, you must ensure that RIP updates are not sent to R3, which is running only IGRP, and ensure IGRP updates are not sent to R2, which is running only IGRP.

Example 8-4 configures passive interfaces to ensure that only RIP updates are sent to R2 and IGRP updates are sent to R3.

Example 8-4   *Passive Interfaces on R1*

```
R1(config)#router rip
!Ensure RIP updates are not sent to R3
R1(config-router)#passive-interface s1/1
R1(config-router)#router igrp 10
!Ensure IGRP updates are not sent to R2
R1(config-router)#passive-interface s1/0
```

Example 8-5 displays the IP routing table on R1.

Example 8-5   *IP Routing Table on R1*

```
R1#show ip route
     9.0.0.0/24 is subnetted, 3 subnets
C       9.1.1.0 is directly connected, Serial1/0
C       9.1.2.0 is directly connected, Serial1/1
I       9.1.3.0 [100/80225] via 9.1.2.2, 00:00:31, Serial1/1
R    10.0.0.0/8 [120/1] via 9.1.1.2, 00:00:15, Serial1/0
```

Currently, the IP routing table on R1 displays network connectivity to R2 and R3. R1 has full IP connectivity to R2 and R3. Also, notice that R1 assumes that the entire Class A network 10.0.0.0/8 is reachable through R2 because R1 does not have any locally connected routes in the 10.0.0.0 network.

Example 8-6 displays the IP routing table on R2.

Example 8-6 show ip route *on R2*

```
R2#show ip route
     9.0.0.0/24 is subnetted, 2 subnets
C       9.1.1.0 is directly connected, Serial1/0
R       9.1.2.0 [120/1] via 9.1.1.1, 00:00:27, Serial1/0
     10.0.0.0/24 is subnetted, 1 subnets
C       10.1.1.0 is directly connected, Ethernet0/0
```

The routing table on R2 in Example 8-6 displays no network connectivity to the LAN segment 9.1.3.0/24 because you have yet to configure redistribution on R1.

To configure redistribution, you must perform the following tasks on R1:

Step 1 Use the **redistribute** command on R1 to specify the routes to be redistributed.

Step 2 Specify the metric to be assigned to any redistributed routes.

Example 8-7 displays the **redistribution** command on R1. You set the metric for redistributing IGRP to RIP to a hop count of 1.

Example 8-7 *Redistributing IGRP into RIP on R1*

```
R1(config)#router rip
R1(config-router)#redistribute igrp 10 metric 1
```

At this stage, you haven't configured redistribution from RIP into IGRP so that R3 has full connectivity to R2. Example 8-8 displays redistribution from RIP to IGRP. The **?** tool is used to displays IGRP metrics. Typically, the metrics used match those on the link from R1 to R2 (using the **show interfaces serial 1/0** command and using the values output from this display).

Example 8-8 *Redistribution from RIP to IGRP on R1*

```
R1(config)#router igrp 10
R1(config-router)#redistribute rip ?
  metric     Metric for redistributed routes
  route-map  Route map reference
  <cr>
R1(config-router)#redistribute rip metric ?
  <1-4294967295>  Bandwidth metric in Kbits per second
```

continues

Example 8-8 *Redistribution from RIP to IGRP on R1 (Continued)*

```
R1(config-router)#redistribute rip metric 128 ?
  <0-4294967295>  IGRP delay metric, in 10 microsecond units
R1(config-router)#redistribute rip metric 128 20000 ?
  <0-255>  IGRP reliability metric where 255 is 100% reliable
R1(config-router)#redistribute rip metric 128 20000 255 ?
  <1-255>  IGRP Effective bandwidth metric (Loading) where 255 is 100% loaded
R1(config-router)#redistribute rip metric 128 20000 255 1 ?
  <1-4294967295>  IGRP MTU of the path
R1(config-router)#redistribute rip metric 128 20000 255 1 1500
```

Examine the IP routing tables on R2 and R3 to ensure IP connectivity by pinging the remote
network 9.1.3.1 as displayed in Example 8-9.

Example 8-9 *IP Routing Table and Ping Request to 9.1.3.1/24 on R2*

```
R2#show ip route
     9.0.0.0/24 is subnetted, 3 subnets
C       9.1.1.0 is directly connected, Serial1/0
R       9.1.2.0 [120/1] via 9.1.1.1, 00:00:09, Serial1/0
R       9.1.3.0 [120/1] via 9.1.1.1, 00:00:09, Serial1/0
     10.0.0.0/24 is subnetted, 1 subnets
C       10.1.1.0 is directly connected, Ethernet0/0
R2#ping 9.1.3.1
Type escape sequence to abort.
Sending 5, 100-byte ICMP Echos to 9.1.3.1, timeout is 2 seconds:
!!!!!
Success rate is 100 percent (5/5), round-trip min/avg/max = 28/29/32 ms
```

Example 8-9 displays the remote network 9.1.3.0 reachable through the next hop address
9.1.1.1, and the metric is 1, as defined by the **redistribution** command in Example 8-7. A
ping to the remote address 10.1.1.1/24 on R3 is successful.

Example 8-10 displays the IP routing table on R3, as well as a ping request and reply to the
remote network 9.1.3.1/24.

Example 8-10 *IP Routing Table and Ping Request on R3*

```
R3#show ip route
     9.0.0.0/24 is subnetted, 3 subnets
I       9.1.1.0 [100/84000] via 9.1.2.1, 00:00:58, Serial0
C       9.1.2.0 is directly connected, Serial0
C       9.1.3.0 is directly connected, Ethernet0
I    10.0.0.0/8 [100/102000] via 9.1.2.1, 00:00:58, Serial0
R3#ping 10.1.1.1
Type escape sequence to abort.
Sending 5, 100-byte ICMP Echos to 10.1.1.1, timeout is 2 seconds:
!!!!!
Success rate is 100 percent (5/5), round-trip min/avg/max = 28/29/32 ms
```

A ping to the remote address 10.1.1.1/24 on R3 is successful because the remote network 10.0.0.0/8 is reachable through the next hop address 9.1.2.1 or through R1.

Next, you configure a new subnet on R3 to make the networks a little more complex. Configure the address 10.1.2.1 as a loopback interface on R3 using a 24-bit subnet mask, and enable IGRP on R3 to advertise the 10.0.0.0 network.

Example 8-11 displays the loopback creation on R3 and the enabling of IGRP to advertise the loopback under IGRP.

Example 8-11 *Loopback Creation on R3*

```
R3(config-if)#interface loopback 0
R3(config-if)#ip address 10.1.2.1 255.255.255.0
R3(config-if)#router igrp 10
R3(config-router)#network 10.0.0.0
```

R3 does not advertise the 10.0.0.0 network to R1. Remember from Example 8-5, R1 had seen the 10.0.0.0/8 network advertised through RIP with an AD of 120 through R2 (RIP). Example 8-12 displays the IP routing table on R1 after an IGRP update is sent from R3 to R1.

Example 8-12 **show ip route** *on R1*

```
R1#show ip route
     9.0.0.0/24 is subnetted, 3 subnets
C       9.1.1.0 is directly connected, Serial1/0
C       9.1.2.0 is directly connected, Serial1/1
I       9.1.3.0 [100/80225] via 9.1.2.2, 00:00:23, Serial1/1
I     10.0.0.0/8 [100/80625] via 9.1.2.2, 00:00:23, Serial1/1
```

R1 changes the path to 10.0.0.0 through R3 because the AD of IGRP is 100, compared to RIP, which is 120. In effect, R1 sends all traffic for the 10.0.0.0 network through R3. Example 8-13 displays a ping request to the IP address 10.1.1.1 (R3's Ethernet interface) and 10.1.2.1 (R3's loopback interface).

Example 8-13 *Ping Request on R1*

```
R1#ping 10.1.1.1
Type escape sequence to abort.
Sending 5, 100-byte ICMP Echos to 10.1.1.1, timeout is 2 seconds:
.....
Success rate is 0 percent (0/5)
R1#ping 10.1.2.1
Type escape sequence to abort.
Sending 5, 100-byte ICMP Echos to 10.1.2.1, timeout is 2 seconds:
!!!!!
Success rate is 100 percent (5/5), round-trip min/avg/max = 12/14/16 ms
```

All packets are sent to R3 because the IP routing table selects IGRP as the preferred path to all networks in the Class A range 10.0.0.0. Of course, this is not the desired solution because you have 10.0.0.0 networks configured on R2 and R3. There are a number of different solutions to this, but in this case, configure R1 to reject any networks in the 10.0.0.0 range because the only trusted information for this Class A network is from the RIP domain.

NOTE   Another method to overcome network connectivity problems is to configure static routes on R1 or enable an interface in the 10.0.0.0/24 range on R1.

Example 8-14 configures a distribution list on R1, rejects all networks in the 10.0.0.0 range, and accepts all other networks.

Example 8-14 *Distribution List on R1*

```
R1(config)#router igrp 10
R1(config-router)#distribute-list 1 in
R1(config-router)#exit
R1(config)#access-list 1 deny 10.0.0.0
R1(config)#access-list 1 permit any
```

The **distribute-list** command, when configured on R1, does not permit the 10.0.0.0 network, as displayed in Example 8-14. Therefore, when 10.0.0.0 is advertised by R3 to R1, R1 does not accept the 10.0.0.0 network.

Example 8-15 confirms the installation on the RIP-discovered route through R2.

Example 8-15 **show ip route** *on R1*

```
R1#sh ip route
        9.0.0.0/24 is subnetted, 3 subnets
C       9.1.1.0 is directly connected, Serial1/0
C       9.1.2.0 is directly connected, Serial1/1
I       9.1.3.0 [100/80225] via 9.1.2.2, 00:00:07, Serial1/1
R    10.0.0.0/8 [120/1] via 9.1.1.2, 00:00:07, Serial1/0
```

Any form of redistribution requires careful filtering. At this point, R1 has lost connectivity to the 10.1.2.0/24. To solve this problem, configure a static route on R1 with a more specific destination pointing to R3.

Example 8-16 displays the static route configuration on R1.

Example 8-16 *Static IP Route on R1*

```
R1(config)#ip route 10.1.2.0 255.255.255.0 Serial1/1
```

Cisco IOS routers, because the AD of static routes is 1 and is lower then RIP at 120, send traffic for the more specific route through Serial 1/1 for hosts in the range 10.1.2.1–254/24.

Example 8-17 displays the IP routing table on R1 and a successful ping request to 10.1.1.1 (to R2) and 10.1.2.1 (to R3)

Example 8-17 **show ip route** *and Ping Request on R1*

```
R1#show ip ro
     9.0.0.0/24 is subnetted, 3 subnets
C       9.1.1.0 is directly connected, Serial1/0
C       9.1.2.0 is directly connected, Serial1/1
I       9.1.3.0 [100/80225] via 9.1.2.2, 00:00:54, Serial1/1
     10.0.0.0/8 is variably subnetted, 2 subnets, 2 masks
S       10.1.2.0/24 is directly connected, Serial1/1
R       10.0.0.0/8 [120/1] via 9.1.1.2, 00:00:36, Serial1/0
R1#ping 10.1.1.1
Type escape sequence to abort.
Sending 5, 100-byte ICMP Echos to 10.1.1.1, timeout is 2 seconds:
!!!!!
Success rate is 100 percent (5/5), round-trip min/avg/max = 16/16/16 ms
R1#ping 10.1.2.1
Type escape sequence to abort.
Sending 5, 100-byte ICMP Echos to 10.1.2.1, timeout is 2 seconds:
!!!!!
Success rate is 100 percent (5/5), round-trip min/avg/max = 12/14/16 ms
```

In a simple three router network, you can determine that with even a few networks, redistribution causes routers to misinterpret information based on network configuration and classful behavior of routing protocols, such as RIP and IGRP. In the scenarios that follow, you apply route maps instead of distribution lists to learn to use other filtering methods. You also use the **passive-interface** command to ensure that a network running route redistribution is configured as efficiently as possible.

Example 8-18 displays R1's full working configuration.

Example 8-18 *R1's Full Working Configuration*

```
hostname R1
!
enable password cisco
```

continues

Example 8-18 *R1's Full Working Configuration (Continued)*

```
!
interface Serial1/0
 ip address 9.1.1.1 255.255.255.0
 clockrate 128000
!
interface Serial1/1
 ip address 9.1.2.1 255.255.255.0
 clockrate 128000
!
router rip
 redistribute igrp 10 metric 1
 passive-interface Serial1/1
 network 9.0.0.0
!
router igrp 10
 redistribute rip metric 128 20000 255 1 1500
 passive-interface Serial1/0
 network 9.0.0.0
 distribute-list 1 in
ip route 10.1.2.0 255.255.255.0 Serial1/1
!
access-list 1 deny   10.0.0.0
access-list 1 permit any
line con 0
line aux 0
line vty 0 4
end
```

Example 8-19 displays R2's full working configuration.

Example 8-19 *R2's Full Working Configuration*

```
hostname R2
!
enable password cisco
!
ip subnet-zero
no ip domain-lookup
!
interface Ethernet0/0
 ip address 10.1.1.1 255.255.255.0
!
interface Serial1/0
 bandwidth 128
 ip address 9.1.1.2 255.255.255.0
!
router rip
 network 9.0.0.0
 network 10.0.0.0
```

Example 8-19 *R2's Full Working Configuration (Continued)*

```
line con 0
line aux 0
line vty 0 4
end
```

Example 8-20 displays R3's full working configuration.

Example 8-20 *R3's Full Working Configuration*

```
hostname R3
!
enable password cisco
!
interface Loopback0
 ip address 10.1.2.1 255.255.255.0
 !
interface Ethernet0
 ip address 9.1.3.1 255.255.255.0
interface Serial0
 ip address 9.1.2.2 255.255.255.0
 bandwidth 125
router igrp 10
 network 9.0.0.0
 network 10.0.0.0
 !
no ip classless
line con 0
line aux 0
line vty 0 4
 !
end
```

Scenario 8-2: Migrating from RIP to OSPF in the Core

In this scenario, you migrate a typical RIP network to OSPF in the core of the network and leave RIP on the edge of the network, where typically, on LAN-based segments, bandwidth is not a major concern.

IP addressing and loopback address assignments have already been completed.

Figure 8-3 displays the current RIP network that you migrate to OSPF.

Loopbacks have been configured in R1, R2, and R3 to populate the IP routing tables. The Class B network, 141.108.0.0, has been subnetted using a Class C mask throughout. Because all RIP-enabled routers have a local interface configured using a Class C mask, network connectivity is maintained.

Figure 8-3 *RIP Topology*

Local IP Addressing:

R1 ranges from 141.108.1.1/24 to
131.108.7.2/24

R2 ranges from 141.108.8.1 to
131.108.15.1/24

R3 ranges from 141.108.16.1/24
141.108.23.1/24

WAN Addressing:

R1/R2 141.108.255.0/24

R1/R3 141.108.254.0/24

R2/R3 141.108.253.0/24

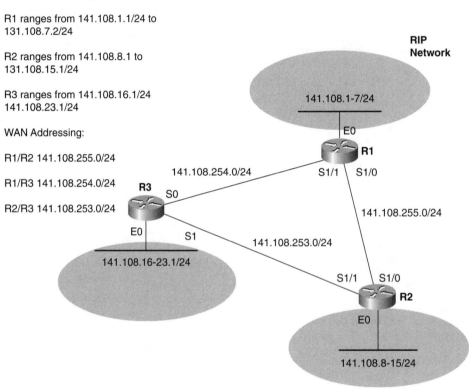

The current IP routing table on R1 is displayed in Example 8-21.

Example 8-21 show ip route *on R1*

```
R3#show ip route
     141.108.0.0/24 is subnetted, 26 subnets
R       141.108.253.0 [120/1] via 141.108.255.2, 00:00:15, Serial1/0
                      [120/1] via 141.108.254.2, 00:00:11, Serial1/1
C       141.108.255.0 is directly connected, Serial1/0
C       141.108.254.0 is directly connected, Serial1/1
C       141.108.1.0 is directly connected, Ethernet0/0
C       141.108.3.0 is directly connected, Loopback1
C       141.108.2.0 is directly connected, Loopback0
C       141.108.5.0 is directly connected, Loopback3
C       141.108.4.0 is directly connected, Loopback2
C       141.108.7.0 is directly connected, Loopback5
C       141.108.6.0 is directly connected, Loopback4
```

Example 8-21 show ip route *on R1 (Continued)*

```
R       141.108.9.0 [120/1] via 141.108.255.2, 00:00:16, Serial1/0
R       141.108.8.0 [120/1] via 141.108.255.2, 00:00:16, Serial1/0
R       141.108.11.0 [120/1] via 141.108.255.2, 00:00:16, Serial1/0
R       141.108.10.0 [120/1] via 141.108.255.2, 00:00:16, Serial1/0
R       141.108.13.0 [120/1] via 141.108.255.2, 00:00:16, Serial1/0
R       141.108.12.0 [120/1] via 141.108.255.2, 00:00:16, Serial1/0
R       141.108.15.0 [120/1] via 141.108.255.2, 00:00:17, Serial1/0
R       141.108.14.0 [120/1] via 141.108.255.2, 00:00:17, Serial1/0
R       141.108.17.0 [120/1] via 141.108.254.2, 00:00:12, Serial1/1
R       141.108.16.0 [120/1] via 141.108.254.2, 00:00:12, Serial1/1
R       141.108.19.0 [120/1] via 141.108.254.2, 00:00:12, Serial1/1
R       141.108.18.0 [120/1] via 141.108.254.2, 00:00:12, Serial1/1
R       141.108.21.0 [120/1] via 141.108.254.2, 00:00:12, Serial1/1
R       141.108.20.0 [120/1] via 141.108.254.2, 00:00:13, Serial1/1
R       141.108.23.0 [120/1] via 141.108.254.2, 00:00:13, Serial1/1
R       141.108.22.0 [120/1] via 141.108.254.2, 00:00:13, Serial1/1
```

Example 8-21 displays over 25 different networks. The main aim of converting the routing algorithm from RIP to OSPF is to enable VLSM in the WAN and summarization among routers to reduce IP routing table sizes.

Example 8-22 displays the current working configuration on R1 running RIP as the primary routing algorithm.

Example 8-22 *R1's RIP Configuration*

```
hostname R1
!
enable password cisco
!
ip subnet-zero
!
interface Loopback0
 ip address 141.108.2.1 255.255.255.0
!
interface Loopback1
 ip address 141.108.3.1 255.255.255.0
!
interface Loopback2
 ip address 141.108.4.1 255.255.255.0
!
interface Loopback3
 ip address 141.108.5.1 255.255.255.0
!
interface Loopback4
 ip address 141.108.6.1 255.255.255.0
```

continues

Example 8-22 *R1's RIP Configuration (Continued)*

```
!
interface Loopback5
 ip address 141.108.7.1 255.255.255.0
!
interface Ethernet0/0
 ip address 141.108.1.1 255.255.255.0
interface Serial1/0
 ip address 141.108.255.1 255.255.255.0
 clockrate 128000
!
interface Serial1/1
 ip address 141.108.254.1 255.255.255.0
 clockrate 128000
!
router rip
 network 141.108.0.0
!
line con 0
end
```

Example 8-23 displays R2's current working configuration.

Example 8-23 *R2's RIP Configuration*

```
hostname R2
!
enable password cisco
interface Loopback0
 ip address 141.108.9.1 255.255.255.0
!
interface Loopback1
 ip address 141.108.10.1 255.255.255.0
!
interface Loopback2
 ip address 141.108.11.1 255.255.255.0
!
interface Loopback3
 ip address 141.108.12.1 255.255.255.0
!
interface Loopback4
 ip address 141.108.13.1 255.255.255.0
!
interface Loopback5
 ip address 141.108.14.1 255.255.255.0
!
interface Loopback6
 ip address 141.108.15.1 255.255.255.0
!
interface Ethernet0/0
 ip address 141.108.8.1 255.255.255.0
```

Example 8-23 *R2's RIP Configuration (Continued)*

```
!
interface Serial1/0
 bandwidth 128
 ip address 141.108.255.2 255.255.255.0
!
interface Serial1/1
 ip address 141.108.253.2 255.255.255.0
router rip
network 141.108.0.0
!
ip classless
!
end
```

Example 8-24 displays R3's current working configuration.

Example 8-24 *R3's RIP Configuration*

```
hostname R3
!
enable password cisco
!
no ip domain-lookup
!
interface Loopback0
 ip address 141.108.17.1 255.255.255.0
!
interface Loopback1
 ip address 141.108.18.1 255.255.255.0
!
interface Loopback2
 ip address 141.108.19.1 255.255.255.0
!
interface Loopback3
 ip address 141.108.20.1 255.255.255.0
!
interface Loopback4
 ip address 141.108.21.1 255.255.255.0
!
interface Loopback5
 ip address 141.108.22.1 255.255.255.0
!
interface Loopback6
 ip address 141.108.23.1 255.255.255.0
!
interface Ethernet0
 ip address 141.108.16.1 255.255.255.0
```

continues

Example 8-24 *R3's RIP Configuration (Continued)*

```
!
interface Serial0
 ip address 141.108.254.2 255.255.255.0
 bandwidth 125
!
interface Serial1
 ip address 141.108.253.1 255.255.255.0
 bandwidth 125
 clockrate 125000
!
router rip
 network 141.108.0.0
!
end
```

To start, add OSPF to the center of the network, and place all the WAN interfaces in area 0. Maintain the Class C mask for now to make redistribution relativity easy to configure. This step is common when migrating from one protocol to another.

Example 8-25 configures R1 for OSPF across the WAN to R1 and R2. You take the same configuration steps on R2 and R3.

Example 8-25 *OSPF Configuration on R1*

```
R1(config)#router ospf1
R1(config-router)#network 141.108.255.0 0.0.0.255 area 0
R1(config-router)#network 141.108.254.0 0.0.0.255 area 0
R1(config-router)#router rip
R1(config-router)#passive-interface serial 1/0
R1(config-router)#passive-interface serial 1/1
```

R1 is configured not to send any RIP updates to Serial 1/0 (to R2) and Serial 1/1 (to R3); this configuration stops the sending of unnecessary updates across WAN links.

At this stage, you have not configured any redistribution, so there is no connectivity among the Ethernet and loopback interfaces. Example 8-26 confirms the status of IP connectivity after the **show ip route** command is entered on R1.

Example 8-26 show ip route *on R1*

```
R1#show ip route
     141.108.0.0/24 is subnetted, 10 subnets
O       141.108.253.0 [110/1562] via 141.108.255.2, 00:00:04, Serial1/0
C       141.108.255.0 is directly connected, Serial1/0
C       141.108.254.0 is directly connected, Serial1/1
C       141.108.1.0 is directly connected, Ethernet0/0
C       141.108.3.0 is directly connected, Loopback1
```

Example 8-26 show ip route *on R1 (Continued)*

```
C        141.108.2.0 is directly connected, Loopback0
C        141.108.5.0 is directly connected, Loopback3
C        141.108.4.0 is directly connected, Loopback2
C        141.108.7.0 is directly connected, Loopback5
C        141.108.6.0 is directly connected, Loopback4
```

The only visible route on R1 is the locally connected routes and the WAN circuit between R2 and R3.

Next, configure redistribution on routers R1, R2, and R3 to advertise the RIP networks to the OSPF backbone.

Example 8-27 displays the RIP to OSPF redistribution on R1. Example 8-27 also displays redistribution from OSPF to RIP to allow communication from R2/R3 Ethernet segments to R1's locally connected network, which, at the moment, is advertised by only RIP. The **?** tool is used to display the available options.

Example 8-27 *Redistribution on R1*

```
R1(config)#router ospf 1
R1(config-router)#redistribute rip metric ?
  <0-16777214>   OSPF default metric
R1(config-router)#redistribute rip metric 100 subnets
R1(config-router)#exit
R1(config)#router rip
R1(config-router)#redistribute ospf 1 metric ?
  <0-4294967295>   Default metric
R1(config-router)#redistribute ospf 1 metric 3
R1(config-router)#distribute-list 1 out
R1(config-router)#exit
R1(config)#access-list 1 deny 141.108.1.0 0.0.0.255
R1(config)#access-list 1 deny 141.108.2.0 0.0.0.255
R1(config)#access-list 1 deny 141.108.3.0 0.0.0.255
R1(config)#access-list 1 deny 141.108.4.0 0.0.0.255
R1(config)#access-list 1 deny 141.108.5.0 0.0.0.255
R1(config)#access-list 1 deny 141.108.6.0 0.0.0.255
R1(config)#access-list 1 deny 141.108.7.0 0.0.0.255
R1(config)#access-list 1 permit any
```

R1 is now configured to redistribute from RIP to OSPF and vice versa. Example 8-27 displays the keyword **subnets** because the Class B network 141.108.0.0 has been subnetted across the network. Without this keyword, only classful networks would not be advertised. (In this case, you are using classless networks on all routers.) Also, the metrics have been set to 100 for all RIP-to-OSPF networks, and the hop count for all redistributed OSPF networks into RIP is set to 3.

Typically, networks have some other paths or back doors between any given routing topologies. To ensure that networks residing on R1 are never advertised by the OSPF backbone, the distribution list on R1 denies any networks residing in 141.108.1.0–141.108.7.255 from being advertised from OSPF to RIP. This ensures that a routing loop cannot occur.

The access list 1, previously defined with seven statements, can be replaced with the configuration in Example 8-28 to deny the range of networks 141.108.0.0–141.108.7.0 and permit all other networks.

Example 8-28 replaces the seven-line access list with two lines of IOS configuration. (The **no access-list 1** command removes the configuration currently present for access list 1.)

Example 8-28 *Access List Configuration on R1*

```
R1(config)#no access-list 1
R1(config)#access-list 1 deny 141.108.0.0 0.0.7.255
R1(config)#access-list 1 permit any
```

Example 8-29 displays the redistribution and filtering required on R2.

Example 8-29 *Redistribution on R2*

```
R2(config)#router rip
R2(config-router)#distribute-list 1 out
R2(config-router)#redistribute ospf 1 metric 3
R2(config-router)#router ospf 1
R2(config-router)#redistribute rip metric 10 subnets
R2(config)#access-list 1 deny 141.108.8.0 0.0.7.255
R2(config)#access-list 1 permit any
```

Example 8-30 displays the redistribution and filtering on R3.

Example 8-30 *Redistribution on R3*

```
R3(config)#router rip
R3(config-router)#redistribute ospf 1 metric 3
R3(config-router)#distribute-list 1 out
R3(config-router)#router ospf 1
R3(config-router)#redistribute rip metric 10 subnets
R3(config-router)#exit
R3(config)#access-list 1 deny 141.108.23.0 0.0.7.255
R3(config)#access-list 1 permit any
```

Confirm IP routing connectivity from R1. Example 8-31 displays the IP routing table on R1 and some sample ping requests that conform IP connectivity.

Example 8-31 **show ip route** *and Pings on R1*

```
R1#show ip route
Codes: C - connected,E1 - OSPF external type 1, E2 - OSPF external type 2, E - EGP
       141.108.0.0/24 is subnetted, 26 subnets
O         141.108.253.0 [110/1562] via 141.108.255.2, 00:00:51, Serial1/0
C         141.108.255.0 is directly connected, Serial1/0
C         141.108.254.0 is directly connected, Serial1/1
C         141.108.1.0 is directly connected, Ethernet0/0
C         141.108.3.0 is directly connected, Loopback1
C         141.108.2.0 is directly connected, Loopback0
C         141.108.5.0 is directly connected, Loopback3
C         141.108.4.0 is directly connected, Loopback2
C         141.108.7.0 is directly connected, Loopback5
C         141.108.6.0 is directly connected, Loopback4
O E2      141.108.9.0 [110/10] via 141.108.255.2, 00:00:51, Serial1/0
O E2      141.108.8.0 [110/10] via 141.108.255.2, 00:00:51, Serial1/0
O E2      141.108.11.0 [110/10] via 141.108.255.2, 00:00:51, Serial1/0
O E2      141.108.10.0 [110/10] via 141.108.255.2, 00:00:51, Serial1/0
O E2      141.108.13.0 [110/10] via 141.108.255.2, 00:00:51, Serial1/0
O E2      141.108.12.0 [110/10] via 141.108.255.2, 00:00:51, Serial1/0
O E2      141.108.15.0 [110/10] via 141.108.255.2, 00:00:51, Serial1/0
O E2      141.108.14.0 [110/10] via 141.108.255.2, 00:00:52, Serial1/0
O E2      141.108.17.0 [110/10] via 141.108.254.2, 00:00:52, Serial1/1
O E2      141.108.16.0 [110/10] via 141.108.254.2, 00:00:52, Serial1/1
O E2      141.108.19.0 [110/10] via 141.108.254.2, 00:00:52, Serial1/1
O E2      141.108.18.0 [110/10] via 141.108.254.2, 00:00:52, Serial1/1
O E2      141.108.21.0 [110/10] via 141.108.254.2, 00:00:52, Serial1/1
O E2      141.108.20.0 [110/10] via 141.108.254.2, 00:00:52, Serial1/1
O E2      141.108.23.0 [110/10] via 141.108.254.2, 00:00:52, Serial1/1
O E2      141.108.22.0 [110/10] via 141.108.254.2, 00:00:52, Serial1/1
R1#ping 141.108.9.1
Type escape sequence to abort.
Sending 5, 100-byte ICMP Echos to 141.108.9.1, timeout is 2 seconds:
!!!!!
Success rate is 100 percent (5/5), round-trip min/avg/max = 16/16/16 ms
R1#ping 141.108.22.1
Type escape sequence to abort.
Sending 5, 100-byte ICMP Echos to 141.108.22.1, timeout is 2 seconds:
!!!!!
Success rate is 100 percent (5/5), round-trip min/avg/max = 12/14/16 ms
```

The next step in migration is to remove RIP and enable OSPF across all interfaces in the networks. Before you complete this migration, look at the routing configurations on Routers R1, R2, and R3.

Example 8-32 displays the IP routing configuration on R1.

Example 8-32 **show running-config** *(Truncated) on R1*

```
router ospf 1
 redistribute rip metric 100 subnets
 network 141.108.254.0 0.0.0.255 area 0
 network 141.108.255.0 0.0.0.255 area 0
 !
router rip
 redistribute ospf 1 metric 3
 passive-interface Serial1/0
 passive-interface Serial1/1
 network 141.108.0.0
 distribute-list 1 out
access-list 1 deny 141.108.0.0 0.0.7.255
access-list 1 permit any
```

Example 8-33 displays the IP routing configuration on R2.

Example 8-33 **show running-config** *(Truncated) on R2*

```
router ospf 1
 redistribute rip metric 10 subnets
 network 141.108.253.0 0.0.0.255 area 0
 network 141.108.255.0 0.0.0.255 area 0
 !
router rip
 redistribute ospf 1 metric 3
 passive-interface Serial1/0
 passive-interface Serial1/1
 network 141.108.0.0
 distribute-list 1 out
 !
ip classless
 !
access-list 1 deny    141.108.8.0 0.0.7.255
access-list 1 permit any
```

Example 8-34 displays the IP routing configuration on R3.

Example 8-34 **show running-config** *(Truncated) on R3*

```
router ospf 1
 redistribute rip metric 10 subnets
 network 141.108.254.0 0.0.0.255 area 0
 network 141.108.253.0 0.0.0.255 area 0
 !
router rip
 redistribute ospf 1 metric 3
```

Example 8-34 **show running-config** *(Truncated) on R3 (Continued)*

```
passive-interface Serial0
passive-interface Serial1
network 141.108.0.0
distribute-list 1 out
!
access-list 1 deny    141.108.16.0 0.0.7.255
access-list 1 permit any
```

Figure 8-4 displays the OSPF area assignment to complete the RIP to OSPF migration.

Figure 8-4 *OSPF Area Assignments*

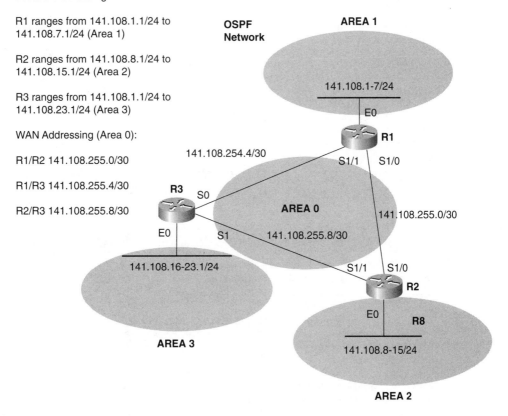

Local IP Addressing:

R1 ranges from 141.108.1.1/24 to
141.108.7.1/24 (Area 1)

R2 ranges from 141.108.8.1/24 to
141.108.15.1/24 (Area 2)

R3 ranges from 141.108.1.1/24 to
141.108.23.1/24 (Area 3)

WAN Addressing (Area 0):

R1/R2 141.108.255.0/30

R1/R3 141.108.255.4/30

R2/R3 141.108.255.8/30

Figure 8-4 displays the OSPF area assignment along with the ability to re-address the WAN circuit to /30 subnets because OSPF understands VLSM.

Example 8-35 displays the removal of RIP on R1 and the OSPF and IP address assignment on R1. Also, note the new IP address assignment for the WAN links with /30 subnets.

Example 8-35 *Removal of RIP on R1 and OSPF/IP Address Assignment*

```
R1(config)#no router rip
R1(config)#router ospf 1
R1(config-router)#network 141.108.255.0 0.0.0.255 area 0
R1(config-router)#network 141.108.0.0 0.0.7.255 area 1
R1(config)#interface s1/0
R1(config-if)#ip address 141.108.255.1 255.255.255.252
R1(config-if)#interface s1/1
R1(config-if)#ip address 141.108.255.5 255.255.255.252
```

Example 8-36 displays the removal of RIP on R2 and the OSPF and IP address assignment on R2.

Example 8-36 *Removal of RIP on R2 and OSPF/IP Address Assignment*

```
R2(config)#no router rip
R2(config)#router ospf 1
R2(config-router)#network 141.108.255.0 0.0.0.255 area 0
R2(config-router)#network 141.108.8.0 0.0.7.255 area 2
R2(config-router)#exit
R2(config)#interface s1/0
R2(config-if)#ip address 141.108.255.2 255.255.255.252
R2(config-if)#interface s1/1
R2(config-if)#ip address 141.108.255.10 255.255.255.252
```

Example 8-37 displays the removal of RIP on R3 and the OSPF and IP address assignment on R3.

Example 8-37 *Removal of RIP on R3 and OSPF/IP Address Assignment*

```
R3(config)#router ospf 1
R3(config-router)#network 141.108.23.0 0.0.7.255 area 3
R3(config-router)#network 141.108.255.0 0.0.0.255 area 0
R3(config-router)#exit
R3(config)#interface serial0
R3(config-if)#ip address 141.108.255.6 255.255.255.252
R3(config-if)#interface serial1
R3(config-if)#ip address 141.108.255.9 255.255.255.252
```

NOTE   Removing RIP from Routers R1, R2, and R3 causes the Cisco IOS to remove any redistribution between RIP and OSPF automatically. Therefore, manual removal of redistribution is not required on Routers R1, R2, and R3.

Now that OSPF is configured across all routers, view the IP routing table on R1. Example 8-38 displays R1's IP routing table.

Example 8-38 *R1's IP Routing Table*

```
R1#show ip route
Codes: C - connected, , O - OSPF, IA - OSPF inter area
      141.108.0.0/16 is variably subnetted, 26 subnets, 3 masks
O       141.108.255.8/30 [110/1562] via 141.108.255.2, 00:00:27, Serial1/0
C       141.108.255.4/30 is directly connected, Serial1/1
C       141.108.255.0/30 is directly connected, Serial1/0
C       141.108.1.0/24 is directly connected, Ethernet0/0
C       141.108.3.0/24 is directly connected, Loopback1
C       141.108.2.0/24 is directly connected, Loopback0
C       141.108.5.0/24 is directly connected, Loopback3
C       141.108.4.0/24 is directly connected, Loopback2
C       141.108.7.0/24 is directly connected, Loopback5
C       141.108.6.0/24 is directly connected, Loopback4
O IA    141.108.9.1/32 [110/782] via 141.108.255.2, 00:00:27, Serial1/0
O IA    141.108.8.0/24 [110/791] via 141.108.255.2, 00:00:27, Serial1/0
O IA    141.108.10.1/32 [110/782] via 141.108.255.2, 00:00:27, Serial1/0
O IA    141.108.11.1/32 [110/782] via 141.108.255.2, 00:00:27, Serial1/0
O IA    141.108.12.1/32 [110/782] via 141.108.255.2, 00:00:27, Serial1/0
O IA    141.108.13.1/32 [110/782] via 141.108.255.2, 00:00:28, Serial1/0
O IA    141.108.14.1/32 [110/782] via 141.108.255.2, 00:00:28, Serial1/0
O IA    141.108.15.1/32 [110/782] via 141.108.255.2, 00:00:28, Serial1/0
O IA    141.108.17.1/32 [110/782] via 141.108.255.6, 00:00:28, Serial1/1
O IA    141.108.16.0/24 [110/791] via 141.108.255.6, 00:00:28, Serial1/1
O IA    141.108.18.1/32 [110/782] via 141.108.255.6, 00:00:28, Serial1/1
O IA    141.108.19.1/32 [110/782] via 141.108.255.6, 00:00:28, Serial1/1
O IA    141.108.20.1/32 [110/782] via 141.108.255.6, 00:00:28, Serial1/1
O IA    141.108.21.1/32 [110/782] via 141.108.255.6, 00:00:28, Serial1/1
O IA    141.108.22.1/32 [110/782] via 141.108.255.6, 00:00:28, Serial1/1
O IA    141.108.23.1/32 [110/782] via 141.108.255.6, 00:00:28, Serial1/1
```

In Example 8-32, the redistributed routes appear as E2 (External Type 2) and OSPF is configured across all three routers. The OSPF type route is displayed as O IA in Example 8-38.

OSPF can support VLSM and network summarization, so configure each router in Figure 8-4 to summarize locally connected routes, which are contiguous. (All routers are ABRs because each router resides in areas 0, 1, 2, or 3.) Example 8-39 displays the summarization for networks 141.108.0.0–141.108.7.0. To summarize internal OSPF routes, the **area** *area-id* **range** *network subnet mask* IOS command is required.

The loopback addresses on R1 reside in OSPF area 1. Example 8-39 displays the **area summary** command on R1.

Example 8-39 *Area Summary on R1*

```
R1(config)#router ospf 1
R1(config-router)#area 1 ?
  authentication  Enable authentication
  default-cost    Set the summary default-cost of a NSSA/stub area
  nssa            Specify a NSSA area
  range           Summarize routes matching address/mask (border routers only)
  stub            Specify a stub area
  virtual-link    Define a virtual link and its parameters
R1(config-router)#area 1 range ?
  A.B.C.D  IP address to match
R1(config-router)#area 1 range 141.108.0.0 ?
  A.B.C.D  IP mask for address
R1(config-router)#area 1 range 141.108.0.0 255.255.248.0
```

The **?** tool is used to display the various options. The mask, 255.255.248.0, encompasses the seven networks ranging from 141.108.0.0–141.108.7.0. You may ask yourself why you are not using 141.108.0.0 on R1 or subnet zero. With large IP networks, the network IP designer should always use all the address space available; subnet zero is a perfect example.

To enable subnet zero, you must configure the global **ip subnet-zero** command on R1.

Example 8-40 enables the use of zero subnets on R1.

Example 8-40 *Subnet Zero Enabling on R1*

```
R1(config)#ip subnet-zero
R1(config-if)#interface loopback 6
R1(config-if)#ip address 141.108.0.1 255.255.255.0
```

Example 8-41 displays the summarization required on R2 to encompass the networks 141.108.8.0–141.108.15.255. (These networks reside in area 2.)

Example 8-41 *Area Summary on R2*

```
R2(config)#router ospf 1
R2(config-router)#area 2 range 141.108.8.0 255.255.248.0
```

Example 8-42 displays the summarization required on R3 to encompass the networks 141.108.16.0–141.108.23.255. (These networks reside in area 3.)

Example 8-42 *Area Summary on R2*

```
R3(config)#router ospf 1
R3(config-router)#area 3 range 141.108.16.0 255.255.248.0
```

Example 8-43 displays the OSPF IP routing table on R1. (Initially, when RIP was the primary routing algorithm, you had 17 RIP entries, as displayed in Example 8-21.)

Example 8-43 **show ip route ospf** *on R1*

```
R1#show ip route ospf
     141.108.0.0/16 is variably subnetted, 13 subnets, 3 masks
O       141.108.255.8/30 [110/1562] via 141.108.255.2, 00:04:57, Serial1/0
O IA    141.108.8.0/21 [110/791] via 141.108.255.2, 00:04:57, Serial1/0
O IA    141.108.16.0/21 [110/782] via 141.108.255.6, 00:01:13, Serial1/1
```

R1 has 3 OSPF network entries as opposed to 17 using RIP.

Now, you can see why networks are converted from classful routing protocols, such as RIP, to classless protocols, such as OSPF. The migration in this scenario demonstrates the powerful use of redistribution and what you should be aware of when configuring metrics. Before looking at another scenario, view the full working configurations of all three routers in Figure 8-4.

Example 8-44 displays R1's full working configuration.

Example 8-44 *R1's Full Working Configuration*

```
Hostname R1
!
enable password cisco
!
ip subnet-zero
interface Loopback0
 ip address 141.108.2.1 255.255.255.0
!
interface Loopback1
 ip address 141.108.3.1 255.255.255.0
!
interface Loopback2
 ip address 141.108.4.1 255.255.255.0
!
interface Loopback3
 ip address 141.108.5.1 255.255.255.0
```

continues

Example 8-44 *R1's Full Working Configuration (Continued)*

```
!
interface Loopback4
 ip address 141.108.6.1 255.255.255.0
!
interface Loopback5
 ip address 141.108.7.1 255.255.255.0
!
interface Loopback6
 ip address 141.108.0.1 255.255.255.0
!
interface Ethernet0/0
 ip address 141.108.1.1 255.255.255.0
!
interface Serial1/0
 ip address 141.108.255.1 255.255.255.252
no ip mroute-cache
 no fair-queue
 clockrate 128000
!
interface Serial1/1
 ip address 141.108.255.5 255.255.255.252
clockrate 128000
!
router ospf 1
 area 1 range 141.108.0.0 255.255.248.0
 network 141.108.0.0 0.0.7.255 area 1
 network 141.108.255.0 0.0.0.255 area 0
!
ip classless
end
```

Example 8-45 displays R2's full working configuration.

Example 8-45 *R2's Full Working Configuration*

```
hostname R2
!
enable password cisco
!
ip subnet-zero
no ip domain-lookup
interface Loopback0
 ip address 141.108.9.1 255.255.255.0
!
interface Loopback1
 ip address 141.108.10.1 255.255.255.0
!
interface Loopback2
 ip address 141.108.11.1 255.255.255.0
```

Example 8-45 *R2's Full Working Configuration (Continued)*

```
!
interface Loopback3
 ip address 141.108.12.1 255.255.255.0
!
interface Loopback4
 ip address 141.108.13.1 255.255.255.0
!
interface Loopback5
 ip address 141.108.14.1 255.255.255.0
!
interface Loopback6
 ip address 141.108.15.1 255.255.255.0
!
interface Ethernet0/0
 ip address 141.108.8.1 255.255.255.0
!
interface TokenRing0/0
 no ip address
shutdown
 ring-speed 16
!
interface Serial1/0
 bandwidth 128
 ip address 141.108.255.2 255.255.255.252
!
interface Serial1/1
 ip address 141.108.255.10 255.255.255.252
!
router ospf 1
 area 2 range 141.108.8.0 255.255.248.0
 network 141.108.8.0 0.0.7.255 area 2
 network 141.108.255.0 0.0.0.255 area 0
!
ip classless
!
end
```

Example 8-46 displays R3's full working configuration.

Example 8-46 *R3's Full Working Configuration*

```
hostname R3
!
enable password cisco
!
no ip domain-lookup
!
interface Loopback0
 ip address 141.108.17.1 255.255.255.0
```

continues

Example 8-46 *R3's Full Working Configuration (Continued)*

```
!
interface Loopback1
 ip address 141.108.18.1 255.255.255.0
!
interface Loopback2
 ip address 141.108.19.1 255.255.255.0
!
interface Loopback3
 ip address 141.108.20.1 255.255.255.0
!
interface Loopback4
 ip address 141.108.21.1 255.255.255.0
!
interface Loopback5
 ip address 141.108.22.1 255.255.255.0
!
interface Loopback6
 ip address 141.108.23.1 255.255.255.0
!
interface Ethernet0
 ip address 141.108.16.1 255.255.255.0
 media-type 10BaseT
!
interface Ethernet1
 no ip address
!
interface Serial0
 ip address 141.108.255.6 255.255.255.252
 bandwidth 125
!
interface Serial1
 ip address 141.108.255.9 255.255.255.252
 bandwidth 125
 clockrate 125000
!
router ospf 1
 network 141.108.16.0 0.0.7.255 area 3
 network 141.108.255.0 0.0.0.255 area 0
 area 3 range 141.108.16.0 255.255.248.0
!
end
```

Scenario 8-3: Redistributing Between EIGRP and OSPF

In this scenario, you configure a five-router topology with four different autonomous systems using two IP routing algorithms: OSPF and EIGRP. The end design goal of this scenario is to ensure full IP connectivity among all interfaces.

The internetwork in Figure 8-5 has an OSPF domain and three EIGRP domains.

Figure 8-5   *OSPF and EIGRP Domains*

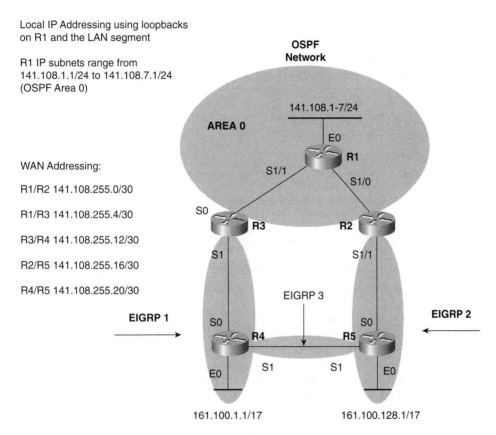

Local IP Addressing using loopbacks
on R1 and the LAN segment

R1 IP subnets range from
141.108.1.1/24 to 141.108.7.1/24
(OSPF Area 0)

WAN Addressing:

R1/R2 141.108.255.0/30

R1/R3 141.108.255.4/30

R3/R4 141.108.255.12/30

R2/R5 141.108.255.16/30

R4/R5 141.108.255.20/30

Routers R1, R2, and R3 are configured in OSPF process 1. (Remember that OSPF has a process ID that is only locally significant.) R4 is configured in EIGRP domain 1, and R5 is configured in EIGRP domain 2. The WAN link between R4 and R5 resides in EIGRP domain 3.

Figure 8-5 details the IP address assignment. Also, notice that a redundant path exists between R4 and R5. Therefore, you must carefully consider any route redistribution to avoid routing loops.

Start by enabling the routing protocols in use, namely OSPF on Routers R1–R3. Figure 8-5 depicts a simple OSPF network with one area, the backbone.

All of Router R1's interfaces reside in area 0; hence, you can use one IOS command to place all R1's interfaces in OSPF area 0 or the backbone.

Example 8-47 places all interfaces on R1 in area 0, the backbone network in OSPF. Figure 8-5 displays the OSPF area assignments required for this topology.

Example 8-47 *R1's OSPF Configuration*

```
R1(config)#router ospf 1
R1(config-router)#network 0.0.0.0 255.255.255.255 area 0
```

Routers R2 and R3 reside in OSPF and EIGRP domains. Example 8-48 configures R2's serial link to R1 to reside in area 0.

Example 8-48 *R2's OSPF Configuration*

```
R2(config)#router ospf 1
R2(config-router)#network 141.108.255.2 0.0.0.0 area 0
```

The inverse mask, 0.0.0.0, configures the IP address 141.108.255.2 into area 0.

Example 8-49 configures R3's serial link to R1 to reside in area 0.

Example 8-49 *R3's OSPF Configuration*

```
R3config)#router ospf 1
R3config-router)#network 141.108.255.6 0.0.0.0 area 0
```

R1 should now have full OSPF adjacency to R2 and R3. Example 8-50 confirms that OSPF has formed a full relationship to R2 and R3.

Example 8-50 shows ip ospf neighbor *on R1*

```
R1#show ip ospf neighbor

Neighbor ID      Pri   State        Dead Time   Address         Interface
141.108.255.17    1    FULL/  -     00:00:38    141.108.255.2   Serial1/0
141.108.255.13    1    FULL/  -     00:00:38    141.108.255.6   Serial1/1
```

R1 is fully adjacent (Full) to R2 and R3, and no designated router (DR) or backup designated router (BDR) is selected over a point-to-point (in this case back-to-back serial connected Cisco routers).

Before you configure redistribution, configure the EIGRP domains on R4 and R5. Example 8-51 configures R4 in EIGRP domains 1 and 3.

Example 8-51 *EIGRP Configuration on R4*

```
R4(config)#router eigrp 1
R4(config-router)# passive-interface Serial1
R4(config-router)# network 141.108.0.0
R4(config-router)#network 161.100.0.0
R4(config-router)# no auto-summary
R4(config-router)#!
R4(config-router)#router eigrp 3
R4(config-router)# passive-interface Ethernet0
R4(config-router)# passive-interface Serial0
R4(config-router)# network 141.108.0.0
R4(config-router)# no auto-summary
```

Automatic summarization is disabled on R4, so you can apply some summary commands later. Also on R4, for interfaces in EIGRP domain 1, you need to apply the **passive** interface command to ensure that no routing updates are sent.

Similarly, in EIGRP domain 3, only one network resides in EIGRP 3, the WAN link to R5.

Example 8-52 confirms the EIGRP interfaces in domains 1 and 3.

Example 8-52 **show ip eigrp interfaces** *on R4*

```
R4#show ip eigrp interfaces
IP-EIGRP interfaces for process 1
                     Xmit Queue   Mean    Pacing Time   Multicast    Pending
Interface   Peers   Un/Reliable   SRTT    Un/Reliable   Flow Timer   Routes
Se0          1         0/0         7         5/194         226         0
Et0          0         0/0         0         0/10          0           0

IP-EIGRP interfaces for process 3
                     Xmit Queue   Mean    Pacing Time   Multicast    Pending
Interface   Peers   Un/Reliable   SRTT    Un/Reliable   Flow Timer   Routes
Se1          0         0/0         0         0/10          0           0
```

Example 8-52 confirms that the Ethernet interface and link to R3 reside in EIGRP 1 and the WAN link to R5 resides in EIGRP 3. The peers on R4 confirm that EIGRP is configured on R3. There is no EIGRP peer to R5 because EIGRP is not enabled on R5 yet.

Example 8-53 configures R5 in EIGRP 2 and EIGRP 3.

Example 8-53 *EIGRP Configuration on R5*

```
R5(config)#router eigrp 3
R5(config-router)# passive-interface Ethernet0
R5(config-router)# passive-interface Serial0
R5(config-router)# network 141.108.0.0
R5(config-router)# no auto-summary
R5(config-router)#!
R5(config-router)#router eigrp 2
R5(config-router)# passive-interface Serial1
R5(config-router)# network 141.108.0.0
R5(config-router)# network 160.100.0.0
R5(config-router)# no auto-summary
```

At this stage, you have not configured any redistribution. Start by configuring redistribution in the EIGRP domains 1, 2, and 3. Redistributing from one EIGRP AS to another does not require you to define a metric because EIGRP conserves the metric. Therefore, you redistribute only networks using the metric from the original AS or domain. You do have to ensure that route maps or distribution lists are used to avoid loops. You configure route maps on R2 and R3, the core routers in the network, later in this chapter.

Example 8-54 configures redistribution from EIGRP domain 1 to 3 on Router R4 and also configures a summary route on R4, advertising the subnet 160.100.0.0/17.

Example 8-54 *Redistribution on R4*

```
R4(config)#interface s0
R4(config-if)#ip summary-address eigrp 1 160.100.0.0 255.255.128.0
R4(config)#router eigrp 1
R4(config-router)#redistribute eigrp 3
R4(config-router)#exit
R4(config)#router eigrp 3
R4(config-router)#redistribute eigrp 1
```

Example 8-55 configures redistribution from EIGRP domain 2 to 3 on Router R5 and also configures a summary route on R4, advertising the subnet 160.100.128.0/17.

Example 8-55 *Redistribution on R5*

```
R5(config-router)#interface Serial0
R5(config-if)# ip summary-address eigrp 2 160.100.128.0 255.255.128.0
R5(config-if)#exit
R5(config)#router eigrp 3
R5(config-router)# redistribute eigrp 2
R5(config-router)#router eigrp 2
R5(config-router)# redistribute eigrp 3
```

To ensure IP connectivity, display the IP routing tables on R2 and R3. Example 8-56 displays the IP routing table (EIGRP only) on R2.

Example 8-56 show ip route eigrp *on R2*

```
R2#sh ip route eigrp
     141.108.0.0/16 is variably subnetted, 13 subnets, 2 masks
D       141.108.255.20/30
           [90/21024000] via 141.108.255.18, 00:01:26, Serial1/1
D EX    141.108.255.12/30
           [170/22016000] via 141.108.255.18, 00:01:26, Serial1/1
     160.100.0.0/17 is subnetted, 2 subnets
D       160.100.128.0 [90/20537600] via 141.108.255.18, 00:01:26, Serial1/1
D EX    160.100.0.0 [170/21049600] via 141.108.255.18, 00:01:26, Serial1/1
```

R2 has the summary route from R4 appearing as an internal EIGRP route (D) because the network resides in the same AS. The second summary route redistributed from domain 3 to 2 appears as an external EIGRP (D EX) route.

Example 8-57 displays the IP routing table (EIGRP) in R3.

Example 8-57 show ip route eigrp *on R3*

```
R3#show ip route eigrp
     160.100.0.0/17 is subnetted, 2 subnets
D EX    160.100.128.0 [170/21529600] via 141.108.255.14, 00:06:21, Serial1
D       160.100.0.0 [90/21017600] via 141.108.255.14, 00:10:12, Serial1
     141.108.0.0/16 is variably subnetted, 13 subnets, 2 masks
D       141.108.255.20/30 [90/21504000] via 141.108.255.14, 00:10:12, Serial1
D EX    141.108.255.16/30 [170/22016000] via 141.108.255.14, 00:07:27, Serial1
```

Similarly, R3 has an internal (D 160.100.0.0) and external summary route (D EX 160.100.128.0) for the remote Ethernet segments on R4 and R5, respectively.

R1's IP routing table does not contain the EIGRP networks because the OSPF routers R2 and R3 (ABRs and ASBRs) have yet to enable redistribution from EIGRP (composite metric) to OSPF (cost metric). Because OSPF and EIGRP use different metrics for routing, you must assign metrics when redistributing and ensure, by using route maps, that no redistributed information causes a routing loop.

Example 8-58 configures R2 for redistributing OSPF routes into EIGRP and EIGRP routes into OSPF. R2 is configured not to permit any routes from R4 advertising networks in the range 141.108.0.0–141.108.7.255 and also the WAN subnets 141.108.255.0/30 (Link R1/R2) and 141.108.255.4/30 (Link R1/R3); this prevents erroneous routing information and routing loops from occurring.

Example 8-58 *Retribution on R2*

```
router eigrp 2
 redistribute ospf 1 metric 1500 2000 255 1 1500 route-map allowintoeigrp
!
router ospf 1
 redistribute eigrp 2 metric 100 subnets route-map allowintoospf
!
route-map allowintoeigrp permit 10
 match ip address 1
!
route-map allowintoospf permit 10
 match ip address 2
! Networks in Access list 1 reside in the EIGRP domain
access-list 1 deny    160.100.0.0 0.0.255.255
access-list 1 permit any
! Networks in Access-list 2 reside in the OSPF domain
access-list 2 deny    141.108.0.0 0.0.7.255
access-list 2 deny    141.108.255.0 0.0.0.3
access-list 2 deny    141.108.255.4 0.0.0.3
access-list 2 permit any
```

R2 is configured to redistribute OSPF networks with a route map named allowintoeigrp, indicating that only networks matching access list 1 are allowed into OSPF. Similarly, when redistributing EIGRP networks into OSPF, the route map named allowintoospf permits all networks matching access-list 2, as shaded in Example 8-58.

Example 8-59 displays the OSPF to EIGRP redistribution on Router R3 with a route map configured to ensure that erroneous information is not sent from either routing domain.

Example 8-59 *Redistribution on R3*

```
router eigrp 1
 redistribute ospf 1 metric 1500 20000 255 1 1500 route-map allowintoeigrp
!
router ospf 1
 redistribute eigrp 1 metric 100 subnets route-map allowintoospf

! Networks in Access list 1 reside in the EIGRP domain
access-list 1 deny    160.100.0.0 0.0.255.255
access-list 1 permit any
! Networks in Access-list 2 reside in the OSPF domain
access-list 2 deny    141.108.0.0 0.0.7.255
access-list 2 deny    141.108.255.0 0.0.0.3
access-list 2 deny    141.108.255.4 0.0.0.3
access-list 2 permit any
route-map allowintoeigrp permit 10
 match ip address 1
!
route-map allowintoospf permit 10
 match ip address 2
```

NOTE   If the WAN link between R4 and R5 goes down, EIGRP domain 3 is isolated. In other
words, R4 won't be able to get to the networks connected to R5 because the 160.100.0.0
network is denied from being redistributed into EIGRP from OSPF. To fix this, you can add
the network 160.100.0.0 as part of the access list. For the purposes of this exercise, assume
the back-to-back serial connections between R4 and R5 never fail.

Now that redistribution is completed and filtered on core routers, examine some IP routing
tables starting from the core router R1 in OSPF area 0, or the backbone. A common technique to ensure network connectivity is to ping IP interfaces.

Example 8-60 displays the IP routing table (OSPF routes only) on R1 and some sample
pings to the remote EIGRP networks 160.100.1.1/25 and 150.100.1.129/25.

Example 8-60 **show ip route ospf** *and Pings on R1*

```
R1#show ip route ospf
     141.108.0.0/16 is variably subnetted, 13 subnets, 2 masks
O E2    141.108.255.20/30 [110/100] via 141.108.255.6, 01:16:02, Serial1/1
O E2    141.108.255.16/30 [110/100] via 141.108.255.6, 01:16:02, Serial1/1
O E2    141.108.255.12/30 [110/100] via 141.108.255.6, 01:16:02, Serial1/1
     160.100.0.0/17 is subnetted, 2 subnets
O E2    160.100.128.0 [110/100] via 141.108.255.2, 01:16:11, Serial1/0
O E2    160.100.0.0 [110/100] via 141.108.255.6, 01:16:02, Serial1/1
R1#ping 160.100.1.1
Type escape sequence to abort.
Sending 5, 100-byte ICMP Echos to 160.100.1.1, timeout is 2 seconds:
!!!!!
Success rate is 100 percent (5/5), round-trip min/avg/max = 28/30/32 ms
R1#ping 160.100.128.1
Type escape sequence to abort.
Sending 5, 100-byte ICMP Echos to 160.100.128.1, timeout is 2 seconds:
!!!!!
Success rate is 100 percent (5/5), round-trip min/avg/max = 28/31/32 ms
R1#
```

Example 8-61 displays the IP routing table on R4.

Example 8-61 **show ip route** *on R4*

```
R4#show ip route

     141.108.0.0/16 is variably subnetted, 13 subnets, 2 masks
C       141.108.255.20/30 is directly connected, Serial1
D       141.108.255.16/30 [90/21504000] via 141.108.255.22, 01:42:25, Serial1
C       141.108.255.12/30 is directly connected, Serial0
D       141.108.255.4/30 [90/21504000] via 141.108.255.13, 01:42:51, Serial0
```

continues

Example 8-61 show ip route *on R4 (Continued)*

```
D EX    141.108.255.0/30 [170/22016000] via 141.108.255.22, 01:42:25, Serial1
D EX    141.108.1.0/24 [170/22016000] via 141.108.255.22, 01:21:46, Serial1
D EX    141.108.0.0/24 [170/22016000] via 141.108.255.22, 01:21:46, Serial1
D EX    141.108.3.0/24 [170/22016000] via 141.108.255.22, 01:21:46, Serial1
D EX    141.108.2.0/24 [170/22016000] via 141.108.255.22, 01:21:46, Serial1
D EX    141.108.5.0/24 [170/22016000] via 141.108.255.22, 01:21:46, Serial1
D EX    141.108.4.0/24 [170/22016000] via 141.108.255.22, 01:21:46, Serial1
D EX    141.108.7.0/24 [170/22016000] via 141.108.255.22, 01:21:46, Serial1
D EX    141.108.6.0/24 [170/22016000] via 141.108.255.22, 01:21:47, Serial1
        160.100.0.0/17 is subnetted, 2 subnets
D EX    160.100.128.0 [170/21017600] via 141.108.255.22, 01:42:27, Serial1
C       160.100.0.0 is directly connected, Ethernet0
```

Full connectivity is displayed on R4, and notice that the shaded routes in Example 8-61 encompass all the routes from 141.108.0.0–141.108.7.255. (These routes are the loopback interfaces on R1.)

Example 8-62 displays a successful ping from R4 to all the remote loopbacks on R1 to ensure that you have network connectivity from the EIGRP domain.

Example 8-62 *Pinging Loopbacks from R4*

```
R4#ping 141.108.0.1
Type escape sequence to abort.
Sending 5, 100-byte ICMP Echos to 141.108.0.1, timeout is 2 seconds:
!!!!!
Success rate is 100 percent (5/5), round-trip min/avg/max = 36/37/44 ms
R4#ping 141.108.1.1
Type escape sequence to abort.
Sending 5, 100-byte ICMP Echos to 141.108.1.1, timeout is 2 seconds:
!!!!!
Success rate is 100 percent (5/5), round-trip min/avg/max = 36/37/40 ms
R4#ping 141.108.2.1
Type escape sequence to abort.
Sending 5, 100-byte ICMP Echos to 141.108.2.1, timeout is 2 seconds:
!!!!!
Success rate is 100 percent (5/5), round-trip min/avg/max = 36/36/40 ms
R4#ping 141.108.3.1
Type escape sequence to abort.
Sending 5, 100-byte ICMP Echos to 141.108.3.1, timeout is 2 seconds:
!!!!!
Success rate is 100 percent (5/5), round-trip min/avg/max = 36/37/40 ms
R4#ping 141.108.4.1
Type escape sequence to abort.
Sending 5, 100-byte ICMP Echos to 141.108.4.1, timeout is 2 seconds:
!!!!!
Success rate is 100 percent (5/5), round-trip min/avg/max = 36/38/40 ms
R4#ping 141.108.5.1
Type escape sequence to abort.
Sending 5, 100-byte ICMP Echos to 141.108.5.1, timeout is 2 seconds:
```

Example 8-62 *Pinging Loopbacks from R4 (Continued)*

```
!!!!!
Success rate is 100 percent (5/5), round-trip min/avg/max = 36/50/100 ms
R4#ping 141.108.6.1
Type escape sequence to abort.
Sending 5, 100-byte ICMP Echos to 141.108.6.1, timeout is 2 seconds:
!!!!!
Success rate is 100 percent (5/5), round-trip min/avg/max = 36/38/40 ms
```

Because R4 and R5 have a redundant path to the OSPF backbone, the EIGRP topology table on R4 and R5 displays feasible successors. Example 8-63 displays the output from the **show ip eigrp topology** command on R4.

Example 8-63 **show ip eigrp topology** *on R4*

```
R4#show ip eigrp topology
IP-EIGRP Topology Table for AS(1)/ID(160.100.1.1)
Codes: P - Passive, A - Active, U - Update, Q - Query, R - Reply,
       r - Reply status
P 141.108.255.20/30, 1 successors, FD is 20992000
        via Connected, Serial1
P 141.108.255.16/30, 1 successors, FD is 21504000
        via Redistributed (21504000/0)
P 141.108.255.12/30, 1 successors, FD is 20992000
        via Connected, Serial0
P 141.108.255.4/30, 1 successors, FD is 21504000
        via 141.108.255.13 (21504000/20992000), Serial0
P 141.108.255.0/30, 1 successors, FD is 22016000
        via Redistributed (22016000/0)
        via 141.108.255.13 (26112000/6826496), Serial0
P 160.100.128.0/17, 1 successors, FD is 21017600
        via Redistributed (21017600/0)
        via 141.108.255.13 (26112000/6826496), Serial0
P 160.100.0.0/17, 1 successors, FD is 281600
        via Connected, Ethernet0
P 141.108.1.0/24, 1 successors, FD is 22016000
        via Redistributed (22016000/0)
        via 141.108.255.13 (26112000/6826496), Serial0
P 141.108.0.0/24, 1 successors, FD is 22016000
        via Redistributed (22016000/0)
        via 141.108.255.13 (26112000/6826496), Serial0
P 141.108.3.0/24, 1 successors, FD is 22016000
        via Redistributed (22016000/0)
        via 141.108.255.13 (26112000/6826496), Serial0
P 141.108.2.0/24, 1 successors, FD is 22016000
        via Redistributed (22016000/0)
        via 141.108.255.13 (26112000/6826496), Serial0
P 141.108.5.0/24, 1 successors, FD is 22016000
        via Redistributed (22016000/0)
        via 141.108.255.13 (26112000/6826496), Serial0
```

continues

Example 8-63 show ip eigrp topology *on R4 (Continued)*

```
P 141.108.4.0/24, 1 successors, FD is 22016000
        via Redistributed (22016000/0)
        via 141.108.255.13 (26112000/6826496), Serial0
P 141.108.7.0/24, 1 successors, FD is 22016000
        via Redistributed (22016000/0)
        via 141.108.255.13 (26112000/6826496), Serial0
P 141.108.6.0/24, 1 successors, FD is 22016000
        via Redistributed (22016000/0)
        via 141.108.255.13 (26112000/6826496), Serial0
IP-EIGRP Topology Table for AS(3)/ID(160.100.1.1)
P 141.108.255.20/30, 1 successors, FD is 20992000
        via Connected, Serial1
        via Reconnected (20992000/0)
P 141.108.255.16/30, 1 successors, FD is 21504000
        via 141.108.255.22 (21504000/2169856), Serial1
P 141.108.255.12/30, 1 successors, FD is 20992000
        via Connected, Serial0
        via Reconnected (20992000/0)
P 141.108.255.4/30, 1 successors, FD is 21504000
        via Redistributed (21504000/0)
        via 141.108.255.22 (22016000/2730496), Serial1
P 141.108.255.0/30, 1 successors, FD is 22016000
        via 141.108.255.22 (22016000/21024000), Serial1
        via Redistributed (26112000/0)
P 160.100.128.0/17, 1 successors, FD is 21017600
        via 141.108.255.22 (21017600/281600), Serial1
P 160.100.0.0/17, 1 successors, FD is 281600
        via Redistributed (281600/0)
P 141.108.1.0/24, 1 successors, FD is 22016000
        via 141.108.255.22 (22016000/2730496), Serial1
        via Redistributed (26112000/0)
P 141.108.0.0/24, 1 successors, FD is 22016000
        via 141.108.255.22 (22016000/2730496), Serial1
        via Redistributed (26112000/0)
P 141.108.3.0/24, 1 successors, FD is 22016000
        via 141.108.255.22 (22016000/2730496), Serial1
        via Redistributed (26112000/0)
P 141.108.2.0/24, 1 successors, FD is 22016000
        via 141.108.255.22 (22016000/2730496), Serial1
        via Redistributed (26112000/0)
P 141.108.5.0/24, 1 successors, FD is 22016000
        via 141.108.255.22 (22016000/2730496), Serial1
        via Redistributed (26112000/0)
P 141.108.4.0/24, 1 successors, FD is 22016000
        via 141.108.255.22 (22016000/2730496), Serial1
        via Redistributed (26112000/0)
P 141.108.7.0/24, 1 successors, FD is 22016000
        via 141.108.255.22 (22016000/2730496), Serial1
        via Redistributed (26112000/0)
P 141.108.6.0/24, 1 successors, FD is 22016000
        via 141.108.255.22 (22016000/2730496), Serial1
        via Redistributed (26112000/0)
```

In Example 8-63, R4 has a number of dual paths to remote networks, as shaded in the output. Because the metric is lower through Serial 1, the chosen path to the remote network 141.108.6.0/24 is through Serial 1, for example. Next, simulate a network failure by shutting down the serial link to R5 on R4. Example 8-64 disables the link to R5.

Example 8-64 *Shut Down S1 on R4*

```
R4(config)#interface serial 1
R4(config-if)#shutdown
04:02:11: %LINK-5-CHANGED: Interface Serial1, changed state to administratively
down
04:02:12: %LINEPROTO-5-UPDOWN: Line protocol on Interface Serial1, changed state
 to down
```

The IP routing table on R4 displays the path to the remote loopbacks and OSPF network through Serial 0. Example 8-65 confirms the IP routing table; note the EIGRP composite metric, which is higher than through Serial 1 to R5 (22016000 compared to 26112000).

Example 8-65 show ip route eigrp *on R4*

```
R4#show ip route eigrp
     141.108.0.0/16 is variably subnetted, 11 subnets, 2 masks
D       141.108.255.4/30 [90/21504000] via 141.108.255.13, 02:53:02, Serial0
D EX    141.108.255.0/30 [170/26112000  via 141.108.255.13, 00:02:07, Serial0
D EX    141.108.1.0/24 [170/26112000] via 141.108.255.13, 00:02:07, Serial0
D EX    141.108.0.0/24 [170/26112000] via 141.108.255.13, 00:02:07, Serial0
D EX    141.108.3.0/24 [170/26112000] via 141.108.255.13, 00:02:07, Serial0
D EX    141.108.2.0/24 [170/26112000] via 141.108.255.13, 00:02:07, Serial0
D EX    141.108.5.0/24 [170/26112000] via 141.108.255.13, 00:02:08, Serial0
D EX    141.108.4.0/24 [170/26112000] via 141.108.255.13, 00:02:08, Serial0
D EX    141.108.7.0/24 [170/26112000] via 141.108.255.13, 00:02:08, Serial0
D EX    141.108.6.0/24 [170/26112000] via 141.108.255.13, 00:02:08, Serial0
     160.100.0.0/17 is subnetted, 2 subnets
D EX    160.100.128.0 [170/26112000] via 141.108.255.13, 00:02:08, Serial0
```

This scenario demonstrates the metric and filtering techniques common in today's large IP networks and the care that you must take when sending networks from one routing algorithm to another. You must pay particular attention to the metric and avoid any routing loops.

Example 8-66 displays R1's full working configuration.

Example 8-66 *R1's Full Working Configuration*

```
hostname R1
!
enable password cisco
!
interface Loopback0
 ip address 141.108.2.1 255.255.255.0
 ip ospf network point-to-point
!
interface Loopback1
 ip address 141.108.3.1 255.255.255.0
 ip ospf network point-to-point
!
interface Loopback2
 ip address 141.108.4.1 255.255.255.0
 ip ospf network point-to-point
!
interface Loopback3
 ip address 141.108.5.1 255.255.255.0
 ip ospf network point-to-point
!
interface Loopback4
 ip address 141.108.6.1 255.255.255.0
 ip ospf network point-to-point
!
interface Loopback5
 ip address 141.108.7.1 255.255.255.0
 ip ospf network point-to-point
!
interface Loopback6
 ip address 141.108.0.1 255.255.255.0
 ip ospf network point-to-point
!
interface Ethernet0/0
 ip address 141.108.1.1 255.255.255.0
!
interface Serial1/0
 ip address 141.108.255.1 255.255.255.252
 clockrate 128000
!
interface Serial1/1
 ip address 141.108.255.5 255.255.255.252
 clockrate 128000
!
router ospf 1
 redistribute connected subnets
 network 0.0.0.0 255.255.255.255 area 0
!
end
```

Example 8-67 displays R2's full working configuration.

Example 8-67 *R2's Full Working Configuration*

```
hostname R2
!
enable password cisco
!
ip subnet-zero
no ip domain-lookup
!
interface Serial1/0
 bandwidth 128
 ip address 141.108.255.2 255.255.255.252
 no ip mroute-cache
!
interface Serial1/1
 ip address 141.108.255.17 255.255.255.252
!
router eigrp 2
 redistribute ospf 1 metric 1500 2000 255 1 1500 route-map allowintoeigrp
 passive-interface Serial1/0
 network 141.108.0.0
 no auto-summary
!
router ospf 1
 summary-address 141.108.0.0 255.255.248.0
 redistribute eigrp 2 metric 100 subnets route-map allowintoospf
 redistribute eigrp 1
 network 141.108.255.2 0.0.0.0 area 0
access-list 1 deny    160.100.0.0 0.0.255.255
access-list 1 permit any
access-list 2 deny    141.108.0.0 0.0.7.255
access-list 2 deny    141.108.255.0 0.0.0.3
access-list 2 deny    141.108.255.4 0.0.0.3
access-list 2 permit any
route-map allowintoeigrp permit 10
 match ip address 1
!
route-map allowintoospf permit 10
 match ip address 2
!
end
```

Example 8-68 displays R3's full working configuration.

Example 8-68 *R3's Full Working Configuration*

```
hostname R3
!
enable password cisco
!
no ip domain-lookup
!
interface Serial0
 ip address 141.108.255.6 255.255.255.252
 bandwidth 125
!
interface Serial1
 ip address 141.108.255.13 255.255.255.252
 bandwidth 125
 clockrate 125000
!
router eigrp 1
 redistribute ospf 1 metric 1500 20000 255 1 1500 route-map allowintoeigrp
 passive-interface Serial0
 network 141.108.0.0
 no auto-summary
!
router ospf 1
 redistribute eigrp 1 metric 100 subnets route-map allowintoospf
 network 141.108.255.6 0.0.0.0 area 0
access-list 1 deny   160.100.0.0 0.0.255.255
access-list 1 permit any
access-list 2 deny   141.108.0.0 0.0.7.255
access-list 2 deny   141.108.255.0 0.0.0.3
access-list 2 deny   141.108.255.4 0.0.0.3
access-list 2 permit any
route-map allowintoeigrp permit 10
 match ip address 1
!
route-map allowintoospf permit 10
 match ip address 2
!
end
```

Example 8-69 displays R4's full working configuration.

Example 8-69 *R4's Full Working Configuration*

```
hostname R4
!
enable password cisco
!
interface Ethernet0
 ip address 160.100.1.1 255.255.128.0
!
interface Serial0
 bandwidth 125
 ip address 141.108.255.14 255.255.255.252
 ip summary-address eigrp 1 160.100.0.0 255.255.128.0 5
!
interface Serial1
 bandwidth 125
 ip address 141.108.255.21 255.255.255.252
 clockrate 125000
!
router eigrp 1
 redistribute eigrp 3
 passive-interface Serial1
 network 141.108.0.0
 network 160.100.0.0
 no auto-summary
!
router eigrp 3
 redistribute eigrp 1
 passive-interface Ethernet0
 passive-interface Serial0
 network 141.108.0.0
 no auto-summary
access-list 1 permit 160.100.0.0 0.0.127.255
access-list 2 permit 160.100.0.0 0.0.127.255
route-map allowtoR3 permit 10
 match ip address 1
!
route-map allowtoR5 permit 10
 match ip address 2
end
```

Example 8-70 displays R5's full working configuration.

Example 8-70 *R5's Full Working Configuration*

```
hostname R5
!
enable password cisco
interface Ethernet0
 ip address 160.100.128.1 255.255.128.0
!
interface Serial0
 ip address 141.108.255.18 255.255.255.252
 ip summary-address eigrp 2 160.100.128.0 255.255.128.0
 clockrate 125000
!
interface Serial1
 ip address 141.108.255.22 255.255.255.252
 no ip directed-broadcast
!
router eigrp 3
 redistribute eigrp 2
 passive-interface Ethernet0
 passive-interface Serial0
 network 141.108.0.0
 no auto-summary
!
router eigrp 2
 redistribute eigrp 3
 passive-interface Serial1
 network 141.108.0.0
 network 160.100.0.0
 no auto-summary
!
ip classless
!
end
```

Scenario 8-4: Route Summarization Using Static Routes

The internetwork in Figure 8-6 displays a simple two-router topology with two routing algorithms in use. This scenario contains only two routers, so you can easily replicate this network with your own set of Cisco IOS routers.

The end goal of this scenario is to ensure full IP connectivity between the two different IP networks. The ability to configure networks from a classless and classful domain and vice versa is critical. This scenario is designed to ensure that you are fully aware of all the potential problems when routing between OSPF (classless routing protocol) and RIP (classful routing protocol).

Figure 8-6   *Routing IP Between RIP and OSPF*

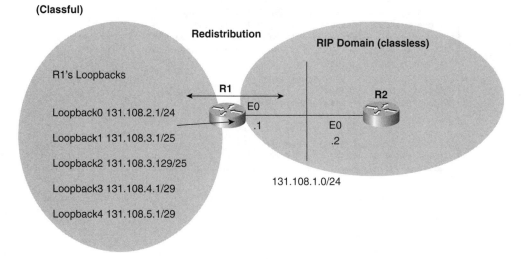

OSPF Domain Area 333

(Classful)

Router R1 has a number of interfaces in OSPF area 333, and R2 is running RIP only.

This scenario uses static routes to ensure connectivity between the classless (RIP) domain to the classful (OSPF) domain.

You configure R1 for redistribution between RIP and OSPF.

Example 8-71 configures R1 for IP addressing and enables OSPF and RIP. Ensure that RIP updates are sent to only the Ethernet interfaces on R1 by configuring R1 with passive interfaces, even on the loopbacks, because OSPF advertises these routes. To ensure that routing resources are not wasted, allow only one routing algorithm to advertise each interface. To do this, you apply passive interfaces where required.

Example 8-71 *R1 Configuration*

```
R1(config)#interface Loopback0
R1(config-if)# ip address 131.108.2.1 255.255.255.0
R1(config-if)#interface Loopback1
R1(config-if)# ip address 131.108.3.1 255.255.255.128
R1(config-if)#interface Loopback2
R1(config-if)# ip address 131.108.3.129 255.255.255.128
R1(config-if)#interface Loopback3
R1(config-if)# ip address 131.108.4.1 255.255.255.248
R1(config-if)#interface Loopback4
```

continues

Example 8-71 *R1 Configuration (Continued)*

```
R1(config-if)# ip address 131.108.5.1 255.255.255.248
R1(config)#router ospf 1
R1(config-router)#network 131.108.2.1 0.0.0.0 area 333
R1(config-router)#network 131.108.3.1 0.0.0.0 area 333
R1(config-router)#network 131.108.3.129 0.0.0.0 area 333
R1(config-router)#network 131.108.4.1 0.0.0.0 area 333
R1(config-router)#network 131.108.5.1 0.0.0.0 area 333
R1(config-router)#router rip
R1(config-router)#network 131.108.0.0
R1(config-router)#pass
R1(config-router)#passive-interface lo0
R1(config-router)#passive-interface lo1
R1(config-router)#passive-interface lo2
R1(config-router)#passive-interface lo3
R1(config-router)#passive-interface lo4
```

Example 8-72 enables IP RIP on R2.

Example 8-72 *RIP Configuration on R2*

```
R2(config)#interface ethernet 0/0
R2(config-if)#ip address 131.108.1.2 255.255.255.0
R2(config-if)#exit
R2(config)#router rip
R2(config-router)#network 131.108.0.0
```

To enable R2 to learn the OSPF loopback interfaces on R1 dynamically, enable RIP-to-OSPF redistribution on R1, by setting the metric to 1 (hop count).

Example 8-73 displays the redistribution on R1 from RIP to OSPF.

Example 8-73 *Redistribution on R1 from RIP to OSPF*

```
R1(config)#router rip
R1(config-router)#redistribute ospf 1 metric 1
```

View the IP routing table on R2 to determine which RIP networks R1 advertises to R2.

Example 8-74 displays the IP routing table on R1.

Example 8-74 **show ip route** *R1*

```
R2#show ip route
     131.108.0.0/24 is subnetted, 2 subnets
R       131.108.2.0 [120/1] via 131.108.1.1, 00:00:06, Ethernet0/0
C       131.108.1.0 is directly connected, Ethernet0/0
```

The only IP network in Example 8-74 is the subnet 131.108.2.0, which is a Class C subnetted route. Because R2 is configured with a classful routing protocol, only 24-bit networks are advertised by R1 and accepted by R2. You can use two methods to solve this scenario. The first is to use static routes, and the second method uses summarization techniques on R1.

Configure R2 with static routes and ensure network connectivity to R1 loopback interfaces.

Example 8-75 configures R2 with four static routes pointing to the next hop destination to R1's Ethernet IP address of 131.108.1.1.

Example 8-75 *Static Route Configuration on R2*

```
R2(config)#ip route 131.108.3.0 255.255.255.128 131.108.1.1
R2(config)#ip route 131.108.3.128 255.255.255.128 131.108.1.1
R2(config)#ip route 131.108.4.0 255.255.255.248 131.108.1.1
R2(config)#ip route 131.108.5.0 255.255.255.248 131.108.1.1
```

R2 is configured with static routing information, even though the remote networks are not Class C subnets. Confirm network connectivity by viewing the IP routing table on R2 and pinging all remote loopback interfaces on R1.

Example 8-76 displays R2's IP routing table and five ping requests to all R1's loopback interfaces.

Example 8-76 **show ip route** *and* **ping** *on R2*

```
R2#show ip route
Codes: C - connected, S - static,R - RIP
     131.108.0.0/16 is variably subnetted, 6 subnets, 3 masks
S       131.108.3.128/25 [1/0] via 131.108.1.1
S       131.108.5.0/29 [1/0] via 131.108.1.1
S       131.108.4.0/29 [1/0] via 131.108.1.1
S       131.108.3.0/25 [1/0] via 131.108.1.1
R       131.108.2.0/24 [120/1] via 131.108.1.1, 00:00:13, Ethernet0/0
C       131.108.1.0/24 is directly connected, Ethernet0/0
R2#ping 131.108.2.1
Type escape sequence to abort.
Sending 5, 100-byte ICMP Echos to 131.108.2.1, timeout is 2 seconds:
!!!!!
Success rate is 100 percent (5/5), round-trip min/avg/max = 1/2/4 ms
R2#ping 131.108.3.1
Type escape sequence to abort.
Sending 5, 100-byte ICMP Echos to 131.108.3.1, timeout is 2 seconds:
!!!!!
Success rate is 100 percent (5/5), round-trip min/avg/max = 1/3/4 ms
R2#ping 131.108.3.129
Type escape sequence to abort.
Sending 5, 100-byte ICMP Echos to 131.108.3.129, timeout is 2 seconds:
```

continues

Example 8-76 **show ip route** *and* **ping** *on R2 (Continued)*

```
!!!!!
Success rate is 100 percent (5/5), round-trip min/avg/max = 1/3/4 ms
R2#ping 131.108.4.1
Type escape sequence to abort.
Sending 5, 100-byte ICMP Echos to 131.108.4.1, timeout is 2 seconds:
!!!!!
Success rate is 100 percent (5/5), round-trip min/avg/max = 1/3/4 ms
R2#ping 131.108.5.1
Type escape sequence to abort.
Sending 5, 100-byte ICMP Echos to 131.108.5.1, timeout is 2 seconds:
!!!!!
Success rate is 100 percent (5/5), round-trip min/avg/max = 1/2/4 ms
R2#
```

Example 8-76 displays IP networks installed in the routing table. Even though RIP is classful, you can use static routes to overcome the limitations of routing between VLSM networks or fixed-length subnet mask (FLSM) networks.

In the next scenario, you configure routing between VLSM and FLSM networks without using static routing.

Example 8-77 displays R1's full working configuration.

Example 8-77 *R1's Full Working Configuration*

```
hostname R1
!
enable password cisco
!
ip subnet-zero
interface Loopback0
 ip address 131.108.2.1 255.255.255.0
!
interface Loopback1
 ip address 131.108.3.1 255.255.255.128
interface Loopback2
 ip address 131.108.3.129 255.255.255.128
interface Loopback3
 ip address 131.108.4.1 255.255.255.248
!
interface Loopback4
 ip address 131.108.5.1 255.255.255.248
!
interface Ethernet0/0
 ip address 131.108.1.1 255.255.255.0
router ospf 1
 network 131.108.2.1 0.0.0.0 area 333
 network 131.108.3.1 0.0.0.0 area 333
 network 131.108.3.129 0.0.0.0 area 333
```

Example 8-77 *R1's Full Working Configuration (Continued)*

```
  network 131.108.4.1 0.0.0.0 area 333
  network 131.108.5.1 0.0.0.0 area 333
 !
 router rip
  redistribute ospf 1 metric 1
  passive-interface Loopback0
  passive-interface Loopback1
  passive-interface Loopback2
  passive-interface Loopback3
  passive-interface Loopback4
  network 131.108.0.0
 !
 end
```

Example 8-78 displays R2's full working configuration.

Example 8-78 *R2's Full Working Configuration (Truncated)*

```
 hostname R2
 !
 enable password cisco
 !
 ip subnet-zero
 no ip domain-lookup
 !
 interface Ethernet0/0
  ip address 131.108.1.2 255.255.255.0
 !
 router rip
 network 131.108.0.0
 !
 ip route 131.108.3.0 255.255.255.128 131.108.1.1
 ip route 131.108.3.128 255.255.255.128 131.108.1.1
 ip route 131.108.4.0 255.255.255.248 131.108.1.1
 ip route 131.108.5.0 255.255.255.248 131.108.1.1
 end
```

Scenario 8-5: Route Summarization Without Using Static Routes

In this scenario, you revisit the topology in Figure 8-6 and use dynamic routing to insert the non-class C networks into R2's routing table.

Example 8-79 removes the static route configuration on R2.

Example 8-79 *Removing the Static Route Configuration on R2*

```
R2(config)#no ip route 131.108.3.0 255.255.255.128 131.108.1.1
R2(config)#no ip route 131.108.3.128 255.255.255.128 131.108.1.1
R2(config)#no ip route 131.108.4.0 255.255.255.248 131.108.1.1
R2(config)#no ip route 131.108.5.0 255.255.255.248 131.108.1.1
```

The IP routing table on R2 now contains only the 131.108.2.0/24 network, as displayed in Example 8-74.

To redistribute the networks in R1's network, you can apply the **summary-address** *network-mask* command.

R1 is an ASBR, so you can use the **summary** command to send an update to RIP with any mask you need. Because all Cisco IOS routers always choose a path with a more specific route, you can advertise all loopbacks on R1 as Class C subnets to R2.

Example 8-80 configures summarization on R1 for the four loopbacks.

Example 8-80 summary-address *Command on R1*

```
R1(config)#router ospf 1
R1(config-router)#summary-address 131.108.3.0 255.255.255.0
R1(config-router)#summary-address 131.108.4.0 255.255.255.0
R1(config-router)#summary-address 131.108.5.0 255.255.255.0
R1(config-router)#redistribute connected subnets
```

The last command in Example 8-80 ensures that all connected routes (in this case, the loopbacks on R1) are redistributed to R2.

Example 8-81 displays the IP routing table on R2.

Example 8-81 show ip route *on R2*

```
R2#show ip route
     131.108.0.0/24 is subnetted, 5 subnets
R       131.108.5.0 [120/1] via 131.108.1.1, 00:00:06, Ethernet0/0
R       131.108.4.0 [120/1] via 131.108.1.1, 00:00:06, Ethernet0/0
R       131.108.3.0 [120/1] via 131.108.1.1, 00:00:06, Ethernet0/0
R       131.108.2.0 [120/1] via 131.108.1.1, 00:00:06, Ethernet0/0
C       131.108.1.0 is directly connected, Ethernet0/0
```

R2 assumes all 131.108.0.0 networks are subnetted as 24-bit networks, as displayed in Example 8-81. To ensure that routing loops cannot occur, R1 sends only the loopbacks interfaces and R2 accepts only routes that are not locally connected.

Example 8-82 configures a route map, called allowout, that permits only the non-class C networks to be advertised to R2.

Example 8-82 *Route Map Configuration on R1*

```
R1(config)#router ospf 1
R1(config-router)#redistribute connected subnets route-map allowout
R1(config-router)#exit
R1(config)#route-map
R1(config)#route-map allowout
R1(config-route-map)#match in
R1(config-route-map)#match interface ?
  Ethernet  IEEE 802.3
  Loopback  Loopback interface
  Null      Null interface
  Serial    Serial
  <cr>
R1(config-route-map)#match interface loopback 1
R1(config-route-map)#match interface loopback 2
R1(config-route-map)#match interface loopback 3
R1(config-route-map)#match interface loopback 4
```

R1 is configured to permit only the loopback interfaces 1–4 to be redistributed into RIP. Loopback 0 is a Class C subnet route, so you do not need to add this interface.

To ensure that R1 never accepts routes that are locally reachable, configure a distribution list that allows only the loopbacks configured on R1.

Example 8-83 configures a distribution list on R2 permitting only loopbacks 0–4 into R2's IP routing table; all other networks are rejected.

Example 8-83 *Distribution List Configuration on R2*

```
R2(config)#router rip
R2(config-router)#distribute-list 1 in
R2(config-router)#exit
R2(config)#access-list 1 permit 131.108.2.0
R2(config)#access-list 1 permit 131.108.3.0
R2(config)#access-list 1 permit 131.108.4.0
R2(config)#access-list 1 permit 131.108.5.0
```

Example 8-84 confirms the IP routing table on R2.

Example 8-84 **show ip route rip** *on R2*

```
R2#show ip route rip
     131.108.0.0/24 is subnetted, 5 subnets
R       131.108.5.0 [120/1] via 131.108.1.1, 00:00:00, Ethernet0/0
R       131.108.4.0 [120/1] via 131.108.1.1, 00:00:00, Ethernet0/0
R       131.108.3.0 [120/1] via 131.108.1.1, 00:00:00, Ethernet0/0
R       131.108.2.0 [120/1] via 131.108.1.1, 00:00:00, Ethernet0/0
```

The same principles applied here can be applied to any number of routers, and as long as route maps and filtering are applied, the network should be free of routing loops and maintain full network connectivity.

Example 8-85 displays R1's full working configuration.

Example 8-85 *R1's Full Working Configuration*

```
hostname R1
!
enable password cisco
!
interface Loopback0
 ip address 131.108.2.1 255.255.255.0
!
interface Loopback1
 ip address 131.108.3.1 255.255.255.128
!
interface Loopback2
 ip address 131.108.3.129 255.255.255.128
!
interface Loopback3
 ip address 131.108.4.1 255.255.255.248
!
interface Loopback4
 ip address 131.108.5.1 255.255.255.248
interface Ethernet0/0
 ip address 131.108.1.1 255.255.255.0
!
router ospf 1
 summary-address 131.108.3.0 255.255.255.0
 summary-address 131.108.4.0 255.255.255.0
 summary-address 131.108.5.0 255.255.255.0
 redistribute connected subnets route-map allowout
 network 131.108.2.1 0.0.0.0 area 333
 network 131.108.3.1 0.0.0.0 area 333
 network 131.108.3.129 0.0.0.0 area 333
 network 131.108.4.1 0.0.0.0 area 333
 network 131.108.5.1 0.0.0.0 area 333
```

Example 8-85 *R1's Full Working Configuration (Continued)*

```
!
router rip
 redistribute ospf 1 metric 1
 passive-interface Loopback0
 passive-interface Loopback1
 passive-interface Loopback2
 passive-interface Loopback3
 passive-interface Loopback4
 network 131.108.0.0
 !
route-map allowout permit 10
 match interface Loopback1 Loopback2 Loopback3 Loopback4
 !
end
```

Example 8-86 displays R2's full working configuration.

Example 8-86 *R2's Full Working Configuration*

```
hostname R2
!
enable password cisco
!
ip subnet-zero
no ip domain-lookup
!
interface Ethernet0/0
 ip address 131.108.1.2 255.255.255.0
 !
router rip
 network 131.108.0.0
 distribute-list 1 in
access-list 1 permit 131.108.5.0
access-list 1 permit 131.108.4.0
access-list 1 permit 131.108.3.0
access-list 1 permit 131.108.2.0
access-list 1 deny   160.100.0.0 0.0.255.255
end
```

Practical Exercise: Redistribution

NOTE   Practical Exercises are designed to test your knowledge of the topics covered in this chapter.
The Practical Exercise begins by giving you some information about a situation and then
asks you to work through the solution on your own. The solution can be found at the end.

Figure 8-7 displays a three-router topology running four routing algorithms, all using /24-bit subnet masks. Loopbacks are used on Routers R1–R3 to populate the network with IP routing entries.

Figure 8-7 *Practical Exercise Topology*

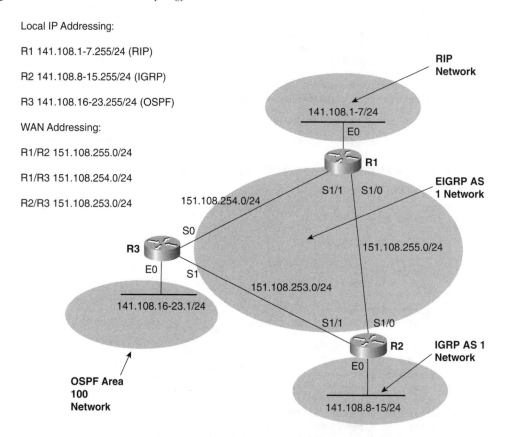

Local IP Addressing:

R1 141.108.1-7.255/24 (RIP)

R2 141.108.8-15.255/24 (IGRP)

R3 141.108.16-23.255/24 (OSPF)

WAN Addressing:

R1/R2 151.108.255.0/24

R1/R3 151.108.254.0/24

R2/R3 151.108.253.0/24

Configure all three routers. Use filtering and make extensive use of passive interfaces to avoid routing loops. Ensure that routing updates are sent to only the relevant interfaces.

Practical Exercise Solution

The issue of FLSM and VLSM is not paramount in this topology because all subnets are /24. So the main issue to be aware of is filtering. Each router is configured for local loopbacks and an interior routing protocol, EIGRP, is configured across the WAN.

After you configure the loopbacks and WAN links are operational, you start by enabling the local LAN interfaces. Then configure redistribution by using filtering wherever required to avoid routing loops. One common troubleshooting scenario is to create a loop by disabling split horizon and then configuring route maps and/or filtering to stop the routing loop— great fun, but only in a practice lab, of course.

The following configurations provide a sample working solution to the network topology in Figure 8-7. You can, however, configure this network many different ways. Static routes are not used in this design.

R1 is configured for RIP and EIGRP. The redistribution on R1 is filtered to deny any locally sourced networks on R1. All other networks are allowed into R1's IP routing table. The shaded portions in Example 8-87 are key configuration commands for filtering.

Example 8-87 displays R1's full working configuration.

Example 8-87 *R1's Full Working Configuration*

```
hostname R1
!
enable password cisco
!
ip subnet-zero
interface Loopback0
 ip address 141.108.2.1 255.255.255.0
!
interface Loopback1
 ip address 141.108.3.1 255.255.255.0
!
interface Loopback2
 ip address 141.108.4.1 255.255.255.0
!
interface Loopback3
 ip address 141.108.5.1 255.255.255.0
!
interface Loopback4
 ip address 141.108.6.1 255.255.255.0
!
interface Loopback5
 ip address 141.108.7.1 255.255.255.0
!
interface Loopback6
 ip address 141.108.0.1 255.255.255.0
!
interface Ethernet0/0
 ip address 141.108.1.1 255.255.255.0
!
interface Serial1/0
 bandwidth 128
 ip address 151.108.255.1 255.255.255.0
 clockrate 128000
```

continues

Example 8-87 *R1's Full Working Configuration (Continued)*

```
!
interface Serial1/1
 bandwidth 128
 ip address 151.108.254.1 255.255.255.0
   clockrate 128000
!
router eigrp 1
 redistribute rip metric 128 20000 255 1 1500
 network 151.108.0.0
 distribute-list 1 in
!
router rip
 passive-interface Serial1/0
 passive-interface Serial1/1
 network 141.108.0.0
!
ip classless
!
access-list 1 deny    141.108.0.0 0.0.7.255
access-list 1 permit any
!
line con 0
line aux 0
line vty 0 4
end
```

Example 8-88 displays R2's full working configuration.

Example 8-88 *R2's Full Working Configuration*

```
hostname R2
!
enable password cisco
!
ip subnet-zero
!
interface Loopback0
 ip address 141.108.9.1 255.255.255.0
!
interface Loopback1
 ip address 141.108.10.1 255.255.255.0
!
interface Loopback2
 ip address 141.108.11.1 255.255.255.0
!
interface Loopback3
 ip address 141.108.12.1 255.255.255.0
!
interface Loopback4
 ip address 141.108.13.1 255.255.255.0
```

Example 8-88 *R2's Full Working Configuration (Continued)*

```
!
interface Loopback5
 ip address 141.108.14.1 255.255.255.0
!
interface Loopback6
 ip address 141.108.15.1 255.255.255.0
!
interface Ethernet0/0
 ip address 141.108.8.1 255.255.255.0
!
interface Serial1/0
 bandwidth 128
 ip address 151.108.255.2 255.255.255.0
interface Serial1/1
 bandwidth 128
 ip address 151.108.253.2 255.255.255.0
!
router eigrp 1
 network 151.108.0.0
 distribute-list 1 in
!
router igrp 1
 passive-interface Serial1/0
 passive-interface Serial1/1
 network 141.108.0.0
!
ip classless
!
access-list 1 deny    141.108.8.0 0.0.7.255
access-list 1 permit any
!
line con 0
line aux 0
line vty 0 4
!
end
```

Example 8-89 displays R3's full working configuration.

Example 8-89 *R3's Full Working Configuration*

```
hostname R3
!
enable password cisco
!
no ip domain-lookup
!
interface Loopback0
 ip address 141.108.17.1 255.255.255.0
```

continues

Example 8-89 *R3's Full Working Configuration (Continued)*

```
!
interface Loopback1
 ip address 141.108.18.1 255.255.255.0
!
interface Loopback2
 ip address 141.108.19.1 255.255.255.0
!
interface Loopback3
 ip address 141.108.20.1 255.255.255.0
!
interface Loopback4
 ip address 141.108.21.1 255.255.255.0
!
interface Loopback5
 ip address 141.108.22.1 255.255.255.0
!
interface Loopback6
 ip address 141.108.23.1 255.255.255.0
!
interface Ethernet0
 ip address 141.108.16.1 255.255.255.0
 media-type 10BaseT
!
interface Ethernet1
 no ip address
!
interface Serial0
 ip address 151.108.254.2 255.255.255.0
 bandwidth 128
!
interface Serial1
 ip address 151.108.253.1 255.255.255.0
 bandwidth 128
 clockrate 128000
!
router eigrp 1
 redistribute ospf 1 metric 128 20000 1 1 1500
 network 151.108.0.0
 distribute-list 1 in
!
router ospf 1
 network 141.108.16.0 0.0.7.255 area 100
!
ip classless
access-list 1 deny    141.108.16.0 0.0.7.255
access-list 1 permit any
!
line con 0
line aux 0
line vty 0 4
!
end
```

Example 8-90 displays the IP routing table on R1, demonstrating full network connectivity.

Example 8-90 show ip route *on R1*

```
R1#show ip route
     141.108.0.0/24 is subnetted, 24 subnets
C       141.108.1.0 is directly connected, Ethernet0/0
C       141.108.0.0 is directly connected, Loopback6
C       141.108.3.0 is directly connected, Loopback1
C       141.108.2.0 is directly connected, Loopback0
C       141.108.5.0 is directly connected, Loopback3
C       141.108.4.0 is directly connected, Loopback2
C       141.108.7.0 is directly connected, Loopback5
C       141.108.6.0 is directly connected, Loopback4
D EX    141.108.9.0 [170/20640000] via 151.108.255.2, 00:06:20, Serial1/0
D EX    141.108.8.0 [170/20537600] via 151.108.255.2, 00:06:21, Serial1/0
D EX    141.108.11.0 [170/20640000] via 151.108.255.2, 00:06:21, Serial1/0
D EX    141.108.10.0 [170/20640000] via 151.108.255.2, 00:06:21, Serial1/0
D EX    141.108.13.0 [170/20640000] via 151.108.255.2, 00:06:21, Serial1/0
D EX    141.108.12.0 [170/20640000] via 151.108.255.2, 00:06:21, Serial1/0
D EX    141.108.15.0 [170/20640000] via 151.108.255.2, 00:06:21, Serial1/0
D EX    141.108.14.0 [170/20640000] via 151.108.255.2, 00:06:21, Serial1/0
D EX    141.108.17.0 [170/25632000] via 151.108.254.2, 00:06:22, Serial1/1
D EX    141.108.16.0 [170/25632000] via 151.108.254.2, 00:06:22, Serial1/1
D EX    141.108.19.0 [170/25632000] via 151.108.254.2, 00:06:22, Serial1/1
D EX    141.108.18.0 [170/25632000] via 151.108.254.2, 00:06:22, Serial1/1
D EX    141.108.21.0 [170/25632000] via 151.108.254.2, 00:06:22, Serial1/1
D EX    141.108.20.0 [170/25632000] via 151.108.254.2, 00:06:22, Serial1/1
D EX    141.108.23.0 [170/25632000] via 151.108.254.2, 00:06:22, Serial1/1
D EX    141.108.22.0 [170/25632000] via 151.108.254.2, 00:06:22, Serial1/1
     151.108.0.0/24 is subnetted, 3 subnets
C       151.108.255.0 is directly connected, Serial1/0
C       151.108.254.0 is directly connected, Serial1/1
D       151.108.253.0 [90/21024000] via 151.108.254.2, 00:06:22, Serial1/1
                      [90/21024000] via 151.108.255.2, 00:06:22, Serial1/0
R1#
```

The redistributed networks from R2 and R3 appear as external EIGRP routes (D EX). Also, because the composite metric to the WAN network 151.108.253.0/24 is the same, EIGRP is load balancing. The EIGRP topology table on R1 confirms the same composite metric.

Example 8-91 displays the EIGRP topology table on R1. The shaded portions display the dual path to 151.108.253.0.

Example 8-91 show ip eigrp topology *on R1*

```
R1#show ip eigrp topology
IP-EIGRP Topology Table for process 1
Codes: P - Passive, A - Active, U - Update, Q - Query, R - Reply,
       r - Reply status
P 151.108.255.0/24, 1 successors, FD is 20512000
        via Connected, Serial1/0
P 151.108.254.0/24, 1 successors, FD is 20512000
        via Connected, Serial1/1
P 151.108.253.0/24, 2 successors, FD is 21024000
        via 151.108.255.2 (21024000/20512000), Serial1/0
        via 151.108.254.2 (21024000/20512000), Serial1/1
P 141.108.1.0/24, 1 successors, FD is 25120000
        via Redistributed (25120000/0)
P 141.108.0.0/24, 1 successors, FD is 25120000
        via Redistributed (25120000/0)
P 141.108.3.0/24, 1 successors, FD is 25120000
        via Redistributed (25120000/0)
P 141.108.2.0/24, 1 successors, FD is 25120000
        via Redistributed (25120000/0)
P 141.108.5.0/24, 1 successors, FD is 25120000
        via Redistributed (25120000/0)
P 141.108.4.0/24, 1 successors, FD is 25120000
        via Redistributed (25120000/0)
P 141.108.7.0/24, 1 successors, FD is 25120000
        via Redistributed (25120000/0)
P 141.108.6.0/24, 1 successors, FD is 25120000
        via Redistributed (25120000/0)
P 141.108.9.0/24, 1 successors, FD is 20640000
        via 151.108.255.2 (20640000/128256), Serial1/0
P 141.108.8.0/24, 1 successors, FD is 20537600
        via 151.108.255.2 (20537600/281600), Serial1/0
P 141.108.11.0/24, 1 successors, FD is 20640000
        via 151.108.255.2 (20640000/128256), Serial1/0
P 141.108.10.0/24, 1 successors, FD is 20640000
        via 151.108.255.2 (20640000/128256), Serial1/0
P 141.108.13.0/24, 1 successors, FD is 20640000
        via 151.108.255.2 (20640000/128256), Serial1/0
P 141.108.12.0/24, 1 successors, FD is 20640000
        via 151.108.255.2 (20640000/128256), Serial1/0
P 141.108.15.0/24, 1 successors, FD is 20640000
        via 151.108.255.2 (20640000/128256), Serial1/0
P 141.108.14.0/24, 1 successors, FD is 20640000
        via 151.108.255.2 (20640000/128256), Serial1/0
P 141.108.17.0/24, 1 successors, FD is 25632000
        via 151.108.254.2 (25632000/25120000), Serial1/1
P 141.108.16.0/24, 1 successors, FD is 25632000
        via 151.108.254.2 (25632000/25120000), Serial1/1
P 141.108.19.0/24, 1 successors, FD is 25632000
        via 151.108.254.2 (25632000/25120000), Serial1/1
P 141.108.18.0/24, 1 successors, FD is 25632000
        via 151.108.254.2 (25632000/25120000), Serial1/1
```

Example 8-91 show ip eigrp topology *on R1 (Continued)*

```
P 141.108.21.0/24, 1 successors, FD is 25632000
        via 151.108.254.2 (25632000/25120000), Serial1/1
P 141.108.20.0/24, 1 successors, FD is 25632000
        via 151.108.254.2 (25632000/25120000), Serial1/1
P 141.108.23.0/24, 1 successors, FD is 25632000
        via 151.108.254.2 (25632000/25120000), Serial1/1
P 141.108.22.0/24, 1 successors, FD is 25632000
        via 151.108.254.2 (25632000/25120000), Serial1/1
R1#
```

Example 8-92 confirms network IP connectivity by pinging all the remote networks from R1.

Example 8-92 *Pinging Remote Networks on R1*

```
R1#ping 141.108.8.1
Type escape sequence to abort.
Sending 5, 100-byte ICMP Echos to 141.108.8.1, timeout is 2 seconds:
!!!!!
Success rate is 100 percent (5/5), round-trip min/avg/max = 16/17/20 ms
R1#ping 141.108.9.1
Type escape sequence to abort.
Sending 5, 100-byte ICMP Echos to 141.108.9.1, timeout is 2 seconds:
!!!!!
Success rate is 100 percent (5/5), round-trip min/avg/max = 16/16/16 ms
R1#ping 141.108.10.1
Type escape sequence to abort.
Sending 5, 100-byte ICMP Echos to 141.108.10.1, timeout is 2 seconds:
!!!!!
Success rate is 100 percent (5/5), round-trip min/avg/max = 16/16/16 ms
R1#ping 141.108.11.1
Type escape sequence to abort.
Sending 5, 100-byte ICMP Echos to 141.108.11.1, timeout is 2 seconds:
!!!!!
Success rate is 100 percent (5/5), round-trip min/avg/max = 16/16/17 ms
R1#ping 141.108.12.1
Type escape sequence to abort.
Sending 5, 100-byte ICMP Echos to 141.108.12.1, timeout is 2 seconds:
!!!!!
Success rate is 100 percent (5/5), round-trip min/avg/max = 16/16/16 ms
R1#ping 141.108.13.1
Type escape sequence to abort.
Sending 5, 100-byte ICMP Echos to 141.108.13.1, timeout is 2 seconds:
!!!!!
Success rate is 100 percent (5/5), round-trip min/avg/max = 16/16/16 ms
R1#ping 141.108.14.1
Type escape sequence to abort.
Sending 5, 100-byte ICMP Echos to 141.108.14.1, timeout is 2 seconds:
```

continues

Example 8-92 *Pinging Remote Networks on R1 (Continued)*

```
!!!!!
Success rate is 100 percent (5/5), round-trip min/avg/max = 16/16/16 ms
R1#ping 141.108.15.1
Type escape sequence to abort.
Sending 5, 100-byte ICMP Echos to 141.108.15.1, timeout is 2 seconds:
!!!!!
Success rate is 100 percent (5/5), round-trip min/avg/max = 16/16/16 ms
R1#ping 141.108.16.1
Type escape sequence to abort.
Sending 5, 100-byte ICMP Echos to 141.108.16.1, timeout is 2 seconds:
!!!!!
Success rate is 100 percent (5/5), round-trip min/avg/max = 12/14/16 ms
R1#ping 141.108.17.1
Type escape sequence to abort.
Sending 5, 100-byte ICMP Echos to 141.108.17.1, timeout is 2 seconds:
!!!!!
Success rate is 100 percent (5/5), round-trip min/avg/max = 12/14/16 ms
R1#ping 141.108.18.1
Type escape sequence to abort.
Sending 5, 100-byte ICMP Echos to 141.108.18.1, timeout is 2 seconds:
!!!!!
Success rate is 100 percent (5/5), round-trip min/avg/max = 16/16/16 ms
R1#ping 141.108.19.1
Type escape sequence to abort.
Sending 5, 100-byte ICMP Echos to 141.108.19.1, timeout is 2 seconds:
!!!!!
Success rate is 100 percent (5/5), round-trip min/avg/max = 16/16/16 ms
R1#ping 141.108.20.1
Type escape sequence to abort.
Sending 5, 100-byte ICMP Echos to 141.108.20.1, timeout is 2 seconds:
!!!!!
Success rate is 100 percent (5/5), round-trip min/avg/max = 12/13/16 ms
R1#ping 141.108.21.1
Type escape sequence to abort.
Sending 5, 100-byte ICMP Echos to 141.108.21.1, timeout is 2 seconds:
!!!!!
Success rate is 100 percent (5/5), round-trip min/avg/max = 12/14/17 ms
R1#ping 141.108.22.1
Type escape sequence to abort.
Sending 5, 100-byte ICMP Echos to 141.108.22.1, timeout is 2 seconds:
!!!!!
Success rate is 100 percent (5/5), round-trip min/avg/max = 12/15/17 ms
R1#ping 141.108.23.1
Type escape sequence to abort.
Sending 5, 100-byte ICMP Echos to 141.108.23.1, timeout is 2 seconds:
!!!!!
Success rate is 100 percent (5/5), round-trip min/avg/max = 16/16/16 ms
R1#
```

Review Questions

The answers to these question can be found in Appendix C, "Answers to Review Questions."

1 How many IP routing tables are there when more than one routing protocol is configured on a Cisco router?

2 Which path is preferred if OSPF and EIGRP have dynamically discovered a remote network?

3 What common methods are used to control routing updates and filtering?

4 What is the metric used by OSPF, and is the lower or higher metric the chosen path?

5 Is a static route always preferred over a directly connected route?

6 Which command stops updates from being sent out of any interface?

7 Which parameter does the Cisco IOS always compare before looking at routing metrics, such as hop count or OSPF cost?

8 Give two examples of classful protocols?

9 Give two examples of classless protocols?

10 What are the three methods commonly applied to avoid routing loops when redistribution is required?

Summary

Redistribution from one routing protocol to another has been extensively covered in this chapter. The issues of routing loops and metric conversion from one routing protocol to another have been demonstrated, and you should now have the skills necessary to enable any form of route redistribution. Routing between classless and classful domains is one of the major learning tools you must master quickly in any IP network. In such a situation, information can be controlled to ensure that the network is routing IP as correctly and efficiently as possible.

Mastering distribution lists, static routing, and route maps enables you to avoid routing loops and ensure that full IP connectivity still exists.

You should now be ready to apply the information in this and all of the previous chapters to the self-study lab in Chapter 9, "CCNP Routing Self-Study Lab."

Table 8-3 summarizes the most important commands used in this chapter.

Table 8-3   *Summary of IOS Commands*

Command	Purpose
area *area-id* **range** *address mask*	Summarizes OSPF network ranges.
router ospf *process id*	Enables OSPF routing. The process ID is local to the router. You can have more than one OSPF process ID running.
router eigrp *autonomous domain ID*	Enables EIGRP routing under a common administrative control, known as the autonomous domain.
no auto-summary	Disables automatic summarization.
show ip route	Displays the complete IP routing table.
show ip eigrp topology	Displays the EIGRP topology table. Useful for determining other paths available on an EIGRP router.
[no] shutdown	Enables or disables an interface. All hardware interfaces are shut down by default.
ping *ip-address*	Tests IP connectivity.
redistribute *options*	Enables redistribution. See Table 8-2 for a complete listing of available options.
passive-interface	Disables updates sent outbound but still listens to updates.

CHAPTER 9

CCNP Routing Self-Study Lab

This chapter is designed to assist you in your final preparation for the Routing exam by providing you an extensive lab scenario that incorporates many of the technologies and concepts covered in this book. The lab presented here requires a broad perspective and knowledge base. This means that any knowledge you have acquired through the practical examples presented in this guide and real-life network implementations will help you achieve the end goal—a routable network according to the set design criteria.

This lab is presented in small sections and provides you a specific amount of time to complete the tasks so that you can ensure that all features are configured in a timely manner, allowing you the ability to tackle any similar Cisco-based certification or real-life network topology configuration.

NOTE The following lab is designed to draw together some of the content described in this book and some of the content you have seen in your own networks or practice labs. There is no one right way to accomplish many of the tasks presented here. The abilities to use good practice and define your end goal are important in any real-life design or solution.

The Ethernet interfaces on all routers are connected to a Catalyst 6509 switch.

Hints are provided to ensure that you are aware of any issues or extra configuration commands required to complete a specific task.

How to Best Use This Chapter

The following self-study lab contains a six-router network with two Internet service provider (ISP) routers providing connections to the Internet. Although on the CCNP Routing exam you do not have to configure six routers running multiple protocols, this lab is designed to ensure that you have all the practical skills to achieve almost any IP routing requirements in real-life networks. More importantly, it tests your practical skill set so you can pass the CCNP Routing examination with confidence.

Full working solutions are provided, along with the configuration of a Catalyst 6509 used to create the LAN-based networks, and the two ISP routers simulating an Internet service.

Following the full configurations in the solution section, a section displays sample routing tables taken from each router, as well as some sample **ping** and **telnet** commands to demonstrate full IP connectivity.

The IBGP and EBGP network connectivity is demonstrated displaying the BGP tables.

Figure 9-1 displays the six-router topology used in this lab.

Figure 9-1   *Router Topology*

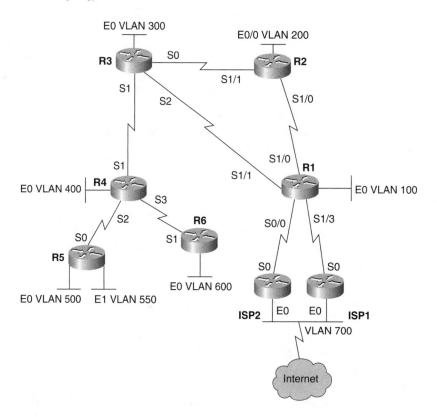

The Goal of the Lab

The end goal of this lab is to ensure that all devices in Figure 9-1 can route to all networks. This ensures, for example, that users on R5's Ethernet networks (E0 and E1) can reach all parts of the network.

Physical Connectivity (1 Hour)

Construct your network as shown on Figure 9-1. All back-to-back serial connections require a clock source.

Use common Cisco defined techniques by using the IOS **description** *name of link* command to provide documentation for all serial links and virtual LANs.

Catalyst Switch Setup 6509 (0.25 Hours)

Configure the Ethernet switch for seven VLANs and cable a catalyst switch for the following VLAN number assignments:

- VLAN 100 is connected to R1 E0/0.
- VLAN 200 is connected to R2 E0/0.
- VLAN 300 is connected to R3 E0.
- VLAN 400 is connected to R4 E0.
- VLAN 500 is connected to R5 E0.
- VLAN 550 is connected to R5 E1.
- VLAN 600 is connected to R6 E0.

Configure the management interface (or sc0) on the switch with the IP address 133.33.1.2/29, and ensure that all routers can Telnet to the switch after you have completed configuring your IGP protocols.

Configure a default route pointing to R1's Ethernet interface, IP address 133.33.1.1/29 on Catalyst 6509.

IP Address Configuration (0.5 Hours)

Use the Class B IP address 130.33.0.0. Configure IP addressing as follows:

- Use a 29-bit mask for VLAN 100 and a 25-bit mask for VLAN 200 and VLAN 300.
- Use a 27-bit mask for VLAN 400.
- Use a 24-bit mask for VLAN 500, VLAN 550, and VLAN 600.
- Use a 30-bit mask for all WAN connections on Routers R1, R2, R3, and R4.
- Use a 24-bit mask for the WAN connection between Routers R4/R5 and R4/R6.

After IP routing is completed, all interfaces should be pingable from any router.

Table 9-1 displays the IP address assignment for Routers R1–R6.

Table 9-1   *IP Address Assignment*

Router Interface	IP Address
R1 E0/0	133.33.1.1/29
R1 S0/0	171.108.1.6/30 (to ISP2)
R1 S1/0	133.33.7.1/30
R1 S1/1	133.33.7.5/30
R1 S1/3	171.108.1.2/30 (to ISP1)
R2 E0/0	133.33.3.1/25
R2 S1/0	133.33.7.2/30
R2 S1/1	133.33.7.9/30
R3 E0	133.33.4.1/25
R3 S0	133.33.7.10/30
R3 S1	133.33.7.13/30
R3 S2	133.33.7.6/30
R4 E0	133.33.5.1/27
R4 S1	133.33.7.14/30
R4 S2	133.33.10.2/24
R4 S3	133.33.11.2/24
R5 E0	133.33.8.1/24
R5 E1	133.33.9.1/24
R5 S0	133.33.10.1/24
R6 E0	133.33.6.1/24
R6 S1	133.33.11.1/24
ISP1 S0	171.108.1.1/30
ISP1 E0	141.108.1.1/24
ISP2 S0	171.108.1.5/30
ISP2 E0	141.108.1.2/24

Loopback IP Addressing: Part I (0.25 Hours)

Configure each router with a loopback interface. Assign the loopbacks on each router using the range of addresses from 133.33.201.0–133.33.206.0 and a Class C mask.

It must be possible to ping and telnet to the loopbacks from any one router. Test IP connectivity by pinging from R1, and ensure that you can telnet to any router within your network after you complete all IGP routing protocol configurations.

Table 9-2 displays the loopback addresses you need to assign to all six routers.

Table 9-2   *Loopback Address Assignments*

Router	Loopback 0
R1	133.33.201.1/24
R2	133.33.202.1/24
R3	133.33.203.1/24
R4	133.33.204.1/24
R5	133.33.205.1/24
R6	133.33.206.1/24

Ensure that all loopbacks in Table 9-2 appear as 24-bit networks in all IP routing tables, by using the interface **ip ospf network point-to-point** command for all routers configured with OSPF.

Loopback IP Addressing: Part II (0.25 Hours)

Create seven loopback interfaces in R1 by using 24-bit network masks in major networks ranging from 133.33.16.0/24–133.33.23.0/24.

Create seven loopback interfaces in R2 by using 24-bit network masks in major networks ranging from 133.33.24.0/24 to 133.33.31.0/24.

Ensure that you perform network summarization of these loopbacks to reduce IP routing table size wherever possible.

Configure a static route on R5 to ensure that all loopbacks ranging from 133.33.16.0 to 133.33.31.0 are encompassed by a single static routing entry. (Hint: The subnet mask for a static route is 255.255.240.0.)

IGP Routing (7 Hours)

This section requires you to configure OSPF, IGRP, and EIGRP across the six routers and ensure that redistribution is used to provide IP connectivity among all routing domains.

IGRP Configuration (1.0 Hour)

Configure IGRP (AS 1) on R4 and R5 to meet the following specifications:

- Configure IGRP on R5 E0/E1 and for the serial link between R4 and R5.
- Ensure proper filtering is configured on R4 to send only networks that do not reside on R5.
- Redistribute the IGRP route into OSPF/EIGRP domain. View the OSPF section for details on redistribution.
- Make sure you can see distributed IGRP routes throughout the topology.
- By using the IOS **passive-interface** command, ensure that only the correct interfaces residing in the IGRP AS are configured to send and receive IGRP updates. This ensures that router resources are not unnecessarily consumed.

EIGRP Configuration (1.5 Hours)

Configure EIGRP on Routers R1, R4, and R6:

- Configure the link between R4 and R6 in EIGRP domain 1.
- Configure VLAN 600 to reside in domain 2.
- Redistribute between EIGRP 1 and 2 and ensure network connectivity.
- Ensure that the IGRP domain and OSPF domain have these networks present in their respective IP routing tables.
- Ensure that VLAN 600 (133.33.6.0/24) and the loopback subnet on R6 (133.33.206.0/24) OSPF cost metric are set to 1000. (Metric type 2 by default is configured when redistributing from any protocol into OSPF.) Hint: Use the **route-map** command to complete this task.
- Configure R6 to set all external EIGRP routes (D EX) in AS 1 with an administrative distance of 90 (the same AD as internal EIGRP routes).

OSPF Configuration (2.5 Hours)

Configure OSPF on R1, R2, R3, and R4:

- Configure the serial back-to-back links between R1/R2, R2/R3, and R1/R3 in the backbone (area 0.0.0.0).
- Configure the serial link between R3 and R4 in OSPF area 350.
- Configure VLAN 100 in area 100.
- Configure VLAN 200 in area 200.
- Configure VLAN 300 in area 300.

- Configure VLAN 400 in area 350.

- Additional areas are not required.

- Ensure that any OSPF areas not connected to area 0 are configured with an OSPF virtual link to ensure IP connectivity. (Hint: No virtual links are required because no OSPF areas are partitioned from the backbone area, or 0.0.0.0.)

- Assign any loopbacks into already existing areas.

- Redistribute OSPF into EIGRP and IGRP to maintain full-network connectivity.

OSPF Modifications (2 Hours)

Configure OSPF to perform the following functions:

- Ensure that R3 is always the DR on VLAN 300 by setting the OSPF priority to 255.

- Change the Hello interval between R1/R3 WAN link to 25 seconds.

- Configure MD5 authentication between R1/R3 WAN link setting the password to ccnp. (Hint: All routers in area 0 require authentication; hence, the serial link between R1/R2 requires MD5 authentication as well.)

- Configure the local names of Routers R1–R6 so that all OSPF-enabled routers can perform an OSPF name lookup (using the loopbacks in Table 9-2 as IP addresses) for all OSPF adjacencies.

- Ensure that the router ID on all OSPF enabled-routers (R1 to R4) match the loopbacks used in Table 9-2. (Hint: Use the **router-id** command under the OSPF process ID.)

- Configure area 200 as a stub area.

- Ensure that the OSPF cost as seen by R1 and R3 for VLAN 200 is 1000.

BGP Routing Configuration (5 Hours)

The aim of this exercise is to configure IBGP among the routers in your IGP network (Routers R1–R6) and minimize the number of IBGP peer sessions for easy configuration. R1 is the focal point for all IBGP peering sessions and has two EBGP connections to the same ISP provided for redundancy purposes. You will also be asked to configure BGP attributes to influence routing decisions made in your IBGP network and also influence which path the Internet ISP routers, ISP1 and ISP2, choose to use for networks residing in your routing domain.

IBGP Configuration (2 Hours)

Configure IBGP (your autonomous system number is 1) within your network to meet the following conditions:

- All routers are configured with minimum number of IBGP peers for scalability; this means you must use route reflectors and configure R1 as the route reflector to R2, R3, R4, R5, and R6 (route reflector clients).

- Use BGP peer groups on R1 to minimize the BGP configuration code required on R1.

- Disable BGP synchronization on all IBGP routers.

- All IBGP routers should receive routing updates from R1 *only*.

- All IBGP connections must be active as long as there is an active path between the routers; hence, use the assigned loopback interfaces as your source and next hop peer address for establishing TCP sessions. (Hint: Because there are redundant paths, the best practice in an IBGP network is to use loopback interfaces as the source and destination addresses for all IBGP peer sessions.)

EBGP Configuration (1 Hour)

- Router R1 has two EBGP connections to the same ISP for redundancy purposes. Configure R1–R6 to meet the following requirements:

- Configure EBGP between R1 (AS 1) and ISP1/ISP2 (AS 1024).

- The Routers ISP1/ISP2 are both connected to AS 1024.

- Configure ISP1 and ISP2 to provide a default route to R1, along with some specific routing destinations using static routes to Null0. Example 9-1 displays the static route configurations on ISP1 and ISP2.

Example 9-1 *Static Routes on ISP1/ISP2*

```
ip route 0.0.0.0 0.0.0.0 Null0
ip route 1.0.0.0 255.0.0.0 Null0
ip route 2.0.0.0 255.0.0.0 Null0
ip route 3.0.0.0 255.0.0.0 Null0
ip route 4.0.0.0 255.0.0.0 Null0
ip route 5.0.0.0 255.0.0.0 Null0
ip route 6.0.0.0 255.0.0.0 Null0
ip route 7.0.0.0 255.0.0.0 Null0
ip route 8.0.0.0 255.0.0.0 Null0
ip route 10.0.0.0 255.0.0.0 Null0
ip route 11.0.0.0 255.0.0.0 Null0
ip route 100.0.0.0 255.0.0.0 Null0
ip route 101.0.0.0 255.0.0.0 Null0
ip route 102.0.0.0 255.0.0.0 Null0
ip route 141.100.0.0 255.255.0.0 Null0
ip route 141.108.0.0 255.255.0.0 Null0
```

Example 9-1   *Static Routes on ISP1/ISP2 (Continued)*

```
ip route 142.100.0.0 255.255.0.0 Null0
ip route 143.100.0.0 255.255.0.0 Null0
ip route 144.100.0.0 255.255.0.0 Null0
ip route 145.100.0.0 255.255.0.0 Null0
ip route 146.100.0.0 255.255.0.0 Null0
ip route 147.100.0.0 255.255.0.0 Null0
ip route 148.100.0.0 255.255.0.0 Null0
ip route 149.100.0.0 255.255.0.0 Null0
```

- The ISP has provided you with the following next hop addresses and your local AS number:

  — The R1 S0/0 next hop address is 171.108.1.1/30, and the remote AS is 1024.

  — The R1 S1/3 next hop address is 171.108.1.5/30, and the remote AS is 1024.

- Configure EBGP on R1 and ensure that all advertised routes from ISP1 and ISP2 are present in R1's BGP table.

Advanced BGP Configuration: Policy Routing (1 Hour)

Using policy-based routing, ensure that all traffic sent from R3 (from users on VLAN 300) meets the following criteria:

- All Internet traffic sent to the default route 0.0.0.0 is sent through R1.
- All ICMP traffic is sent through R2.
- All other traffic is sent through R1.
- Using the IOS **debug ip policy** command, ensure that IP traffic is sent over the correct interface.

Advanced BGP Configuration: Attribute Modification (1 Hour)

Configure R1 to set the following attributes for networks from the ISP routers named ISP1/ISP2:

- Prepend all networks in the range 1.0.0.0 to 9.0.0.0 with the AS_Path 400 300 200 and set the origin attribute to incomplete.
- Set the weight of all networks received from ISP1 to 100 and ISP2 to 200.

Self-Study Lab Solution

The following sample configuration files achieve the desired design criteria. This is by no means the only possible solution. As you have discovered throughout this practical guide, there is not always one right way to accomplish the tasks presented. In fact, the best possible way to learn more is to change the questions to meet your own goals and use **show** and **debug** commands to verify IP connectivity. Presented here are nine configuration files.

Example 9-2 displays R1's full working configuration.

Example 9-2 *R1's Full Working Configuration*

```
hostname R1
!
enable password cisco
!
ip subnet-zero
ip host R6 133.33.206.1
ip host R5 133.33.205.1
ip host R4 133.33.204.1
ip host R3 133.33.203.1
ip host R2 133.33.202.1
ip host r1 133.33.201.1
!
interface Loopback0
 ip address 133.33.201.1 255.255.255.0
 ip ospf network point-to-point
!
interface Loopback1
 ip address 133.33.16.1 255.255.255.0
 ip ospf network point-to-point
!
interface Loopback2
 ip address 133.33.18.1 255.255.255.0
 ip ospf network point-to-point
!
interface Loopback3
 ip address 133.33.17.1 255.255.255.0
 ip ospf network point-to-point
!
interface Loopback4
 ip address 133.33.19.1 255.255.255.0
 ip ospf network point-to-point
!
interface Loopback5
 ip address 133.33.20.1 255.255.255.0
 ip ospf network point-to-point
!
interface Loopback6
 ip address 133.33.21.1 255.255.255.0
 ip ospf network point-to-point
```

Example 9-2 *R1's Full Working Configuration (Continued)*

```
!
interface Loopback7
 ip address 133.33.22.1 255.255.255.0
 ip ospf network point-to-point
!
interface Loopback8
 ip address 133.33.23.1 255.255.255.0
 ip ospf network point-to-point
!
interface Ethernet0/0
 description VLAN 100 (OSPF Area 100)
 ip address 133.33.1.1 255.255.255.248
!
interface Serial0/0
 description Serial Link to ISP2 S0
 ip address 171.108.1.6 255.255.255.252
 no ip mroute-cache
 no fair-queue
 clockrate 125000
!
interface Serial1/0
 description Serial Link to R2 S1/0
 bandwidth 125
 ip address 133.33.7.1 255.255.255.252
 ip ospf authentication message-digest
 ip ospf authentication-key ccnp
 clockrate 128000
!
interface Serial1/1
 description Serial Link to R3 S2
 bandwidth 125
 ip address 133.33.7.5 255.255.255.252
 ip ospf authentication message-digest
 ip ospf authentication-key ccnp
 ip ospf hello-interval 25
!
interface Serial1/2
 shutdown
!
interface Serial1/3
 description Serial Link to ISP1 S0
 bandwidth 125
 ip address 171.108.1.2 255.255.255.252
!
router ospf 1
 router-id 133.33.201.1
 area 0 authentication message-digest
 area 100 range 133.33.16.0 255.255.248.0
 network 133.33.1.1 0.0.0.0 area 100
 network 133.33.7.1 0.0.0.0 area 0
```

continues

Example 9-2   *R1's Full Working Configuration (Continued)*

```
  network 133.33.7.5 0.0.0.0 area 0
  network 133.33.16.0 0.0.7.255 area 100
  network 133.33.201.1 0.0.0.0 area 0
 !
router bgp 1
 no synchronization
 redistribute connected
 redistribute ospf 1
 neighbor ibgpnetwork peer-group
 neighbor ibgpnetwork remote-as 1
 neighbor ibgpnetwork update-source Loopback0
 neighbor ibgpnetwork next-hop-self
 neighbor 133.33.202.1 peer-group ibgpnetwork
 neighbor 133.33.203.1 peer-group ibgpnetwork
 neighbor 133.33.204.1 peer-group ibgpnetwork
 neighbor 133.33.205.1 peer-group ibgpnetwork
 neighbor 133.33.206.1 peer-group ibgpnetwork
 neighbor 171.108.1.1 remote-as 1024
 neighbor 171.108.1.1 route-map setattributes in
 neighbor 171.108.1.1 weight 100
 neighbor 171.108.1.5 remote-as 1024
 neighbor 171.108.1.5 route-map setattributes in
 neighbor 171.108.1.5 weight 200
 no auto-summary
 !
ip classless
ip ospf name-lookup
 !
access-list 1 permit 1.0.0.0
access-list 1 permit 2.0.0.0
access-list 1 permit 3.0.0.0
access-list 1 permit 4.0.0.0
access-list 1 permit 5.0.0.0
access-list 1 permit 6.0.0.0
access-list 1 permit 7.0.0.0
access-list 1 permit 8.0.0.0
access-list 1 permit 9.0.0.0
access-list 2 permit any
route-map setattributes permit 10
 match ip address 1
 set origin incomplete
 set as-path prepend 400 300 200
 !
route-map setattributes permit 20
 match ip address 2
 !
line con 0
line aux 0
line vty 0 4
 !
end
```

Example 9-3 displays R2's full working configuration.

Example 9-3 *R2's Full Working Configuration*

```
hostname R2
!
enable password cisco
!
ip subnet-zero
no ip domain-lookup
ip host R6 133.33.206.1
ip host R5 133.33.205.1
ip host R4 133.33.204.1
ip host R3 133.33.203.1
ip host R2 133.33.202.1
ip host R1 133.33.201.1
!
interface Loopback0
 ip address 133.33.202.1 255.255.255.0
 ip ospf network point-to-point
!
interface Loopback1
 ip address 133.33.24.1 255.255.255.0
 ip ospf network point-to-point
!
interface Loopback2
 ip address 133.33.26.1 255.255.255.0
 ip ospf network point-to-point
!
interface Loopback3
 ip address 133.33.25.1 255.255.255.0
 ip ospf network point-to-point
!
interface Loopback4
 ip address 133.33.27.1 255.255.255.0
 ip ospf network point-to-point
!
interface Loopback5
 ip address 133.33.28.1 255.255.255.0
 ip ospf network point-to-point
!
interface Loopback6
 ip address 133.33.29.1 255.255.255.0
 ip ospf network point-to-point
!
interface Loopback7
 ip address 133.33.30.1 255.255.255.0
 ip ospf network point-to-point
!
interface Loopback8
 ip address 133.33.31.1 255.255.255.0
 ip ospf network point-to-point
```

continues

Example 9-3 *R2's Full Working Configuration (Continued)*

```
!
interface Ethernet0/0
 description VLAN 200 (OSPF Area 200)
 ip address 133.33.3.1 255.255.255.128
 ip ospf cost 200
!
interface TokenRing0/0
 no ip address
 shutdown
 ring-speed 16
!
interface Serial1/0
 description Serial Link to R1 S1/0
 bandwidth 125
 ip address 133.33.7.2 255.255.255.252
 ip ospf authentication message-digest
 ip ospf authentication-key ccnp
 no ip mroute-cache
 no fair-queue
!
interface Serial1/1
 description Serial Link to R3 S0
 bandwidth 125
 ip address 133.33.7.9 255.255.255.252
!
interface Serial1/2
 no ip address
 shutdown
!
interface Serial1/3
 no ip address
 shutdown
!
router ospf 1
 router-id 133.33.202.1
 area 0 authentication message-digest
 area 200 stub
 area 200 range 133.33.24.0 255.255.248.0
 network 133.33.3.1 0.0.0.0 area 200
 network 133.33.7.2 0.0.0.0 area 0
 network 133.33.7.9 0.0.0.0 area 0
 network 133.33.24.0 0.0.7.255 area 200
 network 133.33.202.1 0.0.0.0 area 0
!
router bgp 1
 no synchronization
 neighbor 133.33.201.1 remote-as 1
 neighbor 133.33.201.1 update-source Loopback0
!
ip classless
ip ospf name-lookup
```

Example 9-3 *R2's Full Working Configuration (Continued)*

```
!
line con 0
line aux 0
line vty 0 4
!
end
```

Example 9-4 displays R3's full working configuration.

Example 9-4 *R3's Full Working Configuration*

```
hostname R3
!
enable password cisco
ip subnet-zero
no ip domain-lookup
ip host r1 133.33.201.1
ip host r2 133.33.202.1
ip host R3 133.33.203.1
ip host r4 133.33.204.1
ip host R5 133.33.205.1
ip host R6 133.33.206.1
!
interface Loopback0
 ip address 133.33.203.1 255.255.255.0
 ip ospf network point-to-point
!
interface Ethernet0
 description VLAN 300 (OSPF Areas 300)
 ip address 133.33.4.1 255.255.255.128
 no ip directed-broadcast
 ip ospf priority 255
 ip policy route-map sendtraffic
 media-type 10BaseT
!
interface Ethernet1
 no ip address
 no ip directed-broadcast
 shutdown
!
interface Serial0
 description Serial Link to R2 S1/1
 bandwidth 125
 ip address 133.33.7.10 255.255.255.252
 no ip directed-broadcast
 ip ospf authentication-key ccnp
 fair-queue 64 256 0
 clockrate 125000
```

continues

Example 9-4 *R3's Full Working Configuration (Continued)*

```
!
interface Serial1
 description Serial Link to R4 S1
 bandwidth 125
 ip address 133.33.7.13 255.255.255.252
 no ip directed-broadcast
 fair-queue 64 256 0
 clockrate 2000000
!
interface Serial2
 description Serial Link to R1 S1/1
 ip address 133.33.7.6 255.255.255.252
 ip ospf authentication-key ccnp
 ip ospf hello-interval 25
 clockrate 125000
!
interface Serial3
 shutdown
!
router ospf 1
 router-id 133.33.203.1
 area 0 authentication message-digest
 network 133.33.4.1 0.0.0.0 area 300
 network 133.33.7.6 0.0.0.0 area 0
 network 133.33.7.10 0.0.0.0 area 0
 network 133.33.7.13 0.0.0.0 area 350
 network 133.33.203.1 0.0.0.0 area 0
!
router bgp 1
 no synchronization
 neighbor 133.33.201.1 remote-as 1
 neighbor 133.33.201.1 update-source Loopback0
!
ip local policy route-map sendtraffic
ip ospf name-lookup
!
access-list 1 permit 0.0.0.0
access-list 100 permit icmp any any
access-list 101 permit ip any any
route-map sendtraffic permit 10
 match ip address 1
 set interface Serial2
!
route-map sendtraffic permit 20
 match ip address 100
 set interface Serial0
!
route-map sendtraffic permit 30
 match ip address 101
 set interface Serial2
```

Example 9-4   *R3's Full Working Configuration (Continued)*

```
!
line con 0
line aux 0
line vty 0 4
!
end
```

Example 9-5 displays R4's full working configuration.

Example 9-5   *R4's Full Working Configuration*

```
hostname R4
!
enable password cisco
ip subnet-zero
no ip domain-lookup
ip host R6 133.33.206.1
ip host R5 133.33.205.1
ip host r4 133.33.204.1
ip host r3 133.33.203.1
ip host R2 133.33.202.1
ip host R1 133.33.201.1
!
cns event-service server
!
interface Loopback0
 ip address 133.33.204.1 255.255.255.0
 ip ospf network point-to-point
!
interface Ethernet0
 description VLAN 400 (OSPF Area 400)
 ip address 133.33.5.1 255.255.255.224
!
interface Serial0
 no ip address
 shutdown
!
interface Serial1
 description Serial Link to R3 S1
 ip address 133.33.7.14 255.255.255.252
!
interface Serial2
 description Serial Link to R5 S0
 ip address 133.33.10.2 255.255.255.0
!
interface Serial3
 description Serial Link to R6 S1
 ip address 133.33.11.2 255.255.255.0
 clockrate 125000
```

continues

Example 9-5 *R4's Full Working Configuration (Continued)*

```
!
router eigrp 1
 redistribute ospf 1 metric 128 20000 255 1 1500 route-map allowospf
 passive-interface Ethernet0
 passive-interface Loopback0
 passive-interface Serial1
 passive-interface Serial2
 network 133.33.0.0
 distribute-list 3 out
!
router ospf 1
 router-id 133.33.204.1
 redistribute connected subnets route-map connectedroutes
 redistribute eigrp 1 metric 100 subnets route-map eigrpnets
 redistribute igrp 1 metric 100 subnets route-map igrpnets
 network 133.33.5.1 0.0.0.0 area 350
 network 133.33.7.14 0.0.0.0 area 350
 network 133.33.204.1 0.0.0.0 area 350
!
router igrp 1
 redistribute static metric 128 20000 255 1 1500
 redistribute ospf 1 metric 128 20000 255 1 1500
 passive-interface Ethernet0
 passive-interface Loopback0
 passive-interface Serial1
 passive-interface Serial3
 network 133.33.0.0
 distribute-list 1 out
!
router bgp 1
 no synchronization
 neighbor 133.33.201.1 remote-as 1
 neighbor 133.33.201.1 update-source Loopback0
!
ip classless
ip route 133.33.1.0 255.255.255.0 Null0
ip route 133.33.3.0 255.255.255.0 Null0
ip route 133.33.4.0 255.255.255.0 Null0
ip route 133.33.5.0 255.255.255.0 Null0
ip route 133.33.7.0 255.255.255.0 Null0
no ip http server
ip ospf name-lookup
!
access-list 1 deny    133.33.205.0
access-list 1 deny    133.33.8.0
access-list 1 deny    133.33.9.0
access-list 1 permit any
access-list 2 permit 133.33.205.0
access-list 2 permit 133.33.8.0
access-list 2 permit 133.33.9.0
access-list 2 permit 133.33.10.0
```

Example 9-5 *R4's Full Working Configuration (Continued)*

```
access-list 3 deny    133.33.206.0
access-list 3 deny    133.33.6.0
access-list 3 deny    133.33.11.0
access-list 3 permit any
access-list 4 permit 133.33.206.0
access-list 4 permit 133.33.6.0
access-list 5 deny    133.33.206.0
access-list 5 deny    133.33.6.0
access-list 5 permit any
access-list 6 permit 133.33.204.0
access-list 6 permit 133.33.5.0
access-list 6 permit 133.33.10.0
access-list 6 permit 133.33.7.12
access-list 6 permit 133.33.11.0
route-map igrpnets permit 10
 match ip address 2
!
route-map eigrpnets permit 10
 match ip address 4
 set metric 1000
!
route-map allowospf permit 10
 match ip address 5
!
route-map connectedroutes permit 10
 match ip address 6
!
line con 0
 transport input none
line aux 0
line vty 0 4
 no login
!
end
```

Example 9-6 displays R5's full working configuration.

Example 9-6 *R5's Full Working Configuration*

```
hostname R5
!
enable password cisco
!
ip subnet-zero
no ip domain-lookup
ip host R6 133.33.206.1
ip host R5 133.33.205.1
ip host R4 133.33.204.1
ip host R3 133.33.203.1
```

continues

Example 9-6 *R5's Full Working Configuration (Continued)*

```
ip host R2 133.33.202.1
ip host R1 133.33.201.1
!
interface Loopback0
 ip address 133.33.205.1 255.255.255.0
!
interface Ethernet0
 description VLAN 500 (EIGRP AS 1)
 ip address 133.33.8.1 255.255.255.0
!
interface Ethernet1
 description VLAN 550 (EIGRP AS 1)
 ip address 133.33.9.1 255.255.255.0
!
interface Serial0
 description Serial Link to R4 S2
 ip address 133.33.10.1 255.255.255.0
 clockrate 125000
!
interface Serial1
 shutdown
!
router igrp 1
 network 133.33.0.0
!
router bgp 1
 no synchronization
 neighbor 133.33.201.1 remote-as 1
 neighbor 133.33.201.1 update-source Loopback0
!
ip classless
ip route 133.33.16.0 255.255.240.0 Serial0
!
line con 0
line aux 0
line vty 0 4
!
end
```

Example 9-7 displays R6's full working configuration.

Example 9-7 *R6's Full Working Configuration*

```
hostname R6
!
enable password cisco
!
ip subnet-zero
no ip domain-lookup
ip host R6 133.33.206.1
```

Example 9-7 *R6's Full Working Configuration (Continued)*

```
ip host R5 133.33.205.1
ip host R4 133.33.204.1
ip host R3 133.33.203.1
ip host R2 133.33.202.1
ip host R1 133.33.201.1
!
interface Loopback0
 ip address 133.33.206.1 255.255.255.0
!
interface Ethernet0
 description VLAN 600 (EIGRP AS 2)
 ip address 133.33.6.1 255.255.255.0
!
interface Serial0
shutdown
!
interface Serial1
 description Serial Link to R4 S3
 ip address 133.33.11.1 255.255.255.0
!
router eigrp 1
 redistribute eigrp 2 route-map allowout
 passive-interface Ethernet0
 passive-interface Loopback0
 passive-interface Serial0
 network 133.33.0.0
 distance eigrp 90 90
!
router eigrp 2
 passive-interface Serial1
 network 133.33.0.0
!
router bgp 1
 no synchronization
 neighbor 133.33.201.1 remote-as 1
 neighbor 133.33.201.1 update-source Loopback0
!
ip classless
!
access-list 2 permit 133.33.206.0
access-list 2 permit 133.33.6.0
route-map allowout permit 10
 match ip address 1
!
line con 0
line aux 0
line vty 0 4
!
end
```

Example 9-8 displays ISP1's full working configuration.

Example 9-8   *ISP1's Full Working Configuration*

```
hostname ISP1
!
enable password cisco
!
ip subnet-zero
no ip domain-lookup
!
interface Ethernet0
 description ISP LAN connection to ISP2
 ip address 141.108.1.1 255.255.255.0
!
interface Serial0
 description Serial Link to R1 S1/2
 ip address 171.108.1.1 255.255.255.252
 clockrate 125000
!
interface Serial1
 shutdown
!
router bgp 1024
 redistribute static
 neighbor 141.108.1.2 remote-as 1024
 neighbor 171.108.1.2 remote-as 1
 neighbor 171.108.1.2 default-originate
 no auto-summary
!
ip classless
ip route 0.0.0.0 0.0.0.0 Null0
ip route 1.0.0.0 255.0.0.0 Null0
ip route 2.0.0.0 255.0.0.0 Null0
ip route 3.0.0.0 255.0.0.0 Null0
ip route 4.0.0.0 255.0.0.0 Null0
ip route 5.0.0.0 255.0.0.0 Null0
ip route 6.0.0.0 255.0.0.0 Null0
ip route 7.0.0.0 255.0.0.0 Null0
ip route 8.0.0.0 255.0.0.0 Null0
ip route 10.0.0.0 255.0.0.0 Null0
ip route 11.0.0.0 255.0.0.0 Null0
ip route 100.0.0.0 255.0.0.0 Null0
ip route 101.0.0.0 255.0.0.0 Null0
ip route 102.0.0.0 255.0.0.0 Null0
ip route 141.100.0.0 255.255.0.0 Null0
ip route 141.108.0.0 255.255.0.0 Null0
ip route 142.100.0.0 255.255.0.0 Null0
ip route 143.100.0.0 255.255.0.0 Null0
ip route 144.100.0.0 255.255.0.0 Null0
ip route 145.100.0.0 255.255.0.0 Null0
ip route 146.100.0.0 255.255.0.0 Null0
ip route 147.100.0.0 255.255.0.0 Null0
```

Example 9-8   *ISP1's Full Working Configuration (Continued)*

```
ip route 148.100.0.0 255.255.0.0 Null0
ip route 149.100.0.0 255.255.0.0 Null0
!
line con 0
line aux 0
line vty 0 4
!
end
```

Example 9-9 displays ISP2's full working configuration.

Example 9-9   *ISP2's Full Working Configuration*

```
hostname ISP2
!
enable password cisco
!
ip subnet-zero
no ip finger
no ip domain-lookup
!
interface Ethernet0
 description ISP LAN connection to ISP1
 ip address 141.108.1.2 255.255.255.252
!
interface Serial0
 description Serial Link to R1 S1/3
 ip address 171.108.1.5 255.255.255.252
!
interface Serial1
 shutdown
!
interface Serial2
 shutdown
!
interface Serial3
 shutdown
!
router bgp 1024
 bgp log-neighbor-changes
 redistribute static
 neighbor 141.108.1.1 remote-as 1024
 neighbor 171.108.1.6 remote-as 1
 neighbor 171.108.1.6 default-originate
!
ip classless
ip route 0.0.0.0 0.0.0.0 Null0
ip route 1.0.0.0 255.0.0.0 Null0
ip route 2.0.0.0 255.0.0.0 Null0
```

continues

Example 9-9 *ISP2's Full Working Configuration (Continued)*

```
ip route 3.0.0.0 255.0.0.0 Null0
ip route 4.0.0.0 255.0.0.0 Null0
ip route 5.0.0.0 255.0.0.0 Null0
ip route 6.0.0.0 255.0.0.0 Null0
ip route 7.0.0.0 255.0.0.0 Null0
ip route 8.0.0.0 255.0.0.0 Null0
ip route 10.0.0.0 255.0.0.0 Null0
ip route 11.0.0.0 255.0.0.0 Null0
ip route 100.0.0.0 255.0.0.0 Null0
ip route 101.0.0.0 255.0.0.0 Null0
ip route 102.0.0.0 255.0.0.0 Null0
ip route 141.100.0.0 255.255.0.0 Null0
ip route 141.108.0.0 255.255.0.0 Null0
ip route 142.100.0.0 255.255.0.0 Null0
ip route 143.100.0.0 255.255.0.0 Null0
ip route 144.100.0.0 255.255.0.0 Null0
ip route 145.100.0.0 255.255.0.0 Null0
ip route 146.100.0.0 255.255.0.0 Null0
ip route 147.100.0.0 255.255.0.0 Null0
ip route 148.100.0.0 255.255.0.0 Null0
ip route 149.100.0.0 255.255.0.0 Null0
!
line con 0
line aux 0
line vty 0 4
end
```

Example 9-10 displays the full working configuration of the Catalyst 6509 switch. (The following configuration is also truncated; the #s are comment lines in Catalyst 6500 series software placed by Catalyst IOS).

Example 9-10 *Full Working Configuration of Catalysts Switch 6509*

```
#vtp
set vtp domain ccnp
set vlan 1 name default type ethernet mtu 1500 said 100001 state active
set vlan 100 name VLAN_100_R1E0/0 type ethernet mtu 1500 said 100100 state
  active
set vlan 200 name VLAN_200_R2E0/0 type ethernet mtu 1500 said 100200 state
  active
set vlan 300 name VLAN_300_R3E0 type ethernet mtu 1500 said 100300 state active
set vlan 400 name VLAN_400_R4E0 type ethernet mtu 1500 said 100400 state active
set vlan 500 name VLAN_500_R5E0 type ethernet mtu 1500 said 100500 state active
set vlan 550 name VLAN_550_R5E1 type ethernet mtu 1500 said 100550 state active
set vlan 600 name VLAN_600_R6E0 type ethernet mtu 1500 said 100600 state active
set vlan 700 name VLAN_700_ISP_BACKBONE_ETHERNET type ethernet mtu 1500 said
  100700 state active
set vlan 1002 name fddi-default type fddi mtu 1500 said 101002 state active
set vlan 1004 name fddinet-default type fddinet mtu 1500 said 101004 state
  active stp ieee
```

Example 9-10 *Full Working Configuration of Catalysts Switch 6509 (Continued)*

```
set vlan 1005 name trnet-default type trbrf mtu 1500 said 101005 state active
  stp ibm
set vlan 1003 name token-ring-default type trcrf mtu 1500 said 101003 state
  active mode srb aremaxhop 7 stemaxhop 7 backupcrf off
!
#ip
set interface sc0 100 133.33.1.2/255.255.255.248 133.33.1.7
set ip route 0.0.0.0/0.0.0.0          133.33.1.1
!
#set boot command
set boot config-register 0x102
set boot system flash bootflash:cat6000-sup.5-5-4.bin
!
#mls
set mls enable ipx
!
# default port status is enable
!
#module 1 : 2-port 1000BaseX Supervisor
!
#module 2 empty
!
#module 3 : 48-port 10/100BaseTX Ethernet
set vlan 100  3/1
set vlan 200  3/2
set vlan 700  3/11,3/15
set port name      3/1   R1 E0/0
set port name      3/2   R2 E0/0
set port name      3/3   R3 E0
set port name      3/5   R4 E0
set port name      3/7   R5 E0
set port name      3/8   R5 E1
set port name      3/9   R6 E0
set port name      3/11  ISP2 E0
set port name      3/15  ISP1 E0
set spantree portfast    3/1-48 enable
#module 4 empty
#module 5 empty
#module 6 empty
#module 7 empty
#module 8 empty
#module 9 : 8-port 1000BaseX Ethernet
#module 15 : 1-port Multilayer Switch Feature Card
#module 16 empty
end
Cat6509> (enable)
```

New catalyst software displays only nondefault configurations, as displayed in Example 9-10.

Sample show, ping, and telnet Commands

The following displays are presented here to demonstrate IP connectivity among all six routers. The first command used, **show ip route**, is the most widely used command on Cisco IOS routers. Some ping and telnet requests from each router are also shown. Finally, BGP tables are presented to display BGP attributes and next hop path taken from each router.

Any network designer must use common verification tools to ensure that IP connectivity is achieved. Cisco IOS contains bugs and caveats, so even correct configurations do not always guarantee connectivity. You should familiarize yourself thoroughly with the common **show**, **debug**, **ping**, and **telnet** commands.

This section starts by looking at the IGP network namely, OSPF, EIGRP, and IGRP.

Example 9-11 displays the IP (OSPF) routing table on R1.

Example 9-11 show ip route ospf *on R1*

```
R1#show ip route ospf
          133.33.0.0/16 is variably subnetted, 28 subnets, 6 masks
O IA    133.33.204.0/24 [110/1601] via 133.33.7.6, 00:03:34, Serial1/1
O E2    133.33.205.0/24 [110/100] via 133.33.7.6, 00:03:34, Serial1/1
O E2    133.33.206.0/24 [110/1000] via 133.33.7.6, 00:03:34, Serial1/1
O       133.33.202.0/24 [110/801] via 133.33.7.2, 00:13:17, Serial1/0
O       133.33.203.0/24 [110/801] via 133.33.7.6, 00:13:17, Serial1/1
O IA    133.33.4.0/25 [110/810] via 133.33.7.6, 00:03:34, Serial1/1
O IA    133.33.5.0/27 [110/1610] via 133.33.7.6, 00:03:34, Serial1/1
O E2    133.33.6.0/24 [110/1000] via 133.33.7.6, 00:03:35, Serial1/1
O IA    133.33.3.0/25 [110/1000] via 133.33.7.2, 00:03:35, Serial1/0
O       133.33.7.8/30 [110/1600] via 133.33.7.6, 00:13:18, Serial1/1
                      [110/1600] via 133.33.7.2, 00:13:18, Serial1/0
O E2    133.33.8.0/24 [110/100] via 133.33.7.6, 00:03:35, Serial1/1
O E2    133.33.9.0/24 [110/100] via 133.33.7.6, 00:03:35, Serial1/1
O E2    133.33.10.0/24 [110/20] via 133.33.7.6, 00:02:41, Serial1/1
O E2    133.33.11.0/24 [110/20] via 133.33.7.6, 00:02:42, Serial1/1
O IA    133.33.7.12/30 [110/1600] via 133.33.7.6, 00:03:36, Serial1/1
O IA    133.33.24.0/21 [110/801] via 133.33.7.2, 00:03:36, Serial1/0
```

R1 has an OSPF cost metric to networks 133.33.3.0/24, 133.33.206.0/24, and 133.33.6.0/24 as 1000, as required. The OSPF adjacency on R1 is displayed in Example 9-12.

Example 9-12 show ip ospf neighbor *on R1*

```
R1#show ip ospf neighbor

Neighbor ID    Pri   State        Dead Time   Address       Interface
R2              1    FULL/  -      00:00:36    133.33.7.2    Serial1/0
R3              1    FULL/  -      00:01:37    133.33.7.6    Serial1/1
```

Because R1 is configured with the IOS **ip ospf name-lookup** command and there is a host entry for R2 and R3, the remote neighboring routers are listed as R2 and R3 in Example 9-12.

Example 9-13 displays a ping request to all IP interfaces present in Figure 9-1's interior IP routing network to demonstrate IP connectivity. The loopbacks in Table 9-2 are used to ping from R1.

Example 9-13 *Pinging Local Loopbacks on R1*

```
R1#ping 133.33.201.1
Type escape sequence to abort.
Sending 5, 100-byte ICMP Echos to 133.33.201.1, timeout is 2 seconds:
!!!!!
Success rate is 100 percent (5/5), round-trip min/avg/max = 1/1/4 ms
R1#ping 133.33.202.1
Type escape sequence to abort.
Sending 5, 100-byte ICMP Echos to 133.33.202.1, timeout is 2 seconds:
!!!!!
Success rate is 100 percent (5/5), round-trip min/avg/max = 16/16/16 ms
R1#ping 133.33.203.1
Type escape sequence to abort.
Sending 5, 100-byte ICMP Echos to 133.33.203.1, timeout is 2 seconds:
!!!!!
Success rate is 100 percent (5/5), round-trip min/avg/max = 28/31/32 ms
R1#ping 133.33.204.1
Type escape sequence to abort.
Sending 5, 100-byte ICMP Echos to 133.33.204.1, timeout is 2 seconds:
!!!!!
Success rate is 100 percent (5/5), round-trip min/avg/max = 16/16/20 ms
R1#ping 133.33.205.1
Type escape sequence to abort.
Sending 5, 100-byte ICMP Echos to 133.33.205.1, timeout is 2 seconds:
!!!!!
Success rate is 100 percent (5/5), round-trip min/avg/max = 32/32/36 ms
R1#ping 133.33.206.1
Type escape sequence to abort.
Sending 5, 100-byte ICMP Echos to 133.33.206.1, timeout is 2 seconds:
!!!!!
Success rate is 100 percent (5/5), round-trip min/avg/max = 32/32/32 ms
```

Example 9-14 displays IP connectivity to the remaining IP interfaces as described in Table 9-1. (Note the local interfaces on R1 are not displayed or pinged from R1.)

Example 9-14 *Pinging LAN/WAN Interfaces from R1*

```
R1#ping 133.33.3.1
Type escape sequence to abort.
Sending 5, 100-byte ICMP Echos to 133.33.3.1, timeout is 2 seconds:
!!!!!
Success rate is 100 percent (5/5), round-trip min/avg/max = 16/16/16 ms
```

continues

Example 9-14 *Pinging LAN/WAN Interfaces from R1 (Continued)*

```
R1#ping 133.33.7.2
Type escape sequence to abort.
Sending 5, 100-byte ICMP Echos to 133.33.7.2, timeout is 2 seconds:
!!!!!
Success rate is 100 percent (5/5), round-trip min/avg/max = 16/16/20 ms
R1#ping 133.33.7.9
Type escape sequence to abort.
Sending 5, 100-byte ICMP Echos to 133.33.7.9, timeout is 2 seconds:
!!!!!
Success rate is 100 percent (5/5), round-trip min/avg/max = 16/20/28 ms
R1#ping 133.33.4.1
Type escape sequence to abort.
Sending 5, 100-byte ICMP Echos to 133.33.4.1, timeout is 2 seconds:
!!!!!
Success rate is 100 percent (5/5), round-trip min/avg/max = 28/30/32 ms
R1#ping 133.33.7.10
Type escape sequence to abort.
Sending 5, 100-byte ICMP Echos to 133.33.7.10, timeout is 2 seconds:
!!!!!
Success rate is 100 percent (5/5), round-trip min/avg/max = 28/29/32 ms
R1#ping 133.33.7.13
Type escape sequence to abort.
Sending 5, 100-byte ICMP Echos to 133.33.7.13, timeout is 2 seconds:
!!!!!
Success rate is 100 percent (5/5), round-trip min/avg/max = 28/30/32 ms
R1#ping 133.33.7.6
Type escape sequence to abort.
Sending 5, 100-byte ICMP Echos to 133.33.7.6, timeout is 2 seconds:
!!!!!
Success rate is 100 percent (5/5), round-trip min/avg/max = 28/29/32 ms
R1#ping 133.33.7.14
Type escape sequence to abort.
Sending 5, 100-byte ICMP Echos to 133.33.7.14, timeout is 2 seconds:
!!!!!
Success rate is 100 percent (5/5), round-trip min/avg/max = 16/16/20 ms
R1#ping 133.33.10.2
Type escape sequence to abort.
Sending 5, 100-byte ICMP Echos to 133.33.10.2, timeout is 2 seconds:
!!!!!
Success rate is 100 percent (5/5), round-trip min/avg/max = 16/16/20 ms
R1#ping 133.33.10.1
Type escape sequence to abort.
Sending 5, 100-byte ICMP Echos to 133.33.10.1, timeout is 2 seconds:
!!!!!
Success rate is 100 percent (5/5), round-trip min/avg/max = 32/32/36 ms
R1#ping 133.33.11.1
Type escape sequence to abort.
Sending 5, 100-byte ICMP Echos to 133.33.11.1, timeout is 2 seconds:
!!!!!
Success rate is 100 percent (5/5), round-trip min/avg/max = 32/32/33 ms
R1#ping 133.33.11.2
```

Example 9-14 *Pinging LAN/WAN Interfaces from R1 (Continued)*

```
Type escape sequence to abort.
Sending 5, 100-byte ICMP Echos to 133.33.11.2, timeout is 2 seconds:
!!!!!
Success rate is 100 percent (5/5), round-trip min/avg/max = 16/17/20 ms
R1#ping 133.33.8.1
Type escape sequence to abort.
Sending 5, 100-byte ICMP Echos to 133.33.8.1, timeout is 2 seconds:
!!!!!
Success rate is 100 percent (5/5), round-trip min/avg/max = 32/37/48 ms
R1#ping 133.33.8.2
Type escape sequence to abort.
Sending 5, 100-byte ICMP Echos to 133.33.8.2, timeout is 2 seconds:
!!!!!
Success rate is 0 percent (5/5)
R1#ping 133.33.9.1
Type escape sequence to abort.
Sending 5, 100-byte ICMP Echos to 133.33.9.1, timeout is 2 seconds:
!!!!!
Success rate is 100 percent (5/5), round-trip min/avg/max = 32/32/36 ms
R1#ping 133.33.10.1
Type escape sequence to abort.
Sending 5, 100-byte ICMP Echos to 133.33.10.1, timeout is 2 seconds:
!!!!!
Success rate is 100 percent (5/5), round-trip min/avg/max = 32/32/33 ms
R1#ping 133.33.10.2
Type escape sequence to abort.
Sending 5, 100-byte ICMP Echos to 133.33.10.2, timeout is 2 seconds:
!!!!!
Success rate is 100 percent (5/5), round-trip min/avg/max = 16/16/16 ms
R1#ping 171.108.1.1
Type escape sequence to abort.
Sending 5, 100-byte ICMP Echos to 171.108.1.1, timeout is 2 seconds:
!!!!!
Success rate is 100 percent (5/5), round-trip min/avg/max = 16/16/20 ms
R1#ping 171.108.1.5
Type escape sequence to abort.
Sending 5, 100-byte ICMP Echos to 171.108.1.5, timeout is 2 seconds:
!!!!!
Success rate is 100 percent (5/5), round-trip min/avg/max = 16/16/16 ms
R1#
```

Example 9-15 displays output when the **show ip ospf interface** command is entered on R1.

Example 9-15 show ip ospf interface *on R1*

```
R1#show ip ospf interface
Ethernet0/0 is up, line protocol is up
  Internet Address 133.33.1.1/29, Area 100
  Process ID 1, Router ID 133.33.201.1, Network Type BROADCAST, Cost: 10
```

continues

Example 9-15 *show ip ospf interface* on *R1 (Continued)*

```
      Transmit Delay is 1 sec, State DR, Priority 1
      Designated Router (ID) r1, Interface address 133.33.1.1
      No backup designated router on this network
      Timer intervals configured, Hello 10, Dead 40, Wait 40, Retransmit 5
        Hello due in 00:00:05
      Neighbor Count is 0, Adjacent neighbor count is 0
      Suppress hello for 0 neighbor(s)
   Serial1/0 is up, line protocol is up
     Internet Address 133.33.7.1/30, Area 0
     Process ID 1, Router ID 133.33.201.1, Network Type POINT_TO_POINT, Cost: 800
     Transmit Delay is 1 sec, State POINT_TO_POINT,
     Timer intervals configured, Hello 10, Dead 40, Wait 40, Retransmit 5
       Hello due in 00:00:04
     Neighbor Count is 1, Adjacent neighbor count is 1
       Adjacent with neighbor r2
     Suppress hello for 0 neighbor(s)
     Message digest authentication enabled
         No key configured, using default key id 0
   Serial1/1 is up, line protocol is up
     Internet Address 133.33.7.5/30, Area 0
     Process ID 1, Router ID 133.33.201.1, Network Type POINT_TO_POINT, Cost: 800
     Transmit Delay is 1 sec, State POINT_TO_POINT,
     Timer intervals configured, Hello 25, Dead 100, Wait 100, Retransmit 5
       Hello due in 00:00:18
     Neighbor Count is 1, Adjacent neighbor count is 1
       Adjacent with neighbor r3
     Suppress hello for 0 neighbor(s)
     Message digest authentication enabled
         No key configured, using default key id 0
   Loopback0 is up, line protocol is up
     Internet Address 133.33.201.1/24, Area 0
     Process ID 1, Router ID 133.33.201.1, Network Type POINT_TO_POINT, Cost: 1
     Transmit Delay is 1 sec, State POINT_TO_POINT,
     Timer intervals configured, Hello 10, Dead 40, Wait 40, Retransmit 5
       Hello due in 00:00:00
     Neighbor Count is 0, Adjacent neighbor count is 0
     Suppress hello for 0 neighbor(s)
     Message digest authentication enabled
         No key configured, using default key id 0
   Loopback1 is up, line protocol is up
     Internet Address 133.33.16.1/24, Area 100
     Process ID 1, Router ID 133.33.201.1, Network Type POINT_TO_POINT, Cost: 1
     Transmit Delay is 1 sec, State POINT_TO_POINT,
     Timer intervals configured, Hello 10, Dead 40, Wait 40, Retransmit 5
       Hello due in 00:00:00
     Neighbor Count is 0, Adjacent neighbor count is 0
     Suppress hello for 0 neighbor(s)
   Loopback2 is up, line protocol is up
     Internet Address 133.33.18.1/24, Area 100
     Process ID 1, Router ID 133.33.201.1, Network Type POINT_TO_POINT, Cost: 1
     Transmit Delay is 1 sec, State POINT_TO_POINT,
```

Example 9-15 show ip ospf interface *on R1 (Continued)*

```
   Timer intervals configured, Hello 10, Dead 40, Wait 40, Retransmit 5
     Hello due in 00:00:00
   Neighbor Count is 0, Adjacent neighbor count is 0
   Suppress hello for 0 neighbor(s)
Loopback3 is up, line protocol is up
   Internet Address 133.33.17.1/24, Area 100
   Process ID 1, Router ID 133.33.201.1, Network Type POINT_TO_POINT, Cost: 1
   Transmit Delay is 1 sec, State POINT_TO_POINT,
   Timer intervals configured, Hello 10, Dead 40, Wait 40, Retransmit 5
     Hello due in 00:00:00
   Neighbor Count is 0, Adjacent neighbor count is 0
   Suppress hello for 0 neighbor(s)
Loopback4 is up, line protocol is up
   Internet Address 133.33.19.1/24, Area 100
   Process ID 1, Router ID 133.33.201.1, Network Type POINT_TO_POINT, Cost: 1
   Transmit Delay is 1 sec, State POINT_TO_POINT,
   Timer intervals configured, Hello 10, Dead 40, Wait 40, Retransmit 5
     Hello due in 00:00:00
   Neighbor Count is 0, Adjacent neighbor count is 0
   Suppress hello for 0 neighbor(s)
Loopback5 is up, line protocol is up
   Internet Address 133.33.20.1/24, Area 100
   Process ID 1, Router ID 133.33.201.1, Network Type POINT_TO_POINT, Cost: 1
   Transmit Delay is 1 sec, State POINT_TO_POINT,
   Timer intervals configured, Hello 10, Dead 40, Wait 40, Retransmit 5
     Hello due in 00:00:00
   Neighbor Count is 0, Adjacent neighbor count is 0
   Suppress hello for 0 neighbor(s)
Loopback6 is up, line protocol is up
   Internet Address 133.33.21.1/24, Area 100
   Process ID 1, Router ID 133.33.201.1, Network Type POINT_TO_POINT, Cost: 1
   Transmit Delay is 1 sec, State POINT_TO_POINT,
   Timer intervals configured, Hello 10, Dead 40, Wait 40, Retransmit 5
     Hello due in 00:00:00
   Neighbor Count is 0, Adjacent neighbor count is 0
   Suppress hello for 0 neighbor(s)
Loopback7 is up, line protocol is up
   Internet Address 133.33.22.1/24, Area 100
   Process ID 1, Router ID 133.33.201.1, Network Type POINT_TO_POINT, Cost: 1
   Transmit Delay is 1 sec, State POINT_TO_POINT,
   Timer intervals configured, Hello 10, Dead 40, Wait 40, Retransmit 5
     Hello due in 00:00:00
   Neighbor Count is 0, Adjacent neighbor count is 0
   Suppress hello for 0 neighbor(s)
Loopback8 is up, line protocol is up
   Internet Address 133.33.23.1/24, Area 100
   Process ID 1, Router ID 133.33.201.1, Network Type POINT_TO_POINT, Cost: 1
```

continues

Example 9-15 **show ip ospf interface** *on R1 (Continued)*

```
    Transmit Delay is 1 sec, State POINT_TO_POINT,
    Timer intervals configured, Hello 10, Dead 40, Wait 40, Retransmit 5
      Hello due in 00:00:00
    Neighbor Count is 0, Adjacent neighbor count is 0
    Suppress hello for 0 neighbor(s)
 R1#
```

Example 9-15 displays the area assignments, the OSPF neighbor states, and whether authentication is in use. You can verify OSPF area assignments and other details, such as Hello and dead intervals, with the same command (**show ip ospf interface**).

Example 9-16 displays the IP OSPF routing table on R2.

Example 9-16 **show ip route ospf** *on R2*

```
R2#show ip route ospf
          133.33.0.0/16 is variably subnetted, 37 subnets, 6 masks
O IA    133.33.204.0/24 [110/1601] via 133.33.7.10, 00:06:21, Serial1/1
O E2    133.33.205.0/24 [110/100] via 133.33.7.10, 00:06:21, Serial1/1
O E2    133.33.206.0/24 [110/1000] via 133.33.7.10, 00:06:21, Serial1/1
O       133.33.201.0/24 [110/801] via 133.33.7.1, 17:03:37, Serial1/0
O       133.33.203.0/24 [110/801] via 133.33.7.10, 17:03:37, Serial1/1
O IA    133.33.4.0/25 [110/810] via 133.33.7.10, 00:06:21, Serial1/1
O IA    133.33.5.0/27 [110/1610] via 133.33.7.10, 00:06:22, Serial1/1
O E2    133.33.6.0/24 [110/1000] via 133.33.7.10, 00:06:22, Serial1/1
O IA    133.33.1.0/29 [110/810] via 133.33.7.1, 00:06:22, Serial1/0
O       133.33.7.4/30 [110/864] via 133.33.7.10, 17:03:37, Serial1/1
O E2    133.33.8.0/24 [110/100] via 133.33.7.10, 00:06:22, Serial1/1
O E2    133.33.9.0/24 [110/100] via 133.33.7.10, 00:06:22, Serial1/1
O E2    133.33.10.0/24 [110/20] via 133.33.7.10, 00:05:29, Serial1/1
O E2    133.33.11.0/24 [110/20] via 133.33.7.10, 00:05:29, Serial1/1
O IA    133.33.7.12/30 [110/1600] via 133.33.7.10, 00:06:23, Serial1/1
O IA    133.33.16.0/21 [110/801] via 133.33.7.1, 00:06:23, Serial1/0
```

Example 9-17 displays a successful ping request to all six loopbacks interfaces demonstrating full IP connectivity among all six routers in Figure 9-1.

Example 9-17 *Ping Request on R2 to Remote Networks*

```
R2#ping 133.33.201.1
Type escape sequence to abort.
Sending 5, 100-byte ICMP Echos to 133.33.201.1, timeout is 2 seconds:
!!!!!
Success rate is 100 percent (5/5), round-trip min/avg/max = 16/16/20 ms
R2#ping 133.33.202.1
Type escape sequence to abort.
Sending 5, 100-byte ICMP Echos to 133.33.202.1, timeout is 2 seconds:
```

Example 9-17 *Ping Request on R2 to Remote Networks (Continued)*

```
!!!!!
Success rate is 100 percent (5/5), round-trip min/avg/max = 1/2/4 ms
R2#ping 133.33.203.1
Type escape sequence to abort.
Sending 5, 100-byte ICMP Echos to 133.33.203.1, timeout is 2 seconds:
!!!!!
Success rate is 100 percent (5/5), round-trip min/avg/max = 16/16/16 ms
R2#ping 133.33.204.1
Type escape sequence to abort.
Sending 5, 100-byte ICMP Echos to 133.33.204.1, timeout is 2 seconds:
!!!!!
Success rate is 100 percent (5/5), round-trip min/avg/max = 16/16/20 ms
R2#ping 133.33.205.1
Type escape sequence to abort.
Sending 5, 100-byte ICMP Echos to 133.33.205.1, timeout is 2 seconds:
!!!!!
Success rate is 100 percent (5/5), round-trip min/avg/max = 32/32/36 ms
R2#ping 133.33.206.1
Type escape sequence to abort.
Sending 5, 100-byte ICMP Echos to 133.33.206.1, timeout is 2 seconds:
!!!!!
Success rate is 100 percent (5/5), round-trip min/avg/max = 32/32/32 ms
```

Example 9-18 displays the output from the IOS **show ip ospf interface** command.

Example 9-18 **show ip ospf interface** *on R2*

```
R2#show ip ospf interfac
Ethernet0/0 is up, line protocol is up
  Internet Address 133.33.3.1/25, Area 200
  Process ID 1, Router ID 133.33.202.1, Network Type BROADCAST, Cost: 200
  Transmit Delay is 1 sec, State DR, Priority 1
  Designated Router (ID) 133.33.202.2, Interface address 133.33.3.1
  No backup designated router on this network
  Timer intervals configured, Hello 10, Dead 40, Wait 40, Retransmit 5
    Hello due in 00:00:09
  Neighbor Count is 0, Adjacent neighbor count is 0
  Suppress hello for 0 neighbor(s)
Serial1/0 is up, line protocol is up
  Internet Address 133.33.7.2/30, Area 0
  Process ID 1, Router ID 133.33.202.1, Network Type POINT_TO_POINT, Cost: 800
  Transmit Delay is 1 sec, State POINT_TO_POINT,
  Timer intervals configured, Hello 10, Dead 40, Wait 40, Retransmit 5
    Hello due in 00:00:08
  Neighbor Count is 1, Adjacent neighbor count is 1
    Adjacent with neighbor r1
  Suppress hello for 0 neighbor(s)
  Message digest authentication enabled
      No key configured, using default key id 0
```

continues

Example 9-18 show ip ospf interface *on R2 (Continued)*

```
Serial1/1 is up, line protocol is up
  Internet Address 133.33.7.9/30, Area 0
  Process ID 1, Router ID 133.33.202.1, Network Type POINT_TO_POINT, Cost: 800
  Transmit Delay is 1 sec, State POINT_TO_POINT,
  Timer intervals configured, Hello 10, Dead 40, Wait 40, Retransmit 5
    Hello due in 00:00:08
  Neighbor Count is 1, Adjacent neighbor count is 1
    Adjacent with neighbor r3
  Suppress hello for 0 neighbor(s)
  Message digest authentication enabled
      No key configured, using default key id 0
Loopback0 is up, line protocol is up
  Internet Address 133.33.202.1/24, Area 0
  Process ID 1, Router ID 133.33.202.1, Network Type POINT_TO_POINT, Cost: 1
  Transmit Delay is 1 sec, State POINT_TO_POINT,
  Timer intervals configured, Hello 10, Dead 40, Wait 40, Retransmit 5
    Hello due in 00:00:00
  Neighbor Count is 0, Adjacent neighbor count is 0
  Suppress hello for 0 neighbor(s)
  Message digest authentication enabled
      No key configured, using default key id 0
Loopback1 is up, line protocol is up
  Internet Address 133.33.24.1/24, Area 200
  Process ID 1, Router ID 133.33.202.1, Network Type POINT_TO_POINT, Cost: 1
  Transmit Delay is 1 sec, State POINT_TO_POINT,
  Timer intervals configured, Hello 10, Dead 40, Wait 40, Retransmit 5
    Hello due in 00:00:00
  Neighbor Count is 0, Adjacent neighbor count is 0
  Suppress hello for 0 neighbor(s)
Loopback2 is up, line protocol is up
  Internet Address 133.33.26.1/24, Area 200
  Process ID 1, Router ID 133.33.202.1, Network Type POINT_TO_POINT, Cost: 1
  Transmit Delay is 1 sec, State POINT_TO_POINT,
  Timer intervals configured, Hello 10, Dead 40, Wait 40, Retransmit 5
    Hello due in 00:00:00
  Neighbor Count is 0, Adjacent neighbor count is 0
  Suppress hello for 0 neighbor(s)
Loopback3 is up, line protocol is up
  Internet Address 133.33.25.1/24, Area 200
  Process ID 1, Router ID 133.33.202.1, Network Type POINT_TO_POINT, Cost: 1
  Transmit Delay is 1 sec, State POINT_TO_POINT,
  Timer intervals configured, Hello 10, Dead 40, Wait 40, Retransmit 5
    Hello due in 00:00:00
  Neighbor Count is 0, Adjacent neighbor count is 0
  Suppress hello for 0 neighbor(s)
Loopback4 is up, line protocol is up
  Internet Address 133.33.27.1/24, Area 200
  Process ID 1, Router ID 133.33.202.1, Network Type POINT_TO_POINT, Cost: 1
  Transmit Delay is 1 sec, State POINT_TO_POINT,
```

Example 9-18 show ip ospf interface *on R2 (Continued)*

```
    Timer intervals configured, Hello 10, Dead 40, Wait 40, Retransmit 5
      Hello due in 00:00:00
    Neighbor Count is 0, Adjacent neighbor count is 0
    Suppress hello for 0 neighbor(s)
Loopback5 is up, line protocol is up
    Internet Address 133.33.28.1/24, Area 200
    Process ID 1, Router ID 133.33.202.1, Network Type POINT_TO_POINT, Cost: 1
    Transmit Delay is 1 sec, State POINT_TO_POINT,
    Timer intervals configured, Hello 10, Dead 40, Wait 40, Retransmit 5
      Hello due in 00:00:00
    Neighbor Count is 0, Adjacent neighbor count is 0
    Suppress hello for 0 neighbor(s)
Loopback6 is up, line protocol is up
    Internet Address 133.33.29.1/24, Area 200
    Process ID 1, Router ID 133.33.202.1, Network Type POINT_TO_POINT, Cost: 1
    Transmit Delay is 1 sec, State POINT_TO_POINT,
    Timer intervals configured, Hello 10, Dead 40, Wait 40, Retransmit 5
      Hello due in 00:00:00
    Neighbor Count is 0, Adjacent neighbor count is 0
    Suppress hello for 0 neighbor(s)
Loopback7 is up, line protocol is up
    Internet Address 133.33.30.1/24, Area 200
    Process ID 1, Router ID 133.33.202.1, Network Type POINT_TO_POINT, Cost: 1
    Transmit Delay is 1 sec, State POINT_TO_POINT,
    Timer intervals configured, Hello 10, Dead 40, Wait 40, Retransmit 5
      Hello due in 00:00:00
    Neighbor Count is 0, Adjacent neighbor count is 0
    Suppress hello for 0 neighbor(s)
Loopback8 is up, line protocol is up
    Internet Address 133.33.31.1/24, Area 200
    Process ID 1, Router ID 133.33.202.1, Network Type POINT_TO_POINT, Cost: 1
    Transmit Delay is 1 sec, State POINT_TO_POINT,
    Timer intervals configured, Hello 10, Dead 40, Wait 40, Retransmit 5
      Hello due in 00:00:00
    Neighbor Count is 0, Adjacent neighbor count is 0
    Suppress hello for 0 neighbor(s)
R2#
```

Example 9-19 displays the OSPF neighbors on R2.

Example 9-19 show ip ospf neighbor *on R2*

```
R2#show ip ospf neighbor
Neighbor ID     Pri   State           Dead Time   Address         Interface
R1                1   FULL/   -       00:00:35    133.33.7.1      Serial1/0
R3                1   FULL/   -       00:00:36    133.33.7.10     Serial1/1
```

Example 9-20 displays the IP (OSPF) routing table on R3.

Example 9-20 **show ip route ospf** *on R3*

```
R3#show ip route ospf
     133.33.0.0/16 is variably subnetted, 29 subnets, 6 masks
O       133.33.204.0/24 [110/801] via 133.33.7.14, 00:07:08, Serial1
O E2    133.33.205.0/24 [110/100] via 133.33.7.14, 00:07:08, Serial1
O E2    133.33.206.0/24 [110/1000] via 133.33.7.14, 00:07:08, Serial1
O       133.33.201.0/24 [110/65] via 133.33.7.5, 17:04:09, Serial2
O       133.33.202.0/24 [110/801] via 133.33.7.9, 17:04:09, Serial0
O       133.33.5.0/27 [110/810] via 133.33.7.14, 00:07:08, Serial1
O E2    133.33.6.0/24 [110/1000] via 133.33.7.14, 00:07:08, Serial1
O       133.33.7.0/30 [110/864] via 133.33.7.5, 17:04:10, Serial2
O IA    133.33.1.0/29 [110/74] via 133.33.7.5, 00:07:08, Serial2
O IA    133.33.3.0/25 [110/1000] via 133.33.7.9, 00:07:08, Serial0
O E2    133.33.8.0/24 [110/100] via 133.33.7.14, 00:07:08, Serial1
O E2    133.33.9.0/24 [110/100] via 133.33.7.14, 00:07:08, Serial1
O E2    133.33.10.0/24 [110/20] via 133.33.7.14, 00:06:10, Serial1
O E2    133.33.11.0/24 [110/20] via 133.33.7.14, 00:06:10, Serial1
O IA    133.33.16.0/21 [110/65] via 133.33.7.5, 00:07:09, Serial2
O IA    133.33.24.0/21 [110/801] via 133.33.7.9, 00:07:09, Serial0
```

Example 9-21 displays a successful ping request to all routers by using the names configured on R3. (Refer to the full configuration in Example 9-4).

Example 9-21 *Pinging All Loopbacks Using Names on R3*

```
R3#ping r1
Type escape sequence to abort.
Sending 5, 100-byte ICMP Echos to 133.33.201.1, timeout is 2 seconds:
!!!!!
Success rate is 100 percent (5/5), round-trip min/avg/max = 20/22/24 ms
R3#ping r2
Type escape sequence to abort.
Sending 5, 100-byte ICMP Echos to 133.33.202.1, timeout is 2 seconds:
!!!!!
Success rate is 100 percent (5/5), round-trip min/avg/max = 16/16/16 ms
R3#ping r3
Type escape sequence to abort.
Sending 5, 100-byte ICMP Echos to 133.33.203.1, timeout is 2 seconds:
!!!!!
Success rate is 100 percent (5/5), round-trip min/avg/max = 1/2/4 ms
R3#ping r4
Type escape sequence to abort.
Sending 5, 100-byte ICMP Echos to 133.33.204.1, timeout is 2 seconds:
!!!!!
Success rate is 100 percent (5/5), round-trip min/avg/max = 16/17/20 ms
R3#ping r5
Type escape sequence to abort.
Sending 5, 100-byte ICMP Echos to 133.33.205.1, timeout is 2 seconds:
```

Example 9-21 *Pinging All Loopbacks Using Names on R3 (Continued)*

```
!!!!!
Success rate is 100 percent (5/5), round-trip min/avg/max = 32/33/36 ms
R3#ping r6
Type escape sequence to abort.
Sending 5, 100-byte ICMP Echos to 133.33.206.1, timeout is 2 seconds:
!!!!!
Success rate is 100 percent (5/5), round-trip min/avg/max = 32/32/36 ms
R3#
```

Example 9-22 displays the output when the **show ip ospf interface** command is entered on R3.

Example 9-22 show ip ospf interface *on R3*

```
R3#show ip ospf interface
Ethernet0 is up, line protocol is up
  Internet Address 133.33.4.1/25, Area 300
  Process ID 1, Router ID 133.33.203.1, Network Type BROADCAST, Cost: 10
  Transmit Delay is 1 sec, State DR, Priority 255
  Designated Router (ID) r3, Interface address 133.33.4.1
  No backup designated router on this network
  Timer intervals configured, Hello 10, Dead 40, Wait 40, Retransmit 5
    Hello due in 00:00:04
  Index 1/1, flood queue length 0
  Next 0x0(0)/0x0(0)
  Last flood scan length is 0, maximum is 0
  Last flood scan time is 0 msec, maximum is 0 msec
  Neighbor Count is 0, Adjacent neighbor count is 0
  Suppress hello for 0 neighbor(s)
Loopback0 is up, line protocol is up
  Internet Address 133.33.203.1/24, Area 0
  Process ID 1, Router ID 133.33.203.1, Network Type POINT_TO_POINT, Cost: 1
  Transmit Delay is 1 sec, State POINT_TO_POINT,
  Timer intervals configured, Hello 10, Dead 40, Wait 40, Retransmit 5
    Hello due in 00:00:00
  Index 3/5, flood queue length 0
  Next 0x0(0)/0x0(0)
  Last flood scan length is 0, maximum is 0
  Last flood scan time is 0 msec, maximum is 0 msec
  Neighbor Count is 0, Adjacent neighbor count is 0
  Suppress hello for 0 neighbor(s)
  Message digest authentication enabled
      No key configured, using default key id 0
Serial0 is up, line protocol is up
  Internet Address 133.33.7.10/30, Area 0
  Process ID 1, Router ID 133.33.203.1, Network Type POINT_TO_POINT, Cost: 800
  Transmit Delay is 1 sec, State POINT_TO_POINT,
```

continues

Example 9-22 show ip ospf interface *on R3 (Continued)*

```
    Timer intervals configured, Hello 10, Dead 40, Wait 40, Retransmit 5
      Hello due in 00:00:02
    Index 2/3, flood queue length 0
    Next 0x0(0)/0x0(0)
    Last flood scan length is 1, maximum is 9
    Last flood scan time is 0 msec, maximum is 0 msec
    Neighbor Count is 1, Adjacent neighbor count is 1
      Adjacent with neighbor r2
    Suppress hello for 0 neighbor(s)
    Message digest authentication enabled
        No key configured, using default key id 0
  Serial1 is up, line protocol is up
    Internet Address 133.33.7.13/30, Area 350
    Process ID 1, Router ID 133.33.203.1, Network Type POINT_TO_POINT, Cost: 800
    Transmit Delay is 1 sec, State POINT_TO_POINT,
    Timer intervals configured, Hello 10, Dead 40, Wait 40, Retransmit 5
      Hello due in 00:00:02
    Index 1/4, flood queue length 0
    Next 0x0(0)/0x0(0)
    Last flood scan length is 1, maximum is 9
    Last flood scan time is 0 msec, maximum is 0 msec
    Neighbor Count is 1, Adjacent neighbor count is 1
      Adjacent with neighbor r4
    Suppress hello for 0 neighbor(s)
  Serial2 is up, line protocol is up
    Internet Address 133.33.7.6/30, Area 0
    Process ID 1, Router ID 133.33.203.1, Network Type POINT_TO_POINT, Cost: 64
    Transmit Delay is 1 sec, State POINT_TO_POINT,
    Timer intervals configured, Hello 25, Dead 100, Wait 100, Retransmit 5
      Hello due in 00:00:01
    Index 1/2, flood queue length 0
    Next 0x0(0)/0x0(0)
    Last flood scan length is 1, maximum is 9
    Last flood scan time is 0 msec, maximum is 0 msec
    Neighbor Count is 1, Adjacent neighbor count is 1
      Adjacent with neighbor r1
    Suppress hello for 0 neighbor(s)
    Message digest authentication enabled
        No key configured, using default key id 0
```

R4 is configured for three interior routing protocols: OSPF, IGRP, and EIGRP. Example 9-23 displays the full IP routing table on R4 including the BGP routes.

Example 9-23 show ip route *on R4*

```
R4#show ip route
Codes: C - connected, S - static, I - IGRP, R - RIP, M - mobile, B - BGP
       D - EIGRP, EX - EIGRP external, O - OSPF, IA - OSPF inter area
       N1 - OSPF NSSA external type 1, N2 - OSPF NSSA external type 2
       E1 - OSPF external type 1, E2 - OSPF external type 2, E - EGP
```

Example 9-23 show ip route *on R4 (Continued)*

```
             i - IS-IS, L1 - IS-IS level-1, L2 - IS-IS level-2, ia - IS-IS inter area
             * - candidate default, U - per-user static route, o - ODR
             P - periodic downloaded static route
     Gateway of last resort is 133.33.201.1 to network 0.0.0.0
     B    102.0.0.0/8 [200/0] via 133.33.201.1, 01:12:20
     B    1.0.0.0/8 [200/0] via 133.33.201.1, 01:12:20
          171.108.0.0/30 is subnetted, 2 subnets
     B       171.108.1.4 [200/0] via 133.33.201.1, 01:12:04
     B       171.108.1.0 [200/0] via 133.33.201.1, 01:12:04
     B    2.0.0.0/8 [200/0] via 133.33.201.1, 01:12:20
     B    100.0.0.0/8 [200/0] via 133.33.201.1, 01:12:20
     B    3.0.0.0/8 [200/0] via 133.33.201.1, 01:12:20
     B    101.0.0.0/8 [200/0] via 133.33.201.1, 01:12:20
     B    4.0.0.0/8 [200/0] via 133.33.201.1, 01:12:20
     B    5.0.0.0/8 [200/0] via 133.33.201.1, 01:12:20
     B    141.100.0.0/16 [200/0] via 133.33.201.1, 01:12:20
     B    141.108.0.0/16 [200/0] via 133.33.201.1, 01:12:20
     B    6.0.0.0/8 [200/0] via 133.33.201.1, 01:12:20
     B    142.100.0.0/16 [200/0] via 133.33.201.1, 01:12:20
     B    7.0.0.0/8 [200/0] via 133.33.201.1, 01:12:20
     B    143.100.0.0/16 [200/0] via 133.33.201.1, 01:12:20
     B    145.100.0.0/16 [200/0] via 133.33.201.1, 01:12:20
     B    8.0.0.0/8 [200/0] via 133.33.201.1, 01:12:20
     B    144.100.0.0/16 [200/0] via 133.33.201.1, 01:12:21
     B    147.100.0.0/16 [200/0] via 133.33.201.1, 01:12:21
     B    10.0.0.0/8 [200/0] via 133.33.201.1, 01:12:21
     B    146.100.0.0/16 [200/0] via 133.33.201.1, 01:12:21
     B    11.0.0.0/8 [200/0] via 133.33.201.1, 01:12:21
     B    149.100.0.0/16 [200/0] via 133.33.201.1, 01:12:21
     B    148.100.0.0/16 [200/0] via 133.33.201.1, 01:12:21
          133.33.0.0/16 is variably subnetted, 34 subnets, 6 masks
     C       133.33.204.0/24 is directly connected, Loopback0
     I       133.33.205.0/24 [100/8976] via 133.33.10.1, 00:01:04, Serial2
     D       133.33.206.0/24 [90/2297856] via 133.33.11.1, 02:53:58, Serial3
     O IA    133.33.201.0/24 [110/129] via 133.33.7.13, 00:19:02, Serial1
     O IA    133.33.202.0/24 [110/865] via 133.33.7.13, 00:19:02, Serial1
     O IA    133.33.203.0/24 [110/65] via 133.33.7.13, 00:19:02, Serial1
     O IA    133.33.4.0/25 [110/74] via 133.33.7.13, 00:19:02, Serial1
     S       133.33.4.0/24 is directly connected, Null0
     S       133.33.5.0/24 is directly connected, Null0
     C       133.33.5.0/27 is directly connected, Ethernet0
     D       133.33.6.0/24 [90/2195456] via 133.33.11.1, 02:53:59, Serial3
     O IA    133.33.7.0/30 [110/928] via 133.33.7.13, 00:19:02, Serial1
     S       133.33.7.0/24 is directly connected, Null0
     O IA    133.33.1.0/29 [110/138] via 133.33.7.13, 00:19:02, Serial1
     S       133.33.1.0/24 is directly connected, Null0
     O IA    133.33.3.0/25 [110/1064] via 133.33.7.13, 00:19:02, Serial1
     O IA    133.33.7.4/30 [110/128] via 133.33.7.13, 00:19:02, Serial1
     S       133.33.3.0/24 is directly connected, Null0
     O IA    133.33.7.8/30 [110/864] via 133.33.7.13, 00:19:03, Serial1
```

continues

Example 9-23 show ip route *on R4 (Continued)*

```
I       133.33.8.0/24 [100/8576] via 133.33.10.1, 00:01:05, Serial2
I       133.33.9.0/24 [100/8576] via 133.33.10.1, 00:01:05, Serial2
C       133.33.10.0/24 is directly connected, Serial2
C       133.33.7.12/30 is directly connected, Serial1
C       133.33.11.0/24 is directly connected, Serial3
B       133.33.20.0/24 [200/0] via 133.33.201.1, 01:12:07
B       133.33.21.0/24 [200/0] via 133.33.201.1, 01:12:07
B       133.33.22.0/24 [200/0] via 133.33.201.1, 01:12:07
B       133.33.23.0/24 [200/0] via 133.33.201.1, 01:12:07
O IA    133.33.16.0/21 [110/129] via 133.33.7.13, 00:19:03, Serial1
B       133.33.16.0/24 [200/0] via 133.33.201.1, 01:12:07
B       133.33.17.0/24 [200/0] via 133.33.201.1, 01:12:07
B       133.33.18.0/24 [200/0] via 133.33.201.1, 01:12:07
B       133.33.19.0/24 [200/0] via 133.33.201.1, 01:12:07
O IA    133.33.24.0/21 [110/865] via 133.33.7.13, 00:19:03, Serial1
B*   0.0.0.0/0 [200/0] via 133.33.201.1, 01:12:23
```

R4's IP routing table has entries for OSPF, IGRP, and EIGRP. BGP is supplied a default route from R1, and hence, the gateway of last resort is set.

Example 9-24 displays the output from the IOS **show ip ospf interface** command.

Example 9-24 show ip ospf interface *on R4*

```
R4#show ip ospf interface
Ethernet0 is up, line protocol is up
  Internet Address 133.33.5.1/27, Area 350
  Process ID 1, Router ID 133.33.204.1, Network Type BROADCAST, Cost: 10
  Transmit Delay is 1 sec, State DR, Priority 1
  Designated Router (ID) r4, Interface address 133.33.5.1
  No backup designated router on this network
  Timer intervals configured, Hello 10, Dead 40, Wait 40, Retransmit 5
    Hello due in 00:00:03
  Index 1/1, flood queue length 0
  Next 0x0(0)/0x0(0)
  Last flood scan length is 0, maximum is 0
  Last flood scan time is 0 msec, maximum is 0 msec
  Neighbor Count is 0, Adjacent neighbor count is 0
  Suppress hello for 0 neighbor(s)
Loopback0 is up, line protocol is up
  Internet Address 133.33.204.1/24, Area 350
  Process ID 1, Router ID 133.33.204.1, Network Type POINT_TO_POINT, Cost: 1
  Transmit Delay is 1 sec, State POINT_TO_POINT,
  Timer intervals configured, Hello 10, Dead 40, Wait 40, Retransmit 5
    Hello due in 00:00:00
  Index 3/3, flood queue length 0
  Next 0x0(0)/0x0(0)
  Last flood scan length is 0, maximum is 0
  Last flood scan time is 0 msec, maximum is 0 msec
```

Example 9-24 show ip ospf interface *on R4 (Continued)*

```
    Neighbor Count is 0, Adjacent neighbor count is 0
    Suppress hello for 0 neighbor(s)
Serial1 is up, line protocol is up
   Internet Address 133.33.7.14/30, Area 350
   Process ID 1, Router ID 133.33.204.1, Network Type POINT_TO_POINT, Cost: 64
   Transmit Delay is 1 sec, State POINT_TO_POINT,
   Timer intervals configured, Hello 10, Dead 40, Wait 40, Retransmit 5
     Hello due in 00:00:02
   Index 2/2, flood queue length 0
   Next 0x0(0)/0x0(0)
   Last flood scan length is 1, maximum is 10
   Last flood scan time is 0 msec, maximum is 4 msec
   Neighbor Count is 1, Adjacent neighbor count is 1
     Adjacent with neighbor r3
   Suppress hello for 0 neighbor(s)
```

Example 9-25 displays the output from the IOS **show ip ospf neighbor** command on R4.

Example 9-25 show ip ospf neighbor *on R4*

```
R4#show ip ospf neighbor
Neighbor ID     Pri   State           Dead Time   Address         Interface
r3                1   FULL/   -        00:00:33    133.33.7.13     Serial1
```

Example 9-26 displays the output from the IOS **show ip eigrp interfaces** command.

Example 9-26 show ip eigrp interfaces *on R4*

```
R4#show ip eigrp interfaces
IP-EIGRP interfaces for process 1
                    Xmit Queue    Mean   Pacing Time   Multicast    Pending
Interface    Peers  Un/Reliable   SRTT   Un/Reliable   Flow Timer   Routes
Se3            1      0/0          33      0/15          115          0
```

Example 9-27 displays the output from the IOS **show ip eigrp neighbors** command on R4.

Example 9-27 show ip eigrp neighbors *on R4*

```
R4#show ip eigrp neighbors
IP-EIGRP neighbors for process 1
H   Address              Interface   Hold Uptime   SRTT   RTO  Q  Seq Type
                                     (sec)         (ms)        Cnt Num
0   133.33.11.1          Se3           12 02:58:28   33    200  0  62
```

Example 9-28 displays a ping request from R4 to all IP addresses in Table 9-2 to demonstrate IP connectivity.

Example 9-28 *Pinging Loopbacks on R4*

```
R4#ping 133.33.201.1
Type escape sequence to abort.
Sending 5, 100-byte ICMP Echos to 133.33.201.1, timeout is 2 seconds:
!!!!!
Success rate is 100 percent (5/5), round-trip min/avg/max = 16/16/20 ms
R4#ping 133.33.202.1
Type escape sequence to abort.
Sending 5, 100-byte ICMP Echos to 133.33.202.1, timeout is 2 seconds:
!!!!!
Success rate is 100 percent (5/5), round-trip min/avg/max = 16/16/20 ms
R4#ping 133.33.203.1
Type escape sequence to abort.
Sending 5, 100-byte ICMP Echos to 133.33.203.1, timeout is 2 seconds:
!!!!!
Success rate is 100 percent (5/5), round-trip min/avg/max = 16/17/20 ms
R4#ping 133.33.204.1
Type escape sequence to abort.
Sending 5, 100-byte ICMP Echos to 133.33.204.1, timeout is 2 seconds:
!!!!!
Success rate is 100 percent (5/5), round-trip min/avg/max = 1/2/4 ms
R4#ping 133.33.205.1
Type escape sequence to abort.
Sending 5, 100-byte ICMP Echos to 133.33.205.1, timeout is 2 seconds:
!!!!!
Success rate is 100 percent (5/5), round-trip min/avg/max = 16/16/20 ms
R4#ping 133.33.206.1
Type escape sequence to abort.
Sending 5, 100-byte ICMP Echos to 133.33.206.1, timeout is 2 seconds:
!!!!!
Success rate is 100 percent (5/5), round-trip min/avg/max = 16/16/20 ms
```

Example 9-29 displays the IGRP IP routing table on R5.

Example 9-29 *IGRP IP Routing Table on R5*

```
R5#show ip route igrp
     133.33.0.0/16 is variably subnetted, 34 subnets, 7 masks
I       133.33.204.0/24 [100/8976] via 133.33.10.2, 00:00:44, Serial0
I       133.33.206.0/24 [100/10976] via 133.33.10.2, 00:00:44, Serial0
I       133.33.201.0/24 [100/100125] via 133.33.10.2, 00:00:44, Serial0
I       133.33.202.0/24 [100/100125] via 133.33.10.2, 00:00:44, Serial0
I       133.33.203.0/24 [100/100125] via 133.33.10.2, 00:00:44, Serial0
I       133.33.4.0/24 [100/100125] via 133.33.10.2, 00:00:44, Serial0
I       133.33.5.0/24 [100/100125] via 133.33.10.2, 00:00:45, Serial0
I       133.33.6.0/24 [100/10576] via 133.33.10.2, 00:00:45, Serial0
```

Example 9-29 *IGRP IP Routing Table on R5 (Continued)*

```
I       133.33.7.0/24 [100/100125] via 133.33.10.2, 00:00:45, Serial0
I       133.33.1.0/24 [100/100125] via 133.33.10.2, 00:00:45, Serial0
I       133.33.3.0/24 [100/100125] via 133.33.10.2, 00:00:45, Serial0
I       133.33.11.0/24 [100/10476] via 133.33.10.2, 00:00:45, Serial0
```

R5 is running only IGRP, and because the local interfaces are configured with the Class B network 133.33.0.0 with a Class C mask, R4 has been configured to send all networks as /24, as displayed in Example 9-29.

Example 9-30 demonstrates full IP connectivity by pinging all the loopback interfaces in Table 9-2 and some of the non-Class C networks, such as the subnets 133.33.7.0 and 133.3.1.0/29.

Example 9-30 *Pinging All Loopbacks on R5*

```
R5#ping 133.33.201.1

Type escape sequence to abort.
Sending 5, 100-byte ICMP Echos to 133.33.201.1, timeout is 2 seconds:
!!!!!
Success rate is 100 percent (5/5), round-trip min/avg/max = 32/32/36 ms
R5#ping 133.33.202.1
Type escape sequence to abort.
Sending 5, 100-byte ICMP Echos to 133.33.202.1, timeout is 2 seconds:
!!!!!
Success rate is 100 percent (5/5), round-trip min/avg/max = 32/32/32 ms
R5#ping 133.33.203.1
Type escape sequence to abort.
Sending 5, 100-byte ICMP Echos to 133.33.203.1, timeout is 2 seconds:
!!!!!
Success rate is 100 percent (5/5), round-trip min/avg/max = 28/32/36 ms
R5#ping 133.33.204.1
Type escape sequence to abort.
Sending 5, 100-byte ICMP Echos to 133.33.204.1, timeout is 2 seconds:
!!!!!
Success rate is 100 percent (5/5), round-trip min/avg/max = 16/16/16 ms
R5#ping 133.33.205.1
Type escape sequence to abort.

Sending 5, 100-byte ICMP Echos to 133.33.205.1, timeout is 2 seconds:
!!!!!
Success rate is 100 percent (5/5), round-trip min/avg/max = 1/2/4 ms
R5#ping 133.33.206.1
Type escape sequence to abort.
Sending 5, 100-byte ICMP Echos to 133.33.206.1, timeout is 2 seconds:
!!!!!
Success rate is 100 percent (5/5), round-trip min/avg/max = 32/32/32 ms
R5#ping 133.33.1.1
```

continues

Example 9-30 *Pinging All Loopbacks on R5 (Continued)*

```
Type escape sequence to abort.
Sending 5, 100-byte ICMP Echos to 133.33.1.1, timeout is 2 seconds:
!!!!!
Success rate is 100 percent (5/5), round-trip min/avg/max = 32/32/32 ms
R5#ping 133.33.7.1
Type escape sequence to abort.
Sending 5, 100-byte ICMP Echos to 133.33.7.1, timeout is 2 seconds:
!!!!!
Success rate is 100 percent (5/5), round-trip min/avg/max = 32/33/36 ms
R5#ping 133.33.7.2
Type escape sequence to abort.
Sending 5, 100-byte ICMP Echos to 133.33.7.2, timeout is 2 seconds:
!!!!!
Success rate is 100 percent (5/5), round-trip min/avg/max = 40/40/40 ms
R5#ping 133.33.7.5
Type escape sequence to abort.
Sending 5, 100-byte ICMP Echos to 133.33.7.5, timeout is 2 seconds:
!!!!!
Success rate is 100 percent (5/5), round-trip min/avg/max = 32/32/36 ms
```

Example 9-31 displays the EIGRP routing IP table on R6, which is running EIGRP in two domains: 1 and 2.

Example 9-31 **show ip route eigrp** *on R6*

```
R6#show ip route eigrp
     133.33.0.0/16 is variably subnetted, 26 subnets, 6 masks
D       133.33.204.0/24 [90/2297856] via 133.33.11.2, 00:02:34, Serial1
D EX    133.33.205.0/24 [90/2809856] via 133.33.11.2, 00:02:34, Serial1
D EX    133.33.201.0/24 [90/25632000] via 133.33.11.2, 00:00:35, Serial1
D EX    133.33.202.0/24 [90/25632000] via 133.33.11.2, 00:00:35, Serial1
D EX    133.33.203.0/24 [90/25632000] via 133.33.11.2, 00:00:35, Serial1
D EX    133.33.4.0/25 [90/25632000] via 133.33.11.2, 00:00:35, Serial1
D       133.33.4.0/24 [90/2169856] via 133.33.11.2, 00:02:35, Serial1
D       133.33.5.0/27 [90/2195456] via 133.33.11.2, 00:02:35, Serial1
D       133.33.5.0/24 [90/2169856] via 133.33.11.2, 00:02:35, Serial1
D EX    133.33.7.0/30 [90/25632000] via 133.33.11.2, 00:00:35, Serial1
D       133.33.7.0/24 [90/2169856] via 133.33.11.2, 00:02:35, Serial1
D EX    133.33.1.0/29 [90/25632000] via 133.33.11.2, 00:00:35, Serial1
D       133.33.1.0/24 [90/2169856] via 133.33.11.2, 00:02:35, Serial1
D EX    133.33.7.4/30 [90/25632000] via 133.33.11.2, 00:00:35, Serial1
D EX    133.33.3.0/25 [90/25632000] via 133.33.11.2, 00:00:36, Serial1
D       133.33.3.0/24 [90/2169856] via 133.33.11.2, 00:02:35, Serial1
D EX    133.33.7.8/30 [90/25632000] via 133.33.11.2, 00:00:36, Serial1
D EX    133.33.8.0/24 [90/2707456] via 133.33.11.2, 00:02:35, Serial1
D EX    133.33.9.0/24 [90/2707456] via 133.33.11.2, 00:02:35, Serial1
D       133.33.10.0/24 [90/2681856] via 133.33.11.2, 00:02:35, Serial1
D       133.33.7.12/30 [90/2681856] via 133.33.11.2, 00:02:35, Serial1
D EX    133.33.16.0/21 [90/25632000] via 133.33.11.2, 00:00:36, Serial1
D EX    133.33.24.0/21 [90/25632000] via 133.33.11.2, 00:00:37, Serial1
```

Example 9-32 displays the interfaces configured in EIGRP 1 and 2.

Example 9-32 show ip eigrp interfaces *on R6*

```
R6#show ip eigrp interfaces
IP-EIGRP interfaces for process 1
                    Xmit Queue   Mean   Pacing Time   Multicast     Pending
Interface   Peers   Un/Reliable  SRTT   Un/Reliable   Flow Timer    Routes
Se1           1        0/0        818       0/15         6287          0
IP-EIGRP interfaces for process 2
                    Xmit Queue   Mean   Pacing Time   Multicast     Pending
Interface   Peers   Un/Reliable  SRTT   Un/Reliable   Flow Timer    Routes
Et0           0        0/0         0        0/10          0           0
Lo0           0        0/0         0        0/10          0           0
```

Example 9-33 displays the EIGRP neighbors on R6.

Example 9-33 *EIGRP Neighbors on R6*

```
R6#show ip eigrp neighbors
IP-EIGRP neighbors for process 1
H   Address              Interface   Hold Uptime   SRTT   RTO   Q   Seq
                                     (sec)         (ms)         Cnt Num
0   133.33.11.2             Se1       10 03:06:26  818    4908   0   8
IP-EIGRP neighbors for process 2
```

Note that only one neighbor is pointing to R4. No EIGRP routers exist in domain 2.

Example 9-34 displays a successful ping request to all loopback interfaces in Figure 9-1.

Example 9-34 *Pinging Loopbacks on R6*

```
R6#ping 133.33.201.1
Type escape sequence to abort.
Sending 5, 100-byte ICMP Echos to 133.33.201.1, timeout is 2 seconds:
!!!!!
Success rate is 100 percent (5/5), round-trip min/avg/max = 32/32/36 ms
R6#ping 133.33.202.1
Type escape sequence to abort.
Sending 5, 100-byte ICMP Echos to 133.33.202.1, timeout is 2 seconds:
!!!!!
Success rate is 100 percent (5/5), round-trip min/avg/max = 32/32/36 ms
R6#ping 133.33.203.1
Type escape sequence to abort.
Sending 5, 100-byte ICMP Echos to 133.33.203.1, timeout is 2 seconds:
!!!!!
Success rate is 100 percent (5/5), round-trip min/avg/max = 32/32/32 ms
R6#ping 133.33.204.1
```

continues

Example 9-34 *Pinging Loopbacks on R6 (Continued)*

```
Type escape sequence to abort.
Sending 5, 100-byte ICMP Echos to 133.33.204.1, timeout is 2 seconds:
!!!!!
Success rate is 100 percent (5/5), round-trip min/avg/max = 16/16/16 ms
R6#ping 133.33.205.1
Type escape sequence to abort.
Sending 5, 100-byte ICMP Echos to 133.33.205.1, timeout is 2 seconds:
!!!!!
Success rate is 100 percent (5/5), round-trip min/avg/max = 32/32/32 ms
R6#ping 133.33.206.1
Type escape sequence to abort.
Sending 5, 100-byte ICMP Echos to 133.33.206.1, timeout is 2 seconds:
!!!!!
Success rate is 100 percent (5/5), round-trip min/avg/max = 1/2/4 ms
R6#
```

Telnet from the classful domain on R5 and ensure that you can telnet to all five remote routers. Example 9-35 displays an executive user telneting from R5 to all remote routers using the loopback interfaces in Table 9-2.

Example 9-35 *Telnet into R1, R2, R3, R4, and R6 from R5.*

```
R5>telnet 133.33.204.1
Trying 133.33.204.1 ... Open
R4>quit
[Connection to 133.33.204.1 closed by foreign host]
R5>telnet 133.33.206.1
Trying 133.33.206.1 ... Open
R6>quit
[Connection to 133.33.206.1 closed by foreign host]
R5>telnet 133.33.201.1
Trying 133.33.201.1 ... Open
R1>quit
[Connection to 133.33.201.1 closed by foreign host]
R5>telnet 133.33.202.1
Trying 133.33.202.1 ... Open
R2>quit
[Connection to 133.33.202.1 closed by foreign host]
R5>telnet 133.33.203.1
Trying 133.33.203.1 ... Open
R3>quit
[Connection to 133.33.203.1 closed by foreign host]
R5>telnet 133.33.204.1
Trying 133.33.204.1 ... Open
R4>quit
[Connection to 133.33.204.1 closed by foreign host]
R5>telnet 133.33.206.1
```

Example 9-35 *Telnet into R1, R2, R3, R4, and R6 from R5. (Continued)*

```
Trying 133.33.206.1 ... Open
R6>quit
[Connection to 133.33.206.1 closed by foreign host]
R5>
```

Telnet is an application layer protocol, so if you can telnet from the router, users on connected interfaces routed throughout this network also have full IP connectivity.

View the BGP tables on R1 and R2. Because IBGP is running among R1 (route reflector) and route reflector client, Routers R2–R6, the BGP tables on R3–R6 are exactly the same as R2. Therefore, only R2's BGP table is presented here for your reference.

Example 9-36 displays the BGP table on R1.

Example 9-36 show ip bgp *on R1*

```
R1#show ip bgp
BGP table version is 77, local router ID is 133.33.201.1
Status codes: s suppressed, d damped, h history, * valid, > best, i - internal
Origin codes: i - IGP, e - EGP, ? - incomplete
   Network          Next Hop          Metric LocPrf Weight Path
*> 0.0.0.0          171.108.1.5                       200 1024 i
*                   171.108.1.1                       100 1024 i
*> 1.0.0.0          171.108.1.5            0           200 400 300 200 1024 ?
*                   171.108.1.1            0           100 400 300 200 1024 ?
*> 2.0.0.0          171.108.1.5            0           200 400 300 200 1024 ?
*                   171.108.1.1            0           100 400 300 200 1024 ?
*> 3.0.0.0          171.108.1.5            0           200 400 300 200 1024 ?
*                   171.108.1.1            0           100 400 300 200 1024 ?
*> 4.0.0.0          171.108.1.5            0           200 400 300 200 1024 ?
*                   171.108.1.1            0           100 400 300 200 1024 ?
*> 5.0.0.0          171.108.1.5            0           200 400 300 200 1024 ?
*                   171.108.1.1            0           100 400 300 200 1024 ?
*> 6.0.0.0          171.108.1.5            0           200 400 300 200 1024 ?
*                   171.108.1.1            0           100 400 300 200 1024 ?
*> 7.0.0.0          171.108.1.5            0           200 400 300 200 1024 ?
*                   171.108.1.1            0           100 400 300 200 1024 ?
*> 8.0.0.0          171.108.1.5            0           200 400 300 200 1024 ?
*                   171.108.1.1            0           100 400 300 200 1024 ?
   Network          Next Hop          Metric LocPrf Weight Path
*> 10.0.0.0         171.108.1.5            0           200 1024 ?
*                   171.108.1.1            0           100 1024 ?
*> 11.0.0.0         171.108.1.5            0           200 1024 ?
*                   171.108.1.1            0           100 1024 ?
*> 100.0.0.0        171.108.1.5            0           200 1024 ?
*                   171.108.1.1            0           100 1024 ?
*> 101.0.0.0        171.108.1.5            0           200 1024 ?
*                   171.108.1.1            0           100 1024 ?
```

continues

Example 9-36 show ip bgp *on R1 (Continued)*

```
 *> 102.0.0.0       171.108.1.5             0           200 1024 ?
 *                  171.108.1.1             0           100 1024 ?
 *> 133.33.1.0/29   0.0.0.0                 0         32768 ?
 *> 133.33.3.0/25   133.33.7.2           1000         32768 ?
 *> 133.33.4.0/25   133.33.7.6            810         32768 ?
 *> 133.33.5.0/27   133.33.7.6           1610         32768 ?
 *> 133.33.7.0/30   0.0.0.0                 0         32768 ?
 *> 133.33.7.4/30   0.0.0.0                 0         32768 ?
 *> 133.33.7.8/30   133.33.7.2           1600         32768 ?
 *> 133.33.7.12/30  133.33.7.6           1600         32768 ?
 *> 133.33.16.0/24  0.0.0.0                 0         32768 ?
 *> 133.33.17.0/24  0.0.0.0                 0         32768 ?
 *> 133.33.18.0/24  0.0.0.0                 0         32768 ?
 *> 133.33.19.0/24  0.0.0.0                 0         32768 ?
    Network         Next Hop           Metric LocPrf Weight Path
 *> 133.33.20.0/24  0.0.0.0                 0         32768 ?
 *> 133.33.21.0/24  0.0.0.0                 0         32768 ?
 *> 133.33.22.0/24  0.0.0.0                 0         32768 ?
 *> 133.33.23.0/24  0.0.0.0                 0         32768 ?
 *> 133.33.24.0/21  133.33.7.2            801         32768 ?
 *> 133.33.201.0/24 0.0.0.0                 0         32768 ?
 *> 133.33.202.0/24 133.33.7.2            801         32768 ?
 *> 133.33.203.0/24 133.33.7.6            801         32768 ?
 *> 133.33.204.0/24 133.33.7.6           1601         32768 ?
 *> 141.100.0.0     171.108.1.5             0           200 1024 ?
 *                  171.108.1.1             0           100 1024 ?
 *> 141.108.0.0     171.108.1.5             0           200 1024 ?
 *                  171.108.1.1             0           100 1024 ?
 *> 142.100.0.0     171.108.1.5             0           200 1024 ?
 *                  171.108.1.1             0           100 1024 ?
 *> 143.100.0.0     171.108.1.5             0           200 1024 ?
 *                  171.108.1.1             0           100 1024 ?
 *> 144.100.0.0     171.108.1.5             0           200 1024 ?
 *                  171.108.1.1             0           100 1024 ?
 *> 145.100.0.0     171.108.1.5             0           200 1024 ?
 *                  171.108.1.1             0           100 1024 ?
 *> 146.100.0.0     171.108.1.5             0           200 1024 ?
    Network         Next Hop           Metric LocPrf Weight Path
 *                  171.108.1.1             0           100 1024 ?
 *> 147.100.0.0     171.108.1.5             0           200 1024 ?
 *                  171.108.1.1             0           100 1024 ?
 *> 148.100.0.0     171.108.1.5             0           200 1024 ?
 *                  171.108.1.1             0           100 1024 ?
 *> 149.100.0.0     171.108.1.5             0           200 1024 ?
 *                  171.108.1.1             0           100 1024 ?
 *> 171.108.1.0/30  0.0.0.0                 0         32768 ?
 *> 171.108.1.4/30  0.0.0.0                 0         32768 ?
```

Example 9-37 displays the BGP table on R2.

Example 9-37 show ip bgp *on R2*

```
R2#show ip bgp
BGP table version is 370, local router ID is 133.33.202.1
Status codes: s suppressed, d damped, h history, * valid, > best, i - internal
Origin codes: i - IGP, e - EGP, ? - incomplete

   Network          Next Hop         Metric LocPrf Weight Path
*>i0.0.0.0          133.33.201.1            100      0 1024 i
*>i1.0.0.0          133.33.201.1          0 100      0 400 300 200 1024 ?
*>i2.0.0.0          133.33.201.1          0 100      0 400 300 200 1024 ?
*>i3.0.0.0          133.33.201.1          0 100      0 400 300 200 1024 ?
*>i4.0.0.0          133.33.201.1          0 100      0 400 300 200 1024 ?
*>i5.0.0.0          133.33.201.1          0 100      0 400 300 200 1024 ?
*>i6.0.0.0          133.33.201.1          0 100      0 400 300 200 1024 ?
*>i7.0.0.0          133.33.201.1          0 100      0 400 300 200 1024 ?
*>i8.0.0.0          133.33.201.1          0 100      0 400 300 200 1024 ?
*>i10.0.0.0         133.33.201.1          0 100      0 1024 ?
*>i11.0.0.0         133.33.201.1          0 100      0 1024 ?
*>i100.0.0.0        133.33.201.1          0 100      0 1024 ?
*>i101.0.0.0        133.33.201.1          0 100      0 1024 ?
*>i102.0.0.0        133.33.201.1          0 100      0 1024 ?
*>i133.33.1.0/29    133.33.201.1          0 100      0 ?
*>i133.33.3.0/25    133.33.201.1       1000 100      0 ?
*>i133.33.4.0/25    133.33.201.1        810 100      0 ?
*>i133.33.5.0/27    133.33.201.1       1610 100      0 ?
   Network          Next Hop         Metric LocPrf Weight Path
*>i133.33.7.0/30    133.33.201.1          0 100      0 ?
*>i133.33.7.4/30    133.33.201.1          0 100      0 ?
*>i133.33.7.8/30    133.33.201.1       1600 100      0 ?
*>i133.33.7.12/30   133.33.201.1       1600 100      0 ?
*>i133.33.16.0/24   133.33.201.1          0 100      0 ?
*>i133.33.17.0/24   133.33.201.1          0 100      0 ?
*>i133.33.18.0/24   133.33.201.1          0 100      0 ?
*>i133.33.19.0/24   133.33.201.1          0 100      0 ?
*>i133.33.20.0/24   133.33.201.1          0 100      0 ?
*>i133.33.21.0/24   133.33.201.1          0 100      0 ?
*>i133.33.22.0/24   133.33.201.1          0 100      0 ?
*>i133.33.23.0/24   133.33.201.1          0 100      0 ?
*>i133.33.24.0/21   133.33.201.1        801 100      0 ?
*>i133.33.201.0/24  133.33.201.1          0 100      0 ?
*>i133.33.202.0/24  133.33.201.1        801 100      0 ?
*>i133.33.203.0/24  133.33.201.1        801 100      0 ?
*>i133.33.204.0/24  133.33.201.1       1601 100      0 ?
*>i141.100.0.0      133.33.201.1          0 100      0 1024 ?
*>i141.108.0.0      133.33.201.1          0 100      0 1024 ?
*>i142.100.0.0      133.33.201.1          0 100      0 1024 ?
*>i143.100.0.0      133.33.201.1          0 100      0 1024 ?
*>i144.100.0.0      133.33.201.1          0 100      0 1024 ?
```

continues

Example 9-37 show ip bgp *on R2 (Continued)*

```
   Network          Next Hop         Metric LocPrf Weight Path
*>i145.100.0.0      133.33.201.1          0    100      0 1024 ?
*>i146.100.0.0      133.33.201.1          0    100      0 1024 ?
*>i147.100.0.0      133.33.201.1          0    100      0 1024 ?
*>i148.100.0.0      133.33.201.1          0    100      0 1024 ?
*>i149.100.0.0      133.33.201.1          0    100      0 1024 ?
*>i171.108.1.0/30   133.33.201.1          0    100      0 ?
*>i171.108.1.4/30   133.33.201.1          0    100      0 ?
R2#
```

Example 9-38 displays the BGP peer sessions on R1 in summary format using the IOS **show ip bgp summary** command.

Example 9-38 show ip bgp summary *on R1*

```
R1#show ip bgp summary
BGP router identifier 133.33.201.1, local AS number 1
BGP table version is 77, main routing table version 77
47 network entries and 71 paths using 6455 bytes of memory
10 BGP path attribute entries using 1004 bytes of memory
BGP activity 266/219 prefixes, 533/462 paths

Neighbor        V    AS MsgRcvd MsgSent   TblVer  InQ OutQ Up/Down  State/PfxRcd
133.33.202.1    4     1     182     274       77    0    0 01:48:26           0
133.33.203.1    4     1     182     274       77    0    0 01:48:27           0
133.33.204.1    4     1     182     274       77    0    0 01:48:31           0
133.33.205.1    4     1     182     274       77    0    0 01:48:30           0
133.33.206.1    4     1     146     255       77    0    0 00:18:14           0
171.108.1.1     4  1024     229     322       77    0    0 01:48:17          24
171.108.1.5     4  1024     217     317       77    0    0 01:48:14          24
```

The shaded peers in Example 9-38 are route reflector clients to R1.

Example 9-39 displays the TCP sessions on R1 with the IOS **show tcp brief** command.

Example 9-39 show tcp brief *on R1*

```
R1#show tcp brief
TCB        Local Address         Foreign Address        (state)
812F0240   171.108.1.6.11074     171.108.1.5.179        ESTAB
812EFDC4   171.108.1.2.11073     171.108.1.1.179        ESTAB
8130B85C   r1.11071              r2.179                 ESTAB
812F1F10   r1.11070              r3.179                 ESTAB
813029BC   r1.179                R6.11001               ESTAB
81308298   r1.11069              R5.179                 ESTAB
812F1A94   r1.11068              R4.179                 ESTAB
```

R1 is configured with seven BGP TCP peers, and Example 9-39 confirms that BGP is configured with the TCP port number 179. (BGP uses TCP port 179.)

Summary

You have completed a complex routing topology, and although it may not be a network you will ever need to configure, you have discovered how to route IP with any routing protocol and subnet addressing.

IP routing algorithms are complex, and the ability to configure OSPF or RIP correctly and ensure network connectivity is a rare skill, not found in many engineers.

It is now up to you to take the skills you learned in this book and extend them further, even into areas you thought you could never master. For example, as a further exercise, you could modify the topology in Figure 9-1 and change the routing algorithms in use to see whether you can maintain a fully routable network.

Study Tips

This appendix is a short study guide, but it is by no means the only resource you should use to prepare for any Cisco certification. Provided here are some useful study tips.

Becoming Cisco certified in one of the certification tracks requires much more than simply picking up a manual or book and cramming or learning. Cisco certifications, including the most coveted CCIE examination, are regarded as the most difficult and well-respected IT certification exams in the world. CCNPs are highly regarded in the IT industry.

Taking any Cisco examination is not an exercise you want to do repeatedly. A typical computer-based exam costs approximately $250, so you do not want to attempt an exam more than once if you can help it.

This appendix provides some handy study tips.

Strategies for Cisco Exam Preparation

The first step, particularly if you're a beginner, is to determine your strengths and weaknesses. Self-analysis is one of the most difficult tasks to undertake. Be honest with yourself because the Cisco certification exams will be 100 percent honest with you. The exams require self-study and maybe even classroom training.

Cisco (www.cisco.com/warp/customer/10/wwtraining/training_over/) offers many training courses, so it's best to determine whether you need a training course to help lay the foundations.

Training courses are always packed with other candidates and offer a particular learning style, so you might not get the attention you require. If this is the case, self-study is where you will acquire most of your knowledge.

Cisco certification exams are computer-based. As such, they are constantly evolving and questions are changed, removed, or added at any time. Ensure that you are always updated about exam changes through the Cisco Web site.

Cisco computer-based examinations contain all multiple-choice questions. Typically, you are provided four or five possible answers, and some questions require more than one answer. Any incorrect answer you select results in zero points.

<table>
<tr><td>**NOTE**</td><td>The following link provides all the information you need on the Routing exam, including free sample examination questions:

www.cisco.com/warp/public/10/wwtraining/certprog/testing/current_exams/640-503.html

Download the free challenge test and grade yourself. This simple tool can be useful in determining weak areas before you even book the real examination.</td></tr>
</table>

In any multiple-choice examination, the process of elimination is important. To achieve time-management proficiency and the skills required to answer questions correctly, you must practice with a simulation that places you in an exam situation. (See the previous note for a sample simulation program.)

Typically, the questions have two options that initially appear to be correct, so you can quickly eliminate two or three options. If you can narrow the options to two choices, you give yourself a 50 percent chance of scoring the valuable points. The tests always include easy and hard questions, so if you come across a difficult question, mark the question for later review and move on to the next question. Time management is crucial; if you don't attempt every question, you are at a severe disadvantage because you will not score any points for questions you do not attempt.

Hands-On Experience

Almost all CCIE, CCNP, and CCNA engineers will tell you that hands-on experience with Cisco routers and switches is the most valuable learning tool. If you work daily with routers in your present job, ensure that you utilize your daily access to view how the network is functioning using the techniques presented in this guide.

By building a small practice lab, even with just two routers, you can study any routing algorithm using loopback interfaces, as discussed in several scenarios in this book.

Cisco Systems even provides lab access at various Cisco sites around the world, so you can view the technology and spend time configuring Cisco IOS features for free. Take advantage of this free access to try new configurations and get expert advice from local Cisco engineers. Contact your Cisco representative for more information.

Various Internet sites, too many to mention here, provide tuition and virtual labs. (These labs are called virtual but, in fact, are real Cisco devices.) You can hire and actually configure Cisco IOS routers and switches for a set fee. Point your search engine toward the keywords, Cisco virtual labs. Cisco provides an excellent product called Cisco Interactive Mentor (CIM). CIM is a virtual IOS simulator that enables you to configure a set number of IOS features without having to purchase expensive Cisco routers.

The following link provides more details about this virtual lab program:

www.cisco.com/warp/public/710/cim/index.html

Strategies for the Exam

This section covers some simple things you can do the day before and during the exam.

On the day before the exam, do the following things:

- Call Sylvan Prometrics or whomever is hosting your examination and confirm your seat, the time, and the location of the exam.
- Ensure that you have the correct directions for the testing center.
- Confirm that your photo ID will be accepted; it's best to take your passport so you will not have any problems.
- Have a relaxing evening. Some candidates attempt to cram in too much learning the night before at the cost of a good night's sleep. The examination questions are written by folks who want you to pick the first answer that looks good, so you need to be on your guard mentally.

On the exam day, do the following things:

- Leave plenty of time to get to the testing center; park and take a few moments to relax before the exam. Allow at least an extra hour for any traveling involved. Sometimes, you can go in early, so you can take advantage of your adrenaline rush if you arrive early.
- The testing center provides a pen and some form of writing paper, typically an erasable sheet. You are not allowed anything in the exam room, except a refreshment and the provided writing materials.
- Leave all those heavy books at home.
- Wear loose, comfortable clothing and take a sweater in case the room is too cold.

During the exam, do the following things:

- If you do not know the answer to a question, try answering the question by a process of elimination. Always attempt a question even if you are unsure of the correct answer. Mark questions you are unsure of or didn't answer so that you can return to them with a fresh perspective after you have worked through other questions.
- Use the materials provided to work out the logic of some questions. Typically, two answers will stand out, so try and eliminate the two obviously incorrect answers as soon as you can.
- Try to stay calm. Remember that you can take the exam multiple times, so even if you are struggling, you can use the exam to your advantage by remembering the topics that are not your strengths.

Immediately after the examination, write down the topics you were not comfortable with and the source materials you need to acquire that knowledge, even if you passed. What makes you a CCNP is passing a couple of exams, but what makes you a quality CCNP is the desire to extend your ability with every passing moment.

Cisco Certification Status

As soon as you pass all tests for a given Cisco certification, you attain that Cisco certification status. Cisco also generates transcripts that indicate which exams you have passed and your corresponding test scores. Cisco sends these transcripts to you. In addition, you receive a login ID and password, Cisco certification logos, and more (sometimes even a free shirt).

Tracking Cisco Certification Online

Cisco also provides online tracking, so you can track your status of any certification path at www.galton.com/~cisco/.

This Web site takes about seven days from your examination date to be updated. You can also download Certification logos for use on your business cards, and you can keep your demographic information up to date so you are always informed of any changes.

What to Do After CCNP?

This appendix covers some options for you after becoming a qualified Cisco Certified Network Professional.

You can pursue one more challenging step: the coveted Cisco Certified Internetwork Expert (CCIE) certification. Cisco introduced the CCNA and CCNP certifications so candidates can follow a preferred, gradually building path to the CCIE certification. However, CCNA and CCNP are not prerequisites to attempt the CCIE examination.

NOTE   If you are interested in leading training courses, another difficult certification option is Cisco Certified Systems Instructor (CCSI). This certification is aimed mainly at partners who supply the Cisco course material to the general public. For information, go to www.cisco.com/partner/training/course_channelpartners.shtml.

You need an account to access some of the URLs presented in this chapter. To obtain a guest account, visit www.cisco.com/pcgi-bin/register/main?page=start&relation=clnc.

The guest account also enables you to book a lab seat for the CCIE examination.

CCIE is regarded as the most sought-after certification in the industry today; more and more vendors are devising their own certification programs and trying to catch up to the industry-leading Cisco Systems. While working in the CCIE program every day for the past two years, I have seen the many changes and challenges facing potential CCIEs. As of September 30, 2001, there were approximately 6700 CCIEs. About 110 of these 6700 CCIEs hold more than one CCIE qualification. The majority of CCIEs are located in Europe and North America.

Before you decide to take this step, you need to be aware of the challenges in front of you. You cannot hope to become a CCIE by simply buying a book or a series of books. Hands-on experience is required; at least two years of internetworking experience is critical, and even then you must fully prepare for the difficult examination. Three varieties of CCIE certification are currently available:

- CCIE Routing and Switching (Released 1993)
- CCIE Security (Released August 2001)
- CCIE Communications and Services (Released August 2001)

This discussion concentrates on the Routing and Switching (R&S) certification, as newer certifications generally take months or even years to become well established. The Security examination is one examination you should also consider, especially considering today's climate of Internet firewall frailty and demand for security experts.

NOTE   For more information on the Security track, go to www.cisco.com/warp/customer/625/ccie/certifications/security.html.

For more information on the Communications and Services track, go to www.cisco.com/warp/customer/625/ccie/certifications/services.html.

Recently, four CCIE tracks were retired: ISP Dial, SNA, Design, and WAN Switching.

Steps Required to Achieve CCIE Certification

The CCIE program requires a candidate to perform two qualification steps:

Step 1   Pass a two-hour, computer-based qualification examination consisting of 100 questions. The passing mark is approximately 70 percent, but varies according to statistics and may float between 65-75 percent.

Step 2   Pass an eight-hour lab examination where the passing score is set at 80 percent. Historically, the lab examination was a full two-day lab; that changed in October 2001.

CCIE Qualification Exam Test Format

The CCIE Routing and Switching qualification exam uses the typical certification test format with multiple-choice questions that have one or more correct answers per question. What makes some of questions more difficult on the exam is that more than five answer choices are listed for all or most questions. This reduces the effectiveness of eliminating obviously incorrect answers and choosing from the remaining answers.

The topics tested include the following:

- Cisco device operation
- General networking theory

- Bridging and LAN switching
- Internet Protocol
- IP routing protocols
- Desktop protocols
- Performance management
- WAN (addressing, signaling, framing, and so on)
- LAN
- Security
- Multiservice

The blueprint for this examination is located at www.cisco.com/warp/customer/625/ccie/certifications/rsblueprint.html.

The two-hour, computer-based examination is similar to other Cisco certifications, although it is a little more difficult with many more in-depth questions. You can view some sample questions at www.cisco.com/warp/customer/625/ccie/certifications/sample_routing.html.

NOTE   Occasionally, Cisco announces a beta trial for the Routing and Switching qualification test, and if you book the test, you pay only a small fee compared to the standard fee of approximately $250. The following link has more information:

www.cisco.com/warp/customer/625/ccie/ccie_program/whatsnew.html

---

CCIE Lab Exam Test Format

Passing the qualification examination is the easier part of the CCIE exam journey. To pass the lab exam, your life needs to change dramatically, and you need to study on routers full time for at least three to six months. The good news is that the format of the lab examination has changed from two full days to one day only. You are no longer required to troubleshoot a network (regarded as the true method to test a CCIE's ability to restore a network back to full IP connectivity); you are now required to configure only a set number of features.

After you pass the qualification test, you are eligible to sit for the lab examination. You can book your lab examination online at the following address:

http://tools.cisco.com/CCIE/Schedule_Lab/jsp/login.jsp

The lab examination contains the following devices:

- 2500 series routers
- 2600 series routers

- 3600 series routers
- 4000 and 4500 series routers
- 3900 series Token Ring switches
- Catalyst 5000 series switches

Ensure that you practice with and understand these devices. Practice configuring almost every IOS feature, and fully understand what each IOS command actually enables, instead of relying on limited experience with certain commands. Anyone can configure a Cisco router, but the ability to understand the full consequence of a command is crucial to passing the CCIE Lab Examination.

CCIE Lab Exam Frequently Asked Questions

The following are some frequently asked questions regarding the difficult one-day CCIE Lab Examination:

1 When did the lab format change from two days to one day?

October 2001. All CCIE certification labs around the world are testing candidates in the new one-day format.

2 Where can I take the lab examination?

For locations and contact information, contact the following:

- **For lab locations in North America, South America, Europe, and Africa**

San Jose, California

Research Triangle Park, North Carolina

Halifax, Nova Scotia, Canada

Sao Paulo, Brazil

Brussels, Belgium

Johannesburg, South Africa

E-mail: ccie_ucsa@cisco.com

Tel: 1-800-829-6387 (select option 2) or 1-919-392-4525

Fax: 1-919-392-0166

- **For lab locations in Beijing China, and Singapore**

Tel: +86 10 6526 7777 Ext. 5710

Fax: +86 10 8518 2096

E-mail: ccie_apt@cisco.com

- **For lab locations in Chatswood, NSW, Australia, and Bangalore, India**

  Tel: +61 2 8446 6135

  Fax: +61 2 8448 7980

  E-mail: ccie_apt@cisco.com

- **For lab locations in Tokyo, Japan**

  Tel: +81-3-5324-4111

  Fax: +81-3-5324-4022

  E-mail: ccie@cisco.co.jp

3 What are the maximum score and the passing score required?

The total examination is worth 100 points and the passing grade is 80 percent. The passing rate for first attempts is low, so expect to take the examination more than once. Cisco will not release the passing rate.

4 What if I have a question and cannot find the answer?

E-mail your question to ccie@cisco.com. The CCIE team responds to all questions.

5 What happens after the exam?

You will be escorted outside the lab. You will receive an e-mail notification within 24 hours. The e-mail notification will notify you that the result of your lab attempt is available online at tools.cisco.com/CCIE/Schedule_Lab/jsp/login.jsp.

6 Can I use Notepad and Windows calculator?

Yes you can, but you are not permitted to save any files. You can cut and paste to and from Notepad, however. The calculator is useful for determining subnets and bit boundaries or converting hexadecimal to decimal.

7 How many times can I retake the lab examination?

You must allow 30 days between lab attempts. There is no limit on the number of lab attempts.

8 What happens if I pass?

In addition to becoming a CCIE, you also gain access to an exclusive CCIE chat forum and CCIE merchandise, and you get a CCIE medallion and certificate. Cisco also provides a forum accessible only by CCIE's at www.cisco.com/kobayashi/chat/cciechat.html, which allows you to communicate with other CCIEs from anywhere around the world.

The following URL provides more details on CCIE benefits:

www.cisco.com/warp/customer/625/ccie/recertifications/ccie_information.html

9 What happens if I fail? Am I told in which areas I scored poorly?

Cisco will not tell you specific areas of weakness; that is left to you to decipher from the brief score report. You can, however, pay a fee to have your lab routers re-examined for accuracy. Even with a regrade, no additional information is provided to you; you're provided only a brief score report through e-mail with your new grade, pass or fail.

10 What materials can I bring into the lab?

You are permitted to bring only necessary medication and a dictionary. No other materials are permitted. Cisco provides refreshments at all CCIE lab sites. Lunch is also provided.

11 What is the role of the proctor?

You can seek clarification from a proctor if you do not understand a question or the objective of a question. The proctor will not provide answers but will ensure you understand the question. The proctor may also make any changes required in case of network hardware failures or examination mistakes. At the end of the day, you are provided an electronic feedback form so that you can make any comment on the lab exam or proctor. The proctor is there to ensure that you have the best possible chance of success and should not hinder your ability to pass the test. If you feel otherwise, you can e-mail your concerns to ccie@cisco.com.

12 Where can I find out more about CCIE and all the different certification tracks?

The following URL provides all the material required for any of the three main CCIE tracks:

www.cisco.com/warp/customer/625/ccie/

Answers to Review Questions

This appendix contains the answers to each chapter's review questions. The original questions are included for your convenience. The answers are in bold.

Chapter 1

1 Given the following host address and subnet mask combinations, determine the subnet address and broadcast addresses:

- 131.108.1.24 255.255.255.0
- 151.108.100.67 255.255.255.128
- 171.199.100.10 255.255.255.224
- 161.88.40.54 255.255.255.192

Performing a logical AND reveals the following:

- **Subnet 131.18.1.0 and broadcast address 131.108.1.255**
- **Subnet 151.108.100.0 and broadcast address 151.108.1.127**
- **Subnet 171.199.100.0 and broadcast address 171.199.100.31**
- **Subnet 161.88.40.0 and broadcast address 161.88.40.63**

2 Given the network 141.56.80.0 and a subnet mask of 255.255.254.0, how many hosts are available on this subnet?

Using the formula $2^n-2 = 2^9-2 = 512$ hosts, the subnet mask 255.255.254.0 borrows nine (or n) bits from the subnet mask.

3 What is the broadcast address for the subnet 131.45.1.0/24?

The broadcast address is 131.145.1.255 where 255 represents all binary 1s.

4 What is the purpose of the broadcast address in any given subnet?

The main purpose of a broadcast address in the case of IP is to send out onto the wire a packet that all hosts common to the particular subnets will see and receive. Cisco routers drop broadcasts unless you configure bridging.

5 Given the subnet in binary notation 1111111.11111111.00000000.00000000, what is the decimal equivalent?

The decimal equivalent is 255.255.0.0, or a Class B address.

6 Which routing protocols support VLSM and why?

RIPv2, OSPF, IS-IS, EIGRP, and BGP. These routing protocols support VLSM because the routing protocols send the subnet mask as part of any routing update.

7 Which routing protocols do not support VLSM?

IGRP and RIP I. The only way to overcome this is to use a combination of static IP routes or a default route.

8 Which subnet mask provides approximately 1022 hosts?

$2^{n}-2 = 1022$, or $2^{n}=1024$. The number of bits required in the subnet mask is 10 bits, or the subnet mask 255.255.252.0 (1111111.11111111.11111100.00000000).

9 What is the equivalent subnet mask for the notation 131.108.1.0/24?

The slash notation is common in today's documentation and on Cisco IOS, the slash bit notation represents the number of bits assigned to the subnet mask: /24 means 24 bits. In binary this is 11111111.11111111.11111111.00000000 or 255.255.255.0.

10 Identify the private address ranges defined in RFC 1918?

RFC 1918 defines three major classes for private use, which are address ranges that are not routable in the Internet. The following are the three private ranges:

- **Class A: 10.0.0.0-10.255.255.255**
- **Class B: 172.16.0.0-172.16.255.255**
- **Class C:192.168.1-192.168.255.255**

It is common in large organizations to utilize the private Class A address and use public addresses only on the Internet connection using Network Address Translation (NAT).

Chapter 2

1 What information is stored in an IP routing table as seen by R1?

RIP routing entries and connected routes.

2 Which command do you use to view only RIP routes?

show ip route rip or sh ip ro r.

3 Which command do you use to view only connected routes?

show ip route connected or sh ip ro c.

4 How many subnets are known by R1 using the Class B network 131.108.0.0/16?

There are nine subnets using two masks, 255.255.255.0 (or /24) and 255.255.255.252 (or /30).

5 From R1, a ping test is sent to three remote networks. Is the ping test successful or not? Explain why or why not?

The ping tests to remote networks 131.108.7.0/24, 131.108.8.0/24, and 131.108.9.0/24 are all successful because the 5 ICMP packets are all reachable as displayed by the five ! characters.

6 Why is the command **version 2** configured on each router?

Because you are using two types of masks, or VLSM. RIPv1 does not understand VLSM, so RIPv2 has been enabled to cater to the 30-bit mask between the routers.

7 Each remote routing entry is labeled with the following information: [120/1]. What does the 120 represent and what does the 1 represent?

The 120 is the default administrative distance or trustworthiness of the information, and 1 represents the hop count to reach the remote network. In this case, all the remote networks are 1 hop count away.

8 Besides a ping test, what other methods could you use to ensure connectivity to the remote networks?

You can use the telnet application or the trace command to ensure connectivity.

Chapter 3

1 Which information is stored in an IP routing table as seen by R1?

OSPF routing entries and connected routes.

2 Which command do you use to view only OSPF routes?

show ip route ospf, which can be truncated as sh ip ro os.

3 How many subnets are known by R1 using the Class B networks 131.108.0.0/16 and 141.108.0.0/16?

There are eight subnets using three masks for the Class B address 141.108.0.0. There are nine subnets using three different masks for the Class B network 131.108.0.0.

4 What path is taken to the remote network 141.108.100.1/24?

R1's routing table has no entry for the network 141.108.100.1, and because there is no default network or gateway of last resort, packets to this network are dropped.

5 Why is the remote network 141.108.6.0/32 displayed as learned through the denotation: O IA?

O IA indicates this remote network is learned through OSPF (O) and resides in an area not local to the router (IA). In other words, this is an intra-area OSPF route.

6 What is the cost associated with the remote network 131.108.33.0/24 [110/74]?

The cost is 74 and the administrative distance is 110.

Chapter 4

1 What does the routing entry shaded in Example 4-64 display?

The IP route labeled as R* means that any IP packet designated for a remote destination not specifically listed in the IP routing table is to be sent to the next hop address of 141.108.1.4 (router Simon). This is commonly referred to as the Gateway of Last Resort (GOLR). This is typically Internet-based traffic. The gateway of last resort is also set to 141.108.1.4.

2 In Example 4-64, what is the hop count or metric to the remote network 141.108.2.0/24?

The RIP metric is set to 2. The actual hop count is set by the ASBR (router Simon) in Figure 4-8. Simon is configured to set all networks with a hop count of 2 by using the command redistribute ospf 1 metric 2.

3 What path does the packet sent to the IP subnet 171.108.255.0/24 take?

Because this network is not listed in Sydney's IP routing table, the packet is sent to the default routing entry or the next hop address of 141.108.1.4.

4 What type of OSPF routers are the Routers Simon, Mel, and SanFran?

Simon is a backbone OSPF router in area 0, as well as a router that performs route redistribution (an ASBR).

Mel is contained within one area only and because that area is the backbone, Mel is a backbone router.

SanFran is also a backbone router, but it supplies a default router and can also be classed as an ASBR.

5 Why are static routes injected into the router named Simon?

Static routes are configured on this ASBR to install them into the IP routing table. Because Simon has more specific routing entries, namely 141.108.3.1/29 and 141.108.4.1/28, the longest match rule is used to route packets to the remote networks. Example 4-65 displays the IP routing table on Simon.

Example 4-65 *Simon's IP Routing Table*

```
Simon#show ip route

Gateway of last resort is 141.108.255.2 to network 0.0.0.0

     141.108.0.0/16 is variably subnetted, 10 subnets, 5 masks
C       141.108.255.4/30 is directly connected, Serial2
O       141.108.255.0/24 is a summary, 00:12:23, Null0
C       141.108.255.0/30 is directly connected, Serial3
C       141.108.1.0/24 is directly connected, Ethernet1
S       141.108.3.0/24 is directly connected, Null0
O       141.108.3.0/29 [110/74] via 141.108.255.6, 00:31:46, Serial2
C       141.108.2.0/25 is directly connected, Ethernet0
S       141.108.4.0/24 is directly connected, Null0
O       141.108.2.0/24 is a summary, 00:12:23, Null0
O       141.108.4.0/28 [110/74] via 141.108.255.2, 00:31:47, Serial3
O       141.108.2.0/24 is a summary, 00:12:23, Null0
```

6 How many OSPF neighbor adjacencies do you expect to see on the router named Simon?

There should be two OSPF neighbors: one to SanFran and one to Mel. Configure the command ip ospf domain-lookup in global configuration mode to allow OSPF to assign a name to an IP address.

Example 4-66 displays the OSPF neighbors on the router Simon.

Example 4-66 show ip ospf neighbor *Command on Simo*

```
Simon#show ip ospf neighbor

Neighbor ID     Pri   State        Dead Time   Address         Interface
mel               1   FULL/  -     00:00:30    141.108.255.6   Serial2
sanfran           1   FULL/  -     00:00:30    141.108.255.2   Serial3
```

7 Two methods are used in OSPF to summarize IP networks. What are they and what IOS command is used to provide summarization?

Inter-area summarization with area *area id* range *mask* command.

External summarization with the IOS command summary *network mask* command.

8 Why does creating areas reduce the size of the OSPF database?

Reducing the number of areas leads to the reduction of SPF calculations and, in turn, reduces the topology table. Changes are less likely to occur within a small group of routers than in a large group, leading to fewer SPF calculations as well.

Chapter 5

Example 5-79 displays the detailed paths to the three remote networks, 171.109.1.0, 171.109.2.0, and 171.109.3.0/24, as seen by the router SanFran along with a successful **ping** to the remote networks.

Example 5-79 show ip route *and* **ping** *on SanFran*

```
SanFran#show ip route 171.109.1.0
Routing entry for 171.109.0.0/22
  Known via "eigrp 1", distance 90, metric 409600, type internal
  Redistributing via eigrp 1
  Last update from 131.108.1.2 on Ethernet0/0, 00:13:26 ago
  Routing Descriptor Blocks:
  * 131.108.1.2, from 131.108.1.2, 00:13:26 ago, via Ethernet0/0
      Route metric is 409600, traffic share count is 1
      Total delay is 6000 microseconds, minimum bandwidth is 10000 Kbit
      Reliability 255/255, minimum MTU 1500 bytes
      Loading 1/255, Hops 1
SanFran#ping 171.109.1.1
Type escape sequence to abort.
Sending 5, 100-byte ICMP Echos to 171.109.1.1, timeout is 2 seconds:
!!!!!
Success rate is 100 percent (5/5), round-trip min/avg/max = 1/2/4 ms
SanFran#show ip route 171.109.2.0
Routing entry for 171.109.0.0/22
  Known via "eigrp 1", distance 90, metric 409600, type internal
  Redistributing via eigrp 1
  Last update from 131.108.1.2 on Ethernet0/0, 00:13:32 ago
  Routing Descriptor Blocks:
  * 131.108.1.2, from 131.108.1.2, 00:13:32 ago, via Ethernet0/0
      Route metric is 409600, traffic share count is 1
      Total delay is 6000 microseconds, minimum bandwidth is 10000 Kbit
      Reliability 255/255, minimum MTU 1500 bytes
      Loading 1/255, Hops 1
SanFran#ping 171.109.2.1
Type escape sequence to abort.
```

Example 5-79 **show ip route** *and* **ping** *on SanFran (Continued)*

```
Sending 5, 100-byte ICMP Echos to 171.109.2.1, timeout is 2 seconds:
!!!!!
Success rate is 100 percent (5/5), round-trip min/avg/max = 1/2/4 ms
SanFran#show ip route 171.109.3.0
Routing entry for 171.109.0.0/22
  Known via "eigrp 1", distance 90, metric 409600, type internal
  Redistributing via eigrp 1
  Last update from 131.108.1.2 on Ethernet0/0, 00:13:38 ago
  Routing Descriptor Blocks:
  * 131.108.1.2, from 131.108.1.2, 00:13:38 ago, via Ethernet0/0
      Route metric is 409600, traffic share count is 1
      Total delay is 6000 microseconds, minimum bandwidth is 10000 Kbit
      Reliability 255/255, minimum MTU 1500 bytes
      Loading 1/255, Hops 1
SanFran#ping 171.109.3.1
Type escape sequence to abort.
Sending 5, 100-byte ICMP Echos to 171.109.3.1, timeout is 2 seconds:
!!!!!
Success rate is 100 percent (5/5), round-trip min/avg/max = 1/3/4 ms
```

If you perform a **show ip route** of the network 171.109.4.0/24 on SanFran, you see the output displayed in Example 5-80.

Example 5-80 **show ip route 171.109.4.0** *on SanFran*

```
SanFran#show ip route 171.109.4.0
% Subnet not in table
```

The reason that subnet 4 is not included in the IP routing table is that the summary address configured on the router Sydney includes only the subnets 1, 2, and 3.

1 Example 5-79 displays the IP routing table of the Router SanFran. Which networks does the entry 171.109.0.0/22 embrace?

    The /22 indicates a mask of 255.255.252.0 when applied to the Class B address 171.109.0.0. In binary, 252 is 1111 11100. The last three bits includes the networks 1 (00000001), 2 (00000010), and 3 (00000011). Notice, the last two are not the same, but the first six are (11111100 is 252). Example 5-79 confirms connectivity by displaying detailed IP route entries for the remote networks 171.109.1.0/24, 171.109.2.0, and 171.109.3.0/24 on SanFran.

2 What is the default administrative distance for EIGRP internal routes?

    The default value is 90, which is more trusted than OSPF at 110. Cisco IOS developers figure that their own routing protocol is more trustworthy than OSPF, an industry standard.

3 Which IOS command is used to display the output in Example 5-81?

Example 5-81 *Neighbors Output*

```
IP-EIGRP neighbors for process 1
H   Address             Interface    Hold Uptime    SRTT    RTO  Q   Seq
                                     (sec)          (ms)         Cnt Num
0   131.108.1.2         Et0/0          11 00:18:37    4    200  0   353
```

Example 5-81 displays adjacent EIGRP neighbors with the show ip eigrp neighbors command.

4 Why does EIGRP need to be manually configured to redistribute into another autonomous system?

EIGRP manually redistributes only between IGRP in the same AS. Manual redistribution is required between different autonomous systems or routing domains.

5 When is the EIGRP topology table updated?

Whenever a change occurs in the network, such as a network failure, the EIGRP topology table is updated by update packets sent to all EIGRP routers in the same AS.

6 What is the purpose of the command **no auto-summary**?

The no auto-summary command enables you to transmit subprefix routing information across classful network boundaries, and it disables automatic summarization of subnet routes into network-level routes.

7 What is the **variance** command used for?

The variance command, under the EIGRP process, is used to allow additional paths to a remote destination when the composite metric is not the same.

8 What does the term Stuck in Active mean?

Stuck in Active (SIA) is not a good network condition because the EIGRP router places the network in an active state (in the EIGRP topology table) and sends out a query to a neighbor; a failure to reply leaves the router in an active state. In the end, the EIGRP neighbors are reset, resulting in network down times and the loss of IP data.

Chapter 6

1 Which IOS command clears all BGP sessions on a Cisco router?

clear ip bgp *.

2 Which IOS command is used to enable BGP4 on a Cisco router?

router bgp *as*.

3 Example 6-82 displays the output from the **show tcp brief** command. How many BGP sessions are in use?

Example 6-82 *show tcp brief*

```
R2>show tcp brief
TCB        Local Address          Foreign Address        (state)
613EE508   131.108.255.6.11009    131.108.255.5.179      ESTAB
613ED584   131.108.255.2.11008    131.108.255.1.179      ESTAB
611654BC   161.108.1.1.23         131.108.255.1.11051    ESTAB
```

There are two BGP TCP sessions (the foreign TCP port number is 179). Port 23 (local port) is used by Telnet.

4 Which path is chosen to the remote network 131.108.1.0/24 in Example 6-83?

Use Example 6-83 to answer questions 4-6. Example 6-83 displays the BGP table on a Cisco BGP router.

Example 6-83 show ip bgp

```
R2>show ip bgp
BGP table version is 21, local router ID is 161.108.1.1
Status codes: s suppressed, d damped, h history, * valid, > best, i - internal
Origin codes: i - IGP, e - EGP, ? - incomplete
   Network         Next Hop         Metric LocPrf Weight Path
*  131.108.1.0/24   131.108.255.5      100    200    200 1 ?
*>                  131.108.255.1      100    200    200 1 ?
*  131.108.101.0/24 131.108.255.5      100    200    200 1 ?
*>                  131.108.255.1      100    200    200 1 ?
*> 161.108.1.0/24   0.0.0.0              0           32768 i
```

The path chosen is indicated by > on the left side of the BGP table, which indicates the next hop address 131.108.255.1.

5 Which autonomous system does the network 131.108.101.0/24 originate from?

The path is indicated by 1 ?, or AS 1.

6 What is the metric and local preference for the remote network 131.108.101.0/24?

The metric is set to 100 (lower is preferred) and the local preference is 200 (higher values preferred).

7 Example 6-84 displays the output from the **show ip bgp summary** command for a Cisco BGP-enabled router. What is the BGP autonomous system that R2 resides in? How many BGP sessions are active, and what version of BGP is configured on the router named R2?

Example 6-84 show ip bgp summary *on R2*

```
R2>show ip bgp summary
BGP router identifier 161.108.1.1, local AS number 2
BGP table version is 21, main routing table version 21
20 network entries and 39 paths using 3028 bytes of memory
4 BGP path attribute entries using 432 bytes of memory
BGP activity 61/41 prefixes, 119/80 paths
Neighbor        V    AS MsgRcvd MsgSent  TblVer  InQ OutQ Up/Down  State/PfxRcd
131.108.255.1   4     1    2755    2699      21    0    0 1d20h           19
131.108.255.5   4     1    2755    2699      21    0    0 1d20h           19
```

R2's local AS number is 2 and the number of active BGP sessions is two because the state is blank. The version of BGP in use is 4, the default setting.

8 On a Cisco router, what value is preferred, higher or lower weight, and what is the range of values for weight?

Higher weight values are preferred, and the range of values for weight is 0–294967295. The default value is 0.

9 What are the terms *peer* or *neighbor* used to describe in BGP?

A peer or neighbor indicates a TCP session between two BGP routers.

10 What is the BGP table?

The BGP table is a collection of local and remote network entries describing the next hop address, local preference, weight, and AS path. Based on these entries, networks are inserted into the IP routing table.

Chapter 7

1 What does a route reflector do to nonclient IBGP peers?

A route reflector reflects information to only configured clients. All other peers must be fully meshed.

2 What is a BGP cluster?

***Cluster* is a term used to describe a router reflector and the configured route reflector clients. Route reflectors are used in IBGP networks only.**

3 How is a route reflector client configured for IBGP?

Route reflector clients are configured for normal IBGP peering. The route reflector has additional commands to ensure that updates are reflected from one route reflector client to another.

4 Which IOS command is used to display the following output?

```
BGP table version is 61, local router ID is 131.108.254.4
Status codes: s suppressed, d damped, h history, * valid, > best, i - internal
Origin codes: i - IGP, e - EGP, ? - incomplete

   Network          Next Hop          Metric LocPrf Weight Path
*> 0.0.0.0          171.108.1.5                        0 100 i
*> 141.108.1.0/24   0.0.0.0                0        32768 i
```

This display is a BGP table and is output when the IOS show ip bgp command is used in exec or privileged mode.

5 How many TCP peers are required in a 1000 IBGP network?

The number of peers without the use of route reflectors is n(n-1)/2, where n is the number of BGP routers. For example, with 1000 BGP routers, the number of peers is 1000(999)/2 = 499500. With the use of route reflectors, you would only need 999 peers (use the formulae (n-1) where n is the number of routers), which is only 0.2 percent of the same fully meshed network.

6 Provide the IOS command syntax to enable a default route to be sent to a remote peer.

neighbor *peer ip -address* default-originate.

7 To display route reflector clients, which **show** command(s) can you use, if any?

To view route reflectors, you can use two methods on the route reflector: one is to use the IOS show ip bgp neighbors command, and the second is to view the running configuration with the IOS show running-config command.

8 View the following BGP table. What is the originating AS for the remote preferred path to the remote network 141.108.1.0/24?

```
R5#show ip bgp
BGP table version is 22, local router ID is 171.108.1.2
Status codes: s suppressed, d damped, h history, * valid, > best, i - internal
Origin codes: i - IGP, e - EGP, ? - incomplete

   Network          Next Hop          Metric LocPrf Weight Path
*> 141.108.1.0/24   171.108.1.1          200        2000 100 300 i
*> 151.108.1.0/24   0.0.0.0                0        32768 i
*> 171.108.0.0      171.108.1.1          200        2000 100 ?
```

Cisco IOS always displays the AS path taken, and in this example, the path traversed to reach the remote network 141.108.1.0 is through the AS 2000, then 100, and originating from AS 300.

9 Using a route map, which IOS command sets the weight and local preference attribute to 100?

First, you must define a route map with an arbitrary name (ccnp in this example) and then complete the following set of commands:

```
R5(config)#route-map ?
  WORD  Route map tag

R5(config)#route-map ccnp
R5(config-route-map)#set weight 100
R5(config-route-map)#set local
R5(config-route-map)#set local-preference 100
```

After defining the route map, you must apply it to remote BGP peers on the inbound or outbound direction required.

10 Can you set the BGP attribute **next-hop-self** to both EBGP and IBGP peers?

No. The next-hop-self attribute is used for IBGP peers only. The IOS command to set this attribute to remote peers is neighbor *ip-address* next-hop-self.

Chapter 8

1 How many IP routing tables are there when more than one routing protocol is configured on a Cisco router?

There is only one IP routing table, which can include routing information dynamically discovered using OSPF or RIP. For example, the following indicates all the possible routing methods on a Cisco router:

```
Codes: C - connected, S - static, I - IGRP, R - RIP, M - mobile, B - BGP
       D - EIGRP, EX - EIGRP external, O - OSPF, IA - OSPF inter area
       N1 - OSPF NSSA external type 1, N2 - OSPF NSSA external type 2
       E1 - OSPF external type 1, E2 - OSPF external type 2, E - EGP
       i - IS-IS, L1 - IS-IS level-1, L2 - IS-IS level-2, * - candidate default
       U - per-user static route, o - ODR
```

2 Which path is preferred if OSPF and EIGRP have dynamically discovered a remote network?

The Cisco IOS gives administrative distance first priority given. EIGRP AD is 90 and OSPF is 110. The lower AD is more trustworthy, so the Cisco IOS chooses EIGRP. You can change the default AD values by using the IOS distance command.

3 What common methods are used to control routing updates and filtering?

The main methods are passive interfaces, distribution lists, and route maps.

4 What is the metric used by OSPF, and is the lower or higher metric the chosen path?

OSPF's metric is cost (ranging from 1 to 65535). The lower cost is always preferred to a remote destination.

5 Is a static route always preferred over a directly connected route?

No, directly connected interfaces have an AD of 0, compared to 1 for static routes. Lower ADs are always preferred.

6 Which command stops updates from being sent out of any interface?

passive-interface *interface* **stops updates from being sent, although, updates are still received and processed.**

7 Which parameter does the Cisco IOS always compare before looking at routing metrics, such as hop count or OSPF cost?

Before looking at routing protocol metrics, Cisco IOS chooses any remote path by comparing administrative distance. For example, EIGRP (AD 90) is preferred over OSPF (AD 110) routers. Lower ADs are always preferred.

8 Give three examples of classful protocols.

OSPF, BGP, and IS-IS are common examples.

9 Give two examples of classless protocols?

RIP and IGRP are classless protocols.

10 What are the three methods commonly applied to avoid routing loops when redistribution is required?

The three methods are as follows:

Passive interfaces—A passive interface is a Cisco interface configured for routing, but it does not send any routing information on the outbound interface. Routing information (if any) is still received and processed normally.

Distribution lists—Distribution lists define which networks are permitted or denied when receiving or sending routing updates. Distribution lists require that you configure access lists to define which networks are permitted or denied.

Route maps—Route maps can also be used to define which networks are permitted or denied. Route maps can also be used along with access lists to define which networks are permitted or denied when you apply match statements under any route map configuration options.

CCIE Preparation—Sample Multiprotocol Lab

This appendix is designed to assist you in your final preparation for the most widely sought after certification in the world today, CCIE (Routing and Switching).

Today, many published books describe how to achieve CCIE, but in reality, no matter how many books you purchase, it all comes down to your level of hands-on experience. The strict nondisclosure agreement policed by Cisco ensures that candidates do not share any information about the lab content. Therefore, you'll know little about the lab content before your first attempt. In fact, the FBI has been involved in recent cases in which individuals have been jailed for selling information directly related to CCIE lab examinations.

The CCIE team has approved a sample CCIE multiprotocol lab for inclusion in this book so that you can be aware of the level of difficulty you must prepare to encounter when attempting the CCIE lab. Solutions are not provided in this book per a request from Cisco's CCIE department, so you must research the various solutions on your own.

The end goal of any CCIE lab is a working network solution. You might be restricted in the way you provide a working solution, as you will discover in this sample CCIE lab.

Candidates who prepare for the CCIE lab often ask me how to best prepare for the lab. My answer to them is to practice and configure every feature available and then practice even more. Of course, not every feature is tested, and you are encouraged to read the most up-to-date information on the Web at www.cisco.com/warp/customer/625/ccie/.

You must be able to provide a working solution quickly and adhere to the guidelines stated in the lab. A good analogy is a driving test. Imagine you are asked to drive down a 100-mile length of perfectly straight road. Imagine every 100 feet, a sign indicates a possible action you must take. The exam designer does not necessarily ask about the best solution, and you must have a broad knowledge of all IOS features to configure challenging and difficult scenarios.

The CCIE lab changed dramatically in format in October 2001 from a two-day lab to a one-day lab. A CCIE candidate is no longer required to sit through a separate troubleshooting section but must configure a network in eight hours.

One of the most critical skills in the new CCIE lab format is time management. Therefore, in this guide, each section describes the time constraints within which you should complete that section. This lab is designed to be completed within eight hours. If a section has no time allocation, that section has already been completed for you in the real CCIE lab. For example, this sample lab asks you to physically cable the network. No time allocation is provided, because in the real CCIE lab, the physical cabling is already completed for you.

NOTE   This sample lab incorporates many of the technologies and concepts covered in this guide, but often at an elevated level. Because this appendix covers a sample CCIE lab, the exercises presented in this lab require a broad perspective and knowledge base and experience that goes beyond even the practical examples presented earlier in this guide.

Figures D-1 and D-2 show the topology and assignments for this sample lab.

Figure D-1   *CCIE Lab Topology*

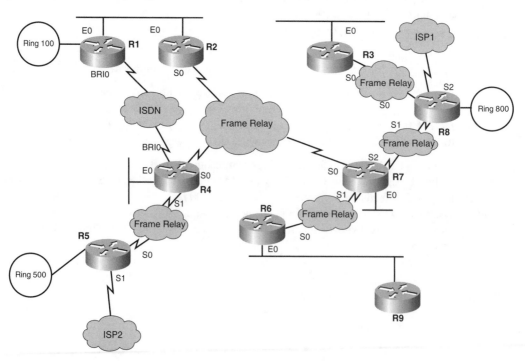

Figure D-2 *Frame Relay DLCI Assignment*

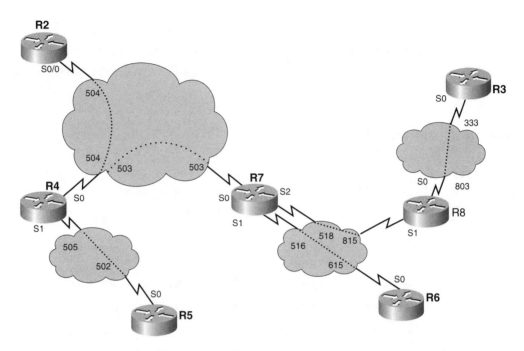

Basic Setup (1 Hour)

Configure the network in Figure D-1 for basic physical connectivity.

Communications Server (0.25 Hours)

Configure the communication server so that when you type the host name of a router on the server, you are connected across the console port to that router:

- Set up the routers as shown in Figure D-1.
- Configure R1 as the communication server by using the **ip host** command.

- Communication server ports 2 through 8 are connected to routers R2 through R8, respectively.
- Communication server port 9 connects to the Catalyst Ethernet switch.
- Communication server port 10 connects to the Catalyst Token Ring switch.
- R9 is a Catalyst 6509 switch with a Multilayer Switch Feature Card (MSFC) module installed.

Physical Connectivity (No Time)

NOTE From October 1, 2001 onward, a CCIE candidate is not required to cable the lab network physically. Therefore, no time allocation is given to this section. This section is added for completeness only.

You network is already physically patched. Construct your network as shown in Figure D-1.

Configure the following characteristics for the topology in Figure D-1:

- All rings should be set to 16 Mbps and should have an MTU size of 1500.
- All serial links between routers are connected through a Frame Relay switch.
- Routers R1 and R4 are connected to an ISDN service with the switch type defined as basic-5ess. R1 connects to number plan 0298017705, and R4 connects to number plan 0296307050.
- Routers R1, R2, R3, R4, R6, and R7 are connected to the Catalyst Ethernet switch (Catalyst 6509 series switch).
- Routers R1, R5, and R8 are connected to the Catalyst Token Ring switch (Catalyst 3900 series switch).

Catalyst Ethernet Switch Setup I (0.25 Hours)

Configure the Ethernet switch for five VLANs:

- VLAN 2, named VLAN_A, is connected to R1 and R2.
- VLAN 3, named VLAN_B, is connected to R3.
- VLAN 4, named VLAN_C, is connected to R4.
- VLAN 6, named VLAN_D, is connected to R6 and R9.
- VLAN 7, named VLAN_E, is connected to R7.

Using VLAN_A, configure the management interface SC0 with the address 131.108.0.2/25. Ensure that all devices in your network can telnet to the switch even if R1 or R2 is down.

Ensure that the switch is configured in the VTP domain Cisc0_vTp and the switch can create and delete VLANs in the future.

Catalyst Ethernet Switch Setup II (0.25 Hours)

Configure the following spanning-tree parameters on the Catalyst 6509:

- Ensure that the switch never becomes the root bridge on VLAN_D.
- Ensure that the switch has the best possible chance of becoming the root bridge in VLAN_E.
- Set all Ethernet ports to forward data immediately after a device is plugged in or activated.
- Set the hello time on VLAN_B to 10 seconds.

Configure the following miscellaneous parameters:

- Disable Cisco Discovery Protocol on ports 3/1-8.
- Ensure that any IP phones installed or connected to Card 3 are supplied inline power.
- Ensure that the switches get a clock source from R1 using NTP.
- Ensure that the only MAC address permitted to access the switch on port 3/3 is the MAC address 2010-2010-2010 or 4000-0000-4000.
- Disable power redundancy on the switch.
- Warn all Telnet clients that any "unauthorized access is not permitted" by displaying a warning message when any Telnet session is activated to the SC0 interface only.
- If any ports become disabled because of hardware errors, ensure that the switch automatically enables the affected ports after 10 minutes.

Catalyst Ethernet MSFC Setup (0.25 Hours)

Configure R9 (6509 with an MSFC card) for IP routing.

Example D-1 displays the hardware profile on the Catalyst 6509 switch.

Example D-1 *show module* *on R9 (MSFC)*

```
Cat6509> (enable) show module
Mod Slot Ports Module-Type          Model               Sub Status
--- ---- ----- -------------------- ------------------- --- --------
 1   1    2    1000BaseX Supervisor WS-X6K-SUP1A-2GE    yes ok
15   1    1    Multilayer Switch Feature WS-F6K-MSFC     no  ok
```

continues

Example D-1 **show module** *on R9 (MSFC) (Continued)*

```
3    3    48     10/100BaseTX Ethernet     WS-X6348-RJ-45     yes ok
9    9    8      1000BaseX Ethernet        WS-X6408-GBIC      no  ok

Mod Module-Name           Serial-Num
--- -------------------   -----------
1                         SAD0413022N
15                        SAD041501U6
3                         SAD04270A8A
9                         SAD03479837
Mod MAC-Address(es)                              Hw   Fw        Sw
1   00-30-96-33-21-7e to 00-30-96-33-21-7f 3.1   5.3(1)    5.5(4)
    00-30-96-33-21-7c to 00-30-96-33-21-7d
    00-d0-01-b0-4c-00 to 00-d0-01-b0-4f-ff
15  00-30-96-33-24-84 to 00-30-96-33-24-c3 1.4   12.1(1)E, 12.1(1)E,
3   00-30-96-34-9b-48 to 00-30-96-34-9b-77 1.1   5.3(1)    5.5(4)
9   00-30-96-2b-e1-f4 to 00-30-96-2b-e1-fb 2.3   4.2(0.24)V 5.5(4)
Mod Sub-Type              Sub-Model            Sub-Serial  Sub-Hw
1   L3 Switching Engine   WS-F6K-PFC           SAD04150DYL 1.1
3   Inline Power Module   WS-F6K-VPWR                      1
```

By using the information displayed in Example D-1, configure the MSFC for IP routing in VLAN 6 using RIPv2 only.

Do not route between any other interfaces.

IP Configuration and IP Addressing (No Time)

NOTE   Because of recent changes to the CCIE exam, the candidate is not required to configure IP addressing; however, the subject is presented here to ensure potential CCIE candidates have a good understanding of IP address spaces and subnetting. Therefore, no time is projected for this section.

Use the Class B subnetted IP address 131.108.0.0 to 131.108.255.255 to design your network. You must use this address space for all addresses unless a different address space is specified in a particular question. Ensure that you read the entire paper before designing your IP address space.

After your IP address space and IP routing are complete, it must be possible to reach all your routers and switches. Set the enable password for all routers and switches to ccieToBe.

Configure IP addresses on your remaining interfaces:

- Use a 25-bit mask for VLAN 2.
- Use a 27-bit mask for VLAN 3.
- Use a 28-bit mask for VLAN D.
- Use a 24-bit mask for VLAN E.
- Use a 26-bit mask for all Token Ring networks.
- Use a subnet with the least number of hosts for the ISDN link.
- Use a 29-bit mask for all Frame Relay connections running classless IP routing protocols.
- Use a 24-bit mask for all Frame Relay connections running classful IP routing protocols.

Assign each router a 24-bit subnet for the loopback address to use. It must be possible to ping and telnet from any one router using the loopback address.

Configure local IP host addresses on each router so that an exec or privilege user can type the router name to ping or telnet without having to type the full IP address.

Frame Relay Setup (0.5 Hours)

Configure IP across your Frame Relay network as displayed in Figure D-2:

- You have to use static maps for each protocol. No dynamic mapping is permitted.
- *No* subinterfaces are allowed on any router.
- Use a most efficient subnetwork for IP addresses on the Frame cloud.
- You may assign a subnet from your Class B range.
- Use LMI type to Cisco only, and do not rely on autosensing the LMI type on any routers. All router interface types are DTE. The Frame port type is DCE.
- Do not use the keyword **broadcast** for the Frame Relay link between R6 and R7 when mapping IP.
- Ensure that you can also ping the local interface from each router configured for Frame Relay.

IGP Routing (3 Hours)

After this section is completed, all routers must have full IP connectivity between every routing domain, including the ISDN backup interfaces when operational.

RIP Configuration (0.5 Hours)

Configure RIP on Routers R6 and R9 only:

- Configure RIP on R6 E0 and R9 E0.
- Ensure that only unicast updates are sent and received.
- Authenticate any RIP packets.
- Redistribute the RIP route into IGRP domain.
- Make sure you can see distributed RIP routes throughout your topology.

IGRP Configuration (0.5 Hours)

Configure IGRP on Routers R6 and R7 only:

- Use 10 as the AS number for IGRP.
- IGRP covers the link between R6 and R7 only.
- Redistribute the IGRP routes into OSPF domain.
- Make sure you can see distributed IGRP routes throughout your topology as Type 1 OSPF routes.
- Redistribute the OSPF and external EIGRP routes with an administrative distance of 199 in the EIGRP domain.

EIGRP Configuration (0.5 Hours)

Configure EIGRP on Routers R3, R7, and R8 only:

- Configure EIGRP in domain 333 between the serial link on R7 to R8, R3 to R8, and Ring 800.
- Summarize as much as possible to reduce the redistributed routes into OSPF, but ensure that all routes appear in the IGRP and RIP domains.
- Ensure that EIGRP is authenticated across the Frame Relay connections.
- Redistribute the EIGRP routes into OSPF domains with a cost metric of 1000 seen on all OSPF routers.
- Ensure that R3 never sends any updates across the Ethernet (E0) segment.

OSPF Configuration (1.5 Hours)

Configure OSPF as described in Figure D-1. Do not create any unspecified OSPF areas:

- Configure the OSPF backbone over the Frame Relay network between the three routers: R2, R4, and R7.

- The ISDN link between R1 and R4 resides in the area 0.0.0.0.
- The link between R4 and R5 is in area 4.
- Ring 100 is in area 100.
- Ring 500 is in area 500.
- The Ethernet segment between R1 and R2 resides in area 1.
- The Ethernet segment on R4 resides in area 0.0.0.40.
- Ensure that all OSPF routes are redistributed and reachable in the IGRP, RIP, and EIGRP domains.
- Ensure that the OSPF backbone in the Frame cloud is authenticated.
- Ensure that R1 will never be the DR on all segments.
- Ensure that R4 is the DR in the OSPF backbone network.
- Ensure that the router ID of all OSPF-enabled routers is the loopback address.
- Do not create any additional areas.
- Set the hello interval between the link R1 and R4 to 25 seconds.
- Set the hello interval on R2 Ethernet segment to 20 seconds.
- Ensure that all loopbacks appear as /24 bit networks on all IP routing tables. Do not use the **redistribute connected** command on any router to accomplish this.
- Ensure that area 0.0.0.40 is configured so that excessive CPU resources are not consumed on Router R4. You can assume no other areas or routers are attached to this segment.

IPX Configuration (1 Hour)

Configure IPX and ensure that IPX connectivity exists on all routers:

- Configure IPX directly on all interfaces *except* all WAN and loopback interfaces.
- All routers must be able to see all other IPX routes and must be able to IPX ping each router.
- You can use IPX EIGRP as your routing protocol.
- Disable IPX RIP wherever possible.
- Configure NLSP between R6 and R7. You cannot configure IPX addressing on the Frame Relay link. Between R6 and R7, do not enable EIGRP IPX.
- Configure two IPX services on R1 named IPXServ1, acting as an IPX server, and IPXPrn1, acting as a printer server. Ensure that all IPX-enabled routers can reach these two server SAPs, except Router R3.
- Ensure that you can IPX ping across your network.

Basic ISDN Configuration (0.5 Hours)

ISDN switch information:

- ISDN switch type: basic-5ess
- ISDN numbering:
  — R1: 0298017705
  — R4: 0296307050
- SPIDS are not required.

Configure the ISDN interfaces on R1 and R4 as follows:

- Only when S0 of R1 goes down, R1 should place an outgoing call to R4.
- R4 cannot call R1 under any circumstances.
- Use PPP encapsulation and the strongest authentication available.
- Ensure that you never bring up more than one B channel to keep costs to a minimum.
- When the Frame Relay link is restored, bring down the ISDN link after 25 minutes.
- When the ISDN is active, all routers must be able to ping and telnet the local ISDN interfaces on R1 and R4.

DLSw+ Configuration (0.75 Hours)

Configure DLSw+ on R1, R3, R5, and R8:

- Rings 100, 500, and 800 should have connectivity to VLAN 2 and 3.
- SNA hosts reside on Rings 100 and 500.
- Hosts on Ring 500 are used only when Ring 100 is not reachable.
- Ensure that all routers peer to R1 and only in a network failure do DLSw+ circuits terminate on R5.
- DLSw+ peers should be active only when user-based traffic (SNA/NetBIOS) is sent or received.
- If IP connectivity exists, ensure that DLSw+ remains established.
- Use a different virtual ring group on each router.
- Configure a filter that blocks NetBIOS packets with the destination name SimonisaCCIE from leaving R5 and R8. Permit all other NetBIOS traffic starting with the name Simonis?***.
- Ensure that remote DLSW+ peers do not send too many queries for the destination MAC address 0200.0200.0200 on Ring 100 or VLAN 2.
- Ensure that VLAN 2 can reach hosts on Ring 100.
- Ensure that the only SAPs enabled on R3 are null SAPs and SAP 08.

Flash Configuration (0.20 Hours)

Your customers accidentally erased router R1's system image in Flash memory. They don't have Cisco IOS Software or an TFTP server on hand. They also have no Internet access. Ensure that the IOS image is restored to the Flash on R1 and then reload R1.

R1 and R2 are running the same IOS code and are the same router hardware type (Cisco 2503 routers).

VTY Changes (0.20 Hours)

Configure all VTY lines so that network administrators do not require local authentication.

Administrators must still use the enable password ccieToBe on all routers to access privilege mode.

To allow nonprivileged users access to R1 and the ability to clear terminal server lines, ensure that all exec users can use the IOS **clear** in exec mode on Router R1 only.

HTTP Server (0.20 Hours)

Configure R1 to act as an HTTP server, but only allow clients from Ring 500.

Catalyst 6509 Password Recovery (0.20 Hours)

The enable password on the 6509 switch has been modified. Assuming you have access to the switch using password recovery on the switch, set the enable password to ccie and the access password to cisco.

Private Address Space Allocation (0.20 Hours)

Some users on VLAN_A have configured their PCs with the Class A addresses ranging from 10.10.1.1 to 10.10.1.255/24. Ensure that the Class A address is never present in any routing table except R1, and allow the users to access the rest of the network.

Ensure that the remaining network can access the host with the IP address 10.10.1.100/24.

BGP Routing Configuration (0.75 Hours)

After finishing each of the following sections, make sure all configured interfaces/subnets are consistently visible on all pertinent routers, even in the event of network failure of any one router.

Basic IBGP Configuration (0.5 Hours)

Configure IBGP on all routers in your network:

- Do not use any WAN IP interfaces for IBGP sessions, as your network is prone to failures across the Frame Relay cloud.
- Configure R5 and R8 as route reflectors, and ensure that all traffic uses a preferred path through router R5.
- Minimize IBGP configurations as much as possible.
- Do not disable BGP synchronization.
- Use AS 2002 on all IBGP routers.
- As long as there is IP connectivity in your network, ensure BGP is active in all routers.
- Using the **network** command only, ensure that all networks are advertised to the route reflectors R5 and R3.
- Do not change the administrative distance on any interior routing protocol.
- Make sure your have full BGP connectivity.
- Ensure that all routers have entries in their IP routing tables.

EBGP Configuration (0.25 Hours)

Configure EBGP on R5 and R8 as follows:

- R5's remote peer is 171.108.1.2/24 and remote AS is 1024.
- R8's remote peer is 191.200.1.2/30 and remote AS is 4345.
- ISP1 and ISP2 are advertising the full Internet routing table.
- Ensure that the only route accepted is a default route and routes of the form 110.100.0.0 to 121.110.255.255.

Set all routes in the range 110.100.0.0 to 121.110.255.255 with the following attributes:

- Ensure that BGP origin is set to IGP.
- Prepend with paths with the AS paths 1000 999 100.
- Set the weight to 1000 for all even networks and 2000 for all odd networks.

INDEX

Symbols

? (question mark), CLI help system, 126

Numerics

2-router BGP topology, configuring, 279–284
4-router BGP topology, configuring, 266, 276–279

A

ABRs (area border routers), 9, 87, 95, 141
    required configuration, 169
    summarization, 164–165
access lists, regular expressions, 366. *See also* prefix lists
ACKs (acknowledgments), 198
active state, EIGRP routing table entries, 203
Active state (BGP), 270
AD (administrative distance), 30–31
    default, 379–380
adjacencies (OSPF), 86
    displaying, 108–109
    DROTHER, 117
    EXSTART/DR state, 111
advanced BGP configuration, practical exercises, 368–373
advanced distance vector routing protocols, 32
    EIGRP, 197–198, 202
        best path selection, 205
        configuring, 56–70, 208–222
        NBMA environments, 206–207
        neighbor relationships, 211–213
        practice exercises, 249–252
        redistribution, 235–245
        route maintenance, 199–202
        route summarization, 207–208, 223–228
        topology table, 202–205
        verifying configuration, 246–249
        VLSM, 229–234
        wildcard masks, 200
advanced BGP, route reflector configuration, 328–340

advanced OSPF
    configuring multiple areas, 140–144
    external type 1 routes, 146
    intra-area routes, 146
    multiple area configuration, 149–161
    network design recommendations, 187–188
    over multiarea NBMA, 147
    summarization, 145–147
        configuring, 162–170
    virtual links, configuring, 152–154
    VLSM, 145–147
Aggregator attribute (BGP), 259
applying
    IP addresses to loopback interfaces, 36–37
    prefix lists to BGP peers, 319
area 0, backbone routers, 141
areas, 86
    configuring, 45–50
    connecting, 140–144
    noncontiguous, virtual links, 98–100
    stub areas, 143–144
AS (autonomous system), 86
AS_Path attribute (BGP), 259
    modifying, 344, 346
ASBR (autonomous system boundary router), 87, 96, 141
assigning
    cost of OSPF routers, 111–112
    IP addresses to EIGRP WAN links, 209–210
    OSFP routers
        to single areas, 88–94
        to multiple areas, 94–104
Atomic attribute (BGP), 259
attributes of BGP, 258–259
    community, applying, 293–301
auto-cost reference-bandwidth command, 111
automatic redistribution, 378
automatic summarization, 8
    disabling, 56, 59
autonomous systems
    clusters, 317
    EIGRP redistribution, 212–214, 235–241

H

I

K–L

M

P

Q–R

S

Hey, you've got enough worries.

Don't let IT training be one of them.

Get on the fast track to IT training at InformIT,
your total Information Technology training network.

 www.informit.com

■ Hundreds of timely articles on dozens of topics ■ Discounts on IT books from all our publishing partners, including Cisco Press ■ Free, unabridged books from the InformIT Free Library ■ "Expert Q&A"—our live, online chat with IT experts ■ Faster, easier certification and training from our Web- or classroom-based training programs ■ Current IT news ■ Software downloads ■ Career-enhancing resources

Cisco Press

ciscopress.com

Committed to being your long-term learning resource while you grow as a Cisco Networking Professional

Help Cisco Press **stay connected** to the issues and challenges you face on a daily basis by registering your product and filling out our brief survey. Complete and mail this form, or better yet ...

Register online and enter to win a FREE book!

Jump to **www.ciscopress.com/register** and register your product online. Each complete entry will be eligible for our monthly drawing to win a FREE book of the winner's choice from the Cisco Press library.

May we contact you via e-mail with information about **new releases, special promotions**, and **customer benefits**?

❒ Yes ❒ No

E-mail address _____

Name _____

Address _____

City _____ State/Province _____

Country _____ Zip/Post code _____

Where did you buy this product?

❒ Bookstore ❒ Computer store/Electronics store ❒ Direct from Cisco Systems
❒ Online retailer ❒ Direct from Cisco Press ❒ Office supply store
❒ Mail order ❒ Class/Seminar ❒ Discount store
❒ Other_____

When did you buy this product? _____ **Month** _____ **Year**

What price did you pay for this product?

❒ Full retail price ❒ Discounted price ❒ Gift

Was this purchase reimbursed as a company expense?

❒ Yes ❒ No

How did you learn about this product?

❒ Friend ❒ Store personnel ❒ In-store ad ❒ cisco.com
❒ Cisco Press catalog ❒ Postcard in the mail ❒ Saw it on the shelf ❒ ciscopress.com
❒ Other catalog ❒ Magazine ad ❒ Article or review
❒ School ❒ Professional organization ❒ Used other products
❒ Other_____

What will this product be used for?

❒ Business use ❒ School/Education
❒ Certification training ❒ Professional development/Career growth
❒ Other_____

How many years have you been employed in a computer-related industry?

❒ less than 2 years ❒ 2–5 years ❒ more than 5 years

Have you purchased a Cisco Press product before?

❒ Yes ❒ No

Cisco Press

c i s c o p r e s s . c o m

How many computer technology books do you own?

❏ 1 ❏ 2–7 ❏ more than 7

Which best describes your job function? (check all that apply)

❏ Corporate Management ❏ Systems Engineering ❏ IS Management ❏ Cisco Networking
❏ Network Design ❏ Network Support ❏ Webmaster   Academy Program
❏ Marketing/Sales ❏ Consultant ❏ Student   Instuctor
❏ Professor/Teacher ❏ Other _____

Do you hold any computer certifications? (check all that apply)

❏ MCSE ❏ CCNA ❏ CCDA
❏ CCNP ❏ CCDP ❏ CCIE ❏ Other _____

Are you currently pursuing a certification? (check all that apply)

❏ MCSE ❏ CCNA ❏ CCDA
❏ CCNP ❏ CCDP ❏ CCIE ❏ Other _____

On what topics would you like to see more coverage?

_____

_____

Do you have any additional comments or suggestions?

_____

_____

Thank you for completing this survey and registration. Please fold here, seal, and mail to Cisco Press.

CCNP Practical Studies: Routing (1-58720-054-6)

Cisco Press

Customer Registration—CP0500227

P.O. Box #781046

Indianapolis, IN 46278-8046

Place
Stamp
Here

Cisco Press

201 West 103rd Street

Indianapolis, IN 46290

ciscopress.com

☐ **YES!** I'm requesting a **free** subscription to *Packet*™ magazine.

☐ No. I'm not interested at this time.

☐ Mr.
☐ Ms.

First Name (Please Print)   Last Name

Title/Position (Required)

Company (Required)

Address

City   State/Province

Zip/Postal Code   Country

Telephone (Include country and area codes)   Fax

E-mail

Signature (Required)   Date

☐ I would like to receive additional information on Cisco's services and products by e-mail.

1. Do you or your company:
- A ☐ Use Cisco products
- B ☐ Resell Cisco products
- C ☐ Both
- D ☐ Neither

2. Your organization's relationship to Cisco Systems:
- A ☐ Customer/End User
- B ☐ Prospective Customer
- C ☐ Cisco Reseller
- D ☐ Cisco Distributor
- E ☐ Integrator
- F ☐ Non-Authorized Reseller
- G ☐ Cisco Training Partner
- I ☐ Cisco OEM
- J ☐ Consultant
- K ☐ Other (specify): _____

3. How many people does your entire company employ?
- A ☐ More than 10,000
- B ☐ 5,000 to 9,999
- c ☐ 1,000 to 4,999
- D ☐ 500 to 999
- E ☐ 250 to 499
- f ☐ 100 to 249
- G ☐ Fewer than 100

4. Is your company a Service Provider?
- A ☐ Yes
- B ☐ No

5. Your involvement in network equipment purchases:
- A ☐ Recommend
- B ☐ Approve
- C ☐ Neither

6. Your personal involvement in networking:
- A ☐ Entire enterprise at all sites
- B ☐ Departments or network segments at more than one site
- C ☐ Single department or network segment
- F ☐ Public network
- D ☐ No involvement
- E ☐ Other (specify): _____

7. Your Industry:
- A ☐ Aerospace
- B ☐ Agriculture/Mining/Construction
- C ☐ Banking/Finance
- D ☐ Chemical/Pharmaceutical
- E ☐ Consultant
- F ☐ Computer/Systems/Electronics
- G ☐ Education (K–12)
- U ☐ Education (College/Univ.)
- H ☐ Government—Federal
- I ☐ Government—State
- J ☐ Government—Local
- K ☐ Health Care
- L ☐ Telecommunications
- M ☐ Utilities/Transportation
- N ☐ Other (specify): _____

CPRESS

PACKET™

Packet magazine serves as the premier publication linking customers to Cisco Systems, Inc. Delivering complete coverage of cutting-edge networking trends and innovations, *Packet* is a magazine for technical, hands-on users. It delivers industry-specific information for enterprise, service provider, and small and midsized business market segments. A toolchest for planners and decision makers, *Packet* contains a vast array of practical information, boasting sample configurations, real-life customer examples, and tips on getting the most from your Cisco Systems' investments. Simply put, *Packet* magazine is straight talk straight from the worldwide leader in networking for the Internet, Cisco Systems, Inc.

We hope you'll take advantage of this useful resource. I look forward to hearing from you!

Cecelia Glover
Packet Circulation Manager
packet@external.cisco.com
www.cisco.com/go/packet

Classless Interdomain Routing Conversion Table

CIDR Prefix Length	Dotted Decimal	Binary	Number of Classful Networks
/1	128.0.0.0	1000 0000 0000 0000 0000 0000 0000 0000	128 Class A addresses
/2	192.0.0.0	1100 0000 0000 0000 0000 0000 0000 0000	64 Class A addresses
/3	224.0.0.0	1110 0000 0000 0000 0000 0000 0000 0000	32 Class A addresses
/4	240.0.0.0	1111 0000 0000 0000 0000 0000 0000 0000	16 Class A addresses
/5	248.0.0.0	1111 1000 0000 0000 0000 0000 0000 0000	8 Class A addresses
/6	252.0.0.0	1111 1100 0000 0000 0000 0000 0000 0000	4 Class A addresses
/7	254.0.0.0	1111 1110 0000 0000 0000 0000 0000 0000	2 Class A addresses
/8	255.0.0.0	1111 1111 0000 0000 0000 0000 0000 0000	1 Class A or 256 Class B addresses
/9	255.128.0.0	1111 1111 1000 0000 0000 0000 0000 0000	128 Class B addresses
/10	255.192.0.0	1111 1111 1100 0000 0000 0000 0000 0000	64 Class B addresses
/11	255.224.0.0	1111 1111 1110 0000 0000 0000 0000 0000	32 Class B addresses
/12	255.240.0.0	1111 1111 1111 0000 0000 0000 0000 0000	16 Class B addresses
/13	255.248.0.0	1111 1111 1111 1000 0000 0000 0000 0000	8 Class B addresses
/14	255.252.0.0.	1111 1111 1111 1100 0000 0000 0000 0000	4 Class B addresses
/15	255.254.0.0	1111 1111 1111 1110 0000 0000 0000 0000	2 Class B addresses
/16	255.255.0.0	1111 1111 1111 1111 0000 0000 0000 0000	1 Class B or 256 Class C addresses
/17	255.255.128.0	1111 1111 1111 1111 1000 0000 0000 0000	128 Class C addresses
/18	255.255.192.0	1111 1111 1111 1111 1100 0000 0000 0000	64 Class C addresses
/19	255.255.224.0	1111 1111 1111 1111 1110 0000 0000 0000	32 Class C addresses
/20	255.255.240.0	1111 1111 1111 1111 1111 0000 0000 0000	16 Class C addresses
/21	255.255.248.0	1111 1111 1111 1111 1111 1000 0000 0000	8 Class C addresses
/22	255.255.252.0.	1111 1111 1111 1111 1111 1100 0000 0000	4 Class C addresses
/23	255.255.254.0	1111 1111 1111 1111 1111 1110 0000 0000	2 Class C addresses
/24	255.255.255.0	1111 1111 1111 1111 1111 1111 0000 0000	1 Class C addresses
/25	255.255.255.128	1111 1111 1111 1111 1111 1111 1000 0000	1/2 Class C address